AGREEING AND IMPLEMENTING THE DOHA ROUND OF THE WTO

Edited by

HARALD HOHMANN

CAMBRIDGE
UNIVERSITY PRESS

CAMBRIDGE UNIVERSITY PRESS
Cambridge, New York, Melbourne, Madrid, Cape Town, Singapore, São Paulo, Delhi

Cambridge University Press
The Edinburgh Building, Cambridge CB2 8RU, UK

Published in the United States of America by Cambridge University Press, New York

www.cambridge.org
Information on this title: www.cambridge.org/9780521869904

First published 2008

Printed in the United Kingdom at the University Press, Cambridge

A catalogue record for this publication is available from the British Library

ISBN-13 978-0-521-86990-4 hardback

CONTENTS

PART TWO Trade policy (including competition) and trade facilitation

PART THREE Reform of the dispute settlement system

PART FOUR Social rights, health, and environment

PART FIVE Conclusions

LIST OF CONTRIBUTORS

Lilia R. Bautista She was the first Philippine Ambassador to the WTO before assuming the chairmanship of the Philippine Securities and Exchange Commission. She is currently a consultant to the Judicial Academy of the Philippine Supreme Court and Director of the Bank of the Philippine Islands (BPI), BPI Capital, RFM Corporation and Transnational Diversified Group.

Andreas Blüthner Former International Law Advisor with BASF AG (Ludwigshafen), Governmental Affairs, and Strategy Co-ordinator for the Global Alliance for Improved Nutrition (GAIN, Geneva). Presently Associate Lecturer for Trade Law (University of Mannheim), Attorney-at-Law (Mannheim) and Strategic Partnership Manager for BASF's business and development activities.

Knut Brünjes Deputy Director General for Trade Policy, WTO, North America, Latin America, and Africa in the Ministry of Economics and Technology, Berlin, Germany.

Paul de Waart Professor Emeritus of International Law at the Free University Amsterdam; member ILA Committee International Law on Sustainable Development; several publications on the United Nations, peaceful settlement of disputes, transfer of technology, international economic order and human rights.

Philippe Duponteil Graduated from the Institut d'etudes Politques de Paris, and Master (PolSci) University of Paris V; Deputy Head of Unit at the European Commission's Directorate General for Trade Policy, previously co-ordinator for Trade & Development in the unit in charge of WTO negotiations at the European Commission.

Petina Gappah Counsel, Advisory Centre on WTO Law, formerly a legal officer in the WTO Appellate Body Secretariat. Graduated from the Universities of Cambridge, Graz and Zimbabwe.

Harald Hohmann Attorney (senior partner) of the law firm *Hohmann & Partner* in Büdingen (close to Frankfurt), advising clients worldwide on international trade law (EC and US export control, customs international contract and WTO law) and national/EC business law, and senior lecturer at the University of Frankfurt/Main, author of several books on international trade and international environmental law.

Faizel Ismail Head of the South African Delegation to the WTO. He joined the new democratic government of South Africa in 1994 and led its trade negotiations with the EU, the Southern African Development Community, the Southern African Customs Union, with a number of bilateral trading partners and the WTO. He joined South Africa's Mission to Geneva in May 2002. He has written numerous articles on trade and development, and he is assistant editor of the *Journal of World Trade*.

Peter Mandelson studied Philosophy, Politics and Economics at St Catherine's College, Oxford; now European Commissioner for Trade. Appointed Labour Party Director for Campaign and Communication in 1985. Labour Party Campaign Manager in May 1997 elections. Elected Member of the British Parliament in 1992. Appointed as Secretary of State for Trade and Industry in 1998 and between 1999–2001 was the Secretary of State for Northern Ireland.

Mitsuo Matsushita Professor Emeritus of Tokyo University. He holds a PhD from Tulane University and a D Jur degree from Tokyo University. He taught at Sophia University, Tokyo University and Seikei University. He was a founding member of the WTO Appellate Body from 1995–2000. He has taught at Harvard Law School, Columbia Law School, Michigan Law School and the College of Europe. He acts as counsel to the international law firm Nagashima Ohno & Tsunematsu in Tokyo. He is also an advisory editor of the *Journal of International Economic Law*.

Karl M. Meessen Professor Emeritus of Jena University. Attorney admitted to the Düsseldorf bar, taking only competition, investment and trade law cases; formerly Professor of Law at the Universities of Jena, Augsburg and Cologne as well as at the Graduate Institute of International Studies in Geneva.

Shinya Murase Professor at Sophia University, Tokyo. Member of the Curatorium of the Hague Academy of International Law; Lead Author of the Fourth Assessment Report of the Intergovernmental Panel on Climate Change (IPCC).

David O'Sullivan Director General for Trade at the European Commission. He previously held the position of Secretary General of the Commission, Head of Cabinet to President Prodi and Director General for Education and Training.

Chiedu Osakwe Director of the Doha Development Agenda Special Duties Division in the WTO Secretariat. Previously, Director, Textiles Division and Director, Technical Co-operation Division. He chaired the WTO Committee on Rules of Origin in 1995 and 1996, the Working Party on Pre-Shipment Inspection in 1997 and the Integrated Framework Working Group for LDCs' Trade Development from 1999–2002. Author of articles and presentations on international trade issues.

Reinhard Quick Director of the German chemical industry's liaison office in Brussels. He teaches international economic law at Saarland University, Saarbrücken, where he has recently been appointed honorary professor.

Asif H. Qureshi Professor of International Economic Law, Law School, University of Manchester, UK. Barrister, Quadrant Chambers, London, UK. Editor-in-Chief of the *Manchester Journal of International Economic Law.*

Debra Steger Professor of Common Law and Executive in Residence at the Faculty of Law, University of Ottawa. An architect of the WTO (former Head of the Secretariat of Appellate Body), and a Member of the Executive of the Canadian Bar Association and the International Law Association. Author and editor of several books on international trade law, and is on the editorial board of the *Journal of International Economic Law.*

Lutz Strack Legal Adviser, Administration of the State Parliament of the Free and Hanseatic City of Hamburg, Germany.

Satoru Taira Professor of Law, LLM (Waseda University), Professor of International Economic Law at the Graduate School of Law, Osaka City University; Faculty Fellow of the Research Institute of Economy, Trade and Industry (RIETI, 2004–2005); Author of '*Kokusai Keizai-ho (International Economic Law)*', Yuhikaku, Tokyo, 2003.

Wolfgang Weiss Professor of Law at University of Erlangen-Nuremberg/Germany. Author of several books and articles on Public International law, WTO law and European law.

Eric White Legal Adviser and Co-ordinator (WTO Affairs), Legal Service of the Commission of the European Community.

FOREWORD

The Doha Round, which is the first major trade negotiation under the new World Trade Organization (established by the GATT Uruguay Round Treaty effective January 1, 1995), has navigated an extraordinarily difficult course. The Third WTO Ministerial Conference in Seattle December 1999 was meant to launch the Round, but this failed because of the important impact of changing membership and the decision-making processes of the WTO (compared to the GATT which had eight trade rounds). The fourth WTO Ministerial Conference held in Doha, Qatar in November 2001 was much more successful and seemed on course to launch the Round, but at the Fifth Ministerial in Cancun, Mexico (September 2003) the process failed, with major confrontations between various groupings of nation members concerning a variety of difficult international economic policy conflicts. The Sixth Ministerial Conference was held in Hong Kong in December 2005, resulting in progress and some optimism, which by the summer of 2006 had turned more negative, resulting, in a 'suspension' of the negotiations. Nevertheless efforts continue to move the process forward, amid considerable optimism that this negotiation has economic and even geopolitical importance to world peace and the increasing alleviation of poverty.

This book is of major importance to international trade law, as it is one of the first major scholarly and practitioner appraisals of the Doha Round to be undertaken with a view to examining the profound impact of the negotiation for the world. It addresses three important issues (or sets of issues) which are central to the Doha negotiations, namely:

- development policy (e.g. special and differential treatment);
- trade policy concerns (e.g. market access to agricultural and industrial goods and access to services, trade facilitation and the improvement of 'rules'); and
- 'trade and issues' (e.g. trade and social rights, trade and environment, and trade and health).

The editor is certainly correct in selecting these issues, as well as addressing the extremely important dispute settlement process (sometimes treated more outside the Doha talks than inside them).

These four subjects are the basic themes of this book and these issues will likely be decisive for the proper-functioning of the WTO system. If the Doha Round is not successful, the multilateral approach of the WTO will be highly endangered, resulting in a set of bilateral and regional efforts. And it is not certain, whether such bilateralism 'could well become the catalyst for further multilateral trade liberalisation in the future' (the assumption of one of the authors) or whether it would destroy the ability of the world community to come to solutions concerning the reduction of poverty, capacity building of developing countries, trade liberalisation, trade facilitation, effective dispute settlement and to secure sustainable development and an environmentally sound and socially just world order.

An important characteristic of this book is the fact that the authors come from three different continents (Europe, America and Asia) and that they are well-known scholars and practitioners who convey insights how the Doha talks developed and what they will mean in practice for the world community. The book treats some of the most crucial aspects of WTO Law in an accessible way and should be warmly welcomed by scholars and practitioners alike as a balanced and very valuable reference tool.

John H. Jackson
Washington D.C.

Introduction

The World Trade Organization (WTO) is a global success story, not least because of its efficiency in dispute settlement. Where else in the world is it possible to solve disputes within sixteen months (for Panel and Appellate Body)? This is especially astonishing in the case of global trade conflicts. Because of the unique efficiency of the WTO dispute settlement system, more and more cases are brought to the WTO panels. However, an efficient dispute settlement alone is not able to solve the crisis of globalisation, for which non-government organisations (NGO) like *Attac* or anti-globalisation campaigns are symbols. They underline that the WTO – especially because of its success up to now – needs more and more justification to correspond to the current aspirations of the world community.

Before the beginning of the Doha Round, *doubts arose whether the WTO was ready for the inclusion of some of the decisive items of globalisation.* The following questions have been asked:

- How can we reduce poverty of developing countries, especially of the least-developed countries (LDC)? How can we support capacity building especially for these countries?
- Is special and differential treatment a *must* to secure the development goals of the least-developed countries? If so, what does it mean in practice?
- Under what conditions will improved access to agricultural and industrial goods[1] and improved access to services be a win–win situation for industrialised and developing countries alike?
- How must trade policy (improved access to agriculture, industrial goods, services) and 'rules' (e.g. on subsidies, anti-dumping) be improved to support trade liberalisation and fairness at the same time? Must competition become a subject of the WTO and what role does trade facilitation play?

[1] The improved access to industrial products is now called NAMA (Non-Agricultural Market Access).

- In case trade liberalisation *per se* cannot be regarded as the main driver for more sustainable development, what additional steps have to be taken for that purpose?
- How can the tension between a judicial and a diplomatic model of dispute settlement be solved? How is it possible to increase the transparency of panel proceedings and to improve the effectiveness of countermeasures? Is funding necessary to improve the access of developing countries (especially LDCs) to the WTO dispute settlement?
- Do the WTO panels or only the WTO Ministerial Conferences have the authority to resolve inconsistencies in the application of various treaty obligations?
- How must the relationship between trade liberalisation and 'non-trade items' like environmental protection, health and human rights/social rights be solved? What does a 'WTO with a human face' mean in practice? Can these 'non-trade items' be included in WTO law by diplomatic processes (e.g. by one of the WTO Rounds) or by WTO panels?

These were some of the most important questions asked at the beginning of the Doha Round, the first major trade round under the new WTO (established 1995), which was launched in 2001 at the WTO Ministerial Conference in Doha. The Doha Round, which focused especially on developmental issues, has also become known as the 'Development Round'. The term *'Doha Development Agenda' – or DDA* – thus refers to the (mandate of the) Doha Declaration, without being specific, whether it also implies reference to other major documents of the Doha Round, namely (1) the Decision adopted by the General Council on 1 August 2004 on the 'Doha Work Programme' – also called the 'July package' and (2) the Hong Kong Ministerial Declaration. DDA is thus a reference to the talks based on the Doha Declaration in light of the further development by these two other main documents of the Doha Round.

In the ***Doha Declaration***, it was agreed to implement several trade issues (e.g. access to agriculture, industrial goods and services, improvement of 'rules', competition policy, trade facilitation, etc; see also paras.13–29 of the Doha Declaration) several development issues (e.g. debts, transfer of technology, technical co-operation/capacity building, LDC, special and differential treatment; see also paras. 35–44 of the Doha Declaration) a few non-trade issues (e.g. environmental protection and social rights, see also paras. 8 and 31–33 of the Doha Declaration) and one dispute settlement issue (e.g. the improvement and clarification of the DSU; see also para. 30 of the Doha Declaration) within the Doha Round.

The Doha Declaration stands for the *'Agreeing'* on the issues of the Doha Round. The *'Implementing'* of these issues started especially with the *Decision by the General Council of 1 August 2004*, since for the first time the Work Programme of the Doha Round was agreed upon (see also the Annexes concerning Agriculture, NAMA, Services, Trade Facilitation). Thus, the WTO needed more than three years to agree on the Work Programme of the Doha Round. When one has in mind that the Doha Round would not run much longer than five years altogether, some time constraints were put on the WTO Members. The *Hong Kong Declaration* has specified how far WTO Members have agreed to implement the Doha Work Programme (e.g. especially the Annexes on Agriculture, NAMA, Services, Rules, Trade Facilitation, Special and Differential Treatment).

The Doha Talks were suspended on 24 July 2006, but this suspension has been lifted and negotiations resumed in February 2007 (and since February–April 2008, there have been some indicators for a Doha success). As *Peter Mandelson* (EC Commission, *Chapter 1a*) and *Chiedu Osakwe* (WTO, *Chapter 1b*) point out there are a lot of indications, that the Doha talks will continue and be resumed in the near future, but there may be questions about the size of the final package. Because of the principle of Single Undertaking, which also applies to the Doha Round, nothing is agreed until everything is agreed. Thus the agreements reached so far in the Doha talks (see *Chapter 1b*) are conditional on the conclusion of the entire DDA negotiations themselves. This is why resuming and concluding the Doha Round is imperative for the world community. However, if a WTO Member wants to implement a few of these agreements, it must not wait until the entire DDA negotiations are legally binding (e.g. the EC is already implementing the 'Everything But Arms' initiative). *Peter Mandelson* (*Chapter 1a*) mentions several risks to the multilateral trading systems in the unlikely event that the Doha negotiations do not resume in the near future.

This book is the *first evaluation of the Doha Round by practitioners and scholars alike.* Its aim is two-fold: first, to make well-known and second, to assess the results of discussions and negotiations reached so far in the Doha Round, in order to analyse their importance for the further development of word trade law. *The book is divided into four parts*:

- Part One: Development policy
- Part Two: Trade policy and trade facilitation
- Part Three: Reform of the dispute settlement
- Part Four: Health, environment and social standards.

The book will stimulate further discussion on how to implement the agreed principles of the Doha Round.

In Part One, **the developmental aspects of the Doha Round** are highlighted by the *WTO Secretariat* (*Chapter 2*), which gives an excellent overview of all the discussions inside the WTO and between the WTO Members. The political assessment of the development aspects in the Doha Round in *Chapter 3a* (*Philippe Duponteil*, EC Commission) and *3b* (*Faizel Ismail* for developing countries) is slightly different: Does the EU 'stand to be the main obstacle to progress in the Doha Round'? (*Ismail*) or 'has the EU from the outset supported a global trade round that is genuinely pro-development'? (*Duponteil*). It is up to the reader to decide. And another quotation from *Duponteil* is worth mentioning: Not so much 'the need for radical agricultural market access, but liberalisation in industrial products and services will be the key for pro-development'. Also the analytical assessments presented by *Ambassador Lilia Bautista* (coming from a developing country) in *Chapter 4* is very valuable for international discussion. She points out that trade liberalisation alone does not guarantee the eradication of poverty, if no adjustment measures are taken inside the developing country. In *Chapter 5*, *Asif H. Qureshi* adds an important aspect of developmental policy, namely the role of special and differential treatment. He is convinced that the dispute settlement system may be the right body for the implementation of this principle.

Part Two analyses **issues of trade policy and trade facilitation**, starting with the political assessments by *David O'Sullivan* from the EC Commission (*Chapter 6a*) and *Knut Brünjes* from the German Ministry of Economy (*Chapter 6b*). Both see the Doha talks at a critical stage – these two chapters were completed in June 2006, but later updated or rewritten – and they concentrate on conditions for further progress for the Doha talks (thus especially *O'Sullivan*: agricultural reforms by the US, changes concerning services and rules, differentiation between developing countries and increased South–South trade) or on the results achieved so far (especially *Brünjes*). In addition, *O'Sullivan* mentions a new EC strategic approach for the future. *Reinhard Quick* (*Chapter 7*) gives a very helpful analysis of what impact the NAMA and the trade–environment negotiations of the Doha Round have for trade in chemicals. He focuses on high bound tariffs for chemicals by emerging countries, two non-tariff barriers (export taxes, double pricing), tariff elimination for environmental goods, the MEA/WTO relationship, and regulatory co-operation (e.g. the EC REACH Regulation). *Harald*

Hohmann (*Chapter 8*) proposes to include additional aspects into the WTO discussion on trade facilitation. After an analysis of the main barriers for global export, import and transit trade and of the recent efforts of international organisations like the WCO, ECE and WTO on this topic, he presents a draft agreement which has enough international support to be accepted by the WTO Members. *Karl Meessen* (*Chapter 9*) proposes to drop competition policy from the Doha talks (see paras. 23–25 of the Doha Declaration), since the informal non-binding inter-agency agreement of the International Competition Network may be a better forum for reaching some convergence of competition law. *Paul de Waart* (*Chapter 10*) finally resumes a discussion of Doha trade liberalisation from the perspective of sustainable development[2] (see para. 6 of the Doha Declaration) and of the legal principle of integration, under which an integrated approach of economic, social, environmental and human rights concerns is needed for current and future generations. From this contribution, which offers insights into new developments of international law and the most recent codification efforts of three committees of the International Law Association (concerning the humanisation of international law), valuable conclusions may be drawn about under what conditions the Doha Round talks may be a win–win situation for industrial and developing countries alike.

Part 3 analyses questions of the **reform of the dispute settlement from three different angles**: (1) improvements and clarifications of the DSU (see para. 30 of the Doha Declaration), (2) the competence of WTO panels in trade–environment disputes (see para. 31 of the Doha Declaration) and (3) technical co-operation and capacity building concerning the use of WTO panels by developing countries (see paras. 38–41 of the Doha Declaration). The first aspect (improvements and clarifications of the DSU) is comprehensively treated by *Eric White* from the EC Commission (*Chapter 11*) and by *Wolfgang Weiss* (*Chapter 12*). Both resume the historical development of the GATT/WTO dispute settlement system and the current DSU review, and comment on proposals concerning transparency, effectiveness of counter-measures, functioning of panels and Appellate Body, flexibility and state control, etc. While *Eric White* pleads for some experimentation with new procedures in order to codify them into a new DSU at a later stage, *Wolfgang Weiss* seems to prefer the codification of a new DSU now. The second aspect (the competence of

2 See the EC Study by the University of Manchester on Sustainable Impact Assessments of the Results of the Doha Round.

WTO panels in trade–environment disputes) is analysed by *Debra Steger* in *Chapter 13*, thus bridging Parts 3 and 4 of the book. She argues as follows: Article 3, para. 2 of the DSU should not be regarded as a broad mandate for incorporation of all principles of international law into the WTO Agreements; inconsistencies between various treaty obligations should be solved by an improved WTO legislative process, rather than asking the Appellate Body for a decision. The third aspect (technical co-operation and capacity building concerning use of WTO panels by developing countries) is the subject of *Chapter 14*. *Patina Gappah's* evaluation of the role of legal aid in international dispute settlements compares the role of trust funds (e.g. concerning disputes at the International Court of Justice) with that of technical assistance from the WTO Secretariat and especially with the role of the Advisory Centre for WTO Law (ACWL). Such an analysis of the work of the ACWL has been missing up to now.

Part 4 of the book summarises the **discussion on the famous non-trade items: the environment, health, social standards and human rights**. First human rights. Again, the paragraphs in the Doha Declaration remain vague: What does: the WTO 'takes note of the work under way in the International Labour Organization (ILO) on the social dimension of globalisation' (para. 8) mean? Is this a legally binding commitment to respect and integrate the binding ILO standards? In *Chapter 15*, *Andreas Blüthner* underlines the practical importance of the inclusion of human rights, labour and environmental standards into trade commitments by summarising the efforts of WTO panels and an ILO Declaration (interpretation of 'social clauses') and by underlining the work of the UN–Global Compact, which may serve as a model for the WTO. Second, Health and food safety. This is another non-trade item, which is not sufficiently treated by the Doha Declaration, except in the more general paragraphs on environmental concerns. In *Chapter 16*, *Mitsuo Matsushita* analyses the conditions (under Art. XX GATT, the SPS and the TBT) under which WTO Members may take protective measures (e.g. for food with GMO content) – one of the questions here is the role of the precautionary principle, especially under Art. 3.2 SPS. Third, the Environment. The three paragraphs of the Doha Declaration (paras 31–33) remain vague, except for some minor aspects (like eco-labels, see para. 32). In *Chapter 17*, *Shinya Murase* gives a very valuable in-depth analysis of the relationship between trade and the environment, first generally, and then by paying particular reference to the Kyoto Protocol on Climate Change. He then describes an alternative regime on climate change under the WTO, by proposing a new framework model treaty according to WTO provisions.

This chapter draws some general observations on the relationship between free trade and environmental protection. The same is true of *Satoru Taira's* analysis in *Chapter 18.* He argues with some principles of the Vienna Convention on the Law of Treaties (good faith, harmonious interpretation with some other rules of international law, *lex specialis, lex posterior*), with four principles developed by the EC, and finally, with the evolutionary interpretation of WTO law. These five chapters are summarised and reviewed in *Chapter 19* by *Lutz Strack.* He compares these visions with the necessary reforms and the results already achieved under the Doha Round thoroughly, in order to find out what will be the most likely result of the Doha Round concerning environment, health, social standards and human rights.

Chapter 20 contains the Conclusions by the Editor. Due to lack of space, the Doha documents are now published electronically at www.cambridge.org/resources, and at www.hohmann-partner.com/wto-law/doha.

Thus, the book gives several insights into the hotly debated topics of international trade law within the WTO. The reader gets a clear analysis of what outcome is to be expected from a resumption of the Doha Round, and what improvements will be possible in the long run.

The book goes partly back to an ILA post-conference (after the ILA-Berlin Conference in August 2004) in the chateau of Büdingen (near Frankfurt/Main, 23–24 August 2004). In addition to conference speakers, some leading scholars and practitioners of WTO Law have been invited to contribute in this book.

My special thanks are due to *Finola O'Sullivan, Richard Woodham, Daniel Dunlavey* and *Paula Devine* (Cambridge University Press) for the publication and final editing of the book, to all the authors who worked very hard to publish the book directly at the end of the Doha Round and who did several updates, to my teacher of WTO Law Professor *John Jackson* for writing the Foreword, to my colleague Attorney *Brigitte Dönges* (Hohmann and Partner) for her support in proofreading, to *Otto Hospes* and *Otto Geneh* (Dutch Ministry of Foreign Affairs) and several members of the WTO Secretariat for valuable recommendations on who to contact, to my colleagues *Satoru Taira* (Osaka City University) and *Eckard Pache* (University Würzburg), who were the co-organisers of the Büdingen conference, and to *Satoru Taira* for organising a research stay at Osaka Law School in April 2006 to discuss several items of the book. I would also like to thank the three sponsors of the Büdingen conference (Dean of the Law School of Osaka City University, BASF AG, Hohmann & Partner

Attorneys) and the participants of this very stimulating conference: Where else does it happen that people from various countries of the world come together in a medieval castle to discuss current topics of WTO Law, allowing an exchange between scholars and practitioners from three different continents? We do hope that the reader will also get this stimulating atmosphere we had during the conference. (Any correspondence concerning the contents of the book may be sent to info@hohmann-partner.com).

This book is dedicated to my daughter Viktoria Letizia Wen-Lin, who came from an emerging developing country to us: she is now four years old and represents the aspirations and requirements of present and future generations as well as globalisation at the same time.

Harald Hohmann
Büdingen, May 2008

P.S. In Geneva on 29 July 2008 the Doha Round of talks seemed close to success. Conflict over certain details of the Special Safeguard Mechanism in the Draft Modalities for Agriculture is not so insurmountable that it should jeopardise the entire process. We think it likely that this second suspension of talks will be lifted in order to allow a successful conclusion of the Doha Round.

1a

Doha *a posteriori*

PETER MANDELSON[1]

Most politicians are understandably reluctant to make predictions. A week, as we are constantly reminded, is a long time in politics. Politics, like the successful outcome of a trade negotiation, is a bet in which there are dozens of variables. So a politician who is also a trade negotiator should be doubly cautious. I am writing this at a time when the Doha Round of negotiations is approaching what is widely recognized as a moment of truth. It is not just another of the multiple moments of truth that all trade rounds pass through on their way to a hard-fought consensus – old hands in Geneva will always remind you that the *Uruguay round was older than Doha is now, when it was successfully concluded.* Rather Doha is approaching a potentially terminal impasse defined by the combination of the US political calendar and the fact that the round has reached a point where the parameters for a final agreement are relatively clear and the gaps to close are political as much as technical. By the time you read this, that moment will have come or gone. I cannot predict what will happen, but I can set out what I believe should happen. Thus, *what follows is either* ***a posteriori*** *defense of the path WTO negotiators have chosen, or it is a measure of lost opportunity, of the deal we may have let slip through our fingers.* As both of those things, it is a guide to some of the political problems that are likely to confront WTO trade rounds and the multilateral trading system in the future.

The package on the table

By November 2007, the Doha negotiation has produced the outlines of a final agreement that, as a whole, would do credit to the multilateral trading system. Especially *in agriculture, there is a package on the table that offers two to three times the outcome of the Uruguay Round*, a package that

[1] The author is EU Trade Commissioner. This Chapter was written on 25 October 2007.

was independently described as “by far the largest liberalization of farm trade in history”.[2] At the centre of this package is the EU’s offer to cut its farm tariffs by an average of 50%, within a banded system that ensures that, unlike the Uruguay Round, the highest tariffs would be cut the most. Alongside these cuts to border protection, the EU is also proposing a cut to overall trade-distorting farm support of at least 70% and the elimination of all export subsidies if others agree to do the same. In the EU market alone, the EU has calculated that its proposed tariff reductions for products like beef would create hundreds of thousands of tonnes of new market access. As the steep drop in trade-distorting support saw EU farmers withdraw from global export markets for products like milk and poultry, these markets would become available for the exports of others, not least farmers in the developing world.

It is easy to forget that Doha *is the first round to treat agriculture seriously*. It is impossible to forget that the politics and economics of agriculture globally are such that it would never have been able to catch up with 40 years of liberalization in manufactured goods trade overnight. Under those circumstances, the offer of a 50% cut in farm tariffs in developed countries and a revolution in trade-distorting farm support is exceptional, far beyond the wildest expectations of negotiators in the Uruguay Round.

Industrial goods negotiations have taken a backseat to agriculture for much of the Doha Round. Yet even here the outline of a potential package is emerging. At least based on the ranges proposed by the chairs of the negotiating groups in Geneva in July 2007, Doha has the potential not only to consolidate the new openness created in the system by liberalization of border protection for industrial goods in emerging economies like India, but also to create new market access for exporters in these same economies. It has the potential to basically eliminate all remaining industrial tariff peaks, and to eliminate virtually all remaining industrial tariffs in developed markets. *In the EU, there would be almost no duties above 5% left*, which would provide new market access for producers in the emerging economies, but also help streamline production within the huge transatlantic marketplace.

This package has substantial economic value in its own right, especially once a moderate but meaningful services agreement, a new rules agreement and greater protection for intellectual property rights in

[2] Polaski, Sandra, *Breaking the Doha deadlock*; Carnegie Endowment for International Peace, January 2007.

agriculture are factored in. It also has the potential to inject some much needed confidence into the global economy and to act as a guard against the reversal of current levels of liberalization. Yet in the autumn of 2007, despite a significant fright in the credit markets, there is still very little sense of the systemic value of a trade deal, both as a confidence builder and as a ratchet in the global economic machine that would stop it sliding backwards.

We hardly need reminding that the current levels of openness in the global economy are not irreversible. Doha's great strength as viewed from 2007 lies in its *ability to lock in the unilateral opening of the last decade and act as an insurance policy against protectionism and trade politicking*, not just in the developed world but also in the emerging economies. Because the chief driver of trade liberalization over the last decade has not been external negotiating pressure but internal economic rationalization and reform, one of the chief functions of a multilateral trade round is to consolidate the gains made in the different parts of the system. The amount of "water" in the system – meaning the often huge difference between the tariff rates that some countries have notified with the WTO, and the rates they actually apply at the border today, especially with regard to the industrial tariffs of the large emerging economies – is evidence of the extent to which tariff bindings have not caught up with the openness of current trade. Inevitably, the currency of trade negotiations is the confrontational language of mutual concessions, and in bilateral negotiations mutual ambition can drive much wider reciprocal opening. But at the multilateral level, where expectations have to be tempered by an intensely complex political balance and a wide range of capacities, the reality is that one of the chief functions of the system is to keep consolidating openness and creating certainty for traders, not necessarily to add it in huge strides. Nevertheless, Doha in November 2007 has the potential to do both.

Above and beyond these things, *the current package has a very substantial potential development component*, much of which may be at risk in the case of failure. In theory, as part of a single undertaking the poorest countries could expect a dramatic increase in their duty and quota free access to the markets of developed countries and the emerging economies, building on the commitments made in Hong Kong in 2005. So long as this is genuinely for all products and all countries in the way that the EU has offered since 2001, then it would act as a way to offset some of the preference erosion that will inevitably result from multilateral tariff liberalization. The trade facilitation stream of the negotiation has the potential to deliver significant benefits by helping standardize customs practice; the biggest winners from which would be the poorer parts of the developing world where red tape and unreliable bureaucracy are currently a serious barrier to trade. We could also expect fast-tracked agreements on ending the serious distortions in the global cotton trade.

The politics of a deal

So why am I unsure that it will happen? First, farm politics. Second, the complex politics of development.

Farm politics

Doha was always going to involve asking farmers in the developed world to accept that trade-distorting farm supports displace developing country products both from global export markets and from the domestic markets of developing countries themselves. *Agricultural trade reform may not be the development panacea as it is sometimes presented, but in this respect at least, there is no question that the developed world has a responsibility to change its practice.* The EU recognized this in 2003 when it began to reform its farm supports. More than 90% of EU direct payments to farmers are now no longer linked to production or support prices. EU farmers have accepted a huge reform agenda, and this agenda, coupled with the tariff cuts offered as part of the Doha negotiation have taken the EU to the very limits of what is politically and economically possible in a single trade round.

The US will inevitably face a similar reform process. Yet the current Farm Bill reverses the downward trend in trade-distorting farm spending before 2002. Challenges through the WTO to US farm supports for cotton and bio-ethanol are a warning that while US legislators understandably don't like the idea of negotiating their Farm Bill in the WTO, they can end up having to *defend* it there when others litigate against them. The experience with cotton suggests that they can lose. *It is arguably better to play reform into a multilateral negotiation* and get something in return, than to reform unilaterally later after litigation and get nothing.

Asking these constituencies to shoulder the burden of change is never easy. It is especially hard when the perception is that change is being demanded by others, and when negotiators encourage the argument that farmers can expect a dollar-for-dollar "compensation" through more market access for the reduction of trade-distorting subsidies. The trade offs will inevitably be more complex than that, and are unlikely to come directly in agriculture, but rather in other parts of the negotiation. Given the development component of the Doha Round, changing the way we support farmers in the developing world is also not something for which we can readily expect to be paid dollar-for-dollar, even if some degree of reciprocity is needed to ensure political support. Global agricultural prices are currently high, and thus programs of price guarantees are unspent. This provides a valuable window for farm reform, although it also removes the external pressure from third countries who don't like seeing developed world farmers subsidized when prices are lower.

Moreover, *it is not the case that US and EU farmers have nothing to gain from Doha*. The EU will provide substantial new export markets for which US farmers will be able to compete. EU farmers are already the biggest exporters in the world, and will have new access to markets for the boutique and high quality produce for which they have considerable comparative advantage. As importantly, the general boost to job creation and incomes in the developing world that would follow from an agreement has been shown to be a bigger determinant of growth in developed world farm exports as any reduction in developing world tariffs. When we create consumers in the developed world, we create customers for our produce.

It certainly makes no sense to make a Doha deal hostage neither to a few billion dollars of US trade distorting farm supports, nor to a maximum expectation of new market access for US farmers. Agriculture makes up 4.5% of US exports. Services and manufacturers make up 90%. Yet, as I write this, that is partly what is happening. Missing from the agriculture package in November 2007 was above all full clarity on the extent to which the US was willing to cut trade-distorting subsidies to its farmers. Despite a welcome US willingness to negotiate on the basis of a range that would see their current ceiling for expenditure fall to below $16.5 billion, sustained high global agricultural prices mean that even the cuts based on the middle of the proposed range would make no impact in current spending on trade distorting farm price guarantees. Based on average spending over the last decade, only a figure of around $15 billion would come close to looking like a real cut: understandably negotiators are looking for a commitment to aim low in the range. Yet the US is also understandably unwilling to table such a final move before the large emerging economies of the G20 provide more clarity on their willingness to cut into applied tariffs for non-agricultural goods.

The complex politics of development

This is the second part of the political log jam. The US is right that a small number of emerging developing countries will have to contribute to the outcome in real world terms. Most of the developing world will not be expected to cut any tariffs or provide any new market access in the Doha Round. This is the political expression of the concept of a development round, even if it is not necessarily based on the best development economics. But negotiators can and should expect limited and proportional cuts from the large emerging economies that are benefiting from the open global trading system. The idea that China or Brazil can expect to contribute nothing to a multilateral trade round in the same way as Benin or Burkina Faso might expect to contribute nothing is obviously untenable.

Yet the emerging economies continue to invoke developing world solidarity at a time when they are rapidly pulling away economically from the poorest economies in the global trading system. *Developed world negotiators and publics will not accept a trade agreement in which the booming emerging economies are perceived to contribute nothing.* But neither should those further down the development ladder. A trade deal that excludes the emerging economies would exclude new opportunities for trade amongst developing countries, which is not only the most protected trade in the global economy, but also a potential source of new economic growth.

In the area of industrial goods, the majority of the emerging economies, are, at most, being asked to bind their existing tariffs rather than lower them. The formula used to cut tariffs only applied to some thirty developing country members of the WTO. These countries were being asked for a modest contribution: bind most of their remaining unbound tariffs; reduce their peak tariffs; consolidate duties to the levels that are actually being applied; and for some countries and some sectors, make limited adjustments of 1 or 2% to the tariffs presently applied – over a period of ten years. For countries like India, that have unilaterally liberalized trade since the launch of the Round, there will be practically no real cuts. In other cases, where tariffs were bound at a very high level and little liberalization has in reality taken place since the end of the Uruguay Round, there will be modest cuts.

No one is arguing for full reciprocity, or in any way diminishing the huge development challenges that are faced in the emerging economies. But the emerging economies are export powerhouses, built on the openness of the international trading system. Some contribution that reflects that growing power and that expectation of openness in others is not unreasonable. *Doha will not be resolved unless the political question of the growing responsibility of the emerging economies is resolved.* Nor will the WTO be properly prepared for the changing politics of the multilateral trading system and future trade rounds, where the current developed world will have eliminated almost all border protection for industrial goods and today's emerging economies will inevitably find themselves on the other side of the table, faced with the demands of those less developed than themselves.

Conclusion: Doha in the balance

If Doha survives as you are reading this chapter, then both of these issues will have been resolved in one way or another. If the round should somehow carry on in stalemate, then its long-term prospects would have to be judged very poor. Even if the winter has passed with the successful agreement on modalities, there will remain significant challenges ahead. The US Presidential election cycle is not the best time to be closing and selling a major international trade agreement, especially one that will require the extension of the departing President's trade promotion authority. The Doha negotiations are complex and they lack a structured negotiating process. The risk of distraction and disengagement is high. *My hope is that political leadership will push negotiators out of entrenched positions and enable them to close the remaining distances.* If it will not, then the multilateral trading system is the worst for it.

1b

The future of the Doha Round after suspension in Geneva and deadlock in Potsdam: Is it all in vain?

CHIEDU OSAKWE[1]

The Doha Development Agenda (DDA) round of negotiations was suspended across the board *de facto* and *sine die* at the informal meeting of the Trade Negotiations Committee (TNC) on 24 July 2006. The General Council noted the suspension on 27 July. A 'soft resumption' was initiated at the technical level of trade negotiators on 16 November 2006. Full scale negotiations resumed in a so called 'hard resumption', based on political commitments emerging from a WTO Mini-Ministerial Meeting on the margins of the Davos World Economic Forum on 27 January 2007. But even with 'full scale' resumption, multilateral negotiating engagement was in slow motion and limbo until April 2007, as Members waited for the exploratory contacts amongst the G4 (Brazil, EU, India and US) to yield results and provide impetus for a breakthrough in modalities for agriculture and industrial products. The G4 process itself, however, ended in deadlock and failure at their Ministerial Meeting in Potsdam, Germany, on 21 June 2007. Prior to this past sequence of 'crisis, suspension and resumption' and 'G4 deadlock, failure and multilateral resumption', the broad pattern of progress in the Doha Round has been its fitful, uncertain and fluctuating evolution (see the Annex to this chapter – DDA Negotiations: 'Calendar of key events'). Neither the suspension nor the G4 Potsdam deadlock and failure will transform the state of the negotiations into *rigor mortis*. The fluctuating pattern of progress and setback is in the nature of trade negotiations. It is a long drawn-out challenging process, because a raft of domestic and multilateral factors intersect in

[1] This chapter was written in October 2006, and was heavily updated in October 2007. The author is grateful particularly to *Marc Auboin* and *Joan Apecu*, who commented on the draft of this chapter. The views expressed and positions taken in this chapter are those of the author and do not necessarily represent either the views of the Secretariat or of its Members.

tightly twisted knots, exacerbated by the effect of multiple audiences in the negotiations.

The negotiations effectively resumed in full multilateral engagement in September 2007 after the circulation of the draft modalities texts in agriculture and non-agricultural market access on 17 July 2007, just prior to the Northern summer break. Significant impetus was provided by the 9 September 2007 Sydney APEC Summit Statement on Trade. APEC Summit leaders, accounting for almost 50% of world trade, agreed to resume negotiations on the basis of the July draft texts in agriculture and non-agricultural market access. This provided a significant boost, signalling further progress.

World leaders understand that the Doha negotiations are more than a mere trade opening. They constitute part of the priority agenda for international co-operation and global order. WTO Members understand what is at stake. In spite of the serious difficulties, the complexity of the negotiations, and the risks associated with the recurring pattern of progress and setback, it is *certain that the negotiations will acquire momentum, and evolve to conclusion, although timing is uncertain.* The questions of 'timing' and 'level of ambition' are indeterminate. The timing is indeterminate because of constraints in more than one country. These constraints, whether they relate, for instance, to the uncertainty regarding renewal of Trade Promotion Authority, or to the content of the 2007 Farm Bill in the United States, or to the judicial decision by the European Court of Justice annulling the new support scheme for cotton,[2] or to comparable developments in any other Member, could constitute a drag on necessary domestic policy reforms and, hence, have strong implications for when the Round would be completed and the level of ambition in multilateral trade liberalisation.

Across the global economy, there is a gathering groundswell for the negotiations to accelerate, *overcome the unresolved issues and evolve to conclusion in the shortest possible time.* Ample evidence abounds. For instance, after the July 2006 suspension of the negotiations, the G20 agreed a 'Statement' on 9 September 2006 in Rio de Janeiro, Brazil, in which they called for the resumption of the negotiations. The force of the resumption call at the G20 Meeting in Rio was enhanced by the presence and participation of the EU, the United States, Japan, and the

[2] Press Release No68/06, 7 September 2006 (Judgment of the Court of Justice in Case C-310/04; *Kingdom of Spain* v. *Council of the European Union*): 'The Court of Justice Annuls The New Support Scheme for Cotton.'

representatives of the least-developed countries (LDCs), Small and Vulnerable Economies, the G33, the Cotton 4, and WTO Director-General Pascal Lamy. This is the leadership that is required. The conviction and determination in the call for resumption were comparable to similar moods in Doha in 2001 at the launch of the DDA itself. The Rio meeting was a strong indication that the resumption and conclusion of the negotiations are not in question. In September 2006 at the Annual Meetings of the World Bank and the IMF, the Development Community called on WTO Members to avoid backsliding and provide trade ministers with the necessary flexibility to resume negotiations by the end of the year;[3] while the IMF International Monetary and Financial Committee (IMFC) called for leadership from the major trading nations to work urgently toward an early resumption of the negotiations, and an ambitious, successful outcome by the end of the year.[4] These are not just optimistic assertions without justification.

At Heiligendamm, in a dedicated 'G8 Trade Declaration' on 8 June 2007, G8 Summit leaders provided strong endorsement for achieving an ambitious, balanced and comprehensive agreement on the DDA. They noted that intensified work could produce convergence to conclude the Round by the end of 2007. Although the deadlock and failure of G4 Trade Ministers occurred barely two weeks later in Potsdam, this latter development did not diminish the strong global consensus for the vital necessity of the DDA to expand global trade, enhance prosperity and reinforce the foundations of the rules-based trading system. Developing countries in particular appreciated the advantages of a rules-based multilateral trading system over and above one-on-one negotiating relationships with the major traders, for which they were apprehensive of the 'law of the jungle' where the strong prevail. This *global consensus on the importance of the DDA* notwithstanding the negotiating gains were strongly re-affirmed at the September APEC Summit in Sydney, Australia. Continuing evidence of policy statements at national and regional levels, demonstrates that the DDA is of collective vital interest in any effort to strengthen global order, promote prosperity, alleviate poverty and improve global governance.

Today, no WTO member questions that a major factor contributing to the growth in global incomes, wealth and prosperity, in the post-war period, have been greater openness, trade integration through successive

[3] Development Committee Communiqué, Singapore, 18 September 2006: paragraph 7.

[4] Communiqué of the International Monetary and Financial Committee of the Board of Governors of the IMF 17 September 2006, at para. 9.

rounds of negotiations. What is uncertain, at this stage, and with the bargaining twists and turns in the negotiations, will be the size of the final package. What will be the degree of ambition? *It is the size of the final package*– the extent of ambition, measured by new market opportunities, global welfare gains, strengthened rules with adequate flexibility for the weakest and the most vulnerable – which will enable an assessment to be made as to whether the round was worth the negotiating effort and the cost of participation, since its launch in 2001.

However, expectations on the final outcome must be tempered with realism and assessed, bearing in mind the Doha Round's pattern of 'progress and deadlock' in the negotiations. The details of the September/October 2007 negotiations in Agriculture and Non-Agricultural Market Access (NAMA) amongst Members illustrate the continuing uncertainty over the final package in the Round, although some judge that this is evidence of the death throes of the Round. In September 2007 in the Room E negotiating process on agriculture, the United States stated their acceptance of the range of between US$13–14.4 billion, for the reduction of Overall Trade Distorting Domestic Support (OTDDS), proposed by the Chairman of the Committee on Agriculture Special Session. This was a significant step forward in the agriculture negotiations. Although some wanted to see the specifics of the reduction to which the US would agree, the vast majority of Members welcomed the US acceptance of the range as the flexibility needed to advance the negotiations. The EU almost instantly proposed to match the US movement with commensurate higher cuts in agricultural tariffs. This created real progress, and also activated a momentum. However, at the 9 October 2007 General Council, a group of developing countries, tabled a proposal on Non-Agricultural Market Access (NAMA)[5] that effectively rejected the coefficient proposed for the reduction of tariffs on industrial products, by the Chairman of the Negotiating Group on NAMA. The US immediately responded that '. . . this proposal could signal the end of the Doha Round'. Assessed against the pattern of the Doha Round and the broader history of trade negotiations, even this particular development does not indicate that the Doha Development Agenda (DDA) will fail. To the contrary, it is further evidence of the difficulties confronting trade negotiators, and the brinkmanship they employ in order to secure what they consider the best possible bargain for their countries and coalitions.

[5] 'Elements of NAMA Modalities that meet the Ministerial Directions', submitted by the ACP Group, the African Group, the NAMA 11 Group of Developing Countries and Small Vulnerable Economies (SVEs), 9 October 2007.

Beyond the guesswork on the future of the Doha Round and conditional calculation about potential gains, there is a non-obvious fact, well worth underlining. There is intrinsic value even in the process of the negotiations *per se.* The proposals presented and the give and take in the course of the negotiations, have served an educational purpose for segments of the broader international community on the benefits of globalisation, coping with adjustment costs, and exposing the self-serving arguments of special interests. Paradoxically, the suspension and the recurrent pattern of progress and setback, with the ever-present, but unlikely risk of total collapse in the Doha negotiations have combined to burnish the value of the DDA. *Instances of crisis,* apparent deadlock, with associated risks of failure, *have led to bursts of considerable progress and created opportunities for yet further progress.*

Initial analysis is useful on the raft of reactions, positions and issues that emerged in relation to the suspension. Reactions ranged from alarm, to conclusions of the onset of a crisis, from varying assessments of its potential impact on the global economy, if it is prolonged and culminated in failure, to speculations regarding its impact on the WTO as an organisation and on the multilateral trading system. The scope of reactions included analysis on the prospects of resumption and the future of the negotiations. Opinions were offered on how to get it right the next time (as if a ready and applicable formula existed for complex trade negotiations). Retrospectively, some suggested that it was a monumental mistake to have named the round a 'Development Round', with others suggesting that the WTO should re-set and return to its core business, namely trade concessions and rule making. Questions have been raised on who was at fault, *a propos* the suspension. There are questions as well on the rationale and logic for suspension.

At this stage of the negotiations the *key objectives are to sort the issues, establish priorities, focus on the essentials in order to achieve a breakthrough* in the modalities for agriculture and non-agricultural market access before the end of 2007. Yet many have stated a need for initial analysis to gain an understanding of the reasons surrounding this pattern of deadlock and suspension, progress and stall, and for initial lessons to be drawn for the balance of the negotiations. *This chapter is an assessment of the negotiation at the current stage.* Any meaningful assessment should consider explanations of outcome, initial lessons drawn, and immediate to long-term prospects in terms of 'deliverables on the Table so far'. At this time and as the negotiations continue to evolve in uncertain ways, what initial primary lessons can be drawn from the July

2006 suspension, January 2007 resumption, and the June 2007 G4 Potsdam Ministerial deadlock and failure, barely a fortnight after the G8 Heiligendamm Summit had committed to conclude the Round by the end of 2007?

Several initial broad lessons can be drawn. First, there are lessons to be drawn from the composition and functioning of groups. Small groups and coalitions are critical parts of the negotiating process. They make effective contributions to process and substance. However, while the G4/G6[6] are 'major traders', significant and pre-eminent drivers of the negotiations, recovery from setbacks in the negotiations and progress towards conclusion can only be energized, not just by a few, or a group, but with the *involvement of the entire membership*. This has been characterised by Director-General Lamy as the 'Geneva, bottom-up, transparent multilateral process'. In the dynamic transformations of country and regional trade shares in the global trading system, multilateral trade policy making is non-substitutable. *All* regions and members have a role to play. Many developing countries still reel from their Uruguay Round negotiating experience from which they concluded that they had signed on to agreements to which they were hardly involved and barely understood. They are determined that this will not reoccur.

Second, the developments in the Doha Round have underlined with crystal clarity the *emergence of China (and India) as major global trading powers*. Without the full integration of China (and India) in the principal negotiating configurations, there will be no deal. It is awkward that China, the third largest trading power in the world, does not participate in meetings of the core drivers: the G6 circle. In a 2006 meeting with Chinese leaders, Director-General Lamy underlined the vital importance of a leadership role by China. The United States reinforced this call. Former WTO Director-General Peter Sutherland has pointed out that the era is long gone when a few developed countries could reach a deal and hand it out to the others for endorsement. This used to be the case. The negotiating inner circle of drivers of the negotiations requires widening. This widening of the circle to include the trade principals is necessary to avoid deadlock and fitful progress. The Statement by President Bush at the APEC Business Summit in Sydney, Australia, reflects an understanding that the days when a few countries could conclude a trade round are in the past. President Bush said: 'No Single

[6] Australia, Brazil, European Communities, India, Japan, and the United States.

Country can make Doha a success, but it is possible for a handful of countries that are unwilling to make the necessary contributions to bring Doha to a halt.'[7] This statement implied the limitations of the major traders, like the US and the EU, to conclude the Round, relative to their preponderant influence in the past in such groupings as the QUAD (US, EU, Japan and Canada).

Third, the *Doha Round will rise and fall on its development outcomes.* The cycle of progress, setback and progress has tended to revolve around divergent interpretations of the development update for the Round. In both form and substance, this is the immovable redline for developing countries, at the core of which is agriculture. Progress towards conclusion of the Round will depend on adhering to the development mandate and *staying the course on the agreed agenda in 2001*, on the basis of the Single Undertaking. Deviation from the 2001 mandate would magnify difficulties. The far-reaching parameters of the 2001 mandate were the price for the consensus to launch the round. The turnover of trade negotiators between Geneva and the capitals continue. But, the present negotiators need to know that chipping away at that mandate would undermine the prospects for a successful conclusion of the round by whatever degree of ambition.

Fourth, more than ever the Doha trade negotiations are entangled with international politics and the *backlash against globalisation.* In this regard, it also appears that although, future trade rounds will be needed to generate growth, check protectionist reversals and safeguard the rules-based system, it does appear that the easier stages of reducing trade barriers may be in the past. Areas in the negotiations with the knottiest challenges relate to agriculture and the behind the border regulatory non-tariff barriers. The going will be tougher not easier. Alan Greenspan argues that, 'In a sense, most of "the low-hanging fruit of trade openings has already been picked".'[8] He suggests that the rate of reducing barriers to trade will almost surely slow as the point is reached of intractable political resistance to further reductions. Mr. Greenspan concludes that: 'Trade liberalization has brought about significant lowering of barriers to movements in goods, services and capital flows. But further liberalization will come with increasing difficulty (as the Doha Round of trade

[7] Statement by President George W. Bush, at the Business Summit of the Sydney Opera House, Sydney, Australia, 7 September 2007.

[8] Greenspan, Alan, *The Age of Turbulence. Adventures in a New World*: (2007) New York: Penguin, p. 315.

negotiations demonstrated).[9] The almost normal pattern of evolution of multilateral trade negotiations is unstable and uncertain. It is almost certain that this pattern will tend to repeat, even as future trade liberalization will become more painful and slower. The solution is more and not less multilateral trade engagement.

What are the prospects? The negotiating pattern of suspension and re-engagement, deadlock and fitful progress carry risks, such as exhaustion, a long stall and limbo, evaporation of the negotiating consensus, modification of the structure and content, or outright failure. But it also carries with it a window of opportunity for rapid progress.

Failure is highly unlikely, although there is serious uncertainty regarding the level of ambition of the final package. If the past is to be of any guide, a rational assumption can be made that members understand what is at stake. Even though Director-General Lamy had been warning for months in advance of what was at stake and pointing to the cost of failure, the deadlock in the negotiations (on the fields of agriculture), still constituted a shock to the system. It was a wake up call. Even before the conclusion of the General Council meeting of 27 July 2006, the realisation finally dawned on the vast majority of the membership that the risk of outright failure could indeed transform into reality. Calculations of the potential cost of failure were made. In the sombreness of the 27 July 2006 General Council, the membership eventually grasped the full meaning of the conclusion by Director-General Lamy, after the decision on the suspension, that 'There are no winners and losers in this assembly. Today, there are only losers'. Before the conclusion of the General Council, individual Members and membership coalitions were already calling for the immediate resumption of the negotiations after the August 2006 summer recess. For instance, Benin, on behalf of the Cotton 4, proposed the resumption of the negotiations in September 2006. All through the month of August, calls for resumption increased from the Asia-Pacific region to Africa, from Europe to North America, South America and in the Caribbean Regional Negotiating Machinery.

Every now and then in the uncertain and fitful progress of the negotiations, Members have realised that they teeter on the edge of the precipice. At such moments, when they have gazed into the void, minds have focused. These cold assessments have not always energised them to leap over the chasm, but they have pulled back. The danger in this trade brinkmanship, is that *a mix of gravitational forces* from below (domestic

[9] *Ibid.*, p. 365.

level forces) are also at work. The risk certainly exists (albeit unlikely) that it could overwhelm the ability of the negotiators in the Geneva multilateral forum to orchestrate and control their actions. Working in favour of the Geneva actors, a better understanding has emerged of what is already on the table 'to be gained', if the negotiations conclude, or 'to be lost' if re-engagement becomes impossible, either due to the absence of leadership, or a lack of understanding of the global issues in question, or because of 'overwhelming' constraints posed by domestic policy interests.

Beyond initial lessons and implications of the 2006 suspension and the G4 Ministerial deadlock and failure is the frequently asked question of 'responsibility; who and what is responsible'. The responsibility for the failure of the negotiations to progress beyond the weekend of 22–23 July 2006 was collective. (This is not the moment to investigate the causes of failure.) But, it would only be someone who has not observed the entrenched positions, or followed the twists and turns, the flanking manoeuvres and counter proposals in the negotiations since 2002 (when effective negotiations began) who could reach a different conclusion. The *cul de sac* in the negotiations and the *decision to suspend were the consequence of a 'collective responsibility'.* This almost 'confessional' expression in the position of several Members at the 27 July Council augurs well for the resumption of the negotiations. It demonstrated the understanding that assigning blame to individual members would neither be 'truthful' nor prudent and that acceptance of a collective responsibility in the consensus building process was *sine qua non* for progress in concluding the negotiations. Yet, there were also specific factors that caused suspension and deadlock. The entrenched positions, the twists and turns, the flanking manoeuvres and counter proposal strategies in the negotiations since 2002 (when effective negotiations began) demonstrate degrees of specific responsibility.

What is currently on the table?

As the Chairman of the TNC, Director-General Lamy has frequently pointed out, significant progress has been made across the board in the negotiations: 'what is already on the table today is potentially worth two to three times more than in previous rounds, whether for developed or for developing countries'. *Several areas of progress are illustrative. In agriculture,* it was agreed in the Hong Kong Ministerial Declaration to eliminate all forms of export subsidies by 2013, ensure that no loopholes exist for continuing subsidisation, and to have effective disciplines on in-kind food aid, monetisation and re-exports as part of modalities. Ministers also agreed to establish a 'safe box' for bona fide food aid, so that the rules do not impede food aid for emergency situations. As difficult and as sensitive as the negotiations on the market access and domestic support pillars remain, demonstrable progress has been made. On the market access pillar of agriculture, there was progress, *inter alia*, with the agreement for four bands for tariff reductions, and the need to converge on relevant thresholds for developed and developing countries. Members also agreed on self-designation for Special Products for developing countries, guided by the criteria of food security, livelihood security and rural development. Further progress was made in the negotiations in September 2007 based on the 17 July 2007 draft modalities text on agriculture. Members engaged with seriousness of purpose to examine and seek to clarify several specific market access details. These ranged over such complex issues as defining sensitive products, designation of special products, the Special Safeguard Mechanism (SSM), tropical and diversification products, tariff escalation, erosion of preference margins, and commodities. Two examples are illustrative. On sensitive products, negotiators are exploring a definition based on 'domestic consumption' (a Cairns Group proposal) and also on 'additional methodologies' (proposed by the EC). In the discussions on Special Products (SPs), enhanced co-operative search for a solution is reflected in the fact that even developing countries, themselves the proponents of SPs, are objectively pointing to the consequences and shortcomings of certain amongst the twelve indicators developed by the G33 countries.[10] Although complex, slow and painful, the negotiations continue to evolve positively. On domestic support at the 2005 Hong Kong Ministerial meeting, there was agreement on three bands for subsidy cuts (in respect of final bound Aggregate Measures of Support – AMS – and overall Trade Distorting Support cuts), with the EU in the top band, the US and Japan in the middle band and all the rest that have to cut domestic support in the last band. In addition, thresholds have been sorted out for the bands. On this, the most intractable of negotiating areas, the progress already made, in 2005 was given significant boost by United States acceptance of the range of between US$13–16.4 billion, proposed by the Chairman of the Committee on Agriculture Special Session in July 2007, for the reduction

[10] Job(07)/35: Committee on Agriculture Special Session: 'G33 Contribution on the Indicators Guiding the Designation of any Agricultural Product as a Special Product (SP) by any Developing Country Member', 27 March 2007.

of Overall Trade Distorting Domestic Support (OTDS). This should not be underestimated. Although conditional on commensurate movements in agricultural market access, tariff cuts in industrial products and improvements in services offers, it represented a departure from the US proposal of October 2005 (before the Hong Kong Ministerial Conference), when they proposed a cap of US$22.3 billion for US domestic support. The negotiating frontiers in agriculture have been pushed beyond any level previously achieved. Nonetheless, the bottleneck that remains is the proportion of the cuts in domestic support and tariffs, and of course the treatment and percentage of tariff lines to be covered under sensitive products.

The *cotton dossier* has emerged as a test of the development outcomes from the Doha negotiations. The mandate provides for the cotton dossier to be addressed on two tracks: the trade policy and the development assistance aspects. The trade policy aspects, which are being addressed under the Single Undertaking, within the Agriculture Negotiations, also registered progress. In the Hong Kong Declaration, Ministers agreed that all forms of export subsidies for cotton would be eliminated by developed countries in 2006; developed countries would provide duty- and quota-free market access for cotton exports from least-developed countries (LDCs) from the start of the implementation period for the agreed reform in agriculture. Ministers also agreed that trade distorting domestic support for cotton production would be reduced more ambitiously than for whatever agreed general formula to be implemented, and over a shorter period of time than generally applicable. The US September 2007 acceptance to work within the range of US$13–16.4 billion proposed, by the Chairman of the Special Session of the Committee on Agriculture, for the reduction of trade distorting domestic support, improved the prospects for a more 'ambitious and specific treatment', as mandated, for the reduction of commodity-specific support for cotton. However, in the continued absence of specific US counter proposals for reduction of domestic support for cotton, the current draft modalities reflect the proposal by the Cotton 4 for an approximate reduction of 82.4% in domestic support based on the cotton correction co-efficient in the proposed formula[11] On the

[11] $$(Rc = Rg + \frac{(100 - Rg) * 100}{3 * Rg}$$

Rc = Specific reduction applicable to cotton as a percentage (the correction coefficient).
Rg = General reduction in AMS as a percentage.
JOB(07)/128: Draft Modalities for Agriculture, 17 July 2007.

development assistance aspects, measurable progress has been made. In quantum and value terms, this is reflected in the commitments for development assistance by the bilateral and multilateral development communities in support of the cotton sector in the Cotton 4 and other African cotton producing and trading countries. At this time, the implementation focus on cotton development assistance is to bridge the wide gaps between donor 'commitments' on the one hand, and actual 'disbursements' on the other hand; accelerate operational follow through; encourage faster domestic sectoral reforms in the recipient countries and, to better synchronise the 'Geneva multilateral process' on cotton development assistance with the 'in-country bilateral process' in the recipient countries.

In Non-Agricultural Market Access (NAMA), Members adopted a Swiss formula (which would cut higher tariffs more). The understanding exists and the proposed July 2007 draft modalities reflect a two co-efficient 'simple-Swiss formula' approach, although there is no agreement yet on the actual coefficients for the reduction of NAMA tariffs, either for developed or for developing countries. Members also agreed on a non-linear mark-up approach for unbound tariffs to determine the base rates for purposes of applying the formula. The non-mandatory nature of sectorals was also clarified by Members in Hong Kong.

In the services negotiations, progress has been made, although wide scope exists for further progress. Pursuant to the Hong Kong Ministerial mandate, Members have intensified and expedited their work using the bilateral request–offer approach as the main method of the negotiations, but also in addition pursuing negotiations on a plurilateral basis. Work has advanced considerably on all three fronts of market access, rules, and special and differential treatment. Assessments of the plurilateral request process have been positive so far. The Hong Kong Declaration also provided a new impetus to the implementation of the LDC modalities for services negotiations and work is proceeding on this front too. The positive evolution of progress is reflected in the prospects for improved commitments in such sectors as banking and insurance, computer services and communications and express delivery. At this stage of the negotiations, there appears to be an essential convergence on the *need for a Services text* (to correspond to the evolution of the negotiations in agriculture and non-agricultural market access). The Chairman of the Council for Trade in Services Special Session has been asked to produce such a text, although a few Members have reservations and have raised questions about the 'necessity' for such a text. This draft text shall be governed by Annex C of the Hong Kong Ministerial Declaration,[12] the least-developed countries modalities for services liberalisation, and by the mandates for the negotiations on General Agreement on Trade in Services (GATS) rules, and domestic regulations. This process is underway in the '*Enchilada Consultations*' by the Chair of the Services negotiations. Characterising the negotiations are the different areas of emphasis between Service *demandeurs*, on the one hand, and developing country groups, on the other. While the former (EC, US, Canada, Japan, Australia, Korea and Hong Kong) negotiate to ensure that the draft Services text reflects a statement on the 'level of ambition' in the services negotiations, the latter (ASEAN, SVEs, African Group, South Africa, China) push for the mandatory parameter of 'progressive liberalisation' and flexibility.

In the rules negotiations, even as the negotiations were in the throes of a crisis in July 2006, Members approved a Decision establishing a Transparency Mechanism for Regional Trade Agreements (RTAS) to be implemented on a provisional basis. This Decision would enable early announcement of an agreement by parties to an RTA. Ministers in Hong Kong mandated the Chairman of the Rules Negotiating Group to prepare consolidated texts in the areas of anti-dumping and subsidies that would be the basis for the final stage of the negotiations. Work in the rules area – anti-dumping and subsidies (including fisheries subsides) – has registered significant progress, although like other areas of the negotiations, progress has been affected by the pace in the linked areas of agriculture and Non-Agricultural Market Access. Nonetheless, at the July 2007 meeting of the Trade Negotiations Committee (TNC), the Chairman of the Rules Negotiating Group announced his intention to circulate texts around the same period that revised texts in agriculture and Non-Agricultural Market Access would be circulated.

Work has advanced rapidly and positively in the *area of trade facilitation*, which holds one of the biggest development pay-offs from the Round. This is an area of the negotiations where developed and developing countries have formed partnerships in presenting proposals. Substantive progress had been made and a compilation of text-based proposals which would form the basis of an eventual agreement had been circulated to Members.[13] Uncertainty on the broader setting of the negotiations (dependent on the Agriculture/NAMA relationship) has not enabled full

[12] Annex C of the Hong Kong Ministerial Declaration sets out the objectives, approaches and time lines for progressively higher levels of services liberalisation.

[13] See *Hohmann*, chapter 8 in this book.

acceleration on the Trade Facilitation negotiations. Nonetheless, Trade Facilitation remains the best example of developed/developing countries co-operation in the Doha negotiations.

Significant and positive progress was made at the Hong Kong Ministerial on *the development aspects* of the negotiations. These include the agreement on the five LDC's Agreement-specific proposals on Special and Differential Treatment; of which the most important was the Decision to grant duty- and quota-free (DFQF) market access to all LDC's products by 2008. There was the proviso that those who found it difficult to provide DFQF for all products, should do so, at least, for 97% of LDCs products, with progressive steps to achieve compliance.

In other areas of negotiations, even though intensive work has been undertaken, the work so far and the possibility for any further progress, all have been held in suspension. These include the areas of anti-dumping, fishing subsidies, and the reduction, or as appropriate, elimination of tariffs and non-tariff barriers on environmental goods and services, dispute settlement and TRIPS.

The concrete advances in the negotiations, in spite of the outstanding issues, are by no means minimal. In several areas, they *are substantial and far-reaching*. All this should not be in vain and should not unravel. It is highly unlikely that members will allow this happen.

Aid for Trade is an area where work has forged ahead and which has not been adversely affected by the fluctuating pattern of progress and setback in the DDA. Work has proceeded pursuant to the mandate in paragraph 57 of the Hong Kong Ministerial Declaration. Much progress has been made. Impetus was provided by the pledges in Hong Kong made by Japan, the United States and the European Union (EU) and its Member States. The Aid for Trade Task Force, established by the Director-General at the February 2006 General Council, met its July 2006 deadline by submitting its recommendations to the Council on the two issues of 'how to operationalise Aid for Trade', and 'how it might effectively contribute to the development dimensions of the DDA'. The recommendations were considered and adopted by Members at the October 2006 Council. Since then, Aid for Trade implementation has evolved with positive rapidity. Three Aid for Trade Regional Review, co-ordinated with the relevant Regional Development Banks and the World Bank, were organised in Latin America (Lima, Peru, 13–14 September 2007), Asia (Manila, Philippines, 19–20 September 2007), and Africa (Dar es Salaam, Tanzania, 1–2 October 2007). The results from these regional reviews will be pulled together at the Annual Global Aid for Trade Review, in the WTO General

Council, 20–21 November 2007. *Aid for Trade is a major step forward.* It has been eminently successful in raising the level of awareness on such critical issues as the imperative of trade infrastructure, providing for the adjustment costs that result from trade liberalisation, and the necessity to reflect trade priorities in national development plans. The latter contribution built on the original idea of the Integrated Framework for 'trade mainstreaming'. Nonetheless, questions still abound about whether Aid for Trade provides 'additionality'. There are still questions about the 'newness' of the concept.[14] There are those who still express the position that it offers nothing new beyond what previously existed. *Aid for Trade implementation is in parallel with the enhancement of the Integrated Framework for the Least-developed countries.* The recommendations for an Integrated Framework are being implemented. The purpose is to enhance the capacity of least-developed countries to mainstream trade into their strategies for poverty reduction or development plans. A Pledging Conference was held for the Enhanced Integrated Framework for LDCs in September 2007 in Stockholm, Sweden. About US$170 million was pledged by twenty-two out of thirty-eight donors over the five-year period 2007 to 2011. A target of US$250 million had been set.

The challenge posed by adjustment costs has been highlighted in the Doha negotiations, much more than in previous rounds. This in itself has been valuable in the sense that members now understand the usefulness in providing assistance to cope with the challenge of some of the transitional costs attendant on multilateral liberalisation. The Aid for Trade mandate is in part an implicit acceptance of this need for a multilateral response. Individual Members now also better understand that multilateral trade liberalisation, own domestic reform and the process of change *per se*, entail costs. A valuable aspect of the discussions in the Aid for Trade Task Force has been greater awareness of coping with adjustment costs. Domestically, countries that embark on policy reforms for growth, better understand that national fiscal outlays are required to cover the costs of adjustments (for instance on the model of the United States Trade Adjustment Assistance). It is essential for national development plans to appropriately account for the distribution of adjustment costs across various sectors, and to re-allocate resources from the uncompetitive to the more dynamic sectors for accelerated growth.

[14] 2007 African Economic Outlook, (AEO), Development Centre of the Organization for Economic Co-operation and Development and African Development Bank, (OECD/African Development Bank), 2007 p. 26.

The Doha Development Agenda (DDA) *is part of a broader global agenda for international co-operation for development.* This fact was evident in the unanimous position by participants at the Johannesburg World Summit on Sustainable Development (WSSD) in 2002, in which over 100 Heads of State and Government participated. At that Summit, there was recognition of the importance of the DDA alongside other global policy priority agenda which had been set, particularly the Rio Declaration on the Environment; the Monterrey Consensus on Financing for Development (FFD); and, the Millennium Development Goals (MDGs). The DDA is now so very firmly wedged into the agenda of broader international cooperation that failure is unlikely, although the outcome of the final package is uncertain.

There is greater appreciation of the fact *that a delayed conclusion, or even an unlikely failure, would entail foregone welfare gains*, efficiency losses, the loss of the opportunity to re-balance the rules and achieve greater rule transparency and predictability, in several areas. Worse, it would erode multilateralism, undermine the prospects of future co-operation and indirectly darken the pall on a current geopolitical environment, which reflect few silver linings. It would be a hard sell for the major trading powers to credibly promote international co-operation for sustainable trade development, if they fail to deliver on the DDA.

In discussing trade and development, *Africa* always deserves special mention. The greatest risks for stalled or failed negotiations would weigh heavily, particularly against Africa and other least developed, and low-income economies. In the past five years, economic performance in Sub-Saharan Africa has been very encouraging. The 2007 African Economic Outlook, jointly prepared by the OECD and the African Development Bank, report that Africa as a whole exhibited real GDP growth. The Continent experienced the highest economic growth in the last two decades. GDP growth rate averaged nearly 5% in the past six years and is expected to attain 6% in 2007 and remain buoyant in 2008. However, this growth still falls short of the 7%–8% essential for achieving the Millennium Development Goal (MDG) of halving poverty by 2015.[15] In spite of this overall positive picture, the picture is varied for individual African economies. Furthermore, there are continuing risks and challenges for growth and expansion in the global economy, which would

[15] 2007 African Economic Outlook (AEO), Development Centre of the Organization for Economic Co-operation and Development, and the African Development Bank, (OECD/African Development Bank), 2007 pp. 13, 30–1.

affect Africa, such as the rise in energy costs and tightening credit triggered by the sub-prime crisis in the US. The situation in many African countries remains precarious and dire, for a variety of reasons. Stalled or failed negotiations would exacerbate the difficulties, deepen poverty, and increase the risk of slowing their integration into the multilateral trading system and the global economy.

An area that points to the risks is the *noticeable increase in the recent spurt of activities for Free Trade Areas (FTAs)*. Comparable to the behaviour by the more dynamic trading countries after the November 2003 failure of the Cancún Ministerial Conference, the immediate aftermath of the 27 July 2006 suspension of the Doha negotiations similarly witnessed suggestions, proposals and an intensified flurry of efforts to negotiate bilateral trade agreements and establish FTAs. Three examples are illustrative. First, Fred Bergsten proposed a Free Trade Area of the Asia Pacific (FTAAP). Such an FTA would embrace the twenty-one Members of the Asia Pacific Economic Co-operation (APEC). It would account for over half of the world economy, and almost half of world trade in goods and services. Second, Japan is in the process of negotiating a free trade arrangement with ASEAN, and at the same time has also proposed the creation of a sixteen-nation free trade zone that would include the ten Members of ASEAN,[16] with China, India, Australia, South Korea, New Zealand and Japan itself. Such a free trade zone would have a total population of 3.1 billion people and a GDP of approximately US$10 trillion a year. ASEAN already has free trade agreements with China and South Korea. Third, in this evolving scenario, initial steps have already been taken, in some cases, for what could possibly lead to the establishment of such FTAs. For example, the US recently signed a Trade and Investment Framework Agreement (TIFA) with ASEAN on 25 August 2006. Significantly, the US has negotiated FTAs, *inter alia*, with Colombia, Panama and South Korea in 2007. These three remain subject to Congressional decision and passage.

There has been an underlying *dual motivation in this rush to conclude bilateral agreements and FTAs*. First, it has been claimed that such agreements, although yet to be corroborated, could trigger a momentum for 'competitive liberalisation' that directly or indirectly would re-vamp multilateral trade negotiations and the system itself, when such negotiations run out of steam. In this strain, it has been argued, in respect of

[16] Brunei, Cambodia, Indonesia, Laos, Malaysia, Burma, Singapore, Thailand, the Philippines and Vietnam.

APEC, for instance, that it could generate much stronger inducement for countries outside APEC to restore the multilateral track; because a broader group of countries would be jolted into supporting the global approach. Second, and more muted, is the motivation that these agreements are sought as 'insurance policies', by the proponents, in the event that multilateral trade negotiations for deeper and more encompassing trade opening either stall for the long term, or fail, or deliver insufficiently ambitious outcomes. Nobody now believes that any preferential agreement in any free trade area could ever deliver ambitious outcomes in agriculture. To deliver ambitious outcomes in agriculture and to strengthen trade rules, *all efforts would have to focus on the multilateral process in Geneva.*

Regardless of the motivation, the fact which should be *of concern for Africa and other low-income economies* is that they are essentially *not part* of these more robust proposals for free trade arrangements with the most dynamic regions and countries in the global economy. A pattern of free trade areas amongst and between the most dynamic economies, would slow the integration of the weaker and more vulnerable countries into the global economy. Apart from the likelihood of the potentially marginalising effect for Africa of free trade areas amongst the more robust economies, there are also the difficulties associated with overlapping and inconsistent free trade areas. Multilateral trade negotiations and outcomes still remain the first best option in the strategies by African countries and the least-developed countries to eliminate barriers to their trade and growth. The cotton issue is without doubt a sharp example.

The good news is that the past six years have made clear a *change in Africa's attitudes to the Round.* The original ambivalence, discomfort and in some cases strong opposition to the efforts to launch in 1999 and later to the Round itself after the launch in 2001, have now given way to Africa's advocacy for an ambitious outcome to a Round that yields significant development pay-offs. When the Director-General met with African Trade Ministers at the African Conference of Trade Ministers in Nairobi in April 2006, they strongly advocated with Director-General Lamy the urgent necessity for an early conclusion of the Round. They were fully supportive of the change in gear by the Director-General to wrap up the Round sooner rather than later. In January 2007, African Heads of State and Government expressed their deep concern and disappointment over the July 2006 suspension and called 'for a prompt resumption and a speedy and successful conclusion of the Doha Round, with its development dimensions given high priority . . .'.[17] Africa also has a leadership role to play. This role needs to be stepped up.

The gains from multilateral trade liberalisation within the set parameters of the DDA mandate would generate more resources for Africa (and other low income economies). The gains would be more significant than compared to conditioned and frequently unpredictable development assistance. Trade commitments to greater openness and liberalisation would enhance the prospects of foreign investment flows. All the analysis so far clearly shows that African countries in particular, would stand to gain considerably from the conclusion and implementation of a *Trade Facilitation Agreement.* At the same time, it needs to be pointed out that a Trade Facilitation Agreement has to be complemented by significant financial resources to produce effective gains at the borders. A successfully and ambitiously concluded DDA would increase efficiency, stimulate greater competitive impetus, and introduce new ideas across borders, with gains in productivity. This should happen, *inter alia*, because new trade rules and expansion in market opportunities would create positive pressure to assist in locking in reforms in those African countries that have embarked on serious and sustained programmes of domestic policy reforms. And here the point is obvious: complementary policies are required for trade opening to work. Trade liberalisation is not a stand-alone magic policy that reduces poverty and conjures up development.

There is *a need to distinguish between the future of the 'Doha negotiations' and 'the future of the WTO'* as an organisation, which is the anchor of the multilateral trading system. Frequently, some have conflated the 'future of the Doha negotiations' with 'the future of the organization'. While there is a relationship, both should be distinguished. Although there is a degree of uncertainty with the 'future of the Doha Development Round' because of the risks associated with the suspension and its causes, *the 'future of the WTO' itself, is not in jeopardy.* Undoubtedly, the organisation and the multilateral trading system would be strengthened and their credibility enhanced with a successful outcome from the DDA. But fatal consequences would not follow for the Organization and the multilateral trading system, in the unlikely event that the Doha negotiations completely unravel or stall for the long

[17] Declaration on WTO Negotiations, African Union (AU) Assembly Heads of State and Government, 29–30 January 2007 (Assembly/AU/Dec.134–164(VIII); and, Assembly/AU/Decl.l. 1 – 6(VIII)).

term. The Organization is an indispensable pillar of the architecture for international co-operation. If it did not exist, there would be a necessity to create it. *Successive cycles of trade negotiations have been necessary for traction and impetus to trade expansion, increased global welfare, keeping protectionism at bay, and ensuring the smooth functioning of the rules-based system.* At this stage, however, existing rules and the dispute settlement system would provide a modicum of stability in the system and provide for continuing trade expansion, even with an uncompleted Round. As noted by several observers, although its credibility would be affected with uncertainty, the WTO would survive and thrive. It will remain essential as a forum for trade negotiations (even in the context of an on-going Round, or a Round held in abeyance). The Organization will continue with the implementation of existing rules, resolution of trade disputes, and managing the integration of acceding members and recently acceded members. The strong varied impact on the global economy of China, India and Brazil, also indicate the necessity of the WTO for managing the rapid dynamic economic transformations of these emergent trade powers. The WTO's function in increasing the transparency and understanding of country's trade policies and practices, by regular monitoring through its Trade Policy Review Mechanism, is another important function. There should be no angst about the future of the WTO. Its existence as a pillar in the architecture of international cooperation will hold, even if the outcome of the Doha Round remains uncertain and indeterminate.

After six years of negotiations, from initial lesson drawn and explanations of particular outcomes, what explains this overall fluctuating pattern of 'progress and failure', 'crisis and deadlock', 'suspension and resumption'? There are many factors in interplay.

A careful review of the facts since 1999 suggests that at the core are the divergent interpretations of the content of a development round, *the aggressive resistance of domestic policy interests* against a perceived increasingly 'intrusive' multilateral trading system that is restrictive of domestic policy space, and the inability of many individual countries to translate global welfare gains from trade liberalisation into individual country benefits that exceed adjustment costs. Variant notions of 'fairness' considerations from previous trade rounds and the current negotiations, with a fundamentally changed negotiating environment have intervened as complicating factors. Explaining the fortunes of the Doha Round also entails an understanding of the technical complexity of the negotiations and significant shifts in contemporary international relations. These factors have played out over the entire Doha Round negotiating agenda. They have influenced group membership and motivated the politics of various changing coalitions. They largely explain the insistence and opposition over issues, and consequently the fluctuating fortunes in the negotiations.

Solutions exist. Overcoming these difficulties will require individual members explicitly linking serious and sustained programmes for domestic policy reforms with multilateral negotiations for trade liberalisation. Domestic reform processes would need to better spread the gains and costs from trade opening across domestic constituencies, including through adjustment assistance as part of annual budgetary processes. Domestic processes for economic policy reform were never designed to work in synchrony with multilateral negotiations for trade reform. Yet, this absence of a lock-step relationship has tended to generate friction, trigger stalls, and explain the swings between progress and slow-down, setback and failure, crisis suspension and resumption of the Doha negotiations. Ignoring the connection between the timing and content of domestic economic processes and multilateral negotiations will be fatal. Wider scope for flexible domestic sequencing of multilateral trade commitments will be necessary because of the low likelihood of success in synchronising different domestic processes with multilateral trade commitments. Steady progress will require a strong, activist and committed pro-reform leadership by the major trading powers and, indeed, by all Members. This leadership will need to face down special interests, at timed moments. Progress in multilateral trade negotiations and stability in the rules-based trading system, will also require the WTO Membership to institutionalise and accept the role of the Director-General as advocate, mediator and arbiter of last resort in the negotiations, particularly at those moments when Members checkmate themselves in the negotiations. The Director-General's role should also be strengthened to actively implement a structured and coordinated agenda for policy coherence with the international financial institutions. Frequently, Members will find themselves in impossible negotiating positions, for a variety of reasons. They will need an impartial, objective and technically sound arbiter to break the logjam. Director-General Lamy has played this role. Progress points in this direction. Along these lines, the conditional gains, the efforts so far and the experience acquired would not be in vain.

Annex 1: DDA Negotiations: Calendar of key events

Events	*Date*
Doha Ministerial Declaration: Launch of the DDA Round[18]	14 November 2001
1st TNC Meeting and establishment of negotiating bodies	1 February 2002
G8 Evian Summit 'Enlarged Dialogue'[19]	1 June 2003[20]
10th TNC Meeting – Burkina Faso President addresses TNC on Cotton	10 June 2003
Decision on TRIPS Agreement and public health	30 August 2003
5th WTO Ministerial Meeting, Cancún, Mexico	10–14 September 2003
G8 Sea Island Summit statement on trade[21]	21 June 2004
1 August 2004 General Council Decision – 'The July Package'[22]	1 August 2004
Establishment of the sub-committee on cotton (SCC)	19 November 2004
G8 Gleneagles Summit paragraphs on the DDA[23]	8 July 2005
6th WTO Ministerial Meeting, Hong Kong, China	13–18 December 2005
Initial Draft Modalities on agriculture and non-agricultural market access	22 June 2006[24]
G8 St Petersburg Summit (Trade outreach session)	17 July 2006
Suspension of Doha Negotiations at informal TNC	24 July 2006
Suspension *noted* by General Council	27 July 2006
Technical/Soft resumption – Informal TNC	16 November 2006
Davos WTO Mini-Ministerial: Political commitment to full/hard resumption of negotiations	27 January 2007
G4 +/− process: Exploratory contacts, but multilateral negotiations in limbo	30 Jan – 7 May 2007
WTO high-level session on cotton[25]	15–16 March 2007
G4 +/− Process: ministerial meeting, New Delhi, India[26]	13 April 2007
Informal TNC – Statement by DG: 'Multilateral process can't wait'.	20 April 2007

[18] WTO/MIN(01)/DEC/1, Ministerial Declaration, Doha, adopted 14 November 2001.

[19] Summit Document: 'Cooperative G8 Action on Trade'.

[20] Prior to the 2003 G8 Evian, France Summit, Director-General Mike Moore participated in the Rome/Genoa G8 Summit, 19–21 July 2001, to make a case relevant to the launch of the Round.

[21] WT/L/576: G8 Leaders' Statement on Trade. Sea Island Summit 2004.

[22] WT/L/579, Decision Adopted by the General Council on 1 August 2004.

[23] The Gleneagles Communiqué, signed version of 8 July 2005: paragraphs: 21, 22(a) and 35.

[24] TN/AG/W/3.

[25] See High Level Session, 15–16 March 2007 – Director-General's Summary Remarks (TN/AG/SCC/W/7). Also see 'Director-General's Evolving Working Table on Cotton Development Assistance', WT/L/684.

[26] TN/C/9: G4 Ministers' Letters Commitment to conclude the Doha Round in 2007.

Annex 1: DDA Negotiations: Calendar of key events (*cont.*)

Events	*Date*
Circulation of agriculture 'First Challenges' paper by Chairman Committee on Agriculture Special Session/ Sub-committee on Cotton[27]	30 April 2007
Circulation of the agriculture 'Second Challenges' paper by Chairman Committee on Agriculture Special Session/Sub-committee on Cotton	25 May 2007
Emergence of bipartisan US trade policy	10 May 2007
G4 process – Brussels Ministerial Meeting (New Delhi Follow-up)	16–17 May 2007
G8 Summit, Heiligendamm, Germany: 'G8 Trade Declaration'	6–8 June 2007
G4 Ministerial in Potsdam, Germany – Deadlock and failure	19–21 June 2007
Draft Modalities texts for agriculture[28] and NAMA[29] negotiations	17 July 2007
Fifteenth APEC Economic Leaders Meeting: 'Statement on the WTO Negotiations',[30] Sydney, Australia	9 September 2007
US acceptance, in 'Room E Process', to work on basis of CoA SS Chairman's proposed range for reducing overall trade distorting domestic support (OTDS) to between US$13–16.4 billion[31]	
EU proposal to match US with commensurate cuts in agriculture tariffs	20 September 2007
ACP + NAMA-11 + African Group + SVE General Council Proposal rejecting NAMA draft modalities paper by Chairman NAMA Negotiating Group	9 October 2007

[27] Discussions of this 'First Challenges Paper', which began on 7 May, signalled full multilateral resumption of 'Geneva, bottom-up, transparent and inclusive process'.

[28] JOB(07)/128: Draft Modalities for Agriculture, 17 July 2007. (Committee on Agriculture, Special Session).

[29] JOB(07)/126: Draft NAMA Modalities (Negotiating Group on Market Access).

[30] APEC Doha Round Statement notably agreed, *inter alia*, 'to resume negotiations on the basis of the draft texts tabled by the chairs of the negotiating groups on agriculture and non-agricultural market access'. APEC economies account for nearly 50% of world trade.

[31] USTR Ambassador Susan Schwab confirmed US acceptance on 4 October, with further precision that acceptance was conditional on others agreeing to commensurate reductions in agricultural tariffs and tariffs for non-agricultural products.

PART ONE

Development policy of the WTO

2

Developmental aspects of the Doha Round of negotiations

WTO SECRETARIAT (*):

I. Introduction

1. At the 54th Session of the Committee on Trade and Development (CTD) on 5 October 2005, Members undertook a review of the developmental aspects of the Doha Round of negotiations based on a background paper prepared by the Secretariat (WT/COMTD/W/143). Discussions continued at the 55th Session on November 28 2005 and the 58th Session on July 6 2006 based on revised versions of the background paper (WT/COMTD/W/143/Rev.1 and Rev.2 respectively). The usefulness of periodic updates to the paper has been widely recognized by Members.

2. The present chapter addresses the developmental aspects in all the subject areas under negotiation in the Round. In addition to providing a brief summary of the status of the negotiations in each area,[1] the chapter attempts to highlight the broad parameters of the development dimension, to identify specific issues of interest to developing countries and to describe the potential gains which could accrue to developing countries from the conclusion of the negotiations. This revised chapter has been prepared under the Secretariat's own responsibility and by no means claims to provide an exhaustive coverage of all the developmental aspects raised in the course of the negotiations. Nor should the chapter be seen as an attempt to prioritize issues, subjects or concerns raised by individual Members or groups of Members. Finally, this paper does not prejudice the right of any Member to raise other concerns or views related to

(*) Reproduced in part from: WTO, Committee on Trade and Development, Document of May 22 2007, WT/COMTD/W143/Rev.3 , by kind permission of the WTO Secretariat.

[1] Relative to an earlier version, the present document takes into account developments in the negotiations up to the end of March 2007.

paragraph 51 of the Doha Ministerial Declaration or the presentation below concerning the areas currently under negotiation in the Doha Development Agenda.

II. Developmental aspects of the Doha development agenda negotiations

A. Agriculture

1. Parameters of the development dimension

3. Agriculture plays an important role in the development of many WTO Members. For a large number of developing and least-developed countries, agriculture makes a significant contribution to their economies, including its direct contribution to gross domestic production, export revenue and employment as well as to rural development and livelihood security. However, many of the world's agricultural producers are currently disadvantaged in the world trading environment because of high tariff barriers and competition from producers that receive high levels of domestic or export-related support. Therefore, a reduction in protection and support can lead to important gains for developing country agricultural producers. The development aspects related to agriculture can be found in each of the three pillars of the agriculture negotiations – market access, domestic support and export competition.

(a) Market access 4. The market access pillar is arguably the most complex and intricate pillar of the agriculture negotiations. Some Members see a link between market access and flexibilities, in particular that an increase in flexibilities (defensive interests) leads to a curtailing of market access (offensive interests). In this regard, the August 1 2004 General Council Decision (WT/L/579) is a delicate balance of the offensive and defensive interests of all Members. Despite its complex nature, the market access pillar has, arguably, the greatest potential to deliver real economic benefits to Members. As tariff barriers are reduced and tariff rate quotas expanded in both developed and developing countries, increased market access opportunities will allow Members to improve welfare by expanding export volumes and revenues and through better access to their markets for imports, while taking account of the sensitivities and development goals in developing countries.

5. A significant reduction in tariffs and the expansion of tariff quotas,

particularly in developed country markets, is being sought by many developing countries in order to assist with the achievement of their development and other trade-related objectives. In addition, some Members also view the reduction of tariff escalation and the implementation of the long-standing commitment to the fullest liberalization of trade in tropical products as being key elements of the development dimension of the Doha Round. At the same time, many developing countries are concerned about the likely impact of tariff reductions on rural livelihood, and consequently on their food security concerns, in particular should domestic support levels remain high in some other countries. Accordingly, they argue for a flexibility in the reduction of tariffs, especially for "Special Products" and through the Special Safeguard Mechanism. Preference-receiving developing and least-developed countries are also concerned that tariff reductions by preference-granting countries will result in significant preference erosion, especially since preferential access arrangements play a vital role in terms of their ability to export and earn foreign exchange, thereby contributing to the development of their economies. However, there are also concerns that the levels of flexibility sought by some negotiating groups would reduce the welfare gains that could arise from improved opportunities for trade between developing countries.

(b) Domestic support 6. Achieving reductions in the high levels of domestic support is a key issue to most developing countries, since such policies distort the agricultural trading environment and contribute to lower world prices, including the decline of commodity prices. This has a negative impact on producers not receiving subsidies, particularly those in developing countries, many of which are keen to see large reductions in trade-distorting support.

7. Reform of domestic support is linked to the market access pillar. Some developing and least developed countries argue that it would indeed be counter to development aims to expect them to further reduce their tariffs while other countries continue to maintain significant levels of spending on Amber and Blue Box subsidies. They are concerned that further market openings could mean increased competition for their domestic producers from subsidized production in other countries.

(c) Export competition 8. Some delegations have stated that export subsidies, of all kinds, are the most egregious form of trade-distorting support. The use of export subsidies ensures that there are more agricultural goods on world markets, resulting in lower world prices than would otherwise be the case. For non-subsidising countries this means artificially high levels of competition in both the domestic market and abroad. Thus, the removal of this form of artificial competition and price suppression would help to improve the ability of Members that do not use such programmes, particularly developing and least-developed Members, to compete.

9. Most developing countries argue for the elimination of all forms of export subsidies, including in the form of export credits, non-genuine food aid or trade-distorting practices of exporting state trading enterprises. However, there are concerns that the elimination of all forms of export subsidies may increase the cost of imported food products for some net-food importing developing countries.

10. At the Sixth Ministerial Conference in Hong Kong, Ministers reaffirmed their commitment to the mandate on agriculture. They agreed, *inter alia*, to a three-band system for reductions in domestic support, with higher linear cuts in higher bands, and to ensure the parallel elimination of all forms of export subsidies and disciplines on all export measures with equivalent effect by the end of 2013. In addition, a safe box for *bona fide* food aid will be provided to ensure there is no unintended impediment to dealing with emergency situations. On market access, four bands were adopted for structuring tariff cuts, with relevant thresholds, including those applicable for developing countries, to be agreed. The Ministerial Declaration also stated that developing countries would have the flexibility to self-designate an appropriate number of tariff lines as Special Products guided by indicators based on the criteria of food security, livelihood security and rural development and have the right to recourse to a Special Safeguard Mechanism based on import quantity and price triggers.

2. Status of the negotiations

11. As the Chairman noted in his report of July 27 2006 to the General Council (TN/AG/23), a wide number of proposals had been received since the Hong Kong Ministerial Crence from various delegations including many from developing country groups like the African Group, the least-developed group of countries, the G-20, the G-33 and the group of small, vulnerable economies (SVEs). In addition proposals were made by groups which include some developing countries such as the Cairns Group and the G-10. Unfortunately, the differences between Members meant that it was not possible to establish modalities and the Chairman's Draft Possible Modalities document (TN/AG/W/3) clearly shows that a lot more work and compromises will be needed before modalities can be finalized. However,

he also pointed out that progress had been made since the Hong Kong Ministerial Conference. Even in areas where differences are most acute, the issues and the background to Member's positions are now clearer. Progress can be made provided Members show the necessary flexibility.

12. On April 30 2007, the Chairman issued a communication outlining his thoughts on a number of negotiating issues. Since not all the issues in the agriculture framework were covered in this communication, he planned to issue a second instalment in due course.

3. Specific issues of interest to developing countries

13. Issues of interest to developing countries are included in all the three pillars of the negotiations. The specific issues of interest to developing countries cover every aspect of market access. Given the different situations in different developing countries their views are often different on specific issues. The various positions include, *inter alia*:

(a) Market access

- Improved market access to developed countries.
- Improved market access to other developing countries (South–South trade) but with less than full reciprocity in the negotiations, including by having to undertake lesser tariff reductions and/or tariff quota expansion commitments relative to those to be undertaken by developed countries.
- Fullest liberalization of trade in tropical agricultural products and for products of particular importance to the diversification of production from the growing of illicit narcotic crops.
- Addressing problems relating to preference erosion.
- Addressing the issues of tariff escalation and the issue of tariff simplification.
- Improving the administration of tariff rate quotas.
- Lifetime of the existing special agricultural safeguard (SSG).
- Appropriate special and differential treatment (S&D) for developing countries, including the flexibility to designate a number of products as "Special Products" (SP) guided by indicators based on the criteria of food security, livelihood security and rural development needs, and the establishment of a Special Safeguard Mechanism (SSM).

(b) Domestic support

- Substantial reductions in trade-distorting support in developed countries.

- Enhanced Blue Box criteria to ensure that this category of support is less distorting than Amber Box support.
- Review and clarification of the Green Box criteria to ensure that such measures have no, or at most minimal, trade-distorting effects on production while ensuring that programmes of developing countries that meet this fundamental requirement are effectively covered.
- Capping of product-specific aggregate measurements of support, in accordance with a methodology to be agreed.
- Appropriate special and differential treatment, including lesser reductions in trade-distorting support and the flexibility to provide certain types of investment and input subsidies.

(c) Export competition

- Elimination of all forms of export subsidies.
- Developing appropriate rules in respect of short-term export credits, export credit insurance or guarantee programmes (export credits, etc. with repayment terms of more than 180 days are to be eliminated), exporting STEs, with special consideration for the monopoly status of STEs in developing countries, and on food aid, whilst ensuring that these disciplines have appropriate provisions for differential treatment of least-developed and net food-importing developing countries.
- Appropriate special and differential treatment, including longer time frames to eliminate all forms of their export subsidies (to those developing countries that have reduction commitments in this area), extension of the provisions contained in Article 9.4 which provides an exemption from reduction commitments for certain types of export marketing and transport costs.

14. In addition to the issues of interest to developing countries highlighted above, S&D will include lower reduction rates and longer implementation periods for developing countries while LDCs will not have to undertake reduction commitments and will have full access to all S&D provisions. The Hong Kong Ministerial Declaration also provided that developed countries and developing countries in a position to do so will provide duty-free and quota-free market access for at least 97 per cent of products originating from LDCs.[2]

[2] Reference is made to the Decision on Measures in Favour of LDCs in Annex F of the Hong Kong Declaration on duty-free and quota-free market access for LDCs, which is treated in the section on "Special and Differential Treatment."

15. Given the importance of cotton for a number of developing countries, especially LDCs, cotton has now its own specificity in the agriculture negotiations through the Sub-Committee on Cotton. While being supported by a wide range of developing countries, the issue is being most actively pursued by the four proponents of the Sectoral Initiative on Cotton: Benin, Burkina Faso, Chad and Mali. The Hong Kong Ministerial Conference agreed that all forms of export subsidies for cotton would be eliminated by developed countries in 2006, and that developed countries would give duty-free and quota-free access for cotton exports from LDCs from the commencement of the implementation period. Members also agreed to the objective of reducing trade distorting domestic subsidies for cotton production more ambitiously than under whatever general formula is agreed in the negotiations and that it should be implemented over a shorter period of time than generally applicable. Since the Hong Kong Ministerial Conference, the Sub-Committee on Cotton has continued its work with additional proposals from the proponents, including TN/AG/SCC/GEN/6 of June 16 2006. These proposals are reflected in the Draft Possible Modalities Document (TN/AG/W/3).

16. A number of recently acceded Members (RAMs), are concerned about the possible negative impact on their agricultural sectors of further significant market access commitments. These Members argue that due to the significant commitments they undertook during their accession process their levels of border protection are already at very low levels, especially compared to the tariff levels of other, more advanced countries.

17. Other issues of concern to various groups of developing countries include monitoring and surveillance mechanisms to ensure implementation of Members's commitments, low prices for commodities, the removal of tariff escalation, the elimination of tariff duties for commodity products under GSP schemes, the elimination of non-tariff barriers and the particular problems facing SVEs.

4. Possible gains for developing countries

18. A successful conclusion of the negotiations would lead to considerable gains for developing countries. Further reform of the world agriculture trading system, would lead Members closer towards the long-term objective they agreed to during the Uruguay Round and which is encapsulated in the Doha Declaration, the August 1 2004 Decision and the Hong Kong Declaration, namely to establish a fair and market-oriented agricultural trading system.

19. Substantial reductions of tariffs, along with a reduction of tariff peaks and tariff escalation, would result in increased market access opportunities. Exports to developed countries would increase and South–South trade would be stimulated. This would not only allow developing countries to export products where they have a comparative advantage, but would also allow for the diversification of production, including value-added processing, and export orientation. Enhanced tariff quotas with an improved tariff quota administration regime would also result in improving market access opportunities. Substantial reductions in trade-distorting domestic support and the elimination of all forms of export subsidies would make world prices more realistic, reduce artificial competition and benefit exporters, especially in developing countries.

20. At the same time, appropriate special and differential treatment, including the flexibility to designate a number of products as "special" and the establishment of a Special Safeguard Mechanism, would go a long way in alleviating concerns that many developing countries have about the possible effect of tariff reductions on their rural development, rural livelihood and food security. Similarly, flexibility in the right to provide some agriculture support, as well as the flexibility to provide certain types of investment subsidies, and to target these subsidies to low-income or resource-poor farmers, would help developing countries in their effort to increase the productivity, and consequently the earning capacity, of their agriculture sector. At the same time, improved market access conditions on a more certain footing can help to increase infrastructure and investment, including foreign direct investment, and therefore increase and improve production and processing standards, employment and standards of living.

B. Non-agricultural market access

1. Parameters of the development dimension

21. Trade in non-agricultural products accounts for more than 90 per cent of world trade in goods and encompasses some key products of export interest to many developing countries. Therefore the NAMA negotiations offer the promise of improved and more secure market access conditions (through new tariff reductions and bindings) in both developed and developing country markets. Some major aspects of these are:

- *Improved access into developed country markets (North–South trade)*: The reduction or elimination of tariff peaks, high tariffs, tariff escalation on products originating in developing countries would open up new valuable market access opportunities in developed countries.

- *Improved opportunities in other developing country markets (South–South trade)*: Since more than 40 per cent of their merchandise exports are directed towards other developing countries, there is a substantial interest in improving market access conditions to each other.
- *Improved market access for LDCs*: LDCs consider improved market access in the form of preferential duty-free/quota-free access is key for their development goals. At the Hong Kong Ministerial Conference it was agreed that developed Members shall, and those developing country Members in a position to do so should, provide duty-free and quota-free market access for at least 97 per cent of products originating from LDCs. [3]

22. Developing country Members in the NAMA negotiations have often called for flexibilities that would allow them to make lower tariff cuts or exempt a number of tariff lines from new bindings or reduction commitments in order to take account of special and differential treatment and the principle of less than full reciprocity in reduction commitments. Some of the main considerations underlying these arguments are listed below.

- *Preserving "policy space"*: Many developing country Members have argued for a degree of flexibility to set their import tariffs in order to pursue their developmental goals, including industrialization and the diversification of their economies. Others have noted that many developing countries have a large binding overhang (difference between the bound duties and the applied duties) and tariff reductions will probably not cut into applied duties as a result of this Round. The idea has also been mooted, that since some developing countries lack the institutional capacity to use trade remedies (i.e. safeguards, antidumping, etc.) they need to preserve high bound duties as a substitute instrument.
- *Protecting infant industries*: Some developing countries have argued for the need to retain tariffs to nurture infant industries because they lack public funds to provide subsidies or other types of incentives for this purpose. Members have discussed the risks of excessive protection

[3] Reference is made to the Decision on Measures in Favour of LDCs in Annex F of the Hong Kong Declaration on duty-free and quota-free market access for LDCs, which is treated in the section on "Special and Differential Treatment."

over extended periods in terms of a potentially negative impact on development. Some have noted that almost all countries have protected nascent industries at some stage of their development.

- *Maintaining unbound duties*: Some Members have made a case for keeping tariff lines unbound, particularly in sensitive sectors. Others have questioned why the establishment of new bound duties, as opposed to their level, should be considered detrimental to any industry. They have also noted that all agricultural tariffs, which are normally considered to be more sensitive, were bound during the Uruguay Round and that several developing countries and LDCs already have full binding coverage.
- *Non-reciprocal preference erosion*: Many developing and least-developed countries have argued that they depend on non-reciprocal preferences, which are granted by developed countries, for a significant share of their exports. They consider that further MFN liberalization should provide for a trade solution that takes this into account and should not lead to further marginalization and de-industrialization of their economies. Other developing countries which benefit to a lesser degree from preferences emphasize the importance they attach to further MFN liberalization precisely in the markets of the preference giving countries and note that non-reciprocal preferences are autonomously granted outside the WTO system. These Members are ready to consider safety-net solutions for preference receiving countries which could be affected by tariff reductions in the developed countries, but outside the NAMA negotiations (e.g. in the context of the Aid for Trade discussions).
- *Preventing the loss of tariff revenue*: Dependence on import tariffs for government revenue has been cited by some developing countries as a reason for preserving tariffs at current levels. While arguing that it is desirable for a country to diversify its tax base over time, others have noted that, since bound and not applied duties are being negotiated, the risk of revenue loss for many developing country Members is low.

2. Status of the negotiations

23. Following a process of intensive meetings and consultations, the Chairman of the Negotiating Group on Market Access (NGMA) put forward in July 2006, on his responsibility, a paper entitled "Towards NAMA Modalities".[4] In this document, he laid out possible modalities language taken from the NAMA Framework[5] supplemented by the Hong

[4] TN/MA/W/80.

[5] Annex B of the Decision Adopted by the General Council on August 1 2004 (WT/L/579).

Kong Ministerial Declaration, language subsequently agreed or language he was proposing on his own responsibility (identified in italics).

24. With regard to modalities for tariff reduction, it was agreed at the Hong Kong Ministerial Conference to adopt a Swiss formula with coefficients that satisfy the mandate in paragraph 16 of the Doha Declaration. Ministers also reaffirmed the importance of special and differential treatment and less than full reciprocity in reduction commitments, including paragraph 8 of the NAMA Framework, as integral parts of the modalities. In July 2006, there continued to be two Swiss formula options on the table: a simple Swiss formula with two coefficients (one for developed and a higher one for developing country Members) and the so-called ABI formula.

25. The different flexibilities contained in the Framework and Hong Kong Ministerial Declaration (i.e. for LDCs, Members with a low binding coverage, SVEs, RAMs and developing countries applying the formula) have been subject of numerous substantive discussions. The tension around this point arises from the trade-off between ambition and flexibilities (particularly paragraph 8 flexibilities), as an increase in the latter (defensive interests) leads to a curtailing of market access (offensive interests). One agreed issue worth highlighting is that LDCs are exempted from tariff reductions and are only expected to increase their bindings substantially, leaving it largely to them to decide on the level and coverage of the bindings.

26. Unbound tariffs have also been an issue of concern to a number of developing countries. At Hong Kong, Ministers agreed to adopt a non-linear mark-up approach to establish base rates for commencing tariff reductions and the NAMA Chairman noted in his July 2006 report that this mark-up was in the range of 5 to 30 percentage points. It should be noted that twelve developing countries with a binding coverage below 35 per cent would be exempted from the application of the formula (the so-called "Paragraph 6" Members) and the application of the non-linear mark-up. Instead, they are expected to bind a certain percentage of non-agricultural tariff lines at an average level that does not exceed 28.5 per cent. The Chairman noted in his July 2006 report that the percentage of tariff lines to bind was in the range of 70 to 100 per cent.

27. The flexibilities for the developing countries applying the formula are described in Paragraph 8 of the NAMA Framework. This paragraph would allow these developing countries to choose between applying less than formula cuts of up to [10] per cent of the tariff lines; or keeping tariff lines unbound or not applying formula cuts for up to [5] per cent of tariff lines. The numbers in brackets are still under negotiation and

both options would be conditioned on not exceeding a certain level of imports.

28. Ministers at Hong Kong noted the concerns raised by SVEs and instructed the Negotiating Group to establish ways to provide flexibilities for these Members without creating a sub–category of WTO Members. The Chairman noted in his July 2006 report that there appears to be broad support on the "trigger" to determine eligibility (i.e. Members having a share of less than 0.1 per cent of world NAMA trade for reference period of 1999 to 2001), but positions remain divided on the possible treatment of these Members. The basic options being considered revolve around a proposal to grant bigger numbers to SVEs under Paragraph 8 and another one which would exempt SVEs from the application of the formula and would entail a Paragraph 6 type of treatment.

29. A number of additional issues have been discussed in the NGMA, including the issue of recently acceded Members (RAMs). The NAMA Framework recognized that these Members shall have recourse to special provisions for tariff reductions in order to take into account their extensive market access commitments undertaken as part of their accession. The Chairman noted in his July 2006 report that there is consensus to grant them additional flexibility in the form of "longer implementation periods." Other flexibilities which have been proposed by the RAMs include a higher coefficient in the formula, greater Paragraph 8 flexibilities and grace periods.

30. The sectoral tariff component of the negotiations is being pursued actively in an informal Member-driven process. Fourteen sectors have been proposed for negotiation, some of which are being pursued by developing countries (e.g. fish & fish products, gems & jewellery and raw materials). Ministers at Hong Kong instructed the Negotiating Group to review proposals with a view to identifying those which could garner sufficient participation to be realized. They agreed that participation should be on a non-mandatory basis. Some developing country Members have indicated that such initiatives may be to the detriment of small Members, as they would erode even further their preferential margins. Other Members consider the sectoral tariff component an essential component of the NAMA negotiations in order to achieve commercially meaningful market access.

31. Another issue which has been discussed intensively is that of non-reciprocal preferences. Ministers at Hong Kong instructed the NGMA to intensify work on the assessment of the scope of the problem with a view to finding possible solutions. Intense discussions have taken place on the

issue based on a preliminary assessment by the Secretariat, and currently the focus is on identifying the possible solutions.

32. Addressing non-tariff barriers (NTBs) is important for many developing countries and LDCs.[6] It has now become clearer that the majority of notified NTBs will be taken up by the Members concerned either in regular WTO committees or in other negotiating groups. The majority of NTBs notified pertain to technical barriers to trade (TBT), trade facilitation, customs valuation and sanitary and phytosanitary (SPS) measures. Ministers at Hong Kong recognized the need for specific negotiating NTB proposals and encouraged participants to make such submissions as quickly as possible. There are currently eight draft vertical and horizontal proposals, one of which is spearheaded by a group of developing countries.[7] This is a very complex area of work in which many developing countries and LDCs have had difficulties in identifying the NTBs affecting their exports.

3. Specific issues of interest to developing countries

33. Summarizing from the preceding section, the specific issues of interest to developing country Members are listed below. It is noted that not all developing countries share the same views on some of these issues and, in some of them, they have conflicting views.

- Bring down tariff peaks, high tariffs and tariff escalation in developed country markets (improve access in developed country markets).
- Bring down tariff peaks, high tariffs and tariff escalation in other developing country markets (improve South–South trade).
- Duty-free and quota-free access for LDCs while ensuring that LDCs are only required to increase their level of bindings and not to apply the formula or to participate at sectorals.
- Reduce or eliminate non-tariff barriers.
- Preserve "policy space."
- Provide adequate protection for infant industries.
- Preserve unbound duties.
- Address non-reciprocal preferences.
- Prevent tariff revenue losses.

[6] See the LDC Group's proposal on rules of origin (TN/CTD/W/30 – TN/MA/W/74 – TN/AG/GEN/20) and the Secretariat note on non-tariff measures on products of export interest to LDCs (WT/COMTD/LDC/W/39 – WT/COMTD/CDC/W/39A1.).

[7] Proposal entitled "Draft Text on Procedures for Resolution of Non-Tariff Barriers" by the NAMA–11 group of developing countries.

4. Possible gains for developing countries

34. In recognition of benefits that accrue from appropriately designed trade liberalization measures, many developing country Members have been reducing their import tariffs autonomously over the years. Several of them have also liberalized in the context of customs unions and regional trade agreements. The importance of developing countries in international trade has been growing. Trade in manufactures – which is a subset of the non-agricultural products accounting for more than 70 per cent of world merchandise exports – provides a good example: the share of developing countries in world exports of manufactures rose from 16.6 per cent in 1990 to 28.1 per cent in 2004.[8]

35. Overall, the gains from NAMA liberalization have been estimated by several institutions to range from US$54.2 billion to US$276.8 billion.[9] Most of these estimates are long-term, in the sense that they assess the impact following full adjustment. Evidence regarding short-term effects is scarce. These estimates need to be considered in light of the following: first, the estimates are based on scenarios which may diverge substantially from any final agreement reached. Second, the models typically do not take proper account of factors such as growth effects, preferences, or supply-side constraints. For example, in order to feel the full benefits of results in the NAMA negotiations, alleviation of supply-side constraints is a necessary condition. Moreover, it is important to note that the estimates of gains from opening up to trade do not take into account any consideration of adjustment costs associated with increased trade competition.

36. The gains that could accrue to individual developing countries would also differ depending on each country's comparative advantage as well as on the extent to which it will liberalize itself. However, in general terms, both North–South and South–South trade are expected to expand as a result of the NAMA negotiations, with the corresponding effect on economic efficiency and growth. Additionally, removing or reducing tariff escalation will give developing countries the opportunity to diversify their export base and to produce and export products with a higher domestic value-added component.

37. Another outcome of the NAMA negotiations is expected to be an improvement in the binding coverage levels which, along with a possible

[8] Source: WTO Secretariat. The term manufactures refers to SITC sections 5, 6, 7, 8 minus division 68 and group 891. It excludes fish and fish products, as well as fuel and mining products.

[9] Piermartini, R. and Teh R. (2005). "Demystifying Modelling Methods for Trade Policy", WTO Discussion Paper No. 10.

reduction in binding overhang, could enhance the predictability and transparency of the trading environment. This could be further reinforced by the requirement that bindings should only take the form of *ad valorem* duties. Problems in the area of non-tariff barriers are also expected to be addressed in the context of the NAMA negotiations and in other negotiating groups. Since the results of the different NTB negotiations will be applied on an MFN basis, the benefits will accrue to the entire Membership. Granting duty-free and quota-free market access to LDCs, whether by developed country Members or other developing Members, would offer this group of countries additional market access.

C. Services

1. Parameters of the development dimension

38. Services production is the dominant economic activity in virtually all countries of the world, regardless of their level of development. The services sector represented 68 per cent of world gross domestic product (GDP) in 2004.[10] Despite many country-specific factors such as natural resource endowments, the share of services tends to be positively related to the level of income or development. This is due to a variety of factors, including a propensity of individuals to spend more on services as their incomes grow and of the services content of production to increase with growing sophistication in industrial production. For example, in 2004, services were estimated to account for 49 per cent of GDP in low income economies, 53 per cent in middle income economies, and 72 per cent in high income economies.[11]

39. Many traditional services, including distribution, construction, or social services are particularly labour intensive. Services thus tend to be an even more important source of employment – and employment creation – than the above figures suggest. By the same token, given the sector's dominant role in total employment, productivity gains are essential for overall economic expansion and welfare. Removing barriers to access and competition among services and service suppliers can lead to lower prices, better quality and a wider choice for consumers. Given their infrastructural role, services such as telecommunications, financial services (including banking and insurance), business services, construction and transport are crucial in shaping overall economic performance.

[10] World Bank (2006), *World Development Indicators.* [11] *Ibid.*

Logistics (packaging, storage, transport, inventories, administration and management) are also an important component of the production and distribution chain, and logistics costs may indeed constitute a particularly heavy burden for developing countries, especially small economies, island economies, and landlocked economies. In sum, there is a common interest across countries at all levels of development in ensuring that their services infrastructure underpins, rather than inhibits, internal economic performance and access to external markets. The quality, availability and price of core producer services are key determinants of competitiveness, and ultimately of growth and development.

2. Status of the negotiations

40. The services negotiations are taking place on two broad fronts: market access and rule-making (Emergency Safeguard Measures, Government Procurement, Subsidies and Domestic Regulation). The market access segment consists of negotiations on new or improved commitments for inclusion in Members' schedules of specific commitments under the General Agreement on Trade in Services (GATS), and the re-negotiation of current MFN exemptions as mandated by the Annex on Article II Exemptions. Appropriate flexibility is to be provided to individual developing countries, which may open fewer sectors and liberalize fewer types of transactions in line with their development situation.

41. The GATS does not recommend or prescribe templates for undertaking commitments. Each Member is free to structure its commitments in line with its national policy objectives and constraints. However, in accordance with GATS Article XIX, Members have adopted specific instruments to guide the negotiations. Among these are the "Guidelines and Procedures for the Negotiations on Trade in Services," which, *inter alia*, recall that the negotiations aim to achieve progressively higher levels of liberalization and increase the participation of developing countries in services trade; reaffirm that the process of liberalization shall take place with due respect for national policy objectives, the level of development and the size of economies of individual Members; require Members to give special attention to sectors and modes of supply of export interest to developing countries; and recognize the right of Members to regulate and to introduce new regulations. Special provision has also been made for LDC participation in the negotiations, affirming the need for greater flexibility in terms of the depth and coverage of LDC commitments, calling for particular attention on the part of other Members in opening up sectors of interest to LDCs, and emphasizing the importance of assist-

ing LDCs to participate more effectively in international trade in services.

42. The Negotiating Guidelines, which govern the negotiations on market access, establish the request-and-offer approach as the main negotiating method. However, the request-and-offer process has only produced limited results so far: by the end of March 2007, only seventy Members (counting the EC as one) had submitted offers, including thirty revised offers.

43. At Hong Kong, Ministers urged all Members to participate actively in the negotiations towards achieving a progressively higher level of liberalization of trade in services, with appropriate flexibility for individual developing countries as provided for in Article XIX of the GATS. LDCs are not expected to undertake new commitments. Ministers expressed their determination to intensify the negotiations in accordance with agreed principles and the objectives, approaches and timelines set out in Annex C of the Ministerial Declaration with a view to expanding the sectoral and modal coverage of commitments and increasing their quality. (However, the timelines foreseen in the Annex were later made redundant by the suspension of all negotiations in late July 2006.) In terms of approaches, Ministers agreed, *inter alia*, that in addition to bilateral negotiations, the request–offer procedure should also be pursued on a plurilateral basis. They also agreed to give due consideration to proposals on the trade-related concerns of small economies, to develop methods for the full and effective implementation of the LDC Modalities, and to provide targeted technical assistance with a view to enabling developing and least-developed countries to participate effectively in the negotiations.

44. Discussions – both formal and informal – have also been conducted on the implementation of the LDC modalities, on the basis of a communication submitted by Zambia on behalf of the LDC Group – "A mechanism to operationalize Article IV:3 of the GATS" (TN/S/W/59). At the meeting of the Special Session of the Council for Trade in Services held on July 14 2006, the EC delegation presented a paper co-sponsored by the US, Japan and Canada. The new proposal provides that all Members notify, by September 2006, how they would grant "Special priority" to LDCs in the negotiations, pursuant to Article IV:3 of the GATS. It also provides that a review of these notifications be conducted and that the Chairman of the Council for Trade in Services in Special Session compile a "list of best practices" in this regard. Intensive discussions on this issue have been held since the resumption of the negotiations in February 2007, although significant gaps remain to be bridged.

45. At the same meeting, the African Group presented a room document regarding S&D proposals. The document calls for the Council for Trade in Services to undertake, before the conclusion of the Doha Round, an evaluation of the extent to which the envisaged services package contributes to the full and effective implementation of Article IV of the GATS. It also proposes, *inter alia*, a regular review of the implementation of Article IV by Members. While the document was generally well received at an informal meeting in March 2007, demandeurs and some other Members differed on certain aspects. The African Group is expected to submit further proposals on S&D treatment.

46. The rule-making negotiations which already started in 1995, are based on the mandates contained in Article VI:4 (Domestic Regulation), Article X (Emergency Safeguard Measures), Article XIII (Government Procurement), and Article XV (Subsidies). Pursuant to the Doha Declaration, they were integrated into the broader agenda of the new round of negotiations disciplines on domestic regulation, and called upon Members to develop text for adoption. Following the informal resumption of the negotiations in late 2006, the Chairman conducted several rounds of informal consultations and finally submitted, in April 2007, a room document containing a draft negotiating text for the Article VI:4 disciplines. The Hong Kong Declaration also called upon Members to intensify their approaches to conclude the respective mandates and timelines. While a number of issues have been raised and discussed in the Working Party on GATS rules since then, overall there was no notable change in long-held positions.

3. Specific issues of interest to developing countries

47. A broad range of developing countries have expressed their negotiating objectives and expectations in written submissions since the start of the services negotiations. Over 40 per cent of the 150 proposals that have been tabled since November 2000 involve one developing country or more (this number excludes most proposals on so-called horizontal issues, but covers basically all proposals on sectors and modes of supply). In total, more than 30 developing country Members have voiced interest in at least one sector or mode of supply under negotiation. Relevant sectors include professional services, computer and related services, telecommunication services, audiovisual services, construction and related engineering services, distribution services, energy services, environmental services, financial services; tourism services and transport services (including logistics).

48. Movements of natural persons (under Mode 4) and, more

recently, the cross-border supply of services (under Modes 1 and 2), have also attracted attention. Proposals on Mode 4, which plays a focal role for many developing countries, have included a call for the harmonization of categories of service suppliers used in scheduling commitments, more commitments on lower-skilled workers, the reduction of barriers involving such matters as nationality, residency and work permit requirements, tax treatment, wage parity requirements, and the duration of stay. The emergence of "off-shoring" activities in recent years has turned the spotlight on crossborder trade. A number of developing countries have recently called for ambitious commitments under both Modes 1 and 2 across a wide range of sectors, including business services, research and development services, computer services, management consulting services, call-centre services, and transfer of financial information and data.

49. Developing-country Members are actively taking part in the plurilateral request–offer mechanism agreed to at Hong Kong. Apart from being recipients of many requests, some of them have also co-sponsored plurilateral requests for market access in areas of specific interest, such as the movement of natural persons, cross-border supply of services, computer-related services, construction and related engineering services, and the removal of MFN exemptions. At the meeting of the Special Session of the Council for Trade in Services held in May 2006, the delegation of Zambia submitted on behalf of the LDC Group a communication presenting their collective request in Mode 4 (JOB(06)/155). The LDC Group requests Members to make commitments in four categories of natural persons, with each category applying to a number of specified sectors of export interest to this group.

4. Possible gains for developing countries

50. Several studies have estimated, with a wide variety of research techniques, the income effects attributable to a reduction in services protection. In general, these gains have been found to dwarf the benefits expected to flow from further trade liberalization in goods. This is due to several factors. First, barriers in many services markets are higher than existing barriers in goods trade, barring particular exceptions such as in the case of agriculture. Second, these barriers normally consist of less transparent and efficient measures – quotas and other non-revenue generating interventions – than tariffs in merchandise trade. Third, as explained above, the costs of services protection, in particular of infrastructure-related services, are spread across, and impose deadweight losses on, a wide array of downstream user industries.

51. Developing countries stand to gain considerably from liberalization of trade in services, both on the part of their trading partners and in terms of their own policy regimes. Bearing in mind the nature of potential economy-wide gains from low-cost, high quality services, benefits to countries from their own liberalization can be considerable. While there are obvious long-term gains associated with services liberalization, there are also adjustment costs involved which may need to be addressed with assistance and capacity-building programs. Obviously much depends on domestic regulatory or institutional reforms to underpin the viability and credibility of the new environment. For example, the absence of clear and predictable market conditions may prompt potential investors to demand risk premiums that are not politically or socially acceptable. If increased entry into financial sectors is not accompanied by adequate prudential supervision, instability may ensue. And the absence of well-designed universal service requirements may result in new, unsustainable burdens being imposed on vulnerable groups or regions. The pace, content and sequencing of liberalization programmes are thus key to avoiding unnecessary frictions and ensuring the efficiency and viability of the new regimes.

52. Even though governments can – and indeed do – initiate reforms of services sectors unilaterally, multilateral commitments under the GATS can be an important catalyst for such liberalization and reform efforts. On the one hand, services negotiations can help to improve export access in areas of developing country interest, such as the movement of natural persons, cross-border supply of services, or in specific sectors. The GATS can also be used to secure access to markets that are already open, and where developing countries are acquiring a comparative advantage, such as the cross-border trade of electronically delivered services. On the other hand, specific commitments can spur and promote investment in the unilaterally liberalized sectors, by making access to the market predictable, secure, and discrimination-free. Moreover, specific commitments can be shaped to take into account eventual adjustment processes and to allow for the development of necessary regulatory frameworks.

D. Trade facilitation

1. Parameters of the development dimension

53. Development aspects have always been at the heart of WTO work on facilitating trade, reflecting the wide-spread recognition of Trade

Facilitation as a fundamental element of a country's trade and growth policy. Having brought down tariff barriers to historically low levels, Members decided to address the remaining obstacles to trade. Negotiations on Trade Facilitation are widely seen as a necessary complement to broader liberalization efforts – essential to reap the full benefits of freer trade.

54. The importance of development aspects is also reflected in the negotiating mandate, listing the enhancement of **technical assistance and capacity building** (TA & CB) as a specific goal of the negotiating exercise. Also to be taken into account is special and differential treatment for the developing country Members with the extent and the timing of entering into commitments being compatible with their implementation capacities. It is recognized that the S&D principle would have to extend beyond the granting of traditional transition periods. The mandate makes clear that developing and least-developed Members would not be obliged to undertake investments in infrastructure projects beyond their means. Far-reaching flexibility is further granted to LDCs, which will only be required to undertake commitments to the extent consistent with their individual development, financial and trade needs or their administrative and institutional capabilities. Development-related aspects are also reflected in the mandate's call for the identification of trade facilitation needs and priorities as an integral part of the negotiations. Each of those aspects has been reflected in various contributions by the Membership, advancing their understanding and outlining possible ways for their practical implementation.

2. Status of the negotiations

55. Based on the modalities set out in Annex D of the July Package and supported by the additional guidance obtained at the Ministerial Conference in Hong Kong, negotiations have proceeded on the basis of Members' contributions, both in written and verbal form. More than 140 submissions, many by developing countries, have been tabled on all issues under negotiation, underlining their commitment to advancing the facilitation of trade. Written contributions have also been made by LDCs, often teaming up with partners from the developed world.

56. Through a series of discussions on all elements of the mandate, members arrived at refining their input from initial ("first generation") proposals over consolidated ("second generation") suggestions to contributions in text form ("third generation").They were all compiled in a

regularly updated document (TN/TF/W/43 with its respective revisions[12]) which came to be the basis of the Negotiating Group's further discussions.[13]

57. Based on the Hong Kong Ministerial recommendation[14] to deepen and intensify the negotiations on the issue of special and differential treatment, Members made particular efforts to advance this pillar of their work with encouraging results. Valuable advances were also achieved at the crucial technical assistance front which had also been highlighted in the Ministerial Declaration as area requiring "special attention."[15] Members submitted substantive proposals on the subject which were subject of intensive discussion in the Negotiating Group. Two proposals were presented in text form. The first originates from a group of developed and developing countries[16] and proposes a staged, need-oriented implementation mechanism of trade facilitation commitments, including key elements for technical assistance (TN/TF/W/137 and subsequent editions). A textual proposal was also submitted by the Core Group of developing countries,[17] (TN/TF/W/142), equally presenting ideas on an implementation mechanism for S&D and TA & CB support. Both submissions represent work in progress with additional ideas on the subject also having been presented by other delegations (albeit not yet in written form).

58. Work also advanced on the important needs assessment area. A corresponding programme, which includes both regional and national activities in all parts of the world, is a joint undertaking by the WTO Secretariat and relevant international organizations (in particular the World Bank, WCO, UNCTAD, OECD and IMF) with the

12 The most recent revision is TN/TF/W/43/Rev.10.

13 At the General Council meeting of July 27–28 2006, the Chairman reported on the state of play in the trade facilitation talks, submitting compilation TN/TF/W/43/Rev.9 as the document "on which negotiations are proceeding" (TN/TF/4). The compilation was referred to as "a reflection of work in progress that represents a significant advance, but not agreement." Reference was also made to it being "without prejudice to the right of Members' to put forward new contributions". The report equally made clear that the proposals required further refinement and negotiation.

14 Annex E of the Hong Ministerial Declaration, para. 7.

15 *Ibid.*, para. 6.

16 Armenia, Canada, Chile, China, Columbia, Costa Rica, Dominican Republic, Ecuador, EC, Georgia, Guatemala, Honduras, Japan, Kyrgyz Republic, Mexico, Moldova, Nicaragua, Pakistan, Paraguay, Sri Lanka, Switzerland and Uruguay.

17 Bangladesh, Botswana, Cuba, Egypt, India, Indonesia, Jamaica, Kenya, Malaysia, Mauritius, Namibia, Nepal, Nigeria, Philippines, Rwanda, Tanzania, Trinidad & Tobago, Uganda, Venezuela, Zambia and Zimbabwe.

support of donors from the government side. It is carried out on the basis of a self-assessment guide specifically developed for that end (TN/TF/W/143[18]).

3. Specific issues of interest to developing countries

59. Apart from TA & CB, much attention has been given to the needs and priorities of developing countries, to cost implications and questions of S&D. Reference was further made to linkages between Annex D's elements and the need for a balanced result. There was also focus on measures to improve and clarify the relevant regulatory framework with a view to expediting and enhancing developing country trade. For landlocked countries (as well as non-landlocked Members of the developing world), transit matters are of particular interest in that regard. Regional approaches to trade facilitation were brought up as an area of interest by a number of small economies[19] (TN/TF/W/129/Rev.1), especially with respect to implementing requirements and the provision of TA & CB. Issues such as economies of scale, maximization of resources and targeted support were stressed as important considerations for the trade facilitation discussions.

60. In the TA & CB area, calls have been made for support both during the negotiations and after their conclusion, with a number of concrete measures proposed for each phase. Such support is recognized as vital for developing and least-developed countries to fully participate in and benefit from the negotiating process. Assistance was requested to be precise, effective and operational, reflecting the trade facilitation needs and priorities of the developing world. Reference was also made to enhancing cooperation and coordination amongst the various aid providers to increase efficiency and avoid duplication of work. The identification of trade facilitation needs and priorities is another issue close to the heart of developing Members, with requests being made for their advancement and support. Work is also requested to continue and intensify on the process of addressing concerns on the cost implications side.

18 The tool was developed by the World Bank in cooperation with the WTO Secretariat and other Annex D organizations. Professor David Widdowson of the Centre for Customs and Excise Studies of the University of Canberra was commissioned by the World Bank to prepare the main draft.

19 The submission was sponsored by Antigua and Barbuda, Barbados, Dominica, Fiji, Grenada, Papua New Guinea, the Solomon Islands, St. Kitts and Nevis, St. Lucia and St. Vincent and the Grenadines.

61. Special and differential treatment is another key pillar of the negotiations and an essential requirement for their success. As in the case of TA & CB, calls have been made for S&D provisions to be precise, effective and operational. Requests were further made to allow for the necessary flexibility in implementing the negotiations' results.

62. Issues raised by developing countries with respect to improving and clarifying the existing regulatory framework cover all relevant GATT Articles. Proposals range from enhanced transparency and non-discrimination initiatives over various measures regarding import/export-related fees and formalities to matters addressing goods in transit. The landlocked countries have been especially active in pursuing some of these issues. Common underlying objectives of those suggestions are increased trading opportunities that take account of the particular needs of the developing world.

4. Possible gains for developing countries

63. Lowering trade-related transaction costs can result in a significant improvement in a country's ability to compete effectively in the global economy. This has been widely recognized by developing countries and LDCs which also acknowledge the importance of trade facilitation for the attainment of their development objectives. While pointing at the need for TA & CB to respond to possible costs of implementing certain measures, developing and least-developed Members have drawn particular attention to the benefits they foresee in terms of increasing the competitiveness of their small- and medium-scale enterprises. This applies in particular to the case of landlocked developing countries and LDCs, for which steps to facilitate transit traffic along with facilitating their own cross-border trade can produce a marked reduction in their import costs and an improvement in their export competitiveness on world markets. National experience papers presented by delegations in the Negotiating Group, as well as numerous studies that have been conducted by relevant international organizations that are collaborating with WTO Members in this area, point to a range of benefits that can be realized by taking measures to facilitate trade, including improving revenue collection, improving border controls and security, lowering administrative costs, encouraging more trade and foreign investment, and enhancing the competitiveness of domestic business in its home market as well as on export markets. Developing countries also stand to benefit greatly from the aspired increase in transparency and predictably of the trading environment.

E. Special and differential treatment

1. Parameters of the development dimension

64. Special and differential treatment is an integral part of the WTO Agreements and reflects a recognition of the diverse nature of WTO's vast membership, asymmetry in their economic strengths and the need to ensure that economic gains from the trading system are well distributed among all Members. While acknowledging that the multilateral trading system has attempted to address some of their concerns through appropriate S&D provisions, most developing countries still feel that more needs to be done to enhance the effectiveness and operationalization of these provisions. One of the main concerns expressed has been that S&D provisions are couched in best endeavor language and merely exhort Members to take certain steps, rather than making this action mandatory and binding.

65. The development dimension of S&D can be best gauged from the different submissions made by the proponents in the CTD in Special Session. The African Group, one of the main proponents on S&D, states that "special and differential treatment shall aim, to address and resolve the imbalances between developed country Members and developing and . . . to support developing and least-developed country Members to undertake adjustments that are necessary for them to meaningfully benefit from the agreements . . . and to secure for them market access in the multilateral trading system that will facilitate their rapid economic development" (TN/CTD/W/3/Rev.2). The African Group has submitted that its experience with implementing S&D provisions has shown that such provisions are best operationalized when they are in the form of binding obligations. The LDCs, which have also played a central role in this work, believe that developing country Members, particularly the LDCs, "experience peculiar problems, which constrain their beneficial participation in the multilateral trading system" (TN/CTD/W/4). They therefore feel that assuming the same types and levels of obligations as undertaken by other Members has prevented them from addressing their development challenges and from participating meaningfully in the international trading system. The LDCs argue that S&D provisions should provide them flexibility to take measures to assist their domestic industries, and that they should be obliged to undertake only such commitments or obligations that are consistent with their trade, development and financial needs.

2. Status of the negotiations

66. Of the eighty-eight agreement-specific proposals submitted in the Special Session mainly by the LDCs and the African Group, thirty-eight proposals had been referred to other negotiating groups and WTO bodies. Of the remaining fifty proposals Members had, by Cancún, agreed in principle to twenty-eight proposals. These proposals, which are yet to be adopted, are contained in Annex C of JOB(03)/150/Rev.2. At the Hong Kong Ministerial Conference, Members adopted the five remaining LDC Agreement-specific proposals. The adopted texts of the five proposals are contained in Annex F of the Hong Kong Declaration.

67. The five remaining LDC proposals adopted at Hong Kong include the decision that developed country Members shall, and developing country Members declaring themselves in a position to do so should, provide duty-free and quota-free (DFQF) market access for at least 97 per cent of products originating from LDCs. Members are to also ensure that preferential rules of origin applicable to imports from LDCs are transparent and simple, and contribute to facilitating this market access.[20] The other adopted decisions in Annex F of the Hong Kong Declaration, *inter alia*, provide the LDCs flexibility in the Agreement on Trade-Related Investment Measures (TRIMs), simplification of the waiver process and improved coherence agreements with other international organizations to ensure more targeted technical assistance and capacity-building programs.

68. In addition, Ministers at Hong Kong instructed the Special Session as well as the bodies in which the Category II proposals are being addressed, to complete the review of all the outstanding Agreement-specific proposals and report to the General Council with clear recommendations for a decision by December 2006. The Special Session was also instructed to resume work on all other outstanding issues, including on the cross-cutting issues and report on a regular basis to the General Council.

69. Since the resumption of the negotiations, work in the Special Session has focused on the 16 remaining Agreement-specific proposals with a view to making clear recommendations on all these proposals in the shortest time possible. The text-based discussions have focused mainly on seven of the remaining proposals, of which on six proposals Members have been able to come up with revised texts. On the

[20] Cross-reference with footnotes 2 and 3 in the "Agriculture" and "Non-Agricultural Market Access" sections respectively.

remaining nine proposals, significant divergences exist and, unless Members are able to put forward new ideas or alternate language, progress will be difficult.

70. During discussions on the Agreement-specific proposals, the LDCs have continued to stress the need for quick and effective implementation of the DFQF market access decision. In this context, the LDCs formally tabled two submissions in the Special Session, one on rules of origin and the other on market access.[21] A number of Members have indicated their intention to implement the decision. Of these, Japan has recently notified the details of its revised GSP scheme to LDCs which has increased the coverage of DFQF market access for LDCs to 98 per cent.[22]

71. On the outstanding issues, while a number of elements have been raised as possibly forming part of the future work on the cross-cutting issues, the Monitoring Mechanism is considered by most Members as an important step in the continuing review of the effectiveness and operationalization of the S&D provisions. Members have therefore agreed that work on the outstanding issues begin with consideration of the possible elements of the Mechanism, including its possible scope and structure. To facilitate discussions, the Secretariat compiled a paper containing all the earlier proposals made on the Monitoring Mechanism.

3. Specific issues of interest to developing countries

72. In the context of the proposals tabled in the Special Session, it can be said that the specific issues of interest to developing countries, include the following:

- Flexibility in the multilateral rules, which reflect their concerns and constraints.
- Transitional arrangements linked to the achievement of developmental objectives.
- Simplifying existing procedures, including for enhanced flexibilities and extended transition periods, so as to provide a timely and effective response to particular concerns.
- Less than full reciprocity in the commitments undertaken by developing countries.

[21] TN/CTD/W/30 and W/31 respectively. [22] WT/COMTD/N/2/Add.14.

- Enhanced and targeted technical assistance and capacity-building programmes that would assist countries to implement WTO rules.
- Measures that would provide additional and predictable market access for products of export interest to developing countries.
- Operationalization of the decision to provide duty-free and quota-free market access to the least-developed countries.
- Making S&D provisions mandatory, in keeping with the concern expressed by many developing countries that most of these provisions are not couched in binding language.
- Improved coherence arrangements to ensure that flexibilities provided in the WTO rules are not diluted because of commitments mandated by other organizations.

4. Possible gains for developing countries

73. While it is difficult to quantify the gains from the S&D work program, mainly because of the lag between adopting and operationalizing any recommendation, it can be said that gains would accrue by making the S&D provisions more precise, effective and binding. Clearly, in order to assist developing countries, especially the LDCs, the S&D provisions must respond to, and be reflective of, their concerns. A number of developing country Members have said that commitments and obligations undertaken by them in the WTO have reduced their flexibility to adopt, what in their view, are pro-development policies and measures. In this context, they have put forward a number of proposals which seek to enhance the existing flexibility in the rules for them, and consequently provide them a certain degree of policy space. They have also sought simplification of cumbersome procedures and/or notification obligations, so that they can divert their resources to other developmental issues and areas.

74. Developing country Members also consider transitional time periods as an important element of S&D treatment; one that provides them with more time to conform with, or fulfil particular obligations. However, many, if not all, of these transition periods have expired and developing countries, especially the LDCs, are seeking a positive consideration of their requests for extension of these transition periods. There are several proposals on the need for technical assistance to be more predictable and targeted to the development needs of developing and leastdeveloped countries. There are also a number of proposals that seek to improve coherence arrangements with other organizations in the delivery of such assistance.

F. Implementation-related issues and concerns

1. Parameters of the development dimension

75. Concerns arising from the implementation of the Uruguay Round Agreements were raised by some developing countries shortly after the establishment of the WTO in 1995. To them, the Uruguay Round Agreements were not balanced and did not contain provisions that would facilitate their integration into the multilateral trading system. In fact, there was the view that some of the Agreements, particularly the Agreement on TRIMs and the Agreement on Subsidies and Countervailing Measures restricted the policy measures that could be implemented by developing countries to attract foreign direct investment and to support their nascent domestic industries. Concerns were also expressed about a wide range of issues, including the back loading of commitments under the Agreement on Textiles and Clothing. There was the additional concern among small and economically weak developing countries that the cost of implementing the Uruguay Round Agreement, particularly the Agreement on Trade-Related Aspects of Intellectual Property Rights (TRIPS) and the Agreement on Customs Valuation was excessive as compared to benefits they had derived from the implementation of the Uruguay Round Agreements. Some developing countries also complained about the abuse of anti-dumping, safeguards and countervailing measures as well as standards, sanitary and phytosanitary measures.

2. Status of work

76. In December 2005, Ministers at Hong Kong reiterated the instruction in the August 2004 Decision to the TNC, negotiating bodies and other WTO bodies concerned to redouble their efforts to find appropriate solutions to outstanding implementation-related issues. Ministers requested the Director-General, without prejudice to the positions of Members, to intensify his consultative process under paragraph 12(b). Specific mention of the issue of the relationship between the TRIPS Agreement and the Convention on Biological Diversity (CBD) was added alongside that of Geographical Indications (GIs) extension. Ministers also instructed the Director-General to report to each regular meeting of the TNC and the General Council on the outstanding implementation issues. The General Council is to review progress and take any appropriate action no later than July 31 2006.

77. At the July 2006 General Council meeting, the Director-General reported that although numerous consultations on GI extension had

been held, the positions of participants in the discussion remained essentially unchanged between those who supported GI extension and those opposed. A key issue on which positions remained divided was whether the current level of protection for GIs for products other than wines and spirits under Article 22 of the TRIPS Agreement was sufficient for protecting such GIs for progress. Other issues concerned the implications of extension for other producers that had been using the terms in question in their own market and in third country markets, and the extent to which extension of the exceptions provisions of Article 24 would meet concerns on this count. As to action to be decided by the General Council, the proponents of GI extension had advocated a clear General Council decision to engage in text-based negotiations aimed at providing for GI extension. Some other delegations had opposed moving to negotiations and argued that the case for extension of additional protection had not been made. However, these delegations had expressed preparedness to envisage further fact-based work on the issue.

78. As regards the relationship between the TRIPS Agreement and the CBD, the consultations had included the examination of a non-exhaustive list of topics on the basis of consultations with delegations. While positions in the detailed consultations on the basis of the topics in the list remained essentially unchanged, the consultations facilitated a more clear-cut identification of the points of divergence and convergence and of the key policy questions that remained to be decided. As to action to be decided by the General Council, the proponents of a new TRIPS disclosure obligation advocated a clear General Council decision to engage in text-based negotiations aimed at providing for such an obligation. Some other delegations had opposed negotiations but had indicated preparedness to envisage further fact-based work on the issue aimed at seeing how the underlying commonly agreed objectives could be best realized. With regard to the other outstanding implementation issues – which related to other TRIPS issues, balance of payments, market access, TRIMs, customs valuation, safeguards and TBT – the Director-General reported that the situation had not evolved and that the ball was essentially in the court of the proponents.

79. Given the impasse in the Director-General's consultations on the outstanding implementation issues, as in the negotiations, the Chairman of the General Council said he could only urge all delegations to seriously reflect on this situation. For his part, he would continue his contacts with delegations and with the Director-General to consider how to take the work forward in this area, although realistically Members should be

under no illusion that these issues could make significant progress until the overall negotiating environment improved.

3. Specific issues of interest to developing countries

80. Although raised under a number of agreements, the outstanding implementation issues can be broadly classified under four main headings:

(a) Proposals intended to give longer transitional periods to developing countries to implement their obligations.
(b) Proposals safeguarding the market access of developing countries and ensuring that they derive benefits under certain Agreements, such as the TRIPS Agreement.
(c) Proposals intended to exempt developing countries from complying with obligations, such as those under the TRIMs Agreement.
(d) Proposals requesting that developing countries be provided with effective technical assistance.

4. Possible gains for developing countries

81. Proponents of the various implementation-related proposals have argued that they would derive economic and development benefits from them. For example, some of the proposals are intended to safeguard the market access of developing countries by requiring developed countries to take account of their interests when applying contingency protection measures. Proponents have said that the proposals relating to technical assistance would strengthen their human and institutional capacities and enable them to participate effectively in the activities of standard-setting bodies. To take another example, the proponents have said that the proposal on Article XVIII of the GATT 1994 would assist them to implement programmes which would put their economies on the path of sustainable growth and development.

82. With regard to the proposals under the TRIMs Agreement, the proponents have said that these would enable them to attract foreign direct investment into certain critical sectors of their economies. They argue that the domestic content requirement would benefit local industries in terms of enhancing their competitiveness and facilitating the transfer of technology. Some other Members argue that if the domestic industries are efficient, most foreign investors would source inputs from them rather than importing them from elsewhere.

83. While useful clarificatory work on GI extension has been undertaken, positions remain divided on the impact of extension on developing countries. Developing countries figure both among the proponents and opponents of extension. Developing country and other proponents maintain that extension would provide stronger and more easily asserted protection of GIs for products other than wines and spirits. As a result, extension would foster development of local rural communities and the value added contingent of a GI would help create new and better opportunities for quality products, especially for smaller, developing country Members. In response, developing country and other opponents have said that it had not been shown that the existing level of protection required for such GIs was inadequate. They have also argued that extension could not in itself make GIs for quality products a valuable marketing tool; nor could GI protection guarantee market access. The opponents have also raised concerns, *inter alia*, on the impact of any extension on producers not located in the area designated by a GI, as well as questions related to administrative costs and burdens. The Secretariat circulated in May 2005 a factual compilation of the issues raised and views expressed on issues related to GI extension since the beginning of the Doha Work Programme (WT/GC/W/546 – TN/C/W/25). This document gives a fuller picture of the debate that has taken place on the matter.

84. Issues relating to the relationship between the TRIPS Agreement and the CBD are being discussed in two contexts. In addition to the consultations undertaken on behalf of the Director-General in the context of outstanding implementation issues, an intensive exploration of substantive concerns and suggestions is being carried out in the regular sessions of the Council for TRIPS, pursuant to paragraph 19 of the Doha Declaration and paragraph 44 of the Hong Kong Declaration. The Secretariat circulated in February 2006 an updated summary note of issues raised and points made on the relationship between the TRIPS Agreement and the CBD (IP/C/W/368/Rev.1) which gives more details on the positions of Members on this subject in the TRIPS Council. With regard to the consultations on outstanding implementation issues carried out on behalf of the Director-General, a group of developing countries, with wide support from other developing countries, have reiterated their proposal on amending the TRIPS Agreement to include a disclosure requirement in patent applications aimed at avoiding erroneous patents and facilitating compliance with national access and benefit-sharing regimes. Developing country proponents have said that a satisfactory outcome on the issue of the relationship between the TRIPS Agreement

and the CBD is critical for the development dimension of the Doha Work Programme. Some others take the view that the case has not been made and that such a proposal is neither necessary nor appropriate in achieving the shared objectives in this area, which can be most effectively realized in other ways without involving the patent system. In between these two positions, support has been expressed for a more limited patent disclosure requirement at the international level, restricted to the origin or source of genetic material and related traditional knowledge and without substantive implications for patentability.

G. Rules

1. Anti-dumping and subsidies and countervailing measures, including fisheries subsidies

(a) Parameters of the development dimension 85. Developing country exports have been the subject of some 45 per cent of all anti-dumping investigations since 1995. Developing country Members also are the main users of anti-dumping, accounting for nearly 60 per cent of all antidumping investigations since 1995. A number of developing country Members have sponsored or co-sponsored proposals aimed at tightening antidumping rules (i.e. reflecting exporter interests). On the other hand, a number of developing country Members (including some that have submitted proposals aimed at tightening anti-dumping rules) have cautioned against making the rules too difficult for developing country investigating authorities to implement, thereby reflecting their interests as users.

86. Disciplines on subsidies are differentiated among developing country Members based on their level of development and certain other factors. This diversity of current treatment is reflected in positions on various proposals concerning whether and how subsidy disciplines might be strengthened, and on proposed changes to the special and differential treatment provisions of the Agreement on Subsidies and Countervailing Measures (SCM). Finally, in the area of fisheries subsidies, certain developing country Members favor very strict disciplines with few exceptions and limited special and differential treatment, while others seek broad exemptions from any new disciplines.

(b) Status of the negotiations 87. Ministers at Hong Kong directed the Negotiating Group on Rules (NGR) to intensify and accelerate the

Negotiating process in all areas of the mandate (on the basis of detailed textual proposals before the Group or on those yet to be submitted and to complete the analysis of proposals by participants on the Anti-Dumping (AD) and SCM Agreements as soon as possible). The Chairman of the Negotiating Group was also mandated to prepare consolidated texts of the AD and SCM Agreements that would serve as the basis for the final stage of the negotiations. Following the Ministerial Conference, and pursuant to the instructions from Ministers, the Negotiating Group intensified its work in respect of all areas of its mandate, in informal plenary sessions as well as in bilateral and plurilateral consultations convened by the Chairman.

88. In his July 27 2006 report to the TNC (TN/RL/19), the Chairman noted that Members individually, and the Negotiating Group collectively, had done what was required to complete the analysis of textual proposals by the June target date that he had set to put him in a position to table his consolidated texts. He observed that it had not proven possible to do so because of conditions elsewhere in the Round. Since that report, the Negotiating Group has continued certain technical work, focusing in particular on fisheries subsidies and horizontal subsidy disciplines, including on new proposals that have been tabled in these areas.

(c) Specific issues of interest to developing countries 89. Most of the proposals on antidumping have been submitted by a group of Members known as the Friends of Antidumping Negotiations (FANs), which includes a number of developing country Members. Developing and developed Members have also submitted proposals individually on various aspects of anti-dumping and countervailing duty measures. The general orientation of the FANs' proposals is to make the rules on using anti-dumping measures stricter, both in respect of the substantive provisions (how dumping margins are calculated, and how injury and causation are established), and in respect of duty application and investigative procedures. In addition, various Members are pursuing some of the implementation and S&D issues pertaining to anti-dumping which were referred to the Negotiating Group. On the other hand, certain proposals by developing country Members reflect concerns that anti-dumping rules are becoming more demanding and that many developing country administrators have difficulty implementing them because of their cost and/or complexity. A final cluster of anti-dumping proposals/issues with implications for developing countries concern transparency and due process in anti-dumping investigations. While certain developing country Members express concerns over a lack of access to information in investigations to which their exporters are subject, others express concern over the increased costs and burdens of any new procedures or mechanisms. Proponents on these issues, however, have stressed the importance that they attach to a high and consistent standard of procedural fairness and transparency on the part of any Member making use of the anti-dumping instrument.

90. A relatively small number of proposals on horizontal subsidy disciplines under the SCM Agreement are under active discussion at present. These pertain to the rules on prohibited subsidies, the meaning of "withdrawal" of a subsidy, the rules on serious prejudice, subsidy calculation issues and countervailing measures. Two proposals, on export credits and export competitiveness, are sponsored by developing country Members. In other fora, including the Dedicated Sessions of the Committee on Trade and Development and the SCM Committee, certain proposals have been tabled to prolong the exemption of certain developing countries from the SCM Agreement prohibition on export subsidies. In addition, early in the negotiations, developed and developing country Members tabled papers referring to S&D under the SCM Agreement. Developing country proposals differ on the question of exemptions from horizontal obligations under the Agreement, with some favoring the prolongation of such exemptions and others expressing concern about their implications for international competition. Finally, certain papers tabled early in the negotiations propose enhanced immunity from countervailing measures for developing country exporters.

91. The main proponents of new, sector-specific disciplines on fisheries subsidies comprise a group called "Friends of Fish." This group includes a number of developing country Members. For the developing country proponents, the main concern is the artificial competitive advantage created by subsidies, which affect access to fish and contribute to the depletion of the resource. Most Members (developed as well as developing) have stressed the need for effective S&D as part of any fisheries subsidies package. Of particular concern in this regard are small-scale, artisanal fisheries and any subsidies thereto, as well as payments that some developing Members receive from foreign governments for access to the fisheries in their waters. Aquaculture is another area of considerable interest to many developing country Members, which seek to ensure that any new disciplines would not interfere with these activities. Certain developing country Members, including a group of small, vulnerable coastal states, have tabled specific proposals addressing the general

framework of possible new disciplines as well as treatment of developing country Members within such a framework.

(d) Possible gains to developing countries 92. An eventual clarification and improvement of any of the rules under negotiation will increase the predictability of the trading system to the benefit of all Members. Moreover, an appropriate balance of rights and obligations will permit developing countries to pursue their development objectives and at the same time guard against practices that have a negative impact on their trade. Another area where balance is crucial concerns trade-offs between the costs and administrative burdens of the contingency protection system and its capacity to ensure fairness and transparency.

2. Regional trade agreements

(a) Parameters of the development dimension 93. In the WTO context, a regional trade agreement (RTA) constitutes a commitment to liberalize trade among a selective number of countries, hence on a preferential and discriminatory basis. While RTAs can foster economic growth and development, such an outcome is not guaranteed. It depends on various factors, most significantly the RTA's design and effective implementation. Studies tend to show that ambitious RTAs among countries with open trade regimes tend to perform better than RTAs that are limited in scope, poorly implemented and employed as an import substitution strategy (i.e. preferential liberalization behind high MFN tariffs). The former type of RTA will minimize the risks of trade diversion and is likely to bring benefits in the form of an improved regulatory environment, enhanced investment flows and increased technology transfers. Such benefits may be further enhanced provided that the RTA commitments are taken as a temporary step to further multilateral trade liberalization, thus benefiting over time third parties and the multilateral trading system as a whole. RTAs based on an open trading regime that envisage the gradual MFN extension of preferences are all the more important at a time when all WTO Members are engaged in an RTA race that inevitably amplifies the level of discrimination in international trade. Clearly, the net losers of this race are those countries, mainly developing ones, that are left out of the preferential trading network being built around the major trading partners. Concerns are mounting over the defensive nature of many RTAs strategically designed at maintaining access to larger markets, locking out competition from other MFN suppliers and locking in investment. If such trends are sustained and not counterbalanced by a successful outcome of the Doha Round, the contribution of an ever-growing number of overlapping RTAs to the economic progress of both parties and non-parties could be negative.

(b) Status of the negotiations 94. The aim of the negotiations in this area is to clarify and improve WTO rules and procedures that apply to RTAs and to take into account RTA's development aspects. The negotiations have proceeded on parallel tracks, considering "systemic" and "procedural" issues. With respect to the latter, the Negotiating Group on Rules has made very significant progress and a decision on a "Transparency Mechanism for Regional Trade Agreements" was adopted by the General Council on December 14 2006 (WT/L/671). The mechanism clarifies and streamlines the existing transparency provisions contained in all the current WTO provisions on RTAs. Its main objectives are to ensure coherence in the treatment of transparency across the relevant WTO provisions and to enhance the provision of RTA information by simplifying Members' reporting obligations and complementing it with technical assistance for developing country Members. The decision also seeks to untangle the current deadlock in the WTO Committee on RTAs (CTRA) by shifting the focus of its *modus operandi* from the present legalistic examination of agreements to a more open transparency exercise. Recognizing the systemic importance of RTA transparency, the decision also applies to RTAs notified under paragraph 2c of the Enabling Clause, although it preserves the Committee on Trade and Development as the WTO body responsible for such RTAs.

95. Discussions on systemic issues have not made as much progress as those on transparency issues. Submissions by participants have focused on the clarification of certain GATT Article XXIV provisions, most notably the "substantially all trade" (SAT) requirement, the length of RTAs transition periods and the inclusion of S&D provisions in Article XXIV of the GATT 1994. Participants have indicated that the scope of any future work in this area should be comprehensive (with specific reference to Chair Roadmaps) and not lead to a dilution of current provisions. It has been reiterated that text-based proposals are at this point essential to advance the process.

(c) Specific issues of interest to developing countries 96. In light of the growing number of RTAs, both South–South and North–South, the scope of the these negotiations is of particular interest to developing countries since any outcome will affect the nature of their WTO obligations with respect to RTAs. In the area of RTA transparency, there was consensus among NGR participants that given the systemic importance of the issues, any such mechanism should apply to all RTAs. Thus, the Transparency Decision clarifies, streamlines and enhances the existing reporting obligations under the relevant WTO provisions. Of interest to developing countries, in particular those availing themselves of the flexibilities offered by the Enabling Clause, is the extent to which the new mechanism adds to existing transparency obligations and whether it adequately addresses their capacity constraints (see subparagraph (d)).

97. The negotiations on RTA systemic issues aim at clarifying existing rules and have to date focused mainly on elements pertinent to Article XXIV of the GATT 1994. This Article does not contain any flexibility for developing countries and it is the only legal cover available to developing countries entering into RTAs with developed countries. In light of the increasing number of North–South agreements, some developing countries have shown an interest in modifying existing provisions by including S&D treatment. As mentioned earlier, the systemic discussions have focused on the concept of SAT, length of transition periods and S&D. The question of flexibility for developing countries has been acknowledged on repeated occasions, though it has also been the opinion of most participants that this issue cannot be adequately dealt with until a more concrete position on SAT and transition periods, among others, emerges. It should also be noted that of the submissions received, very few deal with the S&D question.

(d) Possible gains to developing countries 98. With respect to RTA transparency, the new Transparency Mechanism may have certain implications for developing countries and in particular for those availing themselves of the Enabling Clause. The latter agreements will be subject to transparency obligations on a par with RTAs notified under Article XXIV of the GATT 1994 and Article V of the GATS, thus adding new elements to what is current practice (i.e. a "Factual Presentation" of the RTA prepared by the Secretariat).[23] However, while strengthening the

[23] Parties to RTAs notified under GATT Article XXIV and GATS Article V were previously required to submit a "Standard Format" which was essentially a summary of the agreement. The Factual Presentations relieve Members of such responsibility thus benefiting all Members irrespective of whether they are developed or developing country Members.

transparency obligations, the Transparency Mechanism acknowledges the constraints that some developing countries may face in gathering the required reporting information and it provides for flexibilities with respect to the reporting timeframes and for technical assistance. Of great significance to developing countries is the improved access to RTAs-related information that will result from the operation of the mechanism. Since practically all Members are engaged, or are engaging, in multiple RTAs, the need for adequate transparency has become systemic in a fundamental sense.

99. As for RTA systemic issues, it is generally accepted that a developmental rationale exists for allowing developing countries to engage in progressive asymmetric liberalization with selected partners. However, if transition periods are too long or too many products are excluded from coverage, potential gains from RTAs in terms of growth and development will be foregone. At the same time, it is important to ensure coherence both within the regional arrangement, as well as with the broader goals of the multilateral trading system. Negotiations in this area can deliver important gains for developing countries by shaping the rules in such a way as to reflect RTAs parameters that can better accommodate their development needs and constraints.

H. Trade-related aspects of intellectual property rights[24]

1. Parameters of the development dimension

100. The negotiations regarding the establishment of a multilateral system of notification and registration of geographical indications for wines and spirits (hereinafter "multilateral system") form an integral part of the wider mandate of the Doha Development Agenda. Article 23.4 of the TRIPS Agreement provides that "[i]n order to facilitate the protection of geographical indications for wines, negotiations shall be undertaken in the Council for TRIPS concerning the establishment of a multilateral system of notification and registration of geographical indications for wines eligible for protection in those Members participating in the system." Paragraph 18, first sentence, of the Doha Declaration states that "[w]ith a view to completing the work started in the Council for Trade-

[24] The work undertaken by the Council for TRIPS on the relationship between the TRIPS Agreement and the Convention on Biological Diversity (CBD) pursuant to paragraph 19 of the Doha Ministerial Declaration is treated in the section on "Implementation-Related Issues and Concerns."

Related Aspects of Intellectual Property Rights (Council for TRIPS) on the implementation of Article 23.4, we agree to negotiate the establishment of a multilateral system of notification and registration of geographical indications for wines and spirits by the Fifth Session of the Ministerial Conference," thus extending the mandate of Article 23.4 to cover also spirits.

2. Status of the negotiations

101. Since 2002, a considerable amount of work has been done, involving the tabling of position papers and proposals by delegations. There are three proposals on the table: a proposal from Hong Kong, China (TN/IP/W/8); a Joint Proposal from Argentina, Australia, Canada, Chile, Costa Rica, Dominican Republic, Ecuador, El Salvador, Guatemala, Honduras, Japan, Mexico, New Zealand, Nicaragua, Paraguay, Chinese Taipei and the United States (TN/IP/W/10); and a proposal from the EC (TN/IP/W/11). They have been set out side-by-side in Secretariat document TN/IP/W/12. Co-sponsors of the Joint Proposal consider that the EC proposal is beyond the mandate in Article 23.4 by requiring mandatory participation and by increasing the protection of geographical indications through the use of legal presumptions, a system of reservations and compulsory bilateral negotiations, and restrictions on the use of exceptions. The EC and Switzerland, on the other hand, consider that the Joint Proposal, which proposes an information database, would be insufficient to facilitate the protection of geographical indications for wines and spirits and therefore to meet the mandate.

102. There are two major stumbling blocks. The first is the extent to which the registration of a geographical indication, within the multilateral system, should create legal effects at the national level. The second is about whether participation in the system should by voluntary or mandatory, including whether the legal effects under the system should apply to all WTO Members or only to those opting to participate in the system. In addition to these two key issues, there are other points such as administrative and other burdens of a multilateral system, especially on developing and least-developed countries, and whether the proposals on the table would modify the balance of rights and obligations in the TRIPS Agreement and respect the principle of territoriality. In his July 26 2006 report to the TNC (TN/IP/16), the Chairman of the Special Session remarked that the side-by-side document continued to represent a valid description of the state of the proposals in the Special Session. He observed that progress towards establishing a common basis for the final

negotiating phase would require delegations to be creative in finding new flexibility. In the light of consultations held by the Chairman in December 2006 and in February 2007, a compilation of points raised and views expressed on the three proposals is being circulated as an addendum to the side-by-side document (TN/IP/W/12/Add.1).

3. Specific issues of interest to developing countries

103. While some developing country Members have expressed the view that the EC proposal is the only one that makes a genuine attempt at meeting the requirements of Article 23.4 of the TRIPS Agreement to facilitate the protection under that provision (TN/IP/W/3), others have sponsored or supported the "Joint Proposal" as the only one that fully respects the mandate of Article 23.4. A significant number of developing countries have yet to take a position and are still studying the various proposals, including as they relate to their own development. An issue on which a number of developing countries have expressed particular interest is that of participation, taking the view that the system should be voluntary and not have legal effects for countries opting not to participate in it. Another issue of concern to developing countries relates to the possible costs and other burdens that the system might entail, in particular for non-participating developing countries.

104. Discussion of special and differential treatment has been relatively limited so far. The point has been made that the need for it would depend, to a significant extent, on the nature and complexity of the basic notification and registration system to be chosen – which still remains unclear. Nonetheless, there has been some discussion of this issue. The point has been widely made that the system should be efficient for developing countries, keeping in mind the burdens they are already bearing and the fact that the Doha Round is about development. Other points made relate to: the extent to which S&D in the payment of registration fees might be envisaged for developing countries and LDCs; technical assistance to facilitate participation of developing countries in the system; and transition periods for developing countries and, in the case of LDCs, the need to take account of their overall transition period under the TRIPS Agreement.

4. Possible gains for developing countries

105. The question of possible gains to developing countries has been the subject of some debate among the participants in the negotiations. Some hold the view that a multilateral system's ability to alleviate the costs for

all producers in seeking protection worldwide by allowing them to gain legal standing in third countries via a centralized procedure would help developing country producers in particular, who have less resources to invest in asserting such protection internationally. Others consider that the system would impose considerable administrative burden on developing countries would not necessarily save costs for GI owners and would, in any event, entail burdens that would more than offset any benefits developing countries might obtain, especially as the mandate is for wines and spirits, of which most developing countries are not exporters. It is, therefore, important that the system be simple and voluntary in nature and not entail new obligations.

I. Trade and environment

1. Parameters of the development dimension

106. The negotiations under paragraph 31 of the Doha Declaration, which are undertaken with a view to enhancing the mutual supportiveness of trade and environment, and the negotiations under paragraph 28 of the Doha Declaration on fisheries subsidies,[25] form the "environmental package" of the current negotiations. Paragraph 31 has three main components: paragraph 31(i) mandates negotiations on the relationship between existing WTO rules and specific trade obligations set out in multilateral environmental agreements (MEAs). It states that the negotiations shall be limited in scope to the applicability of such existing WTO rules as among parties to the MEA in question, and that they shall not prejudice the WTO rights of any Member that is not a party to the MEA in question; paragraph 31(ii) mandates negotiations on procedures for regular information exchange between MEA Secretariats and the relevant WTO committees, and the criteria for the granting of observer status; paragraph 31(iii) mandates negotiations aimed at the reduction or, as appropriate, elimination of tariff and non-tariff barriers to environmental goods and services.

2. Status of the negotiations

107. Since the commencement of the negotiations, the Committee on Trade and Environment in Special Session (CTESS) has held several formal and informal meetings, with a significant number of proposals

[25] See the section on "Rules."

submitted by both developed and developing country Members on all three items of paragraph 31 (TN/TE/INF/4/Rev.11).

108. Recent discussions under Paragraph 31(i) focused on a proposal for an outcome that suggested to build on the sharing of national experience in the negotiation and implementation of specific trade obligations in MEAs, which was undertaken in CTESS. The other proposal on the table suggested, *inter alia*, the establishment of core principles to govern the relationship between MEAs and WTO rules, and that WTO committees and panels be called upon to "defer" to the expertise of MEAs on relevant environmental matters.

109. Under paragraph 31(ii), Members continued to explore avenues for enhancing information exchange and cooperation between the WTO and MEA secretariats. In this regard, concrete elements were discussed to improve or complement existing practices and cooperation mechanisms. Various suggestions were also put forward regarding criteria for the granting of observer status to MEA secretariats in relevant WTO Committees. Some delegations have pointed to synergies between paragraphs 31(i) and (ii) of the mandate. It is important also to note that developing countries have participated actively in the discussions under paragraphs 31(i) and (ii) with a number of them tabling submissions to clarify their positions in this area of the negotiations.

110. With respect to paragraph 31(iii), discussions in the CTESS have focused mainly on clarifying the concept of "environmental good." In this context, different approaches to the negotiations have been discussed on the basis of submissions put forward by Members (TN/TE/W/63). One approach proposes that the Committee establish a multilateral list of environmental goods for liberalization. Under this approach, nine members have proposed products for inclusion in the multilateral list. Other approaches have also been considered, including, *inter alia*, the "environmental project approach", which proposes to grant concessions to environmental goods and services required in the context of environmental projects approved by a Designated National Authority (DNA), for the duration of the project; and the "integrated approach," which suggests that the CTESS identify categories of projects and environmental goods that could benefit from tariff reduction or elimination for the period of implementation of the project in which they are used.

111. Members in the CTESS have engaged in technical work to further examine the products, systems or projects that could potentially fall within the scope of the mandate. As part of this exercise, Members have exchanged views on the environmental and developmental credentials

and potential benefits of a broad range of products put forward under different categories. A number of questions were raised in this context, including with respect to product coverage and how to deal with multiple use products. Proposals have also been made on modalities for environmental goods negotiations including, *inter alia*, provisions regarding special and differential treatment for developing countries and the elimination of non-tariff barriers. Most recently, a group of delegations, including eight Members that had earlier tabled lists of environmental goods, have proposed to the CTESS a "Potential Convergence Set" of products as a basis for negotiation and further work among Members.

3. Specific issues of interest to developing countries

112. While positions and interests naturally vary among developing countries, some specific issues of interest to them can be discerned. Many developing countries feel that trade liberalization of environmental goods should offer opportunities for them to increase exports of goods in which they have a competitive advantage. On their part, proponents of lists have generally underlined the importance they attach to achieving a "balanced list" of environmental goods, i.e. a list of products which takes into account areas of trade interest for all Members, including developing countries.

113. Some Members have observed that the export interests of developing countries lie mainly in natural resource-based products. Hence, the definition of environmental goods should cover such products. Furthermore, some concerns have been expressed regarding the existing asymmetries in production capacities, trading volumes and tariff structures for environmental goods. A number of developing countries have questioned the benefits for them of liberalizing trade in environmental goods, commenting that most environmental goods proposed thus far have multiple uses or consist of "hightech" or "end-of-pipe" products of interest primarily to developed countries. Other issues of concern to developing countries include the need to facilitate technology transfer to the developing and least-developed Members and the manner in which non-tariff barriers as well as the principle of special and differential treatment will be taken into account in the negotiations.

4. Possible gains for developing countries

114. There has been little substantive debate among participants in the negotiations on the specific gains that may accrue to developing countries from the negotiations under paragraphs 31(i) and (ii) on the relationship between MEAs and the WTO. Many developing countries have ratified

many of the multilateral environmental agreements considered relevant in the present negotiations. The mandate under paragraphs 31(i) and (ii) affords an opportunity to create positive synergies between the trade and environment regimes, including through more efficient institutional cooperation. As regards paragraph 31(iii), some hold the view that liberalization of environmental goods and services can be beneficial to trade, environment and development. According to them, the negotiations could result in increased trade due to a reduction or elimination of tariffs and non-tariff barriers. They also feel that the negotiations could potentially assist developing countries in obtaining the resources and tools needed to address key environmental priorities. Others, however, question the possible environmental benefits of some of the goods proposed for liberalization. These Members feel that the development gains would be enhanced only if goods which have an unambiguous environmental use are liberalized.

115. Some developing country Members have also argued for the retention of a certain level of policy space in determining which goods may help them meet their nationally prioritized environmental objectives. In this context, they have also stressed that their national interests in these negotiations are mainly directed towards the building-up and development of domestic production capacity in the provision of environmental goods and services. This, in their view, would further contribute to their objective of achieving sustainable development.

J. Dispute settlement understanding

1. Parameters of the development dimension

116. According to paragraph 30 of the Doha Ministerial Declaration, the negotiations on dispute settlement aim to "agree on improvements and clarifications of the Dispute Settlement Understanding (DSU)." Under paragraph 47 of the Doha Declaration, these negotiations are not to be treated as part of a single undertaking. A number of developing country Members highlighted in the early stages of the negotiations the need to have effective access to the dispute settlement procedures. In this context, it was stressed that clarifications or improvements to the DSU should not lead to any reduction in the access of developing country Members to dispute settlement procedures. Although a number of developing country Members have been active users of the dispute settlement procedures, others, in particular African and LDC Members, have had much more limited participation to date. These Members highlighted in their

proposals the significant constraints, including resource constraints, they face in having recourse to the complex and expensive (if outside counsel is used) procedures of the DSU.

117. The interests of developing country Members in the DSU negotiations are, however, not limited to S&D, or indeed to developmental aspects only. The improvement and clarification of the dispute settlement mechanism has an institutional dimension that goes beyond the particular interests of developed or developing countries. A stable, predictable and effective multilateral system to resolve trade disputes benefits the whole WTO membership. Many proposals put forward by developing country Members therefore address systemic concerns and are not intended to secure any particular form of S&D. Some of these proposals may reflect concerns which are of special significance to developing country Members as users of the dispute settlement mechanism (for example, the enhancement of third party rights). Others, however, reflect more general systemic concerns not intrinsically tied to a developmental dimension.

2. Status of the negotiations

118. Since the Hong Kong Ministerial Conference, the work of the Special Session has been based on a Member-driven, "bottom-up" approach to develop areas of convergence based on work in the previous phases of the negotiations. The Chairman has since January 2007 been conducting a series of substantive consultations on DSU review, taking up revised drafting proposals discussed recently in the DSB Special Session. The substantive consultations have been taking place in an informal, smaller group setting. Participation in that group remains open to any interested delegation. Key developing country delegations have been invited regularly.

119. The issues addressed at the three substantive consultations held until the end of March 2007 addressed revised drafting proposals on: (i) remand; (ii) enhanced third party rights in consultations and at the panel and appeal stage; (iii) the protection of strictly confidential information; (iv) transparency, including *amicus curiae* briefs; (v) general provisions in the revised proposal of the Like-Minded Group of developing countries; (vi) sequencing; and (vii) post-retaliation. The substantive consultations are scheduled to continue after the end of March and take up any revised drafting proposals on outstanding issues, such as special and differential treatment, and improving flexibility and Member control. Further, for the sake of transparency and inclusiveness, an informal

meeting of the DSB Special Session has been held after each set of substantive consultations to allow the Chairman to report back to the Membership at large.

3. Specific issues of interest to developing countries

120. Given the systemic dimension of the clarification and improvement of the DSU, virtually all issues under discussion could be said to be of relevance to developing countries as Members of the WTO and potential users of the DSU. The most directly pertinent recent development concerning developing country issues has been the submission by the so-called Like-Minded Group, composed of Cuba, Egypt, India, Malaysia and Pakistan, of a revised drafting proposal on S&D (JOB(06)/222 and Corr.1 and Add.1). The S&D proposals in the LMG paper can be categorized, following the different stages of dispute settlement, as:

- developing country interests in consultations;
- extended timeframes in consultations and panel proceedings;
- litigation costs;
- developing country interests in reasonable period of time (RPT) arbitrations; and
- cross-retaliation.

4. Possible gains for developing countries

121. A strengthened multilateral rules-based dispute settlement mechanism has been heralded as one of the major achievements of the Uruguay Round. The DSU is generally acknowledged to have served WTO Members well so far. Indeed, more than 80 WTO Members (including 65 developing countries) have participated, either as party or as third party, in at least one dispute to date. Since the dispute settlement procedures are in essence an instrument for the protection of Members' substantive rights and obligations under the WTO Agreements, it might be said that the immediate objective of improving and clarifying procedures under the DSU ultimately serves the long-term goal of enhancing the ability of WTO Members, in particular developing country Members, to fully benefit from the trade opportunities they have negotiated in the WTO.

122. The main benefits of improvements and clarifications to the DSU could be expected to come in the form of institutional strengthening of the multilateral trading system and enhanced capacity for all Members to protect their interests in the WTO. To the extent that developing country

Members, especially smaller economies with limited political power to influence the behaviour of larger trading partners, may generally have more difficulty in defending their interests effectively, such enhancements would especially benefit them. A number of procedural improvements are under consideration, that may not have any particular developmental dimension, but that would also, if successfully negotiated, benefit developing country Members as users of the system (e.g. the establishment of remand authority, the clarification of "sequencing" between compliance and retaliation procedures or the elaboration of procedures to address "post-retaliation" situations).

123. Other proposals under consideration address the resource constraints highlighted by a number of developing country Members, in the form of enhanced technical assistance or financial support. While they do not directly affect procedural steps in the dispute, they focus on ensuring that developing country Members have effective access to the procedures in the first place and the means to successfully go through a procedure. Improvements designed to address these resource constraints could facilitate recourse to the procedures by developing country Members and enhance their ability to effectively defend their rights under the WTO agreements, as complainants or defendants.

III. Concluding remarks

124. In an effort to assist Members with their discussion concerning paragraph 51 of the Doha Ministerial Declaration, this document identifies the key developmental aspects raised in the various negotiating bodies. While the issues raised in the paper vary according to subject area, it is clear that developing countries have serious and pressing interests which they wish to see addressed in the Round. These interests also change according to the subject area under discussion and reflect the very diverse interests of developing countries overall.

125. Two conclusions stem from this document: first, development issues suffuse all areas being negotiated, including in the market access and rule-making aspects of the negotiations. Second, a large number of proposals already on the table are aimed at addressing the development aspects of each subject. The possible gains to developing countries would largely depend on the outcome of the ongoing negotiations and manner in which the various proposals are operationalized after being adopted. It is hoped that this paper helps Members in their discussions and negotiations towards a successful conclusion of the Doha Development Round.

3a

Aspects of development policy in the Doha Round – An EC perspective

PHILIPPE DUPONTEIL (*)

1. Introduction

The contribution that trade can make to the integration of developing countries into the world economy has been widely recognised in recent years. In the WTO, Members have explicitly placed development at the heart of the multilateral trade system with the Doha Development Agenda (DDA) which aims at boosting economic growth across the whole developing world, including of course in Africa. It is a widely cited but striking fact that a 1% increase in Africa's share of global trade would deliver much more income every year than the continent currently receives in aid.

Therefore, the EU has from outset supported a global trade round that is genuinely pro-development. It is based on the belief that in the right circumstances, trade can help economic growth, which in turn can contribute to poverty reduction and development. Open economies tend to develop more than closed ones.

But a word of caution. *First, the link between trade and development is not automatic, and not immediate. Good governance and regulatory reforms* need to accompany trade liberalisation to ensure maximum output. *Second, it is wrong to believe that there is a monolithic developing country situation.* The WTO Ministerial Conference in Hong Kong and the Doha Development Agenda have shown significant differences in interests between developing countries – for example between the Least-Developed Countries (LDCs) and other small developing countries; between advanced developing economies such as Brazil or India and small and vulnerable economies (G–90 members); between preference seekers and MFN suppliers; between those developing countries that embrace multilateral rules in order to lock in place their domestic

(*) EC Commission, DG Trade, Brussels. The opinions expressed are personal.

reforms, and those who remain resistant to rule making on grounds of sovereignty or even more misguided reasons. *Third, one highly misleading proposition* is that all that stands between the present situation and a successful, pro-development *conclusion of the Round is the need for radical agricultural market access.* This is simply wrong. World Bank research is sometimes cited to buttress the argument that the greatest benefits in Doha for developing countries will come from freer farm trade. But this research is often misquoted or distorted. The World Bank's own research suggests first that *liberalisation in industrial products and services will be the key*, and that the bulk of benefits from agricultural liberalisation will go to those rich developed countries which have the capacity to exploit it, not to poor developing countries. And within the developing world, new market access would be snapped up by a few highly competitive agricultural exporters, not by countries belonging to the G–90.

2. Why does the DDA matter for developing countries?

The Doha Round of WTO trade talks matters for developing countries, especially for the LDCs and the small and vulnerable in a number of important ways.

First, it is a *key opportunity to stimulate South–South trade*, which represents already 40% of developing countries exports. 62% of tariffs in world trade are paid by developing countries to other developing countries. Doha is a chance to chip away at these and build better trade between developing countries, opening the markets of the large emerging ones to their poorer neighbours.

Second, *it can boost North–South trade*: That is the main reason why the declaration at the WTO Hong Kong Ministerial in December 2005 is to be welcomed, that developed-country Members, and developing-country Members in a position to do so, agree to implement duty-free and quota-free market access for products originating from LDCs.

Third, the Doha Round is a way of ensuring fast action in sectors that are particularly critical for developing countries – most obviously, *cotton*. We also need solutions in difficult sectors such as sugar and bananas where we need to balance tariff cuts with means of supporting countries affected by preference erosion.

Fourth, *the Doha Round can lock in reductions of trade distorting agricultural subsidies* as part of a comprehensive package. The EU is already doing this with the reform of its Common Agriculture Policy (CAP), and is offering to bind its reform in the WTO.

And finally, the opportunity to trade must be linked to the capacity to trade. That means building the infrastructure and the capacity for development. Everybody now recognises that open markets are only half the story for develop countries – these countries need assistance to build infrastructures and develop the means to exploit the market access which will be offered to them by others as a result of the DDA. Which is why the EU is pushing for a significant *Aid for Trade package for developing countries* as part of the final Doha deal.

3. Outcome of Hong Kong

It was against this background that the Trade Ministers from the 149 member states of the WTO met in Hong Kong in December 2005. What did we achieve there for developing countries? While everybody had to adjust their expectations on the core issues of modalities, in Hong Kong limited progress was possible on development issues due to a political push from the EU:

- The agreement to grant duty-free and quota-free access to 97% of all imports from LDCs was welcome, although it regrettably did not match the 100% access already offered by the EU. The measure must now be stamped and sealed as it will offer real benefits for poor developing countries – not least because it is one part of a wider response to the problem of preference erosion in many African countries. The EU and developing countries together now need to maintain pressure on the US, Japan and others to raise this access to 100% over time.
- WTO members also made important progress on access to medicines for African countries. Just before Hong Kong the WTO enshrined in its intellectual property agreements conditions for better access to cheap drugs against pandemics. It also agreed on an exemption for LDC's from the TRIPS Agreement until the middle of 2013, allowing African countries an extended period of time to comply with its requirements. Again, the EU was instrumental in securing this positive outcome.
- On cotton, the results were more disappointing because of US resistance to reform its own domestic agriculture. The EU pushed for the elimination of export subsidies by the end of 2006 and exports from the Least-Developed Countries to be allowed into developed countries without duty or quotas. The EU has argued that these commitments should come into effect from day one of the implementation period of

the final Doha Agreement, reflecting the urgency of the situation faced by cotton producers in West Africa. Ministers also agreed to aim to cut trade-distorting domestic subsidies on cotton by more than would normally apply under the new agreement, and to do so more quickly.

- Finally, a substantial Aid for Trade package for developing countries was adopted in Hong Kong. The EU collectively (EC and member states) offered to increase its effort to more than ⇔2 billion a year for trade-boosting projects (excluding infrastructure). The US announced they would double their effort to US$2.7 billion per year on Trade-Related Assistance and infrastructure projects, and Japan said that it would spend US$10 billion over three years. All of this is vital support in building African and other developing countries' capacity to trade.

But in three core areas of the negotiations – agriculture, industrial goods and services – the results were disappointing. Especially as the bulk of development gains in the Doha Development Round will surely derive from new market access in these sectors (and reduction of trade-distorting subsidies in agriculture). The Director-General of the WTO, Pascal Lamy, has mentioned that 70% of the development gains of the DDA will come from these three areas under negotiation. Progress in trade facilitation and new and improved trade rules will also have positive development implications and must be agreed under a single-undertaking principle that 'nothing is agreed until everything is agreed'.

4. So what would constitute a 'good' development outcome of the Doha Development Agenda?

1. Notwithstanding common assumptions, *most (80%) of the trade of developing countries does not concern agricultural products but industrial goods*, notably in labour intensive sectors like garments and footwear, as well as electronics and fisheries' products. Although tariffs in developed countries have on average already been reduced to a fairly low level in previous WTO Rounds, some products of export interests of developing countries still face significant tariff peaks and tariff escalation. Through the DDA, high tariffs can be substantially reduced, improving developing countries' access to developed countries' markets and untapping the potential for South–South trade. In turn, developing countries liberalising – at least in part – their own trade in goods will allow them to benefit from lower consumer prices, lower prices for inputs for their own industry and services sectors, and more efficient allocation of resources in the domestic

economy. Action on Non-Tariff Barriers (NTBs) can also complement tariff reductions by addressing a range of – usually – behind the border measures that have the tendency to impede developing country exports.

What then would constitute a real pro-development outcome of the DDA on NAMA? Presumably a pro-development outcome should create real new market access in both developed and advanced developing countries, should involve a progressive reduction in developing country tariff protection (gradual enough to enable adjustment to competition), and should ensure that no sectors key to developing country exports are excluded from liberalisation.

There are therefore big potential gains in the NAMA negotiations for all developing countries: developed countries will reduce the most, followed by a few large emerging countries (which are becoming more advanced in certain areas than most so-called developed countries). On the other hand, LDC's need make no commitments, and for others, it will be commensurate with their capacities, but always asymmetrical.

2. Many developing countries still believe though that the DDA *agriculture negotiations* are of critical importance, because the majority of poor people are still living in rural areas and are dependent on agriculture. This importance of agricultural trade for development, including for subsistence farming, income growth, and food security, is reflected in the mandate for the agriculture negotiations.

However, the interests of developing countries in the agriculture negotiations and their perceptions of the development implications of agricultural reform vary greatly. Agriculture is arguably an important 'offensive' interest only for a limited number of competitive agricultural exporting developing countries within the so-called G–20 group, who seek further MFN liberalisation. The situation in the developing world is thus far from unified. *Some developing countries will benefit from a more level playing field in agriculture, others will not*, namely in the G–90. Some producers in developing countries will benefit from higher world market prices resulting from reductions of subsidies and decrease of market access barriers in developed countries, while others will not.

Against this complex background, in which different developing countries have clearly diverse interests, what kind of outcome on agriculture would best serve development? What kind of liberalisation in developing countries themselves would serve development, notably by stimulating South–South trade? What kind of disciplines on food aid should be established to avoid unfair competition and the displacement of local production in receiving countries?

The most straightforward outcome of Hong Kong was a conditional agreement to end export subsidies by 2013. This has a real cost for the EU as it will put export markets out of reach for many European farm producers. Other forms of domestic subsidies that distort trade would be cut by 70%, leading to lower production in Europe. One highly misleading proposition though is that all that stands between the present situation and a successful, pro-development conclusion of the Round is the need for radical agricultural market access. The costs of eroding existing preferential trade arrangements for the poorest developing countries, as tariffs come down, also needs to be taken into account as this issue is a major concern for many developing countries.

3. Developing countries also need fair and transparent multilateral *rules*. The WTO anti-dumping agreement should be amended therefore in order to prevent overzealous, abusive or protectionist use.

4. Trade in *services* can contribute in various manners to the promotion of development. Opening up to international competition of important services sectors such as telecommunication services, computer, construction and financial services is key to strengthening the overall infrastructure of developing countries' economies, as is the introduction of the kind of regulatory practices and structures promoted by the GATS.

In addition, many developing countries enjoy a strong comparative advantage in labour intensive services such as outsourced business services delivered through mode 1 (trade across borders) and many other services delivered through mode 4 (temporary presence of service suppliers). Developing countries also have export potential in several other services sectors such as tourism, transport, business services, professional services, construction services, maritime services, computer services and health services. In the EC view, a more pro-development outcome of the DDA could logically include ambitious market access commitments in services by developed countries and developing countries alike, especially in areas crucial for development (infrastructure services) and of export interest to Developing Countries (outsourcing of services, temporary movement of natural persons).

5. *Implementation* of results of the negotiations in these areas will of course be fundamental. The WTO Agreements contain provisions which give developing countries special rights as well as exemptions to WTO obligations. This '*special and differential treatment*' (SDT) principle can take several forms, including: more favourable market access; safeguards of the interest of developing countries; flexibility when undertaking commitments; transitional periods for implementation of commitments; and

increased technical assistance. The Doha declaration mandated the review of all SDT provisions 'with a view to strengthening them and making them more precise, effective and operational'. Which raises the need to strike a proper balance between, on the one hand establishing well-understood and reasonably stable 'rules of the game' and, on the other, allowing for flexibility when these rules are applied to developing countries and *a fortiori* LDCs. The calls by some developing countries for a broad 'policy space' need to be considered against economic evidence showing that blanket exemptions and high barriers to trade are not in the long-term interest of developing countries. There are also substantial differences of view (and outright rejection by the most advanced developing countries) on the need for 'situational flexibility' (i.e. greater differentiation) between developing countries, including the desirability of characterising some of them (e.g. small and vulnerable economies) as a distinct group. A pro-development DDA outcome should therefore include agreement on a sufficient SDT package, which would need to provide sufficient flexibility to developing countries in implementing their commitments, without creating a two-tier WTO membership.

6. Another area which could bring substantial development benefits is *trade facilitation*. Vast amounts of time and money are wasted worldwide because of outdated customs and border procedures and practices. The cost of such procedures can reach 4 to 5% of the overall cost of trade transactions, which is about the same as the current developed countries' average tariff on trade in industrial goods. The mandate given to WTO members is very pro-development, recognises that technical assistance will be a key issue and that any rule must be suitable to Members' capacity to implement. This will greatly benefit developing countries to help improve customs efficiency and boost customs revenues and decrease the costs to consumers and businesses that arise from delays in trading across borders.

7. This is why the opportunity to trade must be linked to the capacity to trade. There is growing political momentum in favour of doing more '*aid for trade*' and more specifically to increase Trade Related Assistance (TRA) for developing countries, especially the weaker and more vulnerable ones, which require such assistance to address supply-side constraints and enhance the capacity to take advantage of expanded trade opportunities. Based on *Para. 57 of the Hong Kong declaration*, the EU is at the forefront of efforts to make Aid for Trade more operational by improving existing delivery mechanisms and increase funding. Similarly, the EU is fully engaged in the process to enhance the Integrated Framework for LDCs.

5. But is this enough to ensure the DDA promotes development?

Market access will not automatically lead to development. There will be winners and losers. Winners will be the most competitive, the most open to investment, those that have planned ahead the furthest, and those who are the most efficiently governed. *Agricultural reform is also going to have mixed effect.* Similarly, many developing countries (notably ACP countries) fear that the general reduction in tariffs will erode the value of the preferences which they currently receive on large developed country markets. The EU is particularly concerned by these criticisms as it is the most important market for LDCs, the market where they enjoy the largest preferences, and where we have a degree of historic responsibility to help these development partners. A pro-development outcome of the DDA must include launching a coherent set of policy responses by which the affected countries and the international community can address possible adverse consequences of the reduction of preference margins. This package would need to include a combination of trade policy responses – liberalisation of South–South trade to create new markets in advanced developing countries, longer transitional periods for tariff cuts on products that are particularly sensitive for some preference–beneficiary countries, and non-trade policy responses: assistance to economic diversification (reconversion of declining industries and protection/retraining of displaced workers).

And most important of all, the ability to benefit from opportunities of the DDA will depend on the governance of the developing countries – to provide a stable, predictable and transparent climate for trade and investment, to ensure civil society, unions and SME's are fully involved in trade policy decision making, to ensure that the economic growth from trade is shared in an equitable manner throughout society. Without these domestic governance factors trade is unlikely to have a significant impact on an individual country's development.

So the potential gains for developing countries, if there is a successful DDA, are substantial. In today's globalised world, the Doha Round is a unique opportunity for developing countries to shape the global trading system in a way that reflect their needs and their priorities. On the other hand, if WTO members do not make progress in the negotiations, poor developing countries will miss the opportunity of access to the fast growing markets of the larger emerging economies. South–South trade is growing by about 10% a year, which is twice as fast as global trade as a whole. And a multilateral negotiation enables all WTO members to agree levels of new market access for all – something no bilateral negotiation can match. For ACP and G–90 countries, failure in Doha would mean missed opportunities for new trade and missed opportunities to attract new investment and new growth. Success would mean real benefits for the vast majority of WTO members and those most in need.

3b

An Assessment of the Sixth WTO Hong Kong Ministerial Conference from a development perspective

FAIZEL ISMAIL (*)

I. Introduction and background

In the early hours of Sunday morning, on the 18 December 2005, as the negotiations amongst about thirty Ministers began to conclude, the 'grand bargain' that was needed for the WTO Hong Kong Ministerial Meeting to succeed was clearly in sight. However, there were significant differences in the perspectives of these Ministers, on the composition of the key elements of the bargain and the timing of the Doha deal. In this assessment we provide a perspective on the recent Hong Kong Ministerial Meeting and outline the central fault lines of this 'grand bargain'. Some suggestions will be made which could help to advance the negotiations towards the successful achievement of this 'grand bargain'.

The central fault line or principle in the current Doha talks was clearly articulated by the Commissioner of the EU, Peter Mandelson, in his statement after the Hong Kong Meeting.[1] In this statement Mandelson argues that the EU was unlikely to make further concessions in the current Doha negotiations given the paucity of concessions, in his view, that are on offer from the EU's trading partners. He goes on to state that there was no possibility of him using the WTO to push through, further, or early, reforms of the EU Common Agricultural Policy (CAP). Although the EU at its recent summit[2] had decided to review the EU CAP budget in 2008/2009, Mandelson warns that there would be no links between this and the efforts to conclude the Doha negotiations early in 2007.

He argues further that given real incentives in the Doha industrial goods and services negotiations, the EU could provide 'more predictabil-

(*) Head of the South African Delegation to the WTO, Chairman of the WTO Committee on Trade and Development, Geneva. This chapter was written end of January 2006.

[1] See 'Trade chief says EU united on farm stance', *Financial Times*, 21/12/2005, p. 2.

[2] The EU Summit was held on 16 and 17 December. See 'EU, horse-trading was humiliating – but failure would have been worse', *Financial Times*, 19/12/2005, p. 3.

ity and transparency for agricultural exporters' (referring to the demands of the CAIRNS Group, G20 and the US) and show more flexibility in the range of products that the EU has demanded should be deemed 'sensitive'.[3] Mandelson also questioned 'Lamys' view' that further progress could be made by April 2006 ie, the achievement of full modalities in the agriculture and industrial products (NAMA) negotiations.[4] In this regard Mandelson states rather ominously in the same article that 'the EU cannot be pushed into an agreement that simply is not there'.

Mandelson's assessment above sets the stage for the complex post-Hong Kong Doha negotiations. There are *three key issues*, that he has raised, which need to be challenged. *Firstly, the argument that the EU has done enough in making concessions in the agriculture negotiations is simply not true*, as the current EU offer on Market Access made by Mandelson on 28 October, will result in no further real market opening or acceleration of CAP reforms.[5] He has argued that the only possible concessions the EU could make, notwithstanding any possible changes in the EU budget, is some additional flexibility in its demand to continue to maintain the current high levels of protection for its sensitive sectors.

Secondly, his view that other WTO members (especially the so-called 'advanced developing countries') need to make real concessions in industrial goods and services for the EU to make the above additional concessions is an attempt to raise the bar above the heads of the majority of the major developing countries, and thus shift the burden of adjustment in this Round from the major agricultural subsidizers to the major developing countries. Mandelson's argument that the EU needs the major developing countries to make these concessions before the EU can make even some incremental concessions is spurious. There is no discernible major drive by the EU's industrial producers or service providers for additional market access into developing country markets. On the contrary, these interests have voiced their concern with regard to the disproportionate political influence of the EU's agricultural lobbies. There is legitimate suspicion that Mandelson's argument is an attempt to shift

[3] The EU has demanded a so-called 'pivot' in the tariff-cutting formula (i.e. the flexibility to deviate from the agreed percentage cut by a maximum of two-thirds, with a 20% minimum cut, for about 70% of their tariff lines). In addition, the EU insists on designating up to 8% of its tariff lines as being 'sensitive'. The EU intends to make only minimal cuts in these so called 'sensitive products'.

[4] The Hong Kong Declaration has set the deadline for the conclusion of the negotiations for full modalities to be the end of April 2006.

[5] 'Making Hong Kong a Success: Europe's contribution' European Commission. Brussels. 28 October 2005.

the blame for lack of movement in the Doha Round to the major developing countries.

In addition, a group of developing countries[6] have argued that the real danger of a joint push by the EU and other developed countries (notably the US)[7] to seek additional extensive concessions from developing countries in the NAMA and Services negotiations is that the development content of the Round will be turned on its head, with the developed countries making more inroads into developing country markets and with developing countries still facing high levels of protection and distortions in global markets for products of export interest to them. In a paper[8] submitted to the Committee on Trade and Development and the Trade Negotiating Committee of the WTO, developing countries have argued that the strategic objective for this round of negotiations should be for industrial countries to reduce the protection they grant to inefficient sectors that frustrate the growth potential of developing countries. Reflecting on the recent proposals[9] of developed countries they have stated that these demands in NAMA and Services will create enormous and disproportionate burdens of adjustment that developing countries would have to bear in their industrial and service sectors. In sharp contrast, the EU has made insignificant offers to open its markets in the agriculture negotiations, and both the EU and US have proposed a coefficient for developed countries in the NAMA negotiations that will require them to make no real adjustment in their industrial sectors. They have thus argued that the EU and the US are seeking a round for free!

Thirdly, Mandelson's assertion that the EU would not be prepared to make any significant move in offering even the minimal additional concessions that he referred to above, by April 2006,[10] will make the possibility of

[6] See Statement made by South Africa to the 55th session of the Committee on Trade and Development on behalf of Argentina, Brazil, India, Indonesia, Namibia, the Philippines and Venezuela, 28 November 2005.

[7] The US has stated on several occasions that it will work shoulder to shoulder with the EU to seek significant market access in the markets of advanced developing countries in the NAMA and Services negotiations.

[8] 'Reclaiming Development in the WTO Doha Development Round' submission made to the 55th session of the Committee on Trade and Development on behalf of Argentina, Brazil, India, Indonesia, Namibia, Pakistan, the Philippines, South Africa and Venezuela, 28 November 2005.

[9] 'Making Hong Kong a Success: Europe's Contribution.' European Commission. Brussels, 28 October 2005.

[10] The Hong Kong Ministerial Declaration calls for full modalities in Agriculture and NAMA to be agreed by the end of April 2006.

concluding the Doha Round by the end of 2006, or early 2007, even less likely. In addition, developing countries will be reluctant to make significant concessions early in the post-Hong Kong period, unless the EU reflects the political will to make real concessions in the agriculture negotiations that are in line with the Doha Mandate.

There is a second fault line or a secondary set of issues which are of great importance to the majority of the poorer and smaller members of the WTO, and that are a crucial component of the Doha grand bargain. Without a successful resolution of these issues, a Doha deal or grand bargain will simply not be struck. These issues relate to addressing the trade-related development challenges faced by Least-Developed Countries, and the so-called 'small, weak and vulnerable developing countries'. The specific development issues raised by these countries include, the need to provide duty-free quota-free market access to LDCs, cotton, preference erosion, special flexibilities for small, weak and vulnerable economies and development aid.

There was a great deal of posturing on these issues before the Hong Kong Ministerial Meeting. The EU trade Commissioner Peter Mandelson, in a letter to WTO members written in October 2005, challenged Ministers to provide a development package on these issues in Hong Kong.[11] There was great suspicion amongst developing countries that the EU was again trying to divert attention from the core issues of development in the Round, which related to developing country demands for developed countries to remove their trade distorting subsidies and protection of agricultural products. In addition, the US delegation was suspicious that in focusing on these development specific issues, the EU was attempting to divert attention to the US inability to deliver concrete results on the cotton issue and on the issue of duty-free, quota-free market access for LDCs.

II. What happened in Hong Kong?

After six days of intense negotiations in Hong Kong (13–18 December 2005), Ministers managed to cobble together an agreement late on Sunday night, 18 December, several hours past the agreed deadline. For the major developing countries in the G20 the agreement was no major breakthrough,[12] but a small and significant step forward in the Doha

[11] Letter dated 9 October 2005.

[12] Celso Amorim, the Brazilian Minister of Foreign Affairs and Trade and the co-ordinator of the G20 was quoted in the *Financial Times* (19/12/2005) as saying that the decisions reached in the Hong Kong Declaration were 'modest but not insignificant'.

Round. For LDCs and other small, weak and vulnerable developing countries, there were some incremental gains made in the Hong Kong Declaration, but no breakthrough emerged on their major demands. We briefly evaluate the results of the negotiations in Hong Kong below.

1. Agriculture

In Agriculture, the EU had reluctantly agreed to table an offer to eliminate its export subsidies by 2013. After much difficult negotiation in the chairman's consultative group in the final hours of the negotiations, the G20 members in the meeting agreed to this offer provided that 'the substantial part is realized by the end of the first half of the implementation period'. Before the Hong Kong Ministerial Meeting there was great pressure on the EU to decide on this issue in Hong Kong, as the G20, CAIRNS Group, the Africa Group, the ACP, LDC Group and the US, all called for export subsidies to be eliminated by 2010.

There was no substantial advance in the Agriculture negotiations in Hong Kong. In addition to re-stating the decisions already reached in the July Framework agreement, the final draft of the Hong Kong Declaration reflected some significant movements by WTO members in the technical work undertaken in Geneva. These issues related to the conversion of specific tariffs to their *ad valorem* tariff equivalents and some convergences reached to use three bands for cuts in domestic support subsidies and four bands for the tariff cuts envisaged in the market access negotiations.

There was some improvement in the final text on the language on Special Products (SP) and the Special Safeguard Mechanism (SSM) demanded by less competitive developing countries (G33). Agreement was reached that developing countries can self-designate a still-to-be determined percentage of tariff lines as Special Products to be 'guided by indicators based on the criteria of food security, livelihood security and rural development'. There was also agreement that developing countries will 'have recourse to a SSM based on import quantity and price triggers'.[13] The addition of a price trigger was fought for vigorously during the Ministerial Meeting and was a victory for the G33.

[13] See WT/MIN (05)/DEC Para 7 of the 'Ministerial Declaration', Doha Work Programme, 22 December 2005. The July 2004 Framework Agreement already provided for developing countries to self-designate Special Products and utilise a Special Safeguard Mechanism without specifying the criteria to determine SP or the details of the SSM.

2. NAMA

In the NAMA negotiations, several of the major developing countries including South Africa, India and Brazil were of the view that the decisions reached on NAMA at the Hong Kong Ministerial Conference did not represent a roll back of gains made in Doha or in the July 2004 Framework agreement. Indeed some of the gains made in the NAMA negotiations, for example, on flexibilities agreed to in the July 2004 Framework, had been under threat in the past few months in Geneva. Whilst the final draft of the Hong Kong Declaration reflected members' agreement to adopt a Swiss Formula, the option to use different types of Swiss formulae still remain to be decided and have not been foreclosed. *The major advance for developing countries in this text was the decision to link the ambition in the market access negotiations in Agriculture with NAMA*. This allows developing countries to argue that WTO members would need to produce a formula in the market access negotiations in agriculture that is 'balanced and proportionate' to that in the NAMA negotiations. In addition WTO members agreed that the level of ambition in market access for Agriculture and NAMA should be 'comparably high'.[14]

Whilst there was some fragmentation in developing country positions on the formula to be adopted by the WTO on NAMA in the period before Hong Kong, the approach taken by the EU in its 28 October submission caused these countries to create a united front on the *need to defend the flexibilities* that developing countries had succeeded in obtaining in the July 2004 Framework Agreement.[15] This united front was further consolidated in Hong Kong where Ministers of the so-called NAMA 11 presented joint proposals in the negotiations on NAMA.[16] This group was also able to establish a strong link between the level of ambition in NAMA with that in Agriculture in the final text of the Hong Kong Ministerial Declaration.[17]

[14] See WT/MIN (05)/DEC Para 24 of the 'Ministerial Declaration'. Doha Work Programme, 22 December 2005.

[15] See TN/MA/W/65 'Market Access for Non-Agricultural Products. Flexibilities for Developing Countries'. Communication from Argentina, Bolivarian Republic of Venezuela, Brazil, China, Egypt, India, Indonesia, Namibia, Pakistan, Philippines and South Africa, 8 November 2005.

[16] See letter by the above countries, including Tunisia, sent to the Chairman of the Conference and the Director General at the Hong Kong Ministerial Conference.

[17] See WT/MIN (05)/DEC. Para 24 of the 'Ministerial Declaration'. Doha Work Programme, 22 December 2005.

3. Services

On Services, the existing GATS[18] development friendly methodology in the services negotiations were under threat of being fundamentally altered by proposals made in the first draft of the Hong Kong Ministerial text.[19] Developed countries, and a few developing countries were attempting to substantially change the methodology of the services negotiations in an attempt to raise the ambition of the negotiations, in a manner that would increase the pressure on less competitive developing countries. There was widespread opposition to these attempts by the African Group, the ACP and several ASEAN countries.

In the draft Ministerial text that was forwarded to the Ministers,[20] the quantitative targets insisted on by the EU were deleted. A number of countries, including South Africa, still had concerns about this text. Their initial concern was that the chapeau of the Ministerial draft text did not state that the new methodology proposed in the annex (Annex C) was not agreed. Thus, at the insistence of those countries that had substantive objections to some elements of Annex C, the chapeau of the Ministerial text that referred to Annex C was bracketed.

Negotiations in Hong Kong focused on the changes needed by these countries before they agreed to remove the brackets. In the course of the negotiations in Hong Kong these members succeeded in making two significant changes to Annex C. Firstly in the section on Objectives the words 'strive to achieve the following objectives' were replaced with 'should be guided, to the maximum extent possible, by the following objectives'. Most developing countries viewed these objectives as being too ambitious and prescriptive. Secondly, these countries also objected to the prescriptive language of the proposed methodology for plurilateral negotiations in services. The compromise struck in the final text underlined the fact that the existing flexibilities provided for in the GATS and the Negotiating Guidelines would still remain the basis for the negotiations in services.

[18] The current methodology for the negotiations in Services is based on the General Agreement on Trade in Services (2000) and the GATS negotiating guidelines agreed by the WTO in 2001. These agreements call for a positive list approach where countries choose the sectors they wish to make concessions in and the extent to which they wish to open their markets. Secondly, the current negotiating methodology that is largely utilised by members is a bilateral request and offer method, although a plurilateral approach is also provided for by the above guiding documents.

[19] See WT/MIN (05) W/3 'Draft Ministerial Text'. Doha Work Programme, 7 December 2005.

[20] WT/MIN(05) W/3. 'Draft Ministerial Text'. Doha Work Programme, 7 December 2005.

4. *The 'development package'*

There were five key development-specific issues identified by the EU[21] and other members in the period before Hong Kong: a development package for LDCs, cotton, preference erosion, the specific concerns of small, weak and vulnerable countries and the question of an 'Aid for Trade' envelope to support the needs of developing countries. Despite intense negotiations on both the LDC duty-free, quota-free issue and the need for an early harvest on cotton, the *so-called 'development package' proposed by the EU failed to materialize in Hong Kong.*

5. *LDCs*

The compromise offered by the US after six days of intense negotiations, to provide duty-free, quota-free market access for up to 97 percent of tariff lines and to progressively increase this, with no obligation to reach 100 percent, was not acceptable to LDCs. The US argued that it could not offer to extend full product coverage to countries such as Bangladesh and Cambodia which were competitive in some products, such as textiles, as this would displace the existing preferential market access for African countries provided under the US AGOA preferential scheme. Pakistan surprised most members by arguing that it would not accept a deal for LDCs which did not allay its fear that preferential textile exports from Bangladesh, in terms of the proposed deal, could displace a significant part of its exports to the US market.

LDCs were reluctant to accept the US offer as they argued that the 3 percent exemption would allow the US to exclude almost all the products of export interest to them. In the statement made to WTO members at the final plenary on Sunday evening (18 December 2005) the co-ordinator of the LDCs, Minister Patel of Zambia, thus called for the Annex on LDCs to be part of the ongoing negotiations in Geneva and to be used as a basis to develop modalities to conclude the negotiations on LDCs. In a letter sent to the DG and several WTO Ministers subsequent to the Hong Kong Ministerial Meeting, Minister Patel, as co-ordinator of the LDCs, in a reconciliatory tone called for the offer of the US and other developed

[21] See letter by Peter Mandelson sent to WTO Trade Ministers dated 9 October 2005. Mandelson identifies five deliverables for Hong Kong in this letter, including the so-called implementation issues. In their subsequent position paper, dated 28 October (referred to above), the EC supported the need for 'specific actions to overcome the distortions to trade on cotton' and the 'early implementation' of such actions.

members on duty-free, quota-free market access referred to above (in Annex F) to be built upon in the post-Hong Kong Geneva process.[22] In the statement made by the Chair of the conference, Secretary Tsang of Hong Kong, China referred to the section on the duty-free quota-free treatment in Annex F as a 'framework' and urged developed and developing country members in a position to do so, 'to set out by the end of 2006, the means by which they will implement this decision'.[23]

There were four other *Special and Differential Treatment, LDC Agreement Specific proposals* that were agreed to in Annex F. These included an agreement to give 'positive consideration' to requests for waivers by LDCs, and when requested to provide waivers exclusively in favour of LDCs by other members, to decide such a matter expeditiously and 'without prejudice to the rights of other members'. Costa Rica and Paraguay had finally agreed to this compromise. A second agreement called for donors, multilateral agencies and international financial institutions to ensure greater policy coherence with WTO agreements in the conditionalities that they often impose on developing country members. A third agreement re-affirmed that LDCs will only be required to undertake commitments and concessions to the extent that it is consistent with their development needs and capabilities and directed the WTO to coordinate its efforts with donors to 'significantly increase aid for trade-related technical assistance and capacity building'. Finally, of these four, the most significant agreement for LDCs was the decision to provide new flexibilities for LDCs so they did not have to comply with the TRIMS Agreement until 2020. These flexibilities include a transition period of seven years for existing measures and an agreement to give positive consideration to allow any new TRIMS for a period of five years.

6. Cotton

In the cotton negotiations, the four West African cotton-producing countries (C4 countries) pleaded passionately for an early harvest. In response, the US delegation, insisted that they did not foresee any negotiations outside the context of the agriculture negotiations. However, there was some movement by the USTR Robert Portman, when he agreed to

[22] In this letter Minister Patel states, 'I believe that the LDCs managed to get an outcome which, although was not all that we wanted, is a platform upon which we can build in the future.'

[23] Statement made by Secretary Tsang, the Chair of the Conference at the closing plenary meeting of the WTO Hong Kong Ministerial Conference, 18 December 2006.

eliminate the US cotton export subsidies in 2006. Brazil had argued that this was required anyway by the recent WTO Appellate Division decision in the case brought to the WTO by Brazil, on the US-trade-distorting cotton subsidies. In addition, the US agreed to support a decision to provide duty-free, quota-free market access for cotton exports from LDCs from the date of implementation of the Doha deal. These were two incremental advances made on the cotton issue in Hong Kong.

However, on the most significant demand of the C4 countries and other members (i.e. the need to reduce trade-distorting cotton subsidies) the US did not agree to an early harvest. As part of the final agreement, both the USTR and the four West African cotton producers agreed to continue the negotiations in Geneva, in the post-Hong Kong period, with the C4 countries still maintaining their demand for an early harvest not linked to the Doha agriculture negotiations.[24]

7. Erosion of preferences and the needs of small, weak and vulnerable countries

On the issue of erosion of preferences and the needs of small, vulnerable economies, the ACP group succeeded in gaining some further recognition of these concerns in the NAMA negotiations and a commitment to address these issues in the ongoing Doha negotiations.[25]

8. Aid for trade

Finally, on the issue of 'Aid for Trade', the final text[26] called on the Director General of the WTO to create a Task Force and to provide the General Council with recommendations by July 2006.

There was no major breakthrough or early harvest on the five identified development-specific issues in Hong Kong. For LDCs there was some significant advances made on the five agreement-specific proposals that LDCs had prioritized, in the negotiations on Special and Differential Treatment. The agreements reached on duty-free, quota-free market access, and increased flexibilities in WTO rules and capacity building, are

[24] These positions were articulated by both the USTR and Ministers from the C4 countries in their statements made to the final plenary of the Hong Kong Ministerial meeting.

[25] See WT/MIN (05)/DEC Paras. 20 and 21 of the 'Ministerial Declaration'. Doha Work Programme, 22 December 2005.

[26] See WT/MIN (05)/DEC Para. 57 of the 'Ministerial Declaration'. Doha Work Programme, 22 December 2005

significant gains to build on in the ongoing Doha negotiations. Thus, whilst some incremental advances were made on the so-called development package, greater political will is required to advance these issues in the post-Hong Kong period.

In most cases it has become clear that there will, or can, be no major breakthrough or early result on these issues. The political will and capacity of the major countries to deliver depends on the ambition to agree on the core issues in the Doha negotiations regarding agriculture, NAMA, services and the related disciplines. Thus for these countries to make any gains from the Doha Round and advance their issues, there needs to be an early conclusion to the Doha Round as a whole, with the focus on the core issues.[27]

III. The way forward

The post-Hong Kong work programme and the timing for the conclusion of the Doha Round did not obtain much consideration by Ministers in Hong Kong. Ministers simply assumed that the Round should be concluded by the end of 2006. Thus the timetable for the achievement of full modalities in Agriculture and NAMA was decided to be 30 April 2006 and the completion of schedules based on these modalities was set for 31 July 2006.

There was no discussion of how the political will to complete the task of achieving full modalities on Agriculture and NAMA by the end of April 2006, could be developed within the next four months. The EU Commissioner, Peter Mandelson, has already signalled that the EU did not have the will to finalise full modalities in a manner that will require them to make significantly new concessions in the agriculture negotiations (discussed above). Notwithstanding this, the EU will continue to pressure others, particularly the major developing countries, to make additional onerous concessions in the NAMA and Services negotiations.[28] A failure to achieve any real movement on these core issues of the negotiations and to resolve the fundamental fault line in the Doha Round is also likely to have a detrimental effect on any possible resolution of the specific development issues of interest to the majority of least developed and small, weak and vulnerable developing countries.

[27] See also Ismail, F. 'How Can Least-Developed Countries and Other Small, Weak and Vulnerable Developing Countries also Gain from the Doha Development Round?' *Journal of World Trade*, 40, 37.

[28] See statement by Peter Mandelson 'Trade chief says EU united on farm stance', *Financial Times*, 21/12/2005.

Advancing the Doha negotiations in the post-Hong Kong period will require renewed political commitment and political will by the major developed and developing countries. The US will need to play its part in making more significant offers to reduce its trade-distorting subsidies and discipline its farm support in line with new WTO rules. The US will also need to display greater political will to address the needs of the LDCs and the small, weak and vulnerable members of the WTO. Without an ambitious effort by all WTO members to address these specific issues of interest to these members of the WTO, a 'grand bargain' is unlikely to emerge.

The major developing countries represented in the G20 and the 'NAMA 11' have displayed a firm resolve to maintain the high level of ambition of the Round and defend the development content of the Doha Round thus far. They have called for more open and undistorted trade and have signalled their willingness to make a contribution in this regard provided this is proportionate to their level of development and the contribution of the developed countries. In their recent paper they have also committed themselves to making a contribution towards addressing the development challenges of the LCDs and the small, weak and vulnerable countries.[29] Their leadership in advancing these objectives and engaging effectively with developed and other developing countries to build the consensus needed for the round to succeed will be crucial in the year ahead.

There was renewed optimism that developing countries will be able to manage and resolve their differences whilst keeping the pressure on developed countries to deliver on the development content of the Round in Hong Kong when the major developing country groupings including the G20, the G33, the ACP, the LDCs, the African Group and the Small Economies met at Ministerial level. This meeting was called 'historic' by Minister Amorim as it was the first such meeting of Ministers in the WTO and was referred to as the 'G110' (G90+G20). These groups agreed that agriculture is central to the Round and to development and were united in calling for export subsidies to be eliminated by 2010. They all agreed to address the specific development challenges facing developing countries in the Doha Round.[30] The Doha Round 'grand bargain' will also require that in exchange for the strong support of the G20 countries for their

[29] 'Reclaiming Development in the WTO Doha Development Round' submission made to the 55th session of the Committee on Trade and Development on behalf of Argentina, Brazil, India, Indonesia, Namibia, Pakistan, the Philippines, South Africa and Venezuela, 28 November 2005.

[30] See Joint Press Statement issued by the G20, the G33, the ACP, the LDC Group, the African Group and the Small Economies. Hong Kong, 14 December 2005.

concerns in the Round, including that of preference erosion, the LCDs and the small, weak and vulnerable countries should not obstruct or delay the market access needs of the G20 and other more competitive developing countries.

At this stage, however, *the EU stands to be the main obstacle to progress in the Doha Round.* Unless significant political pressure is brought to bear on the EU member states in the next few months the WTO is set to miss its next deadline of achieving full modalities, by April 2006 and will certainly not conclude the Round by the end of 2006. The EU will hope that the resolve of those in the G20, the Cairns Group and the US for further agricultural reform in the EU will wane and that they will settle for a lower ambition from the Doha Round. For the G20 and other developing countries, accepting this will mean that the development content of the Doha Round will have little, if any, meaning and the WTO will continue to be seen to be unfair and imbalanced, having yet again failed to address the needs of developing countries!

4

Capacity building and combating poverty in the WTO

LILIA R. BAUTISTA (*)

Trade liberalization, the main objective of multilateral trade negotiations, is expected to result in economic growth. Faster economic growth can lead to poverty reduction, if not eradication. Today, all over the world, 1.3 billion people live on less than one dollar a day, one-half of the world, or nearly three billion people, live on less than two dollars a day.[1] Approximately 790 million people in the developing world are still chronically undernourished, almost two-thirds of whom reside in Asia and the Pacific.[2] More heart-wrenching is the UNICEF report which states that 30,000 children die daily because of extreme poverty – "and they die quietly in some of the poorest villages on earth, far removed from the scrutiny and the conscience of the world. Being meek and weak in life makes the dying multitudes even more invisible in death."[3] In 2003, 10.6 million died before they had reached five years of age, the same children population in France, Germany, Greece and Italy.[4]

Faced with the existing poverty in developing countries, hope is high that the Doha Round of multilateral trade negotiations, which is supposed to be a development Round, will be true to its name. The Doha declaration clearly states that: "International trade can play a major role in the promotion of economic development and alleviation of poverty . . . In this context, enhanced market access, balanced rules, sustainably financed technical assistance and capacity building programmes have important roles to play."[5]

(*) Ambassador Bautista was the Permanent Representative of the Philippines to the WTO for more than six years.

1 Larry Elliot, A Cure Worse than the Disease, *The Guardian*, January 21 2002.

2 World Resources Institute Pilot Analysis of Global Ecosystems, February 2001 (in the Food Feed and Fiber section).

3 Where and why are 10 million children dying every year? *The Lancet*, Vol. 361, No. 9376, June 28 2003.

4 State of the World's Children, 2005, UNICEF.

5 Paragraph 2 of the DOHA Declaration.

As enunciated by OECD,[6] if developing countries are to maximize the benefits of trade liberalization, market access is of critical importance. This is not enough, however. *Market access must be complemented by domestic policy reforms and trade capacity building.*

I. Market access

In the market access negotiations, developing countries still face roadblocks when trying to penetrate the export market, both in goods and services. Domestic support and export subsidies in developed countries make it difficult for developing countries to compete in the world market. Since negotiations are reciprocal, developing countries must likewise open up. This would require adjustment measures for developing countries due to loss of revenue and loss of jobs in areas where competition is likely to occur because of domestic support and export subsidies to products entering developing countries. The same applies to services.

Before any adjustment measures can be made via domestic policy-reforms and international assistance, market access for developing countries must be there. The developmental aspects of the Doha Round as indicated in the Doha Development Agenda (DDA)7[7] discusses the issues involved in the negotiations of market access:

1. Agriculture

The developing countries are seeking lower tariffs for products of export interest to them, such as tropical products and the expansion of the quota of products subject to the quota system (e.g. the European Union (EU) quota on tuna).

The WTO General Council decision of August 1, 2004 in the area of market access in agriculture states that tariff reduction will be achieved by a tiered formula that takes into account the member's different tariff structures and that progressive tariff reduction will be achieved through deeper cuts in higher tariffs and with flexibilities for sensitive products that are supportive of their development goals, particularly poverty reduction strategies.

[6] OECD Global Forum on Trade Workshop, November 2002.

[7] WT/COMTD/143/Rev 1, the updated document Rev 2 is contained in Chapter 1 of this book.

Since developed countries are likewise seeking tariff reduction and other commitments, the developing countries have proposed the concept of "special products" which will not be subject to further commitments because its liberalization can have an effect on rural livelihoods and, consequently, the food security of developing countries. This, in effect, is special and differential treatment for developing countries. On the other hand, the European Union (EU) has proposed the concept of sensitive products which should not exceed eight percent (8%) of the tariff lines on agricultural products. This would be available to developed and developing countries and, presumably, would be on top of the special products of developing countries. The guidelines on the identification of such products are currently under negotiation.

Reduction in the high level of domestic support is also under negotiation since such a policy distorts the agricultural trading environment and lowers world prices, particularly commodity prices. Developing countries are hoping that there will be at least a sixty percent (60%) reduction of domestic support by developed countries to enable products of developing countries to compete in the world market.

On export competition, as a result of the Hong Kong Ministerial Meeting, the EU has agreed to remove export subsidies by 2013. In the past, there have been internal reforms within the EU which included cutting subsidies, but they have never materialized. The agreed 2013 deadline will enable the EU to push for the elimination of export subsidies because it has become an international commitment. Such commitment, therefore, can truthfully be an accomplishment of the Round, which is the most tangible one at this time.

2. Non-agricultural Market Access (NAMA)

On non-agricultural market products, bound tariffs of developing countries are comparatively higher than developed countries (i.e. on average, thirty-four percent (34%)). On the other hand, applied tariffs of developing countries are much lower than their bound tariffs. Developed countries would like more tariff cuts from developing countries or at least that they bind their applied tariffs.

Unlike agricultural products which talk of bands of tariff levels and cuts depending on whether or not one is in the higher, middle or lower band, the Swiss formula currently under discussion for NAMA has the characteristic of cutting more for higher tariffs and cutting less for lower tariffs. This is for harmonization purposes. Developing country negotiators are fighting hard for a different coefficient for developing countries so that the cuts will not reach their applied rates which are much lower than the bound tariffs. The Hong Kong ministerial accepts coefficients that may be more than one.

The developing countries have asked for a degree of preserving "policy space" in order to pursue their development goals of industrialization and the diversification of their economies. They have argued that since they have no institutional capacity to use trade remedies such as anti-dumping measures, safeguards and the like, they need to preserve high-bound tariffs as a substitute instrument.

Some developing countries have argued that they need to retain tariffs to protect industries that are in their infancy since they have no public funds for their support. Although there is a provision in the present GATT about infant-industry protection, its application is difficult. Developing countries which have claimed such a right have not been successful in their attempts to retain tariffs.

With respect to non-reciprocal preference erosion which would be the result of lowering tariffs, there are suggestions to address the same in the negotiations. Some countries believe, however, that compensation for the erosion of non-reciprocal preference should be addressed outside the WTO. Most of these preferences, such as the Generalized System of Preferences (GSP), for developing countries are granted outside the WTO. According to some countries, to place within the WTO would compromise the MFN liberalization in the GATT and would mean that non-reciprocal preferences enjoyed by developing countries would also require compensation.

These countries are willing to consider safety-net solutions outside the WTO. It would be interesting to see if the solutions which would compensate for this erosion to determine would be meaningful and unconditional.

There is also concern among developing countries as to how to prevent the loss of tariff revenues as a result of tariff reduction. While the long-term solution is the diversification of the country's tax base, it is accepted that there will be immediate loss of tariff revenue as tariffs are reduced, which will result in a loss of income for some developing countries before they can look for other sources of revenue.

The NAMA 11[8] has reiterated *flexibilities for certain tariff lines* to be exempt from further liberalization. They maintain that the developing

[8] Argentina, Venezuela, Brazil, China, Egypt, India, Indonesia, Namibia, Pakistan, Philippines and South Africa.

countries should apply less than formula cuts to up to ten percent (10%) of the tariff lines, provided that the cuts are no less than half of the formula cuts and that these tariff lines do not exceed ten percent (10%) of the total value of a member's import; or keeping as an exception tariff lines unbound or not applying formula cuts to five percent (5%) of tariff lines, provided they do not exceed five percent (5%) of the total value of a member's imports.[9]

On average, tariffs of developed countries are lower than developing countries. However, their tariff peaks and escalation are more than developing countries. The *elimination/reduction of tariff peaks* and escalation is being asked for by the developing countries because tariff escalation in developed countries may inhibit the development of value-added industries in developing countries where they may be more suitably located. Tariff peaks are high tariffs, usually defined as tariffs that are three times the national weighted average. Developed country tariff peaks tend to be higher on products of export interest to developing countries such as textiles, apparel and footwear.[10]

3. *Services*

The importance of services in world trade cannot be understated. For least-developed countries (LDCs), it is forty-four percent (44%) of the GDP, fifty-seven percent (57%) for middle income countries and seventy-one percent (71%) for higher income countries, according to statistics provided by the World Bank for 2002. Truly, the area is wide and can be significant in international trade.

The General Agreement on Trading Services (GATS) provided for progressive liberalization in subsequent rounds on top of what has been offered under the GATS in the Uruguay Round. The developed countries are moving for more service areas to be opened under the Doha Round. Among the four modes of delivering services, the fourth mode (i.e. movement of natural persons in services) is being pushed by some developing countries. While movement of goods and capital have been extensively dealt with in the WTO, the movement of people has met a number of barriers, notwithstanding the labor deficiency in some countries and the labor surplus in others.

[9] TN/MA/W/65.

[10] Now what? Searching for solutions to the WTO Industrial Tariff Negotiations, Santiago Fernandez de Cordoba and David Vanzeth., UNCTAD, p. 3, 2005.

India has a very interesting proposal, based on the highly asymmetric levels of commitments undertaken by Members among the various modes of supply with mode 4, movement of people, being perceived as highly restricted. It is noted that while commitments in mode 4 are mostly horizontal, these are nonetheless subject to many kinds of limitation. Further, these horizontal commitments refer mainly to a small subset of service personnel related to commercial presence (mode 3) and at higher levels at that, with very few commitments extending to the independent movement of individual service suppliers.

More than merely advocating further market access commitments by Members for, specifically, professionals under mode 4, India suggests that from an administrative standpoint, the *temporary movement of labor should be treated separately from the permanent movement of labor*, such that the former need not fall under the purview of immigrations statutes and authorities with their correspondingly stricter eligibility conditions and limitations on length of stay. As a corollary to this, India is proposing the concept of the *"GATS visa" for temporary service providers* under mode 4. India further argues that temporary service providers should be exempt from minimum wage requirements and the payment of social security taxes.

From a classification standpoint, India proposes the dis-aggregation of categories of service providers in the sectoral schedules, to be achieved through the superimposition of the International Labour Organization's International Standard Classification of Occupants (ISCO-88) onto the WTO Services Sectoral Classification List (MTN/GNSIW/120). Moreover, India posits the idea that horizontal schedules should specifically include the category of "individual professionals" in addition to the various categories that currently exist. Through these, India aims to de-link true mode 4 commitments from the mode 3 movement of personnel which requires a commercial presence.

In effect, there is a *call for harmonization of categories of service suppliers* used in scheduling commodities under the GATS, the reduction of barriers involving matters such as nationality, residence, work permits and the commitment of lower skilled workers. It would truly alleviate poverty in developing countries if the labor surplus of developing countries can be utilized by developed countries in need of their services. In some developing countries, workers' remittances to their families reached $8 billion a year.

As the service area opens up further, rules implementing GATS, such as emergency safeguards, is long overdue.

4. *Special and differential treatment (S&D)*[11]

To gain market access, special and differential treatment should be granted to developing countries in the various WTO Agreements.

While it may be argued that reciprocal reduction in tariffs by both developed and developing countries is the essence of trade liberalization, exceptions can be made for developing countries which still need tariff protection.

After all, five of the six fastest-growing developed countries during the Age of Capitalism (1950–1973) were high tariff countries with Japan in the lead with an 8.05 percent growth rate. With its protectionist policies, it developed its car industry with subsidies from the government and a tariff of 35.9 percent.[12] History shows that developed countries have not strictly pursued free trade since the late nineteenth century. Most countries have used protectionism and, in particular, tariffs, to promote their industries from the eighteenth century until 1960, except during the years 1860–1880.[13]

Historically, GATT (the General Agreement on Tariff and Trade) in 1947 was essentially a forum of reciprocal tariff cuts. In 1964, after the birth of a new trade and development organization (UNCTAD) in the United Nations, Part IV was appended to GATT for a limited special and differential treatment. The Uruguay Round expanded it and under the WTO, there are ninety-seven provisions on S&D divided into five (5) categories of special and differential treatment:[14]

1. Provisions intended to increase trade opportunities for developing countries:

(a) Recognition in the preamble of the special needs of developing countries, particularly concerning positive efforts to ensure that developing countries secure a share in the grant in international trade commensurate with their economic development needs.

(b) Provisions that allow developed countries to provide trade preferences to developing countries such as the GSP which is bilaterally negotiated.

[11] See also Qureshi, chapter 5 of this book.

[12] Ha-Joon Chang, Why Developing Countries Need Tariffs, South Centre and Oxfam, pp. 56–8, Nov. 2005. [13] *Ibid.* 87–8.

[14] Working Paper 2, Special and Differential Treatment for Developing Countries, South Centre, Geneva: pp. 1–6, 1999.

(c) Article IV:1 of the GATS, which aims for the increasing participation of developing countries in trade in services which shall be facilitated through negotiated specific commitments and through the liberalization of trade in services in sectors and modes of supply of export interest to them.
(d) Provisions in the Agreement on Textiles and Clothing for more favorable growth rates in quotas for small exporters, new entrants and least-developed countries (LDCs).
(e) Provisions in the Decision on Measures in Favor of LDCs for improving preferential treatment for products of export interest to LDCs, as well as the adoption of positive measures that facilitate the expansion of trading opportunities for LDCs.[15]

The problem with the above provisions is that they are not specific enough to be legally binding. Moreover, assuming a developed country takes positive steps to grant preferential tariffs to developing countries outside the WTO, they may impose conditions with which developing countries may have difficulties in complying. In hearings on GSP, opposition has been premised on non-trade issues such as human rights.

Recently, the EU imposed labor and environmental conditions for the additional availment of GSP.

2. Provisions to safeguard the interests of the developing countries

(a) In the Dispute Settlement of Understanding (DSU) there are provisions to safeguard the interest of developing countries, such as:

- In consultations under the DSU, members should give special attention to the particular problems and interests of developing country members (Article 4.10).
- If a complaint is brought by a developing country, that developing country may choose to apply certain other alternative procedures (Article 3.12).
- When a dispute is between a developing and a developed country, the panel will, if the developing country so requests, include at least one panellist from a developing country member (Article 8.10).

[15] Constantine Michalopolous, Trade and Development in the GATT: The Role of Special and Differential Treatment, p. 19, WTO Documents, February 28 2000.

- In the context of consultations involving a measure taken by a developing country, the parties may agree to extend the periods set for the establishment of panels (Article 12.10).
- Panels shall afford developing countries sufficient time to prepare and present argumentation (Article 12.10).
- Where one or more of the parties is a developing country, the panel's report will explicitly indicate the form in which account has been taken of relevant provisions on differential and more favorable treatment for developing countries under the covered agreements (Article 12.11).
- In surveillance of implementation of recommendations and rulings, particular attention should be paid to matters affecting the interests of developing countries with respect to measures that have been subject to dispute settlement (Article 21.2).
- If the case is brought by a developing country, the Dispute Settlement Body, in considering what appropriate action might be taken, will take into account not only the trade coverage of measures under consideration in the dispute, but also their impact on the economy of the developing country concerned (Article 21.8).
- At all stages of the determination of the causes of a dispute and of dispute settlement procedures involving a least-developed country, particular consideration will be given to their special situation, including the exercise of due restraint by the complaining party, and the offer of good offices, conciliation and mediation by the WTO Director-General or the Chairman of the Dispute Settlement Body (Article 24).
- Special assistance and advice will be made available to developing countries in disputes (Article 27.2).[16]

(b) Under Article 10.1 of the Agreement on Sanitary and Phytosanitary Measures (SPS), developed countries are required to take into account the situation of developing countries in the preparation and application of these measures. It would be very difficult for a developing country to produce evidence that its concerns were not taken into account if the respondent says it has done so.

[16] *Ibid.*, pp. 22–3.

(c) Under the agreement on Technical Barriers to Trade (TBT), Article 12.3 also provides that Members shall, in the preparation and application of technical regulations, standards and conformity assessment procedures, take account of the special development, financial and trade needs of developing country Members, with a view to ensuring that such technical regulations, standards and conformity assessment procedures do not create unnecessary obstacles to exports from developing country Members.

In the case of the above provisions, the developing countries may have a difficult time to claiming S&D if the measure can be for a legitimate objective within the meaning of Article 2 of the TBT.

In the above provisions for SPS and TBT, the obligation of the developed country is to consider the impact on the developing country, but it has no obligation to change the measure even if the developing country can prove the negative impact to its trade interest.

The TBT also provides that:

- "Members shall take such reasonable measures as may be available to them to ensure that international standardizing bodies, upon request of developing country Members, examine the possibility of, and, if practicable, prepare international standards concerning products of special interest to developing country Members." (Article 12.5)
- "Members shall take reasonable measures as may be available to them to ensure that international standardizing bodies and international systems for conformity assessment are operated in a way which facilitates active and representative participation of relevant bodies in all Members, taking into account the special problems of developing country Members." (Article 12.5)

These provisions have led to quite a few problems because the obligation is not a binding one due to lack of specificity and are confined to taking reasonable measures as may be available to them. Moreover, the participation of developing countries in international standards bodies presents difficulties due to financial constraints and lack of technical know-how.

(d) Under Article 15 of the Anti-Dumping Agreement, it is provided that: "Possibilities of constructive remedies provided for by this Agreement shall be explored before applying anti-dumping duties where they would affect the essential interests of developing country Members."

Under this provision, there is no obligation to provide alternative remedies considered as constructive so as not to affect the essential interests of developing countries nor has there been any effort to explore other possibilities before rendering a decision on anti-dumping.

3. Provisions permitting developing countries to assume lesser obligations

(a) In some WTO agreements, developing countries were allowed to undertake fewer commitments than developed countries. Under the Agreement on Agriculture, developing countries were given a longer time-frame to implement their obligations. They are obliged to reduce their tariffs, on average, by 24 percent over ten years, while developed countries are required to reduce theirs by 36 percent over six years. While developing countries are required to make at least a 10 percent reduction on each tariff line, developed countries are expected to make a minimum reduction of 15 percent on each tariff line. With respect to trade-distorting domestic support measures, developing countries are expected to reduce such measures by 13.3 percent over ten years, while developed countries are required to reduce theirs by 20 percent over ten years. Regarding export subsidies, developing countries are expected to reduce their value and volume by 24 and 14 percent, respectively over ten years, while developed countries are expected to reduce theirs by 21 and 36 percent, respectively. Least-developed countries are exempt from making any reduction commitments.

These provisions are legally binding and countries, developing and developed, cannot be compelled to assume more obligations. Monitoring compliance with the obligation herein would be essential to give effect to these provisions.

(b) The Subsidies Agreement also confers S&D treatment on developing countries, least-developed countries and developing countries whose GNP per capita income is less than $1,000. They are exempt from the prohibition against export subsidies, provided that they do not attain export competitiveness in a particular product for two consecutive years. (A country will be deemed to have attained export competitiveness in a given product when its share reaches 3.25 percent of world trade for two consecutive years). Other developing countries are expected to phase out export subsidies within eight years of the coming into force of the WTO Agreement, although upon request, it

> could be extended for a further two-year period. Developed countries were given three years within which to phase out their export subsidies, while countries in transition were given seven years to do so. With respect to import substitution subsidies, least-developed countries, developing countries, countries-in-transition and developed countries were given eight, five, seven and three years, respectively, to phase out such subsidies after the coming into force of the WTO Agreement. Regarding actionable subsidies, while there is a presumption of serious prejudice in the case of certain subsidies provided by governments of developed countries, there is no such presumption in the case of similar subsidies provided by governments of developing countries. Serious prejudice in cases involving subsidies allegedly provided by governments of developing countries must be proved by positive evidence.

Where the provisions of the Agreement are clear, it would seem that S&D provisions can be relied upon by developing countries to defend themselves against alleged violations of the WTO Agreement. However, capacity building measures are necessary for developing countries to be in a position to utilize these tools.

4. Provisions relating to transitional time periods

With the notable exception of the Anti-Dumping Agreement and the Pre-shipment Inspection Agreement, almost all the major WTO Agreements contain longer transitional periods for developing countries to comply with their obligations. The flexibility takes the form of an agreed delay on the part of developing countries, of certain or all provisions of the agreement concerned.[17] Under the Agreement on Agriculture, for example, developing countries were given ten years to implement their obligations, while developed countries were given six years. Under the TRIPS Agreement, least-developed countries, developing and developed countries were given respectively, eleven, five and one year to bring their legislation into conformity with WTO disciplines. A developing country which was not providing product patents under its legislation was given an additional five years to comply with its obligations under the Agreement. The TRIMS Agreement gave least-developed

[17] Laird, n. 22 at p. 23 as cited in Kessie, E. (2000) Enforceability of the Legal Provisions Relating to Special and Differential Treatment under the WTO Agreements, A paper prepared for a WTO Seminar on Special and Differential Treatment for Developing Countries, 7 March, Geneva, p. 13.

countries, developing countries and developed countries seven, five and two years, respectively, after the coming into force of the WTO Agreement to phase out all their inconsistent trade-related investment measures. The Customs Valuation Agreement gave developing countries which were not parties to the Tokyo Round Code on Customs valuation five years within which to comply with their obligations under the Agreement. Developing countries were also given the possibility of delaying the application of the "computed value" method of valuation for a further three years.[18]

5. Provisions relating to technical assistance

A number of the WTO Agreements require the WTO or its developed Members to provide technical assistance to developing countries to enable them to comply with their obligations under the various WTO Agreements and also to help them to participate effectively in the multilateral trading system. The words "agree to facilitate" and "shall consider" would seem to indicate that it was not intended to make the provision of technical assistance obligatory. It is therefore up to a developed Member country to decide whether or not it is going to provide assistance to a particular developing country. The same applies to technical assistance provided by WTO and other multilateral institutions. The provision of technical assistance is usually dependent on the availability of funds.[19]

Most of the above provisions on S&D are not obligatory and others may need rules or guidelines for implementation. Only two (2) of the S&D provisions are categorical, i.e., transition period or longer time-frame and in some aspects have fewer obligations such as in cutting subsidies. Since developing countries can hardly afford to subsidize and the usual five-year transition period has passed, the developing countries have all banded together to *insist on new modalities in these negotiations, such as so-called "special products" in agriculture and "flexibilities to exempt at least five percent (5%) of tariff lines not exceeding five percent (5%)* of the import value of industrial products" for the negotiations. It is believed that in these negotiations, the developing countries are one in seeking special and differential treatment which are not mere exhortations. It is in line with the WTO mandate to increase the share of developing countries in world trade.

It is provided in the Doha Ministerial that S&D should be embedded in all the WTO agreements. At least *for the LDCs*, there is a consensus among

[18] Kessie, *Ibid.* [19] *Ibid.*

WTO members that developed countries should give them duty-free and quota-free entry for their products but the tariff preferences of other developing countries are still under negotiation.

On implementation issues, there are a number of proposed amendments to the WTO agreements which are designed to remove inequities in the implementation of the agreements. There seems to be a strong resistance to the amendment of existing agreements, as this may disturb the balance of negotiated give-and-take in these agreements.

Instead of changes in the wording of the agreements, some countries have proposed the further extension of the delayed commitments of developing countries. In particular, local content programs which developing countries have undertaken, once phased out, may mean the closure of some manufacturing industry since importation would be the order of the day rather than sourcing these parts locally. In this situation, it may be worthwhile to assess the conditions in the particular country invoking the extension. While an across the board extension of the local content program may be counterproductive, there is merit in making some exceptions.

There are proposals to revise certain rules, particularly on dumping. On this issue, forty-five percent (45%) of the cases are against developing countries. It is noted, however, that developing countries are both dumpee and dumper, hence, the difficulty of negotiating amendments to the agreement. Maybe this is an area where special and differential treatment can be given to developing countries in the interpretation and application of the Anti-dumping Code as well as the Subsidies Code, the Sanitary and Phytosanitary Agreement and the Agreement on Technical Barriers to Trade.

For a developing country to avail of a dispute settlement, it must have the necessary resources. A proposed fund for this purpose has been suggested and this should be seriously considered so that developing countries can appoint the necessary counsel to prosecute their claims and ably defend themselves.[20]

New models to enforce the decisions of the Appellate Body should be explored. The usual method, imposing restrictions on exports of a recalcitrant developed country, may not work as a retaliatory measure as exports to the developing country concerned may be quite limited and could be ignored by the developed country.

In sum, for developing countries to benefit fully from S&D, the following must be resolved and implemented as soon as possible:

[20] See also Gappah, chapter 14 of this book.

Guidelines on "special products" under the Agricultural Agreement must be specifically provided for in the revised Agreement. Developing countries must be well equipped to come up with suitable guidelines to cover products critical to them not only for the present, but also for their long-term planning in food security.

Increased leeway is needed for developing countries to exempt certain non-agricultural products from the negotiations. The maximum limit of 5% of the tariff line is much too small for some countries. While as a rule, differentiation among developing countries is not favored, as a compromise, higher limits can be set up for those less industrialized developing countries. Additionally, tariff escalation and tariff peaks should be eliminated/reduced.

Corollary to all the market issues is the application of S&D to all the agreements such as anti-dumping, subsidies, technical barriers to trade, sanitary and phytosanitary and dispute settlement to give meaning to the intent to allow developing countries to catch up. A liberal interpretation and application of the rules in favor of developing countries must be clearly enunciated.

Individual countries that are asking for the extension of time-frames should be examined as to their current stage of development, to see if they merit such an extension.

As to those provisions which are motherhood statements or mere exhortations, it is about time to give flesh to their bones.

5. Impact on poverty reduction

What the developing countries have submitted for differential treatment in the Doha negotiations is some kind of laundry list which must be prioritized. Developing countries must work hard to undertake this *prioritization*. Understandably, this will be a difficult task considering the various stages of development by developing countries. Moreover, developed countries are wary of free riders. While they have reorganized the need for special treatment of LDCs, the less affiuent developing countries are forgotten. There would seem to be *a need to look at the special conditions of some developing countries which are not LDCs.*

If poverty is to be reduced, growth rates must be high enough to impact on poverty reduction and must be continuous for a certain period of time. Some economists believe that a growth rate of less than seven percent (7%) can have little effect on poverty reduction

> One of the most robust results of empirical research in development economics is that rapid and sustained economic growth leads to significant and long-term poverty reduction and that direct pro-poor programs are inefficient and unsustainable. The much-heralded *dynamic development-cum-poverty reduction* of our East and Southeast Asian neighbors is living testimony to this. For example, South Korea, Taiwan, and Malaysia have been able in two decades to bring down their poverty to levels close to those of Western countries. Similarly, Thailand and Indonesia, which had poverty rates of above forty percent (40%) – comparable to that in the Philippines – in the early 1980s, have reduced those rates to less than ten percent (10%) and below twenty percent (20%), respectively, by the early 2000s, while the incidence of poverty in the Phillippines remains at around thirty-three percent (33%).
>
> Several observers and analysts have characterized the economic development of our Asian neighbors as *'pro-poor growth.'* So, what is pro-poor growth? Simply put, it is growth that enables the poor to actively participate in and significantly benefit from, economic activity. This is a departure from 'trickle down' which was the dominant development concept in the 1950s and 1960s. Trickle down means that the benefits of economic growth go to the rich first and the poor gain only indirectly through a vertical flow. Poverty could diminish but only slowly at best . . . .[21]

Using growth rates can be a factor in the enjoyment of special and differential treatment. Per capita income of less than USD1,000 has already been used in the continued practice of granting export subsidies of developing countries in the Subsidies Code. Considering inflation, the benchmark can be increased to USD2,000.

What is clear is that the "one size fits all" treatment of all developing countries may not be acceptable to developed countries. Developing countries must be prepared to accept some differentiation so that all their demands can be considered.

Without market access and the corollary special and differential treatment, developing countries cannot hope to fight poverty within the WTO.

II. Adjustment measures/Domestic reforms

Having dealt with the issue of market access, adjustment measures must be adopted domestically by developing countries. Products which have

[21] Ernest M. Pernia, former lead economist of ADB, Star Science. Philippine Star Science and Technology, B-7, March 9 2006.

no comparative advantage must be examined and the respective areas opened up. Plans to transfer jobs lost to other areas must be provided.

Studies undertaken by UNCTAD[22] covering some developing countries have indicated that while there has been economic growth in these countries, the immediate result, presumably from liberalization, has been unemployment, lower wages, transition costs and obsolescence.

Studies[23] done on the effect of liberalization have netted mixed results. In the case of India, Dr. Veena Jha of DFID–UN found economic growth surged after liberalization, averaging six percent (6%). Poverty indicators have improved, but regional disparities have widened. Both exports and imports grew by fifty percent (50%) between 1998 and 2003, but unemployment rose from six percent (6%) in 1993–1994 to 7.3% from 1999–2003.

It was noted, however, that India's gradual approach to liberalization has helped spread adjustment costs and has ensured better performance. Fiscal, monetary and investment reforms have preceded liberalization.

On the other hand, Malawi's post-liberalization performance has been disappointing. The growth rate has dropped from fifteen percent (15%) in 1994 to two percent (2%) in 2002. A study by Kennedy Vybekeame, showed that manufacturing shrank by thirty percent (30%).

Jamaica's growth rate was only five percent (5%). In Bangladesh, a study by Narum Rahman showed that there was expansion in trade due to garment exports, but there was no other diversification. There was a reduction in poverty, but there was an increase in inequality. With textile quotas being phased out, there is apprehension that there will be little growth.

In Brazil, post-liberalization has been characterized by low rates of growth. Based on a study by Prof. Lia Valls Pereira unemployment rose from 5.7% in 1992 to 7.9% in 1999.

In Bulgaria, Victor Ogrietsev of UNCTAD found a high level of unemployment and poverty indicators have deteriorated.

Based on the above studies, it would seem that no adjustment measures have been undertaken after liberalization. Only in India, which insisted on gradual liberalization, were the results of liberalization positive. One theory is that liberalization is the outcome of development rather than a prerequisite. India and China did not start with liberalization, but followed the historical pattern of liberalizing trade as they grew richer. The other theory is that liberalization must be gradual and selective. Now that

[22] Sam Laird and Santiago Fernandez de Cordoba, UNCTAD, IV, V, 2005. [23] *Ibid.*

most countries are members of the WTO, the latter theory would seem to hold more water. Regardless of what type of liberalization is undertaken, adjustment measures are necessary and should be part of domestic policy reforms.

For other countries, *domestic policy reforms* centered on encouraging foreign investment which accelerated the adjustment to trade liberalization. New industries brought about by foreign investment created employment. The use of foreign investment as a tool should be explored further.

In the private sector, on the labor side of in addition to the cost of unemployment and lower wages, there have been costs due to retrains as well as personal costs such as psychological suffering. On the capital side there is temporarily unemployed capital, the cost of capital rendered obsolete, and transition costs involved in shifting capital from one to the other.[24]

In the public sector, there is the loss of tax revenue, the erosion of benefits from preferential arrangements (as discussed above) efforts to ensure macro-economic stability, unemployment and retraining programs to be supported by government. In some cases, there is a lack of food and additional costs to meet competition.[25]

All these additional costs would have been minimized if developing countries had *unemployment benefits.* Unfortunately, very few of these developing countries have such benefits or if they do, they are not enough to sustain families. Some of the countries surveyed have adopted policies to cope with the adjustment. Richer developing countries have paid for compensation losses for a limited period and governments have provided social policies and safety nets such as unemployment benefits and retraining programs.

On the other hand, countries that have not provided adjustment measures have had difficulty recovering or have been turned off by liberalization. Those who adopted adjustment measures seem to have benefited from liberalization.

III. Capacity building and technical assistance

The WTO technical assistance plan for 2006[26] is meant to guide the secretariat in pursuing the key objectives as allegedly mandated by WTO members. These are to enhance institutional and human capacity in

[24] Sam Laird, Coping with Trade Reforms, UNCTAD, February 10 2006 [25] *Ibid.*
[26] WTO/COMTD/W/142.

beneficiary countries to address trade policy issues and concerns, mainstreaming trade into national policy and poverty reduction policies, facilitating fuller participation of beneficiaries in the multilateral trading system. It allegedly takes into account the priorities set out in the Doha Development Agenda. The DDA recognizes that technical assistance and capacity building are key elements in the development dimension.

According to the WTO, the key features of the technical assistance and training plan are as follows:

Quality oriented: It is important that high quality is assured and that product oriented process and programs are geared towards facilitating the integration of the beneficiaries into the multilateral trading system

- *Development oriented*: geographically balanced to ensure equitable coverage of beneficiaries
- simple and flexible to accommodate specific requests from beneficiaries, particularly LDCs and vulnerable economies
- designed to build and strengthen partnership with beneficiaries and donors.

The Plan has the following products:

(1) General WTO-related Training and Technical Assistance – Geared towards government officials with broad overall WTO responsibility (specialists and technicians)
  (a) Trade policy courses – All agreements in the WTO are covered:
    - Geneva-based trade policy courses – The main purpose is to provide general information about the WTO;
    - regional trade policy courses.
  (b) Geneva-based introduction courses.
  (c) Regional and sub-regional short trade policy courses and DDA advanced training program:
    - basic training – dissemination with regional and sub-regional dimensions;
    - specialized and Advanced Training and Technical Assistance;
    - more in-depth understanding of specific issues.
  (d) Geneva-based specialized courses.
  (e) National technical assistance activities.
  (f) Regional seminars.
  (g) Trade negotiation techniques.
  (h) Outreach activities for parliamentarians and civil society.

(2) Academic support for training and capacity building: An integrated approach – cooperation with learning institutions to promote capacity building
  (a) Regional trade policy courses.
  (b) Workshops for university professors on WTO matters.
  (c) Support program for doctoral studies.
  (d) Program for visiting academics.
  (e) Research collaboration.
  (f) Document dissemination program for universities.

(3) Support training and technical assistance facilities – General and specific support to delegations and beneficiaries in the field and in Geneva
  (a) Geneva-based activities.
  (b) Geneva-based topic-specific symposia.
  (c) WTO introduction days.
  (d) Other forms of Geneva-based support.
  (e) Trainee programs and internships.

(4) Activities held in the field
  (a) Reference centres.
  (b) Technical assistance within the TPRM framework.

(5) Other activities
  (a) Assisting beneficiaries in conducting needs assessment.
  (b) Distance learning and information technology.

As can be seen from the above list, there are *a number of capacity building programs for the benefit of member countries.*

It is noted that despite such a wide-ranging technical courses on the WTO, supposedly to arm negotiators of the developing countries, *specific adjustment measures due to liberalization are not dealt with.* Presumably, this will have to be done on a country-by-country basis taking into account the specific circumstances of each country. The capacity building program of the WTO has helped officials of many countries to understand the WTO. Unfortunately, some countries have not chosen the right person to be trained or may have taught the right person only to have them transferred elsewhere in the government system. In some countries, the officials have not passed their knowledge onto their colleagues, so other workers have not been trained in their turn.

The WTO capacity building program should have a component which is country specific, delving deeply into the problems of a lagging developing country and discussing various options with the country's policy makers. Capacity building for impact assessment and policy research and design are sadly lacking in some developing countries. In this connection, capacity for the right data gathering to support decision making is critical. Technical assistance would be required for a developing country to set up such facility.

In connection with exports of developing countries, studies indicate that *two to three percent (2–3%) of the value of the export products can be reduced if trade facilitation is effected.* Technical assistance for capacity building would be necessary for developing countries to allow the faster release of goods upon arrival at port.

Technical assistance on product design and packaging would help developing countries to be more competitive.

IV. Conclusion

The Doha Round is scheduled to conclude in December 2006 or early 2007. It is expected that this deadline will not be met. Be that as it may, the Hong Kong Ministerial clearly showed that the developing countries have found their voice and they stood together to lay down their demands. It may be appropriate to quote what former Director-General Moore said in his speech on April 23 2001:

> But perhaps more importantly from a WTO perspective, it means that developing countries are now full and active members of the multilateral trading system. And since they are expected to make concessions, they have a right to make demands. Moreover, since they make up the overwhelming majority of the WTO's membership, their demands cannot be ignored. They can set priorities for negotiations and expect to meet many of them. They no longer have to make do with the scraps tossed from the rich man's table.
>
> The older member of the Organization are adjusting to this new world. The big players know they can no longer simply cut deals amongst themselves and expect the rest of the world to fall in line. Developing countries are adjusting, too.[27]

[27] Director-General Moore, The WTO and developing countries: Priorities for negotiations, Berlin, April 23 2001.

Trade agreements can help alleviate poverty and bring about development. History shows that it is difficult, if not impossible, for a technologically backward country to develop without some kind of trade protection of which tariff is one. Trade liberalization should be gradual and selective as part of a long-term industrial policy.[28]

[28] Ha-Joon Chang, above n. 12 p. 101.

5

Integrating development and SDT (Special and Differential Treatment) into the architecture of the WTO – through the operation of its Dispute Settlement System

ASIF H. QURESHI[1]

1. Introduction

A consideration of development in the context of the Doha Round raises many issues. In this chapter the main focus is on Special and Differential Treatment (SDT) as an aspect of development, with particular reference to its integration into the architecture of the WTO through the dispute settlement system.

Thus far there has been no significant overall progress in the work of the Committee on Trade and Development (CTD) on SDT. However, the decisions in *Annex F of the Hong Kong Ministerial Declaration* with respect to Least-Developed Members are to be noted.[2] The deliberations of the CTD generally seem to have started with a focus on detail, and have moved only latterly in terms of general conceptual approaches towards realising the objectives of the negotiations on SDT. The reverse might have been the case. As a matter of general negotiating approach the general thematic clusters and conceptualisation of the issues and potential proposals, should have been sorted out at the outset, in order to allow the issues and proposals raised during the negotiations to be pegged into them. As yet, it is not possible to discern the outline of the pillars of development and SDT in the architecture of the WTO. Some progress may, however, be discerned in terms of a measure of consensus

[1] Law School University of Manchester, Manchester UK. I am grateful to Shishir Priyadarshi from the WTO Trade and Development Division for his assistance.

[2] See Annex F Ministerial Declaration Adopted 18 December 2005 WT/MIN(65)/Dec: Understanding in Respect of Waivers of Obligations under GATT 1994; Decision on Measures in Favour of Least-Developed Countries; Decision on Measures in Favour of Least-developed Countries; Agreement on Trade-Related Investment Measures; Decision on Measures in Favour of Least-Developed Countries.

in relation to the clarification and strengthening of some agreement-specific SDT provisions. Similarly, in relation to cross-cutting issues, the identification of capacity building and measures to improve the implementation of SDT provisions is to be noted – in particular the Monitoring Mechanism proposed by the African Group, which seems to have gained currency.

Whereas the issues and proposals in the deliberations of the CTD generally demonstrate a high level of understanding of the issues, of problems imagination and of foresight – nevertheless the whole process does beg the question of whether developing Members (particularly the LDCs) have been fully empowered to effectively participate at this level of policy in the process. In particular, there appears to be a certain distance between the amount of literature, evidencing analysis and proposals at the academic and civil society level (for the improvement of the development dimension in the WTO) and the deliberations of the CTD.

This outline chapter sets out briefly the state of affairs so far, and proffers some proposals for integrating development and SDT into the architecture of the WTO.

2. Developments with respect to SDT in the Work of the Committee on Trade and Development (Special Session)

The mandate

Para 44 of the Doha Ministerial Declaration provides that the 'provisions for special and differential treatment are an integral part of the WTO Agreements', and that 'all special and differential treatment provisions shall be reviewed with a view to strengthening them and making them more precise, effective and operational'.

Para 12.1 of the Decision on Implementation-related Issues and Concerns[3] directs the CTD:

> (a) to identify those special and differential treatment provisions that are already mandatory in nature and those that are non-binding in character, to consider the legal and practical implications for Developed and Developing Members of converting special and differential

[3] WT/MIN(01)/17 20 November 2001 (Decision of 14 November 2001 of the Ministerial Conference).

treatment measures into mandatory provisions, to identify those that Members consider should be made mandatory, and to report to the general Council with clear recommendations for a decision by July 2002;

(b) to examine additional ways in which special and differential treatment provisions can be made more effective, to consider ways, including improved information flows, in which developing countries, in particular the least-developed countries, may be assisted to make best use of special and differential treatment provisions, and to report to the General Council with clear recommendations for a decision by July 2002; and

(c) to consider, in the context of the Work Programme adopted at the Fourth Session of the Ministerial Conference, how special and differential treatment may be 'incorporated into the architecture of WTO rules'.

CTD work generally

The CTD has met on several occasions. Its focus mainly has been on cross-cutting Issues and agreement-specific proposals and issues.

The cross-cutting issues refer to systemic and institutional issues, for example principles and objectives of SDT; structure of rights and obligations and their effectiveness; policy coherence; technical assistance and capacity building; transition periods; trade preferences, universal or differential treatment, including graduation. On the other hand the agreement-specific issues focus on existing provisions of the various WTO Agreements.

Some eighty-eight agreement-specific proposals have thus far been made. These proposals have been categorised by the Chairperson of the General Council[4] as follows:

- Proposals where there has been agreement in principle, and where there is a greater likelihood of reaching an agreement. Around thirty-five proposals. (Category One.)[5]
- Proposals that fall within current areas of negotiations under the Doha Round, for example, Agriculture, Services, DSU, Rules. Around forty proposals. (Category Two.)

[4] [Job 03]/68.

[5] The proposals are too numerous to set out here in a footnote or as an addendum. In general the proposals purport to strengthen, 'operationalise', interpret and clarify existing SDT provisions – including provisions of the Enabling Clause.

- Proposals in relation to which there are wide differences of opinion. Around fifteen proposals (Category Three.)[6]

State of affairs since March 2002

The first meeting of the CTD in Special Session was held on 5 March 2002. This was followed by a number of subsequent meetings prior to July 2002. During this period a number of proposals on cross-cutting issues were discussed. In particular:

- except in the case of LDCs, preferential treatment should be accorded on a non-discriminatory basis (Paraguay);
- the Monitoring Mechanism (African Group);
- the annual Special Session of the General Council on LDCs participation (LDC Group);
- the Facility under the Doha Development Agenda Trust Fund (African Group);
- the proposals on Technical Assistance and Training (African Group).

were noted.

Of these cross-cutting proposals the Monitoring Mechanism appears to have received general agreement in principle with a recommendation to the General Council that it agree with the establishment of such a mechanism. However, during this period some eighty Agreement-specific proposals were made and discussed, but no agreement was reached.

Between July 2002 and February 2003 the Special Session of the CTD met on a number of occasions. During this period the Agreement-specific proposals were considered, as directed by the General Council, in *thematic clusters*, as follows:

- provisions aimed at increasing the trade opportunities of developing country members;[7]

[6] For example, the proposal that LDCs should be exempt from the disciplines of the Agreement on TRIMs.

[7] For example, proposal from the African Group: 'Developed countries should agree to take measures for encouraging the import of services from developing countries. Various measures can be envisaged, including: (i) reserving a specified portion of services import for government use from developing countries; and (ii) relaxing entry conditions for service providers from developing countries. Special attention should be given to sectors and modes of supply of interest to developing countries.' WT/COMTD/W/77/Rev.1.

- provisions under which WTO Members should safeguard the interests of developing country Members;[8]
- flexibility of commitments, of action, and use of policy instruments;[9]
- transitional time periods;
- technical assistance;
- provisions relating to LDC members;
- proposals not included above.

Agreement in principle within the CTD was reached in relation to some twelve agreement-specific proposals but no recommendation to the General Council for their adoption was made. These proposals do not individually or together constitute much progress in this sphere. In relation to the Monitoring Mechanism some progress was made on some of the issues, but others remained unsettled. Little progress was made on the question of incorporation of SDT into the architecture of the WTO rules.

Between February 2003 and April 2004 there was not much progress. However, in relation to agreement-specific proposals, there was agreement in principle on twenty-eight proposals in the CTD but this was not adopted at the Fifth Ministerial Conference at Cancun, Mexico.

Not much progress was made during July 2004 in this sphere. The General Council's post-Cancun *decision of 1 August 2004* [WT/L/579] did not involve any significant specific decisions, other than general affirmations and directions as to how the negotiations might further proceed in the CTD.

From April 2004 until recently much of the discussion has been around the manner in which the work of the CTD should progress. The principles identified in the CTD[10] as being important in further advancing the work on SDT in relation to Agreement-specific proposals are:

[8] For example, proposal made by CARICOM: 'Safeguards: We endorse the proposal that safeguard measures be included in the GATS. We attach great importance to emergency safeguards for services as a useful instrument for countering negative effects arising from the liberalisation of trade in services. We share the view that multilateral disciplines in this area would encourage the active participation of developing countries.' *Ibid.*

[9] *Ibid.* Hong Kong China: 'Hong Kong, China fully subscribes to the provision of the GATS which provide for flexibility for developing countries to undertake commitments in a progressive manner and with the objectives of Article IV in mind. We believe, however, that the liberalisation of services sectors, provided that appropriate regulatory frameworks are in place, is in the overall benefit of all Members. We thus consider that the best approach to flexibility is to provide for realistic phasing-in periods for commitments for developing countries, rather than to consider the exclusion of sectors from specific commitments.'

[10] See TN/CTD/11.

- effective market access for products of export interest to developing Members;[11]
- flexibility in WTO rules;[12]
- flexibility to be consistent with a multilateral rules-based system;[13]
- enhanced capacity building programmes.[14]

In relation to the cross-cutting issues similar principles have been identified to enable their placement namely:

- flexibility in WTO rules;
- elaboration of the Monitoring Mechanism;
- enhanced capacity building needs;
- coherence in international policy making.

The current *modus operandi* that is being developed in the sphere of SDT that seeks to conceptualise the Agreement-specific and cross-cutting issues and proposals discussed is to be commended, even though it is perhaps late in the day. However, there are three points to note with respect to the deliberations thus far. First, they seems to be focused mainly on existing proposals. Second, they do not differentiate between issues that are concerned with implementation and SDT as such, and others that relate to changes that need to be brought about. Finally, the most important issue, namely how to integrate development into the architecture of the WTO, is not sufficiently focused upon.

As has been noted earlier, and to complete the picture so far, the December *2005 Hong Kong Declaration* has resulted in *five specific proposals*[15] that relate to least-developed countries. These are welcome,

[11] This is seen as a 'means of enhancing' the economic development of developing Members (TN/CTD/11).

[12] For example, transitional arrangements.

[13] Flexibility in WTO rules is qualified by an affirmation of the multilateral disciplines. These disciplines are also needed to support developing countries' efforts to build their competitiveness and integration into the world economy. See TN/CTD/11.

[14] This is in order to facilitate the implementation of WTO rules and 'address supply-side constraints'. See TN/CTD/11.

[15] These are set in Annex F of the Declaration as follows:

> 'Special and Differential Treatment LDC Agreement-specific Proposals
>
> (23) Understanding in respect of waivers of obligations under the GATT 1994
>
> (i) We agree that requests for waivers by least-developed country Members under Article IX of the WTO Agreement and the Understanding in respect of Waivers of Obligations under the GATT 1994 shall be given positive consideration and a decision taken within 60 days.
>
> (ii) When considering requests for waivers by other Members exclusively in favour of least-developed country Members, we agree that a decision shall be taken within

although out of these perhaps the only one of significance appears to be that according market access to duty-free and quota-free products from least-developed Members. This access to markets of developed Members and in some measure to developing Members' markets is not immediate, but starts in 2008, and it does not apply to services. The other decisions

60 days, or in exceptional circumstances as expeditiously as possible thereafter, without prejudice to the rights of other Members.
(36) Decision on measures in favour of Least-Developed Countries
We agree that developed-country Members shall, and developing-country Members declaring themselves in a position to do so should:
(a)(i) Provide duty-free and quota-free market access on a lasting basis, for all products originating from all LDCs by 2008 or no later than the start of the implementation period in a manner that ensures stability, security and predictability.
(ii) Members facing difficulties at this time to provide market access as set out above shall provide duty-free and quota-free market access for at least 97 per cent of products originating from LDCs, defined at the tariff line level, by 2008 or no later than the start of the implementation period. In addition, these Members shall take steps to progressively achieve compliance with the obligations set out above, taking into account the impact on other developing countries at similar levels of development, and, as appropriate, by incrementally building on the initial list of covered products.
(iii) Developing-country Members shall be permitted to phase in their commitments and shall enjoy appropriate flexibility in coverage.
(b) Ensure that preferential rules of origin applicable to imports from LDCs are transparent and simple, and contribute to facilitating market access.
Members shall notify the implementation of the schemes adopted under this decision every year to the Committee on Trade and Development. The Committee on Trade and Development shall annually review the steps taken to provide duty-free and quota-free market access to the LDCs and report to the General Council for appropriate action.

We urge all donors and relevant international institutions to increase financial and technical support aimed at the diversification of LDC economies, while providing additional financial and technical assistance through appropriate delivery mechanisms to meet their implementation obligations, including fulfilling SPS and TBT requirements, and to assist them in managing their adjustment processes, including those necessary to face the results of MFN multilateral trade liberalisation.
(38) Decision on measures in favour of Least-Developed Countries
It is reaffirmed that least-developed country Members will only be required to undertake commitments and concessions to the extent consistent with their individual development, financial or trade needs, or their administrative and institutional capacities.

Within the context of coherence arrangements with other international institutions, we urge donors, multilateral agencies and international financial institutions to coordinate their work to ensure that LDCs are not subjected to conditionalities on loans, grants and official development assistance that are inconsistent with their rights and obligations under the WTO Agreements.
(84) Agreement on Trade-Related Investment Measures

are hortatory and do not appear to significantly add to the existing benefit entitlements of least-developed members.

In conclusion this is not a very happy state of affairs. The progress has been slow and could have been more imaginative. This is a time for the developing Members when the proverbial genie has given them three wishes. Of course, in such a given situation the clever response would involve as the first wish, the wish to have infinite wishes fulfilled! In this light emphasis should be placed on inculcating SDT into the very architecture of the WTO. Thus, emphasis should be placed on the cross-cutting issues. These should facilitate mechanisms that will strengthen SDT provisions long after the end of the Doha Round on an on-going basis.

Footnote 15 (*cont.*)

LDCs shall be allowed to maintain on a temporary basis existing measures that deviate from their obligations under the TRIMs Agreement. For this purpose, LDCs shall notify the Council for Trade in Goods (CTG) of such measures within two years, starting 30 days after the date of this declaration. LDCs will be allowed to maintain these existing measures until the end of a new transition period, lasting seven years. This transition period may be extended by the CTG under the existing procedures set out in the TRIMs Agreement, taking into account the individual financial, trade, and development needs of the Member in question.

LDCs shall also be allowed to introduce new measures that deviate from their obligations under the TRIMs Agreement. These new TRIMs shall be notified to the CTG no later than six months after their adoption. The CTG shall give positive consideration to such notifications, taking into account the individual financial, trade, and development needs of the Member in question. The duration of these measures will not exceed five years, renewable subject to review and decision by the CTG.

Any measures incompatible with the TRIMs Agreement and adopted under this decision shall be phased out by the year 2020.

(88) Decision on Measures in Favour of Least-Developed Countries – Paragraph 1

Least-developed country Members, whilst reaffirming their commitment to the fundamental principles of the WTO and relevant provisions of GATT 1994, and while complying with the general rules set out in the aforesaid instruments, will only be required to undertake commitments and concessions to the extent consistent with their individual development, financial and trade needs, and their administrative and institutional capabilities. Should a least-developed country Member find that it is not in a position to comply with a specific obligation or commitment on these grounds, it shall bring the matter to the attention of the General Council for examination and appropriate action.

We agree that the implementation by LDCs of their obligations or commitments will require further technical and financial support directly related to the nature and scope of such obligations or commitments, and direct the WTO to coordinate its efforts with donors and relevant agencies to significantly increase aid for trade-related technical assistance and capacity building.'

3. The way forward

There appear to be three areas wherein the CTD might need assistance:

(a) Legal and policy issues that have arisen during the course of the negotiations. For example:
- What is the Doha mandate in terms of SDT?
- Can the relationship between trade and development be clarified?
- How should the beneficiaries of SDT be defined?

(b) What are the policy considerations in the formulation of SDT proposals? How can the developing members be empowered to raise their consciousness in developing SDT perspectives?

(c) What are the most effective ways of implementing SDT proposals and provisions?
- Appraisal of the existing state of affairs with a view to suggestions for a way ahead in the negotiations?
- Suggestions for a way ahead in the negotiations?

4. Some suggestions for integrating development and SDT into the architecture of the WTO – in particular through the interpretative and dispute settlement process

- Reformulating the WTO objectives in the preamble to the Marrakesh Agreement and elsewhere clearly affirming development (and SDT as a means to that objective) as an objective of the WTO, and as being integral to the architecture of the WTO. This reaffirmation is needed to dispel doubts about the purposes and nature of the WTO; and to confirm the relationship between development and international trade.

  Note: This will also lead to the interpretation and implementation of provisions of the WTO Agreements being informed by this expressly stated objective – such that developing issues and SDT provisions are not treated as being marginal – but rather that the interpretation and implementation of all the WTO Agreements and their provisions will be informed by this. It will also ensure that development and SDT are not treated as exceptions in the system of the WTO. In the practice of treaty interpretation of exceptions, and despite WTO jurisprudence, exceptions can be prone to being strictly interpreted.
- Express direction that the interpretation of the provisions of the WTO Agreements will be informed by the development objective, and that SDT facilitates that objective. The need for an expressly formulated

teleological approach to interpretation in so far as it relates to development is needed for the effective implementation of SDT provisions and the development objective; and as a response to the generally perceived strict interpretative approach adopted in the practice of the Appellate Body.[16]

Note: This will ensure that greater emphasis is placed in the interpretation of the WTO Agreements on development as an objective. It will also ensure that development and SDT are mainstreamed into the system of the WTO.

- With respect to market access for exports of developing members, the 'non-violation complaint' or some comparable mechanism for the enforcement of SDT should be available, which generally implies the SDT standard into the agreements, where appropriate. This will ensure that SDT is accorded in the limited circumstances where it has not been expressly articulated, but can be reasonably implied as being intended and necessary, so as not to undermine the existing SDT provisions and the spirit of the development objective.

  Note: In the same manner as a non-violation complaint is available where the balance of tariff concessions are being undermined – where a provision is not being applied with sufficient deference to SDT by a developed member and/or an SDT provision is being otherwise undermined – the possibility of a non-violation complaint should be available. This would imply SDT standards where appropriate, and could be available across the developing Membership or limited to LDCs.

In conclusion, the cumulative effect of these proposals would be to cut across the piecemeal approach thus far adopted to building SDT and development into the architecture of the WTO. In particular it would deal with any lapses in the negotiations that might occur in this sphere.

[16] See Asif H. Qureshi *Interpreting WTO Agreements: Problems and Perspectives* (2006) Cambridge: Cambridge University Press.

PART TWO

Trade policy (including competition) and trade facilitation

6a

Trade policy objectives in the Doha Round – A European Union perspective

DAVID O'SULLIVAN (*)

The European Union is a major trade power. In economic terms, it is the world's biggest trading block and it is home to nearly half a billion consumers, with a high average level of income. As such, it is a very attractive market for exporters in other countries. In political terms, it has a decisive influence in shaping the world trade architecture. On trade matters, it speaks with one voice: the European Commission acts as single negotiator on behalf of the twenty seven Member States of the European Union. Also, the EU is the most important donor of both aid and preferential market access to the developing world.

1. Core principles of the EU's common trade policy

The EU's common trade policy is deeply rooted in *a few core principles: liberalisation, open markets, rule of law, sustainable development.* On that basis we have played a leading role in the WTO, built up a network of preferential trade relations and set up a number of autonomous trade policy instruments, such as for instance in the area of trade defence. As a result, the average weighted *level of customs duties* on industrial goods entering the European Union is just 4%. In agriculture, the EU's average tariff - including bilateral and preferential arrangements – is just 10%. A country such as Brazil exports some 37% of its agricultural products to the EU (thanks to MFN Tariff Rate Quotas) and Africa exports more to the EU than to the rest of the OECD taken together. And in the case of poor developing countries, the EU gives (virtually) 100% duty-free access to all forty Least-Developed Countries (LDCs) based on our *'Everything*

(*) Director General for External Trade, European Commission, Brussels. The opinions expressed are personal. This contribution was written in July 2006, and updated in October 2007.

But Arms' initiative. Now, the EU's trade policy is also part and parcel of the external aspects of the EU's Lisbon Agenda for growth and jobs, which aims to harness reforms, to drive competitiveness, and to improve regulation.

As for other aspects of the EU's external policy, *multilateralism is a core value of our trade policy*, which is why the DDA remains the EU's single most important trade priority. The EU has been a staunch promoter of a broad agenda for this Round, covering market access rules and development, as this is the only way to cater for the diverse interests of the Member States, to ensure that the EU's efforts on agriculture be counterbalanced by new opportunities in other sectors and, last but not least, to deliver economic growth and development for all. No number of bilateral deals would have the same widespread effects or benefits. This is what has constantly driven the EU's stance in the DDA, and still does now, even if, as is inevitable in such complex process, we have at several times recalibrated our expectations, while improving our own offer.

2. Doha talks are at a critical stage now

The Doha talks are now at a critical stage. It is not a secret that the DDA has not been an easy ride until now. But one should not forget that these negotiations are taking a place in a difficult environment. Global trade agreements are increasingly hard to achieve. There is the size and structure of the WTO Membership and the changing architecture of multilateral trade relations making the negotiating mechanics extremely complicated; there is a difficult political environment within certain Members, where some sectors of public opinion are increasingly suspicious towards trade liberalisation, notably because of fear of trade-related job losses, or putting the equity of the system into question, making the case of trade liberalisation a difficult one. The fact that *the DDA's launch coincided with anti-globalisation campaigning* and a certain anti-WTO attitude from many Non-Governmental Organisations was hardly propitious. It just shows how much more needs to be done to reposition the multilateral system in response to the anti-globalisation challenge. There is also the fact that many countries around the world, especially developing ones, fear the impact of China, and are concerned that this country would be the main beneficiary of any market opening.

Still, despite all that, there is still a small, but non-negligible, window of opportunity to agree on the broad outlines of a deal. Most of the work is now concentrating on the *so-called 'golden triangle': domestic subsidies in agriculture, agricultural tariffs and industrial tariffs.* A deal on these issues should be feasible, but only under the condition that key players move on those issues on which they are most defensive.

The *EU is prepared to play its part by enhancing its October 2005 agricultural offer, if the circumstances allow* (i.e. (1) if the US makes a meaningful offer on agricultural subsidies and (2) if emerging economies make a meaningful contribution on industrial tariffs, accept cuts into applied tariffs so as to create real new business opportunities). This will need to go together with progress in other key areas for the EU such as services, overall trade rules, the protection of geographical indications and ensuring that Doha delivers on development.

We indeed need a proportionate contribution from those players in a position to contribute. *Emerging developing countries* like China, Brazil and India and the other growing economies of the G–20 are benefiting from the increasingly important role they play in world trade and are, rightly, claiming a prominent role in world politics. But with this role also comes responsibilities.

The EU accepts that developing countries should do less than developed countries and that the poorest and most vulnerable ones should take no or only limited market access commitments. But we expect emerging economies to make a proportionate contribution, by offering real new market access and business opportunities for industrial goods and services. The basis for a deal has to be 'real cuts for real cuts'.

3. Conditions for progress concerning agriculture, services, etc.

In the area of *farm subsidies,* the Round must generate – and bind – a substantial reversal of the negative trend created in the United States by the 2002 Farm Bill. This must involve a real reduction in overall trade distorting farm support as well as a disciplining of the most distortive individual programmes. The EU will substantially reduce its overall spending. We can make a major down payment on agriculture because we have already substantially reformed our Common Agricultural Policy, especially by drastically reducing trade-distorting subsidies; and we already agreed to eliminate all of our export subsidies by 2013. While we are already implementing this, the US has yet to cut a single dollar or dime from its escalating farm spending.

If these conditions are not present, the EU Member States will simply not allow the Commission to improve its offer on agriculture. *EU proposals have a real political and economic price for EU Member States* as they will have a considerable impact on people's jobs and people's lives. European agriculture – cereals, poultry, beef and much besides – will contract and there will be a significant loss of agricultural employment that Member States and the EU will need to cope with. And this applies to all Member States, not only those that are traditionally defensive on agriculture, but also those countries that concentrate on defensive interests like industrial products and services.

But there is more at stake than just agriculture and industrial goods. This is a Single Undertaking, where we need agreement across the board. *In services*, which are a vital part of the global economy and a driver of development, all countries in a position to contribute should offer new commercial opportunities as well as predictability and non-discrimination where services markets are already open to competition. As regards *rules*, we need to improve and strengthening trade rules in areas such as trade facilitation, anti-dumping, as well as stronger protection for *geographical indications*.

4. Development issues and aid for trade

And, last but not least, there are *development issues*. The issue of global social justice is one of the great issues of the twenty-first century. Too many impoverished people around the world have no real stake in the global economy. We need to address this in the WTO negotiations, on the basis of the link between trade & development (**). This is not the whole story though and there are other fora to address development issues and tackle poverty such as the UN or the Bretton Woods institutions. We should be careful not to overburden the DDA with issues on which it has no power to act. The basic tenet that trade liberalisation in the right conditions benefits everyone remains as true as ever. However, not all countries are equipped to benefit from liberalisation at the same pace. *Therefore, a policy of differentiation between developing countries is necessary*. It will enable developing countries themselves to calibrate what they can contribute to the Round according to their means. And the major driver for development will be the creation of new market access opportunities for DCs, including *increased South–South trade*. This is why the EU pays particular attention to identifying a pro-development outcome in each main pillar of the core negotiation issues.

(**) See also Duponteil, chapter 3a in this book.

That means less than full reciprocity and special and differential treatment for the developing countries. But we have to break the politically correct fallacy that developing countries are all alike and have all the same interests. The G–20 and the G–90 do not have identical interests and capacities in trade. Some are now major economic players and exporters on the world stage. Others are small and vulnerable economies, which will need an extra push to make their full integration into the world trading system a success. The acceptance of other developed countries in Hong Kong to follow the EU some of the way in granting duty-free and quota-free entry to products originating in the Least-Developing Countries was an important move.

However, there still remains much to do in *increasing Aid for Trade* and countering the effects of *preference erosion.* There is no single key for addressing preference erosion, and we cannot solve this issue in the WTO alone. But the EU sees the solution as a combination of longer transitional periods for particularly affected products and supply side measures, such as support for capacity building, restructuring, diversification and regional integration. Although Aid for Trade should not be seen as part of the negotiation agenda, nevertheless it is a necessary complement to ensure a pro-development outcome and should be part of the 'final package'. Especially for the poorer developing countries who will find it difficult to take advantage of the new market access opportunities created by the DDA as they are coping with heavy supply side constraints. These countries also need assistance in the implementation of their WTO commitments. And a small group of countries will need support to deal with adjustment problems. This is why European Commission President Barroso pledged at the G8 Summit in Gleneagles to increase EC Aid for Trade effort to €1 billion per year, and EU Member States committed to increase their own effort to a similar amount in Hong Kong.

If we do not manage to find an *ambitious and realistic bargain soon*, we will miss an opportunity and will collectively have to face the consequences of putting off agreement for some time. And these consequences are potentially serious: the principles and process of multilateral trade liberalisation, embodied in the WTO, would be set back, and this may have consequences beyond the trade sphere. Weaker developing countries will be the ones to lose most of course because what is already on the table represents something substantial for them and they need it more than anyone else. Global economies and business confidence will be hit. So we need a vision. This is why the EU is pressing more than ever for a balanced deal.

5. Beyond achieving a successful Doha Round

But our Trade Agenda goes beyond achieving a successful Doha deal. The European Commission in November 2006 defined a new forward-looking agenda that helps to boost our competitive performance in the world: *Global Europe – Competing in the world.* This examines how future trade policy can contribute to our internal competitiveness policies and what are the priority tasks for us to build new and secure global markets for our investment and trade.

This includes *a new strategic approach to market access*, including non-tariff barriers, the *definition of new bilateral and regional relationships and the examination of our political and economic ties with China.*

We also need to be sure that *our trade defence instruments* (TDI) and our use of them take account of the new realities of globalisation. Recent cases such as the anti-dumping investigations on imports of leather shoes from China and Vietnam or energy saving light bulbs from China have highlighted the complexity of global markets, as did textiles in 2005. The European Commission therefore launched a reflection process in December 2006 over how it can update its trade defence instruments to adapt them to new realities, and be sure that the costs of measures do not outweigh their benefits.

Global Europe is not meant to be an alternative for the DDA. Our immediate priority remains to bring about the necessary political engagement by all WTO members to successfully conclude the DDA. However, it provides a complementary track. It can strengthen and deepen the way in which trade policy supports the wider political agenda inside the European Union and beyond its borders among our partners around the world.

6b

The final phase of the Doha Round

KNUT BRÜNJES

Although the history of the Doha round of global trade talks has repeatedly demonstrated the stakeholders' inability to meet self-imposed deadlines, there is **still hope that the talks can be completed by the end of 2008**. A host of economic and political factors indicates that this hope is well founded. No single country has the power to derail the talks and with them the existing multilateral system. On the contrary: most members of the World Trade Organization want to see the talks succeed, a sentiment that has been echoed by numerous heads of major trading countries, including US President Bush, British Prime Minister Brown, German Chancellor Merkel, and Brazilian President Lula da Silva.

The Doha talks are currently moving through their final phase like an undulating procession. It will in the end be not a "marche funèbre" but rather become a low-key victory parade. The outcome of the Doha talks will undoubtedly leave all stakeholders dissatisfied to one degree or another, since it is unreasonable to expect the results of a complex multilateral process requiring the consensus of 150 member nations and customs territories to fit the bill for all concerned. At the same time, the large number of players involved and the widely divergent interests they bring to the negotiating table clearly illustrate why closure for the Doha process has been so long in coming.

Not only political considerations, but **all of the prevailing economic reasons speak for a successful conclusion to the Doha process**. The integration of developing countries into the global trading system remains a top economic and political priority, since this is the most effective known weapon against poverty, terrorism and regional conflicts Economic prosperity and growth work to the benefit of rich and poor countries alike.

As alluded to above, the Doha talks thus far have been marked by missed opportunities and the failure to meet self-imposed deadlines. This tendency was also in evidence during the most recent round of ministerial talks in Hong Kong last December, when no genuine breakthrough was achieved on the biggest trade issues facing the WTO's members. In the wake of the failure last fall to find the common ground needed to reduce tariffs on services, agricultural products, and industrial goods, expectations for the Hong Kong meeting were pegged extremely low. Indeed, there was general agreement among WTO members that it would not be possible to establish all modalities at the Hong Kong meeting. Against this backdrop, Germany set itself the following goals for the event:

- making progress on key market access issues;
- adoption of a negotiation schedule for 2006;
- adoption of the "development package."

Morale at the Hong Kong talks received a boost from Saudi Arabia's accession to the WTO, as well as adoption of a definitive agreement on the granting of compulsory pharmaceutical licenses for nations that do not have their own pharmaceutical industry.

Agricultural issues a major focus

As had been expected, agricultural issues were a major concern at the six-day conference. The debate initially centered on setting a date for the elimination of trade-distorting agricultural export subsidies, which the European Union pledged to do in the "July package" of frameworks and other agreements adopted in 2004. In accordance with European Union wishes, the July package also promulgates parallel elimination, in all other countries, of all forms of trade-distorting export subsidies, as well as disciplines on all export measures. The Hong Kong conference also reached an agreement that sets a deadline for the abolition of all forms of trade-distorting agricultural subsidies by 2013, with a substantial portion of these export subsidies slated for elimination by the end of the first half of the implementation period. The ministerial meeting also fleshed out the criteria for disciplines on export credits, food aid, and exporting state trading enterprises, although a great many details remain to be ironed out by the end of April for further negotiations on agricultural modalities. The Hong Kong conference also defined specific structural elements as the basis for further negotiations. It was agreed that the various countries will fall into one of three reduction "bands" for the elimination of domestic support, that market access will be subject to four bands for which tariff cuts will be set, and that specific thresholds will be adopted for developing countries in connection with these bands. Developing country members won a concession that allows them to self-designate special products that will receive protective status and to institute a special safeguard mechanism based on price and, possibly, quantity triggers. All outstanding agricultural modalities are slated for establishment by April 30 2006. The list of specific commitments, including the actual tariff lines and the exact amounts of reductions in domestic support, will be elaborated by July 31 2006.

Improved market access for industrial goods

The ministerial declaration issued at the conclusion of the Hong Kong meeting calls for the "Swiss formula" to be used as a basis for a treaty on tariff liberalization for industrial goods. But unfortunately, the document also refers to coefficients and thus sidesteps a decision as to which formula will be used for the reductions themselves. In addition to negotiations on tariff reductions, the ministerial declaration also opens up the possibility of conducting sectoral negotiations. Pressure from G20 agricultural export nations led to inclusion of a clause in the declaration to the effect that such negotiations are to achieve a balance between market access levels for agricultural and industrial goods.

A new approach to negotiating a reduction in barriers to trade in services

In the interest of bolstering negotiation dynamics, an additional mechanism aimed at initiating plurilateral negotiations on trade in services was agreed upon. Up till now, service related negotiations have revolved around bilateral exchanges of supply and demand and attempts to narrow the gap between them. However, the plan now is for WTO members with maximally overlapping export interests in trade in specific service sectors to jointly elaborate negotiation requests that will be communicated to specific target countries. If a critical mass of WTO members participates in such sectoral negotiations and is willing to take steps to liberalize market access, a certain amount of progress might well be made in this domain. The European Union's proposal that all WTO members be obligated to enter into such negotiations in accordance with the number of market liberalization service sectors in each country was not adopted. Despite this setback, the trade officials in Hong Kong successfully formulated a strict schedule for further negotiations that calls for concrete results to be achieved in three stages from February to July 2006 until the end of October 2006, and for the required lists of commitments to be exchanged.

The European Union's main concern in terms of the service sector is to codify the current mode 1 and 2 obligations, although the negotiating groups have far greater ambitions for modes 3 and 4. The main goal of mode 3 is to establish foreign subsidiaries and handle foreign investments, whereas mode 4 is mainly concerned with regulations governing limited periods of residence of natural persons in the various treaty countries.

The Hong Kong development package

The duty and quota free access that the European Union granted to least-developed countries (LDCs) under the Everything But Arms Initiative in 2001 has become a model for industrialized and threshold nations around the world. The Hong Kong ministerial declaration stipulates that all industrial countries are to implement this market liberalization initiative for LDCs by 2008 for 97 percent of all tariff lines. In addition, threshold countries are to take increasing responsibility for the strengthening of South–South trade relations and are to document that this responsibility is being exercised in favor of LDCs. Notwithstanding demands by African nations, no agreement has yet been reached on the reduction of export subsidies for cotton, particularly in the US. However, the US has agreed to resolve this problem in the overall context of negotiations on agriculture. The Hong Kong declaration's stipulations on development benefits have been bolstered by concessions pertaining to Aid for Trade, including formation of a task force that will provide recommendations by July 2006 on how Aid for Trade might contribute most effectively to the development dimension of trade cooperation. The industrialized nations also expressed a willingness in Hong Kong to greatly increase their financial support for measures aimed at promoting trade.

Status of the negotiations and the way forward

WTO negotiating activities have ramified outward from the organization's headquarters in Geneva to numerous meetings throughout the world between small groups of high level officials. Despite the greatly increased scope of these negotiations, a breakthrough has yet to be achieved on agriculture and market liberalization for industrial goods, which are the issues of overriding importance. However, the negotiators are unanimous in their view that agreements on market liberalization for industrial and agricultural products and cutbacks in domestic agricultural subsidies can only be achieved at one fell swoop through high level policy decisions, and are not amenable to sequential realization. A strategy involving an incremental series of compromises has been all but ruled out, since the timescale up until June 2006 leaves little room for maneuver. Hence, the stakeholders have come to the realization that the deadlock on the various interconnected issues can only be broken via a "big bang." Marathon negotiations are scheduled for early May with a view to completing the final and critical lap of the Doha process, which will hopefully create a framework for policy decisions regarding a prospective definitive package.

Director General Lamy urges ministers to conduct conclusive negotiations

The first key G6 ministerial meeting was held in London from March 10–12. Unfortunately, trade ministers from the US, Brazil, India, Japan, Australia and the European Union were unable to break the deadlock on agricultural market liberalization, subsidy cutbacks, and the reduction of tariffs on industrial goods. However, possible compromises were adumbrated on the basis of various scenarios.

At the last Trade Negotiation Committee (TNC) meeting on May 1, WTO Director General Pascal Lamy showed disappointment, that the April 30 deadline the ministers had set in Hong Kong for full elaboration of all negotiation modalities for industrial and agricultural goods had been missed. He saw the overall goal of a successful conclusion of the round however still in reach. Mr. Lamy stated that the deadline could not be moved endlessly and that June is the "moment of truth" for the Doha round.

Agriculture negotiations get down to brass tacks

An extensive and detailed technical discussion held at the March meeting of the Trade Negotiation Committee (TNC) offered clear evidence of the delegates' desire to wind up the Doha Round, and at the same time clearly showed that multilateral cooperation can have a positive outcome. There appeared to be room for compromise in only a few areas that are nonetheless critical, giving rise to cautious optimism:

- For the first time since the inception of the Doha process, the US displayed a willingness to consider a mechanism that would prevent a "concentration" of Blue Box payments for individual products.

- The European Union dropped its demand that the ceiling on Blue Box payments not be reduced to less than 5 percent and indicated a willingness to consider a reduction to 2.5 percent by the end of the implementation phase, providing that the US makes genuine concessions in this arena.
- The European Union expressed a willingness to consider the formula for the treatment of sensitive products, and to factor both current goods flows and domestic consumption into tariff quota calculations for products whose export volumes are currently negligible owing to the existence of blanket import tariffs.

US still intransigent on cotton tariffs

Despite the progress that was made in Hong Kong, the cotton issue remains unresolved, particularly the dispute over the reduction of trade-distorting domestic cotton subsidies, in regard to which only the US is under pressure to act. However, the European Union also regards Blue Box payments for specific cotton products in African countries as problematic, and efforts to include severe restrictions on these payments in the current common agricultural policy have been unsuccessful. African nations are also pushing for the creation of a compensation fund.

Non-agricultural market access: in search of a blanket solution

The positions of the parties negotiating a non-agricultural market access (NAMA) agreement have become increasingly entrenched. The negotiations pit WTO member states, which are pushing for ambitious negotiation results and genuinely liberalized markets, against the NAMA 11 Group, which is led by Argentina, Brazil and South Africa. It has assumed a highly defensive stance, and opposes any tariff reductions on "development policy" grounds.

Insofar as the tariff reduction formula is concerned, it is reflected, albeit informally, by the compromise tariff line – "a simple Swiss formula" comprising one coefficient each for developing and industrialized nations. The main source of conflict is the amount of the two coefficients, since they will determine the extent to which tariffs are reduced and hence the scope of genuine market liberalization. Another bone of contention is the proposed flexibility for developing countries in the guise of full or partial exemptions from tariff reductions, the problem being that granting exemptions for major trade sectors could leave the overall tariff reductions toothless. Both of these issues – the amount of the coefficients and the scope of flexibility for developing nations – are pivotal to the establishment of concrete NAMA modalities.

Ambassador Don Stephenson, the newly appointed chairperson of the Negotiating Group on Market Access, has successfully dynamized the negotiating process by integrating a series of NAMA related technical issues, a move that has clarified some issues and moved the two sides closer to a compromise in areas such as the conversion of non *ad valorem* duties to *ad valorem* equivalents, product coverage, and specific developing country flexibility. One of the next steps in this process will be the elaboration of objective criteria for the identification of small, vulnerable economies, and a more precise definition of the term "WTO accession country."

Negotiations regarding the relaxation of trade restrictions enter a new phase

Following the ministerial conference, negotiations on the relaxation of trade restrictions resumed. The negotiating group's positive response to a summary of proposals relating to goods in transit compiled by a group of European Union countries shows that all WTO members are ready to enter into serious negotiations aimed at achieving a draft treaty. Encouraged by this development, the members of the "Colorado Group,"[2] whose members were among the first to endorse the European Union's Singapore objectives, decided that a clearly structured negotiation protocol should be elaborated that classifies the various proposals by subject area. The initial results of this process have already been submitted by Australia, Canada and the US, and the European Union's synthesis will be forthcoming, which means that clustered discussions of these proposals can begin. The tenor and progress of the discussions will serve as a guide to the actual readiness of the stakeholders to negotiate in earnest and will provide a first indication as to whether the July 31 deadline for elaboration of a draft treaty can be met. However, the amount of negotiation that remains to be realized with respect to needs and priority analyses for trade-related technical assistance and capacity building should not be underestimated.

Good start for plurilateral negotiations on trade in services

Twenty plurilateral requests regarding the various sectors and modes of supply of export interest have been elaborated. Twenty plurilateral negotiating groups have been holding meetings since early April to explore these requests and ascertain the extent to which the countries concerned are prepared to take on further commitments. A total of eighty-seven WTO members are participating in this new type of negotiations, although twenty-two of these countries are only involved in one or two negotiating forums. No requests were submitted to less developed countries or very poor developing countries. The European Union, US and Japan are represented in all twenty negotiation forums, mainly as requesters but in some cases also as request recipients.

It is safe to assume that substantial new commitments will only be realized following or in conjunction with an agreement on NAMA and agricultural matters. Once this hurdle has been cleared, it will also be easier to ascertain whether and to what extent a new round of plurilateral talks will begin in May.

"Aid for Trade" moving forward

The first two meetings of the Aid for Trade task force discussed the eponymous subject but did not make any concrete recommendations. A number of issues have yet to be resolved, including the ultimate scope of the Aid for Trade program, as well as how aid assistance in building supply-side capacity and trade-related infrastructure should or can be differentiated from other infrastructure projects.

There is also disagreement regarding the extent to which adjustment costs (primarily resulting from preference erosion) occasioned by a successful Doha Round should be addressed by Aid for Trade. Some Latin American countries fear that Aid for Trade will serve as a pretext for watering down agricultural market liberalization measures. The developing countries have unanimously insisted that the program should serve as an additional, no strings attached support mechanism. In keeping with the slogan "No new debts" some African nations have called for assistance for their government's national budgets. But one thing is certain: The Task Force will have to keep its nose to the grindstone if it is to meet the July deadline for the submission of proposals.

All stakeholders wish to adhere to the schedule pertaining to negotiations on rules

All proposed negotiating rules on antidumping and subsidies (including fisheries subsidies) are to be submitted in draft form by the end of May.

These proposals will hopefully enable the chairperson to formulate a complete draft treaty, including changes in the treaty, by the end of June. The intensity of the negotiations during the March session clearly indicated that all delegations take this final stage of the Doha process seriously. Hence, there appears to be a good chance that the chairperson will be able to elaborate a draft treaty before summer (but not in April as had been quietly suggested by the European Commission). However, the ground covered by the draft will necessarily be limited by continued US intransigence. Extensive efforts are continuing to reach regional agreements regarding transparency by the end of April.

[1] Bolea, December 2007

7

Further liberalisation of trade in chemicals – can the DDA deliver? A summary of the chemical industry's position on the Doha Development Agenda

REINHARD QUICK**

I. Introduction

In December 2005, after four years of difficult and tedious negotiations, the WTO's Sixth Ministerial Conference in Hong Kong decided upon a bare minimum: the negotiations should continue and be concluded by the end of 2006.[1] The ministers avoided complete failure at the conference, but could not make significant progress on the three main negotiating items, namely agriculture, industrial tariffs and services. This chapter will discuss the positions of the European chemical industry[2] on the WTO DDA negotiations and on specific trade policy issues related to these negotiations. It seriously *questions whether the Doha Development Agenda can produce meaningful liberalisation results for a global industry, such as the chemical industry.*

Governments and the press have criticised business for not being active and outspoken enough on the DDA negotiations. It is true that given the narrow mandate of the DDA negotiations the business community is not as active with respect to the DDA as it was with respect to the Uruguay Round. Yet European, Japanese and American business organisations have all adopted strong positions on the negotiations and have made them public. Substantive business positions do exist – the real problem, however, lies in whether governments and the press are interested in these positions.

** Dr. iur., LL.M. Head of the Liaison Office Brussels of the German Chemical Industry's Association (Verband der Chemischen Industrie, eV). The author is grateful to Prof. Marco Bronckers for his thoughtful comments on an earlier draft of this chapter.

[1] Hong Kong Ministerial Declaration, WTO/WT/MIN(05)/DEC of 22 December 2005.

[2] In the following the chapter refers to the positions of the chemical industry either by reference to specific chemical industry position papers or, where the chemical industry supports the overall European industry position, to general European industry position papers.

II. The NAMA[3] negotiations

1. *Industrial tariffs – The industry needs a long breath*

The chemical industry is essential to a broad range of manufacturing and agricultural industries, with virtually every product – from automobiles to zippers – using chemical inputs. Worldwide, the output of the industry is valued at $19 trillion annually. Of that output, forty percent – $792 billion – is traded globally, accounting for more than 10 percent of world merchandise exports in 2003. The chemical industry also employs more than 7 million people worldwide.[4]

In order to understand the industry's position on the NAMA negotiations, namely to eliminate chemical tariffs altogether, one needs to look at the results of the tariff negotiations of the Uruguay Round. During the early Uruguay Round tariff negotiations the approaches chosen by the European Communities[5] and the United States[6] were quite different.[7] Whilst the EU supported a non-linear formula approach to tariff reduction, the US suggested a 'request-and-offer' approach. The industry was not convinced of either approach as it regarded the negotiations as a remarkable opportunity to reduce all chemical tariffs to a harmonised low level at which competitive producers could compete. The EU approach, it feared, would not reduce high tariffs to a competitive level, whilst the US approach would make an industry input impossible. It is, in fact, difficult for industry to find consensus on 'request-and-offer', since companies will always try to exempt certain products from the offers their countries make and will request cuts in products which other countries would like to exempt. Given this situation the European, Japanese, Canadian and US chemical industries initiated a discussion on the harmonisation of chemical tariffs in 1990 which resulted in the adoption by ICCA[8] of the Joint Framework Agreement for Tariff Harmonisation in

[3] NAMA stands for non-agricultural market access (i.e. industrial goods).

[4] Citation from WTO/TN/MA/W/58 of 4 July 2005. Communication on Tariff Liberalisation in the Chemicals Sector made by Canada, Japan, Norway, Separate Customs Territory of Taiwan, Penghu, Kinmen and Matsu, Singapore, Switzerland, and the United States.

[5] The abbreviation EU will be used in the text.

[6] The abbreviation US will be used in the text.

[7] For a description of the different approaches to tariff negotiations taken by the US and the EU in the Uruguay Round see, Hugo Paemen and Alexandra Bensch, From the GATT to the WTO, The European Community in the Uruguay Round, Leuven: Leuven University Press (1995), pp. 110 *et seq.*

[8] International Council of Chemical Associations (ICCA); www.icca-chem.org.

the Uruguay Round[9] in 1991. The ICCA proposal found its way into the final results of the Uruguay Round tariffs negotiations as a so-called sectoral agreement.[10]

The *Chemical Tariff Harmonisation Agreement (CTHA)* of the Uruguay Round provides for the reduction of chemical tariffs to 0%, 5.5% or 6.5% of the Harmonised System of Customs (HS) Chapters 28–39 and includes inorganic and organic chemicals, fertilisers and plant protection products, soaps and cosmetics, and plastics. Chemical tariffs below the harmonised level remained unchanged. The agreement does not allow for any exceptions; instead it provides for three time periods during which CTHA members have to reduce chemical tariffs to the harmonised level: five years for all tariffs which were equal to or below 10%, ten years for all tariffs which were above 10% and below 25%, and fifteen years for all tariffs above 25%. The agreement came into force on 1 January 1995 and is now being applied by fifty WTO members.[11] For pharmaceuticals CTHA was complemented with a Tariff Elimination Agreement which came into force on 1 January 1997 and is being applied by thirty two WTO members.[12] It covers HS Chapter 30 and specific parts of HS Chapter 29, as well as active pharmaceutical ingredients and sole use intermediates. These last two categories must be listed individually, annexed to the tariff schedules and updated every three years.

Given the success of CTHA and the continued globalisation of the chemical industry, *ICCA set itself the goal in 1999 to eliminate chemical tariffs by 2010.*[13] The chemical industry's spirit of continuous trade liberalisation stood in contrast to the difficult birth of the new trade round eventually agreed upon in 2001. By that time it had become evident that the

9 ICCA Position on the Joint Framework Agreement for Tariff Harmonization in the Uruguay Round, 28 October 1991; www.icca-chem.org/section06e.html.

10 Kai-Uwe Schanz, *Der Marktzugang im WTO-Welthandelssystem: Zollsenkungen auf Industrieprodukten und Neuerungen bei den Ausgleichsmassnahmen für Dumping und Subventionen*, in Gatt-Uruguay Round, Thomas Cottier (ed.), Bern, 1995, pp. 107 *et seq.*, 110.

11 Armenia, Australia (de facto), Bulgaria, Canada, Chile (de facto), Ecuador, the European Union (25 members), Hong Kong China, Iceland, Japan, Jordan, Kyrgyzstan, Republic of Korea, Mongolia, New Zealand (de facto), Norway, Oman, Panama, People's Republic of China, Qatar, Singapore, Switzerland, Taiwan, Turkey (de facto), the United Arab Emirates and the United States of America.

12 Australia, Canada, European Union (25), Iceland, Japan, Norway, Switzerland and the United States of America.

13 European Chemical Industry Council (CEFIC). CEFIC comments on a new Multilateral Trade Round of 15 March 1999 can be found at: www.cefic.be/Templates/shwPublications.asp?NID=2&T=3&S=9&P=4.

cosy days of trade negotiations under the GATT were over. The WTO's Seattle disaster not only demonstrated that trade policy had reached the centre stage of politics and was no longer considered a politically unimportant expert topic; it also showed very clearly that the two world trading powers, the EU and the US had lost their leadership and could no longer use their dominant position in world trade to convince others to support their views. This situation still exists today as Cancún and Hong Kong have amply demonstrated that agreement on further trade liberalisation is very difficult if not impossible. The WTO seems to be losing sight of its role, namely to liberalise trade within a rules-based system.

The chemical industry never believed in a WTO without trade rounds and therefore supported a comprehensive new round of trade negotiations as early as 1999.[14] Unfortunately the view of the WTO as a body of permanent negotiations did not materialise; on the contrary, after the successful conclusion of the ITA[15] and the financial services agreement[16] it became clear that the membership was *not ready to negotiate individual items separately, but rather needed a general round with a package of different issues that provided a chance for trade-offs*.

The Doha mandate speaks of reduction or, as appropriate, elimination of tariffs but does not explicitly refer to sectoral tariff elimination.[17] The first such reference can be found in *Annex B of the July 2004 package*[18] which states that sectoral tariff elimination is a key element to achieving the objectives of the NAMA negotiations. The *Hong Kong Ministerial Declaration* goes one step further and asks the negotiating group to identify these sectors specifying that participation in such sectoral initiatives should be non-mandatory.[19] Such a specification has not yet occurred.

In its position on NAMA the chemical industry goes beyond the position of the European industry. Whilst the European industry asks for an ambitious non-linear formula with the highest tariff at a maximum of 15% (bound),[20] the chemical industry asks for a comprehensive chemical

[14] *Ibid.*

[15] Ministerial Declaration on Trade in Information Technology Products of 13 December 1996, WTO/WT/MIN/(96)/16.

[16] See WTO Press Release Press/18 1995: www.wto.org/english/newse/pres95e/addpr3.htm.

[17] Doha Ministerial Declaration, WTO/WT/MIN(01)/DEC1 of 20 November 2001, para. 16, pp. 3, 4. [18] WTO/WT/L/579 of 2 August 2004, para. 7, p. B–7.

[19] See n. 1 above, para. 19, p. 4.

[20] Union of Industrial and Employers' Confederation of Europe (UNICE) Doha Development Agenda, UNICE Position on Non-Agricultural Market Access Negotiations available at: www.unice.org/content/default.asp?PageId=382.

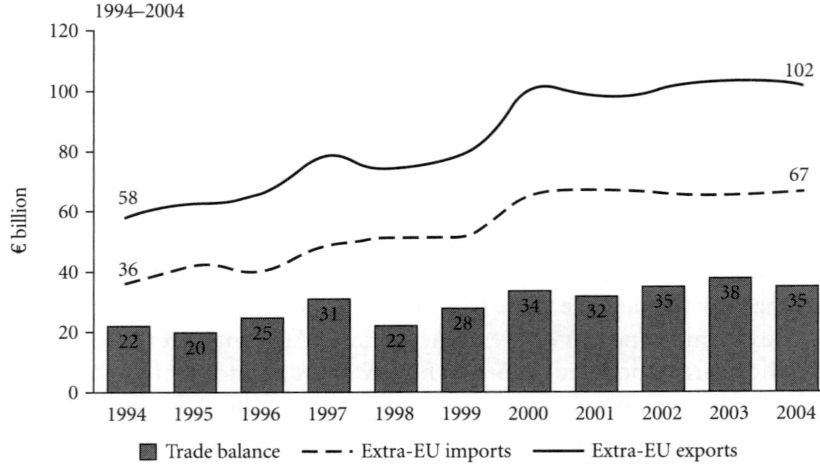

In bn euro	1994	1995	1996	1997	1998	1999	2000	2001	2002	2003	2004
Exports	58	62	66	80	73	79	100	99	101	103	102
Imports	36	42	41	49	52	52	65	67	66	65	67
Balance	22	20	25	31	22	28	34	32	35	38	35

Figure 1 Trade in Chemicals 1994 to 2004

tariff elimination agreement.[21] Given the harmonisation of chemical tariffs agreed in the Uruguay Round, real market access for chemical products should consist of the elimination of chemical tariffs and not a further reduction of tariffs.

Figure 1 shows that, between 1994 and 2004, *trade in chemicals has nearly doubled.* The CTHA was certainly an important factor contributing to this increase. The chart also demonstrates the need to further liberalise trade in chemicals as most of them are inputs for the production of other goods. If countries want to have a competitive manufacturing sector they should not burden it with extra costs, i.e. the tariffs on the imported chemicals, but rather strive to eliminate them. To give an example: in 2005 German chemical exports to the US amounted to €9.2 billion. If we take the CTHA tariffs applicable in the US and exclude the pharmaceutical exports from this figure (€3.8

[21] ICCA, Market Access for the Doha Development Agenda, May 2005 available at: www.icca-chem.org/section06e.html.

Figure 2 Average applied/bound chemical tariffs

EU	4.5% applied	bound 4.6%
US	3.2% applied	bound 2.9%
Japan	2.5% applied	bound 2.0%
China	6.8% applied	bound 6.7%
Korea	5.8% applied	bound 5.8%
Malaysia	3.8% applied	bound 11.9%
Indonesia	5.4% applied	bound 38.1%
Thailand	6.7% applied	bound 29.4%
India	29.3% applied	bound 39.6%
Brazil	8.4% applied	bound 21%
Argentina	9.6% applied	bound 21.6%

Source: WTO World trade Report 2005, Tariffs Profiles Table IV

billion) we see that US importers of German chemicals paid roughly €176 million into the US budget, a considerable amount of money.

Today the *average bound chemical tariffs are relatively low in industrialised countries but quite high in emerging countries.* Figure 2 contains the average applied and bound rates of important chemical producer and user countries. It clearly shows the problem of the NAMA negotiation for chemicals: how can the high bound average tariffs of the emerging countries be reduced significantly enough so as to allow for competition?

The *discrepancy between bound and applied tariff rates in emerging countries is at the centre of the debate in the NAMA negotiations.* Since the negotiators have decided that the tariff cuts will be calculated on the basis of the bound rates one can easily imagine that some countries will only agree to cuts on paper, but not in the applied rates. This leads to a dilemma: the already low average tariffs in the industrialised world will be reduced even further while the high average industrial tariffs in emerging countries will not be reduced to a level which can be overcome by competitive industries. The goal of getting real market access in emerging countries will not be achieved. After the DDA results are implemented, the industrialised world will have no bargaining chips left to obtain further tariff cuts in emerging countries. Therefore the industrialised world, fully supported by business, *expects the emerging countries to make substantial tariff concessions now.*

This position of the industrialised world has been heavily *criticised by the emerging countries*, particularly India and Brazil, who claim that their tariff cuts should not be as significant as the cuts of the industrialised countries. As a justification for their claim they refer to the Doha Declaration which says: The negotiations shall take fully into account the special needs and interests of developing and least developed country participants, including *through less than full reciprocity in reduction commitments*. . . .[22]

It is interesting to note that the coalition of emerging, developing and least-developed countries has, so far, been very successful in blocking the NAMA requests made by the industrialised countries. The WTO membership seems to have enormous difficulty in agreeing on a liberalisation package which produces real cuts in applied industrial tariffs and at the same time is in line with the development aspect of the negotiations.[23] The question boils down to whether the emerging countries should benefit from the development exceptions or not. Since the DDA should result in increased South–South trade and should enable all WTO-members, but in particular developing countries, to benefit from such trade,[24] industrialised and emerging countries have to open their markets. Hence *emerging countries cannot insist on the flexibilities provided for by the NAMA package.*

The *Hong Kong Declaration* has not solved, but rather postponed, this conflict. The modalities have not been properly addressed. As a result, the negotiators are expected to find the magic tariff-cutting formula and the coefficients on the one side, whilst agreeing on flexibilities and exceptions on the other. The declaration simply repeats these elements without indicating the way forward; it further complicates the negotiations by requiring that market access for agriculture and NAMA should have a comparatively high level of ambition.[25] Given this situation it is not surprising that the negotiators did not meet the April 2006 deadline set out in the Hong Kong declaration.[26]

22 Paragraph 16 of the Doha Ministerial Declaration, see n. 17 above.

23 For an overview of all submissions made by 4 April 2006, see WTO/TN/MA/S/16/Rev.4 of 5 April 2006, List of Documents, Note by the Secretariat.

24 For an interesting study on how the high and often unbound industrial tariffs in countries such as India, Brazil, Egypt, Malaysia, South Africa and Turkey constitute an obstacle for trade between those countries see, the NFTC Report: *NFTC WTO Tariff Analysis Project, Making the Case for Ambitious Tariff Cuts in the WTO's Non-agricultural Market Access Negotiations*, May 2005 available at: www.nftc.com.

25 Paragraph 24 of the Hong Kong Declaration; see n. 1 above.

26 *Ibid.*, para. 23; see n. 1 above. See also WTO/TN/MA/18 of 26 April 2006: Negotiating Group on Market Access, Progress Report by the Chairman, Ambassador Don Stephenson, to the Trade Negotiations Committee.

The sectoral tariff negotiations are part of this complicated picture. The way forward is not clear and some emerging countries particularly India and Brazil, oppose them.

For the chemical industry *the problematic issues of the sectoral negotiations are*:

- country coverage;
- exceptions; and
- special and differential treatment.

As to *country coverage*, the industry suggests that all WTO members with a viable chemical industry participate (*'viable' meaning a domestic chemical production of $3 billion per year*). This is a new benchmark in the WTO which in the past looked at shares of world trade and not at domestic production. However chemical production is a more accurate indicator, since it includes countries that have considerable domestic production even if they do not trade. A future agreement should also contain a provision specifying that countries which have reached this threshold should join. According to the latest industry figures about thirty countries (EU = 1) would be covered by the threshold and should, therefore, be part of the sectoral tariff elimination agreement (see Table 1).

As to *exceptions*, the ICCA follows the CTHA format and suggests product coverage (HS Chapters 28–39) without exceptions. Flexibility will be introduced by distinguishing between CTHA members and non-CTHA members and through phasing (i.e. the elimination of tariffs in three steps). CTHA countries should eliminate their chemical tariffs within five years, countries not participating in CTHA should reduce their tariffs within ten years for tariffs which are lower than 25% and within fifteen years for those which are higher than 25%. The reductions should be accomplished annually.

Special and differential treatment will be acknowledged by the $3 billion threshold and the longer phasing period for non-CTHA members. CTHA members will have to reduce their tariffs faster than non-CTHA members and will therefore offer developing countries more market access. Furthermore, only the most important chemical producing nations would have to sign the agreement, thus leaving approximately ninety WTO members free to decide whether to join or not. ICCA supports the idea of a 'round for free' for the least-developed countries.

Table 1 Global chemical industry rankings, 2004

Countries and Regions	*Sales*	*Export*	*Import*
€ billions			
EU 25	585.738	455.133	383.765
USA	415.186	87.928	90.839
Japan	185.567	38.854	28.370
China	137.400	18.650	43.628
Korea Republic	52.589	15.423	12.785
Brazil	47.748	4.760	11.657
India	47.619	6.324	6.463
Switzerland	37.242	32.021	19.083
Taiwan	31.161	12.249	11.565
Canada	28.865	15.003	21.924
Saudi Arabia	17.793	3.530	3.489
Singapore	15.850	8.916	6.350
Australia	14.921	3.079	8.137
Mexico	13.600	3.824	8.031
Russia	13.217	4.939	7.499
Indonesia	11.200	3.176	4.447
South Africa	8.813	2.538	3.347
Turkey	8.449	3.292	13.276
Malaysia	8.365	4.286	5.533
Thailand	5.875	4.417	6.591
Iran	5.734	410	2.532
Argentina	5.444	1.817	3.040
Philippines	5.350	332	2.695
Norway	5.180	4.070	4.876
Chile	3.900	1.299	1.859
Israel	3.897	3.362	2.524
Colombia	3.890	1.215	2.651
Egypt	3.695	481	1.664
Pakistan	3.104	199	2.088

The *sectoral negotiations* have not yet progressed very far. In July 2005 several countries suggested the elimination of chemical tariffs.[27] For the

[27] See WTO document, n. 4 above; see also WTO/TN/MA/W/15/Add.2 of 4 March 2003, Japan's Submission on 'Zero-for-Zero' and, 'Harmonisation' as well as WTO/TN/MA/W/8/Add.1 of 1 February 2006, Communication by Singapore on an Update on the Negotiations on the Sectoral Tariff Component.

timebeing the EU is not engaging actively in these negotiations[28] as it fears that this could undermine its goal for ambitious horizontal tariff cuts. Once the horizontal modalities are agreed upon, however, the EU will have to catch up with the other WTO Members that have already started their discussions and have elaborated on their proposals.[29] It is subject to speculation whether the WTO will be able to conclude the NAMA negotiations and indeed the whole DDA Round successfully. Too many deadlines have been missed so far and the political will to liberalise trade further is still lacking. Also, even if the DDA is concluded, *it is not guaranteed that the results will include a chemical sector tariff elimination agreement at all, let alone its contents.*

2. Non-tariff barriers (NTBs) – How to address them?

The main issue for business in the NAMA negotiations is improved market access, which can be impeded by tariffs and non-tariff barriers. The WTO membership has *listed some 2000 NTBs, a few of which require a negotiated solution.* Some NTBs relate to an agreement which is part of the DDA negotiations (e.g. the anti-dumping and the subsidy/CVD agreements); others relate to, or are even covered by, existing agreements which are not part of the DDA negotiations (e.g. customs valuation, import licensing, preshipment inspection); still others are not covered by the above categories and could therefore be the *subject of negotiations.* These are: *tariff classification, export duties and export restrictions, double pricing schemes, 'buy national' campaigns, fiscal incentives and tax and duty exemptions.*[30] However, it is important to note that the WTO membership is quite divided on these NTBs. There are objections made on principle (i.e. the NTB is not covered by the DDA mandate) and there is also disagreement on how to address and regulate these NTBs.[31]

28 The EU did however host a meeting on chemical tariff elimination on 2 November 2005 in Geneva which was attended both by the ICCA and by eleven other WTO members.

29 See, e.g., WTO/TN/MA/W/18/Add 13 of 4 April 2006, Progress Report: Sectoral Discussions on Tariff Elimination in the Chemical Sector, Communication from the United States. This report gives an overview of the discussions held so far and of the issues surrounding a sectoral chemical tariff elimination agreement; see also, WTO/MA/W/72 of 15 May 2006, Communication on Tariff Liberalisation in the Chemical Sector by Canada, Norway, Singapore, Switzerland, the Separate Customs Territory of Taiwan, Penghu, Kinmen and Matsu, and the United States. It is interesting to note that Japan has not co-signed this Communication. Japan did however co-sign the Communication mentioned in n. 4 above.

30 See WTO/TN/MA/9/Rev.1 of 29 October 2004, Overview of Proposals Submitted, Non-Tariff Barriers, Note by the Secretariat, p. 2.

31 *Ibid.*, p. 13.

In the following, two issues will be addressed: the first concerns a procedural suggestion to deal with NTBs and the second concerns the issue of export taxes and double pricing of natural resources.

(a) The NTB problem solving mechanism – A business initiative

NTBs can be addressed through the Trade Policy Review Mechanism (TPRM) and the Dispute Settlement Mechanism (DSM). Furthermore the TBT and SPS Agreements give the membership the right to raise concerns about, and consult on, new technical or SPS regulations. These mechanisms are useful and valuable tools which can deal with some NTBs; yet they can only partially solve the problem because of the inventiveness of WTO members to create and adapt NTBs. Often business cannot wait several years for a WTO dispute settlement case to be decided and fully implemented; it is interested in tackling existing barriers expeditiously. Instead of looking for a negotiated solution for all NTBs, business has *suggested that an NTB problem-solving mechanism is established at WTO level*.[32] This mechanism would *result in a mediation exercise over the alleged NTB and would be voluntary.* Recourse to the mechanism would be triggered by a request from one WTO member to another member and the responsible WTO body. The responding WTO member could decide within an agreed time (e.g. thirty days) whether to participate in the mediation process. If there is agreement between the two sides, the *WTO would appoint a mediator* who, in co-operation with the parties concerned, would come forward with a final proposal within a clearly defined time limit (e.g. three months). The final proposal should reflect the letter and the spirit of the relevant WTO rules and would be non-binding. The report would be seen as a problem-solving tool rather than an instrument of enforcement. If not accepted, recourse to dispute settlement would remain open. Coverage for the mechanism should be broad and include all NTB relevant rules and agreements; the mechanism would also be ideally suited to deal with new agreements for example, trade facilitation. Business is aware that this mechanism cannot solve all problems relating to NTBs, but considers it a useful and pragmatic tool for removing trade barriers in an efficient and non-adversarial manner. Given its simplicity it could easily be used by developing countries who often feel that they are being excluded from developed country markets because of their burdensome regulations. *In April 2006 the EU submitted*

[32] UNICE Initial Views on a WTO Problem-Solving Mechanism for Implementation-Related Non-Tariff Barriers of 10 December 2005 available at: www.unice.org.

a proposal to Geneva on how to facilitate the resolution of NTBs using a mediation process.[33]

(b) Export taxes and double pricing – How to tackle trade distortive government practices?

The DDA mandate explicitly refers to the reduction or elimination of tariff escalation. *Tariff escalation* is the practice of charging higher import tariffs on processed goods than on unprocessed goods. It has long been held that tariff escalation in developed countries may hinder the development of high value-added industry in developing countries. Yet, given the already low average tariffs on industrial goods in developed countries it is doubtful whether the degree of tariff escalation still existing today may discourage the development of a processing industry in developing countries.

With reference to tariff escalation in the developed world, *developing countries have justified export duties or export taxes for certain commodities.*[34] These measures are thought to promote the development of downstream processing industries and encourage foreign direct investment whilst at the same time being a reliable source of revenue. As mentioned above, export duties have been notified as NTBs in the DDA NAMA negotiations. Export duties or export taxes are customs duties on exports often levied on commodities by exporting developing countries for fiscal or industrial policy reasons. Economically speaking they are the reverse-side of tariff escalation, as they make it more difficult for developed countries to process these commodities.

WTO disciplines on export duties are not clearly defined, hence the discussions in the DDA.[35] On the other hand, these measures are prohibited by some regional trade agreements and have also been dealt with in some accession negotiations (e.g. China and most recently Russia).[36]

33 WTO/TN/MA/W/11/Add. 8 of 1 May 2006, Negotiating Proposal on WTO Means to Reduce the Risk of Future NTBs and to Facilitate their Resolution, Communication from the European Communities.

34 See OECD Document TD/TC/WP(2002)54/Final of 31 January 2003, Analysis of Non-tariff Measures: The Case of Export Duties, p. 14.

35 See for example, WTO/TN/MA/W/46/Add.12 of 24 May 2005, Non-tariff Barrier Notifications, Addendum by the European Communities, p. 2.

36 See n. 34 above, p. 11, n. 20 which reads: *In the accession process of Russia export duties on minerals, petrochemicals, natural gas, raw hides and skins, ferrous and non-ferrous metals and scraps are discussed. Members argue that in the case of dominant supplier in Russia, third country buyers would suffer from increased cost and encounter an insufficient supply of the goods. They point out that the loss of relative competitiveness in the global market for downstream products vis-à-vis Russian products should be taken into account.*

The economic implications of export duties are well known:[37]

> The economic effects of export duties need to be assessed with regard to their objectives as well as their overall effects on the economies of the trading partners concerned.
>
> When the purpose of export duties is essentially revenue, it may be asked whether alternative internal taxation measures could be equally effective and also less trade distortive. In making such an assessment it should be recognised that developing and least-developed countries may need technical assistance to help modernise and improve the efficiency of their tax systems.
>
> When the objective is primarily the promotion of downstream industries, the economic implications vary according to the extent to which the exporting country can affect the world market price of the taxed product. However, whether or not there is such an effect, an export duty would create a differential between a price available to domestic processors and the price charged to foreign processors. This differential would provide a competitive advantage to domestic downstream processors. This could be justified by the 'infant industry' argument, i.e. to provide an initial incentive for the development of a processing industry. It would also improve the overall terms of trade of the country, benefiting its balance of payments. However the net result could be a welfare loss in that it would penalise exporters of the taxed product while benefiting downstream processing industries which in turn would have a reduced incentive to become truly competitive internationally. In this sense an export duty acts as an implicit subsidy for the domestic processing industries, providing them with an artificial competitive advantage both in the domestic markets of the country and in export markets.

Given these negative effects it is not surprising that *the EU attacks export duties as 'beggar-thy-neighbour' policies and insists that these measures be first bound, then substantially reduced and eventually eliminated.*[38] The European business community fully supports this approach. It is difficult to predict whether the DDA will eventually agree on some discipline concerning export duties given the WTO membership's fundamental disagreement on the issue.[39] Yet it is clear that the conceptual justification in favour of export taxes (in the developing world) with the existence of tariff

[37] *Ibid.*, p. 15. A recent WTO study also supports these findings. See Roberta Piermartini, *The Role of Export Taxes in the Field of Primary Commodities* (2004) WTO.

[38] See WTO/TN/MA/W/11 Add. 6 of 27 April 2006, Negotiating Proposal on Export Taxes, Communication from the European Communities.

[39] India, for example, considers that export duties are not part of the Doha mandate; Note by the Secretariat, n. 30 above, p. 13. The EU's proposal on export taxes (see n. 38 above) was sharply criticised by several developing countries including Argentina, Brazil, India,

escalation (in the developed world) is difficult to make when the average tariff for industrial products (in the developed world) is as low as it is.

Double pricing schemes for natural resources are another non-tariff trade barrier which have considerable trade distortive effects. These measures are practised in particular by Russia and Saudi Arabia with respect to natural gas. A double pricing scheme provides the natural resource cheaper internally than after export:[40] the government has a monopoly over the natural resource, so it can fix the price. The economic effects of a double pricing system are the same as those of an export duty. The countries practising these schemes justify them as being a WTO-compatible investment incentive. In fact the double pricing system of Saudi-Arabia has triggered many capital intensive investments in the petrochemical sector. The capacities already built in Saudi Arabia and those expected over the next years exceed the demand of the region by far. They are aimed at supplying the world market[41] and can thus be seen as a threat to the European petrochemical industry.

The EU has attacked these practices for a long time, but it failed to have them eliminated in its bilateral WTO accession treaties with both countries: in 2003 the EU concluded an agreement with Saudi Arabia[42] and in 2004 one with Russia.[43] Initially the issue looked as though it might have a positive outcome with Saudi Arabia,[44] i.e. Saudi-Arabia undertook to eliminate double pricing. However in the negotiations with Russia the EU did not insist on such elimination. As a consequence Saudi Arabia[45] withdrew its original commitment in the final WTO accession negotiations. *This means that both countries can continue to practise a double pricing*

Indonesia, Malaysia and Venezuela. See *Bridges Weekly Trade News Digest*, (2006) Vol. 10, No. 14, p. 8.

40 See for example, WTO/WT/ACC/SAU/61 of 1 November 2005, Report of the Working Party on the Accession of the Kingdom of Saudi Arabia to the World Trade Organization, pp. 12–13. See also Ulrich Klaus, *Russlands Erdöl und Erdgas im Kontext der WTO Rechtsordnung*, in Der Beitritt Russlands zur Welthandelsorganisation, Chritian Tietje (ed.), Beiträge zum Transnationalen Wirtschaftsrecht, Heft 44, 2005, Martin Luther Universität, Halle-Wittenberg, p. 48.

41 See CHEManager 5/2006 pp. 1–3. See also *Chemistry and Industry*, Issue 6 of 20 March 2006, p. 16.

42 EU Press Release IP/03/1188 of 30 August 2003: Accession of Saudi Arabia to the WTO: Conclusion of the EU-Saudi Arabia Bilateral Market Access Deal.

43 EU Press Release IP/04/673 of 21 May 2004: Russia – WTO, European Union Russia Deal Brings Russia One Step Closer to WTO Membership.

44 See n. 42 above. The Press Release clearly refers to the elimination of the double pricing practice by Saudi Arabia.

45 WTO Press/420 of 11 November 2005, WTO General Council successfully adopts Saudi Arabia's terms of Accession.

system. The EU' s lack of enthusiasm to combat double pricing practices in the context of WTO accession can only be explained in political and geopolitical terms. WTO membership of Russia and Saudi Arabia was considered more important than solving the petrochemical industry's problems with double pricing.[46]

The trade distortions caused by these schemes persist and are now being addressed in the DDA negotiations. It is interesting to note that both the EU and the US consider double pricing schemes *as an issue to be dealt with in the 'rules' and not in the NAMA negotiations.*[47] Legally speaking double pricing schemes are not subsidies within the meaning of the WTO Agreement, since they are not 'specific',[48] but rather confer a general benefit; therefore they cannot be attacked under the existing WTO-regime.[49] Given their intrusive nature and the trade distortions they create, both the EU and the US have suggested categorizing these schemes as prohibited subsidies. This would solve the issue of specificity, since prohibited subsidies are irrebuttably presumed to be specific.[50]

III. The trade and environment negotiations

1. Tariff elimination for environmental goods – Win–Win or lose–lose?

Rumour has it that when Commissioner Lamy suggested that the WTO should start negotiations on the relationship between WTO and MEAs at

46 The issue of double pricing amply demonstrates the difficulty of bridging the gap between the external aspects of competitiveness and general political considerations. On this issue see UNICE Position Paper dated 9 March 2005 on Competing for Growth and Jobs in a Global Market, UNICE's Preliminary Views on the External Dimension of the Lisbon Agenda, p. 3 available at: www.unice.org.

47 WTO/TN/RL/W/78 of 19 March 2003, Subsidies Discipline Requiring Clarification and Improvement, Communication from the United States, p. 3; see also WTO/RL/GEN/94 of 16 January 2006, Expanding the Prohibited 'Red Light' Subsidy Category, Paper from the United States; or the Submission of the European Communities on Subsidies WTO/TN/RL/GEN/135 of 24 April 2006.

48 On the specificity requirement of the Subsidies Code, see Christian Pitschas, *Das Übereinkommen über Subventionen und Ausgleichsmaßnahmen*, in WTO Handbuch, Hans-Joachim Priess, Georg Berrisch (eds.) (2003) München, pp. 457 *et seq.*; see also Marc Benitah, The Law of subsidies under the GATT/WTO System (2001) The Hague, London, New York: pp. 87 *et seq.*, p. 88 fn. 191.

49 '*In the EC's experience, the current ASCM discipline does not permit theses practices to be tackled effectively . . . To that effect, a possible solution would be to introduce a specific prohibition*'. See EC Submission, n. 46 above. See also Klaus, n. 40 above, p. 48.

50 See Pitschas, n. 48 above, p. 458.

the Doha Ministerial Conference, USTR Zoellick insisted that the negotiations should also deal with tariff elimination for environmental goods. And so it was decided that both subjects would be part of the negotiations. *Paragraph 32 of the Doha Ministerial Declaration* foresees negotiations on 'the reduction, or, as appropriate, elimination of tariff and non-tariff barriers to environmental goods and services'.[51]

Apparently, the WTO membership agrees that if environmental goods are traded freely and without any tariff or non-tariff barriers, everybody wins. Trade liberalisation in this area can bring economic, environmental and development benefits, in other words a win–win–win situation.[52] Yet the negotiations have not made much progress. On the contrary, the WTO membership continues to be deeply divided over this issue: so much so, that *at the Hong Kong Ministerial, the subject has barely been mentioned.*[53]

Business in general and the chemical industry in particular has been very critical of these negotiations.[54] At the heart of the discussions are not only the controversial suggestions made by the EU, but also the more general systemic question of whether the tariff system should be used to deal with socio-economic considerations. Business is concerned that these particular negotiations could result in discrimination between like products as well as placing an additional burden on the customs administration. They would also introduce into the WTO the highly controversial issue of non-product related process and production methods (the *so-called PPMs*) through the back door.

Some commentators and negotiators[55] see no reason for not advancing the negotiations rapidly. However the subject remains controversial since the WTO membership has been unable to address the conceptual problem of these negotiations: namely, what is the function of a tariff?

51 Paragraphs 31 and 32 of the Doha Ministerial Declaration, see n. 17 above.

52 Gary Sampson, The WTO and Sustainable Development, Tokyo, New York, Paris, UN 2005, pp. 63–4. See also Commission Paper *Trade and Environment, Post-Hong Kong Paper for 133 Committee* of 7 February 2006, p. 4. See also OECD Trade Policy Studies, Environment and Energy Products, The Benefits of Liberalising Trade, OECD 2006.

53 Paragraph 32, Hong Kong Ministerial Declaration, see n. 1 above.

54 UNICE Preliminary Position on the Reduction and/or Elimination of Tariffs and Non-tariff Barriers to Environmental Goods, 23 January 2003; www.unice.org. ICCA Position on Tariff Elimination for Environmental Goods, June 2003; www.icca-chem.org.

55 See Gary Sampson (see n. 52 above) or the EU (see, the part Objectives contained in WTO/TN/TE/W/47, 17 February 2005, Market Access for Environmental Goods, Communication from the European Communities) and more recently, the Commission Paper mentioned in n. 52 above.

What, then, *is* the function of a tariff? Based on the tradition of the GATT the WTO accepts tariffs as a means to protect domestic industry. At the same time it requires its membership to pursue negotiations on substantial tariff reductions to foster its overall goals of *'raising standards of living, ensuring full employment and a large and steadily growing volume of real income'*.[56] The eight GATT rounds of multilateral trade negotiations have indeed achieved remarkable progress in this particular area. Tariffs also have a revenue function which is, however, more incidental than purposeful since it is the goal of the WTO to liberalise trade and therefore to eventually eliminate this function. The question remains as to whether tariffs should serve any other purposes. For example, *should the WTO also encourage its membership to use the tariff system to pursue other policy objectives, such as public health or environmental policies*? This would entail the notion that the tariff structure should, in effect, be used to distinguish between 'good' and 'bad' goods. Following the logic of the Doha mandate, according to which tariffs should be eliminated for environmental goods, it could be argued that they should be increased for non-environmental goods.

One can assume that the WTO membership would categorically reject this logic thus accepting tariff elimination for 'good' goods but rejecting tariff increases for 'bad' goods. In other words, the membership itself has doubts about whether to use the tariff system to promote certain policy objectives. The tariff system is neutral with respect to products. It classifies them, but it does not reflect societal values about them.

Apart from these conceptual considerations the subject requires answers to many practical questions. Looking at these negotiations from a sectoral point of view one has to define product coverage, country coverage and exceptions.

Contrary to typical sectoral negotiations, such as the ITA or indeed the CTHA, where the product coverage is relatively easy to define, the product coverage for environmental goods requires explanation. *There is no agreed definition of what constitutes an environmental product.* One could of course describe environmental goods as those goods that 'measure, prevent, limit, minimise, or correct environmental damage to air, water and soil as well as problems related to waste, noise and eco-systems',[57] yet

[56] Preamble of the Marrakesh Agreement Establishing the World Trade Organization.

[57] See Sampson, n. 52 above, p. 64 referring to OECD/Eurostat, *The Environmental Goods and Services Industry: Manual on Data Collection and Analysis*, OECD, Paris 1999 p. 10.

this definition is insufficient for the categorisation of these products for the purpose of tariff elimination.[58]

The following examples demonstrate the complexities of the discussions. Chlorine is used to sanitise water; used in the correct way it will help to save the lives of many people, used carelessly it can kill! Is chlorine therefore an environmental good? Polystyrene is used to produce insulation panels which increase the energy efficiency of houses and therefore serve an environmental purpose. However, polystyrene can be used for other purposes, such as coffee cups. It is generally traded in small pallets, but the customs officer does not know what these pallets will eventually be used for. Is polystyrene an environmental good? Also, polystyrene panels are in direct competition with insulation panels made of natural fibres. Are both panels environmental goods or should only natural fibres be considered? To complicate things even further, assume that the EU awards an eco-label to a product that has been produced using renewable energy. *Should eco-labelled products be considered environmental goods*?

The negotiators are aware of these difficulties. They started to address the definitional aspect, but soon recognised that they could not solve the problem.[59] Given that the negotiations are aimed at contributing to the objective of sustainable development,[60] which means finding a balance between economic, ecological and social issues, the negotiators should at least have considered subjecting all products identified as environmental goods to a life-cycle assessment. Such an approach would have been complicated and burdensome, yet it would have produced a more objective assessment.

The EU made an attempt to define environmental goods by proposing some 'Guiding Principles'.[61] However, the text is rather 'woolly' and purposefully unclear. The EU states for example that:

> 'environmental goods should be defined in order to contribute to the fulfilment of national and internationally agreed environmental priorities' or that 'finding a generally acceptable definition of environmental goods, while not always easy, is not insuperable. Pragmatic and innovative approaches will certainly enable Members to develop technically workable

[58] See also Ronald Steenblik, *Liberalising Trade in Environmental Goods: Some Practical Considerations*, OECD Trade and Environment Working Paper No. 2005–05; OECD/COM/ENV/ TD(2003)34/Final. [59] *Ibid.*, p. 5.

[60] See para. 5 of the Doha Ministerial Declaration, n. 17 above.

[61] See EC Communication n. 55 above.

definitions solutions that ensure the possibility of living up to the commitments entered into to the benefit of sustainable development'.

With two notable exceptions,[62] the negotiators adopted a pragmatic approach by submitting lists of environmental goods.[63] Referring to the works undertaken by OECD and APEC they wanted to use the lists drawn up by these institutions as a basis for the discussions.[64] Since the APEC list was drawn-up for the purpose of tariff elimination it was considered to be more appropriate than the OECD list which focused on the particular industrial usage of these goods.[65]

In general the lists are based on the following environmental categories[66]:

- Air pollution control;
- Recycling systems;
- Solid hazardous waste management;
- Heat/energy management;
- Potable water treatment;

[62] India wishes to concentrate on an 'environmental project approach' and would like customs officers to decide on a case-by-case basis whether the project can be considered 'environmental'. See WTO/TN/TE/W/51 of 3 June 2003, An Alternative Approach for Negotiations under Paragraph 31 (iii), Submission by India. India is very critical with respect to the approaches suggested by other members since it feels that '*there is a growing feeling that the directions of the negotiations so far have focused on goods which are likely to give highly industrialized countries a comparative advantage*'. India reiterated its approach in WTO/TN/TE/W/54 of 4 July 2005. Argentina has suggested an integrated approach: the WTO should agree a list of environmental goods in principle, but these would only qualify for tariff reductions if included in a project contributing to a domestic environmental objective. It is highly unlikely that the suggestions made by India or Argentina will be chosen by the negotiators as they are quite bureaucratic and could result in high transaction costs and non-tariff barriers which, in turn, would offset the tariff reduction/elimination.

[63] For a list of submissions, see WTO/TN/MA/7Add. 1 of 10 October 2005: Environmental Aspects in the Negotiation Group on Market Access for Non-agricultural Products, Update by the Secretariat. A complete list can also be found in WTO/TN/TE/W/63 of 17 November 2005, Synthesis of Submissions on Environmental Goods, Informal Note by the Secretariat.

[64] WTO/TN/MA/S/6 of 7 October 2002 contains both the APEC and the OECD lists of environmental products.

[65] See WTO/TN/MA/W/18/Add. 4 of 19 June 2003, Liberalising Environmental Goods in the WTO: Approaching the Definition Issue, Submission by the United States. Concerning PPM, see also Taira, chapter 18 in this book.

[66] See WTO/TN/MA/W/18/Add.7 of 4 July 2005, Initial List of Environmental Goods, Submission by the United States.

- Waste water management;
- Environmental monitoring, analysis and assessment;
- Remediation/clean-up of soil and water;
- Noise/vibration abatement;
- Renewable energy plant;
- Environmental preferable products based on end-use or disposal characteristics;
- Natural resource protection.

The list of products submitted mostly cover products that are used in pollution control and resource management.[67] Some members also have included *environmentally preferable products (EPPs)*. The latter are defined as 'products that cause significantly less environmental harm at some stage of their life-cycle than alternative products serving the same purpose'.[68] It is believed that developing countries are net exporters of EPPs.[69] The EU has added a further very controversial category, namely goods with a high environmental performance/low environmental impact,[70] which could also be identified as EPPs.

Without an objective definition of environmental good the *use of lists entails the risk of arbitrariness and discrimination.* If one compares the guiding principles suggested by the EU with its suggested lists,[71] one notes that the list mainly consists of machinery classified in HS[72] Chapter 84 and other products listed in HS Chapters 68, 69, 73, 86, 87, 90. In other words the EU list contains the 'hardware' to deal with environmental issues. At the same time the 'commodities' needed to make the 'hardware' work, for example many chemicals, are not mentioned. The chemical industry produces a vast range of products without which environmental protection would be impossible. These products range

67 The Update by the Secretariat, see n. 63 above, lists documents submitted by the WTO-membership containing a reference to environmental goods. See also the Synthesis made by the Secretariat, n. 63 above.

68 See Synthesis by the Secretariat, n. 63 above, p. 9, referring to a UNCTAD definition of EPPs, UNCTAD/COM/70 (1995) Environmental Preferable Products (EPPs) as a Trade Opportunity for Developing Countries. 'Less environmental harm' should be defined according to the following criteria: (a) use of natural resources and energy; (b) amount of hazardousness of waste generated by the product along its life-cycle; (c) impact on human and animal health; (d) preservation of the environment.

69 *Ibid.*, p. 9. See also Chapter 1 of the OECD Publication mentioned in n. 52 above.

70 See EC Submission, n. 55 above; see also WTO/TN/TE/W/56 of 5 July 2005, EC Submission on Environmental Goods, Submission by the European Communities.

71 See EC Submission, n. 55 above.

72 HS = Harmonised System. For a description of HS see Steenblik, n. 58 above, p. 9.

from kits for environmental analysis to films used in solar panels for an efficient production of renewable energy. Why, one wonders, do the EU's 'Guiding Principles' not apply to these products?

The *EU' s list* classifies waste water treatment plants as environmental products. These plants cannot function without chemicals: they need lime and hydrochloric acid for a correct Ph value and iron and aluminium salts for phosphate precipitation. They also need polyacrylamides which act as flocculants or coagulants to condition sludge, to clarify raw water and to treat effluent streams from sewage plants. The EU risk assessment for polyacrylamides says that the largest use of this product is in the treatment of municipal drinking water and waste water. Approximately 500,000 tons of polyacrylamides are used per annum.[73] The EU has not included these products as environmental goods, yet some of them can be found in the suggestions made by other WTO-members.[74]

The EU's list also contains a reference to pipes for drinking water, HS 681091.[75] The US list[76] contains HS 391721 (ethylene polymers pipes and tubes), 391722 (propylene polymers pipes and tubes) and 391723 (polyvinylchloride pipes and tubes). The tariff schedules list many pipes and tubes: ceramic, cement, plastic, steel, nickel, copper, and aluminium. All these could be used for drinking water. But will the negotiators classify all of them as environmental?

The *APEC list*, one could argue, does not contain many 'commodities' either. The discussions on environmental goods were part of the APEC's Early Voluntary Sectoral Liberalization (EVSL)[77] initiative which covered fifteen sectors including chemicals. It was therefore unnecessary for APEC to address the issue of chemical commodities in the context of environmental goods since these products had already been covered by another sectoral initiative.

[73] See: http://ecb.jrc.it/DOCUMENTS/Existing-Chemicals/RISK_ASSESSMENT/REPORT/acrylamidereport011.pdf.

[74] See Synthesis made by the Secretariat, n. 63 above, p. 14.

[75] See EU list, n. 55 above.

[76] See US list, n. 66 above.

[77] In 1997, APEC Economic Leaders agreed to Early Voluntary Sectoral Liberalisation (EVSL) in fifteen important areas to facilitate efficient reductions to trade barriers and to ultimately open markets. The fifteen areas are: environmental goods and services; fish and fish products; forest products; medical equipment and instruments; telecommunications mutual recognition arrangement (MRA); energy sector; toys; gems and jewelry; chemicals; oilseeds and oilseed products; food sector; natural and synthetic rubber; fertilizers; automotive; and civil aircraft. See www.apec.org/apec/apec_groups/committees/committee_on_trade/early_voluntary_sectoral.html.

Apart from the aspect of discrimination the discussions on product coverage need to address the issue of end use. *Should only those products which have an environmental end use be considered to be environmental or should one also consider dual-use products?* The latter could be identified as environmental goods using an end-use certificate which would probably solve the above mentioned case of polystyrene pallets used in insulation panels. Deeming them impractical, the APEC participants refused end-use certificates.[78] It is interesting to note that the ITA also rejected end-use certificates.[79]

A related issue to end use is the product coverage of HS six-digit headings which normally contain a basket of products. The US has given a specific example for HS 841360 'pumps for liquids'. It does not consider all pumps for liquids to be environmental goods, only 'submersible mixer pumps to circulate water in waste water treatment process; sewage pumps, screw type'.[80] European business has suggested that if one product within a six-digit tariff line is considered to be environmental, the whole line should be reduced to zero.[81] Business does not want to inflate the tariff by introducing new distinctions. The negotiators will probably draw the line '*if all or the core of the products within the category are considered environmental*'.[82] If only some products are covered, but not the whole basket, they will normally be 'ex-ed out', i.e. be identified specifically in a narrower national eight- or nine-digit level.[83] However, this will introduce yet another distinction which will make the tariff more difficult to apply.

The most contentious issue of the debate is the *suggestion put forward by the EU that goods produced in an environmentally friendly manner should also be covered.* The EU has drawn up a list of goods with high environmental performance/low environmental impact.[84] This list also contains the suggestion to include products with an eco-label. Although not explicitly mentioned by the EU, this approach arguably introduces a tariff distinction between goods based on their (non-product related) process and production methods. Some commentators have suggested using such a PPM-based distinction to classify environmental goods,[85] and others have shown that a differentiation on the basis of PPMs is possible for

78 See US Submission, n. 66 above, p. 4. 79 *Ibid.* 80 *Ibid.*

81 See UNICE Position, n. 54 above.

82 See for example the US explanations of the APEC approach, US Submission, n. 65 above.

83 See also Steenblik, n. 58 above, p. 8. 84 See EU list, n. 55 above.

85 See for example Robert Howse and Petrus B. van Bork, *Options for the Liberalisation of Trade in Environmental Goods in the Doha Round*, International Centre for Trade and

statistical and therefore also for classification purposes.[86] In the WTO, the reaction to the EU's suggestion was hostile.[87] The US argued that APEC had refused to include such a category of goods because of the practical and WTO legal issues surrounding tariff discrimination on the basis of PPM-criteria.[88]

Categorisation of goods in the tariff schedule on the basis of their production process leads to a *discussion of 'like products'*. The WTO applies the well-established GATT criteria of physical properties, end-use, tariff classification and consumer tastes and habits[89] to answer the question of whether products are like. If identical products were classified in different tariff categories because of the difference in their production processes they could be considered different within the meaning of GATT. A WTO member could therefore treat the 'environmentally unfriendly' product differently than the 'environmentally friendly' product, thus introducing a different treatment of identical products by way of a tariff classification exercise. Would such a treatment, if attacked in WTO lead to a finding that identical products are to be considered 'unlike'? Without analysing the legal issue of this case, and in particular the question of whether such a broad interpretation of GATT Article III would render GATT Article XX superfluous,[90] it suffices to say that, for the purposes of this article, this

Footnote 85 (*cont.*)
Sustainable Development, Geneva, 2005; available at: www.trade-environment.org/page/theme/goods.htm. [86] See Steenblik, n. 58 above, p. 12.

[87] '*The EC Submission on environmental goods (TN/TE/W/47) met with the greatest resistance, in particular its suggestion to not only include goods used in pollution control and resource management but also goods that have a high environmental performance or low environmental impacts. The EU acknowledged that some of these products might need to be defined through standards, which require clarification, and proposed using schemes included in the existing international Global Eco-labelling Network. The proposal was widely rejected by many developing countries, which resisted the inclusion of process and production method (PPM) based environmental goods as well as eco-labels. The EU expressed disappointment with the unfavourable reception, noting that at this point few alternatives had been put forward. They also stressed that not all environmentally preferable products would necessarily be distinguished on the basis of the process through which they had been produced*'. *Bridges Weekly Trade News Digest*, (2005) Vol. 9, No. 7.

[88] See US Submission, n. 65 above, p. 3.

[89] *European Communities – Measures Affecting Asbestos and Asbestos Containing Products*, WT/DS135/AB/R, paras 84 *et seq.*, referring to the GATT Working Party Report *Border Tax Adjustments* of 2 December 1970, BISD 18S/97.

[90] For a legal analysis on whether identical products can be considered unlike for the purposes of GATT Article III, see Reinhard Quick and Christian Lau, *Environmentally Motivated Tax Distinctions and WTO Law: The European Commission's Green Paper on*

controversial proposal could 'have consequences for the multilateral trading system as a whole'.[91] Similar reasonings to those for PPMs can also be developed for eco labels.[92]

The country coverage for a sectoral agreement on environmental goods seems easy. If these goods are considered to be good for the environment then all WTO members should participate. Business has suggested that no exceptions should be made.[93] It remains to be seen whether the negotiators will apply a strict environmental approach when it comes to country coverage or whether they will also calibrate the environmental goods modalities and apply the principle of less than full reciprocity.[94]

To summarise, the negotiators are deeply divided and the issue itself creates numerous problems. Whilst many commentators and negotiators consider that these problems can be resolved in a pragmatic way, business wonders whether these negotiations should be pursued. Instead of introducing a difference between 'good' and 'bad' goods and distinctions and discriminations between products based on end use, the business community considers it more efficient to substantially reduce and eventually eliminate tariffs for all industrial goods. *Environmental aspects should be dealt with nationally or internationally but should not be introduced into the tariff structure.* Business is concerned that the negotiators are concentrating on making this structure even more complicated and burdensome instead of facilitating trade altogether. If the exercise, agreed by Ministers in the Doha mandate, leads to an arbitrary and discriminatory result thereby putting the main purpose of the WTO in doubt, namely to liberalise trade for all goods, then the ministers should perhaps reverse their decision.

2. The relationship between WTO and MEAs – An inconclusive mandate prohibiting real negotiations

The WTO/MEA relationship has been part of the trade and environment discussions initiated in 1994 by the Ministerial Decision[95] taken at the

Integrated Product Policy in Light of the 'Like Product' and 'PPM' Debates, (2003) *Journal of International Economic Law* (2), 419–58. [91] Steenblik, n. 58 above, p. 12.

[92] Manoj Joshi, *Eco-Labels and WTO Agreements*, (2004) *Journal of World Trade*, 38(1), 69–92, 87. [93] See UNICE Position, n. 54 above.

[94] WTO/TN/MA/W 1 of 24 June 2002, Market Access for Non-Agricultural Products, Communications from the European Communities, para. 12, p .3.

[95] Marrakesh Ministerial Decision on Trade and Environment; LT/UR/D-6/2 of 15 April 1994.

Marrakesh conference and further elaborated on by the first report of the Committee on Trade and Environment[96] adopted in 1996. Although there are about 200 MEAs *only twenty of them contain trade measures*,[97] for example, the Convention on International Trade in endangered Species of Wild Fauna and Flora (CITES),[98] the Basel Convention on the Control of Transboundary Movements of Hazardous Wastes and their Disposal,[99] the Montreal Protocol on Substances that Deplete the Ozone Layer,[100] the Convention on Biodiversity,[101] the Cartagena Protocol on Biosafety,[102] the Rotterdam Convention on the Prior Informed Consent Procedure for Certain Hazardous Chemicals and Pesticides[103] and the Stockholm Convention on Persistent Organic Pollutants.[104]

Paragraph 31(i) of the Doha Declaration[105] foresees negotiations on the relationship between existing WTO rules and specific trade obligations set out in multilateral environmental agreements (MEAs). It clarifies that the negotiations shall be limited in scope to the applicability of such existing WTO rules among parties to the MEA in question and furthermore states that the negotiations shall not prejudice the WTO rights of any Member that is not a party to the MEA.

Paragraph 31(i) contains a number of limitations to the WTO/MEA negotiations and explicitly excludes the issue of non-MEA members. One wonders though whether there is a real need for a set of new rules on the specific relationship if the states are both members of the WTO and the MEA in question. Even if there were an alleged conflict[106] between the obligations contained in the two agreements would such an issue really be brought to the WTO or the MEA dispute settlement processes and would such a process then result in the finding that the obligations contained in both agreements cannot be complied with simultaneously? In other words, would it not be likely that the judge would construe the provisions

[96] Report of the Committee on Trade and Environment; WTO/WT/CTE/1 of 12 November 1996.

[97] See WTO/WT/CTE/W/160/Rev.2, TN/TE/S/5 of 25 April 2003, Matrix on Trade Measures Pursuant to Selected Multilateral Environmental Agreements, Note by the Secretariat.

[98] CITES: www.cites.org.

[99] Basel Convention: www.basel.int.

[100] Montreal Protocol: www.unep.org/ozone/index-en.shtml.

[101] Biodiversity Convention: www.biodiv.org.

[102] Cartagena Protocol: www.biodiv.org/biosafety.

[103] PIC Convention: www.pic.int.

[104] POPs Convention: www.pops.int.

[105] See n. 17 above.

[106] On the concept of conflict in international law see Wolfram Kall, *Treaties, Conflict Between*, in Encyclopedia of Public International Law, Rudolf Bernhardt (ed.), 1984, p. 468.

of one agreement in such a way so as not to create conflict with the rules of the other agreement?[107]

Paragraph 32 of the Doha Declaration contains a further limitation for the negotiations. It requires that the WTO/MEA negotiations 'shall be compatible with the open and non-discriminatory nature of the multilateral trading system, *shall not add to or diminish the rights and obligations of Members under existing WTO agreements*, in particular the SPS Agreement, nor alter the balance of these rights and obligations'. (emphasis added).

The limitations contained in paragraphs 31(i) and 32 have tied the hands of the WTO members. A *solution to the MEA/WTO relationship can probably only be found through an Interpretative Understanding*[108] since this instrument will not change the existing rules nor add new substantive provisions to the WTO textbook, but will only interpret the already existing rules.

The European business community adopted several positions on the different issues of the trade and environment debate and published them as a contribution to the WTO High-level Symposium on Trade and Environment held in March 1999.[109] European business considered that the WTO/MEA relationship had to be addressed.[110] Being aware and afraid of a possible attack by a WTO member against an MEA trade measure taken by another WTO member and fearing that such a case could put into question the objective of the MEA, business urged the

[107] See WTO/TN/TE/W/61 of 10 October 2005, The Relationship Between WTO Rules and MEAs, Submission by Switzerland. The EU/Chile Swordfish dispute could have been a very interesting legal case on whether two international agreements were in conflict with each other, or could have been construed so as to create no conflict. The case was not decided but suspended. See Jan Neumann, *Die materielle und prozessuale Koordination völkerrechtlicher Ordnungen, Die Problematik paraller Streitbeilegungs-verfahren am Beispiel des Schwertfisch-Falls*, 38 ZaöRV 2001, pp. 529–76. The *Swordfish* case could be considered as an example that parallel dispute settlement may render judicial attempts to avoid conflicts impossible.

[108] According to Article IX paragraph 2 of the Marrakesh Agreement Establishing the World Trade Organization.

[109] UNICE Positions on Trade and Environment, Brussels, 1999, to be found at: www.unice.org/content/default.asp?PageId=382.

[110] UNICE Position on the Relationship Between the Provisions of the Multilateral Trading System and Trade Measures for Environmental Purposes, Including those Pursuant to Multilateral Environmental Agreements (MEAs) of 22 July 1996. Update of UNICE Position on the Relationship Between the Provisions of the Multilateral Trading System and Trade Measures for Environmental Purposes, Including Those Pursuant to Multilateral Environmental Agreements of 15 February 1999; www.unice.org/content/default.asp?PageId=382.

WTO membership to address and resolve the WTO/MEA relationship. It suggested that the WTO adopt an Interpretative Understanding containing the *presumption of compatibility of MEA trade measures with GATT and in particular with GATT Article XX.*[111] European business felt that no hierarchy existed between WTO rules and MEAs and that both legal instruments should be mutually supportive.[112] The Interpretative Understanding should underline the principle of mutual supportiveness by stating that states have a duty to fulfil their obligations from one agreement without violating their other obligations. No hierarchy means that each system can only function if there is deference to the other. In other words *WTO rules are informed by MEA rules and have to be interpreted accordingly. Vice versa, MEA rules are informed by WTO rules.*[113] European business also wanted to extend the presumption of compatibility to those MEA trade measures that were authorised against non-members. An attack in the WTO against such measures would be possible; however the WTO member attacking the MEA trade measure would be faced with a higher burden of proof. Mutual understanding and the reversal of the burden of proof should allow the negotiators of an international environmental agreement to adopt trade measures which are necessary from an environmental proportional and from a trade point of view. The Understanding should also contain a reference that the underlying environmental objective of the agreement is based on science and that a global participation in the MEA is encouraged. It should also deal with dispute settlement and provide for a hierarchy in favour of MEA dispute settlement. A case arising from an MEA trade measure should first and foremost be dealt with by the MEA and not by the WTO. The exception to this rule would be an MEA trade measure against a non-party. Since the non-party is not bound by the MEA

[111] Switzerland also supports such a reversal of the burden of proof; see WTO/TN/TE/W/16 of 6 November 2002, Statement by Switzerland at the CTE Special Session on 10 October 2002.

[112] The Plan of Implementation of the World Summit on Sustainable Development (WSSD) contains the following wording: *States should promote mutual supportiveness between the multilateral trading system and the multilateral environmental agreements, consistent with sustainable development goals, in support of the work programme agreed through WTO, while recognizing the importance of maintaining the integrity of both instruments*: UN/A/CONF/199/20*, United Nations Report of the World Summit on Sustainable Development, Johannesburg, South Africa, 26 August–4 September 2002, para. 98, pp. 56–7.

[113] UNICE Letter to the Commission dated 23 May 2003 on the MEAs/WTO Relationship; available on request.

the trade measure taken against it has to be regarded as any trade measure taken by one WTO member against another. Given that the WTO Appellate Body found in *Shrimps-Turtle*[114] that the unilateral trade measure based on a 'non-product related process and production requirement' (PPM) was compatible with WTO, it could well be that an MEA trade measure against a non-party would also be found WTO-compatible. The business community considered that the Interpretative Understanding would provide environment negotiators with considerable leeway to adopt trade measures which would not be scrutinised by the WTO. A case would only succeed if the trade measure was truly discriminatory or arbitrary and did not contribute to achieving the environmental objective. Of the existing MEA trade measures only one provision of the Basel Convention would probably be held to be incompatible with the WTO and that provision is not yet in force.[115]

The WTO membership held extensive discussions on paragraph 31(i), based on many submissions in the early years of the DDA negotiations[116] but lately, the subject has not been advanced much. Certain progress has been made with respect to the *information exchange between MEA Secretariats and the relevant WTO committees* (as provided for by *paragraph 31(ii) of the Doha Declaration*) and on the issue of observer status of those secretariats.[117] On all the other issues the WTO membership is deeply divided. The *Hong Kong Declaration*[118] merely reaffirms the mandate and recognises the progress achieved by the negotiators.

[114] *United States – Import Prohibition of Certain Shrimp and Shrimp Products*, WT/DS58/AB/R of 12 October 1998 as well as *United States – Import Prohibition of Certain Shrimp and Shrimp Products, Recourse to Article 21.5 of the DSU by Malaysia*, WT/DS58/AB/RW of 22 October 2001. Concerning this case, see also Taira, chapter 18 in this book.

[115] Article 4A in conjunction with Annex VII of the Basel Convention contains a ban on exports for recycling of dangerous waste to non-OECD countries. The distinction between OECD and non-OECD members is probably well meant, since one could assume that non-OECD members probably do not have recycling facilities at an ecological level of OECD members, but this distinction nevertheless constitutes an arbitrary and unjustifiable discrimination. The Basel ban violates GATT Article XI and could probably not be justified with in GATT Article XX. Suppose a non-OECD country has built an advanced ecological recycling facility. Should an OECD country not be allowed to send its waste to this recycling facility? The Basel ban does not refer to the issue of whether a country is capable, in an ecological sense, of recycling dangerous waste, it just discriminates between OECD and non-OECD countries.

[116] See for example WTO/TN/S/3/Rev.1 of 24 April 2003, Compilation of Submissions under Paragraph 31(i) of the Doha Declaration, Note by the Secretariat.

[117] See Trade and Environment at the WTO, Background Document at: www.wto.org/english/tratope/envire/envirbackgrnde/contentse.htm.

[118] Paragraph 31, see n. 1 above.

However, it seems that there is more disagreement now than there was on the adoption of the first trade and environment report in 1996.

The most contentious issues are (a) what constitutes a *specific trade obligation* and how the WTO should accommodate them? (b) the meaning of *among parties to the MEA in question* and (c) whether there should be a hierarchy in dispute settlement. Nor is the outcome of the negotiations in any way clear: will it be an Interpretative Understanding or new substantive provisions notwithstanding the limited mandate?

The EU has started the debate on specific trade obligations by suggesting four categories.[119] (1) mandatory trade measures explicitly provided for under MEAs; (2) trade measures not explicitly provided for nor mandatory under the MEA itself but consequential of an 'obligation of result' of the MEA (this category covers cases where an MEA identifies a list of potential policies and measures that parties could implement to meet their obligations); (3) trade measures neither identified in, nor mandatory under the MEA, but consequential of the 'obligation of result' although not listed in the MEA, which gives the party more scope as regards the measure it wishes to deploy to achieve the objectives of the MEA; and (4) trade measures neither identified in nor mandatory under the MEA, but which parties can decide to implement. Many countries have submitted comments on the EU's suggestion[120] but the views on the relationship between WTO rules and the specific MEA trade obligations vary considerably. Some countries would like to accommodate categories (1) and (2),[121] others only category (1)[122] and others see no need to deal with this issue at all but consider national co-ordination to be more important than an accommodation via specific trade obligations.[123]

[119] See WTO/TN/TE/W/1 of 21 March 2002, Multilateral Environmental Agreements (MEAs): Implementation of the Doha Development Agenda, Submission by the European Communities.

[120] See Background Document, n. 117 above, pp. 18–34.

[121] For example, Switzerland: see WTO TN/TE/W/4 of 6 June 2002, Multilateral Environmental Agreements (MEAs): Implementation of the Doha Development Agenda, Submission by Switzerland; see also TWTO/TN/TE/W/58 of 6 July 2005, The Relationship Between Existing WTO Rules and Specific Trade Obligations (STOS) set out in Multilateral Environmental Agreements (MEAs); Submission by Switzerland.

[122] For example, Malaysia: see WTO/TN/TE/W28 of 30 April 2003; Paragraph 31(i) of the Doha Ministerial Declaration – Submission by Malaysia.

[123] For example, the US: see WTO/TN/TE/W/20 of 10th February 2003, Subparagraph 31(i) of the Doha Declaration, Submission by the United States; Contribution of the United States on Paragraph 31 (i); see also WTO/TN/TE/W/40 of 21 June 2004, Subparagraph 31(i) of the Doha Declaration, Submission by the United States.

European business has submitted the view that only those specific trade obligations of category (1) should be accommodated by the WTO.[124] They are, in fact, the object of multilateral understanding and consensus and have been negotiated openly and tailored in such a way as to meet both environmental and trade implications. A challenge of such measures between MEA parties in the WTO is highly unlikely. If a dispute should arise in spite of its likelihood, the parties to the MEA should, in principle, try to settle it within the MEA and not in the WTO.[125] All the other categories involve a national decision and should therefore be treated like any other domestic decision by the WTO. Unilateral interpretations of MEA obligations should not override multilaterally agreed rules. European business has suggested that MEAs should have a binding dispute settlement mechanism. Such a system would take the pressure off the WTO since it would provide for an authoritative interpretation of the MEA obligation and would have a 'chilling effect' on legally possible WTO cases. *The Interpretative Understanding could provide that specific trade obligations of categories (1), (2) and (3) should first be dealt with by the MEA and not by the WTO.* Such provision could also solve the difficult legal issues which arose in the EU/Chile *Swordfish* case.[126] Specific trade measures of category (4) should be regarded as unilateral actions having no direct relation to the MEA in question and should therefore be treated as such.

Since specific trade measures of category (1) taken against non-parties cannot be dealt with by the MEA, the non-party can only have the dispute solved by the WTO. Yet even if it is not possible to deal with this issue in an Interpretative Understanding because of the limited mandate, the WTO's judicial system will not ignore public international law as the Appellate Body has demonstrated that WTO obligations cannot be interpreted in 'clinical isolation'. One can therefore expect that MEAs will inform the WTO and that the WTO obligations could be interpreted in the light of internationally agreed upon environmental rules.[127]

[124] See UNICE letter, n. 113 above.

[125] This recommendation was also made in the First Report of the CTE, n. 96 above, para. 178.

[126] See Neumann, n. 107 above; see also WTO Background Document, n. 117 above.

[127] In *European Communities – Measures Affecting the Approval and Marketing of Biotech Products*, WT/DS 291/292/293/interim of 7 February 2006, not yet publicly available but nevertheless to be found on the Internet, the Panel addressed the relationship between the Biosafety Protocol and the WTO. The case was interesting in so far as the complainants had not ratified the Biosafety Protocol. Relying on Article 31(3(c)) of the Vienna Convention on the Law of Treaties which provides that the interpreter of a treaty should take into account, together with the context, *any relevant rules of international law*

Is it the Appellate Body's judicial activism, though, which raises the question on whether the WTO needs to negotiate the WTO/MEA relationship at all? The inability to solve a hotly disputed subject through negotiations provides the 'judge' in a system of a binding dispute settlement mechanism with an enormous opportunity and burden. *Instead of blaming the judge, one should rather encourage the rule-makers to assert their power.*

IV. Regulatory co-operation – A solution for REACH or a goal beyond reach?

In October 2003 the European Commission adopted a controversial proposal for a new EU regulatory system for chemicals, the so-called REACH Regulation.[128] REACH stands for Registration, Evaluation and Authorisation of Chemicals. It will require companies that manufacture or import chemicals in quantities of one tonne or more per year to register these chemicals, to assess the risks arising from their manufacture and use and to take the necessary measures to manage any risk they identify through the whole supply chain. The registrants will have to submit specific information to a central agency, which will evaluate the submitted data and will closely scrutinize 'substances of concern'. These might then be subject to a restriction process or an authorisation procedure. REACH is 'big' in every aspect: the draft Regulation and its annexes fill 1,200 pages to which several thousand pages of implementation and

Footnote 127 (*cont.*)
applicable in the relations between the parties, the Panel held that it was not required to take into account the Biosafety Protocol since the complainants to the dispute were not members of the said agreement (emphasis added). See Interim Report pp. 294 *et seq.* See also Hohmann, *Der Konflikt zwischen freiem Handel und Umweltschutz in WTO und EG*, Recht der Internationalen Wirtschaft 2000, p. 88 *et seq.* and Steger and Matsushita, chapters 13 and 16, in this book.

[128] Proposal for a Regulation of the European Parliament and the Council concerning the Registration, Evaluation, Authorization and Restriction of Chemicals (REACH), establishing a European Chemicals Agency and amending Directive 1999/45/EC and Regulation (EC) (on Persistent Organic Pollutants, COM(2003) 644 final). (*Note from editor*: Now adopted as EC Regulation 1907/2066 of 18 December 2006.) For an overview of the REACH proposal see Horst von Holleben and Hartmut Scheidmann, *Das europäische Chemikalienrecht im Umbruch*, Zeitschrift für Stoffrecht, 2004, pp. 16 *et seq.* For a discussion of the chemical industry's positions on REACH, see the websites of CEFIC or VCI at: www.cefic.be; or: www.vci.de. For a discussion of the NGOs position of REACH see, for example Greenpeace at: www.greenpeace.org/international/campaigns/toxics/chemicals-out-of-control/chemicals-regulation; or WWF at: www.panda.org/about_wwf/what_we_do/toxics/ our_solutions/chemical_reform/index.cfm.

handling guidelines as well as technical guidance documents will be added;[129] the obligations on companies are heavy and costly[130] and REACH *affects not only the chemical industry, but the entire manufacturing sector since chemicals can be found in each and every product.*[131] Given its scope, it is not surprising that REACH has been the subject of a very powerful lobby campaign by industry, NGOs and foreign governments.[132]

With a turnover of more than €600 billion per year, the European chemical industry has a share of 35% of the world's production of chemicals followed by North America with 28% and Asia with 27%. Europe exports chemicals worth €165 billion and imports €95 billion. The chemical industry is one of the great contributors to the European export surplus. Europe's biggest trading partner in chemicals is the United States. About 40% of the transatlantic exports and imports in chemicals are intra-company.[133]

129 For more information on the so-called REACH Implementation Projects see: http://ecb.jrc.it/REACH/RIP_PROJECTS/.

130 See KPMG-Study, *REACH – Further Work on Impact Assessment – A Case Study Approach*, July 2005, to be found at: www.europa.eu.int/comm/enterprise/reach/docs/reach/kpmgfinalreport.pdf. *Platts Commodity News* of 7 June 2005 writes about the KPMG Study: 'The European REACH legislation will mean companies are likely to have to rationalize their portfolios as registration cost are up to 20% of turnover', Jan van der Kolk, manager at KPMG, the Netherlands, said Tuesday, at a conference in Frankfurt. 'Simply to find the money to carry out the REACH regulations will be difficult for smaller companies' said the analyst, adding that this could lead to an 'uncontrolled rationalization within chemical companies'. The criteria for rationalization will be the profitability, of the substance concerned, strategic importance customer relations as well as the life cycle of the products. 'Almost all vulnerable substances are found in the smaller than the 100 tonnes bracket. So the cost is relatively high with a view to the volumes of chemicals' said van der Kolk. This would, in turn, impact significantly the cost of downstream products.

131 REACH is therefore of interest to industry in general; see for example, the UNICE Position Papers on REACH to be found at: www.unice.org, such as the 'Position Paper on REACH' dated 1 September 2004 or the paper 'An EU industry recommendation to improve the efficiency and workability of REACH' of 17 January 2005.

132 Many third countries participated in the European Commission's Internet Consultation on REACH held from May–July 2003; Chile, Singapore, Australia, Canada, United States, Brazil, China, Japan, Thailand, Chinese Taipei and Cuba also submitted comments on REACH in the WTO TBT context after the EU had notified its draft regulation to the WTO TBT Committee. The references to the TBT discussions, the documents as well as the European Communities response to the comments can be found at: http://europa.eu.int/comm/enterprise/tbt/index.cfm?. On 8 June 2006 the diplomatic missions of Australia, Brazil, India, Israel, Japan, Korea, Malaysia, Mexico, Singapore, South Africa, Thailand and the United States to the European Union issued a joint press statement requesting for further improvements to REACH, see: http://useu.usmission.gov/.

133 For a reference to the figures used in the text see: CEFIC Facts and Figures 2005 and the CEFIC Study *Horizon 2015* at www.cefic.be. See also William Storck, *Much Needless Ado About Trade Balance, Business Insights* (2001) 79(45), 20.

The European chemical industry is an active supporter of closer economic relations between the European Union and the United States. Since the early 1990s many transatlantic initiatives have been under taken, whose purpose is to bring the two sides closer together on a wide range of political, economic and societal issues.[134] An ambitious agenda of co-operation exists, requiring intensive dialogue and extensive preparation and culminating in an annual EU/US summit.[135] Of particular importance from a business point of view is the Action Plan of the 1998 Transatlantic Economic Partnership covering many issues ranging from the WTO to technical barriers to trade as well as biotechnology, environmental and intellectual property.[136] This initiative should further transatlantic economic integration, spur innovation and job creation and realise the competitive potential of both economies.[137] While the exercise falls short of liberalising transatlantic trade in the traditional sense – due to the fact that an EU/US free trade agreement is, unfortunately, not on the political radar[138] – it goes way beyond free trade in that it aims, *inter alia*, for an approximation of technical regulations and standards through mutual recognition, technical convergence and outright harmonisation.

Parallel to these political initiatives the late US Secretary of Commerce Ron Brown and Commissioner Martin Bangemann initiated a dialogue structure to encourage the different stakeholders to become more involved in closer transatlantic co-operation. In 1995 the Transatlantic Business Dialogue (TABD)[139] was launched to help to establish a barrier-free transatlantic market. The business community adopts its recommendations on EU/US issues and presents them to the annual EU/US Summit.[140]

[134] Transatlantic Declaration on EC–US Relations, 1990; New Transatlantic Agenda, 1995; Joint Action Plan, 1995; Transatlantic Economic Partnership 1998, EU–US-Economic Initiative 2005 as well as the latest Commission Communication on a Stronger EU–US Partnership and a more Open Market for the 21st Century of 18 May 2005. These documents can be found at: http://europa.eu.int/comm/external_relations/us/intro/docs.htm#core.

[135] The Summit Declarations can be found at http://ec.europa.eu/comm/external_relations/us/intro/summit.htm.

[136] See the documents mentioned in n. 134 above.

[137] EU–US 2005 Summit Declaration of 20 June 2005, see n. 135 above.

[138] The chemical industry is one of the few supporters of a EU/US FTA; see the letter by Reinhard Quick to the *Financial Times*, *Let the EU and US truly open up transatlantic trade*, *Financial Times*, 12 April 2006, p. 12. The industry is convinced that a real FTA would increase industry's competitiveness.

[139] For further information on TABD, its mission statement, working methods and functioning see www.tabd.com.

[140] The different TABD CEO Reports can be found at the website mentioned in n. 139 above.

A barrier-free transatlantic market requires the elimination of trade, regulatory and investment impediments. This is, of course, more easily said than done and transatlantic regulatory co-operation is still in a very early phase. Duplication and diverging technical regulations are a fact of life in transatlantic business. They will not be easily abolished, converged or harmonised since they have been adopted by democratically elected parliaments who are learning how to co-operate.

A first step, though, has been made and both sides are committed to the process. The enthusiasm of the early years which can be characterised by the TABD slogan '*approved once, accepted everywhere*'[141] has given way to a more pragmatic approach which should bring tangible results aiming at 'effective mechanisms to promote better quality regulation, to minimise unnecessary regulatory divergences to facilitate transatlantic trade and investment and increase consumer confidence in the transatlantic market'.[142] In 2002 the two sides adopted Guidelines on Regulatory Co-operation and Transparency[143] and in 2005 they adopted a *roadmap for EU-US Regulatory Co-operation*[144] with work plans in fifteen specific areas, including chemicals.

Given the importance of the chemical industry on both sides of the Atlantic, one would assume that regulatory co-operation on chemicals was high on the political agenda. A closer look at the results obtained so far shows how difficult it is to produce a substantive result and how much political commitment and work are still needed to achieve a transatlantic market in chemicals.[145] The two sides discuss REACH instead of working on a joint approach to chemicals legislation and putting such joint action

[141] See for example the 1999 TABD CEO Conference Conclusions of 30 October 1999, p. 1 to be found at www.tabd.com.

[142] 2005 EU-US Summit Declaration, see n. 135 above.

[143] See: http://europa.eu.int/comm/external_relations/us/sum0402/me0285.htm.

[144] See Results of the 2005 EU–US Summit, n. 135 above.

[145] This becomes apparent when looking at the 2005 Roadmap for US–EU Regulatory Co-operation which states with respect to chemicals: **Objective:** Pursue informal co-operative dialogue, in the spirit of the US–EU Guidelines on Regulatory Co-operation, between the US Environmental Protection Agency (EPA), DG Environment, DG Enterprise and Industry and DG Health and Consumer Protection and relevant agencies on chemicals related interest of mutual interest. **Progress/Result:** the US EPA hosted the second transatlantic environmental conference on chemicals which addressed the EU's proposed REACH legislation, the globally harmonised system (GHS) for the classification and labelling of chemicals, pollution prevention techniques, access to information and genomics. EPA hosted EC experts on its approach to the risk assessment of new chemicals and integrated QSAR modelling programmes. Further exchange of experience and training programmes could be explored for respective staff. The US EPA and the European Commission are also collaborating in the OECD framework on the

into effect. The idea of a joint legislative approach to chemicals should not be considered a dream but a necessity. It makes sense from a consumer, environmental and economic point of view. Yet it seems that *the EU' s unilateral move on REACH*[146] *has put the whole idea of transatlantic co-operation into doubt.* Reading the 2002 Guidelines one cannot but conclude that they have been completely ignored by the European Commission when adopting the REACH proposal in 2003.[147]

REACH could have been a good basis for co-operation and a demonstration on how to achieve regulatory convergence. Instead it will probably lead to a WTO case against the EU.[148] The judicial system will be called upon to find a balance between 'regulatory autonomy' and 'violation of WTO obligations'.[149] REACH will probably be a very interesting case from a legal point of view since it raises many questions which, so far, have not been addressed in detail by the WTO. On top of the list is the issue of whether the REACH requirements for 'substances', 'preparations', 'polymers' and 'substances in articles' are necessary or whether they are, in effect, 'discriminatory' or an 'unnecessary obstacle to international trade' and therefore violate Articles 2.1 and 2.2 of the TBT Agreement or the respective GATT provisions of GATT Articles III or XI without falling under the general exception of GATT Article XX. Although the WTO has already decided several trade and environment

Footnote 145 (*cont.*)
development of the Global High Production Volume (HPV) chemicals information Portal. **Next Steps:** The EC and the US will continue dialogue on the development on the Global HPV Portal. See, http://europa.eu.int/comm/enterprise/enterprisepolicy/govrelations//interntlregulcoopeuus/index.htm.

[146] Some commentaters blame the EU for wanting to become the 'World's Regulator', see *Wall Street Journal*, of 3 April 2006.

[147] It suffices to cite the first objective of the Guidelines: 'The objectives of these Guidelines are to improve co-operation between regulators and to promote transparency to the public in establishing and amending regulations, and, in particular, to: (a) Improve the planning and developing of regulatory proposals, leverage resources for regulations development, improve the quality and level of technical regulations, pursue, as appropriate, harmonised, equivalent or compatible solutions, and take appropriate steps to minimise or, where appropriate, eliminate unnecessary divergence in regulations through a more systematic dialogue between regulators, involving increased co-operation at all phases at the regulations development process', (emphasis added); see n. 143 above.

[148] Japan was so concerned about the implications of REACH for international trade that it has publicly been quoted as considering a legal challenge if the REACH proposal will not be amended. See Tokyo opposes draft EU chemicals law, *Financial Times*, 22 February 2005.

[149] For a discussion of the different WTO arguments against REACH see: AmCham EU–CEFIC–FEEC Discussion Paper on the Trade Impact of REACH of 30 November 2004 at www.cefic.be. See also Marco Bronckers and Pablo Charro, *REACH Reviewed Under*

cases and there exists quite an important body of case law concerning the application of GATT Article XX,[150] the Appellate Body has not yet dealt with the obligations contained in Articles 2.1 and 2.2 TBT. Will the Appellate Body, for example, give the necessity test contained in Article 2.2 TBT a different reading than the one it has developed so far with respect to 'necessity' under GATT Article XX?[151] Other important legal issues of REACH are (a) data protection, and here, in particular, the compatibility of REACH with Article 39 TRIPs[152] and (b) the protection of confidential business information in general.

The REACH example also shows that the WTO itself is probably not ready to discuss the limits of 'regulatory autonomy' and to come to grips with those new trade barriers lying behind and not at the border. Regulatory convergence will eventually become a subject for the WTO. Until then the business community will have to be patient reminding the governments of their political commitments and trying to achieve convergence via a bilateral and not a multilateral route.

V. Conclusions

The chemical industry has made far-reaching and controversial liberalisation proposals to the negotiators. *It would like to eliminate tariffs on chemicals, prohibit some distortive non-tariff barriers which affect the industry's competitiveness, introduce a mediation mechanism on NTBs and*

WTO Law, JEEPL 31/2005 pp. 184 *et seq.*; Christian Tietje and Sebastian Wolf, REACH Registration of Imported Substances – Compatibility with WTO Rules, Beiträge zum Transnationalen Wirtschaftsrecht, Martin-Luther-Universität Halle-Wittenberg, Heft 42, July 2005; Harald Hohmann, *Zur Frage der Vereinbarkeit der REACH Verordnung der EG mit höherrangigem EG- und WTO-Recht*, Zeitschrift für Stoffrecht 2006, pp. 67 *et seq.*

150 For a general discussion of GATT Article XX see Petros C. Mavroidis, The General Agreement on Tariffs and Trade, (2005) New York: Oxford University Press, pp. 184 *et seq.*; see also WTO/WT/CTE/W/53 Rev.1/Corr. 1* of 30 November 1998, GATT/WTO Dispute Settlement Practice Relating to Article XX, Paragraphs (b), (d) and (g) of GATT. This note is an excellent summary of the different interpretations given by the Appellate Body.

151 For an overview of the relationship between GATT and TBT see Gabrielle Marceau and Joel P. Trachtmann, *The Technical Barriers to Trade Agreement, the Sanitary and Phytosanitary Measures Agreement, and the General Agreement on Tariffs and Trade* (2002) 36 JWT 811 *et seq.*, 824–32.

152 Marco Bronckers and Petr Ondrusek, *Protection of Regulatory Data in the EU and WTO Law – The Example of REACH*, 2005 8(5), *Journal of World Intellectual Property*, 579 *et seq.*; see also Marco Bronckers and Petr Ondrusek, *Schutz von Registrierdaten im EU- und WTO-Recht: Das Beispiel von REACH*, Zeitschrift für Stoffrecht (2005) 1(2) 2 *et seq.*

solve the MEA/WTO issue in a pragmatic way. The industry remains sceptical whether the Doha mandate on environmental goods will attain its goals. In the transatlantic context, the industry aims at liberalisation going beyond WTO, namely to achieve regulatory convergence through co-operation.

Given the magnitude of difficulties the DDA is faced with, it is probably not too pessimistic *to assume that the round will not deliver a 'grand' liberalisation of trade in chemicals.* It is already questionable whether the negotiators will be able to bridge the 'triangular gap',[153] i.e. market access in agriculture, substantive reduction of domestic support in agriculture and real market access for industrial products. A non-ambitious result or even a failure of the round will provoke a shift from the multilateral to the bilateral level with a focus on Asia. From a business point of view, bilateral agreements with the most important economic partners are a feasible alternative to the multilateral process notwithstanding the many problems they create.[154] Business cannot wait idly and hope that the multilateral process will deliver a specific result. It will have to jump on the bilateral bandwagon so it does not suffer from discrimination. Bilateral agreements should not be rejected out of hand: they can contribute positively to growth and employment provided they do not contain too many exceptions. If the WTO membership is not willing to engage in further liberalisation now, the much criticised bilateralism could well become the catalyst for further multilateral trade liberalisation in the future.

[153] See speech by WTO Director General Pascal Lamy, *The WTO and the Doha Round: The Way Forward*, 6 April 2006, New Dehli, to be found at www.wto.org/english/news_e/sppl_e/sppl23_e.htm.

[154] For a discussion of the multilateral/bilateral relationship see the so-called Sutherland Report, *The Future of the WTO: Addressing the Institutional Challenges in the new Millennium*, 17 January 2005, available at www.wto.org. For a discussion of the report's conclusions, see the articles contained in (2005) *Journal of International Economic Law*, 8(5), 287 *et seq.*

8

Trade facilitation within the Doha Round: A critical review of recent efforts of the WTO and other international organizations (1996–2007)(*)

HARALD HOHMANN(**)

I. Introduction

The export of goods via ship from one continent to another requires "200 kilograms of documents" for customs, transport, financing and insurance.[1] Trade facilitation is therefore an urgent need !

The *term "Trade Facilitation"* is often defined as "the simplification and harmonization of international trade procedures," with trade procedures being the "activities, practices and formalities involved in collecting, presenting, communicating and processing data required for the movement of goods in international trade."[2] This definition relates to "a wide range of activities, such as import and export procedures (e.g. customs or licensing procedures), transport formalities, and payments, insurance and other financial requirements."[3]

This topic is not a totally new issue in international trade. Some aspects of it were already on the agenda in the League of Nations in 1923. "The main strategy before the globalisation of the post 1950s was primarily to establish *mutual recognition between different regimes* and at the most to harmonise the various independent national systems, a process that in

(*) Heavily updated, amended and revised version of an article published two years earlier in the *Manchester Journal of International Economic Journal* (MJIEL) Vol. 2 Issue 2 (2005), at pp. 44 *et seq.* The article was written in September 2006, with several updates as of September 2007.

(**) Senior Partner, *Hohmann & Partner Attorneys*, Büdingen (close to Frankfurt/Main), and Senior Lecturer, University of Frankfurt/Main. The author thanks *Nora Neufeld* (WTO Secretariat, Geneva) and *Tadatsugu Matsudaira* (WCO, Technical officer, Brussels) for their discussions and modification proposals. All errors are of course mine.

1 Luzius Wasescha, in: Reginhard Henke (ed.), *Beförderungen – Präferenzen – Trade Facilitation* (Annual EFA Basel Symposium 2002), Aachen 2003, at 127.

2 The WTO training package on Trade Facilitation, Market Access, Slide no.52, available at www.wto.org/english/thewto_e/whatis_e/eol/e/wto02/wto2_69.html.

3 The WTO training package on Trade Facilitation (fn. 2).

many aspects still is very important."[4] The work by the ECE, the World Customs Organization (WCO), the World Bank, numerous NGOs and most recently by the WTO, especially since the Doha Round, have all contributed to the current international legal discussion on trade facilitation.

"Trade facilitation" was added to the WTO agenda in December 1996, when the Singapore Ministerial Declaration directed the Council for Trade in Goods "to undertake exploratory and analytical work, drawing on the work of other relevant organizations, on the simplification of trade procedures, in order to assess the scope for WTO rules in this area."

According to the *Doha Declaration*,[5] "trade facilitation" has the following impacts:

> Recognizing the case for further expediting the movement, release and clearance of goods, including goods in transit, and the need for enhanced technical assistance and capacity building in this area, we agree that negotiations will take place after the Fifth Session of the Ministerial Conference on the basis of a decision to be taken, by explicit consensus, at that session on modalities of negotiations. In the period until the Fifth Session, the Council for Trade in Goods shall review and, as appropriate, clarify and improve relevant aspects of Articles V, VIII and X of the GATT 1994 and identify the trade facilitation needs and priorities of members, in particular developing and least-developed countries. We commit ourselves to ensuring adequate technical assistance and support for capacity building in this area (para. 27).

From the Doha Declaration we can conclude that: "trade facilitation" means the simplification of export, import or customs barriers in order to expedite the clearance of goods, and especially simplifications regarding freedom of transit of goods (Art. V GATT), reduction of custom fees and custom procedures (Art. VIII GATT), and more transparency of trade restricting norms (Art. X GATT). Up to now, the topic was often reduced to facilitation of *customs* procedures. We will show, that some *export control* restrictions must also be made subject to "trade facilitation" aspects.

[4] Marcus Hellqvist, Trade Facilitation: Impact and Potential Gains *Swedish National Board of Trade*, April 2003, available on the website of the Center for International Development at Harvard University, www.cid.harvard.edu/cidtrade/issues/tradefacpaper.html. For the evolution of Trade Facilitation see also Carolin Bolhöfer, *Trade Facilitation – WTO-Recht und dessen Reform zur Erleichterung des internationalen Warenhandels*, Witten (EFA-Schriftenreihe vol. 27) 2006.

[5] WTO-Ministerial Doha Declaration of November 14 2001, in *ILM* 41 (2002), 746 *et seq.*, also reproduced electronically, see also the Editor's Introduction.

In this chapter we will discuss, first what the main items in need of "trade facilitation" are (II.), then we will propose a Draft Agreement on trade facilitation and compare it with the current discussions (III.), in order to find out, how much international support there is for these proposals, especially by the WTO since the Doha Round, and then we will conclude (IV.) what the most likely outcome of the Doha Round will be, by proposing a Revised Draft Agreement.

II. The main items in need of "trade facilitation"

As some of the main items which are in need of trade facilitation, we want to mention the following 12 items, based on our experience in consultations on export trade issues:

(a) *Trade restrictions for trade with other Member States of the EC* According to German export law, an export license is required, if listed goods – or in some cases also non-listed goods – are shipped from Germany to France or to other EC Member States and the exporter is aware that the final destination of the goods is outside of the EC Single Market (sect. 7 paras 2, 3 and 4 AWV, German Export Trade Ordinance). In more than 60% of all export activities in Germany – intra-Community trade represents at least 60% of German exports – undue bureaucratic trade barriers are raised in the form of Intra-Community "transfer licenses".[6] In the EC Single Market, such additional national trade barriers are excessive, since they cannot be justified by the legal reasoning of the EC Single Market,[7] and they will result either in forum shopping, or in the movement of company headquarters or stocks to those EC Members with the lowest export level or in near-shore outsourcing.

(b) *Purely national export restrictions without any foundation under (EC or similar regional trade law) and under WTO law* Regulations like those in Germany under AWV, ss 5(c) or (d), which require export licenses for non-listed goods, if the exporter is aware that the goods could be used for military purposes or for nuclear power plants in a country listed by sect.5 c or by sect.5 d AWV, are purely national export restrictions. These are not used by other EC

[6] Harald Hohmann, *Angemessene Außenhandelsfreiheit im Vergleich*, Tübingen 2002, 325, and John, *Zeitschrift für Zölle* 1993, 377.

[7] Hohmann, (n. 6), at 498. The only open question may be, whether the WTO is willing to discuss questions which might be regarded as being intra-EU questions.

member states outside Germany.[8] The same conclusion may be drawn for sect.5 German AWV, adding purely national positions on the EC list of dual-use goods requiring an export license, or for General Prohibition 6 of US Export Law as foreseen in the EAR, requiring export licenses for the export of goods to countries, which have been declared embargo countries unilaterally by the USA. These unilateral regulations have no legal foundation, neither under EC or similar regional trade law (e.g. NAFTA), nor – even more importantly – under WTO law.[9] The result of such disproportionate regulations will be as under (a): forum shopping, transboundary movement of company headquarters or stocks or near-shore outsourcing.[10]

(c) *Frictions between regional agreements and WTO law*
Considering the current trend to regional and bilateral agreements, there is an urgent need for the WTO to solve the friction between regional free-trade zones and multilateral WTO rules: At present, more than 250 free-trade areas, custom unions and regional agreements are limiting the multilateral scope of the WTO rules.[11] These regional agreements should be harmonized under the WTO (within a regional agreement and across different regional agreements). Otherwise, questions will arise such as: How should the principle of most-favored-nation treatment be interpreted, in the multilateral sense of the WTO, or in the higher regional level that has to be given to all other WTO Member States?

(d) *National export restrictions ignoring foreign availability*
National export restrictions should be lifted when the critical goods concerned are available in the country of destination (US principle of foreign availability).[12] Proportionality requires the integration of

[8] Under Art. 4, para. 2 of EC Regulation 1334/2000 concerning the export of dual-use goods, an export license is required for the export of non-listed goods which may be used for military purposes in one of the multilaterally imposed (UN and EC) arms embargo states. Under s 5(c) AWV, Germany unilaterally adds further states to this EC arms embargo list, because an export for military purposes to one of the two listed states (country group K) also requires an export license. There is a similar situation with regard to AWV, s 5(d) since the ten countries listed here are not under EC export control – only Germany regards these ten countries as suspicious concerning nuclear proliferation.

[9] Hohmann, (n. 6) especially at 325. At least, these regulations may be regarded as excessive.

[10] Hohmann, at 324.

[11] Petersmann/Mavroidis, in International Trade Law, *Report for the Conference of the International Law Association at Berlin (2004)*, at notes 50–3. For the recent trend to regionalism, see also Osakwe, Chapter 1b in this book

[12] Hohmann, (n. 6), at 158.

the whole world market into the analysis, whether there is a risk of non-proliferation or not. Concentrating this analysis on the isolated national market alone would not be sufficient. If the principle of foreign availability is introduced in order to make export licenses in those cases unnecessary, evidence is required by the exporter that the exported goods are freely obtainable in the country of final destination or on the world market.[13]

(e) *No harmony and not enough transparency of regulations*

More transparent and more harmonized export control provisions (e.g. *de minimis* levels like the German general licenses AG 12 und AG 13, and the US general license LVS), and more harmonization and transparency concerning regulations on Limitations and Restrictions[14] (i.e. trade regulations or standards based on health, consumer protection, security, public order, intellectual property, ecology, etc.) are indispensable. Example 1: *De minimis* levels regulated by statutes are transparent,[15] however, those that were granted by the German administration without any clear authorization (by statute or EC Law) are not.[16] A more transparent – and in any case a more harmonized – way would be to regulate these cases by EC Regulation 1334/2000 on the export of dual-use goods, which would especially avoid that license exceptions under this Regulation are applicable in only one of twenty-seven EC Member States. Example 2: More transparency is required, concerning regulations on limitations and restrictions as these are usually incomplete in national collections of trade statutes.[17] Consequently, even internationally exporting companies ("international players") are often not aware of all the export or import restrictions resulting from chemicals, food, or environmental law. This transparency could be realized e.g. by listing all of them on

[13] *Ibid.*

[14] This terminology is used by EC Law, cf. Art. 58 para. 2 of the EC Regulation on the Customs Code (ZK), and sect. 1 para. 3 of the German Customs Administration Act (*Zollverwaltungsgesetz*).

[15] In Germany this is done in AWV s 5c para. 4, 5d para. 4 and 7 para. 6 (German Export Ordinance), regulating a *de minimis* level of ⇔2,500 or 5,000, and also in s 19 AWV, naming other cases, where no control interests are at stake.

[16] In Germany this is done by general licenses AG 12 and AG 13: AG 12 covers listed goods exported under Art. 3 of the Dual-Use Regulation 1334/2000, up to ⇔2,500, and AG 13 covers other cases under the Dual-Use Regulation, where no export controls are at stake. Cf. Hohmann, *op.cit* (n. 6)., at 239 and at 179.

[17] In Germany, only a small part can be found in the collection of trade statutes by the German Minister of Economy ("*Vorschriften der Finanzverwaltung, VSF*"). The same result could be found in other states, like Japan or the US.

the website of the national customs agencies or of the national export licensing agency. Even more important is the harmonization of these regulations: Non harmonized standards for health and consumer protection may possibly be regarded as the biggest burden for exports e.g. in the US, more than 2,700 agencies are regulating standards which are often contradictory[18]

(f) *Few general licenses*

At present, there are only few general licenses for trade activities of EC Member States (e.g. EU 001). New general licenses should be introduced and those in existence should be extended. For example, there is no control interest, when a good is delivered to seven non-proliferation States which are recognized by the EC (the US, Canada, Japan, Australia, New Zealand, Norway and Switzerland); thus, the exception list to general license EU 001 should be removed. Only very few German general licenses[19] are accepted for trade between EC countries; given the far-reaching license requirements for trade between EC Member States, more general licenses for intra-Community trade would be preferable. In addition, more general licenses should be introduced to cover exports to destinations, which are either well-recognized non-proliferation States or where the risk of proliferation is not very likely.

(g) *Few bulk licenses*

Bulk licenses should be extended to cover international stocks of goods. National bulk licenses regularly ignore this aspect of globalisation; instead, they are regulating only the export from country A to specific clients in country B. They allow the export of a variety of goods to reliable clients in a few countries, without requiring any prior export license – instead they require the notification of data on exports, provided that not only the goods but also the clients in a few countries are approved by the national export agency and that the exporter is accepted as reliable.[20] More and more international players are now organizing their export trade with the help of international stock, from where they carry out the exports world wide. National bulk licenses should also be extended to cover exports from international stocks.

(h) *Not enough trade facilitation based on audits or registered compliance procedures*

[18] Hohmann, (n. 6), at 200.

[19] General licenses 18, 19 and 21, concerning very few defence articles.

[20] The German regime under the bulk license SAG, cf. Hohmann, (n. 6), at 243.

Audits or registered compliance procedures should be used to facilitate export clearance. If they are implemented, the national export agency can always assume, that the exporter is reliable: The *Japanese METI model* for checking reliability of exporters seems to be more successful and more convincing than the German strategy (concerning the bulk license SAG). Instead of a large number of export licenses received (in Germany), in Japan an auditing takes place. After companies have been registered, they follow the compliance program developed by METI and its half-private subsidiary CISTEC. They are then regarded as reliable by all customs agencies – more than 850 Japanese companies have done this.[21] Without this audit Japanese customs officials may not trust the information given by export companies. This Japanese experience could and should be used as a prototype for a risk management and for the simplification of export controls based on low risks ("authorized traders"), in which reliability can be derived from the fact, that a company has implemented a registered compliance program developed by national export agencies.

By contrast, currently it is not clear enough whether the *Authorized Economic Operator* (AEO), which is binding in EC Law since 2008,[22] will trigger this kind of trade facilitation. At the moment, especially the duties imposed on companies in order to be certified as AEO are clear – precise provisions are missing specifying what kind of trade facilitation will be available, in spite of some current legal provisions on trade facilitation.[23]

(i) *Disproportionate black lists*

US sanction lists and EC lists of potential supporters of some terrorist organizations (under EC Regulations 881/2002 and 2580/2001) could partly be regarded as problematic under privacy laws and the rule of law, as they sometimes list individuals or companies who cannot be precisely identified, who are supposed to have violated export duties or to have supported terrorism, while any evidence to support this is

[21] Hohmann, at 300.

[22] Arts. 5a and 5b of the EC Customs Code and Art. 3 of EC Regulation 1875/2006.

[23] The proposal by Chinese Taipei, the EC and Switzerland of April 4 2006 (TN/TF/W/87) concerning duties and trade facilitation for Authorized Traders. See however the following new development which may modify our point: under the Modernized Custom Code EC Regulation 450/2008 of the EC, the existence of all current and future trade simplification will depend on the question, whether the applicant fulfils most requirements of the AEO (Art. 116). However a similar provision should also be introduced into the new draft of the Dual Use Regulation as of 18 December 2006; see our critique in EC document, Working Party Dual Use Goods, DS 21/2/2007 Rev. 2 of 24 April 2007, at 38–40.

often scarce. Especially problematic is the listing of "related persons" on the US Denied Persons List (DPL) – these are often trade partners of exporting companies, which have possibly violated US export law, and these trade partners are often very surprised to be named on the DPL as "related persons." The Entity List in US export law partly contains the names of companies where some "red flags" for possible violations of export law are available,[24] but treats them as if it has always been proven that they have violated US export law. These unspecific and legally not well-founded "critical" persons should be removed from the lists to avoid undue barriers to international trade. Instead, such black lists should be limited, by restricting them only to those individuals/companies, who can be clearly identified and where there is well-founded evidence about their export violations or their support for terrorism available.

(j) Not sufficient simplified customs procedures

All possible procedures to simplify customs procedures – including the harmonization, standardization, mutual recognition of equivalent procedures/tests and regional customs cooperation – should be introduced. For example, the customs notification procedure under Art. 253 of the Customs Code Implementation Order (ZK-DVO) could also be used for an export license procedure; and the requirements of the reliability check needed to use the simplified customs procedure of customs notification in advance (AWV, s.13 ZK-DVO, Art. 289)[25] should be reduced and made more transparent. In contrast, *pre-shipment customs notifications*, as required under the EC Customs Code, should only be introduced, if this leads to a quick customs clearance (pre-arrival clearance to facilitate the movement of low-risk goods); currently, this result is not clear: the electronic EC customs clearance is not yet working, and binding provisions for simplified customs clearance are still missing. The global cooperation of customs agencies of regions (e.g. that of European customs agencies) and the electronic transfer of customs clearance should be harmonized and improved. The prototype should be the *"single window" approach*: "A Single Window is a facility that allows

[24] The German early warning list, indicate by red flags, that the companies mentioned could possibly be interested in proliferation activities. However, under German or EC export trade law, this listing leads only to some "red flags," but not to a licensing requirement. For flaws concerning the listing of some persons on the anti-terror lists see Hohmann, in: Puschke (ed.) *Basiswissen Sanktionslisten*, Cologne 2008, chapter 5, quoting case law of the ECJ.

[25] Hohmann, n. 6 at 237–38.

parties involved in international trade and transport to lodge standardized information and documents with a single entry point to fulfill all import, export, customs and transit-regulatory reuirements."[26]

(k) *Restrictions on transit trade*
Transit trade[27] could and should be simplified (e.g. by not requiring a transit license among OECD countries). Currently, Germany has a license exception for the seven non-proliferation countries recognized by the EC and for the EC Members.[28] This should be extended to all OECD countries. In addition, a *de minimis* exception and other exceptions should be introduced to lessen restrictions on transit trade.

(l) *Restrictions on imports*
Import procedures should be harmonized and standardized, by using electronic or other automatic information exchange, instead of using hundreds of different paper documents, which often have to be personally signed.[29] Imports should be more fully liberalized, and the lists of non-liberalized goods should be made transparent, by publishing them on the website of the national import or customs agencies. A 100% scanning of import articles by customs should be regarded as excessive – instead scanning should be based on risk management. In addition, no undue notification requirements for imports should be created, as is now foreseen under the REACH-Regulation on production and trade with chemicals.[30] It requires very expensive notification procedures for production in the EC or the import of chemicals into the EC, so hundreds of jobs in the chemical industry may be endangered. These notification requirements should be restricted to the absolute minimum, and the EC principle of *mutual recognition of tests*, notifications and licenses should avoid the need for additional notification in each additional Member State of the EC.

[26] Economic Commission for Europe ECE, Recommendation 33 on Establishing a Single Window, New York/Geneva 2005, at p. 2. "Single Window" does not cover customs procedures alone, but all kind of trade transactions.

[27] The definition in s. 4, no. 8 of the German Export Trade Ordinance AWV: "transaction where uncleared goods that are located outside Germany are acquired by <German> residents from noo-residents and are sold to non-residents."

[28] AWV, s. 40, para. 1.

[29] ECE, Recommendation 13: Facilitation of identified legal problems in import clearance procedures, Geneva 1979.

[30] EC Regulation 1907/2006, 644; see von Holleben, *Stoffrecht* 2005, at 64 *et seq.*, and Hohmann, *Stoffrecht* 2006, at 67 *et seq.*

III. Our draft Agreement, compared with the current international discussion

1. Our proposal: the draft agreement

Based on this provisional analysis of these main items in need of "trade facilitation," we assume, that the following WTO Draft Agreement (or WTO Draft Declaration) could be a proper solution:

> *Draft WTO Agreement (Declaration) on Trade Facilitation*
> Under the Ministerial Declaration of Doha, we have committed ourselves to expedite the movement, release and clearance of goods, including goods in transit; for these reasons, we agree as follows:
>
> 1 We will reduce all purely national export restrictions to a minimum, by giving priority to regional or multilateral restrictions.
> 2 We will endeavour to harmonise national duties or duties under bilateral and regional agreements with international duties (especially under WTO Law, UN or WCO conventions), and we will reduce export restrictions within bilateral and regional agreements which may otherwise endanger the implementation of our WTO duties.
> 3 We will endeavour to lift all export restrictions, if the critical goods are freely available on the world market or in the country of final destination.
> 4 We will publish all rules (including penalties) on international trade and we will endeavour to harmonise and make more transparent *de minimis* levels for export controls, and we will endeavour to harmonise and make more transparent national technical standards and national rules on Limitations and Restrictions (i.e. regulations or standards based on health, consumer protection, security, public order, etc.).
> 5 We will endeavour to extend all simplified export procedures, like general licenses and bulk licenses, which in principle should become available to all WTO Member States.
> 6 We will endeavour to offer auditing schemes or registered compliance programs in order to facilitate export and customs clearance.
> 7 We will offer sufficient instruments for simplification and harmonisation of customs procedures, for regional customs co-operation and for electronic transfer of customs clearance, and we will endeavour to follow a "Single Window"-approach for this.
> 8 We will simplify, harmonise and make more transparent transit, import and export procedures, and we will endeavour to follow a "Single Window"-approach for this. We will endeavour to publish the list of non-liberalised goods, to limit transit regulations and to limit notification requirements to the absolute minimum, by giving due regard to harmonised or equivalent notifications and standards.

9 We will endeavour to limit all blacklists of persons – persons, with whom no trade is allowed – to the absolute minimum, based on precise identity and on well-founded legal proof for export violations or for terrorism support.

2. *International support for these proposals in our draft agreement*

The question arises, how much international support may be found for such a Draft WTO Agreement. To answer this question, we will check as to how far these nine proposals have been accepted by the international legal community, especially by international organizations and NGOs.

(a) WCO, ECE and other international organizations

The *World Customs Organization (WCO)* has often emphasized our proposal 7 (simplified customs procedures)[31] and also our proposal 6 (facilitation of customs inspections, if best practices are met). The 33 Recommendations by the *ECE* on Trade Facilitation are remarkable. They give support especially to our proposals 4, 7 and 8. Recommendation 13 (1979) requires the simplification of import procedures (our proposal 8), its Recommendation 18 (1980, amended 2001) requires the simplification, harmonization and standardization of procedures and documents, by including information technology and by publishing all rules and regulations (our proposal 4: publications of all rules, and our proposals 7 and 8, simplified customs and export procedures). Finally, its Recommendation 33 (2005) requires the "Single Window" approach (our proposal 8). Other international organizations currently discussing Trade Facilitation include APEC, the OECD and the World Bank.

(b) International NGO and national governments

From the various NGO, we will concentrate on the *European Business Trade Facilitation Network*, which proposed, in 2002, a very interesting rules-based trade facilitation agreement, with compulsory core commitments and optional provisions.[32] This agreement is focused on the

[31] See WCO, *Framework of Standards to Secure and Facilitate Global Trade*, June 2007. Its core elements are: harmonization of the advance electronic cargo information requirements, a risk management approach to address security threats, facilitation of customs inspection needs if minimal supply chain security standards and best practices are met. See also the Revised Kyoto Convention (WCO, 1999) which provides a very thorough basis for trade facilitation.

[32] Peter Wilmott, in: R. Henke, (n. 1), at 15 *et seq.*

simplification of customs and transit procedures, *inter alia*, by transparency, information technology, consultative arrangements between border agencies and trade representatives, reduction of formalities, and appeals. It proposes optional audit-based controls and more *de minimis* levels. Thus, our proposals 4, 6, 7 and 8 are emphasized.

The *German government's program "Globally Active"* (on p. 5) mentions two of our nine proposals: simplification of customs clearance (our proposal 7), and "strengthening the self-responsibility principle for reliable exporters and importers," which may support our proposal 6.[33]

Concerning proposals of other governments see (c).

(c) The current WTO discussion

(aa) Before and at the beginning of the Doha Round Within the *WTO*, before the beginning of the Doha Round, discussions were more complicated, since some developing countries and the US originally wanted to limit trade facilitation to customs facilitation.[34] Europeans wanted to include broader issues, like services, intellectual property, rules of origin, insurance, etc. Originally, developing countries did not prefer any specific WTO agreement, but referred to the work done by other organizations, like UNCTAD, ECE and WCO; they insisted that capacity building of developing countries and technical assistance should be the main focus.[35]

After the start of the Doha Round, this picture became more and more differentiated. Most developing countries are now in favor of a WTO Trade Facilitation Agreement, among others because they successfully included clauses of special and differentiated treatment – leading to longer transition periods for developing countries (and especially for LLDC) – and technical assistance and capacity building. Now developing countries (e.g. the African countries) feel that they would gain considerably from the conclusion and implementation of a WTO Trade Facilitation Agreement.[36]

[33] The position paper of the German Association of Export Trade of November 2001, supporting reduction of customs duties and of regulations on "Limitations and Restrictions" in favor of harmonized standards, simplification of customs procedures and strict observance of Art. XXIV GATT, which has strict requirements for the acceptance of regional free-trade areas; here, our proposals 2, 4 and 7 are supported.

[34] Luzius Wasescha, in R. Henke, at 128.

[35] *Ibid.* See the text proposal by twenty-two countries and the EC on Special and Differential Treatment, Capacity Assessment and other Implementation Matters, WTO Doc. TN/TF/W/137.

[36] Osakwe, Chapter 1b in this book.

(bb) The Council Decision of August 2004 The *General Council Decision on a Doha Development Program* (so-called "July Package") of August 1 2004[37] did not answer the question of what aspects of trade have to be facilitated. Instead, Annex D of this program formulates: "As an integral part of the negotiations, Members shall seek to identify their trade facilitation needs and priorities" (no. 4). Under the mandate contained in this Annex D, the WTO Negotiation Group on Trade Facilitation developed a Work Plan (TN/TF 1) and a questionnaire in July 2005.[38] From this Work Plan and questionnaire, it is possible to derive what possible contents a draft agreement by the WTO may have. These fifty-nine questions addressed the following items:

- transparency of regulations (questions 1–10, our proposal 4),
- appeal against customs decisions (questions 11–12),
- uniform administration of custom and other agencies, *inter alia*, concerning fees (questions 13–19),
- reduction and harmonization of export/import formalities (questions 20–23, cf. our proposals 7 and 8),
- simplification of customs procedures, based on the concept of a "single window" (questions 24–33, our proposal 7),
- simplified export procedures (questions 34–41, our proposals 5 and 6),
- limitation of transit and transport regulations (questions 43–59, our proposal 8).

(cc) The Hong Kong Declaration (December 2005) The Ministerial Declaration of the Sixth Hong Kong Ministerial Conference, the *Hong Kong Ministerial Declaration* of December 18 2005,[39] adopted in its Annex E the Report of the Negotiation Group on Trade Facilitation, which listed up the measures proposed by some WTO Members, especially the thirteen sets of measures which follow:

A. "Publication and Availability of Information" (publication of trade regulations and of penalty provisions, internet publication, notification of trade regulations, etc.)
B. "Time Periods between Publication and Implementation (interval between publication and entry into force)"
C. "Consultation and Comments on New and Amended Rules" (including information on policy objectives sought)

[37] WT/L/579 of August 2 2004. [38] WTO Questionnaire of July 28 2005, TN/TF/W/59.
[39] WT/MIN(05)/W/3/Rev.2, also reproduced electronically.

D. (Provision of) "Advanced Rulings"
E. "Appeal Procedures (right of appeal, release of goods in event of appeal)"
F. "Other Measures to Enhance Impartiality and Non-Discrimination (uniform administration of trade regulations, maintenance and reinforcement of integrity and ethical conduct among officials)"
G. "Fees and Charges connected with Importation and Exportation" (publication and reduction of fees)
H. "Formalities connected with Importation and Exportation" (including periodic review of formalities, reduction/limitation of formalities, use of international standards, automation, Single Window, elimination of pre-shipment inspection, phasing out mandatory use of customs brokers)
I. "Consularization (prohibition of consular transaction requirement)"
J. "Border Agency Cooperation"
K. "Release and Clearance of Goods ((1) Expedited/simplified release and clearance of goods: pre-arrival clearance, expedited procedures for express shipments. risk management, authorized traders, etc., (2) Establishment and publication of average release and clearance time)"
L. "Tariff Classification (Objective criteria for tariff classification)"
M. "Matters Related to Goods in Transit (Strengthened non-discrimination, disciplines on fees and charges, disciplines on transit formalities, improved co-ordination, operationalization and clarification of terms)."

(dd) Specification of the Hong Kong Declaration by WTO Member Proposals (June 2006) A specification of these thirteen sets of measures can be derived from a recent WTO compilation of Members' proposals,[40] although it should be emphasized that these proposals represent only "the universe of ideas", and it must be seen which of them will crystallize into "black letter" rules of soft or hard law:

A. *"Publication and availability of information"* means to:

(1) publish all laws, regulations, judicial decisions and administrative rulings of general application (including, *inter alia*, "procedures of border agencies, rate of duties imposed on or in connection with importation or exportation, decisions and examples of customs classification, import and export restrictions, fees and charges

[40] WTO document TN/TF/W/43/Rev.7 of June 6 2006 (hereafter: n. 40a) and additionally now TN/TF/W/43 Rev.11 of June 27 2007 (hereafter: n. 40b).

imposed on or in connection with importation or exportation, penalty provisions against breaches of import and export formalities, appeal procedures, agreements with any other country relating to these issues")[41] in official gazettes or on internet websites, which are available to all WTO Members or to any interested parties at no cost or at limited cost;[42] and to

(2) notify new or amended trade rules at the earliest possible stage in one of the WTO official languages to the WTO Secretariat, with the information then being available to all WTO Members (e.g. through the WTO website) and to establish enquiry points or trade desks, providing information on trade rules and trade measures.[43]

B. *"Time periods between publication and implementation (interval between publication and entry into force)"* would mean to:
Publish all new or amended trade rules, including final draft regulations, at a reasonable time before their enforcement, so as to allow time for traders to become acquainted with and become well prepared for compliance, while taking into account the restraints accruing to differing legislative and administrative situations among WTO Members.[44]

C. *"Consultation and comments on new and amended rules"* would mean to:

(1) give WTO Members concerning all new or amended trade rules and regulations – and also private parties (especially traders) concerning at least the core measures of these new or amended trade rules – the right to comment on them and to take these comments into account, either by amending these trade rules or regulations or by explaining as to why their comments have not been taken into account,[45] and

(2) to establish a regular consultative mechanism on trade rules and procedures with representative private sector bodies, including importers, exporters, carriers, chambers of commerce, customer liaison groups, advisory bodies etc.; and possibly to hold regular consultations between border agencies and traders.[46]

[41] Especially the proposal by Chinese Taipei, Costa Rica, EC, Japan, Mongolia, New Zealand, Singapore and Switzerland, TN/TF/W/96.

[42] WTO document *loc. cit.* (n. 40a) at pp. 12–6 and n. 40b at p. 8s.

[43] Cf. WTO document (n. 40a) at pp. 18–21 and n. 40b, at p. 10.

[44] Cf. WTO document (n. 40a) at pp. 22–23 and (n. 40b), at p. 12.

[45] *Ibid.*, n. 40a at pp. 23–26 and (n. 40b) at p. 12.

[46] *Ibid.*, n. 40a at pp. 23–26.

D. (Provision of) "advanced rulings" would mean to:
issue a written ruling on matters such as tariff classification, applicable duties or taxes, tariff preferences or rules of origin to a person with justifiable cause (an exporter, importer or producer) that has made written request accompanied by relevant factual and supporting material, which remains valid at least a specified time, provided the relevant rules, facts and conditions remain the same.[47]

E. "Appeal procedures (right of appeal, release of goods in event of appeal)" would mean to:

(1) provide for affected traders[48] a non-discriminatory legal right of appeal against customs or other trade agency rulings and decisions, initially within the same agency or body and subsequently to a separate judicial or administrative body; there should be a standard time set for these appeals, and there should be the right of affected companies to be represented at all stages of appeal by an agent or a legal representative;[49] and
(2) release goods that are the subject of an appeal, based on duty payments to be left in abeyance, for which a guarantee, a surety or a deposit may be requested.[50]

F. "Other measures to enhance impartiality and non-discrimination (uniform administration of trade regulations, maintenance and reinforcement of integrity and ethical conduct among officials)" would mean to

(1) establish a central body within the government with the primary responsibility to interpret trade regulations such as those relating to customs classification etc, and/or publication of casebooks on interpretation of these rules, and customs staff trained based on such casebooks;
(2) publish a code of conduct for customs service, spelling out the rights and obligations of these public servants, appoint officials in charge for providing adequate training to relevant officials and to introduce computerized systems in order to reduce the discretion exercised by officials with respect to basic customs decisions;[51]

[47] *Ibid.*, n. 40a at pp. 26–29 and (n. 40b) at p. 13s.
[48] Some WTO Member proposals remain vague, as to whether this should be a right only of affected traders, or a right of all "interested parties." In the latter case, it could possibly also cover other WTO Members e.g. because their comments on new or amended trade regulations were not sufficiently taken into account.
[49] WTO document (n. 40a) at pp. 29–31 and (n. 40b), at p. 15.
[50] *Ibid.*, n. 40a at p. 31.
[51] For both issues, see WTO document (n. 40a) at pp. 31–4.

(3) allow a second confirmatory test of a sample, where the first test result has given an adverse finding, and to accept the results of confirmatory test carried out in one member state of a customs union in all other member states.[52]

G. "Fees and charges connected with importation and exportation" (publication and reduction of fees) would mean to

(1) establish objective criteria for the application of fees and charges by WTO Members to import and export operations; and the fees and charges should only be imposed for services provided in direct connection with the specific importation or exportation in question, and the fees and charges should not exceed the appropriate cost of the service provided;
(2) publish all information on the application of fees and charges concerning import or export operations (including the reason – i.e. the provision of service – for the fee or charge, the responsible authority, the fees and charges that will be applied, and how and when payment is made) especially on the websites of the WTO Members and to prohibit the collection of unpublished fees and charges;
(3) periodically review the appropriateness of the amount and the number of fees and charges imposed on importation or exportation, with a view to consolidating them and reducing their number and diversity, and to allow automated payment of fees and charges.[53]

H. (Reduction of) "formalities connected with importation and exportation" would mean to

(1) apply non-discrimination in the design, application and effect of export and import procedures and formalities imposed on the goods and like products of all WTO members – except that objective risk assessment criteria or special and different treatment allow a different treatment;[54]
(2) periodically review the appropriateness of export and import formalities with a view to minimize them to the least trade restrictive level, and for this taking into account new developments – like new business practices, new techniques or new regulations; according to

[52] *Ibid.*, n. 40a at p. 35 (based on the proposal of India alone) and (n 40b) at p. 17; cf. also India's proposal of Import Alerts/Rapid Alerts (n. 40b), at p. 16.
[53] Concerning all three points cf. WTO document (n. 40a) at pp. 35–40 and (n. 40b) at p. 19.
[54] WTO document, n. 40a at pp. 40–2 (based on the proposal of the EC alone).

one WTO Member (Hong Kong), this minimization duty would require to apply "the necessity test (in terms of the administrative burden brought by, and trade restrictiveness of, the measures) and a balance against reasonableness (having regard to the need for measures to achieve certain legitimate objectives, e.g. implementation of international conventions) with regard to the objectives of applying the formalities and requirements; the second benchmark is to ensure that measures are applied efficiently so as to reduce transaction costs and processing time for traders, if not for the authorities."[55] Other WTO Members have mentioned that the formalities should be least trade restrictive, thus indicating some necessity test, while this one WTO Member clearly requires this two-balanced necessity test;

(3) use international standards for simplified or standardized import and export procedures to the extent possible, where other international organizations already have set up international standards – like the WCO with the Kyoto Convention on Harmonization and Simplification of Customs Procedures or with the International Convention on the Harmonized Commodity Description and Coding System (1983, HS Convention), or international standards organizations concerning format and contents of documentation and data requirements (e.g. the UN Layout Key Guidelines – now ISO standard 6422 – or UN/CEFACT Recommendations for standard documents, or UN EDIFACT = UN Electronic Data Interchange for Administration, Commerce and Transport), except where such international standards would be an ineffective or inappropriate means to fulfill the legitimate objectives sought;[56]

(4) introduce by a customs union a uniform customs code (or aligned customs legislation) as well as a single import and export declaration and one administrative message or data set;[57]

(5) identify cases, in which copies (and not originals) of documents are accepted, and to require only those documents (and their translation) if this is necessary to carry out the customs operation, except some justifiable cases, and to introduce automated and EDI (electronic data interchange) based electronic systems which shall replace paper-based procedures across customs and trade agencies;[58]

[55] Cf. WTO document (n. 40a), at pp. 42–5. The Hong Kong proposal is contained in TN/TF/W/31 – and (n. 40b) at p. 20.

[56] *Ibid.*, n. 40a at pp. 45–8, and (n. 40b), at p. 21s.

[57] *Ibid.*, WTO document (n. 40a), at pp. 48–9 (based on the proposal only of the EC).

[58] *Ibid.*, n. 40a at pp. 49–51 and (n. 40b), at p. 23.

(6) establish a "single window" agency – if possible with efficient computer back-up – which would act as a clearing house for all documents and data submission traders would then need to submit data only once to one agency on the basis of streamlined documentation formats, namely to the single window agency administrating all information on the document;[59]
(7) eliminate any requirements for the mandatory use of pre-shipment inspections and to phase out any requirement for the mandatory use of customs brokers over time;[60]
(8) apply uniform standards, procedures, test methods, forms and documentation requirements for export and import clearance within a customs union.[61]

I. "Consularization (prohibition of consular transaction requirement)" would mean to:

prohibit the procedure of "consular transaction," including any fee or charge, in connection with the importation of any good; "consular transaction" means obtaining from a consul of the importing Member in the territory of the exporting Member or in the territory of a third country a consular invoice or a consular visa for commercial invoices, manifests, shippers' export declarations, or consul "verification" of other elements of customs documentation required in connection with importation, such as valuation or origin.[62]

J. "Border agency cooperation" would mean to:

(1) promote the compatibility or standardization of customs, import or export data requirements of various agencies (inter-agency cooperation at one place within a country and cross-border cooperation), so as to allow importers and exporters to present all required data to only one border agency, and to coordinate procedures and formalities that ensure cooperation between customs authorities and other interested agencies and to establish technical and regulatory measures to regulate the functioning of integrated border controls, among others the alignment of working hours and the development of common customs facilities;

59 *Ibid.*, n. 40a at pp. 51–3 and (n. 40b), at p. 23.
60 *Ibid.*, n. 40a at pp. 54–5 and (n. 40b), at p. 24.
61 *Ibid.*, at pp. 55–6 (based on the proposal only of India) and (n. 40b), at p. 24s.
62 WTO document (n. 40a), at pp. 56–7 and (n. 40b) at p. 25.

(2) strive to establish, to the extent possible, to a "one-stop shop", i.e. a single location for one-time documentary or physical verification of goods, where required, by all concerned authorities and agencies.[63]

K (Expedited/simplified) "release and clearance of goods" would mean to:

(1) introduce pre-arrival notifications ("pre-arrival processing") for examining customs and other importation documents prior to the arrival of goods, so that importers may claim their goods immediately after their arrival , as long as they are not selected for physical examination or for similar border controls based on risk assessment, and to provide for specific expedited procedures for express shipments;[64]
(2) conduct documentary and physical customs examination based on objective criteria of risk management to concentrate on the examination of high-risk goods and facilitate the movement of low-risk goods, for which international standards and practices (e.g. the Revised Kyoto Convention and the WCO Risk Management Guide) should be used, and in addition, to design and apply simplified import, export and customs formalities for traders which meet specific criteria ("authorized traders") – also for the assessment of any application for authorized trade status, objective risk management techniques should be used;[65]
(3) expedite customs clearance by different means (e.g. a post-clearance audit for the goods of a few companies based on a risk analysis or release of goods from customs prior to payment of duties, if a sufficient guarantee/security is provided for by the trader, or other simplifications, like customs clearance at the premises of companies or periodical declarations/periodical duty payment instead of separate declarations/payments for individual transactions, based on the results of risk management);[66]
(4) establish and publish average times for the release and clearance of goods, based on common standards such as the WCO Time Release Study, and continuously to endeavor to reduce the average release time.[67]

[63] For both points, see WTO document (n. 40a) at pp. 57–8 and (n. 40b), at p. 25.
[64] *Ibid.*, n. 40a, at pp. 59–61 and (n. 40b) at p. 25s.
[65] WTO document (n. 40a), at pp. 61–4 and (n. 40b), at p. 27s (cf. especially proposals by EC, Chinese Taipei, Switzerland, India and Korea).
[66] *Ibid.*, n. 40a at pp. 65–8 and (n. 40b), at p. 28s.
[67] *Ibid.*, n. 40a at pp. 68–9 and (n. 40b), at p. 29s.

L "*Tariff classification*" would mean to:

require objective criteria for the tariff classification of goods, especially by using international standards, such as the WCO HS-Convention.[68]

M "*Matters related to goods in transit*" would mean to:

(1) strengthen non-discrimination between means of transport, between carriers, between routes chosen and between types of goods or their origin for the transit of goods, while transit Members are encouraged to provide landlocked developing Members with national treatment;[69]
(2) publish fees and charges for transit, to prohibit application of unpublished transit fees and charges, to periodically review the transit fees and charges with the aim for their limitation, to limit the transit fees and charges so that they are strictly related to transport costs or services rendered, and to exchange with neighboring authorities in order to discuss the new transit fees and charges;[70]
(3) limit transit formalities and procedures by various means: by publishing and periodically reviewing them with a view to consolidating and reducing their impact on trade, by using electronic and internationally standardized procedures (including pre-arrival clearance and risk management see also Specific Annex E of the Revised Kyoto Convention, the UN TIR Convention and the ATA Convention/Istanbul Convention), by promoting regional transit arrangements, by giving preferential clearance for "perishable goods" and "normal low-risk goods" (and normal clearance for high-risk goods, as well as for some dangerous or sensitive goods), by generally mutually accepting inspections of neighboring states concerning the same shipment, by generally not investigating sealed goods, by cooperating with other authorities involved in traffic in transit leading to coordinated documentation requirements, and by introducing bonded transport system that would allow goods to be transited in the territory of a Member without payment of custom or transit duties, accompanied with a provision of appropriate security;[71]

68 *Ibid.*, n. 40a at pp. 69–70 and (n. 40b), at p. 30.
69 *Ibid.*, n. 40a at pp. 70–2 and (n. 40b), at p. 32.
70 *Ibid.*, n. 40a at pp. 72–5, and (n. 40b), at p. 33.
71 *Ibid.*, n. 40a at pp. 72–83 and (n. 40b), at pp. 34–7.

(4) cooperate as far as possible among authorities of WTO Members, from the simple harmonization of border crossing procedures and working hours to shared infrastructures ("one-stop border posts") and delegated competences, so that exit and entry formalities are handled by the same authority, and jointly clarify the terms of Art. V GATT, like freedom of transit, "route most convenient for international transit", "unnecessary delays", "administrative expenses" etc.[72]

Other aims of the negotiations are enhanced capacity-building/technical assistance and closer customs cooperation.

IV. The most likely outcome of the Doha Round

The role of the driving force for an agreement on trade facilitation has been shifted from the WCO (and the ECE) to the WTO at the end of the Doha Round. Although the Doha talks had been suspended – this suspension has been lifted and negotiations resumed in February 2007 – it is likely that WTO Members will take several steps to conclude a WTO Agreement on Trade Facilitation as soon as possible.[73]

The analysis of the most recent WTO Member proposals, based on the Hong Kong Declaration, shows, that nearly all our proposals have been accepted to some extent, with the exception of proposal 3 (principle of foreign availability) and proposal 9 (limitation of blacklists) – nevertheless, they should be integrated into the Agreement. There is also some uncertainty as to how much support there is for our proposal 1 (reduction of all purely national export restrictions), but there is support for a similar idea, which should be used as an alternative: the duty to periodically review all national export, import or customs restrictions with the aim of standardization and minimization to the least trade restrictive level. If we go more into detail, we can draw the following conclusions:

The WCO and the ECE have especially emphasized our proposals 4, 6, 7 and 8 (4: publication and harmonization of trade rules, 6: facilitation of customs procedures if best practices are met, 7: simplified and harmonized customs procedure, based on Single Window, and 8: simplified and harmonized export, import and transit procedure, based on Single Window). After the events of September 11 2001, more and more

[72] *Ibid.*, n. 40a at pp. 83–6 and (n. 40b), at p. 37s.

[73] See also Peter Mandelson, speech of 25 July 2006 (A Deal Can Still be Salvaged from the Ashes of Doha).

national governments are following the US and EC example to require "authorized traders"/ "Authorized Economic Operators" to join a "custom-trade partnership (against terrorism)" (C-TPAT and AEO), with strict export control, customs, book-keeping/logistics and security duties being sticks and trade facilitation being the carrots

If we again go through the WTO Members proposals, we can draw the following conclusions:

A to C: Here we find some additional aspects to our proposal 4: not only the publication of all trade rules, but also a time period before implementation are required, and especially consultation and comments on new and amended trade rules by other WTO Members. The latter idea is taken from (1) international environmental law, which requires that at least neighboring States or all possibly affected States should be given a chance for consultation (and eventually also of legal redress) before potentially hazardous activities are started,[74] and (2) from the "comments and consultation" mechanism of the TBT and SPS Agreements of the WTO. To transfer this idea from international environmental law or from SPS/TBT to WTO law in general is interesting and will have some merit, however, it may be difficult to implement it, if it would limit national sovereignty severely.

D to E: Here we find the principle of legal redress and of advanced rulings, which are not yet contained in our proposals; this will be new principle 10.

F to G: Here we find two new principles (uniform administration of trade regulations, objective criteria for fees and charges), which are not yet contained in our proposals; these will be new principles 11 and 12.

H: Here proposals 7 and 8 are supported; some new aspects are mentioned in aspect (2) (periodically reviewing the duties), (7) (end of mandatory use of pre-shipment inspections and of customs brokers) and (8) (application of uniform standards – an alternative would be: mutual recognition of equivalent standards, procedures, tests and documents); these additional aspects should be included in proposals 7 and 8.

J: Here our proposals 2, 7 and 8 are supported; the picture of a "one-stop shop" could be mentioned in our proposals.

K: Aspects (1) and (2) clearly support our proposal 6 (the pre-shipment notifications and the risk management should be integrated

[74] Harald Hohmann, *Precautionary Legal Duties and Principles in Modern International Environmental Law*, London 1994, at pp. 196 *et seq.*

into our proposal 6), aspect (3) supports proposal 5 (simplified export procedures), and aspect (4) proposals 7 and 8.

L: Here we find a new principle (objective criteria for classification of goods), which is not yet contained in our proposals; it should be integrated as a new principle 13.

M: Here we find much support for proposal 8 (simplification of transit procedures), while a few additional aspects (non-discrimination, measures for limiting formalities, shared infrastructures) could be worth mentioning in proposal 8.

Now chances seem to be very good, that there could be a WTO Agreement on Trade Facilitation in the near future, like our proposed Revised Draft Agreement in the annex of this Chapter 8. The world has now a realistic chance to overcome some of the national barriers of international trade; all WTO Members, supported by business associations – the International Chamber of Commerce and national business associations[75] – and lawyers associations – the International Bar Association or the International Law Association – should now work hard to agree on such a WTO Agreement on Trade Facilitation and to implement it later.

Revised Draft WTO Agreement (Declaration) on Trade Facilitation

Under the Ministerial Declaration of Doha, we have committed ourselves to expedite the movement, release and clearance of goods, including goods in transit; for these reasons, we agree as follows:

1 *We will reduce all purely national export restrictions to a minimum, by giving priority to regional or multilateral restrictions, or: we will periodically review all national export, import or customs restrictions with the aim to standardize or minimize them.*

2 *We will endeavor to harmonize national duties or duties under bilateral and regional agreements with international duties (especially under WTO Law, UN or WCO conventions), and we will reduce export restrictions within bilateral and regional agreements which may otherwise endanger the implementation of our international duties.*

3 *We will endeavor to lift all export restrictions, if the critical goods are freely available on the world market or in the country of final destination.*

[75] In Germany e.g. the Bund der Deutschen Industrie, Verband der Chemischen Industrie, etc.

4 *We will publish all rules and regulations (including penalties, possibly also some judicial decisions and administrative rulings of general application) on international trade, we will notify new or amended trade rules at the earliest possible stage to the WTO Members via the WTO Secretariat in order to give all WTO Members a chance to send some comments before the enactment of these new or amended trade rules, and we will endeavor to harmonize and make more transparent them (e.g.* de minimis *levels for export controls, or national technical standards and rules on Limitations and Restrictions, i.e. those based on health, consumer protection, security, public order, etc.).*

5 *We will endeavor to extend all simplified export procedures, like general licenses and bulk licenses, which in principle should become available to all WTO Member States.*

6 *We will endeavor to offer auditing schemes or registered compliance programs and also pre-shipment customs notifications in order to facilitate export and customs clearance of low-risk goods, based on audits or risk management.*

7 *We will offer sufficient instruments for simplification and harmonization of customs procedures, for mutual recognition of equivalent standards, procedures or test methods, for regional customs cooperation (*inter alia, *by promoting the compatibility or standardization of customs, import or export data requirements for various agencies of the countries involved, with a view to come, to the extent possible, to a "one-stop shop," i.e. a single location for one-time documentary or physical verification of goods of all concerned agencies) and for electronic transfer of customs clearance, and we will endeavor to follow a "Single Window" approach for this; and we will eliminate any requirements for the mandatory use of pre-shipment inspections or of the mandatory use of customs brokers.*

8 *We will simplify, harmonize and make more transparent transit, import and export procedures,* inter alia, *by periodically reviewing the appropriateness of export, import or transit formalities with a view to minimize them to the least trade restrictive level or by mutual recognition of equivalent standards, procedures or test methods, and we will endeavor to follow a "Single Window" approach and a close cooperation with customs agencies of other WTO Members for this; and we will eliminate any requirements for the mandatory use of pre-shipment inspections or of the mandatory use of customs brokers. We will endeavor to publish the list of non-liberalized goods, to limit transit fees and charges and to limit notification requirements to the absolute minimum, by giving due regard to harmonized or equivalent notifications and standards.*

9 *We will endeavor to limit all blacklists of persons – persons, with whom no trade is allowed – to the absolute minimum, based on precise identity and on well-founded legal proof for export violations or for terrorism support.*

10 *Affected traders will have a non-discriminatory legal right of appeal against customs or other trade agency rulings and decisions within standard times set, initially within the same agency or body and subsequently in a separate judicial or administrative body, and they will have a right to advanced rulings in such matters as tariff classification, applicable duties or taxes, tariff preferences or rules of origin.*

11 *We will enhance the uniform administration of national customs and trade regulations, e.g. by establishing a central body within the government with the primary responsibility to interpret the trade regulations or by publishing a code of conduct for customs service and providing adequate training to relevant customs officers.*

12 *We will establish objective criteria for the application of fees and charges for import and export operations, we will publish all relevant information on the application of these fees and charges, prohibit the collection of unpublished fees and charges, and we will periodically review the appropriateness of the amount and the number of fees and charges imposed on importation or exportation, with a view to consolidating them and reducing their number and diversity.*

13 *We will require objective criteria for the tariff classification of goods, especially by using international standards.*

9

ICN accompanied convergence, instead of WTO imposed harmonization, of competition laws

KARL M. MEESSEN*

I. Change of forum

Competition had a short-lived career in the WTO negotiations. It was identified as one of the four new subjects at the Singapore Ministerial Conference in 1996[1] and was unloaded from the agenda of the Doha Round in the aftermath of the Cancún Ministerial Conference in 2003.[2] Whether competition will be given a second chance as a WTO subject after the conclusion of the Doha Round is doubtful. *Pascal Lamy*, while Trade Commissioner of the EC one of its main promoters, first seemed determined to take it on board again despite its contributory role to the debacle of the Cancún meeting.[3] Having become Secretary General of WTO, he may now have other more pressing concerns.[4] Above all, *the worldwide expansion of competition law has meanwhile found a more accommodating forum: the International Competition Network* (ICN).[5]

This chapter will first outline what the ICN is about and then discuss which of the functions originally to be assigned to the WTO the ICN can be expected to fulfil and whether there are functions that still need to be entrusted to the WTO, possibly at a later stage. The balance, it will be

* Attorney-at-law Düsseldorf (Germany); formerly Jean Monnet Professor at the Friedrich-Schiller University Jena (Germany).

[1] WTO: Singapore Ministerial Declaration of 13 December 1996, 36 *Int'l Leg. Mat.* 218.

[2] See e.g. *Financial Times* of September 30 2003, p. 15, c. 6; a formal decision on slimming down the agenda of the Doha Round in response to the Cancún Ministerial Conference was taken by the WTO General Council on August 1 2004, para. 1(g). www.wto.org.

[3] Letter of EC Commissioners Lamy and Fischler to the "Ministers responsible for trade in all WTO countries" of May 9 2004, http://trade-info.cec.eu.int/doclib/docs/2004/may/tradoc117097.pdf.

[4] For a skeptical assessment of the future of the Doha Round see Everett, The World Trade Organization Ministerial Conference in Hong Kong, What Next?, 40(2) *Journal of World Trade* 221 (2006).

[5] For an informative account see Todino, International Competition Network, The State of Play after Naples, 26 (2) *World Competition* 283 (2003).

shown, is clearly *in favour of a continued primary involvement of the ICN.* Instead of being burdened by another potentially controversial subject, the WTO should devote its considerable energies to its core functions of promoting trade liberalization, especially in the fields of agriculture, services and public procurement.

II. The ICN as an information exchange agreement

Unlike business enterprises and hence without incurring any risk of being prosecuted as a cartel, competition law enforcement agencies may exchange information and even personnel, to allocate enforcement functions and to develop and apply new models of joint enforcement. For once, it is not an international convention (whose negotiation and ratification process might have consumed decades) that provides the legal basis but *an informal non-binding inter-agency agreement.* Legal concerns may at most be raised to the extent information on particular enterprises are sporadically exchanged in violation of applicable national laws on business secrets and legal privilege.[6] ICN member agencies did not commit themselves to cooperation in particular cases but, like businesses operating under an information exchange agreement, agency representatives have plenty of occasions for such cooperation at or after ICN meetings. The official discussion of matters of general interest at those meetings, however, gives potential contraveners of competition law no reason to complain. They are just being exposed to better coordinated, hence more effective, enforcement.

According to the "*Statement of Mission and Achievements,*" which forms part of the materials preparing the Capetown Conference of May 3–5 2006, the ICN was launched by fourteen jurisdictions (a term to include supranational organizations in addition to states) in 2001.[7] It now comprises eighty-five jurisdictions. Most of them have enacted competition legislation. Those jurisdictions are represented by 103 member agencies. The "*Memorandum on the Establishment and Operation of the International Competition Network,*" published as part of the materials of the Capetown Conference, emphasizes the *"consensus-based" character of the group and the non-binding effect of its decision making.* The required

[6] For the problem see K. Meessen, Economic Law in Globalizing Markets, 2004, at p. 251 *et seq.*

[7] That statement and the other ICN materials cited in this paper may be found at www.internationalcompetitionnetwork.org.

consensus can be established at every annual conference to be attended by all of the members. Annual conferences are prepared by the Steering Group of fifteen members, whose Chair rotates on an annual basis, and by ad hoc meetings of Working Groups and their subgroups. As follows from the "*International Competition Network Operational Framework,*" last revised on December 1 2004 and also contained in the Capetown Conference materials, the ICN website, which is controlled by the Steering Group Chair, serves as the prime vehicle of communication among members and with the outside world.

An explicit disclaimer in para. 1, subpara. 5 of the Memorandum mentioned above provides that the ICN *will not exercise any "rule-making function."* Nonetheless, its *indirect* contribution to competition member jurisdictions improving domestic law making can hardly be overstated. Again looking at the Capetown Conference materials, one finds an "*Implementation Handbook*" on mergers, a "*Merger Guidelines Workbook*" and all sorts of reports. One of those reports is on collecting and discussing the particular experiences of young agencies, (i.e. the sixty agencies established during the last fifteen years).[8] Only twenty of them found the time to respond to the questionnaire, which had been circulated. However, since the spread of responding agencies reached from the administratively experienced Netherlands to venues such as Barbados, that report offers a representative account of activities and problems. The contents will be referred to towards the end of the following section.

III. Aiming at a worldwide spread of competition law

Already *Adam Smith*, while focusing on the liberalization of cross-border trade, did not fail to recommend the dismantling of internal restraints to competition, such as those resulting from guild-type regulation.[9] In that same vein, the drafters of the Havana Charter of 1948, having lived through the mercantilist experience of the two world wars and the inter-war period, sought to make international competition law part of their venture to reopen the world's markets.[10] As is well known, only the cross-border part of the Havana Charter became provisionally

[8] See n. 17 below.

[9] A. Smith, An Enquiry into the Nature and Causes of the Wealth of Nations, 5th edn. (1789), at p. 118 *et seq.*, 128, 420 *et seq.* (1937).

[10] Articles 46–52 of the Havana Charter for the International Trade Organization of 24 March 1948, (US) Department of State Publication No. 3206, Commercial Policy Series No. 114, 1948.

applicable for nearly half a century under an agreement concluded already in 1947 and made it into formally binding treaty law as part of the Marrakesh Agreement of April 15 1994.[11] Further attempts to establish a body of universally applicable rules of competition law by the United Nations' ECOSOC, the GATT itself and most famously by the UNCTAD, were either not formally adopted (ECOSOC, GATT),[12] or met with benign neglect (UNCTAD).[13] Regional efforts were more successful, especially the 1957 Treaty Establishing the European Economic Community which matched the gradual abolition of inter-member-state trade barriers by rules of competition law, whose scope of application, was, and is, limited to cases liable to affect the trade between member states (Arts. 85 and 86 of the EC Treaty) or to cases that have a "Community dimension" (Article 1 of the EC Merger Control Regulation).

With the European experience in mind, a group of competition law and trade law experts met in Munich *in 1993* to *draft an International Antitrust Code.* Ever since, members of the group have individually advocated the adoption of the project in numerous publications.[14] Indeed, their proposal led to the – presently suspended – move of the EC to make competition law a new WTO subject at the Singapore Ministerial Conference as mentioned above.

Adopting rules of global competition law may make sense in economic theory, less so in legal theory. From a legal perspective, there is a fundamental difference between trade law and competition law.[15] Trade

[11] Final Act Embodying the Results of the Uruguay Round of Multilateral Trade Negotiations of April 15 1994, 33 *Int'l Leg. Mat.* 1140 (1994).

[12] K. Meessen, Völkerrechtliche Grundsätze des internationalen Kartellrechts, 1975, at p. 37 *et seq.*

[13] P. Kather, Der Kodex der Vereinten Nationen über wettbewerbsbeschränkende Geschäftspraktiken, 1986; Rahl, An International Antitrust Challenge, 10 *Nw. J. Int'l L. & Bus.* (5) (1989).

[14] See e.g. Fikentscher, Competition Rules for Private Agents in the GATT/WTO System (with annex reproducing the draft code), 49 *Aussenwirtschaft* 281 (1994); Petersmann, International Competition Rules for the GATT, 27 *J. World Trade* 35, 78 *et seq.* (1993); Fox, Competition Law and the Millenium Round, 2(4) *J. Int'l Econ. L.* 665 (1999); Immenga, Der Wettbewerbskodex von 1994 – Relikt oder Referenzmodell?, in: Konvergenz der Wettbewerbsrechte – Eine Welt, ein Kartellrecht, 2002, p. 13; for a different draft see J. Basedow, Weltkartellrecht, 1998; for a critical assessment see the Munich draft, e.g. Hauser and Schoene, Is There a Need for International Competition Rules?, 49 *Aussenwirtschaft* 205, 217 (1994); Gifford, The Draft International Antitrust Code Proposed at Munich, Good Intentions Gone Awry, 6 *Minn. J. Global Trade* 1 (1997).

[15] For an elaboration see Meessen (n. 6), p. 101 *et seq.*

law aims to abolish any legal rule that directly or indirectly impedes cross-border trade. Competition law, by contrast, aims to set up counterintuitive standards for business conduct. Businesses, if allowed to follow their intuition, would always prefer to collect monopoly rents by agreeing on prices at the expense of customers, by exploiting dominant positions through excessively high prices or by acquiring whatever player is, or threatens to become, a serious competitor.

The making of competition law requires not only setting positive standards of conduct so as to control profit making at the expense of customers, but also to fit those standards into the respective legal environment. The legal environment varies from state to state. It always reflects a complex web of economic and social facts as well as political aspirations of equal complexity. Competition law has so far only been made inside nation states or inside such supranational organizations as have achieved a certain degree of homogeneity with regard to the aforementioned factors. That observation may also explain the continuous failure of worldwide law making in the field of competition law, on the one hand, and the astounding success of competition law making in a regional context, on the other. In many respects, the EC can serve as a model for WTO development. But there are exceptions. Competition law is one of them.[16]

ICN practice corroborates the theoretical findings. By way of example, it is proposed to take a closer look at the report of Subgroup 2 on "*Lessons to be learnt from the experiences of young competition agencies*" prepared for the Capetown Conference of the ICN on May 3–5 2006.[17] A recurring theme is that a "one-size-fits-all" policy rarely exists within a single country and is even less likely to be shared by various jurisdictions.[18] That conclusion is, *inter alia*, derived from the need to coordinate competition policy – other government departments pursue different policies under different laws without being inclined to take competition policy aspects into account.[19] The enactment of legislation, even if accompanied by a set of serious sanctions, does in no way suffice to decisively restrain anticompetitive practices. What is needed is a radical change in attitudes towards competition[20] (i.e. to develop a "*competition culture*" linked to both the

[16] Todino (n. 5), 299; but see Petersmann (n. 14), 64.

[17] International Competition Network, Competition Policy Implementation Working Group, Subgroup 2, Lessons To Be Learnt From The Experiences of Young Competition Agencies, May 3–5 2006, www.internationalcompetionnetwork.org.

[18] *Ibid.*, at p. 8, 48. [19] *Ibid.*, at p. 18. [20] *Ibid.*, at p. 39.

"overall social-economic development" of the respective country and its "experience in regard to the observance of law and order").[21] To build up such competition culture, young agencies appreciate working with consultants and experts from international organizations or with a staff from more experienced agencies.[22] Indeed, consultation-on-demand is probably the most efficient way to transfer the necessary administrative know-how.

IV. Supplementary need for internationally binding obligations?

The long-time spontaneous proliferation of competition laws, since 2002 supported by the ICN, makes one wonder *whether that process would be further accelerated and enhanced if it was supplemented by a multilateral or plurilateral agreement on a set of principles, or detailed rules, of competition law within the WTO framework.* In 2000, this author drew up a list of pros and cons to find the cons to have slightly more weight.[23] He now feels that *some of the pros lost validity.* They have been satisfactorily taken care of by the ICN while, among the cons, the then question mark over the institutional capacity of the WTO now has to be replaced by a definite warning that the WTO not jeopardize its primary task of liberalizing cross-border trade. In the following, it may be permitted to run down, and comment upon, that earlier list of factors militating partly for or partly against imposing international law obligations of competition law and entrusting their enforcement to the WTO.

1. Pros invalidated

Giving institutional *support to newcomers* in the community of market economy states, especially to developing states and transformation states, could in the past be cited in favor of laying down international obligations to adopt competition laws and providing the transfer of the necessary know-how.[24] That task, however, has now been entrusted to the

[21] *Ibid.*, at p. 46. [22] *Ibid.*, at p. 17.

[23] Meessen, Das Für und Wider eines Weltkartellrechts, 50 Wirtschaft und Wettbewerb 5 (2000); for an English language update see Competition in the Doha Round of Trade Negotiations, in: N. Schrijver and F. Weiss (eds.), International Law and Sustainable Development, Principles and Practice, 2004, p. 217.

[24] See e.g. Jenny, Globalization of Competition and Trade Policy, in: R. Zäch (ed.), Toward WTO Competition Rules, 1999, pp. 2, 25.

International Competition Network. The horizontal measures to support the spontaneous convergence it offers are preferable to coerced harmonization under a top-down approach. They respect the sovereignty of the target states and appeal to their sense of responsibility. Neither developing states nor transformation states are particularly keen on being schoolmastered by the staff of an international organization, let alone by representatives of its principal member states. Thus, proceeding by coercion would be bound to delay the process of internalization necessary to build up the competition culture critical for effective enforcement.

Cases of *multiple jurisdiction* abound in globalizing markets. Understandably, worldwide harmonization continues to be advocated from time to time as a means to diminish the transaction costs of business and to avoid jurisdictional conflicts.[25] Since jurisdictional conflicts can hardly be avoided by realistically conceivable harmonization, one is left with technical harmonization so as to diminish transaction costs at least; nowadays however, that kind of harmonization, can be taken care of by the ICN.[26]

Only a small minority of the multiple jurisdiction cases give rise to conflicts of jurisdiction. The usual pattern of conflicts is: one or more foreign states, though largely following the same competition policy goals, have very specific objections against the state applying its law. In the recent *Vitamins case*, for instance, Germany and Switzerland did not complain about the fining of cartel participants BASF of Germany and Hoffmann-LaRoche of Switzerland under US antitrust law. They only complained about their companies being sued for treble damages before US courts with regard to the damages that allegedly arose outside the United States. The respective treble damage action was eventually dismissed by the US Court of Appeal for the District of Columbia Circuit on remand by the US Supreme Court.[27]

That type of conflict can, however, *only be avoided by total harmonization of the applicable competition laws* including related private law

[25] For a recent statement to that effect see Haucap, Müller and Wey, How to Reduce Conflicts over International Antitrust? 23 *Conferences on New Political Economy* 207 (2006); for a critical "Comment" see Meessen, *ibid.*, 339.

[26] For an elaboration see Meessen, Antitrust Jurisdiction Under Customary International Law, 78 *Am. J. Int'l L.* 783 (1984); reprinted in: Reisman (ed.), Jurisdiction in International Law, 1999, p. 395; see also *idem* (n. 23).

[27] *Empagran S. A.* v. *F. Hoffmann-LaRoche Ltd.*, 417 F. 3d 1267 (D.C.C. 2005); 124 S. Ct. 2359 (2004); for a summary account Meessen, Schadensersatz bei weltweiten Kartellen, 55 *Wirtschaft und Wettbewerb* 1115 (2005).

remedies. Even total uniformity fails to totally preclude jurisdictional conflicts as long as decentralized decision-making of various national agencies under different national court systems allows for diverging outcomes of parallel proceedings in one and the same case. With regard to conflict avoidance, harmonization short of full uniformity of laws and full integration of decision-making processes is a straitjacket that is both utopian and undesirable as will be explained below. Hence one is left with the need to save transaction costs before a background of continued diversity of competition laws.

In that respect, technical harmonization is helpful, such as agreeing on the data to be submitted (not forgetting the forms to be filled out) when a merger of multinationally operating corporations has to be notified in a number of jurisdictions. Preparatory work of the ICN, agreeing on "*Recommended Merger Practices*,"[28] might before long lead to the adoption of a non-binding recommendation on a uniform form on the notification of mergers. At least (and that removes the point from the list of the pros) there is no institutional framework better qualified to save of transaction costs in that way than the ICN.

2. A con re-enforced

The WTO drew unnecessary fire by extending its jurisdiction to environmental matters and to matters of social policy. This became apparent at the Ministerial Conferences in Seattle (1999) and Cancún (2003), which did not leave the standing of the organization untarnished, and Hong Kong Ministerial Conference in 2005 failed to mark an unequivocal return to better times.[29] *Entrusting therefore the WTO with monitoring obligations of competition law*, be it under a multilateral or a plurilateral agreement, *would increase that burden* since it would frequently give occasion to intervene in another central policy field of Member States. The interstate structure of the WTO, as compared to the inter-agency structure of the ICN, is far too heavy-handed to be spared the type of resentment the International Monetary Fund is regularly exposed to when granting loans under the condition that specific economic policies are adopted.[30] A similar caveat would have to be made if, instead of the WTO,

[28] Recommended Practices for Merger Notification Procedures as approved during the Second Annual Conference in Mérida (Mexico) of 23–25 June 2003, www.internationalcompetitionnetwork.org. [29] For an account see Evenett (n. 4).

[30] For the policy context Meessen, IMF Conditionality and State Sovereignty, in: D. Dicke (ed.), Foreign Debts in the Present and a New International Economic Order, 1986, at p. 117.

any other intergovernmental organization was put in charge of competition policy. The low profile of cooperation among enforcement agencies is well suited to accompany the spontaneous convergence in the adoption and implementation of competition laws, especially if one considers that any intergovernmental organization set up to harmonize competition law would be bound to absorb and thereby put an end to the loosely structured, but highly efficient, International Competition Network.

3. Remaining non-issues

For the sake of completeness, it should be remembered that some considerations, though occasionally still brought forward in favor of harmonizing world competition law, were actually moot right at the beginning. There are three such non-issues.

Governments may try to circumvent binding obligations of trade law by sponsoring business practices that foreclose *market access.*[31] *Kodak/Fuji* is a case in point. The US lost the WTO panel proceedings, in which it had claimed that the Japanese government supported Fuji so as to deprive Kodak of a commercially viable opportunity to distribute its products in Japan.[32] From a trade law perspective, the outcome might have been different if the GATT had then been, or as now, amended to clearly cover circumventive action, supposing there was one in the *Kodak/Fuji case*, through government-sponsored restrictive business practices. From a competition law perspective, the effects principle of international law permits the home state of the company trying to export its products to extend its domestic competition law so as to cover restrictive practices that preclude access to the target state's market.[33] At any rate, *an isolated incident* – the US "Strategic Impediments Initiative" addressing alleged Japanese practices of that kind was silently dropped after a while[34] – *does not justify making competition law a matter of international law.* To proceed in that way would be an overreaction.

[31] See e.g. Brill and Carlson, U.S. and Japanese Antimonopoly Policy and the Extraterritorial Enforcement of Competition Laws, 33 *Int'l Lawyer* 75, 118 (1999).

[32] Japan – Measures Affecting Consumer Photographic Film and Paper, WTO Panel Report of March 31 1998, WT/DS44/R. [33] Meessen (n. 6), p. 135.

[34] Saxonhouse, A Short Summary of the Long History of Unfair Trade Allegations against Japan, in: J. Bhagwati and R. Hudec (eds.), Fair Trade and Harmonization, vol. 1, pp. 471, 491 *et seq.* (1997); for a cautious review by a government installed committee see International Competition Policy Advisory Committee to the Attorney General and Assistant Attorney General for Antitrust, Final Report of 28 February 2000, at p. 211 *et seq.*

Market access therefore is a non-issue in the context of creating world competition law, whereas some strengthening of GATT disciplines in the form of TRAMs (Trade Related Antitrust Measures), as they were dubbed,[35] may well be worth considering in the light of the *Kodak/Fuji case*.

Anti-dumping surely designates a sore point of trade liberalization.[36] In that case, the best remedy would be to suppress the dumping and thereby pre-empt the need to impose protectionist antidumping sanctions. One way of doing this would be to effectively prohibit the state subsidies or the government procurement practices that allow low pricing with the intention of recouping the losses, and making a profit, once competitors have been put out of business in a second phase.[37] The prospect of collecting such rewards during a second phase can, also be curtailed by the importing state applying its own competition law to such predatory pricing. Genuine antidumping cases (most of them are not genuine) therefore *can be handled by national competition law*. Even if one or the other national competition law needs to be amended to that effect, there is no good reason to overreact by setting up an additional body of competition law rules in international law.[38]

Export cartels have also been cited as a reason to set up international obligations of competition law.[39] To be sure, it looks somewhat selfish when states vigorously enforce their own competition law on import cartels while exempting pure export cartels from the purview of the domestic rules prohibiting restrictive practices. Altruistically pursuing export cartels, however, may not always be welcome in target states where, for example, market entry can be so costly that, in the absence of the helping hand of an export cartel, it would not be reached by any supplies.[40] Furthermore, the target state is free, and ideally positioned, to pursue the very cartel exempted under the exporting state's law, as an

[35] For the term TRAMs see Graham and Richardson, Conclusions and Recommendations, in: E. Graham and J. Richardson (eds.), Global Competition Policy (1967), p. 547, 558; for a survey see Cadot, Grether and de Melo, Trade and Competition Policy, Where do we Stand?, 34(3) *J. World Trade* 1 (2000); S. Evenett, A. Lehmann and B. Steil (eds.), Antitrust Goes Global (2000).

[36] Meessen (n. 6), p. 103 *et seq.*; for the intention to substitute world competition law for trade law rules on antidumping see e.g. Matsushita, Reflections on Competition Policy Law in the Framework of the WTO, *Ann. Proc. Fordham Corp. L. Inst.* 31, 47 *et seq.* (1998).

[37] Meessen (n. 6), p. 104.

[38] See also Meessen (n. 23), 2004, p. 223 *et seq.*

[39] See e.g. Drexl, Trade-Related Restraints of Competition, in: R. Zäch (ed.), Toward WTO Competition Rules, Bern: Staempfli 1999, p. 246.

[40] For an elaboration see Meessen (n. 23), 2004, p. 223 *et seq.*

import cartel under its own competition law.[41] It may be added that *the ICN is now ready to support enforcement through both exchanging information and giving advice to enforcement agencies of such target states as are less experienced in the administration of competition law.*

4. *Continuing the competition of competition laws as the decisive point*

In view of WTO-imposed harmonization, it is a *con*; otherwise, it is a *pro*: to refrain from imposing competition law obligations through a multilateral or plurilateral WTO agreement precisely avoids the one-size-fits-all solution to problems that vary from state to state and in the course of time. Put positively, the absence of harmonization allows every state to tailor its competition law to its own needs and to adjust whatever legislative solution it adopts to both changing needs and changing perceptions of the problem. The making of competition law would then continue to take place in a competitive context. The resulting "competition of competition laws"[42] is just one instance of economic law-making in the competition of systems that prompts states and supranational organizations to compete for the best legal solution of any problem in order to make their respective economies perform better, to attract more inward investment and to provide for more jobs than their peers.[43] The outcome is an open-ended process of dynamic competition apt to improve the competition-law-and-enforcement product to the benefit of consumers and to welfare at large.

V. The ICN as the market place

The ICN was characterized as a well-functioning market information system. It is not a cartel. It would, however, become one if the states represented by their enforcement agencies formally agreed to subscribe to rules of competition law. With regard to the rules that become internationally binding in that way, the contracting states would abandon competition law as a parameter in the ongoing competition of systems and would then be responsible for all the common evils of cartelized conduct, such as desisting from further improvement of the legislative product.

[41] *Ibid.*, 224.

[42] For the term and the concept see Meessen, Competition of Competition Laws, 10 *Northwestern J. Int'l & Bus* 17 (1989).

[43] For the concept and for references see Meessen (n. 6), p. 7 *et seq.*

Since amendments to international conventions are difficult to bring about, it would no longer make sense to question the wisdom of the agreed rules. They would simply have to be applied. Changes of legal standards, like the one when the European Union replaced the market dominance test in merger control by the "significant impediment to effective competition" test,[44] could no longer be expected to occur.

However, as long as the ICN continues to operate as it did during its first five years of existence, it will enliven the competition of competition laws. All the agencies will exchange information, and some of them will try hard to innovate while others will monitor outcomes so as to imitate whatever legislative or administrative yield proves successful. This author is not aware of any other field of law, in which the *transnational approach*[45] of comparing legislation, administrative acts and judicial decisions has found a more efficient forum. The ICN may therefore be characterized as the market where the ongoing competition of competition laws takes place.

[44] Article 2 (2) and (3) Council Regulation (EC) No 139/2004 of January 20 2004 on the control of concentrations between undertakings, O.J. L 24/1 (2004); for an explanation see Considerations 23 – 26 of the Preamble to that regulation and Riesenkampff & Lehr, Article 2, nos 53 *et seq.*, in: U. Loewenheim, K. Meessen and A. Riesenkampff (eds.), Kartellrecht, Kommentar, vol. 1: Europäisches Recht, 2005.

[45] For the transnational theory of today's economic law see Meessen (n. 6), p. 322 *et seq.*

10

Legal principle of integration in the Doha Round: Embedding a social order in the global market

PAUL DE WAART(*)

The stone age Capaukoos – a Papuan people in former Netherlands New Guinea – were smart enough to fully understand the principle of one good turn deserves another. When Dutch missionaries stopped in the middle of the last century to reward the Sunday church attendance with cigarettes, the Capaukoos simply stopped coming: "No tobacco, no hallelujah."[1] The same *mercantile spirit* moved the ministers from Australia, Brazil, the European Union, India, Japan and the United States when they let the Doha Negotiation Round wreck: "No development round, no market access round."[2] WTO Director-General Pascal Lamy sighed at his press conference: "We have missed a very important opportunity to show that multilateralism works."[3] His frustration was shared at the time by member's comments blaming the inadequacy of proposals to cut in domestic support in agriculture. By accident, the WTO almost simultaneously launched the 2006 World Trade Report "Exploring the links between subsidies, trade and WTO." According to the Report, government subsidies can be useful instruments in correcting market failures

(*) Professor Emeritus, VU (Free University) of Amsterdam. This chapter was written in September 2006 with updates as of September 2007.

[1] Mathhieu Smedts, *No tobacco, no hallelujah; a tale of a visit to the stone age Capaukoos*, W. Kimber London (1955). The failure of the WTO ministerial conference in Cancun in September 2003 elicited from the principal EU diplomat the hard judgment that the Doha Negotiations Round and the WTO are medieval and in urgent need of reform. See John H. Jackson, *Sovereignty, the WTO, and Changing Fundamentals of International Law*, Cambridge University Press (2006), p. 103.

[2] Jane Nalunga, Trade and Development at the WTO Conference in Hong Kong: An Assessment from a Southern NGO, *Global Governance*, 12/2, April–June 2006.

[3] Statement WTO Director-General Pascal Lamy, WTO News-DDA June/July Modalities: Summary July 24 2006. But see his report to the General Council on July 27 2007: "We have come a long way since the start of this Round. What we have now in sight represents a very significant package of trade opening and rule-making, and a strong collective commitment to work for a more development-friendly trading system."

and working towards social objectives but can also distort trade and provoke strong responses from trading partners.[4] In so doing, it left no doubt that "[F]rom an economic perspective, it is far from obvious that agriculture subsidies in rich countries are any more defensible than subsidies on manufactures in developing countries. The different treatment is therefore probably most easily understood in terms of asymmetries in negotiating power (. . .).[5] *A ray of hope, however, is an increasing attention in international trade law for human rights and for sustainable development in the global market.* A case in point is the discussion in the Committees on International Trade Law (ITLC) and on International Law on Sustainable Development (ILSDC) at the 72nd Conference of the International Law Association (ILA) in Toronto, Canada, June 4–8 2006.

I. Humanization of international law

International law is becoming increasingly humanized under the impact of the *integration of human rights in international law.*[6] This humanization paves the way for globalization with a human face under the aegis of international law.[7] The ILA has accepted the challenge to fit out international law better for this task. This appears from the present schedules of activities of the ITLC, the ISDLC and the Committee on International Human Rights Law and Practice, hereafter referred to as IHRLC. *A suitable clue for bridging the gap between neo-liberal globalism and social sustainable globalizations is the principle of integration*, the discussion of which has caused

[4] WTO Press Releases, Press/447 July 24 2006.

[5] World Trade Organization, *World Trade Report 2006 Exploring the links between subsidies, trade and WTO* (2006), p. 194.

[6] See Theodor Meron, *The Humanization of International Law*, Martinus Nijhoff Publishers Leiden (2006). Meron was from 2003–2005 President of the International Criminal Tribunal for the former Yugoslavia (ICTY), on which he now serves as a judge. His book demonstrates "that the influence of human rights and humanitarian norms has not remained confined to one sector of international law, and that its influence has spread to many other parts, though to varying degrees" (Introduction). It does so on the basis of the following scheme: The Humanization of the Law of War (chapter 1); Criminalization of Violations of International Humanitarian Law (chapter 2); The Law of Treaties (chapter 3); Humanization of State Responsibility: From Bilateralism to Community Concerns (chapter 4); Subjects of International Law (chapter 5); Sources of International Law (chapter 6); International Courts (chapter 7); and UN Institutions and the Protection of Human Rights (chapter 8).

[7] Willem van Genugten, Kees Homan, Nico Schrijver & Paul de Waart, *The United Nations of the Future: Globalization with a Human Face*, KIT Publishers Amsterdam (2006). See also Eva Nieuwenhuys (ed.), *Neo-Liberalism and Social Sustainable Globalisation*, Brill Leiden, (2006).

much action at every level of government and in literature.[8] For that reason the present chapter discusses the effect of the principle of integration upon sustainable development law, WTO jurisprudence, international trade law and the global market.

1. International trade law and human rights

The ITLC Report raised the question whether the ILA should adopt a Declaration on International Trade Law and Human Rights.[9] The second report of the ILSDC focused on the principle of integration as a core principle of international law on sustainable development.[10] Moreover, the ILHRC intends to submit its final report on the topic to the 2008 ILA Conference in Brazil.[11] A somewhat embarrassing complication for the ITLC is that the latter Committee preferred "to work towards a succinct doctrinal statement on the relationship between general international law and international human rights law" over and above commenting on the constitutional and human rights dimensions of international trade law.[12] However, it agreed in Toronto to hold a joint meeting with the ITLC before the next ILA Conference in Brazil in 2008. It will depend therefore whether the draft doctrinal statement will discuss international law on sustainable development and human rights dimensions of international trade law.

Against such an inclusion may speak the *experience of the ILC* in preparing the draft on state responsibility. The ILC could only finish its draft after abandoning the study of particular subjects – *in casu* responsibility for injuries to aliens – and opting for focusing "on the 'secondary' rules of state responsibility as an abstract area of its own."[13] Even then it took almost

[8] The second report of the ILSDC (2006) focused on that principle, part 1 Introduction. The reports of ILA Committees and the resolutions adopted by the Toronto Conference in June 2006 can be read at the ILA website www.ila-hq.org/committees. See also ILA Report of the Seventy-Second Conference held in Toronto in 2006, hereafter the Toronto Report.

[9] Seventh Report of the ITLC (2006), Part VI Human Rights and International Trade, Toronto Report, pp. 279–91.

[10] Second Report of the ILSDC (2006), Part I, Introduction, Toronto Report, pp. 468–72.

[11] Interim Report on the Relationship between general international law and international human rights law (2006), Introduction and Preliminary Findings sub 8, Toronto Report, pp. 457–8 and 461–2.

[12] *Ibid.*, Preliminary findings, paragraph 8, and International Trade Law, paragraph 57, Toronto Report, pp. 292.

[13] Peter Malanczuk, *Akehurst's Modern Introduction to International Law*, Routledge New York (7th revised edition 1997), pp. 254–5.

forty years before the ILC could submit the draft to the UN General Assembly in 2001 In doing so, the ILC recommended a period for reflection and experience to the General Assembly before deciding whether to send the draft to a diplomatic conference.[14] Nevertheless, the ILHRC unanimously agreed to take as the point of departure for the draft that international human rights law is part of general international law and that the two branches should be reconciled with each other as much as possible.[15] Moreover it noted that other specialized areas of international law such as international trade law and international environmental law gave rise to the same question of whether special rules applied in the areas.[16]

2. Sustainable development law

According to Sands, international agreements reflect four legal principles in respect of the concept of *sustainable development*:[17]

1. The need to preserve natural resources for the benefit of future generations (the principle of *intergenerational equity*).
2. The aim of exploiting natural resources in a manner which is "sustainable" or "prudent" or "rational" or "wise" or "appropriate" (the principle of *sustainable use*).
3. The "equitable" use of natural resources which implies that use by one state must take account of the needs of other states (the principle of *equitable use, or intra-generational equity*).
4. The need to ensure that environmental considerations are integrated into economic and other development plans, programmes and projects, and that development needs are taken into account in applying environmental objectives (the *principle of integration*).

These principles gave guidance to the work of the successive ILA Committees on Legal Aspects of Public International Law relating to a

[14] Robert Rosenstock, 'The ILC and State Responsibility', *American Journal of International Law* 96/4 (2002), pp. 796–7.

[15] ILA Toronto Conference (2006) 'International Human Rights Law and Practice', Preliminary findings, paragraph 3, Toronto Report, p. 460.

[16] *Ibid.*, paragraph 7. It was therefore suggested that "a comparison of the 'specialized' application of selected general rules of international law in one or other of these fields (e.g. the rules of treaty interpretation in WTO dispute settlement procedures) might be useful in exploring the nature of the application of general rules in the field of human rights." See Toronto Report, p. 461.

[17] Philippe Sands, *Principles of International Environmental Law*, Cambridge University Press (2003), p. 253.

New International Economic Order – NIEO Committee (1979–1992), chaired by Kamal Hossain (Bangladesh) – Legal Aspects of Sustainable Development (1992–2002), also chaired by Kamal Hossain – and International Law on Sustainable Development (since 2003), chaired by Nico Schrijver (the Netherlands).

The ILA Declaration on the Progressive Development of Principles of Public International Law relating to a New International Economic Order, adopted by the Sixty-Second ILA Conference held in Seoul 1986 – the *Seoul Declaration* – stated that the principles are interrelated and that therefore each principle should be construed in the context of the other principles, in particular the principles of equity and solidarity and the entitlement to development assistance; the duty to cooperate for global development; permanent sovereignty over natural resources, economic activities and wealth; the right to development; common heritage of mankind; equality and non-discrimination; participatory equality of developing countries in international economic relations; substantive equality, including the preferential and non-reciprocal treatment of developing countries in international economic relations; and the right of every state to benefit from science and technology.[18]

II. The legal principle of integration

As of 1992 legal issues related to development, dealt with by the ILA NIEO Committee, has formed part of the mandate of its successor Committee (i.e. the ILA Committee on Legal Aspects of Sustainable Development).[19] On the proposal of this Committee the Seventieth ILA Conference held in New Delhi, April 2–6 2002, adopted the *New Delhi Declaration of Principles of International Law relating to Sustainable Development.*

1. ILA New Delhi Declaration

The New Delhi Declaration lays down *seven principles*, i.e. the duty of states to ensure the sustainable use of natural resources; the principle of equity and eradication of poverty; the principle of common but differentiated

[18] ILA, Report of the Sixty-Second Conference held at Seoul, August 24–30, 1986, Resolution Legal Aspects of a New International Economic Order (1987), pp 1–12.

[19] ILA, Report of the Sixty-Fifth Conference, Cairo 1992, Resolution 12 Legal Aspects of a New International Economic Order/Legal Aspects of Sustainable Development (1993), pp. 12–13.

responsibilities; the principle of the precautionary approach to health, natural resources and ecosystems; the principle of public participation and access to information and justice; the principle of good governance and the principle of integration and interrelationship, in particular to human rights and social, economic and environmental objectives.[20] The latter principle reads:

> 7.1 The principle of integration reflects the interdependence of social, economic, financial, environmental and human rights aspects of principles and rules of international law relating to sustainable development as well as of the interdependence of the needs of current and future generations of humankind.
> 7.2 All levels of governance – global, regional, national, sub-national and local – and all sectors of society should implement the integration principle, which is essential to the achievement of sustainable development.
> 7.3 States should strive to resolve apparent conflicts between competing economic, financial, social and environmental considerations, whether through existing institutions or through the establishment of appropriate new institutions.
> 7.4 In their interpretation and application, the above principles are interrelated and each of them should be construed in the context of the other principles of this Declaration.

2. *Framework for integration*

The new ILA ILSD Committee included as the very first element of its work program "the current status in international law and further implementation of the principle of integration as a key aspect of the international law-making process in the field of sustainable development, both in substantive and institutional terms."[21] The second report of the Committee submitted to the ILA at the Toronto Conference was entirely devoted to the principle of integration. The Committee decided in Toronto to prepare and disseminate a questionnaire, to analyze and evaluate the questionnaire findings, and to organize a seminar for dis-

[20] ILA, Report of the Seventieth Conference, New Delhi 2002, Resolution 3/2002, pp. 22–30. See also the Fifth and Final Report of the Committee "Searching for the Contours of International Law in the Field of Sustainable Development", *ibid.*, pp. 380–99. This search induced the ILA to establish a new Committee on International Law of Sustainable Development in 2003.

[21] First Report of the ILSDC, Report of the Seventy-First Conference, held in Berlin August 16–21 2004 (2004), p. 586.

Integration

Systematic integration	*Institutional integration*	*Legal integration*
Sustainable development *qua* systematic integration	intra-institutional *v.* inter-institutional (horizontal and vertical)	Normative integration: intra-treaty inter-disciplinary intra-disciplinary
Idealistic imperative *v.* real-life trade-offs	level-specific: project policy programmatic organizational	integration as a judicial reasoning tool

cussing findings and known examples of State/organizational practice for preparing the third report, which will be submitted to the Seventy-Third ILA Conference to be held in Brazil in August 2008. The following framework for integration has been drafted for developing a theory on the principle of integration:[22]

As for systematic integration the report underlines that it is not only concerned with bringing together the *three pillars of sustainable development – economic growth, environmental protection and social development –* but also with the imperative that sustainable development must be achieved without undermining any of these pillars. In respect of institutional integration, the report made it very clear that integrative decision making is the backbone for achieving sustainable development at all levels of projects, policy-making, programs and organizations. The report considers legal integration to differ sufficiently from institutional integration because of normative interrelationships and judicial reasoning.

In explanation of the framework the report further notes that despite the somewhat artificial division of integration in systematic, institutional and legal integration and of their respective subdivisions, it "may at least assist in clarifying the range of issues under discussion, something that is arguable less feasible when considered from the perspective of Principle 4 alone."[23] Two members of the Committee give a good taste of what this could mean in practice: Tomer Broude (Israel) in

[22] Second Report of the ILSDC (2006), paragraph 1, Toronto Report, p. 471.

[23] *Ibid.* Principle 4 of the 1992 Rio Declaration reads: "In order to achieve sustainable development, environmental protection shall constitute an integral part of the development process and cannot be considered in isolation from it."

his comment "Elements of the Principle of Integration in WTO Jurisprudence: Another Look at the *Shrimp* Cases" and Joyeeta Gupta (the Netherlands), dealing with integration of international environmental law in climate change and in the water regime.[24] The latter's preliminary conclusion is that political realities may be major obstacles to comprehensive integrative exercises such as the study of the potential for clustering international environmental treaties or pursing the idea of promoting a hierarchic global environmental organization. The former argues that the principle of integration has been indirectly applied or followed in WTO-jurisprudence. This view has been heard in some recent studies of WTO law.[25]

The World Trade Report 2006 refers to integration albeit not as a legal principle but in the context of integration of countries in the world economy and that incidentally. The same applies to the *two reports* presented on 16, June 2006 at a meeting *on trade sustainability impact assessments (SIA) of WTO/DDA* (Doha Development Agreement), i.e. SIA on Fisheries and Trade SIA on the Final Global Overview of DDA.[26] More than that, the latter study does not include Principle 4 of the Rio Declaration in the key sustainable development principles relevant to trade liberalization.[27] The same fate has fallen to Principle 7 of the ILA New Delhi Declaration.[28] Admittedly, both SIA studies were prepared by the Institute for Development Policy and Management of the University of Manchester and do not represent any official view of the Commission of the European Communities, which financed the publication, let alone of the WTO. Nevertheless, it is striking that a search for the Rio principle of integration and the ILA New Delhi principle of integration and interrelationship, in particular in relation to human rights and social, economic and environ-

[24] *Ibid.*, Annex II and Annex III, Toronto Report, pp. 500 and 510–13.

[25] Peter van den Bossche, *The Law and Policy of the World Trade Organization: Texts, Cases and Materials*, Cambridge University Press (2005), chapter 3 WTO Dispute Settlement, pp. 172–307; Jackson, *op. cit.* n. 1, chapter 5. The WTO dispute settlement system, pp. 134–211; Giorgio Sacerdoti, Alan Yanovich and Jan Bohanes (eds.), *The WTO at Ten: The Contribution of the Dispute Settlement System*, World Trade Organization/Cambridge University Press (2006).

[26] See www.sia-trade.org/FinalPhaseFinalReports.shtml. See also WT/CTE/W/245 of June 4 2007, list of Environmental Reviews.

[27] Final Global Overview Trade SIA of the Doha Development Agenda, July 2006, p. 7, paragraph 3.2 Analytical Framework, Box and p. 66. Table 5.16: Consistency of NAMA liberalization with sustainable development principles. On the core character of Principle 4 of the Rio Declaration for sustainable development law (*supra* n. 23), see Sands, *op. cit.* n. 17, p. 55 and 259/260, ILSDC, second report, paragraph 1 (*supra* n. 10).

[28] ILA resolution 3 (2002), su*pra* n. 20, published as UN Doc. A/57/329 of August 31 2002.

mental objectives at the WTO website does not give a single hit, although the latter declaration has been officially distributed, by way of exception, as an official UN document.[29]

3. WTO law and policies

The Toronto report of the ITLC dwells upon human rights and international trade. The chairman of this ILA committee, Ernst-Ulrich Petersmann, derives the relevant paragraph from the recently published study on reforming the world trading system.[30] Petersmann discusses in his contribution to the study three aspects of the legal relevance of human rights for WTO law and policies (context for the interpretation of WTO rules, increasing inadequacy of the utilitarian output-legitimacy for democratic approval of WTO agreements and complementarity of human rights and liberal trade rules). He underlines that the European Court of Justice had to construe EC Treaty rules in light of the human rights obligations long before human rights provisions were included in the EC Treaty. In view of the human rights obligations of every WTO member, it is only a matter of time before "WTO dispute settlement bodies will have to respond to legal claims or questions."[31] To that end *the ITLC suggested six political principles for a WTO Ministerial Declaration on WTO and Human Rights*, expressing:[32]

(a) the commitment of WTO members to ensure the consistency of WTO rules and politics with universal human rights;
(b) the support of WTO members for the clarification by human rights bodies of the impact of these rights on trade and policies;
(c) the need to harness the complementary functions of WTO rules and human rights for welfare-increasing cooperation among free citizens in international trade;

29 Sébastien Jodoin, "The Principle of Integration and Interrelationship in Relation to Human Rights and Social, Economic and Environmental Objectives", a legal working paper of the Centre for International Development Law (CISDL), Montreal, March 2005, published at www.cisdl.org/pdf/sdl/SDL_Integration.pdf, p. 3.

30 Ernst-Ulrich Petersmann (ed.), *Reforming the World Trading System: Legitimacy, Efficiency, and Democratic Governance*, Oxford University Press (2005). The book is the result of three international conferences on "Preparing the Doha Development Round: WTO Negotiators meet the Academics" (*ibid.*, p. 3).

31 *Ibid.* Chapter 17 "The 'Human Rights Approach' Advocated by the UN High Commissioner for Human Rights and by the International Labour Organization; Is it Relevant for WTO Law and Policy", pp. 357–81 at 361–2.

32 Seventh Report of the ITLC (2006), paragraph 45, Toronto Report, p. 18.

(d) the possibility that international treaty interpretation requires WTO bodies to take into account human rights obligations of WTO members;
(e) the conviction that the objectives, principles and exception clauses of WTO agreements are flexible enough to implement WTO rules in conformity with the obligation of WTO members to promote and protect the human rights of their citizens;
(f) the urgency that WTO dispute settlement bodies "fully respect the margin of appreciation which any WTO member may legitimately claim in designing its domestic human rights laws and policies in conformity with its international obligations and in response to the democratic preferences and social needs of its citizens."

Van den Bossche points out that the *present WTO dispute settlement system is still unbalanced* as regards "effectiveness and impact between the political, rule-making bodies and processes *and* the quasi-judicial, dispute settlement bodies and processes of the WTO."[33] This "must not be fixed by weakening the WTO dispute settlement system but by strengthening the WTO political system." Jackson, who is a member of the ITLC, also warns that the relative success of the WTO dispute settlement system, "when compared sometimes with the apparent paralysis of the diplomatic/political side of the WTO, has led to some concern that this power imbalance could be detrimental to the system longevity of the WTO and trade institutions."[34] He shares the view of Van den Bossche that this concern should not result in cutting back on the effectiveness of the dispute settlement process.[35]

Knowing who it is dealing with, the ITLC doesn't pin much faith in the room for maneuver of political WTO bodies for risking their neck by speaking openly about the impact of human rights on WTO rules and policies. As in the case of interpreting and applying international customary law, it will therefore depend on the ability and willingness of WTO dispute settlement bodies to avail themselves of the judicial reasoning tool for integrating human rights in international trade law. The ITLC rightly states that it is the responsibility of the ILA to assist WTO dispute settlement bodies in doing so, either *through a Declaration on International Trade Law and Human Rights* or, when failing to reach agreement on such a Declaration, by promoting a worldwide discussion on "synergies between international trade law

[33] Van den Bossche, n. 25, p. 304. [34] Jackson, n. 1, p. 207. [35] *Ibid.*, p. 208.

and human rights."[36] To some extent the ILA anticipated this responsibility by resolving that:[37]

> Governments are urged to refrain from using bilateral and regional trade negotiations and agreements to limit or eliminate flexibilities in the WTO Agreement on Trade-Related Aspects of Intellectual Property Rights which are recognized in the Doha Declaration on the Trips Agreement and Public Health to support the protection of public health and to promote access to medicines for all.

It remains to be seen whether this will fall on deaf ears. A bad omen is the *recent explosion of regional, bilateral, and preferential trade arrangements.* The former Director-General of the GATT and the WTO and former European Commissioner, Peter Sutherland, worries about it not only because the explosion deeply affected the Doha Round, but also because "the WTO appears incapable of policing – or even monitoring – such agreements."[38]

III. Social sustainable globalization

A lot of missionary work has to be done by the ITLC and other related ILA Committees, particularly the ILSDC and the ILHRC, in respect of social sustainable globalization. After all, Jackson did not include sustainable development in the index of his book and Van den Bossche did so only three times and only in respect of the Appellate Body in the *Shrimps* case.[39] *Reforming the World Trading System* compares favorably with the former books to some extent.[40] For, referring to the 2002 World Summit on Sustainable Development, it argues at least that identifying specific areas of potential collaboration between the WTO and UN Agencies is essential to complement political declarations of good intent.[41] *The key question is whether the present fair wind for neo-liberalism,* built as it is in the vein of Adam Smith, still the predominant individualistic and

[36] Seventh Report of the ITLC, paragraphs 48 and 49, Toronto Report, pp. 284–6.

[37] ILA Toronto Conference, Resolution No. 3/2006, Toronto Report, p. 20.

[38] Peter Sutherland, "The Doha Development Agenda: Political Challenges to the World Trading System – a Cosmopolitan Perspective, in Petersmann, *op. cit.* n. 30, p. 47. See also the speech of WTO Director General Pascal Lamy of 10 September 2007: "Proliferation of regional trade agreements breeding concern" in opening the conference "Multilateral Regionalism" at www.wto.org/english/news_e/spple/sppl67_e.htm.

[39] Jackson, n. 1, p. 360; Van den Bosche, *ibid.*, p. 732.

[40] Petersmann, n. 30, p. 569.

[41] Gary P. Sampson, senior counsellor to the WTO, "Is There a Need for Restructuring the Collaboration among the WTO and UN Agencies so as to Harness their

utilitarian approach, *is able to secure freedom from fear and want for everyone everywhere in the world for present and future generations* that the late American President Franklin D. Roosevelt had in mind.[42]

1. Liberal globalism and ESOCUL rights

According to John Rawls, the basic features of liberal or well-ordered peoples are a reasonable just constitutional democracy, unity by common sympathies and a moral nature.[43] He based the rule of law in (inter)national trade on two main principles: (1) Each person and well-ordered people should have an equal right to the most extensive liberty compatible with a similar liberty for other individuals and well-ordered peoples; (2) Social and economic inequalities should be arranged so that they are both (a) reasonably expected to be to the advantage of every person and well-ordered people, and (b) attached to positions/offices open to all persons and well-ordered peoples.[44] "Well-ordered peoples" refer to reasonable liberal peoples and decent peoples, i.e. "non-liberal societies whose basic institutions meet certain specific conditions of political rights and justice (. . .) and lead their citizens to honour a reasonably just law for the Society of Peoples."[45] Rawls even surmises "that democratic peoples engaged in commerce would tend not to have occasion to go to war with one another."[46] He thus followed, as it were, in the footsteps of Adam Smith, according to whom states with the greatest degree of free trade were most enriched by foreign trade.[47]

Since the fall of the Berlin Wall in 1989 extreme views surfaced again such as that "economic and social rights do not constitute rights (as properly understood) at all. Treating them as rights undermines the enjoyment of

Footnote 41 (*cont.*)
Complementarities?", in Petersmann n. 30, p. 524. Such areas are the TRIPS Agreement, the Convention on Biological Diversity, core labor standards and dispute settlement cases dealing with the environment and public health, *ibid.*, pp. 524–8.

42 Nieuwenhuys, n. 7, pp. 2–3; Van Genugten et al., n. 7, pp. 23–5.

43 John Rawls, *The Law of Peoples*, Harvard University Press (1999), pp. 23–5.

44 John Rawls, *A Theory of Justice*, Harvard University Press (1971), p. 60 in conjunction with *The Law of Peoples*, pp. 120–1. See also Paul J.I.M. de Waart, Sustainable Development through a Socially Responsible Trade and Investment Regime, in Nico Schrijver and Friedl Weiss (eds.), *International Law and Sustainable Development: Principles and Practice*, Brill Leiden (2004), pp. 274–7; and Van Genugten *et al.*, n. 7, pp. 21–2.

45 Rawls, n. 43, pp. 3–4. 46 *Ibid.*, p. 46.

47 Adam Smith, *The Wealth of Nations* [1776], The Modern Library (The Cannan edition 1937), p. 636.

fundamental freedoms, distorts the functioning of free markets, and provides an excuse to downgrade the importance of civil and political rights."[48] It is even said that in liberal globalism, as a universal ideal for all people and all nations, there can be no room for economic, social and cultural (ESOCUL) rights. Judicial review would imply that the judiciary should need to step into the shoes of the legislative or the executive as it implies substituting politics for law and infringing the budgetary right of the legislative. A judicial review of ESOCUL rights would thus undermine the democratic idea, based as it is on the separation and balance of state powers. For that reason such rights can be no more than directive principles of state policy.[49] This opinion meshes with Smith and Rawls idea of "invisible hands" – that every individual in employing his capital is led by an invisible hand to promote an end which was no part of his intention, but appears nevertheless, to be the best one from the standpoint of social justice.[50]

It may not be taken for granted that liberal globalism really is a universal ideal for all peoples and nations, particularly if it is identified with a Western-style separation of powers within states. Moreover, such a separation of powers does not exist at the global level (i.e. between states). For that reason states have committed themselves to take steps to achieve progressively the full realization of the rights recognized in the International Covenant on Economic and Social Rights (ICESCR) by all appropriate means, including particularly legislative measures.[51] Moreover, the end of the political and ideological conflict between command economies and free market economies have exactly increased attention for the protection of the economically and socially vulnerable by emphasizing good governance and by strengthening the monitoring system.[52] It may be no coincidence that the UN concern for the quality of life increased in the

[48] Henry J. Steiner and Philip Alston, *International Human Rights in Context: Law, Politics, Morals*, Oxford University Press (2nd edn, 2000), pp. 237–8.

[49] Paul Cliteur. "Liberal Globalism: A Defence", in Nieuwenhuys, *op. cit.* n. 7, p. 29.

[50] Smith, *op. cit.* n. 47, Chapter II "Of restraints upon the importation from foreign countries of such goods as can be produced at home", p. 423; Rawls, *op. cit.* n. 44, p. 57.

[51] ICESCR, Article 2.1.

[52] Van Genugten *et al.*, chapter 5 "On Rights and Responsibilities: The Integration of Vulnerable Groups", *op. cit.* n. 7, pp. 71–89. See also Matthew Craven, *The International Covenant on Economic Social and Cultural Rights: A Perspective on its Development*, Clarendon Press (1995), pp. 352–8: Martin Scheinin, Economic and Social Rights as Legal Rights, in Asbjørn Eide, Catarina Krause and Alan Rosas, *Economic, Social and Cultural Rights – A Textbook*, Martinus Nijhoff Publishers (1995), p. 62: The acknowledgment of the 'justiciability' of economic, social and cultural rights "gives new impetus to a general understanding of their legally binding nature and, hence, also to the realisation of positive state obligations flowing from them."

1990s, albeit only with the somewhat reluctant support of the rich states. After all, the disruption of the command economies deprived the market economies of a competing economic ideology, which they may blame for their own failures in respect of producing wealth – command economies – or distributing wealth: free market economies.[53]

2. *Redistributive justice*

Rawls' liberalism does not oppose the concept of ESOCUL rights. According to this liberalism a reasonably just constitutional democratic society combines and orders three characteristic principles: enumerating basic right and liberties of the kind familiar from a constitutional regime (1); assigning these rights, liberties and opportunities a special priority especially with respect to claims of the general good and perfectionism values (2); and ensuring for all citizens the requisite primary goods to enable them to make intelligent and effective use of their freedoms (3).[54] As for the latter principle Rawls left no doubt that the first two are without it "an impoverished form of liberalism – indeed not liberalism but libertarianism."[55] A libertarian regime does not have stability, for it lacks important requirements for such stability. These requirements are a certain fair equality of opportunity, especially in education an training; a decent distribution of wealth and income; society as employer of last resort through general or local government, or other social and economic policies; basic health care assured for all citizens; and public financing of elections and ways of assuring the availability of public information on matters of policy.[56]

In sum, libertarianism is not liberalism. It is rightly said that "if libertarians want equal and substantial freedom they should accept socio-economic rights as very important in that these rights are aimed at protecting the freedom of peoples to live their own lives."[57] The WTO

[53] Paul J.I.M. de Waart, "Participants and their role in the development of international development law", in International Development Law, *Encyclopedia of Life Support Systems (EOLSS)*, Developed under the Auspices of the UNESCO, EOLSS Publishers (2005), paragraph 5.1 available at www.eolss.net.

[54] Rawls, n. 43, p. 14. See also John Skorupski, *Why Read Mill Today?*, Routledge, (2006), p. 105: "(. . .) Mill's own view is strongly redistributive: he wanted to eliminate fortunes that are large in relation to general wealth, not to preserve them."

[55] *Ibid.*, p. 49.

[56] *Ibid.*, p. 50.

[57] Rob Buitenhuis, "Individual Freedom and ESOCUL Rights: The Illusions of Libertarianism", in Nieuwenhuys, *op. cit.* n. 7, p. 95.

should accept the importance of these rights for its own performance appraisal. For that reason it should labor for the cause of a social sustainable globalization by making redistributive justice among states and people(s) through the global market the theme of present and future trade negotiations. Its challenge is to do so in a world system of political units, which are not coextensive with the boundaries of the market economy.[58] The well-known American sociologist Immanuel Wallerstein is of the opinion that this difficulty cannot be overcome without a kind of socialist world government.[59] Based as it will be on a command economy, such a world government and the WTO can hardly be combined. Rawls resolves the difficulty by including in *The Law of Peoples* the duty of well-ordered peoples to assist peoples living under unfavorable conditions that prevent them to have a just or decent political and social regime.[60]

Rawls' solution may become the result indeed of an effective integration of universal human rights in trade negotiations. Heads of state and government use to show their awareness of the necessity to do so when they attend UN summits, albeit too non-committal as yet. Moreover, the effect thereof is still hampered by the fact that they have kept deliberately the WTO at arm's length from the UN system from its very beginning. Nevertheless, it is significant that the 2005 World Summit Outcome launched the global partnership for development. In doing so, the heads of state and government affirmed their

> commitment to sound policies, good governance at all levels and the rule of law, and to mobilize domestic resources, attract international flows, promote international trade as an engine for development and increase international financial and technical cooperation for development, sustainable debt financing and external debt relief and to enhance the coherence and consistency of the international monetary, financial and trading systems.[61]

[58] Immanuel Wallerstein, *The Capitalist World Economy*, Cambridge University Press 1979, pp. 66 and 73. See also *The Modern World System I: Capitalist Agriculture and the Origins of the European World-Economy in the Sixteenth Century*; Academic Press (1974) and *The Modern World System II: Mercantilism and the Coordination of the European World Economy, 1600–1750*, Academic Press (1980).

[59] Immanuel Wallerstein in the public debate of February 28 2002 on "What good is globalization for developing countries?" which opened the programme of public debates in 2002 under the title of "Beyond Development? Meeting New Challenges", organized by the Institute of Social Studies (ISS) The Hague, on the occasion of its fiftieth anniversary. See also De Waart, n. 44, paragraph 1.3.: Redistributive Justice, pp 278–80.

[60] Rawls, n. 43, pp. 37 and 112.

[61] A/60/L.1. of 15 September 2005, paragraph 21.

Moreover, they resolved:[62]

> That the increasing interdependence of national economies in a globalizing world and the emergence of rule-based regimes for international economic relations have meant that the space for national economic policy, that is, the scope for domestic policies, especially in the areas of trade, investment and industrial development, is now often framed by international disciplines, commitments and global market considerations. It is for each Government to evaluate the trade-off between the benefits of accepting international rules and commitments and the constraints posed by the loss of policy space. It is particularly important for developing countries, bearing in mind development goals and objectives, that all countries take into account the need for appropriate balance between national policy space and international disciplines and commitments.

This ambitious decision contrasts somewhat sharply with the simple and vague promise "to work to accelerate and facilitate the accession of developing countries and countries with economies in transition to the World Trade Organization consistent with its criteria, recognizing the importance of universal integration in the rules-based global trading system."[63] The suspension of the Doha Development Agenda negotiations should be taken as a warning to the Doha trade talks that the time of "never say die" in the political WTO bodies has passed by. This may be an improvement if the negotiators accept it as a challenge to go to the bottom of the realization of redistributive justice within the world system of sovereign states through the integration of human rights in the global free market.

IV. Embedding a social order in the global market

The few references to administration of justice, law and lawyers in the index of *The Wealth of Nations* suggests that Adam Smith had no high opinion about their significance in the context of trade.[64] Discussing the expense of justice he puts down the separation of the judicial power from the executive power, for instance, to the fact that "the sovereigns and the great lords came universally to consider the administration of justice as an office, both too laborious and too ignoble for them to execute in their own persons. They universally, therefore, discharged themselves of it by appointing a deputy, bailiff, or judge." Moreover, the judiciary should be

[62] *Ibid.*, paragraph 22(d). [63] *Ibid.*, paragraph 31. [64] Smith, n. 47, p. 940.

rendered as independent as possible in order "to make every individual feel perfectly secure in the possession of every right which belongs to him."[65]

Discussing that wages vary with the probability of success, Smith states: "Put your son apprentice to a shoemaker, there is little doubt of his learning to make a pair of shoes: But send him to study the law, it is at least twenty to one if ever he makes such proficiency as will able him to live by the business."[66]

1. *Rule of law in trade*

All in all, *The Wealth of Nations* does hardly support a plea for embedding the rule of law in trade. Quite the reverse, for every individual can judge:[67]

> much better than any statesman or lawgiver can do for him. The statesman, who should attempt to direct private people in what manner they ought to employ their capitals, would not only load himself with a most unnecessary attention, but assume an authority which could safely be trusted, not only to no single person, but to no council or senate whatever, and which would nowhere be so dangerous as in the hands of a man who had folly and presumption enough to fancy himself fit to exercise it.

Up to the present day, Smith's invisible hand in the international economic order goes hand-in-hand with Vattel's sovereign equality of states as the cornerstone of the international legal order.[68] The fundamental rejection of world authority by the two contemporaries from the Age of Reason is still well supported by states and individuals and plays tricks on the Doha negotiators,[69] and in such a way that the resulting lawlessness recently provoked a public outcry from the well-known international environmental lawyer Philippe Sands.[70] It's true that he poured out vials of wrath over Bush and Blair's illegal war in Iraq. But that war was the straw that broke the camel's back. This is apparent in his chapters "Global Warming: Throwing Precaution to the Wind"; "Good Trade, Bad Trade, Cheap Shrimp"; and "A Safer World for Investors."

[65] *Ibid.*, pp. 680–1. [66] *Ibid.*, p. 106. [67] *Ibid.*, p. 423.

[68] Emery de Vattel, *Le droit des gens ou principes de la loi naturelle appliqués à la conduite & aux affaires des Nations et des Souverains*, A Leyde, Aux dépens de la Compagnie, MDCCLVIII, para 18.

[69] Van Genugten *et al.*, n. 7, chapter 2 "Hegemonic Power *versus* Civil Society", pp. 27–37.

[70] Philippe Sands, *Lawless World: America and the Making and Breaking of Global Rules*, Penguin Books (2005).

Sands hits the mark by focusing attention on the far-reaching changes in international law in the 1990s. In those years, he writes, the state lost its monopoly with regard to the creation of international law. International law became the subject of discussion in the boardrooms of large corporations, in periodicals and Internet actions of lobbying non-governmental organizations and on the front pages of newspapers.[71] This increasing involvement of non-governmental actors may contribute to the integration of international law and human rights law in international trade indeed. Sands gives four arguments as to that.[72] The first one is that globalization implies the interest of countries in what other countries do to the environment, or to the human rights of their citizens. Secondly, the impact of technological innovation on communications and the environment changed the perception of the importance of the international legal order for everyone everywhere in the world. Thirdly, the weaving of democratization into international legal consciousness makes people aware of the fact that international law and organizations should serve people and not governments. Finally, deregulation and privatization enhance the interest of non-governmental actors in the enforcement of international law. These four factors "not only pose challenges to the established system, they help to transform it."[73]

2. Legal protection of property

Shortly, according to Sands, there will be no globalization without proper international law. In this connection a study of the Institute for Liberty and Democracy in Lima, Peru, is worth mentioning. In the first year of the present millennium the director of that institute, Hernando de Soto, published *The Mystery of Capital.* The highly praised study examines why capitalism triumphs in the west and fails everywhere else.[74] The answer lies in the effective *legal* protection of property in the west. De Soto concludes from facts and figures, collected by his research team in the South that:[75]

> most of the poor already possess the assets they need to make a success of capitalism. (. . .) Because the rights to these possessions are not adequately documented, these assets cannot readily be turned into capital, cannot be traded outside of narrow local circles where people know and trust each other, cannot be used as collateral for a loan, and cannot be used as a share

[71] *Ibid.*, p. 15. [72] *Ibid.*, pp. 15–22. [73] *Ibid.*, p. 19.

[74] Hernando de Soto, *The Mystery of Capitalism: Why Capitalism Triumphs in the West and Fails Everywhere Else*, Basic Books (2000). [75] *Ibid.*, pp. 5–6, 218–19.

> against an investment. (. . .) In brief, capital results from the ability of the West to use property systems to represent their resources in a virtual context. Only there can minds meet to identify and realize the meaning of assets for humankind. The revolutionary contribution of an integrated property system is that it solves a basic problem of cognition.

The failure of agricultural reform programs in the South results from a legal property system that does not facilitate the people's needs and ambitions. The same holds true for extra-legal real estate in shantytowns. The total value of real estate "held but not legally owned by the poor of the Third World and former communist nations is at least $9.3 trillion."[76] De Soto's message is that capitalism is the only system that provides individuals and mankind with the tools required to create massive surplus value. The Third World represents the marvellous challenge of combating poverty by "making a transition to a market based capitalist system that respects people's desires and beliefs."[77] The 2005 World Summit Outcome makes a start on that in the resolve of the heads of state and government to promote gender equality and eliminate gender pervasive discrimination by, amongst others, guaranteeing the free and equal right of women to own and inherit property and ensuring secure tenure of property and housing by women; promoting women's equal access to labor markets, sustainable employment and adequate labor protection; and ensuring the equal access of women to productive assets and resources, including land, credit and technology.[78]

The right to own property is part of the human rights system as appears from a number of human rights instruments at the international and regional levels.[79] The International Bill of Human Rights is a

[76] *Ibid.*, p. 35. See also pp. 168–9. The following example is telling: "When I [i.e. De Soto, de W]. began studying the possibility of giving the poor access to formal property in Peru in the 1980s, every major law firm I consulted assured me that setting up a formal business to access capital would take only a few days. (. . .) So my colleagues and I decided to set up a two-sewing-machine garment factory in Lima shantytown. To experience the process from the point of view of the poor, we used a stop-watch to measure the amount of time it took to get through the red tape. We discovered that to become legal took more than three hundred days, working six hours a day. The cost: thirty-two times the monthly minimum wage." (*Ibid.*, chapter 6 "The Mystery of Legal Failure": Taking the Perspective of the Poor, pp. 190–4.

[77] *Ibid.*, p. 228. [78] A/60/L.1., paragraph 58.

[79] UDHR (1948), Article 17; American Declaration of the Rights and Duties of Man (1948), Article XXIII; ECHR Protocol No. 1 as amended by Protocol No. 11 (1950), Article 1; American Convention on Human Rights (1969), Article 21; African Charter on Human and Peoples' Rights (1981), Article 14; Cairo Declaration on Human Rights in Islam (1990), Article 15; Arab Charter on Human Rights (1994), Article 25; Charter of Fundamental Rights of the European Union (2000), Article 17 See also Convention

remarkable exception as for the ICCPR and the ICESCR but that only because of a difference of opinion between communist and capitalist countries as to the interference with private property for reasons of public interest.[80] The UDHR could lay down the right to own property because it dealt with both civil and political rights and economic, social and cultural rights. Moreover the UDHR recognized everyone's entitlement to a social and international order in which the rights and freedoms set at therein can be fully realized and that in the exercise of his rights and freedoms everyone shall be subject to such limitations to meet the just requirements of morality, public order and the general welfare in a democratic society.[81] In other words, the right to own property should not be at odds with other human rights by protecting property in such a way that it obstructs a fair (re)distribution of wealth and income.[82]

V. Globalization under the aegis of international law

The WTO argues that the world trading system has not destroyed jobs or worsened poverty.[83] Consumers are increasingly insisting that the market sells goods which are produced in a socially responsible way.[84] Nevertheless, *the Doha trade talks had to be suspended because the WTO members could not agree on a fair balancing of agriculture market access – the poorer South – and non-agriculture market access: the richer North.* The main cause is that no quarter of the world is yet sufficiently imbued with the conviction that trade talks must take human rights seriously. The necessary change of this regrettable situation will only

Footnote 79 (*cont.*)
Relating to the Status of Refugees (1951), Articles 13 and 14; Convention Relating to the Status of Stateless Persons (1960), Articles 13 and 14; International Convention on the Elimination of All Forms of Racial Discrimination (1966), Article 5; International Convention on the Protection of the Rights of All Migrant Workers (1990), Article 15; [80] Catarina Krause, 'The Right to Property', in Eide, n. 52, p. 144.

[81] UDHR, Articles 28 and 29.

[82] Robert Devigne, *Reforming Liberalism: J.S. Mill's Use of Ancient, Religious, Liberal and Romantic Moralities*, Yale University Press (2006), pp. 59, quoting Mill on equal justice: "While the rules of modern justice promote self-interested activities that yield commercial benefits, those who defend justice and equality only to protect property will fail to maintain justice itself."

[83] WTO leaflet *10 common misunderstandings about the WTO* (2003): "Finally, while about 1.5 billion people are still in poverty, trade liberalization since World War II has contributed to lifting an estimated 3 billion people out of poverty."

[84] COM (2001) 366 final of July 18 2001, Green Paper *Promoting a European framework for Corporate Responsibility* (presented by the Commission), paragraphs 3.4.

happen when all participants in the globalization process – i.e. states and their organizations, peoples, people and their organizations at national and international levels – *accept that their thinking and doing in the globalization process should serve the promotion and protection of both civil and political rights*, protecting the freedom of people against the state – shortly freedom rights– *and economic, social and cultural rights*: solidarity rights because they require national and international cooperation to realize these rights.

1. Legal force of solidarity rights

Modern adherents of liberalism still have difficulty not so much with the moral force of ESOCUL rights as with their legal force, because that force would prevent Smith's invisible hand from leading the individual employment of capital to the best possible social justice in the global market. This problem is the connecting theme of the authors on trade negotiations and dispute settlement in *The WTO at Ten, The Contribution of the Dispute Settlement System*, recently published to commemorate the tenth anniversary of the WTO dispute settlement system and the Appellate Body.[85] Weiss concludes from GATT and WTO practice that "the *reconciliation of conflicting goals of trade liberalization and labour standards and environmental regulation, let alone public morals, has hitherto proved elusive*." He argues that if trade negotiators fail and thus negotiated standards do not materialize:[86]

> An increasingly self-confident Appellate Body might take up the challenge and, by default, as it were, articulate carefully crafted harmonizing approaches of conflicting goals of trade liberalization, on the one hand, and labour standards and environmental regulation, on the other hand, as well as with non-trade issues.

[85] See n. 25. The twenty-nine contributions of practitioners, scholars, officials, members of the Appellate Body and judges from international tribunals, are divided into five parts: The WTO at Ten (I); Trade Negotiations and Dispute Settlement: What Balance between Political Governance and Judicialization? (II); Form Initiating Proceedings to Ensuring Implementation: What needs Improvement? (III); Ten Years and Sixty-three Cases Later: The Contribution of the Appellate Body to the Development of International Trade Law (IV); Treaty Interpretation of International Law: Comparing the Appellate Body with the Courts in The Hague, Hamburg and Luxembourg (V).

[86] Friedl Weiss, The limits of the WTO: facing non-trade issues in Sacerdoti *et al.*, n. 25, pp. 189 and 190 (italics added by this author).

Francioni warns that no clear-cut answer has been provided yet at the political level with regard to coordinate, let alone, integrate, human rights and environmental standards with WTO law. Because of this he presents to the Appellate Body a framework for integrating international human rights and environmental law in the dispute settlement just in case it will have to deal with claims or defenses based thereupon.[87] Petersmann expects that nature will be stronger than nurture. He foresees that WTO jurisprudence will learn that:[88]

> even, though 'public morals' and national human rights traditions may legitimately differ from country to country, the WTO rules on the protection of 'public morals' and 'public order' already include 'social clauses' and 'human rights clauses' that protect the right of WTO Members to ensure respect for labour standards and human rights inside their countries.

This does not mean that the impact of the legal principle of integration does not need to be extended to the negotiating bodies. On the contrary, if the Doha trade talks fail, the integration of international sustainable development law and human rights law by the Appellate Body run the *risk of bringing the WTO dispute settlement system in the danger zone of judge-made law without a political cover.* Politicizing dispute settlement in the WTO "is both an inappropriate and a counterproductive means of responding to the challenge of political renewal."[89]

2. Basic needs

The final demise of communism has challenged the UN family and the WTO to a political renewal by bringing state and market into line with each other to make the production and the distribution of wealth

[87] Francesco Francioni, WTO Law in context: the integration of international human rights and environmental law in the dispute settlement process, in Sacerdoti, n. 25, p. 150.

[88] Ernst-Ulrich Petersmann, "From 'member-driven governance' to constitutionally limited 'multi-level trade governance' in the WTO", in Sacerdoti, n. 25, pp. 106–7. See also Paul de Waart, "Quality of life at the mercy of WTO Panels: GATT's Article XX an empty shell", in Friedl Weiss, Erik Denters and Paul de Waart, *International Economic Law with a Human Face*, Kluwer Law International (1998), pp. 109–33.

[89] Robert Howse and Susan Esserman, The Appellate Body, the WTO Dispute Settlement system, and the politics of Multilateralism, in Sacerdoti, n. 25. See also Hélène Ruiz Fabri, "Drawing a line of equilibrium in a complex world", *ibid.*, pp. 139–40: "The WTO judge has opted for a judicial policy that is centred on the balance and cohesion of the system, without isolating it from the rest of international law. This choice implies that states be treated not only as members of the WTO, but also as members of the international community."

instrumental in implementing the hard core of human rights for everyone everywhere in the world. The definition of the hard core of human rights – the so-called basic needs – is quite a challenge to states, international organizations and the civil society. To that end the heads of state and government committed themselves in 1995 in Copenhagen to:[90]

> Focus our efforts and policies to address the root causes of poverty and to provide for the basic needs of all. These efforts should include the elimination of hunger and malnutrition; the provision of food security, education, employment and livelihood, primary health-care services including reproductive health care, safe drinking water and sanitation, and adequate shelter; and participation in social and cultural life. Special priority will be given to the needs and rights of women and children, who often bear the greatest burden of poverty, and to the needs of vulnerable and disadvantaged groups and persons.

The 2000 Millennium Declaration and the result of the 2005 World Summit do not refer to basic needs any more. However, the political commitment remains consistent. Moreover, courts are in a better position to judge efforts in concrete situations. For it is typically a judicial task to determine in concrete cases whether or not the basic needs of people or peoples are fulfilled. The legal principle of integration of sustainable development law and human rights law in trade negotiations *implies that the Appellate Body of the WTO is now able to deal with claims or defences in respect of the basic needs approach without running the risk of stepping into the shoes of political bodies.* After all, in such cases the decision making should take into account the significance of national and regional particularities and various historical, cultural and religious backgrounds.[91] This holds even more true since the Appellate Body, like national and international monitoring and supervisory bodies in general, has at its disposal increasingly reliable and highly detailed data on world development and human development, provided by, amongst others, the annual reports of the World Bank and UNDP. Above the level of basic needs the main responsibility in respect of integrating sustainable development law and human rights *remains with the legislator.* Such an implementation of the legal principle of integration may guide the present generation

[90] UN Doc. A/CONF 166/9 of April 19 1995 Copenhagen Declaration on Social Development and Programme of Action of the Social Summit, para 29, Commitment 2, sub b. See Van Genugten *et al.*, n. 7, pp. 17–18.

[91] UN Doc. A/CONF.157/23 of July 12 1993, Vienna Declaration and Programme of Action, paragraph 5.

and future generations to make true for themselves Roosevelt's Four Freedoms in their mutual dependency.

VI. Conclusions

Roosevelt's freedoms still provide an adequate and almost comprehensive framework for assessing the continuous efforts of states and IGOs as well as civil society to make every effort for a social and international order, in which the global market will secure that at least the basic needs of everyone everywhere in the world will be met. Such a world can be made by integrating sustainable development law and human rights law in the Doha trade talks. The ILA is in a unique position to make a valuable contribution as to that. After all, it has a membership of roughly 4,000 international lawyers from all over the world. They represent the main forms of civilization as well as the principal legal systems of the world. Besides, they come from all branches of law and have a great experience not only in academia but also in public service and trade and industry. The ILA should declare itself openly in favor of the legal force of solidarity rights in addition to the right to freedom and in favor of the legal principle of integration for sustainable development law and human rights law in present and future trade negotiations. The globalization may then begin to show a human face under the aegis of international law.[92] It will show at long last that absolute poverty, as defined by the World Bank, is not so much the result of an "Act of God" but of human selfishness in the global market![93]

[92] Van Genugten *et al.*, n. 7, pp. 189–91.

[93] Unlike last year WTO Director-General Pascal Lamy is now "completely convinced that we have it within our means, politically and technically, to finish the Doha Round this year." See his intervention at the International Monetary and Financial Committee on 12 April 2008 in Washington (WTO News: Speeches – DG Pascal Lamy).

PART THREE

Reform of the dispute settlement system

11

Reforming the dispute settlement system through practice

ERIC WHITE*

1. Introduction

The present chapter is a brief reflection on the lack of progress in the negotiations on the reform of the WTO *Understanding on Rules and Procedures Governing the Settlement of Disputes* (DSU) and suggests an alternative to their continuation at this stage.

2. A brief history of the dispute settlement system

The original basis for dispute settlement in the GATT is Article XXIII (which is still in force), entitled 'Nullification or Impairment'. Paragraph 1 of this provision states that:

> If any contracting party should consider that any benefit accruing to it directly or indirectly under this Agreement is being nullified or impaired or that the attainment of any objective of the Agreement is being impeded . . .
>
> . . .
>
> the contracting party may, with a view to the satisfactory adjustment of the matter, make written representations or proposals to the other contracting party or parties which it considers to be concerned. Any contracting party thus approached shall give sympathetic consideration to the representations or proposals made to it.

Paragraph 2 goes on to provide that:

> If no satisfactory adjustment is effected between the contracting parties concerned within a reasonable time . . . the matter may be referred to the CONTRACTING PARTIES. The CONTRACTING PARTIES shall promptly investigate any matter so referred to them and shall make appropriate recommendations to the contracting parties which they consider to be concerned, or give a ruling on the matter, as appropriate. . . . If the

* Head of Trade Team, Legal Service, EC Commission Brussels. The opinions expressed are personal.

> CONTRACTING PARTIES consider that the circumstances are serious enough to justify such action, they may authorize a contracting party or parties to suspend the application to any other contracting party or parties of such concessions or other obligations under this Agreement as they determine to be appropriate in the circumstances.

The term 'CONTRACTING PARTIES' written in capital letters means the GATT contracting parties acting collectively as a body. Accordingly, the entire membership was to investigate and rule on the dispute. It was then to authorise (where the violation is considered serious enough) the remedy (suspension of such concessions or other obligations as appropriate in the circumstances).

The contracting parties soon started to set up working parties (later called 'panels') to do the investigating and to propose recommendations, but the adoption of final decisions was left to the contracting parties themselves. Since decisions of the contracting parties were always taken by consensus, the process could always be blocked by one of the parties to the dispute at various stages. First, by blocking the decision to refer the matter to a panel. Second by blocking the adoption of the panel report. And finally, by refusing to agree to the suspension of concessions against it.

The GATT dispute settlement process nonetheless worked surprisingly well and the proceedings became gradually more 'legal' in character over the years. A body of procedural practices and customs grew up. Subsequent panels tended to follow past panels not only in procedural matters (where there were at first no written rules) but also on substantive matters relating to the meaning of the various provisions of the GATT. Also, parties found it difficult to block reasoned reports finding an inconsistency, at least in cases that were not politically sensitive.

One of the purposes of the Uruguay Round reform was to agree improvements in the dispute settlement system. There was a sense of frustration at the failure of some proceedings to resolve disputes where the offending party was determined to resist.

At the mid-term review of the Uruguay Round, held at the ministerial conference in Montreal in 1989, a package of improvements, known as the '*Montreal Package*' was adopted.[1] It was essentially a codification of past practice and the main reform was that GATT contracting parties

[1] Improvements to the GATT Dispute Settlement Rules and Procedures, Decision of 13 April 1989 (L/6489), BISD 36S/61.

agreed to cease blocking the establishment of panels (although they could still block adoption of the reports).

The real revolution occurred with the *adoption of the DSU* at the end of the Uruguay Round. This built on the Montreal Package but made access to the system a right and decisions binding. The power to block decisions disappeared through the device of providing that certain decisions would be deemed taken unless the membership decided 'by consensus' not to take them (the so-called *'reverse consensus' rule*):

That the Members agreed to this is remarkable. Some have called it a miracle. During the negotiations, the United States was at first an enthusiastic proponent of making dispute settlement obligatory, believing that it was others (notably the European Communities) that failed to respect their obligations. The EC Member States, among others, were reluctant to give up so much sovereignty. However later on the European Communities were converted when they saw the advantages of a 'rule-based' rather than a 'power-based' system, especially against US 'unilateralism' (Sec. 301). The inclusion of a 'peace clause' in the Agreement on Agriculture played an important role in reassuring agricultural interests in the European Communities. The United States, on the other hand, started to realise that that the new system might lead to binding decisions being taken against it and later became reluctant. The introduction of an Appellate Body was most important in reassuring Members that the decisions taken would be 'correct'.

3. The DSU review

The misgivings concerning the introduction of compulsory and binding dispute settlement were such that it was only introduced provisionally, in the sense that it was *to be reviewed after four years.* The Decision on the Application and Review of the Understanding on Rules and Procedures Governing the Settlement of Disputes annexed to the Uruguay Round Final Act states that:

> Ministers . . . *Invite* the Ministerial Conference to complete a full review of dispute settlement rules and procedures under the World Trade Organization within four years after the entry into force of the Agreement Establishing the World Trade Organization, and to take a decision on the occasion of its first meeting after the completion of the review, whether to continue, modify or terminate such dispute settlement rules and procedures.

The DSU could have been simply terminated by a decision of the Ministerial Conference at its meeting in Seattle in 1999! However no-one suggested during this review that the system should be terminated. The European Communities, among others, made detailed proposals for its improvement.[2] This mandate to review the DSU has now expired. There was no outcome – except the implicit decision not to terminate the understanding.[3]

Having failed to agree on any improvements to the DSU in Seattle, the Ministerial Conference decided to continue the work. This is now called '*DSU reform*' so as to distinguish it from the expired mandate to review (and possibly terminate) the DSU.

The first deadline that was set for the DSU reform was 31 March 2003. A Chairman's text of tentative improvements was drawn up, but there was no agreement.[4] A second deadline was set for 31 March 2004 but hardly any further progress was made. There was simply an agreement to continue negotiating but with no deadline.[5] The report of the (next) Chairman of the negotiating group, submitted to the Hong Kong Ministerial Conference is extraordinary being less than a page simply reporting that work has continued and proposing that it continue to continue.[6] It is in stark contrast to the report of the previous Chairman to the Cancún Ministerial Conference referred to above which ran to nineteen pages and made specific proposals. One has the impression that the *negotiations have gone backwards* and that the sole result of over two years of continued negotiations was to jettison the work that had been done previously.

It would seem that there is limited enthusiasm in the membership as a whole for a reform of the DSU. This may reflect the sentiment that 'if it ain't broke, don't fix it' or reluctance to improve further a mechanism that makes the workings of the negotiating methods of the WTO appear

[2] Proposed Amendment of the Dispute Settlement Understanding, Communication, dated 16 November 1999, from Canada, Costa Rica, Czech Republic, Ecuador, the European Communities and its Member States, Hungary, Japan, Korea, New Zealand, Norway, Peru, Slovenia, Switzerland, Thailand and Venezuela (WT/MIN(99)/8 and WT/MIN(99)/8/Corr.1).

[3] Ministerial Conference, Third Session, Seattle, 30 November–3 December 1999; Summary Record of the Eighth Meeting (WT/MIN(99)/SR/8 of 14 January 2000 (Restricted)).

[4] Report by the Chairman to the Trade Negotiations Committee (TN/DS/9 of 6 June 2003).

[5] Doha Work Programme, Decision adopted by the General Council on 1 August 2004 (WT/L/579).

[6] Document TN/DS/14 of 25 November 2005.

ineffective.[7] In part, the failure to make progress may also be due to the fact that improving the DSU is in the general interest of all, whereas the mercantilist culture of negotiations at the WTO encourages Members to refrain from pushing such proposals for fear of being asked to 'pay' by accepting unwanted requests from other Members. This is especially so since the dispute settlement system *is currently used by only a minority of Members.* Many developing, and especially least developed countries, do not use it through lack of confidence in its utility a perception that resort to dispute settlement will be perceived as a hostile act, lack of courage and lack of capacity.

The result is that there are a lot of good ideas on the table for reforming the system (and a few not so good ideas) many of which have little prospect of ever being adopted. The DSU reform process seems to have become the victim of hostage taking and simple obstructionism.

Many consider that there is a chance that some of the less controversial proposals could be adopted if there is an agreement on the Doha Round (although DSU reform is not formally part of the 'single undertaking'). But there may never be an outcome to the Doha Round. There are very serious divisions, particularly between developing and developed countries, about the objectives of the negotiations.

4. The way forward

In the light of the difficulties of agreeing changes to the DSU, it is worth considering whether another approach should be taken.

The Dispute Settlement system is a permanent experiment. New conventions and procedures are constantly evolving. There is little in the way of binding procedural rules. Working Procedures are set out in Appendix III to the DSU but are not binding (Article 12.1). A panel can draw up different Working Procedures. Many new working procedures have developed over the years. Some are standard in almost all procedures (e.g. rules on service of documents; written replies to questions; and preliminary rulings) and others are brought in when needed (e.g. on confidential documents and appointment of experts). The Appellate Body has the explicit right to draw up its own working procedures and to amend them (Article 17.9).

[7] Indeed Mr Pascal Lamy, then the Commissioner for Trade of the European Communities, described the organisation as 'medieval' following the failure of the Cancún ministerial conference.

Even the binding rules of the DSU leave many gaps that have been filled by case law. For example, the admissibility of *amicus curiae* briefs,[8] the power of panels to rule on their jurisdiction[9] and the rights of third parties in implementation panels under Article 21.5 DSU.[10]

Also, it is possible to circumvent to a large extent even the binding rules of the DSU by agreement. Thus, the Appellate Body has recognised that parties may agree not to hold consultations.[11] Time limits that appear fixed are regularly changed by agreement.[12]

One particular manifestation of the flexibility built into the DSU (as well as of its lacunae) is the possibility for parties to *enter into procedural agreements.*[13]

This technique is particularly useful to resolve what is perceived to be the most serious defect in the DSU – the problem of '*sequencing*'. This is a problem created by the United States, which insisted that it could decide whether new EC legislation on bananas was in conformity with the WTO and could proceed directly to retaliation without having to obtain a new panel ruling (on the basis of the accelerated procedure provided for in Article 21.5 DSU).[14]

These *procedural agreements* raise a number of fascinating legal questions that are yet to be resolved. In particular, what is their legal base and

[8] *United States – Import Prohibition of Certain Shrimp and Shrimp Products*, Appellate Body Report, WT/DS58/AB/R, paras. 79 ff (DSR 1998: VII, 2755) and *United States – Imposition of Countervailing Duties on Certain Hot-Rolled Lead and Bismuth Carbon Steel Products Originating in the United Kingdom*, Appellate Body Report, paras 36ff, WT/DS138/AB/R, paras 36 ff (DSR 2000:V, 2595).

[9] Appellate Body Report, *European Communities – Regime for the Importation, Sale and Distribution of Bananas*, WT/DS27/AB/R, adopted 25 September 1997, DSR 1997: II, 591.

[10] Appellate Body Report, *United States–Tax Treatment for 'Foreign Sales Corporations' – Recourse to Article 21.5 of the DSU by the European Communities*, WT/DS108/AB/RW, adopted 29 January 2002, DSR 2002:I, 55.

[11] Appellate Body Report, *Mexico–Anti-Dumping Investigation of High Fructose Corn Syrup (HFCS) from the United States–Recourse to Article 21.5 of the DSU by the United States*, WT/DS132/AB/RW, adopted 21 November 2001, DSR 2001:XIII, 6675.

[12] Appellate Body Report, *United States–Anti-Dumping Measures on Certain Hot-Rolled Steel Products from Japan*, WT/DS184/AB/R, adopted 23 August 2001, DSR 2001:X, 4697.

[13] A good example of a procedural agreement is that concluded by the European Communities, and six other complainants (China, Japan, Korea, New Zealand, Norway and Switzerland with the United States in their case against the US safeguard measures on steel products. Document WT/DS248/13, WT/DS249/7, WT/DS251/8, WT/DS252/6, WT/DS253/6, WT/DS254/6, WT/DS258/10 of 22 July 2002.

[14] Statement by DSB chairman of 1 February 1999 available at. www.wto.org/english/newse/news99e/lo010299.htm.

are they binding? It is of interest to note that a number of countries seem to assume that procedural agreements are not by themselves binding and thus propose to the DSB to adopt a decision implementing the agreement. A good example of this development is the decision adopted by the DSB on 6 December 2005[15] at the joint request of the European Communities and the United States[16] to prolong the deadline for appeal in the *US–Zeroing* case (in order to facilitate the work of the Appellate Body over the Christmas period).

The parties presumably did not consider it sufficient to simply agree to prolong the time period (perhaps fearing that one may claim that the agreement is non-binding and that the appeal is out of time). However, although the DSB is tasked in Article 2 of the DSU with 'administering' the rules of the DSU, paragraph 4 of the same provision also suggests that the DSB may only take a decision where a power to do so is given to it in the DSU. It may be therefore that the DSB has no more power than the parties to a dispute to change the time periods and other rules laid down in the DSU.

However, as a practical matter, procedural agreements between parties to a dispute (whether blessed by a decision of the DSB or not) are respected by all concerned and provide a useful mechanism for adjusting the rules of the DSU as well as for filling gaps and resolving ambiguities.

If parties (and the DSB) can modify and complete the rules of the DSU in particular disputes, why should they not do so generally for all disputes that they may have – present and future?

One can easily imagine that a WTO Member may not wish to agree a modification of the rules in one case (e.g. a commitment to resort to an implementation panel before retaliating) if it believes the other party might refuse a similar favour in a similar situation when the roles are reversed.

To take another example, if two countries were persuaded that the public should be entitled to observe a panel proceeding (just like a court proceeding in most countries) would it not be easier to agree to allow this as a rule, rather than seek to agree it in each proceeding? There will always be one party (usually the complainant) that has more of an interest in public access than the other.

[15] See WT/DSB/M/201, 25 January 2006.

[16] For the request see document WT/DS294/11 of 25 November 2005.

Examples of the procedural issues that could be regulated more completely or better in this way include:

- sequencing;
- transparency – publication of submissions and opening of panel hearings to the public;[17]
- timetables;
- acceptance of panellists from a defined list (or 'permanent roster');
- waiver of the nationality rule;
- procedures for multiple appeals;
- compensation procedures;[18]
- costs.

After a period of experimenting with new procedures, they will no doubt be improved, refined and new procedures developed. At an appropriate time *they could be codified into a new DSU*. (The existing DSU is after all mainly a codification of practices developed in the GATT.) And certain matters that cannot be achieved by agreement such as the creation of a permanent panel body could be added at that time.

Indeed, once it is realised by the wider Membership (and in particular non-users) that the Dispute Settlement System is here to stay and will evolve whether they like it or not and whether they participate in its development or not, they may then realise that it is better to participate and seek to influence events rather than allowing others to do so.

5. Conclusion

An agreement to change the text of the DSU is of course desirable and some reforms can only be made that way. But dispute settlement is a continuous experiment conducted in a context where solutions have to be found. So a lack of agreement will not stultify the Dispute Settlement System. The Dispute Settlement System is evolving and will continue to evolve in future.

[17] See the agreement between the EC, US and Canada to open the hearings in the Hormones Retaliation case to the public evidenced in the communication from the Chairman of the Panel circulated as document WT/DS320/8 and WT/DS321/8 of 2 August 2005.

[18] See for example the agreement to establish the level of nullification or impairment by arbitration in *United States–Section110 (5) of the US Copyright Act* so as to facilitate an agreement on compensation. See document WT/DS160/15 of 3 August 2001.

Reforming the Dispute Settlement Understanding

WOLFGANG WEISS*

Abstract

The Dispute Settlement Understanding has been under continuous review since its inception. The WTO members confirmed in the current negotiations on the DSU, as set out in the Framework Agreements agreed at the end of July 2004 (the so-called July Package) and in the Hong Kong Ministerial Declaration that the review process should continue and be successfully concluded by the end of 2006, but this did not happen. This chapter intends to give an overview over the reform debate and its history, and comment on current developments of the reform process under the Doha Development Agenda. The reasons for review and the main issues of the debate shall be identified, and possible results of the continuing negotiation process assessed. It will be shown that the intrinsic tension in the dispute settlement mechanism between a legal model and a diplomatic model of settling disputes not only featured at the inception of the review process, but still is decisive for the tabled proposals. This fragile equilibrium between adjudication and diplomatic flexibility will colour the outcome, and is worth maintaining. However, the proposals on improving compliance like introducing financial compensations or collective retaliation that are in the particular interest of developing countries, should be considered more strongly.

I. Introduction

The Dispute Settlement Understanding (DSU) is a legally binding agreement committing WTO members to settle their disputes in an orderly and rule-oriented fashion. It is one of the most significant achievements

* The author is Professor in International Law at Oxford Brookes University, Oxford and Professor at the German University of Administrative Sciences, Speyer, Germany. A first version was published in 1 *Manchester Journal of International Economic Law* 2004 (2) p. 97 *et seq.*

of the Uruguay Round, as it is the first system for the binding settlement of trade disputes between states vested with an unprecedented degree of power, and a key component for the effective operation of the WTO. The DSU establishes a framework within which WTO members seek binding determination as to whether another WTO member has failed to comply with its WTO obligations, and within which WTO members apply remedies for a breach of WTO law. In the ten years of its existence, panels and the Appellate Body being the interpretative organs of the dispute settlement process established by the DSU, have produced a significant body of jurisprudence which increasingly has attracted the attention of not just trade law experts. Despite severe criticism the system is a story of success: it is frequently used, provides guidance for the interpretation of the WTO obligations, and its compliance rate is quite high, though compliance may take long.[1] Nevertheless, since its inception the DSU has been under review. Although the DSU only provides for detailed procedures and steps to be taken by WTO members for resolving disputes (procedural law) and does in general not provide for substantive obligations of the WTO members, the way the DSU is applied and interpreted has repercussions to the substantive WTO law provisions.[2] For example, the rules on burden of proof or the applied standard of review have an impact on the extent and consequences of substantive WTO law provisions. This is also true for the interpretative methods applied by panels and the Appellate Body in their interpretation of substantive WTO law obligations. To the extent substantive WTO law provisions are unclear and need clarification, panels and the Appellate Body have to fill the gaps. Thus, to a certain extent they have to work as a kind of legislature – a function that has attracted lots of criticism,[3] and has to be attributed to an imbalance between the efficient dispute settlement system and the rather weak political decision-making processes in WTO.[4] If the WTO agreements cannot be clarified through negotiations, dispute settlement

[1] For a comprehensive evaluation see *W. Davey*, The WTO Dispute Settlement System: The First Ten Years, 8 *JIEL* (2005) 17; *R. Yerxa/B. Wilson* (eds.), Key Issues in WTO Dispute Settlement. First Ten Years, 2005. *Davey ibid.* 47 points to an implementation rate of 83%.

[2] See also *H. Hauser/T. A. Zimmermann*, The Challenge of Reforming the WTO Dispute Settlement Understanding, 38 *Intereconomics* (2003) 241 at 244.

[3] See *J. Greenwald*, WTO Dispute Settlement: An Exercise in Trade Law Legislation?, *JIEL* (2003) 123.

[4] *C. -D. Ehlermann*, Reflections on the Process of Clarification and Improvement of the DSU, in F. Ortino/E. -U. Petersmann (eds.), The WTO Dispute Settlement System 1995–2003, 2004, 105 (106); *T. Zimmermann*, WTO Dispute Settlement at Ten: Evolution, Experiences, and Evaluation, 60 *Aussenwirtschaft* (2005) 27 (38 *et seq.*).

might be a surrogate for successful negotiations.[5] This applies even more to the current negotiations on the reform of the DSU. Thus, the way the dispute settlement mechanism works influences the material scope of substantive WTO obligations. For these reasons, negotiations about the further development of substantive WTO law provisions are closely linked with negotiations about the change of the dispute settlement system. Therefore, it is easily understandable why the reform of the DSU is progressing very slowly. Hopes have been expressed that DSU negotiations will gain momentum if there was a breakthrough in other negotiation areas.[6]

This contribution will give a general overview over the reform debate and comment on current developments of the DSU reform process under the Doha Development Agenda. The deliberations will focus on the reasons for the continuous review process, and on the main issues of the reform debate before possible results of the DSU review will be assessed. Prior to this, the history of the DSU review negotiations briefly shall be summarised.

II. Negotiating history: The reform of the DSU as a never-ending story?

Reviewing the DSU has been an undertaking that started as early as 1995, this means at the same point in time when the DSU was launched, and by now could be called a never-ending story. When the WTO Agreements were adopted at the Ministerial Conference in Marrakesh in April 1994, the Ministers of the Contracting Parties took a decision on the review of the DSU,[7] which challenged the Ministerial Conference to complete a full review of the new dispute settlement system established by the DSU within four years after the entry into force of the WTO Agreement, which was 1 January 1995. The Ministerial Conference was mandated to decide whether to continue, modify or terminate the DSU. During the review several members proposed possible improvements and clarifications to the agreement. By January 1999, however, the review was not at all completed. Even after extending the deadline for the review to the end of June 1999, members could not agree on any result.The review discussions in

5 *D. McRae*, What is the future of WTO Dispute Settlement?, 7 *JIEL* (2004) 3.

6 See DSU Update, 8 *Bridges Weekly Trade News Digest* (2004) No. 19.

7 Decision on the Application and Review of the Understanding on Rules and Procedures Governing the Settlement of Disputes, www.wto.org/english/docs_e/legal_e/53-ddsu_e.htm (last visited 31 January 2006).

the Dispute Settlement Body continued without success as they suffered from the failure of the Seattle Ministerial.[8]

The *Doha Ministerial Declaration* launching the Doha Development Agenda in November 2001 reconfirmed the need for 'negotiations on improvements and clarifications of the Dispute Settlement Understanding'. The mandate given to the review process no longer mentioned the possibility of terminating the DSU – an indication that overall the WTO members were satisfied with the functioning of the system. At least it appears that they had no idea of a totally different dispute settlement system that could work better than the current system.

The Doha Ministerial Declaration recognised that 'negotiations should be based on the work done thus far as well as any additional proposals by members'.[9] The Ministerial Conference, after several years of ongoing debate, missed the chance to agree on a core list of improvements, and to identify the remaining issues that needed more discussion. Thus, the mandate could have been limited thereby enabling an acceleration of the process. After the Doha Ministerial the negotiations took place in the Special Session of the DSB established by the Trade Negotiations Committee in February 2002. The discussions were expected to be concluded by 31 May 2003. Due to the decisive role of the DSU for the whole of WTO law more member governments have participated actively in these talks than in any other negotiation under the Doha mandate (except for agriculture). Well over eighty WTO members have subscribed to *far more than ninety proposals*, each of which contains several suggested changes, covering virtually all stages of the dispute settlement system. In the meetings, the work progressed from a general exchange of views to a discussion of conceptual proposals touching upon virtually all provisions of the DSU, and by the second half of 2002 to an issue-by-issue thematic discussion. Since the beginning of 2003, the work has focused on discussing specific draft legal texts proposed by WTO members.[10] As the deadline of May 2003 came close, attempts were undertaken to agree on a minimum reform of the DSU dealing only with a core list of issues on which consensus was likely in time for the deadline ('early harvest'). They

[8] See *T. Zimmermann*, What directions should the DSU take? Negotiations and Proposals to Review and Reform the DSU, 2004, 92 *et seq.*

[9] See Doha Ministerial, WT/MIN(01)/DEC/1, para. 30.

[10] See the report by the Chairman to the TNC, TN/DS/9, para. 2. For more details on the negotiating history see *E. Kessie*, The 'Early Harvest Negotiations' in 2003, in F. Ortino/E. -U. Petersmann (eds.), The WTO Dispute Settlement System 1995–2003, 2004, 115 (117 *et seq.*).

failed, however. In April and May 2003 the then chairmen of the Special Session of the DSB, the Hungarian Ambassador *Peter Balas* first presented a Framework Document that included all tabled suggestions and then a revised draft legal text[11] under his own responsibility, which reflects the most striking compilation of the progress of the ongoing negotiations. It summarised and regrouped members' amendments to the DSU on a *number of most promising issues*, including enhancing third-party rights; introducing an interim review and 'remand' (referring a case back to a panel) authority at the appeal stage; clarifying and improving the sequence of procedures at the implementation stage (the so-called sequencing problem[12]); enhancing compensation; strengthening notification requirements for mutually agreed solutions; and strengthening special and differential treatment for developing countries at various stages of the proceedings.[13] This text did not include a number of other proposals due to the absence of a sufficiently high level of support. The latter proposals covered issues such as accelerated procedures for certain disputes; improved panel selection procedures; increased control by members over panel and Appellate Body reports; clarification of the treatment of *amicus curiae* briefs; and modified procedures for retaliation, including collective retaliation or enhanced surveillance of retaliation. The Balas text however did not find consent although some members felt that it captured the essential elements for a final agreement; others felt that there were serious omissions. There was not even

[11] For the revised version see the annex to the report, TN/DS/9; for a comment on the Balas text see *H. Hauser/T. A. Zimmermann*, The Challenge of Reforming the WTO Dispute Settlement Understanding, 38 *Intereconomics* (2003) 241 and *E. Kessie*, The 'Early Harvest Negotiations' in 2003, in F. Ortino/E. -U. Petersmann (eds.), The WTO Dispute Settlement System 1995–2003, 2004, 115 (123 *et seq.*).

[12] See *D. Palmeter/P. Mavroidis*, Dispute Settlement in the WTO, 2nd edn 2004, 278–286. The problem of 'sequencing' arises from a lack of clarity in the DSU text as to the correct order (sequencing) in which two phases of the procedure should occur in a situation where the complainant claims that the defendant has failed to comply fully with the DSB decision. According to Article 21:5 DSU, a so-called compliance panel examines the dispute within ninety days in case the two parties to a dispute disagree whether the decision has been implemented or not, whereas Article 22:2 DSU states that if the defendant fails to implement, the complainant can ask the DSB to authorise retaliation within thirty days from the end of the implementation period; such decision can be challenged according to Article 22.6 DSU; the panel then has to decide within sixty days. Currently, the DSU is ambiguous as to the right of the complainant to seek authorisation to retaliate according to Article 22 DSU *before* a compliance panel according to Article 21:5 DSU has determined that the defendant had actually failed to implement the DSB decision.

[13] See TN/DS/9, para. 5.

agreement among the WTO members on whether further negotiations should only focus on the draft legal text of the then Chairman.

After these attempts did not succeed, the DSU negotiations were extended for another year to May 2004[14] – a deadline which could not be met, and the members agreed to extend to an undetermined deadline.[15] On 31 July 2004 the WTO's then 147 member governments in the General Council approved a package of framework and other agreements[16] which was supposed to greatly enhance members' chances for successfully completing the Doha negotiations. Therein, the General Council adopted the Trade Negotiations Committee's (TNC) recommendation that work in the Special Session of the Dispute Settlement Body should continue on the basis set out by the chairman of that body in his report to the TNC.[17] Thus, as regards dispute settlement, the July Framework simply reaffirms continuing the negotiations.

Negotiations continued after the July Package alongside the proposals already present since most new proposals submitted after the July package referred to suggestions made earlier being revised in the light of the reactions they received.[18] Negotiations were resumed in autumn 2004 with a much-anticipated package deal proposed by Argentina, Brazil, Canada, India, New Zealand and Norway covering the issues of *sequencing, remand authority of the Appellate Body and post-retaliation procedures for the removal of the authorisation to suspend concessions.* These suggestions seek to codify the practice according to which the compliance procedure under Art. 21.5 DSU should be exhausted before recourse to retaliation and to Art. 22.6 can be made. They also proposed a remand procedure according to which the Appellate Body may describe in a detailed way the findings required to complete the analysis. The parties may then request the Appellate Body to send the issue back to the original panel. Third, the proposal indicated procedures that allow to address a panel after retaliation was authorised in case the parties disagree as to whether the measure adopted by the defending party in order to implement the findings of the panel/Appellate Body

[14] At its meeting on 24 July 2003, the General Council agreed to extend negotiations from 31 May 2003 to 31 May 2004.

[15] See the minutes of the meeting of the Special Session of the Dispute Settlement Body of 28 May 2004, TN/DS/M/19.

[16] WT/L/579.

[17] WT/DS/10.

[18] See for more detail Developments in the WTO DSU Review Negotiations since July 2004, in 1 *The South Centre Quarterly on Trade Disputes* 2 (2005) 14 *et seq.* (available at www.southcentre.org/info/scquarterlytradedisputes/TradeDisputesQtrly2005q2.pdf, visited 25 January 2006).

complies with WTO law.[19] Although these proposals were relatively non-contentious and had pre-appeared in the Balas text, no consensus could be found. Some developing countries were disappointed since their concerns were not considered.[20] Further contributions by the EU, the US and Japan, for example, dealt with enhanced third-party rights, panel composition, time-saving streamlined dispute settlement procedures, additional guidance to panels and the Appellate Body, and transparency. The negotiations in 2005 centred on those topics[21] and gained momentum. The new approach by the chairman *David Spencer* (Australia) to encourage informal meetings outside the Special Sessions of the DSB might have contributed to this. The Hong Kong Ministerial decision in December 2005 confined itself to take note of the progress in the Dispute Settlement Understanding negotiations and to direct the Special Session to continue to work towards a rapid conclusion of the negotiations.[22]

Although the negotiations on the reform of the DSU are not part of the single undertaking[23] so that they could be concluded irrespective and independent of the success or failure of the negotiations on substantive issues, the negotiations on DSU review will not be finished before the negotiations in other areas. Substantive and procedural issues are closely interlinked, and the states will invest their negotiation powers in the issues which are more important to them and which need greater attention, like agriculture and market access for non-agricultural goods since the dispute settlement mechanisms work well enough. Thus, clarification of the dispute settlement procedures is not the most pressing concern of the members. The last deadline for the negotiations set by the Hong Kong Ministerial was the end of 2006, but observers expected June 2007 to be the *de facto* time limit for the completion of the Doha Round being the date of expiry of the Trade Promotion Authority of the US Bush administration.

19 This issue is raised by the beef hormone dispute where panels (WT/DS320 and WT/DS321) now have to rule on the procedures for removing authorised sanctions, see 9 *Bridges Weekly Trade News Digest* (2005) 30. The final reports of the panels are scheduled for October 2007, see WT/DS320/7 and WT/DS321/7.

20 See Doha Round Briefing Series: Review of the Dispute Settlement Understanding, December 2004.

21 See the November 2005 report by the chairman David Spencer to the Trade Negotiations Committee, TN/DS/14. For a summary of the 2005 DSU negotiations see the Doha Round Briefing Series: Review of the Dispute Settlement Understanding, November 2005, (available at www.ictsd.org/pubs/dohabriefings/index.htm, visited 26 January 2006).

22 WT/MIN (05)/DEC, para. 34.

23 See para. 47 of the Doha Ministerial.

Some delegations even assume that an agreement on more effective safeguards on the compliance with panel and Appellate Body rulings will be postponed to an even later date as this area is particularly contentious. Currently, negotiations also on DSU gained momentum.

III. Reasons for reviewing the DSU

It might be astonishing that – as mentioned above – the WTO members, when launching the newly negotiated DSU agreement, instantly provided for the beginning of a review process. Such an in-built agenda, however, is not a peculiarity of the DSU, but can be found in other WTO trade agreements as well (e.g. in TRIPS (see Article 71)). The existence of in-built agendas is understandable in agreements that are new or introduce new subjects and mechanisms to international law and world trade law in particular, because the proper functioning of the new elements has to be monitored. In-built agendas take care of a certain degree of automaticity of the review process of new procedures or obligations. They contribute to the workability of the world trade law, at least for the future. For this reason, it is not surprising that agreements like TRIPS, GATS or the DSU that did not exist before the Uruguay Round, but play a pivotal role in the new multilateral trading system, contain such provisions. The WTO members could not know in advance how panels and the Appellate Body would apply the DSU rules, as experience with multilateral dispute settlement in the new fields of trade in services and intellectual property rights was limited.[24] Furthermore, WTO law contains special dispute settlement provisions (Art. 17 of the Antidumping Agreement is one of the most eminent examples) that could lead to developments differing from those under the general dispute settlement rules.[25] Besides, the history of the development of the dispute settlement under GATT 1947 was always characterised by a step-by-step development. There has been a dialectic interaction between dispute settlement practice and periodic review and agreed clarifications of procedures since the inception of GATT. This was expected to continue in the WTO.[26] This expectation is confirmed when looking at recent develop-

[24] *E. -U. Petersmann*, The Dispute Settlement System of the World Trade Organization and the Evolution of the GATT Dispute Settlement System since 1948, *CMLRev* (1994) 1157 at 1228. [25] *Ibid.*, at 1239.

[26] *E.-U. Petersmann*, WTO Negotiators Meet Academics. The Negotiations on Improvements of the WTO Dispute Settlement System, 6 *JIEL* (2003) 237 at 239, 248.

ments in dispute settlement. *New developments like the admission of amicus curiae briefs, increased public transparency of panel proceedings*[27] *or the circumvention of the intricate issue of sequencing by procedural agreements were pushed by practice.*[28]

Nevertheless one might wonder whether the in-built agenda for the reform of the DSU echoes certain doubts and suspicions of the WTO members as to the results of their own negotiations during the Uruguay Round. This touches upon the question whether the negotiators finally got what they wanted.[29] On the eve of the Uruguay Round the old dispute settlement system, although quite successful[30] did not work to the full satisfaction of the contracting parties, in particular in the field of agriculture, antidumping and subsidies.[31] It did not sufficiently take care of a sound implementation of GATT obligations, and satisfying enforcement procedures for the full implementation of panel reports were lacking.[32] It was one of the crucial aims of the Uruguay Round negotiations to create an effective and efficient dispute settlement mechanism that allows for speedy procedures, binding results and that is rule-oriented instead of

27 In this regard a milestone in the development of transparency in dispute settlement was the decision of the panels hearing the EU's challenges against the retaliatory sanctions on its exports imposed by the US and Canada (WT/DS320; WT/DS321), to open the panel hearings to the public, following a request by all parties. See 9 *Bridges Weekly Trade News Digest* (2005) No. 29.

28 See also *T. Zimmermann*, WTO Dispute Settlement at Ten: Evolution, Experiences, and Evaluation, 60 *Aussenwirtschaft* (2005) 27, (50-52).

29 In this regard see *A. Stoler*, The WTO Dispute Settlement Process: Did the Negotiators get What They Wanted?, 3 *World Trade Review* (2004) 99.

30 Cf. *R. Hudec*, Enforcing International Trade Law. The Evolution of the Modern GATT Legal System, (1993) London: Butterworths 353.

31 See *G. Horlick*, Dispute Settlement Mechanism, 29 *Journal of World Trade* 2 (1995) 163 at 164 *et seq.*; *E.-U. Petersmann*, *CMLRev* (1994) 1157 at 1193; *idem*, International Competition Rules for the GATT-WTO World Trade and Legal System, in *Journal of World Trade* 5 (1993) 35 at 68 *et seq.*; 73 *et seq.*; *A. Stoler*, The WTO Dispute Settlement Process: Did the Negotiators Get What They Wanted?, 3 *World Trade Review* (2004) 99 at 100 *et seq.* For the deficits of the GATT 1947 dispute settlement see also the *Leutwiler Report* of 1985 (Trade Policies for a Better Future) and *T. Stewart/C. J. Callahan*, Dispute Settlement Mechanisms, in T. Stewart (ed.), The GATT Uruguay Round. A Negotiating History, Vol. II, 1993, 2663 at 2721.

32 For example, the possibility of authorising the suspension of concessions provided for in Article XXIII: 2 GATT 1947 was used only once as the consensus even of the Contracting Party against whom the report was directed was necessary. That led to rising recourse to unilateral sanctions, see *E.-U. Petersmann*, *CMLRev* (1994) 1157 at 1185, 1203 *et seq.* The 1980s witnessed an increase in non-compliance with dispute settlement rulings, *R. Hudec*, Enforcing International Trade Law. The Evolution of the Modern GATT Legal System, London: Butterworths 1993, at 354.

33 *GATT, GATT Secretariat*, Ministerial Declaration, Punta Del Este, Geneva 1986, 20.

power-oriented. The Punta Del Este Declaration[33] that initiated the Uruguay Round called for prompt and effective dispute resolution, strengthened procedural rules and adequate arrangements for monitoring the compliance with adopted recommendations. These objectives certainly have been met, although the settlement mechanism cannot be called a judicial procedure. The DSU is a controversial instrument of compromise.[34] It is quasi-judicial in character as there is on the one hand, room for political flexibility in resolving disputes and, on the other hand, it takes care of legal integrity, legal security and predictability of WTO law.[35] Conciliation and adjudication methods are mixed in the DSU.[36] This is not only caused by an intermingling of diverse models and rules in the DSU itself, but is also a consequence of the very often quite vague and generous terms of substantive WTO law provisions with their lack of clarity, their ambiguity and the need for improvements and clarifications. The shortcomings of substantive WTO law provisions colour the functioning of the WTO dispute settlement. The uneasy deficient relationship[37] between power and politics on the one hand, and law on the other hand, inherent in world trade law and international law in general, culminates in the dispute settlement system that is supposed to function properly, which facilitates the settlement of trade disputes between states. Due to this ambiguity the functioning of the new dispute settlement mechanisms had to be looked at diligently.

In the Uruguay Round negotiations on dispute settlement there existed two groups of negotiators. Whereas the one group preferred a flexible model of dispute resolution that gives leeway to the states, the other group wanted a judicial system with clear-cut rules. These divergent interests are reflected in the final outcome.[38] The negotiators wanted to

[34] *R. MacLean*, The Urgent Need to Reform the WTO's Dispute Settlement Process, *International Trade Law and Regulation* (2002) 137.

[35] See Art. 3:2 DSU. For more detail see *W. Weiß*, Security and Predictability under WTO law, 2 *World Trade Review* (2003) 183.

[36] *L. Wang*, Some Observations on the Dispute Settlement System in the WTO, 29 *Journal of World Trade* 2 (1995) 173 at 175.

[37] *A. von Bogdandy*, Law and Politics in the WTO – Strategies to Cope with a Deficient Relationship, 5 *Max Planck Yearbook of United Nations Law* (2001) 609.

[38] See e.g. with respect to a mutually agreed solution in Art. 3:7 and Art. 22:8 DSU, the possible influence of the parties to the dispute on the recommendations of the panels in the interim review or the rather long implementation periods for compliance with DSB decisions according to Art. 21:3 DSU (as allowing delay is a form of accommodating the defendant and making dispute resolution softer, *M. Reisman/M. Wiedman*, Contextual Imperatives of Dispute Resolution Mechanisms, 29 *Journal of World Trade* 3 (1995) 5 at 22) on the one hand and the independent position of panelists and AB members, their

overcome the old system that was coined by too much diplomacy and dependence on the political will of the states.[39] Instead, they aimed for compelling integrated and uniform mechanisms leading to binding and enforceable decisions. This was in conformity with an observable trend towards judicialisation and legalisation in international law.[40] Finally, the rule-orientation of the dispute settlement could be strengthened by the Uruguay Round results. Nevertheless, the WTO members still have influence in the dispute settlement mechanism and its results. Diplomacy still has a role to play as consensual solutions are favoured (see Article 3:7 DSU), and may be reached even until the last phase of dispute settlement. The *quasi-judicial characteristic* made the DSU system a unique and novel process for settling international trade disputes. It was this inherent 'systemic'[41] *tension between a judicial model and a diplomatic model* of dispute resolution that created the need for an instant launch of a review process of the DSU. Due to its complexity and its innovations (like extended scope, short deadlines, automaticity in the establishment of panels and in the adoption of panel/Appellate Body reports by negative consensus requirements, appellate review) the proper functioning of the novel mechanisms which has been called the great test of the new WTO[42] could not be taken for granted but had to pass the test of dispute settlement practice.[43]

The US administration when implementing the Uruguay Round Agreements was prepared to monitor the future functioning of the dispute settlement mechanisms in particular as regards panel reports adverse to the US to eventually withdraw from the WTO. It expressed unease about the possibility that the dispute settlement mechanisms

task to examine the relevant WTO provisions and to clarify them in accordance with customary rules of interpretation (see Art. 3:2, 7:1 DSU) and the probability that legally insufficient panel findings are rejected by the appellate body on the other hand. See also the differentiated enumeration of political and legal methods of dispute settlement in the DSU by *E.-U. Petersmann*, *CMLRev* (1994) 1157 at 1210.

39 The Contracting Parties e.g. could block the institution of a panel or could veto the adoption of panel reports. Although that happened only rarely, the mere possibility of blocking stagnated the pre-Uruguay dispute settlement system, see *E. Vermulst/B. Driessen*, An Overview of the WTO Dispute Settlement System and its Relationship with the Uruguay Round Agreements, 29 *Journal of World Trade* 2 (1995) 131 at 135.

40 See *E. -U. Petersmann*, *CMLRev* (1994) 1157 at 1169, 1187; *E. Vermulst/B. Driessen*, An Overview of the WTO Dispute Settlement System and its Relationship with the Uruguay Round Agreements, 29 *Journal of World Trade* 2 (1995) 131 at 153.

41 *E.-U. Petersmann*, *CMLRev.* (1994) 1157 at 1225.

42 *G. Horlick*, Dispute Settlement Mechanism, 29 *Journal of World Trade* 2 (1995) 163 at 168.

43 *E.-U. Petersmann*, *CMLRev.* (1994) 1157 at 1224.

could prove not to be accountable and fair. Panels could exceed their authority. When the DSU was launched, concerns were raised as to whether the DSU is not too ambitious in particular as regards the tight deadlines and the use of the new regime on countermeasures. Furthermore, as the WTO members can no longer block the adoption of a panel report, it was expected that pressure on the dispute settlement system would shift to the implementation stage tempting WTO members to refuse compliance,[44] all the more as the implementation stage is less automatic. And indeed, looking at the dispute settlement mechanism almost ten years after its inauguration this threat appears to have materialised. WTO members do not openly oppose adopted panel reports they do not want to comply with but try to postpone full compliance as long as possible and frequently block, or at least impede, the adoption of countermeasures. Very often they want to fight everything out to the last step.[45] On the other hand, and as a reaction to that, WTO members are tempted not to await authorisation for countermeasures, but to proceed unilaterally.

Although it is shared conviction amongst all members that in general the DSU has served them well,[46] it is still the tension between rule orientation and power orientation and the preference of the WTO members for one of the two models that influence the reform proposals. The evaluation of the functioning of the dispute settlement mechanism and the determination of its possible weaknesses is affected by, if not to say completely depends on, the standpoint and pre-setting of each WTO member in this regard. There is no consensus on which of the two models to continue.[47] Those that see the rule orientation to be the decisive element of the new dispute settlement mechanism want to strengthen, for example, the expertise of the panels and the powers of the Appellate Body or want to improve enforcement or adjust the procedure more fully to that of

[44] *E. Vermulst/B. Driessen*, An Overview of the WTO Dispute Settlement System and its Relationship with the Uruguay Round Agreements, 29 *Journal of World Trade* 2 (1995) 131 at 153.

[45] As one of the most striking example, the dispute on the US Foreign Sales Corporation Act can be named, *R. MacLean*, The Urgent Need to Reform the WTO's Dispute Settlement Process, *Int. TLR.* (2002) 137 at 138. Another example is the beef hormone dispute between the US and the EC.

[46] Since the DSU started operating in January 1995 more than 300 complaints have been brought by members within about ten years; this compares to the final total of 300 cases filed with about 115 panel reports during the entire forty-seven years of the former GATT.

[47] See also *H. Hauser/T. A. Zimmermann*, The Challenge of Reforming the WTO Dispute Settlement Understanding, 38 *Intereconomics* (2003) 241 at 243.

domestic courts (e.g. by allowing for remand procedures) in order to minimise the political element of the dispute settlement; whereas others that are on the side of diplomacy want to increase the influence of the state parties to the disputes, and to limit the role of the WTO secretariat, whilst being less concerned about improving the legal quality of the panel reports.

IV. Main issues of reform

In the review debate, very diverse proposals covering almost all DSU provisions have been presented by WTO members[48] some of which are very divisive, for example, the proposals to increase transparency or to create more effective ways of implementing WTO rulings. All of them are in line with the mandate of the Doha Ministerial to improve and clarify the dispute settlement mechanisms. Not one WTO member proposed the termination of the DSU. The country positions try to further develop the DSU and to remove its shortcomings.[49] None of the proposals calls for a fundamental change of the whole dispute settlement mechanism although the determination and evaluation of failures and the necessary remedies varies within membership. *A synopsis of the main proposals made by the WTO members* can be found at the homepage of the Institute of International Economic Law of the Georgetown University.[50]

The proposals put on the table either represent minor, more or less technical clarifications of the dispute settlement mechanism by fine tuning of the modalities and by streamlining the procedures, or call for major improvements and modifications that tackle structural deficits of the DSU.[51] Some, however, could alter the essence of the dispute settlement by dramatically changing the functioning of the dispute settlement system.

48 They have the document number TN/DS/W/* and can easily be found at www.docsonline.wto.org.

49 For the flaws, for example, of the existing remedies see *M. Bronckers/N. van den Broek*, Financial Compensation in the WTO. Improving the Remedies of WTO Dispute Settlement, 8 *JIEL* (2005) 101 at 102 *et seq.*

50 www.law.georgetown.edu/iiel/research/projects/dsureview/synopsis.html. See also *Y. Gouhua/B. Mercurio/L. Yongjie*, WTO Dispute Settlement Understanding: A Detailed Interpretation, 2005, 504–68; *T. Zimmermann*, What Directions should the DSU Take? Negotiations and Proposals to Review and Reform the DSU, 2004, 111–93.

51 See also *R. MacLean, Int. TLR* (2002) 137. *E.-U. Petersmann*, 6 *JIEL* (2003) 237, identifies eight categories.

A. Technical clarifications

The proposals tabled by some states contain minor changes that address, for example *housekeeping issues* like terminating inactive cases which remained dormant for several years or propose to enhance the protection of *confidential business information*.[52] Other proposals call for a strengthening of the accepted principle of *special and differential treatment* in favour of developing countries. According to them, legal assistance by the WTO secretariat to developing countries must be increased. If a developing country is party to a dispute, the panel must contain at least one national from a developing country, consultations are to take place in the capitals of-least-developed countries and time periods have to be extended or – maybe an even fundamental change – litigation costs have to be refunded to developing country members where the dispute does not end with a finding against the developing country.[53]

Many proposals take care of a *fine-tuning of panel or Appellate Body procedures*. Some propose expedited procedures for certain measures, for example for measures already held inconsistent with WTO law[54] or for safeguard and anti-dumping measures.[55] Others want to oblige panellists to deliver separate opinions,[56] to raise the expertise of panels and to improve their selection procedures. They also propose to alter the time periods currently provided for in the DSU,[57] or to enhance rules on multiple complaints and to improve the working procedures of panels for more consistency. Time saving proposals for a faster start-up process by establishing panels at first request and speeding the selection of panellists were also put forward.[58] According to some proposals, the Appellate Body should be enlarged to respond to the increasing work load[59] and the

[52] TN/DS/W/41, proposal made by Canada to attach, *inter alia*, an Appendix 5 to the DSU on procedures governing confidential business information.

[53] See e.g. TN//DS/W/47 by India, Cuba, Dominican Republic, Egypt, Honduras, Jamaica, Malaysia. For more detail *D. Sarooshi*, The Future of the WTO and its Dispute Settlement System, 2 *International Organizations Law Review* (2005) 129 at 13–41.

[54] Proposal by Brazil, TN/DS/W/45/Rev.1.

[55] Proposal by China, TN/DS/W/51/Rev.1 and Canada, TN/DS/W/49: introduction of a new Art. 8bis DSU. Cf. *B. Mercurio*, Improving Dispute Settlement in the WTO, 38 *JWT* (2004) 795 at 816. On the need for speedy dispute settlement procedures as regards safeguards see *W. Davey*, The WTO Dispute Settlement System: The First Ten Years, 8 *JIEL* (2005) 17 at 49.

[56] Haiti TN/DS/W/37, Kenya TN/DS/W/42.

[57] Some advocate, *inter alia*, a prolongation of the time limit for Appellate review to ninety days, TN/DS/W/52.

[58] By Canada, TN/DS/W/49.

[59] TN/DS/W/30 Thailand; DS/W/32 Japan.

possibility of reappointment should be abolished to strengthen the independence of the Appellate Body.[60]

Maybe the biggest bloc of mainly technical improvements and clarifications dealt with proposals regarding Art. 21 and 22 DSU concerning *implementation* of adopted reports and *countermeasures*. This area can be perceived as the one posing the greatest problems to the functioning of the dispute settlement system. It is no surprise, therefore, that most proposals address this area. The *sequencing* problem related to Articles 21 and 22 and caused by the current ambiguity of the DSU needs further clarification. Japan proposed an amendment to the DSU which would require a compliance panel to decide disagreements over measures taken to implement a panel or Appellate Body ruling before WTO members can request WTO authorisation to impose retaliatory trade sanctions. Thus, the complaining party could request authorisation to suspend concessions under Art. 22:2 DSU only after a panel found that the WTO member concerned failed to bring its measures into conformity.[61] Also the EC stated that completing the procedure under Art. 21:5 DSU is a pre-requisite for invoking the provisions of Art. 22 DSU in case the parties disagree about implementation.[62] In contrast, the US in the beginning disagreed with the rest of the WTO's members. It refused to give up its alleged right to impose sanctions before the WTO-compatibility of a contested revised regime has been examined by a WTO panel. Another contentious issue involves *carousel sanctions*.[63] Some want to limit them.[64] Further proposals dealt with enhanced *compliance panel procedures*. Contentious issues in this regard were whether prior consultations are mandatory,[65] whether appellate review is available also for compliance panel reports, and whether the infringing party has a right to enjoy any further implementation period. The introduction of a

60 TN/DS/W/47, India *et al.*

61 WT/GC/W/410. See *D. Palmeter/P. Mavroidis*, Dispute Settlement in the WTO, 2nd edition 2004, 287.

62 TN/DS/W/1. See also Canada's proposal TN/DS/W/49 to introduce new Art. 21:5*bis* DSU.

63 The DSU neither obliges the retaliating country to submit a list of products targeted for sanctions nor contains any mention of whether or not the retaliating country can change its selection of targeted products. The word 'carousel' refers to the possibility of systematically changing the list of products targeted for retaliation as and when the country wants, so long as it stays within the authorised level of retaliation.

64 Australia proposed that the list of goods subject to retaliation measures, as well as any subsequent changes to the list, should be approved by the DSB.

65 See e.g. TN/DS/W/19.

procedure for lifting sanctions allowing the DSB to *withdraw the authorisation* of countermeasures was proposed by Canada. Furthermore, strengthened *notification and examination standards* for mutually agreed settlements,[66] and more detailed obligations to *report on the status of implementation* of adopted reports were requested in order to strengthen the rule-orientation. Others wanted to promote *mutually agreed settlements*. Some called for *arbitration* procedures that determine the level of nullification or impairment at early stage, and for enhanced rules on *compensations*, for example by enabling – eventually even retroactive – monetary compensation for developing countries.[67] The possibility of the WTO members to *delay the implementation* of reports is also identified as a problem.

B. Major improvements and advancements

Those proposals that address structural deficiencies can be grouped under four subheadings: They call for an increase of the *effectiveness of countermeasures*,[68] plead for greater reforms in the way of the *panels and* the *Appellate Body function* and for more *transparency and participation*; and want to *improve flexibility and member control* over the dispute settlement mechanisms.

1. Effectiveness of countermeasures

Regarding the effectiveness of countermeasures, *far-reaching proposals advocate collective coercion, improvements in particular for developing country members that lack sufficient retaliatory power*,[69] and measures that

66 TN/DS/W/18 by India *et al.*; TN/DS/W/22 by Japan; regarding examination of mutually agreed solution the EC proposed the introduction of a new Art. 22*bis* DSU, TN/DS/W/1.

67 See TN/DS/W/9 by Ecuador and TN/DS/W/23 by Mexico.

68 For doubts on their effectivity see e.g. *M. Matsushita/T. Schoenbaum/P. Mavroidis*, The WTO, 2003, 92 *et seq.*; *B. O´Connor*, Remedies in the WTO Dispute Settlement System – The *Bananas* and *Hormones* Cases, 38 *JWT* (2004) 245–66 addressing the Doha negotiations at 261 *et seq.*

69 This issue turned up in the Banana dispute when Ecuador discovered that the amount of pressure it can exercise is negligible, see WT/DS/27/ARB/ECU. A recent case is the Gambling dispute where Antigua and Barbuda forced the US to allow the supply of gambling services via internet as panel and Appellate Body found a breach of GATS by the US. The US trade officials, however, hinted that it does not intend to change its rules to comply with the rulings, see 8 Bridges *Trade News Digest* Weekly (2004) 40. Later, the US announced its intention to implement the rulings, 9 Bridges *Trade News Digest Weekly* (2005) 19.

fasten the implementation of adopted reports. Mexico proposed to introduce the possibility of transferring an authorisation to retaliate to other WTO members. Thus, remedies would become negotiable.[70] In addition, Mexico favoured a retroactive calculation of the level of the suspension of concessions from the date of imposition of the illegal measure. This proposal intends to render the use of possibilities to retard the implementation of the rulings less attractive for the defendant. In line with this, Haiti proposed that if a least-developed country is complainant, and compensation cannot be agreed upon, the DSB shall grant authorisation to all WTO members to suspend concessions in order to promote the effective implementation of rulings made in favour of least-developed countries.[71]

Furthermore, *provisional, preventive measures* were suggested to remedy problems linked with the lack of retrospective application of the dispute settlement. A dispute settlement system that does not provide for interim measures until panels rule, loses credibility as foreign business actors in practice are locked out for at least one year, which enables local competitors to take over. Therefore, according to Mexico's proposal,[72] if a dispute was 'causing or threatening to cause damage which it would be difficult to repair', the complainant is entitled to request the panel to ask the defendant to suspend the measure during the proceedings. If the defendant refuses, the panel should, under 'exceptional circumstances', allow the complainant to 'take measures to prevent the damage'. As regards developing countries, a proposal provided for a special consideration of the specific constraints for such countries regarding suspension of concessions was made.

2. Functioning of panels and the Appellate Body

Perhaps the most far-reaching proposal concerning the composition of panels and the Appellate Body was made by the EC to *establish a permanent panel body*.[73] This proposal met with many concerns as members feared a loss of control over panel selection, doubted the necessary

70 TN/DS/W/23 and TN/DS/W/40. For a comment on the Mexican proposal see *M. Diego-Fernandez/R. Rios Herran*, The Reform of the WTO Dispute Settlement Understanding: A Closer Look at the Mexican Proposal, 1 *MJIEL* (2004) 4.

71 TN/DS/W/37.

72 TN/DS/W/40, amending Art. 12 DSU by new paragraphs 6*bis* and 6*ter*.

73 TN/DS/W/1. Regarding this very contentious proposal see the Mini Symposium on the Desirability of a WTO Permanent Panel Body, *JIEL* (2003) 175–235 with contributions by *W. Davey, T. Cottier, A. Shoyer, J. Bourgeois, M. Cartland, S. Who Chang, L. Wasescha, J. Lacarte and F. Roessler.*

expertise in a group of 24 or so panellists and felt that a roster of permanent panellists might engage in law making.[74] Others proposals, in particular by the US, regarding the functioning of the adjudicating bodies also favour an *interim review procedure in the appeal stage.* Currently, parties to a dispute have a right to see and comment on a draft of the panel report before it is finalised, but they do not see the draft Appellate Body report. Under the US proposal, parties to a dispute would have the right to see and comment on an Appellate Body report before it is made final. This is supposed to help ensure the best possible final report, since parties would have the chance to provide useful clarifications on the facts and the law, prior to the issuance of the final report.[75] By that way it allegedly could be avoided that 'panel and Appellate Body reasoning and findings . . . go beyond those aspects of the dispute that the complainant and respondent parties consider necessary to resolve the dispute'.[76] Finally, a remand authority was proposed that would enable the Appellate Body to refer cases back to the original panel if a factual issue arose at the appeal stage which had not been examined by the panel.[77]

3. Transparency and participation

Many proposals called for more (external) transparency and public participation in the dispute settlement mechanism. *Transparency of the dispute settlement procedures is one of the points of discussion in which country positions differ the most.*[78] New steps, such as an early release of reports or public access to party submissions and panel/Appellate Body hearings have been asked for in particular by the EC,[79] as in recent years WTO rulings have touched on sensitive public health and environmental concerns. *Amicus curiae briefs* (i.e. unsolicited submissions by non-parties of the dispute, *inter alia*, NGOs) were another contentious issue. The US and the EC favoured a non-state actors' right to submit *amicus curiae* briefs to panels.[80] The US as well – and less forcefully – proposed that non-governmental actors should participate as observers in dispute

[74] For other objections see *B. Mercurio*, Improving Dispute Settlement in the WTO, 38 *JWT* (2004) 795 at 813.

[75] http://usinfo.state.gov/ei/Archive/2003/Dec/31-428260.html.

[76] Proposal by US and Chile TN/DS/W/28 and TN/DS/W/52.

[77] The EC proposal TN/DS/W/38 introduced a new Art 17*bis*; see also TN/DS/W/56 by Jordan.

[78] See *B. Mercurio*, Improving Dispute Settlement in the WTO, 38 *JWT* (2004) 795 at 804 *et seq.*

[79] But also by others like e.g. Canada, TN/DS/W/41.

[80] TN/DS/W/1. The EC proposed a new Art. 13*bis* DSU on *amicus curiae* submissions. See also *D. Palmeter/P. Mavroidis*, Dispute Settlement in the WTO, 2nd edn 2004, 39.

settlement proceedings. The issues of transparency and of *amicus* briefs, however, appear to be so sensitive that no change to the system is likely. The Balas text did not provide for any changes to the DSU in this respect. In particular the proposals on *amicus curiae* briefs met resistance by developing countries as they feared that such a procedure could put developing countries at a disadvantage.[81] Surprisingly, however, the hearings in the *Beef Hormone* arbitrations were open to public. This practice of generating transparency by panel decisions granting a request by the parties might overtake the ongoing negotiations on this issue and coin the future dispute settlement practice of panels irrespective of a formal change from the DSU.

4. Flexibility and state control

Less contentious were proposals to increase *flexibility and member control of the dispute settlement* to foster the influence of the WTO members on the dispute settlement mechanisms. Those proposals intend to strengthen the diplomacy model of dispute settlement. For example, the EC[82] wants greater weight to be given to consultations through more flexibility in the determination of the reasonable implementation period according to Art. 21:3 DSU, and through new rules on the determination of compliance. Furthermore the EC wanted to give more flexibility by allowing the complainant to withdraw requests for consultations, or for the establishment of a panel at any point in time before the issuance of the final report. As soon as the request was withdrawn, the authority of the panel should lapse, and the panel should be terminated. In the same way the US[83] aimed to give parties to a dispute more control over the process to facilitate the settling of disputes and give greater flexibility to settlement process. Under the proposal, parties would be able to suspend appeal proceedings, and they have an enhanced ability to suspend panel proceedings.[84] WTO members currently have a limited ability to suspend dispute settlement proceedings. Panel proceedings can be suspended only if the panel accepts a request from a complaining party. Appeal proceedings cannot be suspended. The additional time could be important to allow parties to continue progress to reach a solution, but the current rules in

[81] TN/DS/W/47 adding a new footnote to Art. 17:6 DSU: 'The Appellate Body shall neither seek nor accept information from anyone other than the parties and third parties to a dispute'. [82] TN/DS/W/1 and W/38.

[83] http://usinfo.state.gov/ei/Archive/2003/Dec/31-428260.html.

[84] TN/DS/W/52 amendment of Art. 12:12 DSU: '*The panel shall suspend its work where the parties so agree*'.

Art. 12:12 DSU make it more difficult to do so once panel proceedings have begun. One may welcome that proposal as it does not adversely affect the authority and independence of panels and of the Appellate Body.[85]

The US and Chile also proposed to *counter-balance the automaticity of the adoption of panel/Appellate Body reports* in order to rebalance the judicial and political elements of the dispute settlement process by more flexibility for the parties if the reasoning and findings of reports go 'beyond what the parties consider to be necessary to resolve the dispute, or, in some circumstances, may even be counterproductive to resolution of the dispute. It is proposed that there should be mechanisms that would enhance the parties' flexibility to resolve the dispute and WTO members' control over the adoption process'. Therefore, a mechanism for parties had to be provided that allows the deletion by mutual agreement of findings in the report that were not necessary or helpful. This might also allow the parties to retain control over the terms of reference. Following this suggestion, WTO members would get the ability to reject specific aspects of reports that hinder settlement or do not accurately reflect the obligations that were agreed on by the negotiators.[86] At present, dispute settlement reports are a 'take it or leave it' proposition where WTO members must accept or reject dispute settlement reports in their entirety, without modification. The already mentioned proposal of an interim review at appeal stage also belongs to this category as it gives the chance to the parties to influence the final report.

In conformity with this, a *procedure for partial adoption of panel/Appellate Body rulings by the DSB* was proposed.[87] This is said to be already state of play in the DSU.[88] The possibility for the parties to mutually agree which findings of a report should not be adopted derives from the wish to control over the terms of reference, but goes beyond that and allows the parties to delete uneasy parts of the report. Such attempts have to be regarded very suspiciously.[89]

[85] As does *C. -D. Ehlermann*, 6 *JIEL* (2003) 695 at 706.

[86] See the proposed amendment to Arts. 12:7 and 17:13 DSU: 'The panel/Appellate Body shall not include in the final panel report any finding, or basic rationale behind a finding, that the parties have agreed is not to be included' and to Arts 16:4 and 17:14 DSU: 'However, the DSB may by consensus decide not to adopt a finding in the report or the basic rationale behind a finding.'

[87] Introduction of a new Art. 17*ter* DSU.

[88] *C. -D. Ehlermann*, 6 *JIEL* (2003) 695 at 707.

[89] *Ibid.* at 707 *et seq.* rejects this proposal.

Furthermore, according to the US and Chilean proposal '*some form of additional guidance to WTO adjudicative bodies* [should be provided] concerning (i) the nature and scope of the task presented to them (e.g. when the exercise of judicial economy is most useful) and (ii) rules of interpretation of the WTO agreements'.[90] This proposal derives from concerns regarding the standard of review applied by panels and the Appellate Body, and from deliberations as to how to limit the power of panels and the Appellate Body. Doubts have been expressed as to whether the Appellate Body and panels do not infrequently exceed the permitted scope of review. Such excess could result in the imposition of obligations that do not derive from the Uruguay Round texts but would create new legal obligations.[91] In particular in disputes regarding safeguard and antidumping measures such concerns have been raised.

Closely interlinked with the above-mentioned transparency issue,[92] but also connected to the attempts to enhance the role of WTO members in dispute settlement, is the reform on the role of third parties. Increased third-party rights contribute to more (internal) transparency and strengthen the position of WTO members in the dispute settlement. Until now, states interested in following the dispute settlement process only could do this if they took part as third parties, due to the confidentiality of the procedure. But third parties to a dispute are supposed not only to have an interest in the process but also in the outcome of the dispute. The EC and others[93] aim at strengthening and clarifying the rights of other WTO members who have substantial interests in a case.

V. Possible outcome: The most promising proposals

As the negotiations still continue, it is difficult to judge which of the above proposals might be accepted, all the more so some proposals appear to be motivated by an attempt to improve the position of

90 US and Chile TN/DS/W/28 and TN/DS/W/52.

91 See the statement of Senator *Max Baucus* in April 2002, http //usinfo.state.gov/ei/Archive/2003/Dec/31-318688.html (visited 31 January 2006) and *C.-D. Ehlermann*, Reflections on the Appellate Body of the WTO, 6 *JIEL* (2003) 695 at 701 *et seq.*

92 See *D. McRae*, *JIEL* (2004) 3 at 10 *et seq.*

93 See, e.g. the proposal by Taiwan on third-party participation in consultation, TN/DS/W/36 or of Costa Rica, TN/DS/W/12/Rev.1 supported by the EC, TN/DS/W/38 on time limits for third-party positions.

the particular member within the system rather than to improve the functioning and legitimacy of dispute settlement within the WTO.[94] Looking at the negotiations from outside and considering the Balas text, *it seems quite clear that those ideas that require major changes to the DSU and even tend to change the core of the dispute settlement will not find agreement.* Examples appear to be the proposals on external transparency and participation, on collective sanctions and on a permanent panel body, and some ideas on increased flexibility like the partial adoption of panel/Appellate Body reports, or the guidance to the panels/Appellate Body. *In contrast, other suggestions that allow for suspension or termination of procedures might get consent.* The rationale behind this attitude might be that the majority of the WTO members feel that the tension between power and rule orientation of the current dispute settlement mechanism[95] could be resolved to one of the two sides of dispute settlement which is unsuited to them. The current shape of this tension, which could be described as a fragile equilibrium, will be maintained as there is no consensus in which direction the DSU has to be developed. Maintaining this fragile balance is difficult though necessary against the backdrop of the unresolved core problem of WTO, *the poor and ineffective political decision-making procedures which contrast to the comparatively effective adjudication.* This systemic problem cannot and should not be solved by changes solely within the dispute settlement system. The introduction of a permanent panel body, for example, might put a strain on rule orientation, as the professionalisation of panellists could mean more law-making by panels, and would reduce the impact of the parties on the composition of the panels. In contrast, certain proposals on flexibility and improved implementation might increase the influence of the WTO members too much (e.g. the US providing panels/Appellate Body with more guidance; this proposal appears to be a reaction to the increasing number of cases lost by the US which means that the US stance is more defensive[96]). It would shift the balance between power orientation and rule orientation and

[94] *Y. Gouhua/B. Mercurio/L. Yongjie*, WTO Dispute Settlement Understanding: A Detailed Interpretation, 2005, 569.

[95] For a categorisation of the different proposals under the categories of power orientation versus rule orientation see *T. Zimmermann*, WTO Dispute Settlement at Ten: Evolution, Experiences, and Evaluation, 60 *Aussenwirtschaft* (2005) 27 at 50.

[96] *T. Zimmermann*, WTO Dispute Settlement at Ten: Evolution, Experiences, and Evaluation, 60 *Aussenwirtschaft* (2005) 27 at 44, 46.

might – by weakening adjudication – reintroduce problems of the GATT 1947 era.[97]

In light of this explanation, proposals that carefully *advance the current dispute settlement process* appear to be acceptable. The *proposal to raise the number of members of the Appellate Body*, for example, was welcomed due to an expected increase in the workload of the Appellate Body, as more than half of the panel reports are appealed. The *remand procedure at appeal stage* also seems to be acceptable, as it is a logical and necessary advancement of the quasi-judicial procedure with one adjudicative body being limited to issues of law. The proposal to avoid delay by establishing panels at first request was broadly welcomed. Proposals for fine-tuning and speeding up panel procedures and for enhanced third-party rights are also widely supported. All of these amendments have become necessary as a result of the success of the established dispute settlement mechanism. It made its own call for amendments to the DSU.

Other proposals that strengthened the influence of the parties, such as the suspension and termination of procedures, reflected a very careful approach, and therefore might be acceptable. Although the effect of the introduction of an *interim review mechanism at appeal stage* is doubtful as the Appellate Body only deals with matters of law, not of fact, and factual allegations of the parties cannot be cross-checked by the Appellate Body, this proposal seems to find agreement among negotiators. Such an interim review – though forcing the Appellate Body to discuss the law with the parties – would not oppose its independence.[98]

The *sequencing* issue will be cleared in conformity with the *ad hoc* solutions of the current DSU practice[99] that makes a compliance panel a usual pre-requisite for the authorisation of sanctions. The difference in opinion that particularly divided the EC and the US on that point is likely to be overcome.

Regarding the *clarifications of the compliance panel procedure*, agreement seems within reach that the report of the compliance panel can be appealed (see Art. 21*bis*:8 of the Balas text) and that, after the adoption of

[97] *A. von Bogdandy/M. Wagner*, The 'Sutherland Report' on WTO Reform – A Critical Appraisal, 4 *World Trade Review* (2005) 439 at 443; *B. Mercurio*, Improving Dispute Settlement in the WTO, 38 *JWT* (2004) 795 at 818 *et seq.*; *P. Sutherland et al.*, The Future of the WTO, 2004 (the so-called Sutherland report), para. 255 (though endorsing in para. 251 the suggested establishment of a special expert group of the DSB to provide criticism).

[98] *D. McRae*, Comments, 6 *JIEL* (2003) 709 at 715. Contra *C.-D. Ehlermann*, 6 *JIEL* (2003) 695 at 707.

[99] See *D. Palmeter/P. Mavroidis*, The WTO Dispute Settlement, 2nd edn 2004, 284 *et seq.*

the compliance ruling by the DSB, the 'reasonable period of time' for implementation of the decision would not be allowed (see Art. 21*bis*:9 Balas text); the complainant could go straight to the authorisation to suspend concessions according to Art. 22 of the DSU.

As developing countries argue that the DSU' s *special and differential treatment* provisions in favour of developing countries[100] have not yet produced the benefits hoped for, there certainly will be an improvement in this regard. Although the requests for the creation of an independent unit to provide legal assistance to developing countries have lost momentum since the establishment of the Advisory Centre on WTO Law in July 2001, nevertheless the WTO secretariat is likely to be strengthened to meet demands from developing country members which also called for dispute settlement funds. Other issues of particular importance for the developing countries, in particular their concerns about the effectiveness of the current retaliation instruments for small countries, appear not to find acceptance, all the more since those proposals that suggest retroactive remedies, monetary compensation or joint retaliation were not intensively discussed during last year.

VI. Conclusion

The tension between the judicial model of dispute resolution and the diplomatic model is inherent in WTO dispute resolution and will continue to be meaningful and important. Both sides of the dispute settlement process have to be maintained.[101] The diplomatic side of the dispute settlement is necessary as not all WTO disputes can be appropriately resolved through judicial decision making.[102] On a more domestic level, alternative means of dispute resolution, such as mediation are progressing, thereby amending or partly replacing mere adjudication.[103] This tension was not only decisive for the inception of a DSU review process, it is also decisive for the individual suggestions received during the review process and ultimately, for its outcome. Therefore, the success of the diverse proposals for review will depend on the extent to which they help to keep the tension between the two sides of a dispute settlement mecha-

[100] Cf. Qureshi, chapter 5 of this book.

[101] See also *J. Pauwelyn*, The Transformation of World Trade, 104 *Michigan Law Review* 1 (2005) 1 at 45 *et seq.*

[102] *S. Essermann/R. Howse*, The WTO on Trial, 82 *Foreign Affairs* (2003) 130 at 136; *D. McRae*, 7 *JIEL* (2004) 3 at 19.

[103] See *D. McRae*, 7 *JIEL* (2004) 3 at 9 *et seq.*

nism (either mere adjudication or mere diplomacy) under control. Proposals that do not try to resolve this tension in one direction either because they are merely technical clarifications or cautious advancements, or because they can be counterbalanced by other proposals might prove to be acceptable to the community of WTO members. It is to be expected that the review process will lead to very carefully considered improvements which will not bring dramatic changes.[104] Thus, the mandate of the Doha Agenda to improve and clarify the DSU certainly will not be stretched too far. It is doubtful, however, whether such careful advancement of the dispute settlement mechanism will be a lasting and sustainable success. *In particular the problem of safeguarding sound implementation of DSB decisions which require efficient countermeasures and compliance mechanisms will remain on the agenda as novel and more ambitious suggestions in this regard* (e.g. collective retaliation, retroactive monetary compensation, tradeable rights to suspend concessions) *will not be accepted.* This is particularly regrettable[105] since the Doha Round was called a development round. *These suggestions which were of particular interest to the developing countries have no chance of being realised*, contrary to the alleged development purpose of the Doha Round. The development purpose is also endangered in this area of the Doha Round.

[104] See also *B. Mercurio*, Improving Dispute Settlement in the World Trade Organization, 38 *JWT* (2004) 795 at 798, 851 *et seq.*; *P. Sutherland et al.*, The Future of the WTO, 2004 (the so-called Sutherland report), para. 214, 254.

[105] Accord *W. Davey*, The Sutherland Report on Dispute Settlement, 8 *JIEL* (2005) 321 at 322–5; *B. Mercurio*, Improving Dispute Settlement in the WTO, 38 *JWT* (2004) 795 at 825, 845, 854. Cf. also *M. Bronckers/N. van den Broek*, Financial Compensation in the WTO. Improving the Remedies of WTO Dispute Settlement, 8 *JIEL* (2005) 101 at 109 *et seq.*, 121 *et seq.*

13

The WTO dispute settlement system: Jurisdiction, interpretation and remedies

DEBRA STEGER (*)

I. WTO – An integral part of public international law

WTO law does not exist in a *vacuum*; it is part of international law. The Appellate Body emphasised, in its very first case, that the provisions of the *Marrakesh Agreement Establishing the World Trade Organization* (the *WTO Agreement*) are not to be read in 'clinical isolation' from public international law.[1] What status does 'non-WTO law' – customary international law, general international law or treaties between parties to a dispute – have in WTO dispute settlement? Can WTO panels and the Appellate Body take 'non-WTO' international legal rules into account in deciding a case under the WTO Agreement, and if so, what status should they be accorded?

II. Jurisdiction of the WTO

In the WTO, the *Understanding on Rules and Procedures Governing the Settlement of Disputes* (the 'DSU') applies only to 'disputes brought pursuant to the consultation and dispute settlement provisions of the agreements listed in Appendix 1 to the Understanding' (the 'covered agreements'). Therefore, under the DSU, WTO panels and the Appellate Body have *jurisdiction* to hear cases involving 'claims' brought under the dispute settlement provisions of the covered agreements. Claims may be based on allegations of violations of specific obligations contained in the covered agreements or involve so-called 'non-violation' complaints or 'situation' complaints.

The WTO is one of the few international dispute resolution mechanisms that has compulsory jurisdiction over disputes arising under

(*) University of Ottawa, Faculty of Law; former Director, WTO Appellate Body Secretariat

1 *United States–Standards for Reformulated and Conventional Gasoline*, WT/DS2/AB/R, adopted 20 May 1996, at p. 17.

its covered agreements. A panel will be established by the Dispute Settlement Body of the WTO (the 'DSB') upon the request of a complaining party, unless there is a consensus to the contrary. Furthermore, rulings of panels and of the Appellate Body are legally binding upon the parties – a losing party cannot block a panel or Appellate Body report from being adopted by the DSB. Moreover, Article 23 of the DSU requires that when a WTO Member seeks redress of a violation of obligations or nullification or impairment of benefits under the covered agreements, it must use the procedures of the DSU. Thus, the WTO dispute settlement system has both *compulsory jurisdiction* and *exclusive jurisdiction* over matters arising between WTO Members under the covered agreements.

III. Applicable law

Professor Joost Pauwelyn in his book, 'Conflict of norms in public international law: How WTO law relates to other rules of international law',[2] takes the view that once a complainant has made specific claims relating to provisions of a WTO-covered agreement, a defendant may invoke defences based on other 'non-WTO' international law, including customary international law, treaties and other legal instruments legally in force between the parties to the dispute. Although he states that a complainant may only rely on the rules in WTO agreements as the legal basis for its claims, he contemplates the possibility that a complainant may base a 'non-violation' claim, in part, on 'non-WTO' law, in particular, bilateral treaties or instruments binding on the parties to the dispute.

His arguments are complex, and I will not attempt to summarise all of them. The crux of his thesis is that in disputes about government measures that have both trade and non-trade aspects, in which the parties to the dispute have legally binding, mutual obligations under the WTO and also under other international agreements and instruments, if there is a conflict between a WTO obligation and a non-WTO obligation, general international law rules should be applied to determine which obligation takes priority. In a case, for example, involving a measure that violates a WTO rule against prohibition of imports of certain products, and that at the same time, is required by a mandatory provision in an environmental treaty, if there is a conflict between the two obligations, Professor Pauwelyn would apply the *lex specialis* and *lex posterior* rules to determine

[2] Joost Pauwelyn, Conflict of Norms in Public International Law: How WTO Law Relates to Other Rules of International Law, Cambridge University Press, 2003.

which obligation takes priority. If the environmental treaty was concluded subsequent to the *WTO Agreement*, deals with the more specific subject matter and is legally binding on both parties to the dispute, a WTO panel and the Appellate Body, in his view, should apply the rules in the environmental treaty over the conflicting rules in the WTO Agreement (*lex posterior*).

Although the *pacta sunt servanda* principle requires that States must perform all of their international obligations in good faith, there is nothing in the *WTO Agreement* that indicates that panels and the Appellate Body constitute a court of general jurisdiction for determining and enforcing all international obligations between Members of the WTO. To the extent that there is an international court with general jurisdiction, it is the International Court of Justice, not WTO panels and the Appellate Body. And, the ICJ does not have compulsory jurisdiction. The practical fact that there is compulsory jurisdiction in the WTO, although it may create certain inequities with respect to enforcement of obligations under other treaties, is not sufficient, in itself, to extend the jurisdiction of WTO panels and the Appellate Body into areas of international law they were never intended, and are not competent, to adjudicate. One cannot simply infer from the principle of *pacta sunt servanda* that WTO Members consented to grant jurisdiction to WTO panels and the Appellate Body to adjudicate on obligations arising under treaties other than the *WTO Agreement*.

The *WTO Agreement* deals with the relations of WTO Members 'in the field of trade and economic endeavour'.[3] *The WTO is not, and cannot, deal with issues relating to the protection of the environment, human rights, labour standards or public health until and unless its Members agree to extend its mandate into these areas. This is not likely to occur in the foreseeable future.* In the Doha Ministerial Declaration, WTO Members agreed to commence negotiations on certain specific issues related to the relationship between the *WTO Agreement* and the multilateral environmental agreements[4] and to clarify certain exceptions in the *Agreement on Trade-Related Intellectual Property Rights* to allow greater access to medicines in the poorer countries of the world, but they did not agree to negotiate more generally on issues related to the environment, public health, labour standards and human rights. Although WTO Members are

[3] Preamble to the *Marrakesh Agreement Establishing the World Trade Organization*, first paragraph.

[4] See Murase and Taira, chapters 17 and 18 in this book.

cognisant that there are overlapping areas of jurisdiction between the WTO and other international treaties, and are aware that there have been some problems arising from the interaction between obligations under these various instruments, they have not as yet given their consent to allow the adjudicative bodies, the panels and the Appellate Body, the mandate to determine rights and obligations as between these various international legal instruments.

A close examination of the rules and procedures of the DSU demonstrates that WTO Members intended that disputes should be resolved pursuant to the rights and obligations contained in the WTO covered agreements. Article 3(2) of the DSU provides, first, that the dispute settlement system of the WTO 'serves to preserve the rights and obligations of Members under the covered agreements, and to clarify the existing provisions of those agreements in accordance with customary rules of interpretation of public international law'. It also stipulates that: 'Recommendations and rulings of the DSB cannot add to or diminish the rights and obligations provided in the covered agreements.' Reference is made three times in paragraph 3(2) to 'rights and obligations' or 'provisions' under the 'covered agreements'. Similarly, throughout the other General Provisions of Article 3, and repeatedly in the rest of the DSU, there are repeated references to 'rights and obligations' under the 'covered agreements'.

A party may request consultations or the establishment of a panel relating only to matters arising under the 'covered agreements'.[5] Panels are usually established with standard terms of reference pursuant to Article 7(1) and (2) of the DSU which require them to 'examine, in the light of the relevant provisions in (name of the covered agreement(s) cited by the parties to the dispute), the matter referred to the DSB . . . and to make such findings as will assist the DSB in making the recommendations or in giving the rulings provided for in that/those agreements'.[6] Panels are also directed to 'address all relevant provisions in any covered agreement or agreements cited by the parties to the dispute'.[7] (Emphasis added.)

Article 11 of the DSU is an important provision setting out the 'Functions of Panels'. It stipulates that a panel is required to 'make an objective assessment of the matter before it, including an objective

[5] See Articles 4(2) and 6 read together with Article 7 of the DSU, as well as the many cases on the specificity of panel requests under Article 6(2) of the DSU.

[6] DSU, Article 7(1).

[7] *Ibid.*, Article 7(2).

assessment of the facts of the case, and the applicability of and conformity with the relevant covered agreements, and make such other findings as will assist the DSB in making the recommendations or in giving the rulings provided for in the covered agreements'.

Professor Pauwelyn accords great weight to the phrase 'and to make such other findings as will assist the DSB' that appears in Articles 7(1) and 11 of the DSU. He infers from this language that WTO Members clearly intended to include all international law as 'applicable law' in WTO disputes brought pursuant to claims relating to the covered agreements. However, in doing so, he conveniently ignores two clear obligations on panels, in both Articles 7 and 11, to examine whether a measure is consistent with the relevant provisions of the relevant covered agreements and to make recommendations and rulings as 'provided for in the covered agreements'.

We also cannot ignore the express language in the DSU relating to the kinds of rulings and recommendations that panels and the Appellate Body may make. In Article 19, panels and the Appellate Body are told that when they conclude that a measure is inconsistent with a covered agreement, they 'shall recommend that the Member concerned bring its measure into conformity with that agreement'. This is consistent with the language in Article 3(4) requiring that 'recommendations or rulings made by the DSB shall be aimed at achieving a satisfactory settlement of the matter in accordance with the rights and obligations under this Understanding and under the covered agreements'. To emphasise the importance of this obligation, Article 19(2) repeats the rule in Article 3(2) that the findings and recommendations of panels and the Appellate Body, which are adopted as the rulings and recommendations of the DSB, 'cannot add to or diminish the rights and obligations provided in the covered agreements'.

Professor Pauwelyn argues that panels and the Appellate Body would not 'add to or diminish' the rights and obligations in the *WTO Agreement* by applying other international law in force between the parties to a dispute because that other international law is also binding on those parties. However, his analysis, once again, ignores the clear wording in two provisions of the DSU which emphasise that panels, the Appellate Body and the DSB do not have the legal authority to 'add to or diminish' the 'rights and obligations provided in the covered agreements'. If ever there was a clear statement as to the applicable law in WTO dispute settlement, Articles 3(2) and 19(2) confirm that WTO disputes must be decided pursuant to the provisions of the covered agreements. This does not allow WTO cases to be decided on the basis of provisions of other treaties, for example, regional trade agreements or environmental treaties between the same parties.

IV. Taking account of international law

Having said that WTO panels and the Appellate Body may not determine Members' rights and obligations *on the basis* of provisions of other treaties and legal instruments, this does *not* mean that they should not take other international law *into account* in deciding disputes arising under the *WTO Agreement* or seek guidance from the experience and practice of other international tribunals in dealing with matters of practice and procedure.

The Appellate Body has often referred to public international law, including other treaties and legal instruments in force between the parties, in *interpreting* provisions of the *WTO Agreement*. Article 3(2) directs panels and the Appellate Body 'to clarify the existing provisions of those agreements' in accordance with customary rules of interpretation of public international law, and Articles 31 and 32 of the *Vienna Convention on the Law of Treaties* (the *Vienna Convention*) have been consistently applied as a tool in interpretation of those obligations.[8] Neither Article 3(2) of the DSU nor Articles 31 and 32 of the *Vienna Convention* provide that all international legal obligations in force between the two States must be examined and applied by a treaty interpreter determining whether a WTO Member has acted consistently with its obligations under the *WTO Agreement*. Those provisions do not prescribe the applicable law in a dispute brought under the *WTO Agreement*. Rather, they set out a method of interpretation of the provisions of a treaty.

Professor Donald McRae has emphasised that, in his view, Article 3(2) of the DSU is not a broad mandate for incorporation of all principles of public international law into the *WTO Agreement*. 'Principles of customary international law', he has maintained, 'do not leapfrog into treaty regimes and add to substantive obligations under those regimes. They exist alongside of and are relevant to the interpretation and application of substantive treaty rules'.[9]

[8] For the interpretation under Art. 31 para. 3 *lit.* c Vienna Convention 'in harmony with other applicable international law'. See also Hohmann, 46 Recht der Internationalen Wirtschaft (2000), at 88 *et seq.*, on the one hand and Taira, in chapter 18 of this book, on the other.

[9] Donald McRae, 'Comments on Presentation by Claus-Dieter Ehlermann's Presentation on the Role and Record of the Dispute Settlement Panels and the Appellate Body of the WTO', 6:3 *J of Int'l Econ L* 709, at 713 (September 2003).

In the same way, international obligations under treaties other than the WTO may influence and inform the process of interpretation and clarification of WTO rights and obligations. For example, in *United States–Import Prohibition on Shrimp (Article 21.5 Malaysia)*, the Appellate Body referred to the Inter-American Convention for the Protection and Conservation of Sea Turtles as a benchmark to guide it in its interpretation of the chapeau to the general exceptions in Article XX of the GATT 1994. In that case, the Appellate Body did not *apply* the provisions of the Inter-American Convention as WTO law, however, it referred to them as evidence of a factual benchmark in its interpretation of Article XX of the GATT 1994.

As Judge Rosalyn Higgins has counselled, rather than the WTO Appellate Body interpreting and applying rules of other international agreements, 'the better way forward . . . is for us all to keep ourselves well informed'.[10] The WTO Appellate Body should continue doing as it has done, keeping up-to-date with the case law of the International Court of Justice as well as of the European Court of Justice and the tribunals of other regional and international agreements. But *being aware* of the rulings of other international tribunals, and *keeping informed and cognisant* of the obligations under other treaty regimes and international instruments, is not the same as applying rules, obligations and decisions from non-WTO sources of international law in deciding rights and obligations under the *WTO Agreement.*

V. Filling in gaps: The special case of remedies

While panels and the Appellate Body only have the jurisdiction to consider claims raised under the provisions of the covered agreements, they have often referred to international law when interpreting and applying WTO rules. The Appellate Body has also, in several cases, referred to customary international law and the practice of other international tribunals when it was faced with issues relating to procedure or practice on which the DSU and the other covered agreements are silent. An example is *European Communities–Regime for the Importation, Sale and Distribution of Bananas*, in which the issues of standing and representation by private counsel were decided after reference to customary international law and the practice of international tribunals.[11] Other early examples

[10] Rosalyn Higgins, 'The ICJ, the ECJ and the Integrity of International Law', 52 *International and Comparative Law Quarterly* 1, at 20 (2003).

[11] *EC–Bananas*, WT/DS27/AB/R, adopted 25 September 1997, at paras. 133 and 10.

were: *United States–Measure Affecting Imports of Woven Wool Shirts and Blouses from India*, in which the issue of burden of proof first arose,[12] and *India–Patent Protection for Pharmaceutical and Agricultural Chemical Products*, in which the Appellate Body referred to an ICJ case in deciding how to treat municipal law.[13] In such cases, it is entirely appropriate for the Appellate Body to look to customary international law and to the practice of other international tribunals for guidance.

Panels and the Appellate Body may be called upon, in future, to make rulings on another important subject that is critical to the efficacy of the WTO dispute settlement system, that is, remedies. The DSU has some provisions dealing with remedies, but they are ambiguous and incomplete.[14] Should panels and the Appellate Body have recourse to customary international law, which has extensive rules on remedies, to fill in the gaps that exist in the DSU and the other covered agreements? There is a real problem in cases under the WTO agreements relating to anti-dumping, safeguards and countervail, in particular, in that prospective remedies really provide no remedy at all in those cases. In my view, panels and the Appellate Body should look to customary international law to help design remedies under covered agreements in situations in which the DSU and the agreements concerned are silent and when resort to the 'usual' WTO prospective remedy would deny the complaining party any 'real' remedy.

Is there an obligation under WTO law and/or under international law to comply with the recommendations and rulings of the DSB in a WTO dispute settlement case? Related, but also difficult, issues are what constitutes compliance and what remedies are available in the WTO?

Article 19.1 of the DSU requires a panel or the Appellate Body, when it finds that a Member has acted inconsistently with its WTO obligations, to *recommend* that the Member concerned bring its measures into conformity with the agreements. This paragraph provides '[i]n addition, the panel or Appellate Body may suggest ways in which the Member concerned may implement the recommendations'.

Most recognised legal experts agree that a 'recommendation' in an adopted panel or Appellate Body report is a legally binding order in international law. Professor Robert Hudec has stated:

> Despite the softer connotation of the word 'recommendation', the traditional understanding of the word 'recommendation' in GATT/WTO

[12] *US–Wool Shirts and Blouses*, WT/DS33/AB/R, adopted 23 May 1997, at p. 14.

[13] *India–Patents*, WT/DS50/AB/R, adopted 16 January 1998, at para. 66.

[14] See Articles 3.7, 19.1, 21 and 22 of the DSU.

jurisprudence has been that, when approved by the plenary body acting for the full membership, it is a legally binding order.[15]

Professor John Jackson has maintained, moreover, that there is an international legal obligation to remove a measure found to be inconsistent with a Member's WTO obligations, contrary to the view, shared by a number of WTO Members, that a Member may choose between withdrawing the measure, offering compensation, or risking retaliation for non-compliance.[16] Professor Christine Gray, in examining the practice of the International Court of Justice as compared to that of the WTO, has stated that, in her view, the argument that after a finding of breach of its obligations, a Member is free to choose whether to comply or not to comply and to pay compensation or risk retaliation is 'hardly a serious argument'.[17]

There is a WTO 'mantra' that remedies are 'prospective', that is, that they apply as from the date of expiry of the reasonable period of time. While it is true that the majority of WTO panels, consistent with the experience under the GATT 1947 and the Tokyo Round Agreements, have simply recommended that Members bring their measures into conformity with their obligations, there is no provision in the DSU, in the GATT 1947 or 1994, or in any of the other covered agreements that stipulates that remedies must be applied prospectively. There have been some cases, in particular, dealing with safeguards, textile safeguards, anti-dumping and countervailing duties, in which panels have suggested or ruled that orders be revoked and duties refunded.

In public international law, not all remedies are prospective. Specific remedies are not necessarily provided for in treaties, as this is a subject that is generally understood to be within the discretion of the judicial

[15] Robert E. Hudec, 'Broadening the Scope of Remedies in WTO Dispute Settlement', in Friedl Weiss & Jochem Wiers, (eds.), Improving WTO Dispute Settlement Procedures: Issues and Lessons from the Practice of other International Courts and Tribunals, (Cameron May 2000) 345–77.

[16] John H. Jackson, 'The WTO Dispute Settlement Understanding – Misunderstanding on the nature of legal obligation', 91 *Am. J. Int'l. L.* 60 (1997); cf. Judith Hippler Bello, 'The WTO Dispute Settlement Understanding – Less is more', 90 *Am. J. Int'l. L.* 416 (1996); T. M. Reif and M. Forestal, 'The revenge of push-me, pull-you: The implementation process under the WTO dispute Settlement Understanding', 32 *The International Lawyer* 755 (1998); R. H. Yerxa and D. J. Marantis, 'Assessing the New WTO Dispute Settlement System: A US Perspective', 32 *The International Lawyer* 795 (1998).

[17] Christine Gray, 'Types of Remedies in ICJ Cases: Lessons for the WTO?', in Friedl Weiss & Jochem Wiers (eds.) Improving WTO Dispute Settlement Procedures: Issues and Lessons from the Practice of other International Courts and Tribunals, (Cameron May 2000) 411.

bodies. In the *Chorzow Factories* case, the Permanent Court of International Justice (the predecessor of the International Court of Justice) stated that:

> . . . it is a principle of international law that a breach of an engagement involves an obligation to make reparation in an adequate form. Reparation therefore, is the indispensable complement of a failure to apply a convention and there is no necessity for this to be stated in the convention itself.[18]

There is considerable customary international law on the question of remedies, which is being codified by the International Law Commission (ILC). The ILC Draft Articles on State Responsibility (ILC Draft Articles) have been quoted favourably by the WTO Appellate Body and panels in recent cases and seem to be generally recognised as expressing accepted principles of customary international law. The ILC Draft Articles deal only with remedies where an internationally wrongful act has been committed; they are applicable, therefore, only in cases involving violation complaints in the WTO.

According to the ILC Draft Articles 41 and 42, a State which has committed an illegal act has two obligations:

(a) to cease the illegal act ('cessation of wrongful conduct'); and
(b) to provide reparation to the injured party(ies).

The first obligation appears to be recognised in Article 19.1 of the DSU in that panels and the Appellate Body are obligated to recommend that the Member concerned bring its measure into conformity with its obligations. Once the panel and/or Appellate Body reports are adopted by the DSB, moreover, those recommendations become legally binding on the Member concerned. In international law, this obligation to cease the illegal act exists whether or not the injured party requests such a ruling or recommendation in the particular case.

One could argue that an obligation to provide reparation exists in customary international law and, as it has not been superseded by any specific provision in the DSU or any other covered agreement, therefore, it could be applied in the WTO. In order to be awarded the remedy of reparation, however, an injured party must specifically claim it in the case at hand. In such a case, the judges or the arbitrators have the discretion to decide whether or not to grant reparation. Reparation can take many

[18] 1929 PCIJ Series A, No. 8, 4, at 21.

forms: *restitutio in integrum*, restitution by equivalent (compensation), satisfaction, and/or guarantees for non-repetition.

Articles 43 and 44 of the ILC Draft Articles establish that *restitutio in integrum*, or bringing the situation back to the state that existed before the wrongful act was committed, is the preferred course of action. This is a retrospective remedy. Where it is not feasible to reinstate the previous situation, then compensation in an equivalent amount through, *inter alia*, damages for losses sustained, may be awarded.

Article 3.7 of the DSU sets up the following hierarchy:

> . . . the first objective of the dispute settlement system is usually to secure the withdrawal of the measures concerned if these are found to be inconsistent with any of the provisions of the covered agreements. The provision of compensation should be resorted to only if the immediate withdrawal of the measure is impracticable and as a temporary measure pending the withdrawal of the measure which is inconsistent with a covered agreement. The last resort which this Understanding provides to the Member invoking the dispute settlement procedures is the possibility of suspending the application of concessions or other obligations on a discriminatory basis vis-à-vis the other Member, subject to authorization by the DSB of such measures.[19]

The first obligation in the WTO hierarchy is to 'withdraw' or remove the inconsistent measure. Withdrawal of an inconsistent measure, moreover, when read in the context of the second sentence of Article 3.7 above, is required to be 'immediate', and compensation may be resorted to only in cases in which immediate withdrawal is impracticable. In *Australia–Subsidies Provided to Producers and Exporters of Automotive Leather: Recourse by the United States to Article 21.5 of the DSU*, the panel held in the context of Article 4.7 of the Subsidies and Countervailing Measures Agreement (SCM Agreement) that a recommendation to 'withdraw the subsidy' is '**not** limited to prospective action only but may encompass repayment of the prohibited subsidy'.[20] The panel did not accept the parties' arguments that only the 'prospective' part of the benefit should be withdrawn. Rather, the panel found that there was no basis for repayment of anything less than the full subsidy in the circumstances of that case.[21] A major consideration for that panel was that withdrawal of the

[19] This language in the DSU is almost a verbatim extract from the 1979 Understanding Regarding Notification, Consultation, Dispute Settlement and Surveillance.

[20] *Australia–Automotive Leather: Recourse to Article 21.5*, WT/DS126/RW, adopted 11 February 2000; DSR 2000:III, 1189, at para. 6.39 (emphasis in the original).

[21] *Ibid.*, at paras. 6.45 and 6.49.

subsidy was intended by the drafters of the *SCM Agreement* to be a specific and effective remedy for violations of the prohibited subsidy obligations.

While it has been the general practice of GATT and WTO panels to recommend only that Members 'bring their measures into conformity with their obligations', that language in and of itself does not preclude the possibility of retrospective application. Indeed, what 'withdrawal' or 'bringing a measure into conformity' means in a particular case should depend very much on the nature of the measure concerned. In a simple example, where the measure at issue is legislation, 'bringing that measure into conformity' may call for repeal of the legislation (and possible replacement with another measure). In *U.S.–1916 Anti-dumping Act*, the panel recommended that the United States bring its legislation into conformity with its WTO obligations and suggested that one way to do that would be to repeal the statute.[22] The panel in *Australia–Leather: Recourse to Article 21.5* was correct in emphasising that the effectiveness of the remedy should be an important consideration in determining whether a Member has complied with its obligations.

The following conclusions can be drawn from the foregoing analysis. First, recommendations and rulings of the DSB in dispute settlement cases are binding legal orders in international law. Second, there is a legal obligation to comply by withdrawing or revoking the measure found to be inconsistent with a Member's obligations. Whether or not the Member concerned decides to replace the inconsistent measure with another measure does not change the legal requirement to revoke or repeal the original measure found to be inconsistent.[23] A Member does not have a choice to revoke the inconsistent measure or to offer compensation to the complaining party or to risk suspension of concessions. There is an obligation to comply, and compliance usually involves withdrawing or revoking the inconsistent measure. Compensation or suspension of concessions are available only when immediate compliance is not practicable, and are only temporary (not permanent) measures intended to encourage compliance.

[22] WT/DS136/R, WT/DS162/R (complaints by EC and Japan), adopted 26 September 2000, at para. 6.292.

[23] The replacement measure may also be challenged in an Article 21.5 proceeding if there is a disagreement as to whether or not it is consistent with the Member's obligations, however, the replacement measure is a different measure from that which was found to be inconsistent in the first place. It is important to separate out these two measures in any analysis of whether or not the recommendations of the DSB have been followed.

Finally, while Members are of the general view that remedies are prospective, there is nothing in the DSU, in the GATT 1994, or in any of the other covered agreements that explicitly requires this. It is true that most GATT and WTO panels have simply recommended that the Member concerned bring its measure into conformity with its obligations under the covered agreements, but this does not mean that panels do not have the authority to make other, more specific recommendations and suggestions. Article 19.1 was clarified in the Uruguay Round to provide that panels may make suggestions as to the ways in which a Member should implement the recommendations of the DSB. The fact that few panels have exercised this authority does not mean that it does not exist.

Customary international law relating to remedies, furthermore, may apply to WTO disputes, particularly in areas where the DSU and the other covered agreements are silent. Despite the perceptions of Members as to 'usual GATT practice', unless it can be demonstrated that there is such a practice, there should be room to argue that customary international law relating to remedies applies in WTO cases. This has not been tested as yet in any real sense. If such arguments were to be made, it is likely that the first instance panels might take a conservative view in keeping with the general views of WTO Members, but the Appellate Body may take a different view based on public international law.

Except for the explicit provisions of the DSU, remedies are generally within the discretion of panels and the Appellate Body. As each WTO agreement is unique, to be effective, different remedies could be designed for different agreements.

VI. Conclusion

The WTO is a specialised treaty regime dealing with trade and economic relations among its Members. Its dispute settlement system exists to resolve disputes relating to obligations under the WTO covered agreements, it is not an international court of general jurisdiction.

The Appellate Body has recognised that the WTO Agreement does not exist in 'clinical isolation' from public international law. The WTO is an integral part of international law. Recognising this, the Appellate Body has frequently looked to public international law, including decisions of other international and regional tribunals, for guidance in interpreting and applying WTO obligations.

As some questions of practice and procedure are not expressly provided for in the DSU, the Appellate Body has sought guidance from the practice of other international legal systems and tribunals. What the Appellate Body has done in these cases, however, is to seek guidance from, or to be informed by, international law and the practice of other tribunals. Where it finds consistent interpretation or practice, the Appellate Body has some measure of comfort that it is proceeding in the right direction. By continuing to inform itself of the law and practice of other international tribunals, the Appellate Body can encourage more harmony in the interpretation and application of international law.

There are limits, however, on what a specialised international tribunal, created by the Members of a treaty regime, can and should do. There is a role as well for the legislative bodies of the WTO. The WTO Ministerial Conference and the General Council have the exclusive authority to adopt binding interpretations or to waive obligations under the *Marrakesh Agreement Establishing the WTO*. There are also complex and specific amendment procedures provided in that *Agreement*.

It is not the role of the WTO panels and Appellate Body to resolve inconsistencies in the application of various treaty obligations. That is the responsibility of the WTO Members themselves. If the means for taking decisions and amending the agreements are too cumbersome, ways must be sought to improve the WTO legislative process to make it more effective, rather than ask the Appellate Body to carry the responsibility for the system as a whole.

14

An evaluation of the role of legal aid in international dispute resolution with emphasis on the Advisory Centre on WTO Law

PETINA GAPPAH*

Access to international justice should not be impeded by financial inequality.

H.E. Judge Gilbert Guillaume, President of the International Court of Justice[1]

Today, and within the framework of the WTO dispute settlement system, the Advisory Centre for WTO Law takes another, almost revolutionary, step forward in international adjudication, by establishing itself as the first true centre for legal aid within the international legal system.

Michael Moore, Former Director of the WTO[2]

I. Introduction

The Advisory Centre on WTO Law (the 'ACWL') is the only international organisation that was created specifically to provide dedicated legal assistance to developing countries and least developed countries.[3] As the ACWL's Management Board noted in a recent Report, when the founders

* Counsel, Advisory Centre on WTO Law (www.acwl.ch). The views expressed in this chapter are the personal views of the author and do not necessarily represent the views of the Advisory Centre on WTO Law. The author is grateful to Frieder Roessler and Niall Meagher for their comments on this chapter.

[1] Part of a speech delivered to the General Assembly of the United Nations, 30 October 2001, See www.icj-cij.org/icjwww/ipresscom/ipress2001/ipresscom2001-31_GA_20011030.htm, last visited 11 May 2005.

[2] Part of a speech delivered on the occasion of the inauguration of the ACWL, 5 October 2001. See www.acwl.ch, last visited 11 May 2005.

[3] The ACWL was also established to provide assistance to countries with economies in transition. The term developing countries in this chapter therefore includes those countries. Further, the term developing countries in this chapter includes WTO customs territories that have developing country status.

of the ACWL decided to create an intergovernmental organisation designed to enhance the credibility of the WTO dispute settlement system and to ensure that developing and least developed countries could participate effectively in that system by providing legal aid in WTO dispute settlement proceedings and WTO law generally, they implemented an idea that had never previously been tried in practice in international relations.[4]

The ACWL is the only organisation in international law that exclusively provides legal assistance to developing countries and least developed countries. Legal aid has been provided through other schemes to enable poor countries to litigate and thus defend and pursue their interests. Thus, trust funds have been set up by various tribunals to assist litigants and secretariats have been tasked with providing technical and legal assistance.

This chapter (i) examines the problems and constraints faced by developing countries in international dispute resolution, and especially, in the multilateral trading system, (ii) discusses the need for legal aid in international dispute resolution, (iii) describes some of the challenges that have been encountered in providing this legal aid and (iv) discusses the unique role of the ACWL in the multilateral trading system.

II. The need for legal aid

A. Problems and constraints of developing countries

Many countries provide legal aid to those unable to pay for the services of lawyers in their domestic legal systems. These services have been recognised as a legal right by some domestic courts, which have taken the view that the provision of legal aid constitutes an important component of the right to equal protection under the law.[5] At regional level, the European

[4] The ACWL After Four Years: A Progress Report by the Management Board, para. 2, ACWL/GA/2005/1, ACWL/MB/2005/1, available on the ACWL website www.acwl.ch (the 'ACWL Progress Report').

[5] See for instance: *Airey* v. *Ireland* (1979) where the European Court on Human Rights declared a right to counsel in civil cases based on the 'fair hearing' guarantee of the European Convention on Human Rights and Fundamental Freedoms; *New Brunswick* v. *J.G.* (1999) where the Supreme Court of Canada declared constitutional the right to counsel in civil cases relating to child custody; and *Nkuzi Development Association* v. *Legal Aid Board* (2001), where the Land Claims Court of South Africa declared that the right to a 'fair hearing' in the South African Constitution requires the government to provide indigents with free counsel in proceedings under the Land Tenure Act.

Court of Human Rights, the European Court of Justice and the Court of the European Free Trade Area all have legal assistance funds for the benefit of individuals seeking recourse to those *fora*.

Access to the law by all members of a society is considered an important measure of the legitimacy of that society's legal order. Similarly, in the international legal system, the participation of developing countries in international dispute resolution, and their engagement and participation in the system is central to the acceptability of legal norms, and the primacy of the rule of law.[6]

The resource and access disparities that necessitate legal aid at the domestic or regional levels also exist at the international level. International legal regimes are often complex and generally understood only by specialised legal experts. Therefore, only countries that either have the necessary legal expertise themselves or are in a position to purchase the required legal services can effectively assert their rights under these regimes. The fact that developing countries lack this expertise is reflected in the fact that most of the lawyers who represent them before international tribunals are not nationals of those countries. This is true, for instance, at the International Court of Justice (the 'ICJ').[7] In contrast to the situation of developing countries, many developed countries have entire departments dedicated to overseeing the enforcement of international legal norms, and they often have separate departments for different treaty regimes.

Least-developed countries are at a particular disadvantage. There are many least-developed countries in which only one civil servant (who is often not a lawyer) is responsible for compliance with several different international legal issues.

[6] This view has been expressed in the context of the multilateral trading system. Professor Claus-Dieter Ehlermann, former Chairman of the Appellate Body said the following in his remarks on the inauguration of the ACWL:

> Ultimately, the [ACWL] will benefit the 'rules-based' multilateral trading system, and strengthen the notion that the dispute settlement system of the WTO is available to the economically weak as much as it is available to the economically strong.

See speech delivered on the occasion of the inauguration of the ACWL, 5 October 2001, available at www.acwl.ch, last visited 11 May 2005.

[7] A 2002 survey revealed that 'lawyers from only six developing countries have pleaded before the [ICJ], as contrasted to 142 developed-country lawyers appearing a total of 265 times'. See Cesare Romano, International Justice and Developing Countries: A Qualitative Analysis, The Law and Practice of International Courts and Tribunals, Vol. 1, No. 2, August 2002, p. 559.

The typical lack of resources in developing and least-developed countries may sometimes have an impact on international dispute resolution, and ultimately, on the delivery of justice. The cost of the legal services required to plead a case before an international tribunal can be prohibitive for many developing countries. In addition to the complexity of the substantive international law, the complexity of the litigation process in international tribunals makes international dispute settlement proceedings a daunting task for many developing countries. This is particularly true in a multilateral trading system. The WTO panel in the dispute in *India–Quantitative Restrictions on Agricultural, Chemical and Industrial Products* used the vivid expression the 'thickening of legality' to articulate the process by which law and the rule of law have become essential components of the multilateral trading system. The panel said:

> Under the WTO, the rule of law has been strengthened through increased automaticity of dispute settlement and detailed integrated dispute procedures. All the more so in this context of thickening of legality. . . .[8]

Busch and Reinhardt explained the implications of this 'thickening of legality' when they observed:

> By adding 26,000 pages of new treaty text, not to mention a rapidly burgeoning case law; by imposing several new stages of legal activity per dispute, such as appeals, compliance reviews and compensation arbitration; by judicialising proceedings and thus putting a premium on sophisticated legal argumentation as opposed to informal negotiation; and by adding a potential of two years to the defendants' legally permissible delays in complying with adverse rulings, the WTO reforms have raised the hurdles facing [developing countries] contemplating litigation.[9]

Proceedings before the judicial organs of the WTO are particularly complex and time-consuming. In accordance with the Understanding on Rules Governing the Settlement of Disputes (the 'DSU'), challenged measures may be subject to successive reviews in different proceedings by an initial Panel, by the WTO Appellate Body, which reviews decisions of

[8] Panel Report, WT/DS90/R, adopted 22 September 1999, para. 5.101.

[9] Marc L Busch and Eric Reinhardt, *Testing International Trade Law: Empirical Studies of GATT/WTO Dispute Settlement* (Paper presented at the University of Minnesota Law School Conference on the Political Economy of International Trade Law, 15–16 September 2000) This view is shared by many developing country Members of the WTO. The WTO's African Group has described the dispute settlement system as 'complicated and overly expensive'. See Negotiations on the Dispute Settlement Mechanism Understanding, Proposal by the African Group, TN/DS/W/15, 25 September 2002.

panels, by the arbitrator determining the reasonable period of time to comply with the rulings of the panel or Appellate Body, and possibly even further review by the Panel and Appellate Body to determine whether the defending Member has properly come into compliance with its WTO obligations. All of these proceedings take a considerable amount of time. While these three-stage procedures take their course, the complainant must bear the economic consequences of any WTO-inconsistent action by the defending Member. Under the WTO dispute settlement procedures, no compensation is due to the complainant for any trade damage incurred during the course of the proceedings. Effectively therefore, the complainant has no procedural remedy until the end of the implementation period. Only then, and only if the defendant does not implement the rulings, may the complainant request compensation or authorisation to suspend the application of concessions or other obligations.

Appealing a Panel report and forcing a complainant to request an arbitrator to determine the length of the implementation allows the respondent to violate – effectively unscathed – WTO obligations for considerable periods of time simply by requiring the adversely affected Members to resort to the DSU. *The fact that no compensation is due for the damage caused during the WTO proceedings gives the respondent an incentive to make use of every opportunity to complicate the dispute settlement process.*[10]

The problems faced by developing countries in the WTO are accentuated by the income and resource disparities among the WTO Members. The most active participants in the WTO dispute settlement system include dominant trading partners such as the US, the European Communities, Canada and Japan – developed countries with significant technical and financial resources. These WTO Members have highly qualified and experienced lawyers. They also have more sophisticated private industries that also contribute resources to assist the government in defending the country's interests in the dispute settlement system. This, combined with the complexity of the WTO dispute settlement

[10] As a result, the lawyer's invoice at the end of a complete, three-stage WTO proceeding can easily amount to $500,000 and more. In the context of the reform of the DSU, a group of developing country Members proposed that in disputes where developing countries are involved, the losing developed country Member should be required to meet the litigation costs of the developing country Member 'to the tune of US$500,000 or actual expenses, whichever is higher'. See Dispute Settlement Understanding Proposals: Legal Text, Communication from India on behalf of Cuba, Dominican Republic, Egypt, Honduras, Jamaica and Malaysia, WT/DS/W/47, 11 February 2003.

proceedings, has resulted in *developing countries being at a distinct disadvantage in WTO dispute settlement.*

B. The limitations of special and differential treatment in WTO dispute settlement proceedings

The drafts of the DSU attempted to provide for legal aid and technical assistance using provisions that accord procedural privileges to developing countries and least-developed countries. These include Article 3.12, according to which developing countries are given the right resort to the good offices of the Director-General and the application of expedited panel procedures in accordance with a decision adopted in 1966 under the GATT 1947 in disputes brought against developed countries. Other provisions according developing countries procedural privileges are Articles 21.2, 21.7 and 21.8, according to which the WTO Dispute Settlement Body (DSB) shall take into account the interests of developing countries in its task of reviewing the implementation of recommendations and rulings.

Provisions granting special and differential treatment in the dispute settlement proceedings have not been effective in addressing the resource constraints of developing countries. One commentator has observed that there appears to be reluctance on the part of developing countries to invoke the DSU provisions according them privileges, in part because they wish to face developed countries as equals in legal proceedings, and in part because they may also fear that the application of procedural provisions biased in their favour may detract from the legitimacy of the result of the procedures and hence reduce the normative force of the rulings they are seeking.[11] Moreover, it is doubtful whether the special and differential provisions address the real disparity of resources. The African Group in the WTO has commented that these provisions of the DSU have 'not fully and coherently addressed the core difficulties developing country Members face in seeking to use the WTO dispute settlement system'.[12]

[11] Frieder Roessler, 'Special and Differential Treatment of Developing Countries under the WTO Dispute Settlement System' in F. Ortino and E.-U Petersmann (eds): The WTO Dispute Settlement System 1995–2003 (The Hague: Kluwer Law International, 2004), pp. 87–90.

[12] Negotiations on the Dispute Settlement Mechanism Understanding, Proposal by the African Group, TN/DS/W/15, 25 September 2002. See also Text for the African Group Proposals on Dispute Settlement Understanding Negotiations, Communication from Kenya, TN/DS/W/42, 24 January 2003. The African Group reiterated the position discussed at the beginning of this paper when it said that 'the difficulties relate to lack of shortage of human and financial resources'.

III. The Limitations of Existing Legal Aid mechanisms

A. Trust funds

One approach to addressing the existing resource constraints of developing countries has been to provide trust funds from which they are provided with money to hire legal experts. To ensure that the burden of cost should not be a factor for states in deciding whether to pursue peaceful means of settling disputes, financial aid has been provided directly to qualifying applicant states. The ICJ, the Permanent Court of Arbitration at the Hague and the International Tribunal for the Law of the Sea all have trust funds that were established to assist states involved in litigation before those tribunals.

In 1989, the Secretary-General's Trust Fund to Assist in the Settlement of Disputes through the International Court of Justice (the '*ICJ Trust Fund*') was established in recognition that there are 'occasions where the parties concerned are prepared to seek settlement of their disputes through the International Court of Justice, but cannot proceed because of the lack of legal expertise or funds'.[13] The ICJ Trust Fund was conceived as a 'practical means of overcoming financial obstacles to the judicial settlement of disputes by offering financial assistance to indigent states for expenses incurred in connection with a dispute'.[14] Under the terms and conditions of the ICJ Trust Fund, legal assistance is available only to states that have accepted the Court's jurisdiction, and only in respect of disputes where there is special agreement as to the Court's jurisdiction or disputes relating to the execution of a judgment resulting from such an agreement. Contributions to the ICJ Trust Fund are made on a voluntary basis by states, intergovernmental organisations, national institutions and non-governmental organisations, as well as natural and juridical persons. The Fund is managed by the UN Secretary-General, and falls under the Office of Legal Affairs within the UN Secretariat. It is governed by the Terms and the Financial Regulations and Rules of the United Nations and is audited annually with a report being sent to the General Assembly.

Money is provided directly to successful applicant states to defray costs related to litigation including fees for counsel, agents, advocates, experts,

[13] Terms of ICJ Trust Fund, para. 3.

[14] A Study and Evaluation of the UN Secretary-General's Trust Fund to Assist States in the Settlement of Disputes through the International Court of Justice, Report by Dr Pieter Bekker, Special Rapporteur, *Chinese Journal of International Law*, 245.

witnesses, research fees, costs relating to oral proceedings, producing materials and execution of judgments. The choice of agent or counsel rests with the applicant state. Grants are made only after expenditure against receipts evidencing actual expenditure, so that the money is disbursed only after the proceedings have been completed.

A similar scheme exists under the United Nations Convention on the Law of the Sea of 1982 ('UNCLOS'), which, like the Charter of the United Nations, commits states to settle disputes in a peaceful manner, including through recourse to the International Tribunal for the Law of the Sea ('ITLOS'). The International Tribunal of the Law of the Sea Trust Fund (the '*ITLOS Trust Fund*') was set up in August 2001 pursuant to a UN General Assembly resolution.[15] Unlike the ICJ Trust Fund, the ITLOS Trust Fund is not limited to developing countries: applications for assistance may be submitted by any state that is a party to the Law of the Sea Convention.[16] Like the ICJ Trust Fund, the ITLOS Trust Fund relies on voluntary contributions from states, intergovernmental and non-governmental organisations, national institutions and natural and juridical persons.[17]

Finally, the Permanent Court of Arbitration, established under the 1899 and 1907 Hague Conventions for the Pacific Settlement of Disputes, has a similar trust fund to assist parties involved in litigation. In December 1995, the Administrative Council of the Permanent Court established a Financial Assistance Fund for Settlement of International Disputes (the '*Financial Assistance Fund*').[18] This helps states to meet costs relating to fees and expenses of members of an arbitral body entitled with settling the dispute, expenses of implementing an award or other decision, payments to agents, counsel, experts and witnesses, and operational or administrative expenses connected with oral and written proceedings.[19] To qualify for legal assistance, states must be parties to the Conventions of 1899 or 1907. Institutions or enterprises owned and controlled by such states may also qualify for assistance.

B. Technical assistance from a Secretariat

The second form of legal aid is the provision of technical assistance by an established Secretariat. In the multilateral trading system, the WTO recognises that developing countries have a particular need for technical

[15] UNGA Res. 55/7, Annex I, Terms of Reference and Guidelines, para. 2. [16] *Ibid.*
[17] *Ibid.* [18] *Ibid.* [19] *Ibid.*

assistance to assist them in litigation. Article 27 of the DSU recognises that '. . . there may also be a need to provide additional legal advice and assistance in respect of dispute settlement to developing country Members'. Accordingly, the WTO Secretariat is required to '. . . make available a qualified legal expert from the WTO technical cooperation services to any developing country Member which so requests'. The WTO Secretariat has put Article 27 into practice by providing dedicated legal experts who are employed by the WTO to advise developing countries on legal matters. The Legal Affairs Division of the WTO Secretariat therefore advises developing countries on an *ad hoc* basis. In addition to providing technical support on request, as required by Article 27.2 of the DSU, the Secretariat also conducts special training courses on the dispute settlement procedures. This training is carried out by officials from the Legal Division, the Technical Cooperation Division and the WTO Training Institute.

C. Evaluation of existing mechanisms

The three trust funds discussed above have the same purpose – to facilitate recourse to international dispute settlement by making funds available to litigants to meet litigation costs. Financial assistance has the advantage that it provides a direct benefit to the recipient countries and leaves it to those countries to choose the legal experts. Further, the direct provision of financial aid allows the recipient to determine how best to use the funds. The choice of counsel, agents or experts is left in the control of the litigant country. This contrasts with the use of a Secretariat or an independent organisation as a source of legal aid, where countries do not have a choice in who assists or represents them.

All three of the trust funds discussed above rely on voluntary contributions. Without strict mandatory requirements for contributions, it may be difficult to sustain an adequate level of funding. *Both the ICJ and ITLOS trust funds are under-funded*, and consequently, there are annual calls for more contributions to both trust funds.[20] A further drawback to this form of legal assistance is that the disbursement of legal aid requires control, which must be exercised by an independent institution or panel

[20] See A Study and Evaluation of the UN Secretary-General's Trust Fund to Assist States in the Settlement of Disputes through the International Court of Justice, Report by Dr Pieter Bekker, Special Reporter, *Chinese Journal of International Law*, 249. See also the Report of the Secretary General on the ICJ Trust Fund, which shows that contributions to the Fund totalled just over $1 million dollars, with contributions ranging from $1,000 to $69,000.

of experts. Finally, while the provision of direct financial assistance may meet the short-term ends of litigant countries, in the longer term, it is not a solution that builds capacity in the recipient states. As discussed in the first section of this chapter, one of the primary constraints that developing countries face is a lack of the necessary human resources. Providing financial assistance so that developing countries can hire lawyers from developed countries does not address this problem.

There are also limits to the extent that developing countries can rely on the technical assistance provided by international Secretariats. Their staff must be neutral and serve the interests of the organisation as a whole, not just individual members. Thus, Article VI:2 of the WTO Agreement states that:

> The responsibilities of the Director-General and the staff of the Secretariat shall be exclusively international in character. In the discharge of their duties, the Director-General and the Staff shall not seek or accept instructions from any government or any other authority external to the WTO.

Under Article 27 of the DSU, the WTO Secretariat is required to provide legal support without compromising its impartiality. Secretariat staff cannot act as counsel for developing countries, or represent them before panels or the Appellate Body. Anecdotal evidence, as well as interviews with Secretariat officials, indicate that this has sometimes put WTO officials in the unfortunate position of being asked to advise on whether a particular dispute should be brought before a dispute settlement panel, when those same officials may later have to advise on the merits of the case. WTO officials have generally avoided these conflicts of interest by providing legal information rather than legal analyses that might be considered to be favouring one legal argument over another. Once a case has been brought, Secretariat officials have also sometimes been requested to comment on submissions brought to them, and to advise on procedure. Secretariat Officials do not themselves draft submissions for parties.

The consequences of this 'arms' length' approach is *that the role of the Secretariat is effectively limited to providing training and information*, and does not extend to providing the much-needed legal analysis and advice about the substance of the dispute itself. This is compounded by the fact that, as explained above, in the WTO, the same Division advises

The largest donors were Austria, Finland, France, Iran, Japan, Luxembourg, Mexico, Spain, Sweden and the United Kingdom.

developing countries involved in disputes, also advises the panellists adjudicating the disputes. For this reason, some WTO Members have proposed that a separate institution be established within the WTO to assist developing countries.[21]

The requirement that the staff of the WTO Secretariat 'shall assist the developing country Member in a manner ensuring the continued impartiality of the Secretariat' effectively makes it impossible for them to act as an advocate for one Member in a legal proceeding against another, and, in practice, they have not done so. Developing countries have therefore had no option but to turn to sources outside the WTO for legal assistance in WTO proceedings. An increasing number of law firms are able to give legal advice on WTO law, particularly in the field of trade remedies. However, the cost of this advice is prohibitive for many developing countries.

In the light of these considerations, *a group of WTO Members decided to establish the ACWL as an independent international organisation* that would provide high-quality legal services at a fraction of the cost of law firms, and as an organisation independent of the WTO.

IV. The Advisory Centre on WTO Law[22]

A. The mandate and institutional structure of the ACWL

1. The mandate

The ACWL was established on the occasion of the Third (Seattle) Ministerial Conference of the WTO on 1 December 1999, by a group of WTO Members who signed the Agreement Establishing the Advisory Centre on WTO Law (the 'Agreement Establishing the ACWL').[23] By creating a standing institution with the mandate to provide legal aid in WTO

[21] See Communication from the European Communities, Developing Countries and the WTO Dispute Settlement Mechanism, WT/DS/W/148 24 February 1999.

[22] This section on the ACWL is based on a report prepared by the ACWL's Management Board, and on the ACWL Report on Operations 2005.

[23] The original signatories were: Bolivia, Canada, Colombia, Denmark, Dominican Republic, Ecuador, Egypt, Finland, Guatemala, Honduras, Hong Kong China, Ireland, Italy, Kenya, Netherlands, Nicaragua, Norway, Pakistan, Panama, Paraguay, Peru, Philippines, Sweden, Thailand, Tunisia, the United Kingdom, Uruguay, Venezuela and Zimbabwe. The Agreement Establishing the ACWL on WTO Law entered into force on 15 July 2001. Subsequently, India and Latvia also became signatories to the Agreement.

dispute settlement proceedings and WTO law generally, the Members of the ACWL implemented an idea that had never previously been tried in practice.[24]

In creating this unique organisation, its Members addressed several of the perceived problems with developing country access to, and use of, the dispute settlement system. As explained in the ACWL's Management Board's review of the first five years,[25] the ACWL Members chose the current structure of the organisation because they wanted to:

- enable the developed countries to provide technical assistance aid through the ACWL without undermining the independence and hence the credibility of the ACWL's legal advice, and to thereby ensure that the developing countries would not be wary of the advice given by an institution financed in large part by countries that were their potential opponents in WTO dispute settlement proceedings;
- ensure that the ACWL's legal aid would not be wasted on frivolous dispute settlement proceedings that would impose an inappropriate burden on the system;
- enable developing countries to rely on the ACWL for legal assistance in *all* WTO dispute settlement proceedings, including disputes in which they face each other as opposing parties, and to ensure that the ACWL provides assistance to both sides without exposing its legal staff to conflicts of interest; and
- make the ACWL's services easily accessible to least developed countries without imposing on them the financial and administrative burdens of membership in the ACWL.

Each of these issues is addressed in the Agreement Establishing the ACWL. The Agreement entered into force on 15 July 2001 and the ACWL became operational on 17 July 2001. The preamble to the Agreement Establishing the ACWL emphasises that a proper balance of rights and obligations under the WTO agreements can only be maintained if all Members of the WTO have a full understanding of their rights and obligations under the WTO agreements and an equal opportunity to resort to the WTO dispute settlement procedures. The preamble further recognises that the credibility and acceptability of the WTO dispute settlement system can only be ensured if all members of the WTO can participate in the system. For those reasons, the ACWL was established to 'provide legal

[24] The ACWL Progress Report, para. 2. [25] *Ibid.*

training, support and advice on WTO law and dispute settlement procedures, in particular the least developed among them, and countries with economies in transition'.[26] Thus, the ACWL was established both to assist the countries entitled to its services and to advance the credibility and acceptability of both the WTO system generally and the WTO dispute settlement procedures in particular. In this manner, both developed and developing countries benefit from the operations of the ACWL.

2. Membership

Pursuant to Article 16 of the Agreement Establishing the ACWL, any Member of the WTO and any State or separate customs territory in the process of acceding to the WTO may become a Member of the ACWL by accession on mutually agreed terms and conditions, subject to the approval of the General Assembly of the ACWL. Membership of the ACWL is open to all WTO members and countries and customs unions in the process of accession to the WTO. WTO Members wishing to join the ACWL must use the accession procedure.[27] Nine developed country members of the WTO were original signatories to the Agreement establishing the ACWL.[28] These Members have since been joined by Switzerland, which acceded to the ACWL on 5 December 2004.

Twenty developing countries were original signatories of the Agreement.[29] Seven other developing countries have since acceded to the Agreement: Jordan, Oman, Mauritius, Turkey, El Salvador, Indonesia,

[26] Agreement Establishing the ACWL, Article 2.1. Membership of the ACWL is open to countries with economies in transition and countries in the process of acceding to the WTO. Latvia initially joined the ACWL but withdrew upon its accession to the European Union. It has remained the only country with an economy in transition to have joined the ACWL.

[27] There are currently twenty-five members of the ACWL. These are: Canada, Denmark, Finland, Ireland, Italy, the Netherlands, Norway, Sweden, United Kingdom, Hong Kong, China, Colombia, Egypt, Pakistan, Philippines, Thailand, Venezuela, Dominican Republic, Ecuador, Guatemala, Honduras, Kenya, Nicaragua, Panama, Peru, Tunisia, India, Latvia and Jordan.

[28] Canada, Denmark, Finland, Ireland, Italy, the Netherlands, Norway, Sweden, Switzerland and the United Kingdom.

[29] The original signatories, with their member categories indicated in brackets, are Bolivia, Colombia, Dominican Republic, Ecuador, Egypt, Guatemala, Honduras, Hong Kong, China, India, Kenya, Nicaragua, Pakistan, Panama, Paraguay, Peru, Philippines, Thailand, Tunisia, Uruguay, and Venezuela. The following is a list of the Members that acceded to the ACWL, together with their member categories in brackets, listed according to the dates of their accession. Jordan (20 January 2002), Oman (25 April 2003), Mauritius (11 June 2003), Turkey (17 August 2003), El Salvador (4 March 2004), Chinese Taipei (13 May 2004) and Indonesia (28 April 2004).

and Chinese Taipei. Costa Rica and Sri Lanka are currently in the process of joining the ACWL. *Two-thirds of the developing countries that have participated in the WTO dispute settlement proceedings as complainant or respondent have decided to become Members of the ACWL.* The ACWL has been particularly attractive for those developing countries that have actively participated in the WTO dispute settlement proceedings, but not sufficiently often to have acquired substantial experience. Once Costa Rica is a Member of the ACWL, all of the developing countries and customs territories that have participated in WTO dispute settlement proceedings more than twice but fewer than eighteen times will have joined the ACWL.[30] The only developing countries that have been active in the dispute settlement process but have *not joined the ACWL* are Argentina, Chile, Brazil, Mexico, and Korea, all with extensive experience in the dispute settlement system and in using the resources available through private law firms before the ACWL was established.[31]

In addition, the forty five WTO Members and countries in the process of acceding to the WTO that have been designated by the United Nations as least developed countries *('LDCs') are entitled to the services of the ACWL without having to take any steps to become a member of the ACWL.*[32] Least developed countries may therefore become members, but they can also enjoy the full benefits of membership without taking any steps to become members. Thus, the Agreement addressed the concerns of the Members that it should not be onerous for the least developed countries to seek recourse to the ACWL. Since the DSU began operating, only one LDC has been a complainant in a WTO dispute settlement proceeding.[33] That country – Bangladesh – was represented by the ACWL in that dispute, in which a settlement has now been reached. Bangladesh has stated publicly that it would not have brought the case if it had not had access to the ACWL's legal aid.[34]

30 See the table showing participation by developing countries in the WTO dispute settlement system listed as an Annex to the Progress Report by the Management Board.

31 The ACWL Progress Report, para. 2.

32 Afghanistan, Angola, Bangladesh, Benin, Kingdom of Bhutan, Burkina Faso, Burundi, Cambodia, Republic of Cape Verde, Central African Republic, Chad, Democratic Republic of Congo, Djibouti, Federal Democratic Republic of Ethiopia, Gambia, Guinea, Guinea Bissau, Haiti, Lao People's Democratic Republic, Lesotho Madagascar Malawi, Maldives, Mali, Mauritania, Mozambique, Myanmar, Nepal, Rwanda, Samoa, Sao Tome and Principe, Senegal, Sierra Leone, Solomon Islands, Niger, Republic of Sudan, Tanzania, Togo, Uganda, Vanuatu, Yemen and Zambia.

33 *India–Anti-dumping Measure on Batteries from Bangladesh* (DS 306).

34 See for instance, Daniel Altman, *An unlevel playing field within the WTO*, *International Herald Tribune*, 3 May 2006, in which the Ambassador of Bangladesh to Geneva confirmed that the ACWL's assistance was crucial to Bangladesh proceeding with the case.

3. Services offered by the ACWL

ACWL members enjoy the ACWL's services at preferential rates and receive priority over non-members in the allocation of the ACWL's resources. *The services of the ACWL are available **exclusively** to developing countries and least developed countries.* Developed countries that are members of the ACWL cannot avail themselves of the services of the ACWL. The ACWL provides legal advice, legal training and support in dispute settlement proceedings. Thus the ACWL gives legal advice on request from the ACWL members and least developed countries; organises seminars on WTO jurisprudence; offers training and internships for government officials from developing countries and least-developed countries and represents its members and the least-developed countries throughout WTO dispute settlement proceedings, including representation before WTO panels and the Appellate Body.

With the exception of services rendered in connection with WTO dispute settlement proceedings, the *ACWL provides its services free of charge to members of the ACWL and to least developed countries.* However, the Management Board of the ACWL *may establish a maximum number of hours of free legal advice.* The fees charged are intended to ensure that the ACWL' s legal aid is not wasted on frivolous complaints, but do not prohibit Members with genuine cases from approaching the ACWL. As explained in the proposal on the establishment of the ACWL, the charging policy is based on the ability of countries to pay and 'attempts to strike a balance between the desire to create incentives for WTO Members to become . . . members of the ACWL and the need to avoid frivolous cases'.[35] The fees are charged on the basis of the ability of members to pay, so that least developed countries pay the least, while category A members such as Hong Kong China and Chinese Taipei pay the most.

Where two members approach the ACWL for services in respect of the same dispute, the ACWL operates on a first-come-first-served basis. A member who is unsuccessful in securing the services of the ACWL is nonetheless entitled to support from a lawyer paid for by the ACWL and selected from a roster of external legal counsel. *Twelve law firms and five legal experts* have agreed to provide legal support on pre-determined conditions in cases in which two WTO Members entitled to the services of the ACWL are involved in the same case and pursue conflicting interests

[35] Proposal on Establishing an Advisory Centre on WTO Law, April 1999, para. 44.

and have been included in the ACWL's roster of external counsel. This ensures that the ACWL provides high-quality assistance to both sides without exposing its legal staff to conflicts of interest.

4. Funding and budget

The ACWL is funded by both its developed and developing country members who have made contributions to the ACWL's Endowment Fund. For the purposes of these financial contributions, the membership of the ACWL is divided into four categories, determined on the basis of their share of world trade with an upward correction reflecting their per capita income. Thus, developed country members each made a contribution of CHF 1.6 million, while developing countries pay CHF 486,000, CHF 162,000 and CHF 81,000, depending on their category of membership. The Agreement specified that contributions from developed countries would finance the annual budget through the first five years of the ACWL's operations.

As explained above, the ACWL also derives income from the comparatively low fees that it charges for providing support in WTO dispute settlement. This funding mechanism, which combines an endowment fund with user fees, was selected to ensure that the operation of the ACWL was not influenced by financial considerations. One-off, or multi-year contributions from developed country members ensure that these countries can provide aid through the ACWL without undermining its independence. This in turn means that developing countries can continue to rely on the credibility of legal advice provided by the ACWL, even though it is financed in large part by countries that are potential opponents in WTO dispute settlement proceedings. The ACWL's independent status also means that its advice and policies are not affected by financial or issue-specific concerns.

5. Institutional matters

The General Assembly is the highest decision-making body of the ACWL, and is composed of representatives of the members of the ACWL and representatives of least-developed countries. Its primary responsibility is to evaluate the performance of the ACWL and to adopt its annual budget. The ACWL has a management board composed of seven persons: three nominated by members that are developing countries or countries with economies in transition; two nominated by the developed country members; one nominated by the least developed countries; and the executive director who serves in an *ex officio* capacity.

The ACWL's management board takes the decisions necessary to ensure the efficient and effective operation of the ACWL. The board consists of six persons acting in their personal capacity who have been selected on the basis of their professional qualifications in the field of WTO law or international trade relations and development. One member of the board is nominated by the least developed countries. The ACWL's eight lawyers are of eight different nationalities. Four of them are from developing countries. The legal staff consists of the executive director, the deputy director, two senior counsel, two counsel, and two associate counsel.

B. Activities from 2001–2006

Since its establishment, *the ACWL has provided support to developing countries and one least-developed country in a total of twenty-two different dispute settlement proceedings*, including eleven disputes that have gone at least to the panel stage and seven disputes that have gone to the Appellate Body.[36] Further, since the ACWL began its operations, there have been a total of thirty-one different dispute settlement proceedings involving countries entitled to the services of the ACWL as either complainant or respondent. This figure excludes disputes involving countries such as Argentina, Brazil, Chile, Korea and Mexico who have been heavily involved in the WTO dispute settlement system and are generally not perceived to be dependent on legal aid. In fifteen of the thirty-one cases, the countries entitled to the services of the ACWL have obtained legal assistance. Of the remaining sixteen cases, where the ACWL's services were not utilised, fourteen were apparently resolved at the consultation phase and did not go through the Panel process. There have therefore only been two cases out of a total of thirty-one in which countries that might have been expected to use the services of the ACWL have not done so.[37]

[36] In one of these cases, *EC–Tariff Preferences*, the ACWL simultaneously assisted six different countries. The ACWL directly represented India, which was the complainant, during the Panel, Appellate Body and implementation phases. The ACWL directly provided assistance to Paraguay, a third party, during the Panel phase of this case. The ACWL also indirectly provided assistance to Bolivia, Colombia, Ecuador, Peru and Venezuela, all of which were third parties, through external legal counsel during the Panel phase of this case. In 2005, the ACWL also provided support to the Dominican Republic in the arbitration under Article 21.3(c) of the DSU in *Dominican Republic–Import and Sale of Cigarettes* through an external legal counsel.

[37] These cases were (i) the *US–Gambling* case, brought by Antigua and Barbuda; and (ii) the *US–Steel Safeguard* case, brought by Chinese Taipei. In both instances, the ACWL

The ACWL has also provided more than 400 legal opinions to developing countries and least-developed countries. The legal opinions are provided entirely free of charge.

Legal opinions have concerned either (i) measures taken or contemplated by the member seeking the advice; (ii) measures taken by other WTO Members affecting the member seeking the advice; or (iii) legal advice relating to systemic issues of WTO law. During 2005, about half of the requests for legal advice concerned general systemic or procedural issues. In these cases, the ACWL provided the legal analysis that allowed the requesting country to participate more effectively in WTO decision-making and negotiations. About one-quarter of the requests for legal opinions concerned measures taken or under consideration by the LDC or Member seeking the advice, including proposed domestic legislation. In these cases, the ACWL's aim was to assist the LDC or Member in achieving its trade policy objectives in a manner consistent with WTO law. In some of these cases, the request was prompted by an internal conflict between the proponents and opponents of a proposed measure. In the remaining requests, the requesting LDC or member sought an assessment of the viability of a complaint against measures taken by another WTO Member. In these cases, the ACWL aimed to enable the LDC or Member to make an informed decision on whether to bring a WTO challenge.[38]

The ACWL' s legal advice has covered a broad range of topics. In addition to opinions regarding the core rights and obligations under the GATT 1994, the ACWL has provided advice on more specialised issues as diverse as pre-shipment inspection, services issues, customs valuation matters, and all types of trade remedy issues. Many of these opinions include requests for advice on the drafting of measures to implement the WTO agreements.[39]

The ACWL has also delivered three rounds of annual courses under its legal training programme for officials from developing countries and least-developed countries. The ACWL also conducts *ad hoc* seminars on topical issues in WTO law. In 2005, the ACWL also launched a Secondment Programme for Trade Lawyers under which government officials work with the lawyers of the ACWL before they resume service with their home governments.

understands that the complainants' legal assistance was provided by the private stakeholders affected by the dispute. See the discussion in the ACWL Progress Report, paras. 32–40.

[38] ACWL Report on Operations, paras. 9–13. [39] *Ibid.*, para. 11.

C. Evaluating the role of the ACWL

1. General comments on the role and achievements of the ACWL

While the ACWL is perhaps best known for its support of developing countries in dispute settlement proceedings, Article 2 of the Agreement places equal emphasis on providing legal advice, providing support in dispute settlement proceedings and training government officials in WTO Law. *Thus, developing human resources capacity is one of the aims of the ACWL*. One observer has said that:

> [The ACWL] . . . has created a precedent that will be difficult to ignore for other international bodies. First, unlike the trust funds created for the ICJ and the ITLOS, and other forms of legal aid, it concentrates on providing human resources, not cash, to defray litigation costs. Second, it is an independent organ, external to the organization and its judicial body, thus reinforcing its credibility as an impartial player. Third, it brings together developing countries and developed countries into a partnership, rather than leaving the financial support of the endeavour to gratuitous contributions by developed countries. Finally, it is partially sustained by user-pays fees, which help reduce waste and unnecessary litigation, and it reinforces the commitment of the parties to the case.[40]

The ACWL has thus been complimented *for not being a purely 'donor-driven' initiative*: by making contributions to the endowment fund, all members, including developing countries, ensure that they have an equal stake in its operations. Thus, the ACWL provides a unique model for donor/aid recipient relationships. Those who pay the least for the ACWL's service benefit the most because they cannot otherwise afford legal advice. At the same time, the fact that developing country members have to contribute an admittedly small amount means that countries have a stake in the operation of the ACWL and an incentive to avoid wasting its resources with unnecessary requests for legal advice and frivolous complaints.

The ACWL has also found its independence from the WTO to be valuable to its operation. Unlike the WTO Secretariat, which, of necessity, exists to serve the interests of its Members, the ACWL is independent of WTO panels and the Appellate Body. There are two aspects to this independence: it guarantees the ACWL's impartiality, and it also means that

[40] *Cesare Romano*, International Justice and Developing Countries: A Qualitative Analysis, The Law and Practice of International Courts and Tribunals, Vol. 1, No. 2, August 2002, 565.

the members of the ACWL could create an organisation best suited to their needs, without having to accommodate it within the structure established by the WTO Agreement. The former Director of the WTO, Michael Moore, emphasised the importance of this independence when he said:

> The [ACWL], however, can go beyond the point at which Secretariat assistance to developing countries had to stop, and provide full-fledged, high-quality, legal aid in all stages of the DSU procedure, including the Panel and Appellate Body stages.[41]

Further, the ACWL offers not only high-quality legal services of the kind provided that are offered by law firms, *but also builds capacity through training government officials.* Professor John Jackson has emphasised the 'capacity-building' function of the ACWL, stating that:

> One of the ingenious facets of the procedures established by the new Advisory Center is that it combines its assistance for advocacy with a moderate mission of training. Part of this training can be accomplished by asking an assisted country to provide a person who will be a sort of 'intern', working with the Advisory Center staff on the case for his or her country, and thus receiving experience in that process. This type of capacity-building is certainly welcome, and some people believe that the Advisory Center will also engage in some other types of training activities along the same lines.[42]

Further, unlike law firms, the ACWL does not rely on fees, so it is able to give advice that is unaffected by purely commercial considerations.

The only aspect of the ACWL's institutional structure which may cause some concern is its structure as an international organisation. The process of accession may seem unduly burdensome as it requires members to ratify an international agreement. The ACWL was established as an international organisation mainly for reasons related to Swiss law and relationship with the Swiss authorities. The members of the ACWL have calculated that the incentives outweigh the cost associated with the membership process. In practice, the ACWL has overcome this in the case of Costa Rica's protocol of accession by inserting a clause in the protocol that entitles Costa Rica to the services of the ACWL even before

[41] Part of a speech delivered on the occasion of the inauguration of the ACWL, 5 October 2001. See www.acwl.ch, last visited 11 May 2005.

[42] Perceptions about the WTO Trade Institutions, Keynote Address at the Inauguration of the ACWL, 5 October 2001.

it ratifies the treaty. As accession to the ACWL is on terms that are agreed between the ACWL General Assembly and the acceding member, this precedent could also be followed in the future.

The possibility that Members could request the ACWL to provide services beyond the niche that it has carved for itself had already been anticipated by observers. Thus, Professor John Jackson warned that:

> [I]n carrying out its responsibilities, particularly in connection with the broader institutional setting of the WTO and providing expertise in relation to proposals for reforms, the Advisory Center will necessarily need to separate its advocacy role rather strongly from its policy preferences. It has an obligation to its clients under professional ethics (some of which will be newly developed as part of the procedures of the WTO) to be a vigorous advocate, and utilize strong arguments on behalf of its clients. But it will need to consider, probably on a case-by-case basis, the degree to which its advocacy role is consistent with expressions of policy preferences or suggestions about reform of the dispute settlement system.[43]

The ACWL is obliged by its Agreement to remain within its narrow niche of giving advice on trade law and legal issues arising from negotiations and other systemic issues, leaving issues of negotiation strategy and trade policy to the organisations that were set up specifically to assist developing countries with those issues. It should be emphasised that the ACWL operates in an environment in which developing countries and least developed countries receive advice from organisations such as The South Centre, the International Centre for Trade and Sustainable Development, the International Agency for International Trade Information and Cooperation, the United Nations Conference on Trade and Development, the Quaker United Nations Office, and the Third World Network. Of these, the ACWL is the only organisation that provides *only* legal advice.

Finally, it should be noted that some WTO Members have taken the view that the ACWL should not preclude other forms of legal aid. In 2002, when the ACWL had been in operation for scarcely more than a year, the African Group at the WTO noted that not all WTO developing country members were members of the ACWL, and that therefore, the activities of the ACWL should be supplemented by the establishment of a permanent fund financed by the WTO membership to help developing

[43] See Jackson above, Perceptions about the WTO Trade Institutions, Keynote address on the occasion of the inauguration of the ACWL.

countries overcome the institutional and human constraint they face in using the complex DSU procedures.[44]

2. The evaluation of the ACWL by the Ministry of Foreign Affairs in the Netherlands

In June 2004, the Policy and Operations Department of the Ministry of Foreign Affairs of the Netherlands conducted an evaluation of the ACWL, as well as two other Geneva-based organisations, as part of its evaluation of the Netherlands' trade-related technical assistance efforts (the 'IOB Evaluation').[45] This was intended to assist the government of the Netherlands in determining whether the ACWL had helped to realise their specific policy objectives, rather than an evaluation of how the ACWL had pursued all of the objectives that it was created to pursue. The IOB Evaluation is nevertheless of interest in evaluating the ACWL, because it included a survey of the countries that had used its services. It is the only current source, other than anecdotal evidence, which assesses the ACWL from the perspective of its Members.

The IOB Evaluation rated the ACWL's staff positively and, in surveys, the users of the ACWL's services compared the ACWL's experience and expertise favourably with that of private law firms.[46] In the IOB Evaluation, the ACWL received positive reviews for the legal opinions it provided to its members: 'All interviewed delegates appreciated the legal service. Both the quality of the advice and the fast response to requests were highly valued.'[47]

The IOB Evaluation noted that many countries that have used the ACWL's services in dispute settlement proceedings felt that the ACWL provided *as good or even better services than private law firms*: 'The respondents felt that the ACWL has built up a lot of expertise and experience over recent years. Most respondents therefore felt that ACWL could provide support in the dispute settlement process at least as well as other private law firms, and many respondents even felt ACWL was better, because ACWL works on WTO issues all the time and has therefore built up a lot of expertise over the last few years.'[48] These countries indicated that they would use the ACWL's services in dispute settlement proceedings in the

[44] See Negotiations on the Dispute Settlement Mechanism Understanding, Proposal by the African Group, TN/DS/W/15, 25 September 2002

[45] The other organisations included in the IOB Evaluation were the Agency for International Trade Information and Cooperation (AITIC) and the Quakers United Nations Office (QUNO).

[46] IOB Evaluation, p. 23.

[47] *Ibid.*, p. 21.

[48] IOB Evaluation, p. 23.

future: 'The appreciation for ACWL is also reflected in its expected future involvement in new dispute settlement cases. Most delegates indicated that they are likely to ask for the support of ACWL in all future disputes in which they may become involved. Only a few delegates noted that in some cases they would perhaps seek additional support from private law firms. Nonetheless, even in most of these cases the countries would also ask ACWL for advice.'[49]

The ACWL' s *training activities have received positive feedback* from the ACWL' s membership: the IOB Evaluation notes that all participants surveyed found the training programmes very useful and had increased their knowledge and understanding of dispute settlement in the WTO.[50]

V. Conclusion

Trust funds that provide direct financial funds to developing countries to litigate individual disputes may meet the short-term litigation needs of developing countries, but do not contribute to the development of a human resources capacity. Further, the success of these schemes depends on the continued availability of funds. As discussed in this chapter, assistance from an international Secretariat on legal issues is limited by the requirement that the Secretariat be neutral in its activities. In contrast, the ACWL's achievement in enabling developing countries and least-developed countries to participate on equal terms in disputes, its achievement in becoming the internal law office for developing countries through its legal advice, and its success in training delegates of developing countries and least-developed countries have been achieved with fewer drawbacks and scarcely greater expenditure than the other forms of legal aid discussed above.

In conclusion, it is important to emphasise that this chapter does not take the view that the existence of legal aid schemes through the ACWL and other schemes, is the major factor in determining whether countries will seek recourse to dispute settlement. Nor does this chapter propose that the cost of litigation is the only consideration that countries weigh before seeking recourse to international dispute resolution. Cesare Romano has written that the decision to litigate does not depend only on the material resources available to a country, but also factors such as the stakes, the chances of success, how long the judicial body will take to decide the case and availability of remedies and enforcement procedure. Romano also

[49] *Ibid.* [50] *Ibid.*, p. 23–4.

writes that '. . . [a]nother set of factors, perhaps the most fundamental one, is . . . the willingness to utilise international judicial bodies'.[51]

This chapter takes the view that all other things being equal and the cost of litigation being the consideration which prevents poor countries from seeking recourse to international dispute resolution, legal aid schemes can assist such countries in getting relief and thus contribute to the acceptability of primacy of international legal norms. The experience of the ACWL shows that legal aid has worked for the benefit of both developing and least-developed countries and has thus contributed to the delivery of justice in the WTO and to the effective participation of these countries in the multilateral trading system.

Selected bibliography

ACWL, The ACWL After Four Years: A Progress Report by the Management Board, ACWL/GA/2005/1, ACWL/MB/2005/1, available at: www.acwl.ch.

ACWL, Executive Director's Report on Operations 2005, January 2006, available at: www.acwl.ch.

Peter Bekker, International Legal Aid in Practice: The ICJ Trust Fund, 87 *American Journal of International Law*, 659.

Peter Bekker, A Study and Evaluation of the UN Secretary-General's Trust Fund to Assist States in the Settlement of Disputes through the International Court of Justice, Report by Dr Peter Bekker, Special Reporter, *Chinese Journal of International Law*, 245.

Marc L Busch and Eric Reinhardt, Testing International Trade Law: Empirical Studies of GATT/WTO Dispute Settlement. Paper presented at the University of Minnesota Law School Conference on the Political Economy of International Trade Law, 15–16 September 2000.

Julio Lacarte-Muro and Petina Gappah, Developing Countries and the WTO Legal and Dispute Settlement System: A View from the Bench, *Oxford Journal of International Economic Law*, 2000, 395.

Mary Ellen O'Conell, International Legal Aid: The Secretary General's Trust Fund to Assist States in the Settlement of Dispute through the International Court of Justice. In Mark W Janis (ed.) *International Court for the Twenty-First Century*, 235.

Cesare Romano, International Justice and Developing Countries: A Quantitative Analysis, *The Law and Practice of International Courts and Tribunals*, Vol. 1 No. 2, August 2002, 375.

[51] *Cesare Romano*, International Justice and Developing Countries: A Qualitative Analysis, The Law and Practice of International Courts and Tribunals, Vol. 1, No. 2, August 2002, 551–2.

(2002) International Justice and Developing Countries: A Qualitative Analysis, *The Law and Practice of International Courts and Tribunals*, Vol. 1 No. 2, August 2002.

Kim Van der Borght, The Advisory Centre on WTO Law: Advancing Fairness and Equality 2(3) *Oxford Journal of International Economic Law*, 1999, 723.

PART FOUR

Social rights, health, and environment

15

Trade and human rights at work: Next round, please . . .? Regulatory and cooperationist approaches in the context of the Doha Round

ANDREAS BLÜTHNER[1]

I. Introduction

The Doha Round, which began with much ambition and great expectations as the 'Development Round' in the context of the tragic incidents of September 11 2001, has been suspended without agreement in June 2006. Notwithstanding the lack of agreement, a significant commitment to development was demonstrated. One example was the *commitment to abolish tariffs for least-developed countries (LDCs) under the 'Everything but Arms' initiative* within the European Union (EU) Generalised System of Preferences (GSP). Improved market access for agricultural exports from developing countries today appears more closely connected to conflict prevention than it was before September 2001. The Doha Round has the potential to contribute to raising standards of living and openness in yet-closed societies in certain parts of the world. Trade can stimulate economic integration between countries and cultures that have been in conflict – European economic integration after World War Two is an often-cited example for how trade can, in the long run, substitute aid which was initially provided under the Marshall Plan.

The ongoing round of trade negotiations, though currently on hold, is likely to survive and be shaped by the experiences gained from the previous round. The Uruguay Round, that ultimately gave birth to a bundle of new agreements and set up the World Trade Organization (WTO) – both unique achievements in the history of world trade – had to overcome

[1] Associate Lecturer International Economic Law (MCL) at University of Mannheim and Coordinator Strategy Development with the Global Alliance for Improved Nutrition (GAIN), Geneva. This chapter exclusively reflects the personal opinion of the author and is based on *Blüthner*, Andreas: Welthandel und Menschenrechte in der Arbeit (Studien zum Internationalen, Europäischen und Öffentlichen Recht), Frankfurt am Main 2004. The author would like to thank Professor Marc Cassell (Kent State University) and Monique Bianci, LLB, LLM (University of Adelaide) for comments on an earlier draft of this chapter.

many breaks and took eight years before it was successfully completed. Contrary to the claim that anything but a rapid consensus will harm the WTO institutionally, *the delay is an opportunity to take a breath and rethink positions, constellations and potential areas for consensus building.*

'Trade and human rights' is not on the agenda of the Doha round.[2] Despite this fact, it is one of the topics that has received a lot of academic attention in recent years. The issue can be approached from different perspectives with diverging intentions. However, from a constitutional viewpoint it has been argued, that a legitimate and lasting world economic order should be underpinned by shared global values absent from protectionist tendencies.[3] From a historical perspective, the example of the European Community illustrates how economic integration can spill over into shared values, political coherence and harmonisation between participating countries, ultimately paving the way towards constitutional tendencies.

Whatever ideological position one takes regarding social development, so called 'human rights at work' are in fact the most 'trade-related' of all human rights, since they matter for competition, including so called cross-border institutional competition.[4] At this point it is helpful to clarify, that *this chapter does not advocate for an inclusion of human rights at work in the Doha agenda. Instead, it outlines and compares potential political and legal options*, de lege lata *and* de lege ferenda, *in case the issue returns to the agenda.* This means clarifying how an inclusion of human rights at work in the WTO system can best be achieved technically so as to contribute to human rights implementation without putting the current WTO system on the slippery slope of protectionism. Ultimately, the discussion of a rigid regulatory approach geared towards inserting human rights at work into the trade law system is put in context with the *UN Global Compact. This initiative offers a 'softer' steering mechanism at the interface of law and economics*, that is based on the same internationally

[2] The issue of 'trade and labour standards' was mentioned in preparatory documents for the WTO Ministerial Declaration in Doha, see WTO-Doc. JOB(01)/140, p. 3, para. 6, the document is accessible online at www.ictsd.org/ministerial/doha/relevantdoc.htm (accessed 15 August, 2006).

[3] See also *Petersmann*, Ernst-Ullrich (2000) The WTO Constitution and Human Rights, *Journal of International Economic Law* 3 (1), 19–25. Cf. also *Hohmann*, Harald, Angemessene Außenhandelsfreiheit im Vergleich, Tübingen 2002, at 4 *et seq.*

[4] For the economic nexus between trade and human rights see *Blüthner*, Andreas (fn. 1), pp. 230–79, with reference to economic literature concluding that there is rather no evidence of a so-called regulatory '*race to the bottom*' in labour legislation caused by trade liberalisation, but instead a positive interrelation.

recognised rights, but is fuelled by aspirational principles for business, rather than pushing for regulation of governments through trade measures.

II. Human rights at work and the WTO system

This first section addresses the questions if, to what extent, and how human rights at work could be considered within the current WTO negotiations, without driving the world trade system onto the slippery slope of protectionism.

A. Just history repeating (from 1927 until today) . . .?

It has become a classic debate in international trade and economics, to what extent liberal trade can and should be complemented by fundamental social standards. The thesis, that maximising human welfare depends on a strengthened conjunction between liberal trade and certain minimum social standards was articulated six decades after Adam Smith and David Ricardo's theoretical paradigm of absolute and comparative advantages.[5] Jérome Blanqui, a French economist, stated in 1839 that respect and progress in fundamental labour legislation between countries that maintain open trade relations depends on a harmonised approach to labour regulation.[6]

Since then diverse forms of 'social clauses' highlighting the interdependence of trade and social development have been debated and introduced in international trade agreements. Part XIII of the Peace Treaty of Versailles, where the foundation of the International Labour Organization (ILO) was agreed on, reads:

> *the failure of any nation to adopt humane conditions of labour is an obstacle in the way of other nations which desire to improve the conditions in their own countries.*

In 1927, the *World Economic Conference of the League of Nations* dealt with the issue and recommended fair labour conditions with a view to

[5] Cp. *Smith*, Adam: Der Wohlstand der Nationen – Eine Untersuchung seiner Natur und seiner Ursachen (1776). Reprint: München, 1974, S.16ff., *Ricardo*, David: On the Principles of Political Economy and Taxation (1817). Reprint: Hildesheim, 1977, S.158ff.

[6] *Blanqui*, Jérome A.: Cours d'Écononomie Industrielle, Paris, 1838/39, p. 4, quoted from *Hansson*, Göte: Social Clauses and International Trade, London, 1983, p. 90.

raising productivity.[7] Two decades later, in Havana, the social dimension of international trade, underscored already by the title *UN Conference on Trade and Employment*, resulted in the stillborn Charter of the International Trade Organization (ITO). The fragment of Chapter IV dealing with liberal trade was brought into force by twenty-three Members as the GATT. The stillborn section of the Charta, namely Article 7, addressed the issue of 'fair labour standards':

> *[M]embers recognize, that unfair labour conditions, particularly in production for export, create difficulties in international trade and accordingly, each Member shall take whatever action may be appropriate and feasible to eliminate such conditions within its territory.*

Since then, international commodity agreements, such as sugar (1953), tin (1954), cacao (1975) and rubber (1979), employed 'soft' programmatic clauses on fair labour standards, such as

> *in order to avoid the depression of living standards and the introduction of unfair competitive conditions in world trade, [parties] will seek maintenance of fair labour standards in the sugar industry.*[8]

In parallel, starting in the 1950s, a regulatory approach addressing the social dimension of international trade was a reccurring topic on GATT's agenda. In 1953 the US Commission on Foreign Economic Policy proposed a draft GATT provision that sought to create a link with the language of the GATT dispute settlement provision of Art. XXIII in stating, that '*unfair labour conditions [. . .] create difficulties in international trade which nullify or impair benefits under this agreement*'.[9] A decade later, the GATT Tokyo Round negotiations addressed the matter again, but arrived at the conclusion, that labour standards are not a question to be dealt with in the international trading system.[10]

In 1986, another attempt to position the issue of labour standards on the trade agenda was undertaken by the US, when proposing the following paragraph as part of the mandate for the Uruguay-Round:

[7] League of Nations: Report and Proceedings of the World Economic Conference (1927), p. 49; quoted from *Charnowitz*, Steve: The Influence of International Labour Standards on the World Trade Regime. A Historical Overview (1987) *International Labour Review* 126 (5), 565.

[8] The text of the International Sugar Agreement is published in United Nations: Treaty Series (1957) Vol. 258, No. 3677, 159.

[9] US Commission on Foreign Economic Policy: Staff Papers, February 1954, p. 437, quoted from *Charnowitz*, Steve (fn. 7), p. 574.

[10] See *Charnowitz*, Steve (fn. 7), p. 565.

> *[T]he negotiations should review the effect of denial of workers rights on contracting parties, and the relationship of worker rights to GATT Articles, its objectives and related instruments, and consider possible ways of dealing with worker rights issues in the GATT so as to ensure that expanded trade benefits all workers in all countries.*[11]

Since other Members objected to such an extension of the mandate, the US reintroduced the issue in a very late stage of the Uruguay Round, namely in 1994. At that point in time, a few weeks before the first WTO Ministerial in Marrakech was about to conclude eight years of negotiations, this move was more a tactical introduction of a bargaining chip to be traded off against other objectives, than a serious search for consensus on the issue itself.

Two years later the US administration succeeded in pushing the issue of labour standards back on to the agenda of the newly established WTO at the Ministerial Conference in Singapore. The declaration stated, that the '*ILO is the competent body to set and deal with [labour] standards*', Members '*reject the use of labour standards for protections purposes*' and '*the WTO and the ILO will continue their existing collaboration*'.[12]

In 1998, the ILO took up this ambivalent statement by unanimously adopting the *Declaration on Fundamental Principles and Rights at Work.*[13] This document complemented the WTO Singapore Declaration and highlighted *four fundamental labour standards*:

- freedom of association and collective bargaining,
- the abolition of forced labour,
- the abolition of child labour and
- non-discrimination in employment.

This move put the ball back in the WTO's court, since the ILO, as the authorative organisation setting and dealing with human rights at work now defined the scope of essential social standards.

In advance of the fourth Ministerial Conference in Seattle, the EU proposed a WTO/ILO '*joint standing forum*', whereas the US advocated a '*working party*'. Both proposals were strongly opposed by the 'Group

11 GATT Doc. PREP.COM (86) W/43 (25 June 1986).

12 Singapore Ministerial Declaration, WTO-Doc. WT/MIN(96)/Dec/W (18 December 1996).

13 For the negotiating history of the ILO Declaration on Fundamental Rights at Work see ILO, Report VII, ILC, 86th Session, 'Consideration of a Possible Declaration of Principles of the International Labour Organization concerning Fundamental Rights and Its Appropriate Follow-up Mechanism' (Geneva, ILO, 1998). Available online at www.ilo.org/public/english/standards/relm/ilc/ilc86/rep-vii.htm (accessed 15 August 2006).

of 77' that represents the developing nations and is traditionally concerned about these countries' competitive advantage from cheap labour costs. In this tension-filled context prior to Seattle, US President Bill Clinton announced his support for labour standards as part of every trade agreement. Clinton also expressed support for a trade systems '*in which sanctions would come for violating any provision of a trade agreement*'.[14]

Despite this provocative statement, an informal working group composed of thirty-five WTO Members and chaired by Costa Rica met on 3 December 1999 in Seattle. The state of the negotiations is reflected by a section for the draft *Ministerial Decision on Trade, Globalization, Development and Labour*, which was never adopted due to the premature end of the Ministerial Conference. This informal document recommended that the WTO and other international organisations '*conduct an in-depth discussion on trade, globalization, development and labour*'.[15]

Despite the fact that the ILO took up the issue in the broader context with its 'World Commission on the Social Dimension of Globalization',[16] human rights do not form part of today's mandate and agenda for the Doha Round. However, the question of the social dimension in world trade is a topic with the potential to reappear on the trade agenda at any time. In addition, as agriculture constitutes the bottleneck for the flow of current trade negotiations, it is not hard to imagine a situation in which developed countries reintroduce the issue.

How such a reintroduction of trade and labour standards would impact the Doha Round depends on the negotiation strategy and partners. The issue has the potential to be used either as a roadblock, bargaining chip or key for the currently deadlocked negotiations. On the one hand, developing countries with a strong stake in liberalising trade in agriculture are traditionally opposed to the inclusion of human rights at work as part of a trade agenda. On the other hand, those administrations and stakeholders in developed countries most concerned with the social impact of agricultural liberalisation are traditionally in favour of introducing minimum social standards to trade in goods. In this situation, one would not be surprised to witness history repeating itself in the sense that the *topic of trade and human rights at work would be brought back to the multilateral trade negotiations by some developed countries*. It remains to

[14] Seattle Post Intelligencer, 1 December 1999, p. A1.

[15] This document is reprinted in *Blüthner* (see fn. 1), Annex I.

[16] The full text of the Commission's report can be downloaded at: www.ilo.org/public/english/fairglobalization/report/index.htm (accessed 15 August 2006).

be seen if this would ultimately serve as roadblock, bargaining chip or stimulus within the Doha Round negotiations that so far is focused on agriculture.

B. The situation de lege lata

Whereas the topic of trade and the environment has kept the WTO dispute settlement system busy over recent years, the issue of human rights has hardly been brought to litigation. *To what extent market access can be differentiated on the basis of human rights compliance has yet not been tested in GATT/WTO dispute settlement.* The exception is the recent landmark case on the EU Generalised System of Preferences (GSP), in which the Appellate Body confirmed, that a positive conditionality between tariff preferences and environmental and human rights compliance principally is in line with WTO Law. This section, therefore, starts with a brief analysis of the GSP case, before taking a closer look on the principle question of a differentiation of market access on the basis of human rights at work.

1. Generalised systems of preferences

In April 2004, the WTO dispute settlement ruled on the GSP of the European Union following a complaint filed by India in March 2002.[17] The Appellate Body decided that differential treatment based on criteria such as environment or labour standards can be principally brought in line with WTO law, as long as similar treatment is applied to all similarly situated GSP beneficiaries.

The EU preference system grants developing countries special and differential tariff incentives based on good governance criteria, such as labour and environmental standards. The additional benefits for compliance were firstly, duty-free treatment instead of just tariff preferences for some 3,600 product groups, and secondly, an expanded scope of an additional 316 products benefiting from the scheme.

The differential tariff treatment of the EU scheme resulted in a three-layer differentiation of imports: first, imports from developed countries that are principally not subject to the scheme; second, imports from developing countries that are subject to the general GSP preference

[17] *EC–Conditions for the Granting of Tariff Preferences to Developing Counties*, Panel Report: WTO Doc. WT/DS246/R (1 December 2003) and Appellate Body Report: WTO Doc. WT/DS246/AB/R (7 April 2004).

scheme; and, third, imports from developing countries that are subject to particular GSP benefits arising from compliance with environmental and labour standards.

With regard to Art. I:1 GATT, any tariff scheme that results in treating '*like products*' from one country less favourably than another constitutes a violation of the basic rule of most-favoured-nation (MFN) treatment. Preference schemes show an intention to differentiate according to nature and purpose and therefore, violate the MFN clause contained in Art. I:1 GATT.[18]

The legal basis suitable to justify differential treatment under preference schemes otherwise inconsistent with GATT Art. I:1 is the so-called Enabling Clause.[19] There is little dispute that the Enabling Clause allows preference schemes which treat developing countries identically or, in other words, only differentiate on the basis of the developing country status. The relevant issue at stake is any additional differentiation between developing countries based on additional criteria, such as human rights.

The requirements for such a justification are set out in Enabling Clause, para. 2(a), footnote 3, and para. 3(c). Para 2(a), footnote 3 defines justifiable GSPs as '*generalised, non-reciprocal and non-discriminatory preferences beneficial to the developing countries*'.

Preference schemes such as the EU GSP are '*generalised*' and also '*non-reciprocal*', since compliance with environmental or social standards by a beneficiary cannot be seen as reciprocal to the granted tariff preferences, at least in the technical sense of WTO law.[20]

The criterion of *non-discrimination* was at the heart of the Appellate Body's decision. The key question was: To what extent do differential tariff preferences based on good governance standards constitute discrimination under para. 2(c) of the Enabling Clause?

[18] See also Panel Report *European Community–Tariff Treatment on Imports of Citrus Products from Certain Countries in the Mediterranean Region*, 7 February 1985, GATT Doc. L/5776, para. 4.11; for non-tariff preferences see *United States–Denial of Most-Favoured-Nation Treatment as to Non-Rubber-Footwear from Brazil*, 19 June 1992, GATT Doc. DS/18/R, reprinted in BISD39S/128, 1993, para. 6.14.

[19] Decision on '*Differential and More Favourable Treatment, Reciprocity and Fuller Participation of Developing Countries*', GATT Doc. L/4903, 28 November 1979, reprinted in BISD 26S/203 (1980). The Enabling Clause substituted the 'Waiver for Generalised Systems of Preferences', GATT Doc. L/3545, 25 June 1971, that was granted on a case-by-case basis so as to exceptionally justify MFN violations of preference differentiations.

[20] *Blüthner*, Andreas (see fn. 1), p. 474 different to *Hilpold*, Peter, Das neue allgemeine Präferenzschema der EU, in EuR 31 (1996) 1, p. 99 who arrives at a violation of the non-reciprocity requirement of para. 2(a) of the Enabling Clause.

At a glance, one might arrive at the interpretation of the Panel, that non-discrimination demands '*identical tariff preferences under GSP schemes be proved to all developing countries without [further] differentiation*'.[21] One strong argument for this restrictive interpretation is that the Enabling Clause is an exception to the basic obligation of Art. I:1 of the GATT according to the customary rules of interpretation in public international law – Art. 3:2 of the Dispute Settlement Understanding (DSU), Art. 31:1 of the Vienna Convention on the Law of Treaties – and thus needs to be interpreted narrowly.

The Appellate Body reversed the Panel's conclusion on differentiation of trade preferences among GSP beneficiaries and found that the term 'non-discriminatory' does not require identical tariff treatment among all developing countries. Rather, para. 2(a) needs to be interpreted in light of para. 3(c) Enabling Clause, that states:

> *Any differential treatment and more favourable treatment provided under this clause [. . .] (c) shall in the case of such treatment accorded by developed contracting parties to developing countries be designed and, if necessary, modified, to respond positively to the development, financial and trade needs of developing countries.*

The Appellate Body found, in contrast to the Panel's view, that para. 3(c) of the Enabling Clause does not preclude differential treatment among developing countries based on their compliance with environmental or labour standards. As long as a preference-granting scheme responds positively to developmental needs, which are not necessarily common or shared among all those countries, a differential treatment can be in line with the requirements set out in the Enabling Clause. The Appellate Body also ruled that this differentiation must not be applied arbitrarily but according to an objective standard based on beneficiaries 'development, trade and financial needs'.[22]

The Appellate Body's finding can further be reasoned with particular reference to the terms '*development, trade and financial needs*'. First, by giving additional reference to 'developmental needs as a criterion', the enumeration of para. 3(c) of the Enabling Clause seemingly goes beyond the welfare generating effect of trade liberalisation. When read in light of the principle of 'sustainable development' mentioned in para. 1 of the Preamble to the WTO Agreement, which calls for a balanced approach of

[21] Panel Report *EC–Tariff Preferences* (see fn. 17) para. 7.176.

[22] Appellate Body Report *EC–Tariff Preferences* (see fn. 17) paras 146 ff.

economic, social and environmental development, *it would seem systematically incoherent to argue that social development cannot be seen as 'developmental need' under the Enabling Clause.* If para. 3(c) of the Enabling Clause was meant to be limited in a narrow sense to trade and economic needs, the enumeration beyond those terms would appear to be redundant.[23]

Despite the fact that the Appellate Body identified certain substantive and procedural failings in the EU's preference scheme, the ruling sets out the principle criteria under which a differentiation of trade based on a countries' social standards is legally possible. *In sum, well-designed preference schemes can be applied so as to foster compliance with human rights at work in developing countries in line with current WTO law and jurisdiction.* Before considering or advocating for any further means of implementation of human rights within the current trading system, this option seems a preferable and feasible way to constructively promote human rights in the global trading system.

2. Human-rights-based conditionality of market access

This section considers to what extent a broader conditionality of market access and human rights compliance would be in line with WTO law *de lege lata*, which has not been yet tested in litigation. Provided there would be a legally sound track towards implementing human rights *de lege lata*, there would be little necessity to consider any regulation *de lege ferenda*, no matter what viewpoint one takes ideologically on the issue.

The question to be considered is two-fold: first, to what extent does the implementation of human rights at work through trade measures violate basic trade law obligations? and, what exceptional provision could eventually justify such a violation?

This legal analysis depends on what type of measure is applied by the importing country. Measures that are likely to be considered are: a non-discriminatory *sales ban* for domestic and imported goods produced in non-compliance with human rights; a *ban of all imports* that do not comply with human rights standards and, finally, a country could raise (bound) tariffs to penalise 'human rights unfriendly' imported goods.

(a) Basic substantive obligations The limited scope of this chapter only allows for a summary of what substantive obligations would be violated by the three hypothetical cases outlined above.[24]

[23] See *Blüthner*, Andreas (fn. 1), pp. 476 *et seq.*

[24] *Ibid.*, pp. 279–375 with further references.

The first case of a *sales ban* for domestic and imported products would violate Art. II:4 (in conjunction with Art. II *note ad*) and Art. I:1 GATT, because '*like products*' would be differentiated on the basis of non-product-related processing and production methods (PPMs).[25] Art. 2.1 of the Technical Barriers to Trade (TBT) Agreement is not applicable to PPM-based measures.[26]

The second case, an *import ban*, clearly violates Art. XI GATT, whereas Art. XIII GATT is not applicable.[27]

Thirdly, the alternative of 'punitive' tariffs on imports originating from countries that do not comply with human rights at work violates either Art. II: 1(a) GATT in the case of bound tariffs, or Art. I:1 GATT. In addition, all of these measures would contradict the spirit of Art. XXXVII:1(b) GATT which prohibits trade restrictions on products of particular interest to less developed countries.

In sum, restrictions of market access aimed at implementing human rights at work would violate basic GATT rules and would depend on a legal justification under an exception, particularly Art. XX GATT.

(b) Justification under Art. XX GATT? Since the Appellate Body's Report *US–Gasoline*, trade lawyers know that the analysis of Art. XX is *two-tiered.*[28] A measure at issue must first pass a 'provisional justification' through meeting one of the ten enumerative exceptions listed in Art. XX. (a) to (j) – also called 'legitimate policy objectives'.[29] Second, further appraisal of the same measure under the introductory clause of Art. XX GATT, also known as 'chapeau' or 'head note', is required.

The two segments of Art. XX – justifications and the chapeau – represent two fundamental antagonists in international trade law. On one side is national sovereignty and, on the other, the fundamental principles of WTO law and the rights of other Members to comply with them (*pacta*

[25] The treatment of non-product-related PPMs under Art. I, III and XI GATT with regard to the 'like product' concept has created a broad and intense debate: see for example, *Howse*, Robert/*Regan*, Donald: The Product/Process Distinction – An Illusory Basis for Disciplining 'Unilateralism' in Trade Policy, *European Journal of International Law* (2000) 11(2), 256 (with further references), creatively arriving at a non-violation of Art. III GATT through narrowly interpreting this basic obligations in light of the policy objectives of the exceptional provision of Art. XX GATT.

[26] See *Blüthner*, Andreas (fn. 1), p. 284. [27] *Ibid.*, p. 304.

[28] Appellate Body Report *United States–Standards for Reformulated and Conventional Gasoline*, WTO Doc. WT/DS2/AB/R (20 May 1996), p. 21.

[29] Appellate Body Report *United States–Import Prohibition of Certain Shrimp Products*, WTO Doc. WT/DS58/AB/R (12 October 1998), para.149.

sunt servanda).[30] The 'legitimate policy objectives' are reservations of *national sovereignty* that allow WTO members to seek preliminary justification for trade restrictive measures *necessary* to protect these goals. Whether a certain goal should be pursued and what the appropriate level of protection is are to a great extent sovereign decisions of the respective member state. In a second step, the flow through this loophole is filtered by the so-called necessity test and ultimately, the chapeau.

There, preliminary-justified measures need to be applied in a least trade restrictive way and must neither constitute means of 'arbitrary or unjustifiable *discrimination*', nor a 'disguised restriction of trade'. These criteria reflect the fundamental principle of non-discrimination, most prominently embraced under Art. I and Art. III GATT.[31]

With respect to the first tier, measures that would differentiate market access on the basis of a countries' compliance with human rights at work would need to meet one of the provisional justifications of Art. XX, namely either for measures *necessary to protect public morals*, Art. XX(a) GATT, or *relating to products of prison labour*, Art. XX(e) GATT.[32]

III. Art. XX(e) GATT

Due to the textual reference to working conditions outside the jurisdiction of the importing country, one might be tempted to first take a closer look at Art. XX(e). If trade restrictive measures relating to prison labour are explicitly permitted, one might argue, worse labour practices such as forced or child labour must also be implicitly covered through an interpretation *a majorem ad minus*. However, this would mean expanding language beyond its ordinary meaning, and, as the International Court of Justice (ICJ) has put it, '*if the relevant words in their natural and ordinary meaning make sense in their context, this is an end of the matter*'.[33]

30 Appellate Body Report *US–Gasoline* (see fn. 28), p. 22.

31 *Jackson*, John: The World Trading System: Law and Policy of International Economic Relations, 2nd edn, Cambridge MA 1997, p. 234 has therefore called the chapeau a 'soft MFN obligation'.

32 In selected circumstances, for example in the case of the worst forms of child labour or hazardous working conditions, the exception Art. XX *(b)(necessary to protect human [. . .] life or health)* might also apply. For a discussion of this provision in the context of human rights at work see *Blüthner*, Andreas (fn. 1), pp. 333 *et seq.* with further references.

33 *United Nations*: Report of the International Court of Justice, New York, 1950, p. 8.

However, seemingly some latitude for interpretation with respect to the *context* of this provision exists, since prison labour is regulated but allowed in most WTO member countries and by the ILO. By contrast, forced labour in most countries and in international human rights law is prohibited. The draft history of this provision reveals an economic, and not humanitarian legal purpose, namely to outlaw competition based on distorted market prices for labour, which is also the case with forced labour.[34]

However, Art. XX GATT is an exception to the treaty's purpose in that it needs to be interpreted narrowly according to customary rules of public international law.[35] It remains to be seen whether dispute settlement litigation will interpret prison labour to include forced labour, but it appears unlikely given the view articulated in Art. 3:3 DSU that '*rulings of the DSB cannot add or diminish the rights and obligations provided in the covered agreement*'. In any event, Art. XX(e) will not provide a solid legal basis for even a preliminary justification of measures aimed at fostering compliance with all relevant human rights at work (e.g. non-discrimination in employment or freedom of association).

IV. Art. XX(a) GATT

Article XX(a) of the GATT allows measures 'necessary to protect public morals'. Measures aimed at improving compliance with internationally recognised human rights might be a matter of 'public morals'. Other examples that have been discussed under this justification include child labour,[36] the denial of fundamental human rights at work[37] or even trade in furs from leg-hold traps[38] and dolphin-unfriendly fishing practices for

[34] *Diller*, Janelle M./*Levy*, David A.: Child Labour, Trade and Investment: Towards the Harmonization of International Law *American Journal of International Law* (1997) 91(4) 684, para. 182 citing an Interpreting Note to an International Trade Agreement of the League of Nations. [35] *Supra*, p. 392.

[36] *Charnowitz*, Steve: The Moral Exception in Trade Policy, *Virginia Journal of International Law* (1998) 38(4) 740.

[37] *Torres*, Raymond: Labour Standards in Trade, *The OECD Observer* (1996) 202, 10.

[38] *Quick*, Reinhard: The Community's Regulation on Leg-Hold Traps: Creative Unilateralism Made Compatible with WTO Law through Bilateral Negotiations? *New Directions in International Economic Law: Essays in Honour of John H. Jackson M. Bronckers and R. Quick.* (eds.) The Hague, 2000, pp. 239–57.

tuna.[39] *Thus it is for good reason that leading trade scholars understand human rights as such as 'moral rights'*.[40]

The public morals clause of GATT Art. XX(a) has not yet been invoked in WTO litigation. However, the analogue exception of Art. XIV(a) GATS has been recently tested for the first time in the *US–Gambling* case. There, the Appellate Body noted the similarities between Art. XX GATT and Art. XIV GATS that allow one to take into account respective case law of both provisions[41] – a finding that can be applied here *vice versa*.

In *US–Gambling*, the Appellate Body upheld the Panel's definition of '*public morals*' based on the ordinary textual meaning, namely, that public morals '*denote standards of right and wrong conduct maintained by or on behalf of a community or nation*'.[42] When reviewing the US measures, the Appellate Body did not pass on the question *of whether* the supply of internet gambling services is socially beneficial or morally desirable. Rather it found it sufficient, that US congressional reports and testimony were *considering* moral standards of conduct, such as money laundering, organised crime, fraud, underage and pathological gambling.[43]

Expecting a country to undertake considerations on public morals, rather than reviewing the national authorities' substantial judgment, reflects the two-tier structure of Art. XX GATT, particularly the checks and balances between provisional justification and chapeau.[44] In addition, setting a standard of substantial review for public morals would have easily overstretched the Appellate Body's authority and capacity with a view to potential issues in future cases. For example, to what extent is the import of beef to India in conflict with Hindu religion? Does

[39] Opinion issued by Australia as third-party submission in Panel Report *United States–Restrictions on Imports of Tuna* (unadopted), GATT Doc. DS29/R 16 June 1994, para. 4.4.

[40] *Petersmann*, Erst-Ullrich: Human Rights and International Environmental Law in the 21st Century: The Need to Clarify their Interrelationships, *Journal of International Economic Law* (2001) 4(1), 18.

[41] Appellate Body Report *US–Measures Affecting the Cross-Border Supply of Gambling and Betting Services*, WTO Doc. WT/DS285/AB/R (7 April 2005), para. 291.

[42] Appellate Body Report *US-Gambling* (see fn. 41), para. 296. For a similar definition see also *Feddersen*, Christoph T. See Focusing on Substantive Law in International Economic Relations: The Public Morals of GATTs Art. XX(a) and Conventional Rules of Interpretation, *Minnesota Journal of Global Trade* (1998) 7(1), 96; *Blüthner*, Andreas (see fn. 1), p. 342.

[43] Panel Report *US–Measures Affecting the Cross-Border Supply of Gambling and Betting Services* WT/DS285/R (10 November 2004) para. 6.486; Appellate Body Report *US–Gambling* (see fn. 41), paras 296, 298.

[44] *Supra*, p. 396.

importing pork conflict with the morals of Islamic or Jewish populations? Alternatively, where does market access for fashion media end and pornography begin? With the standard of review chosen in *US–Gambling* the Appellate Body wisely circumvented the situation of slipping into the role of moral adjudicator.

In sum, the Appellate Body refrained from substantially reviewing the moral judgments of its members. At the same time it ruled that 'public morals' can be determined by national authorities and found it sufficient that *standards of right and wrong* have been considered by relevant national authorities.

Based on these findings, *it is hard to imagine that future WTO litigation would exclude measures concerning internationally recognised human rights from the scope of public morals clauses in WTO law.* Human rights at work are by definition internationally agreed standards that distinguish between conduct that is right and wrong. Art. XX(a) GATT will apply in a given case, if respective national authorities took into account and seriously considered moral aspects such as the protection of children, unfair labour practices abroad or gender discrimination. It would not be a matter of public morals if respective trade measures were just driven by protectionism such as restricting competition from countries with low labour costs. *In sum, trade measures concerning human rights could pass the provisional justification of GATT Art. XX(a).*

V. Necessity test

Before passing on the chapeau of Art. XX GATT, provisionally justified measures under Art. XX(a) GATT must comply with the so-called '*necessity test*'.

The necessity of a measure, according to Appellate Body Report *Korea–Various Measures on Beef*, is determined through 'a process of weighing and balancing a series of factors'.[45] Since then, the so-called *necessity test* has been significantly modified and refined in comparison to early GATT/WTO dispute settlement practices. In *Thailand–Cigarettes*, measures were only considered *necessary*, if there was 'no alternative measure consistent with the GATT, or less inconsistent with

[45] Appellate Body Report, *Korea–Various Measures on Beef*, WT/DS121/AB/R (12 January 2000), para. 164.

it, which [can] be expected to employ to achieve [the] policy objectives'. In a nutshell, *the Appellate Body looked to see if a country had chosen the least trade restrictive measure to achieve its policy objective.*

Since *Korea-Beef*, the Appellate Body has characterised the necessity test as a process of 'weighting and balancing' that:

> *[. . .] comprehended in the determination of whether a WTO-consistent alternative measure which the Member concerned could 'reasonably be expected to employ' is available, or whether a less WTO-inconsistent measure is 'reasonably available'.*[46]

This process begins with an assessment of the 'relative importance' of the interests or values furthered by the challenged measure.[47] The Appellate Body identified two factors that are relevant in most cases[48] One factor is the contribution of the measure to the realisation of the ends pursued by it; the other factor is the restrictive impact of the measure on international trade. Through a 'weighing and balancing' comparison of measures, taking into account the interests or values at stake, it is decided whether a measure is 'necessary' or, alternatively, whether another, WTO-consistent measure is 'reasonably available'.[49]

The necessity test reflects the joint understanding of members that substantive GATT obligations should not be deviated from casually. An alternative measure will be only found 'reasonably available', where it is not merely theoretical in nature, or where the alternative imposes an undue burden on the Member, such as prohibitive costs or substantial technical difficulties. In sum, a reasonable alternative must be a measure that would preserve the Member's right to achieve its desired level of protection with respect to the objective pursued.[50]

Accordingly, a range of factors should be taken into account when applying the '*necessity-test*' to measures geared towards implementing human rights at work, such as:

- the relative importance of the policy objective, namely the implementation of human rights at work;

[46] Panel Report, *Thailand–Restrictions on Importation of and Internal Taxes on Cigarettes*, Adopted 7 November 1990, para. 75, para. 166.

[47] *Ibid.*, para. 162. See also Appellate Body Report, *EC–Measures Affecting Asbestos and Asbestos-containing Products*, WTO-Doc WT/DS135/R (12 March 2001) para. 172.

[48] Appellate Body Report, *Korea–Beef* (see fn. 45): para. 164.

[49] *Ibid.*, para. 166.

[50] Appellate Body Report, *EC–Asbestos* (see fn. 47): paras. 172–4. See also Appellate Body Report, *Korea–Beef* (fn. 45): para. 180.

- the effectiveness of the measure with regard to the human rights objective, namely, reaching the exporting sectors that are in non-compliance with human rights at work and providing positive change,
- the practical availability of less-trade-restrictive alternatives that can be expected to be effectively employed, such as labelling schemes, incentives provided within GSP-schemes,[51] human rights conditionality within government procurement,[52] other multilateral implementation schemes, such as ILO-monitoring, or possibly even corporate citizenship initiatives, such as the UN Global Compact;[53]
- the 'collateral damages' for international trade and commerce, namely industries and sectors that comply with respective human rights standards, but are non-intentionally affected by the measure.

A decisive factor is the burden of proof – namely to what extent the defending party succeeds in establishing a *prima facie* case for the necessity of a measure. This means putting forward evidence and arguments that enable a panel to assess the challenged measure in light of the relevant factors to be 'weighed and balanced' in a given case. A measure will ultimately be considered 'necessary' when the weighing and balancing process reveals that it is 'significantly closer to the pole of "indispensable" than to the opposite pole of simply "making a contribution to"'.[54]

In sum, *the necessity test imposes high hurdles for trade-restricting measures aimed at fostering human rights at work. It remains to be seen whether such a measure will pass this roadblock on the way towards a justification under Art. XX GATT.*

VI. Chapeau

The focus of the chapeau rests on the application of a measure.[55] Its purpose is to ensure that the rights of other members are not frustrated

[51] *Supra*, p. 391.

[52] For a further elaboration of this option and its compatibility with WTO law see *Blüthner*, Andreas (fn. 1), p. 459 with additional references.

[53] See *infra*, p. 410.

[54] Appellate Body Report, *Korea–Beef* (see fn. 45), para. 161.

[55] Appellate Body Report *US–Gasoline* (see fn. 28), p. 22; Appellate Body Report *US–Gambling* (fn. 41), para. 339.

through measures that are otherwise justified under Art. XX(a)–(j) GATT.[56]

Passing the necessity test would not prejudge a measure's review under the chapeau. Here, the key questions are whether the GATT permits trade measures with *'extrajurisdictional effect'* – meaning with effect outside the jurisdiction of the importing country. If so, what are the requirements regarding coherence in human rights implementation arising from the chapeau's 'soft non-discrimination' requirements? Would a differentiation between countries where, regarding human rights, *the same conditions prevail* constitute an *arbitrary discrimination?* Would it be *unjustifiable* to demand compliance with human rights at work abroad, if these standards are not respected domestically?

A. Arbitrary or unjustified discrimination

Reflecting the principle of non-discrimination contained in the substantial provisions of Arts I, III and XIII of the GATT, the chapeau cannot logically refer to the same standards by which a violation of a substantive rule has been determined to occur.[57]

In *US–Gambling*, the Appellate Body confirmed the interpretation which had been proposed by literature,[58] namely, that '*arbitrary or unjustifiable discrimination*' defines a standard of consistency for the application of measures with regard to the objectives contained in the general exception.[59] Without further distinguishing between the criteria 'arbitrary' and 'unjustified', the Appellate Body in *US–Gambling* reviewed the non-discriminatory restriction of domestic *and* remote

[56] Appellate Body Report *US–Gasoline* (see fn. 28). *Ibid.*

[57] Appellate Body Report *US–Gasoline* (see fn. 28), *Ibid.*; Panel Report *US–Gambling* (see fn. 43), para. 6.578; Appellate Body Report *US–Shrimp* (see fn. 29), para. 150, which states: [under the chapeau, first,] . . . the application of the measure must result in *discrimination.* As we stated in *United States–Gasoline*, the nature and quality of this discrimination is different from the discrimination in the treatment of products which was already found to be inconsistent with one of the substantive obligations of the GATT 1994, such as Articles I, III or XI. Second, the discrimination must be *arbitrary* or *unjustifiable* in character (original emphasis).

[58] *Blüthner*, Andreas (see fn. 1), pp. 353, 374.

[59] With regard to Art. XIV GATS, see Panel Report *US–Gambling* (see fn. 43), paras. 6.578–6.581, where the Panel discusses Appellate Body decisions relating to the chapeau of Article XX of the GATT 1994.

gambling services under US legislation. In so doing, the Appellate Body applied the chapeau as a '*soft national treatment*' obligation.

When stepping back from *US–Gambling* and taking a more principled look on the legal interpretation of the terms 'arbitrary' and 'unjustifiable discrimination', they seem to refer to different dimensions of 'consistency'. These dimensions are reflections of the fundamental principles of 'most-favored-nation' and 'national treatment'.

On the one hand, '*arbitrary*', in its ordinary textual understanding means an '*unrestrained exercise of the will, caprice or preference* [. . .] *based on random or convenience or choice rather than on reason or nature*'.[60] 'Reason' with regard to exceptional measures under the chapeau needs to be understood with respect to the policy objective at stake. A measure under the chapeau is not based on reason if it does not contribute consistently to the policy objective put forward. Interpreted in the context of the chapeau's term '*discrimination between countries where the same conditions prevail*' a measure needs to be applied consistently to countries that are similar with regard to the *respective policy objective. This sets up the requirement to treat countries with similar human rights conditions similarly–and countries with a different human rights situation differently*, or in other words, provide MFN treatment with regard to human rights. For example, conditionality between market access and forced labour would result in arbitrary discrimination if applied only to some countries (e.g. not Myanmar (Burma), that is suspended as ILO member due to persistent forced labour).

On the other hand, '*unjustified*' can be understood as complementing 'soft national treatment obligation' with regard to legitimate policy objectives. This understanding accords with the Appellate Body's application of the chapeau in *US–Gambling* for Art. XIV GATS. 'Justifications' within Art. XX GATT are the policy objectives of paras. (a)–(j). Measures are therefore 'unjustified' if they require human rights compliance for imports, but are not equally applied domestically, if the same conditions prevail.

In sum, the proposed interpretation of the chapeau's terms 'arbitrary and unjustifiable discrimination' sets up a consistency test that is two-fold: first measures otherwise inconsistent with the GATT must be applied non-discriminatorily regarding domestic and imported goods; and, second, these measures must not discriminate between imports from third

[60] *Webster's Third New International Dictionary*, Vol. 2, London, 1966, p. 110.

countries with regard to the policy objective at stake – in our case, human rights at work.

B. Disguised restriction of international trade

A human rights-based measure that has passed both the necessity and the consistency test under the chapeau, is still prohibited if it is a 'disguised restriction of international trade'. This requirement may appear to be redundant as the criteria set out in Art. XX GATT already aim at detecting protectionist restrictions of international trade hiding behind legitimate policy objectives.

However, the Appellate Body has also seen the chapeau as an expression of the principle of good faith without particularly referring to the term 'disguised restriction of international trade'. The principle of good faith is a general principle of international law, also known as the doctrine of *abus de droit*, which prohibits the abusive exercise of states rights.[61]

Here, the main issue for human rights-based trade measures is their intended 'extrajurisdictional' effect: At the end of the day, these measures force other members to change their human rights policies within their jurisdiction, even though measures are applied at the borders of the importing country.

Early GATT dispute settlement panels argued, 'extrajurisdictional' measures *as such* would seriously impair the objectives of the GATT since a country could unilaterally determine policies from which other countries could not deviate without jeopardising their rights under the Agreement.[62] The GATT obligations would then only bind countries with identical internal regulations.[63] Based on these arguments measures with an extrajurisdictional effect, even if otherwise justified, can constitute an *abus de droit* and a 'disguised restriction of international trade' and are therefore *per se* not permitted under the GATT.[64]

[61] Appellate Body Report *US–Shrimp* (see fn. 29), p. 61, para. 158.

[62] Panel Report *US–Tuna II* (see fn. 39), para. 5.38.

[63] Panel Report *United States–Restrictions on Imports of Tuna* (not adopted), GATT Doc DS21/R (3 September 1991), para. 5.27.

[64] Panel Reports *US–Tuna I* (see fn. 63) and *US–Tuna II* (fn. 39), systematically hardly convincing, addressed this issue either under Art. III GATT or the provisional justifications of Art. XX (a)–(j).

Under WTO litigation, the issue of 'extrajurisdictionality' has not been explicitly addressed. The Appellate Body in *US–Shrimp* circumvented to rule on the matter. The case concerned a US measure with 'extrajursdictional' effect – namely fishing practices in Thailand that endangered sea turtles. Instead of passing on 'extrajurisdictionality', the Appellate Body noted that '*sea turtles are highly migratory animals, passing in and out of waters* [*subject to*] *the* [. . .] *jurisdiction of various costal states*, [including] *waters subject to United States jurisdiction. We note only that in the specific circumstances of the case before us, there is a sufficient nexus*'.[65]

A closer look into the Appellate Body's reasoning in the *Shrimp* case is needed in order to understand the extent that such a 'sufficient nexus' could potentially arise between an importing country and the human rights situation abroad.

First, it was noted by the Appellate Body, that sea turtles, are protected under CITES,[66] a *de facto* universally agreed environmental agreement.[67] The protection of sea turtles, one might argue, is therefore not just a domestic, but a universally accepted, policy goal.

Second, the physical migration of the turtles was a decisive factor in the conclusion of a 'sufficient nexus'. The protection of the global sea turtle population was therefore not an exclusive concern of a single WTO member.[68] Some might argue that particular human rights have either an *erga omnes* effect or even constitute *jus cogens*. Even though the beneficiaries of these rights are not migratory in a physical sense like sea turtles, matters of fundamental human rights can, however, equally reach beyond the jurisdiction and concern of a single member state.

A third aspect the Appellate Body addressed in the *US–Shrimp* case was the requirement to enter into 'serious, across-the-board negotiations' with the objective of achieving a bilateral or multilateral agreement to solve the according policy objective.[69] The Appellate Body saw it as a necessity and a matter of good faith, to negotiate before enforcing import restrictions against the exports of other countries.[70] In *US–Gambling*, the Appellate Body watered down the necessity to negotiate when it ruled that

65 Appellate Body Report *US–Shrimp* (see fn. 29), para.133 (emphasis added).

66 Convention on International Trade in Endangered Species of Wild Fauna and Flora, published in *ILM* (1973) 12, 1058.

67 See *Sand*, Peter H. Whither CITES? The Evolution of a Treaty Regime in the Boarderland of Trade and Environment, *European Journal of International Law* (1997) 8(1), 29.

68 Similarly Appellate Body Report *US–Shrimp* (see fn. 29), para. 133.

69 *Ibid.*, para. 166. 70 *Ibid.*, para. 172.

'*consultations are by definition a process, the results of which are uncertain and therefore not capable of comparison with the measures at issue in this case*'.[71] With regard to human rights-related measures it remains to been seen if either exhaustive consultations within the human rights system, or separate negotiations about the measure at stake will be required.

Even though one interprets the latest Appellate Body rulings so as to no longer categorically prohibited 'extrajurisdictional' measures, the set of positive criteria required do not make Art. XX GATT a sound basis for fostering human rights through the world trading system de lege lata.

In summing up, this section discussed to what extent a human rights-based conditionality of market access can be brought in conformity with the GATT *de lege lata.* The exercise of thinking through such a hypothetical case illustrates, that on the basis of the current treaty practice *there is hardly a sound legal basis for a trade-based enforcement of human rights at work.* Even if it would be possible to provisionally justify those measures under Art. XX(a) GATT, *the necessity test sets up an initial high hurdle on the way to GATT conformity.* In addition, even if one reads the *US–Shrimp* decision as having turned the principal denial of 'extrajurisdictional' measures into a list of ambitious but positive criteria ('sufficient nexus test'), there is no reliable path for human rights enforcement through Art. XX GATT *de lege lata.*

VII. De lege ferenda

Assuming the topic of human rights at work returns on the negotiation tables of a revived Doha-Round, opponents and advocates would confront the question of the legal design of a 'social clause' *de lege ferenda.* This section discusses two options based on two fundamental premises, namely, that options *de lege ferenda* must:

- conform to the WTO system, in particular be 'protectionism-proof'; and,
- effectively implement human rights at work.

The options to be assessed on the basis of these premises are:

- amending the GATT through an exceptional provision for the protection of human rights at work, mostly proposed for Art. XX GATT;[72] and

[71] Appellate Body Report *US–Gambling* (fn. 41), para. 316.

[72] *Trebilcock*, Michael J./*Howse*, Robert The Regulation of International Trade, London 1995, p. 411; *Willers*, Dietrich: Sozialklauseln in Internationalen Handelsverträgen

- a new WTO Agreement on Trade-Related International Labour Rights (TRILs).

A. A 'social clause' exception under Article XX GATT?

The strength of a 'social clause' under Art. XX GATT, which most likely would be realised through an interpretative agreement (Art. X:2 GATT) on Art. XX GATT as a whole, results from its relative conformity with the objective to effectively implement human rights, which appeals to human rights advocates. It provides individual WTO Members with a *carte blanche* for unilateral trade measures. Since there is no need for prior authorisation of exceptional measures through the WTO or other bodies, market access restrictions necessary to achieve human rights objectives could be applied on short notice, which has been found to maximise the economic force of sanctions on a target country.[73]

The weakness of this approach is its lack of system conformity. The threat for the WTO system results from the unilateral character of exceptions, which interferes with the legal principle of reciprocity. Furthermore, exceptional measures open loopholes towards the slippery slope of protectionism and power politics. A country targeted by sanctions is limited to look for *ex post* remedy under dispute settlement. Even with judicial success, implementation depends on the availability of effective countervailing trade measures, which are not at the disposal of developing countries with marginal import markets. Without addressing the downsides of this approach, the judicial bodies of the WTO would be left to fix this shortcoming through judicial activism.

B. A new TRILs Agreement?

The strength of a self-standing TRILs Agreement is that *de lege ferenda* is laterally reversed to a 'social clause', – it conforms to the WTO system. A multilaterally negotiated TRILs Agreement could be legally designed to achieve coherence with core pillars of the trading system and the interests of developing countries. Also this 'legislative' way of building prior consensus between Members on a new agreement is preferable to shifting the

[Social Clauses in International Trade Agreements], in Weltfriede durch Soziale Gerechtigkeit, Baden-Baden, 1994, p. 169; *Leary*, Virginia: Workers Rights in International Trade: The Social Clause (GATT, ILO, NAFTA, US Laws), in Fair Trade and Harmonization (Vol. 2, Legal Analysis), *Bhagwati* Jagdish/*Hudec*, Robert E. (eds.) Cambridge MA, 1996, p. 182.

73 See *Hufbauer*, Gary/*Schott*, Jeffrey/*Elliott*, Kimberly Economic Sanctions Reconsidered, History and Current Policy, Washington, 2nd edn (1990), p. 100 *et seq.*

burden to the jurisdiction, as would be the case under GATT Art. XX. In addition, implementation under a TRILs Agreement would ensure *ex ante* compliance with WTO law through dispute settlement. A TRILs would include human rights at work as a legal obligation – as is the case for intellectual property rights under TRIPs – instead of as a unilateral legal exception – the case under GATT Art. XX. A Member who sought to enforce TRILs would first need to win a case against the Member violating human rights before trade measures could be authorised. Such implementation through dispute settlement reduces the risk of disguised protectionism and avoids an erosion of the rule of law through unilateral power politics.

The main weakness of a TRILs relates to the present concept of 'nullification and impairment', contained in the WTO dispute settlement provisions. 'Nullification and impairment' reflects the core principle of economic reciprocity in the trading system in restricting implementation measures to the value of 'nullified' benefits resulting from a breach of WTO law. On the one hand, provided a TRILs would have to comply with this principle, the implementation is limited to the level of 'nullification' of trade benefits arising the 'impairment' of human rights at work. In other words, there would be no implementation in cases where a TRILs violation does not result in measurable negative economic consequences to the complaining party. If WTO Members agree on qualifying the principle of 'nullification and impairment' to principally cover fundamental human rights violations, the TRILs Agreement would be an option to harmonise the conflicting demands of system conformity and human rights effectiveness.

VIII. The Global Compact – an alternative way

A. Introduction

This section aims to present and elaborate *a 'cooperationist' policy model addressing the social dimension of globalisation: the UN Global Compact* (GC).[74] This initiative, kicked-off by UN Secretary General Kofi Annan in 1999, is based on cooperation rather than choosing a regulatory approach for realising universally accepted values, including human rights at work.

[74] For the emerging literature dealing with the Global Compact see *Nowrot*, Karsten: The New Governance Structure of the Global Compact, in *Essays in Transnational Economic Law* (2005) 47,5, fn. 4 with further references.

This section will provide a basic understanding of this initiative and its context, where it comes from, what it is, and what it is not. One point of emphasis will lie on how substantive principles and procedural mechanisms fuel implementation in comparison to the implementation of human rights at work under the WTO system.

B. Background and context

The emergence of the GC can best be understood in the context of the growing institutional co-operation between stakeholder groups in globalisation. The UN has been working with the private sector for more than fifty years (e.g., through the procurement of goods and services). Since then, the UN and business have been interacting through intergovernmental processes and policy networks. In addition, non-governmental organisations (NGOs) co-operate with the UN both in the field and at the political level. In 1999 more than 44 000 NGOs existed (in 1991 there were 23,600) and around 3,500 enjoy an official consultative status within the UN.[75]

However, thirty years ago the relevant UN bodies perceived business for their aim and work as part of the problem, rather than part of the solution. Accordingly, rigid rules for corporate behaviour were the means of early UN approaches to business. In the 1970s, the UN Center for Transnational Corporations (CTC) drafted a 'UN Code of Conduct' aimed at setting minimum behaviour standards for multinationals.[76] Since member states did not come to an agreement, the code was never adopted and the CTC was closed down some years ago.

In this context, the approach of the GC can be seen as a change of paradigms. At the beginning of the new century, the UN and world societies were facing increasingly complex and particularly interconnected economic, social, and environmental challenges that call for co-operation. To respond to these new challenges Secretary General Annan's starting point was the recognition that business should be perceived as part of the solution, and not part of the problem.

[75] *Nelson*, Jane: Building Partnerships: Cooperation between the United Nations System and the Private Sector, New York, United Nations 2001, p. 19.

[76] For more information on the work of the CTC, see United Nations, Center on Transnational Corporations, '*The CTC Reporter*', a periodical that ran from 1976–1991; and United Nations, Department of Economic and Social Development: Transnational Corporations and Management Division, Advisory Studies, New York (1987–90), online at http://unctc.unctad.org/aspx/ctcTitle.aspx (accessed 15 August 2006).

Accordingly, he underscored that the UN and business share common goals, even though diverging interests might drive them. For example, the UN contributes to the 'soft infrastructure' for business by advocating respect for public goods and universal values, such as human rights, peace and stability.[77] The private sector can contribute to these goals not only through philanthropic action or community projects but also through the way good corporate citizens conduct their business, including sound social and environmental investments.

On the macro level, Secretary General Annan was aware that the globalisation process is not irreversible, as proclaimed by some in the late 1990s.[78] He saw the threat of a backlash to globalisation, if it did not become more inclusive and sustainable. Accordingly, nine months before the failure of the Seattle WTO ministerial conference, he proposed a compact based on universally shared values to the stakeholders of globalisation gathering in Davos. The overriding goal he had in mind for this compact was to offer a framework that helps to fill the gap between global economic governance, which is underpinned by strong rules and appropriate enforcement through the WTO, and social and environmental pillars, which are not.[79]

C. *How the Compact came about*

The first high-level meeting on the Global Compact was held on 26 July 2000, in the rooms of the General Assembly at the UN Headquarters in New York.[80] This was the official 'kick-off' for the GC. In a forward-looking speech at the World Economic Forum in Davos on 31 January

77 For further research in international cooperation and global public goods from a US perspective, see *Nye*, Joseph S. American National Interest and Global Public Goods, in *International Affairs* (2002) 78(2), 233–44.

78 This statement expresses what political scientists call a 'weak globalization thesis', which sees 'globalization' as nothing entirely new compared to traditional 'economic integration' that still allows a range of viable policy alternatives. However, this chapter does not aim to analyse or contribute to the already fuzzy definition of 'globalization'. On globalisation, its definition problems, and the role of business, see *Leisinger*, Klaus M. Globalization, Minima Moralia of Multinational Companies. Available online at www.novartisfoundation.com/en/articles/business/globalization_multinational_companies.htm (accessed 15 August 2006).

79 *Kell*, Georg Dilemmas in Competitiveness. Paper presented at the Community and Citizenship Business and Human Rights Seminar at Toward Universal Business Principles, London School of Economics and Political Science, London, 22 May 2001. Available online at www.unglobalcompact.org/NewsAndEvents/speeches_and_statements/index.html (accessed 15 August 2006).

80 A wealth of information on the New York meeting and the Global Compact, including UN documents, the commitments of participants, case studies, speeches, press information

1999, UN Secretary General Kofi Annan addressed the following words to the gathering of world business leaders:

> *Let us choose to unite the power of markets with the authority of universal ideals. Let us choose to reconcile the creative forces of private entrepreneurship with the need of the disadvantaged and the requirements of future generations.*[81]

Forty-four founding participants initially took up this proposal from various business sectors. The GC includes such major global players $$as Asea Brown Bovery (ABB), BASF, DaimlerChrysler, Dupont, Nike, Union de Banques Suisse (UBS), and Volvo. Furthermore, a significant number of selected small and medium-sized enterprises and associations are lending their support to the GC. The range of civil society organisations (CSOs) represented in the GC includes leading human rights organisations such as Amnesty International and Human Rights Watch, major environmental groups like the World Wildlife Fund (WWF), and social initiatives (e.g. Business for Social Responsibility and Transparency International).[82] Additionally, the International Organisation of Employers and the International Confederation of Free Trade Unions are actively supporting the GC.

IX. Substantial pillars of the Compact

The GC is based on ten principles, which were drawn from three universally accepted UN declarations in the area of human and labour rights

and the full text of papers can be accessed from the homepage www.unglobalcompact.org (accessed 15 August 2006). For a four-page special section on the Global Compact, see *International Herald Tribune*, 25 January 2001. The work on the Global Compact within the United Nations, however, started as early as 1998. For one of the first presentations of the concept, see *Kell*, Georg/*Ruggie*, John Global Markets and Social Legitimacy: The Case of the 'Global Compact'. Paper presented at the conference Governing the Public Domain beyond the Era of the Washington Consensus: Redrawing the Line between the State and the Market, York University, Toronto, Canada (4–6 November 1999), p. 7. Available online at www.unglobalcompact.org/NewsAndEvents/speeches_and_statements/index.html (accessed 15 August 2006).

81 Secretary-General Annan's speech in Davos (UN-Doc. SG/SM/6881/Rev.1) is accessible online at www.un.org/News/Press/docs/1999/19990201.sgsm6881.r1.html. (accessed 15 August 2006).

82 A list of all participants of the Global Compact is available online at www.unglobalcompact.org/ParticipantsAndStakeholders/index.html (accessed 15 August 2006). Delegates from eighteen countries were also present at the New York meeting as observers, including developed countries like the US, Germany, and Norway and developing countries like India, Pakistan, and Thailand.

and environment, including the ILO Declaration on Fundamental Human Rights at Work from 1998.[83] These principles were translated from state duties to promotional principles addressing the business community and read as follows:

A. Human rights

1. World business should support and respect the protection of internationally proclaimed human rights within their sphere of influence, and
2. Make sure they are not complicit in human rights abuses.

B. Labour

3. Businesses should uphold freedom of association and the effective recognition of the right to collective bargaining.
4. The elimination of all forms of forced and compulsory labour.
5. The effective abolition of child labour, and
6. The elimination of discrimination in respect of employment and occupation.

C. Environment

7. Businesses should support a precautionary approach to environmental challenges.
8. Undertake initiatives to promote greater environmental responsibility, and
9. Encourage the development and diffusion of environmentally friendly technologies.[84]

These original nine principles were on the occasion of the 2004 Global Compact Summit 2004 supplemented with a tenth principle, namely:

10. Businesses should work against all forms of corruption including extortion and bribery.

Human rights make up the first pillar of the GC, as participants have committed themselves to promoting human rights within their sphere of influence and not being complicit in their violation. The commitment to human rights may be particularly beneficial for the purpose of

[83] *Supra*, p. xx8.

[84] The full version of the Global Compact principles is available online at www.unglobal compact.org/AboutTheGC/TheTenPrinciples/index.html (accessed 15 August 2006).

economic and social rights.[85] Through their products, companies can make a vital contribution towards meeting economic and social needs. They have expertise and resources at their disposal, which could efficiently be deployed in implementing, for example, the human rights to food and health.[86] Additionally, it is interesting to note that the UN is starting to clarify the human rights content of the GC by linking it with existing voluntary and legally nonbinding instruments like UN Codes of Conduct.[87] Further, relevant UN treaty bodies are starting to directly refer to the GC and its participants in official UN documents and regulations.[88]

Human rights at work constitute the second pillar of the GC. These labour principles of the GC correspond to the ILO Declaration on Fundamental Principles and Rights at Work.[89] This historical second-ever declaration by the ILO clarified which of the 183 ILO Standards are 'core labour rights' because of their human rights dimension and at the same time correspond to the debate of trade and human rights at work within the WTO.

The third pillar of the GC, which holds the environmental principles, can be traced back to the Rio Declaration of 1992.[90] Among the ecological principles, the spread of environmentally sound technologies seems of

85 For more information on the three dimensions of human rights, see *Riedel*, Eibe H. 'Menschenrechte der dritten Dimension' ('Third Dimension Human Rights'), *EuGRZ* (1989) 16(1), 9–21.

86 For an innovative approach to engage business into combating vitamin and mineral deficiencies as a matter of the human right to food, see www.gainhealth.org (GAIN – The Global Alliance for Improved Nutrition; accessed 15 August 2006).

87 For example, the UN Code of Conduct for Law Enforcement Officials, available online at www.unhchr.ch/html/menu3/b/h_comp42.htm (accessed 15 August 2006), is referred to by different Global Compact publications. Due to the flexible and project-based approach of the Global Compact and its structural differences compared to Codes of Conduct, this approach seems to be questionable.

88 See for example, 'Draft Responsibilities of Transnational Corporations and other Business Enterprises with Regard to Human Rights' UN Doc. E/CN.4/Sub.2/2002/13, available online at www1.umn.edu/humanrts/links/NormsApril2003.html (accessed 15 April 2006). 89 *Supra*, p. 3xx.

90 The text of the Rio Declaration and other milestones in international environmental law are online at www.un.org/documents/ga/conf151/aconf15126-1annex1.htm (accessed 15 August 2006). Further, it is interesting to note that Murphy, David F. African Enterprises and the Global Compact: Adding Value through Human Relationships, Tunis, Tunisia: New Academy of Business (2001), available online at www.new-academy.ac.uk/research/africanenterprise/report.pdf (accessed 15 August 2006), traces the environmental principles of the Global Compact back to African values as described already in the late 1950s.

particular significance for the aim of Sustainable Development (SD),[91] since it likewise addresses economical, ecological and developmental policy needs.[92] The seventh principle of the GC contains the precautionary principle, also enshrined at the Rio Conference, which might be seen as representing the time dimension in the concept of SD.[93]

The concept of SD provides the unwritten and underlying concept of the GC and its ten principles. Due to its integrative effect, SD can provide a common ground for an initiative of partners with divergent backgrounds and particular interests. As the GC embraces a liberal and open world economy, but at the same time addresses social and environmental aspects, the initiative aims to foster basically all three pillars of sustainability on the global level. Also, the composition of participants represents economic, social and environmental interests, which perfectly suits the integrative imperative and the threefold approach of SD. Consequently, the GC was incorporated in the 2002 World Summit on Sustainable Development (WSSD) in Johannesburg ('Rio plus 10') and the Rio process as a whole.[94]

To sum up, *the GC contains ten principles drawn from universally accepted UN treaties covering the areas of human and labour rights, environmental policy and promoting practices geared towards reducing bribery and corruption.* Sustainable development may be seen as the underlying common sense building the bracket between the divergent range of stakeholders engaged in this initiative.

[91] Environmentally Sound Technologies (ESTs) as defined by Agenda 21 'protect the environment, are less polluting, use all resources in a more sustainable manner, recycle more of their wastes and products, and handle residual wastes in a more acceptable manner than the technologies for which they were substitutes. (ESTs) are not just individual technologies, but total systems, which include know-how, procedures, goods and services, and equipment as well as organizational and managerial procedures'.

[92] Sustainable Development is commonly defined as 'development that provides economic, social and environmental benefits in the long-term, having regard to the needs of living and future generations'. Cp. *Gilpin,* Alan Dictionary of Environment and Sustainable Development, Chichester 1996, p. 35. For the foundation of the concept of Sustainable Development, see the so-called 'Brundtland Report', *World Commission on Environment and Development*: Our Common Future, New York: Oxford University Press 1987.

[93] See *Ruggie,* John The Global Compact as Learning Network, available online at www.ksg.harvard.edu/cbg/research/j.ruggie_global.governance_global.governance.net.pdf (accessed 15 August 2006). The essence of the precautionary approach is described in Principle 15 of the Rio Declaration, which states: 'Where there are threats of serious or irreversible damage, lack of full scientific certainty shall not be used as a reason for postponing cost effective measures to prevent environmental degradation'.

[94] The Results of the World Summit on Sustainable Development in Johannesburg (WSSD +10) are available online at www.un.org/events/wssd/ (accessed 15 August 2006).

X. Procedural pillars of the compact

In addition to the ten substantive principles, the GC is also characterised by important procedural components, and two formal obligations for participants that ensure due progress of the initiative.

First, participation depends on a letter signed by the CEO and sent to UN Secretary-General Kofi Annan proclaiming that the company will embrace and promote actively the principles and objectives of the GC. The CEO commitment meanwhile corresponds with the strategic importance the GC has for some businesses. It allows a top-down approach for the internal implementation of the GC based on the top management's decision.

From an international relations perspective, the CEO letter and the Secretary-General's response confirming the participation can be seen as a very 'soft' institutional agreement on jointly promoting the GC's principles. So far corporations have not been recognised as legal subjects in public international law.[95] Meanwhile, a compact nearly 3,000 CEOs and the Secretary-General of the UN agreed on, might be seen as the birth of an innovative form of engagement in international relations.

Second, once a year the participants have to publicly prove concrete undertakings in promoting the principles of the compact on the GC web portal.[96] This procedural element of the GC ensures enduring engagement and concrete action towards implementing the substantial principles. This is necessary to avoid free-riding, namely just signing a letter and taking advantage of being part of this high-profile initiative (e.g. enjoying the privilege of active participants to undertake corporate communication with the GC logo). Free riders not fulfilling this requirement are regularly criticised by NGOs for 'blue washing' their image with help of the UN, (i.e. whitewashing their image with the legitimacy of the UN's blue flag).

In practice, the obligation to communicate progress results in constructive competition as a driving force for implementation of the nine principles through exchanging best practices between the participants. Best practices within the GC incorporate the economically, ecologically or socially applied capacity of companies, most prominently through the realisation

[95] Beside the cases of so-called state contracts, which are treaties between states and the private sector, mostly on subjects regarding business opportunities in the country, like investment or extraction of raw materials and natural resources. As a starting point for further research, see Maniruzzaman, A. F. M. State Contracts in Contemporary International Law: Monist versus Dualist Controversies, in *European Journal of International Law* (2001) 12(2), 309–28, discussing different forms of state contracts.

[96] Online at www.unglobalcompact.org (accessed 15 August 2006).

of concrete projects. Publishing such best practices serves as a stimulus or yardstick to other participants.

Beyond these entry requirements, *the procedural structure of GC itself rests on three core elements: dialogue, learning and projects.*

First, multi-stakeholder '*policy dialogues*' are held on the contemporary challenges of globalisation and corporate citizenship, aimed at providing a key platform for substantive discourse. Participation in these dialogues is voluntary and open to all GC stakeholders: business, labour and civil society organisations. Drawing on the core strength of the UN and its convening power, GC dialogues offer a unique, added feature: proximity to governments and operational entities of the UN. This allows results coming out of dialogues to influence both the policy-making level and the operational activities on the ground. The overall objective is to facilitate mutual understanding, create a climate of collaboration and a culture of innovative, but concrete, solutions.

Second, since the GC was launched in July 2000, learning has been an integral part of both its vision and day-to-day operations. *Learning* is aimed at helping the participants in internally applying ideas and experiences from dialogues and project co-operation. At the heart of the GC learning network is the Learning Forum, which operates as a web-based forum and database and convenes meetings of participants presenting their concrete undertakings with a view to the nine principles. *The Learning Forum invites the participants to share good practices* and to identify and fill knowledge gaps around issues related to the GC. The goal is to establish a rich and useful repository of both corporate practice and fundamental research – a platform of knowledge that integrates the views of all relevant stakeholders, while simultaneously increasing the transparency of companies' activities. On a global level, the Learning Forum aims to inform local and regional learning structures.

Third, *the participants will join UN specialised agencies in public–private partnership projects (PPPs).* The GC is an expression of shared values that allow the identification of common of goals between participating companies, UN agencies, labour (unions) and civil society organisations. These common goals, once agreed on, have led to hundreds of partnership projects that contribute to the achievement of the GC's principles. Through partnership projects, GC participating companies can complement their knowledge, expertise and resources with public institutions participating in the GC.

Even before the birth of the GC, a number of UN organisations co-operated successfully with the private sector on a project basis and therefore have the relevant experience with PPS on the operational level.[97] Accordingly, participants of the GC were already implementing partnership projects in many countries, before the GC arose. However, the GC further encouraged participating businesses to increase the number of projects worldwide, particularly in developing countries. At the same time, it offers companies a communication platform and the organisational and technical services of UN agencies – particularly through the UN Development Programme (UNDP). Recently, the GC Office in close co-operation with UNDP developed the following *project criteria*:

1. The project objective(s) support(s) one or several UN Millennium Development Goals and correspond with one or more GC Principles.
2. Partners and beneficiaries participate in drafting, implementing, monitoring and evaluating the project.
3. Partners and beneficiaries contribute financially or with their work to the implementation of the project.
4. In their design, projects follow the concept of sustainability and capacity building.
5. The partnership project produces measurable results corresponding with its objective(s).
6. The project has the potential to be replicated elsewhere, within the project country or outside.
7. Innovative and successful partnership projects are replicated by becoming part of regional or national sector policies.
8. Project activities continue after funding from external sources ceases, that is, projects are institutionally sustainable.

These criteria underscore that entering into partnerships with other participants based only on financial sponsorship instead of incorporating corporate expertise and resources into concrete projects constitutes a second-best engagement. Due to the divergent interest groups, a crucial

[97] The ILO, for example, has a great deal of experience of co-operation with transnational companies; see, for example, the decent work programme online at www.ilo.org/public/english/decent.htm (accessed 15 August 2006). Also worth mentioning are the partnership programs of the UNIDO that aim to improve the interface between transnational companies and their SME suppliers in developing countries, available online at www.unido.org/doc/4364 (accessed 15 August 2006). An overview of the relations between the UN and business is online at www.un.org/partners/business/index.asp (accessed 15 August 2006).

factor for the overall success of the GC is whether, and to what extent, the partners are willing and able to enter in to concrete and sustainable co-operation at the project level. This is crucial, not only because implemented projects are the means of the concrete implementation of the ten principles, but also because project co-operation provides the opportunity for mutually beneficial learning and organisational development. It is important to note that the opportunities for mutual learning through the GC are not only for the benefit of business participants, but also for NGOs and particularly for the envisaged reform of the UN. As UN Secretary General Kofi Annan underscored: 'I see the Global Compact as a chance for the U.N. to renew itself from within, and to gain greater relevance in the twenty-first century'.[98]

To sum up, the *GC is based not only on ten substantial principles but also on a range of procedural mechanisms.* There are two requirements for participating, namely the letter of commitment by the CEO and the annual 'going public' – providing at least one example of how the nine principles have been implemented. Second, the GC itself is based on three procedural elements: dialogue, learning and projects. 'Policy Dialogues' create a climate of mutual understanding and collaboration, the 'Learning Forum' provides resources for applying ideas and experience from dialogues and project cooperation and finally, partnership projects provide concrete action on the implementation stage.

XI. What the Global Compact Is not

The co-operationist policy model of the GC will become even clearer if one considers what the GC is not. First of all, the ten principles of the GC are not designed as and do not constitute minimum standards. Minimum standards define a general behavioural baseline. Their content is fixed and they are directed to prohibit worst practices, like employing child labour.

In contrast, *the content of the GC is structured in the form of promotional obligations, representing flexible guidelines and aspirational benchmarks*

[98] The paragraphs are based on official and informal information provided by the Global Compact Office. For further reading, see *Blüthner*, Andreas: Der Global Compact – Ein Globalisierungspakt über Werte und Effizienz (The Global Compact: A Globalization Pact on Values and Efficiency), in Kooperation oder Konkurenz Internationaler Organisationen. Eine Arbeitstagung zum Verhältnis von Vereinten Nationen und Europäischer Union am Beginn des 21. Jahrhunderts, Baden-Baden, Nomos 2001, pp. 72–9.

directed to foster best practices, (e.g. projects supporting the education of former child labourers). One pragmatic reason for the flexible content of the ten principles is that, due to the wording, there is no precise consensus about the meaning of the principles yet. So it seems hardly possible to define the 'precautionary principle' for diverse industry sectors or to draw a clear line where the corporate sphere of influence on human rights begins or ends. The aspirational approach of the GC necessarily has considerably greater flexibility and openness than is the case with concepts based on minimum standards or fixed rules.[99] For putting the principles into practice, the GC relies on *the 'patchwork effect' of specific individual projects and not on rigid regulation*.

Some, therefore, may be left wondering whether the GC lacks the teeth to convert the principles into practice. Anyone who arrives too hastily at this conclusion is overlooking the fact that the GC is not a classical regulatory control instrument. It relies on setting the right incentives, the effect of voluntary transparency, the willingness of business to respond to constructive competition and a changing market environment that increasingly rewards good corporate citizenship.

Finally it should be stressed that the GC is not intended to replace governmental action or other forms of governance in the areas of human rights, labour rights, and environmental protection, nor can it do so. *While governmental regulations usually set minimum standards, best practices within the GC aim to go beyond these. Due to the project nature of the GC, concrete action on the operational level can so far only offer a positive complement to governmental action*. Accordingly, many governments have declared their support for the GC, even if they are not directly involved in its actions.

XII. Reasons why the Global Compact delivers

The GC still is a new and innovative, but also much disputed initiative. However, there are a number of reasons explaining why this initiative is still rapidly growing, developing and providing significant results at the project level.

1. The United Nations has experience and core competence as a neutral broker. It is capable of resolving communication problems and

[99] For the nature of principles and their distinction to rules, see *Dworkin*, Ronald: Taking Rights Seriously, London, Duckworth 1977, pp. 22–6; *Alexy*, Robert: On the Structure of Legal Principles, in *Ratio Juris* (2000) 13(3), 294.

achieving consensus and co-operation between unequal partners on an international level. This negotiating expertise will be valuable to companies not only in the actual implementation of the ten principles, but also as they enter into more constructive relations between stakeholders in the globalisation process.

2. The UN and business might have different and sometimes diverging interests, but they share some common goals. By providing peace and promoting human rights, for which the UN and its Secretary General were awarded the Nobel prize, the UN is also creating the 'soft infrastructure' companies, with their global business operations, depend on. This becomes even more clear with regard to the increasing length, complexity and transnational interdependence of business value chains. Therefore 'positive peace' has become a public good also demanded across borders by companies operating globally. At the macro level, the overlapping goals and interdependent interests of the UN and business became strikingly evident through the terrorist attacks of 11, September 2001, and their negative impact on stability, world peace, and the world economy.
3. As producers and investors, companies are already playing a part in putting the universal principles of the UN into practice. Products delivered by companies can contribute to realising human rights (e.g. the right to food and the right to health). There would appear to be scope for increasing the potential held by companies, not just through technological progress, but also through partnership projects under the GC.[100]
4. Economic and development policy goals coincide. Sustainable economic development, which companies can best contribute through foreign direct investment, reduces poverty and poverty diminishes, this creates markets for companies.[101]
5. Companies are aware of how to use market forces and by doing so, to create values efficiently. The GC is the first global initiative so firmly based on the creative and constructive potential of markets and their actors.

[100] Secretary-General Kofi Annan asked world business to support the UN in its combat against HIV within the framework of the Global Compact, see 'Another Five Years at the UN Helm for Annan, of Course', *International Herald Tribune*, 27 June 2001.

[101] Jürgen Strube, as Chairman of the BASF Executive Board of Directors on the occasion of accession to the Global Compact, said the following, 'We regard it as a matter of principle to act in a socially responsible manner. Anything that benefits society ultimately benefits business, and when business prospers, society prospers as well. The Global Compact addresses this win-win situation on the global level'.

6. Political steering potential is moving towards companies. The participants of the GC have demonstrated through embracing globally shared values and through their project efforts that they are responsively executing their growing importance as good corporate citizens.
7. A strategic strength of the GC lies in the '*best practices approach*', which puts emphasis on the advantages of the individual partners. This approach paves the way for detecting synergies and win–win situations and stimulates a results-oriented climate for projects.
8. Last, but by no means least, *the success of the GC backs the maintenance and development of the liberal world trading system, as it decreased the pressure to deal with human rights, labour rights and environmental standards within the WTO.*

XIII. The Global Compact and the world trading system

With a view to the long-standing and sometimes harsh debate about the social and environmental dimension of globalisation, the GC as platform for constructive co-operation in these areas of global governance came to birth at the right point of time for those having a stake in the functioning of the liberal trading system.

Free trade increases the *overall* welfare of all partners involved. The fundamental validity of this basic tenet of liberal trade theory is scarcely disputed today. But supporters of liberal trade are often asked whether the prosperity created for trading partners in total, ultimately generates societal values in a specific country or for particular societal groups and individuals. Development policy advocates often question whether the effects of prosperity gained through liberal trade actually trickle down to all levels of society. With a view to the ongoing Doha Round, the 'development question', including the question of social development, remains to some extent open to the WTO.

In the recent past, the world trading system has faced 'new issues', prominently the interdependence between trade on the one side with environmental policy and human and labour rights on the other. The issue of implementing social and environmental standards through trade measures necessarily causes an intervention in the market. The implementation of labour rights and environmental policies within the WTO is at least to some extent based on the credible threat of trade sanctions. This easily could erode not only the economic basis for environmental and social progress in the targeted country, but also the basic consensus between WTO members about open markets. Accordingly, supporters of liberal trade tend to recognise these 'trade ands' as a threat to liberal trading system, increasing the risk of new trade disputes and protectionism for the WTO. These 'not-only-trade-related' issues will presumably not disappear from the trade agenda in the long-run; or – as discussed above – they might return to the agenda of trade negotiations sooner than expected.

The GC aims to realise these values that cannot be without risks addressed within the WTO and through trade instruments.[102] As stated by UN Secretary General Kofi Annan, *the GC is based on the recognition that liberal trade is a necessary prerequisite for the realisation of the ten principles and economic development.*[103] Accordingly, *the GC is based on the assumption of a positive nexus between liberal trade and the universal values of the United Nations.* By setting incentives for the realisation of environmental and social goals, its instruments not only are compatible with, but also build upon market forces and rely on co-operation. On the contrary, the various proposals on tying up trade with labour and environmental goals mainly function because of pressure, compulsion and ultimately might cause confrontation.

Finally, a fundamental difference between the WTO and the Global Compact occurs when comparing the addressees of the universal principles and their realisation. Regarding human rights at work, implementation through the WTO system depends on a domino-chain of legal force: first a member country needs to force another through trade measures, second the target country would need to change and enforce its domestic labour legislation that finally would need to result in compliance at the level of concrete business operations. Instead, the Global Compact is straightly directed to where the realisation of good workplace practice happens – or not, namely: concrete business operations worldwide. Such straight road towards the addressees promises not only faster implementation, but also reduces welfare losses caused by economic sanctions and rigid regulatory systems that interfere with markets instead of directly stimulating market actors.

To sum up, the approach of the GC constructively addresses the concerns of stakeholders in liberal trade regarding the enforcement of environmental and social standards within the WTO. *The Global Compact enables businesses to actively strengthen the legitimisation of a liberal trading system through a voluntary and market-based approach towards*

[102] For the relationship between the Global Compact and the WTO, see Kell and Ruggie (fn. 80). [103] Quoted from Kell (see fn. 79).

putting human rights principles into practice. The Global Compact, in particular with regard to its constantly improving governance structure and rapidly increasing participation,[104] offers a significant potential to fill gaps in the non-economic areas of global governance.

[104] For the recently improved internal governance structure of the Global Compact see *Nowrot*, Karsten (fn. 74), p. 1.

16

Food safety issues under WTO Agreements

MITSUO MATSUSHITA*

I. Relevant provisions of WTO Agreements relating to food safety issues

1. Overview of WTO Agreements relevant to food safety issues

Several Agreements in the WTO regime can be applied to food safety issues. The GATT 1994 generally prohibits quantitative restrictions of trade by way of import quota or any other form (Art. XI GATT) and the imposition of tariffs above the concession rate (Art. II GATT). It also prohibits Members from imposing a measure favoring its own products in discrimination of products of another Members if those products are "like products" (especially Art. III, para. 4 GATT). This principle is called the national treatment principle. A Member is prohibited from imposing a measure which favors a product of another Member in discrimination of products of third Members if those products are like products. This principle is called the most-favored-nation treatment (Art. I GATT). A state may engage in restrictions of import of foods for food safety reasons and, if that state is a Member of the WTO, this creates a tension between this measure and the above provisions of the GATT. However, Article XX of the GATT 1994 provides certain exceptions from the above prohibitions even if a measure falls under one of such prohibitions provided that the requirements of Article XX are satisfied. Therefore, as regards the GATT 1994, a critical question is to decide the conditions under which a measure which restricts trade but is designed to protect food safety is exempt from the disciplines of the GATT 1994.

There are several other Agreements within the framework of the WTO which have a bearing on food safety issues. One is the SPS Agreement,[1]

* Professor Emeritus of Tokyo University and former member of the WTO Appellate Body; the author thanks the editor for some updates. Revised and updated version of an article published in the *Manchester Journal of Internat. Economic Law* 2 (2005) issue 2, 7–17

[1] The Agreement on Sanitary and Phytosanitary Measures will be referred to as "SPS."

which permits Members to take national measures to protect the life and health of humans, animals and plants. But Members may do so only to the extent necessary for this purpose; the measure must be scientifically justifiable and based on sufficient scientific evidence (Art.2.1 and 2.2 SPS).

Another is the TBT Agreement.[2] This Agreement deals with labeling and representation of products and enforcement of mandatory and optional product standards. This Agreement mandates that the principles of national treatment and most-favored-nation treatment apply to products imported from another Members with regard to TBT measures. Mandatory product standards should not be more restrictive than necessary to secure national security, prevent fraud and misrepresentation and protect human and animal life and health (Art. 2.1 and 2.2 TBT). The SPS is a special law in relation to the TBT and when both a provision of the SPS and a provision of the TBT are applicable to the same subject matter, the provision in the SPS prevails over the provision in the TBT.

The TRIPS[3] is designed to protect intellectual property rights such as patent, copyrights, trademarks, geographical indications and trade secrets by setting up the minimum requirements for protecting those rights and for the procedures of enforcement of such rights. Although the TRIPS provides that all products should be patentable, Article 27.2 allows Members to exclude inventions from patentability if it is necessary to protect the public order and good morals and this includes the protection of life and health of humans, animals and plants and also the prevention of serious damage to the environment.

Although all of those Agreements are applicable to food safety measures taken by a Member, provisions of the GATT 1994 and those in the SPS are most frequently applied. Therefore, we will examine some of the relevant provisions of those two Agreements.

2. The GATT 1994

As mentioned earlier, the GATT 1994 prohibits the imposition of import and export restrictions and discriminatory measures regarding products. When a Member of the WTO intends to impose restrictions on imports of a certain foodstuffs which the state regards as involving hazards to life and health, this may create a tension or conflict with provisions of the GATT 1994. If, for example, a Member prohibits the import of a certain

[2] The Agreement on Technical Barriers to Trade ("TBT").

[3] The Agreement on Trade-Related Aspects of Intellectual Property Rights ("TRIPS").

kind of foodstuff because there are additives in that foodstuff which the Member deems hazardous to the life and health of humans, this may be challenged by another Member under Article XI of the GATT which generally prohibits the imposition of restrictions on exports and imports. Also if such a prohibition only applies to imports from a certain Member, this is an infringement of Article I (most-favored-nation treatment) or Article III (national treatment) of the GATT 1994.

However, Article XX of the GATT provides for exceptions and, as long as a measure of a Member which falls under the prohibition of the GATT satisfies the requirements of exceptions, it enjoys the immunity from the disciplines of the GATT.

Article XX consists of the introduction (often referred to as the "chapeau") and ten exceptions (a)–(j). If a measure falls under one or more of items (a)–(j), the measure is exempt from the prohibition of the GATT on restrictions of trade. However, the chapeau provides for the conditions that the measure must meet in order to enjoy exemption. Among the items included in Article XX of the GATT, Article XX(b) is most relevant. Article XX(b) exempts a measure which is necessary to protect life and health of humans, animals and plants.

In the past, several GATT dispute settlement cases dealing with food safety issues interpreted Article XX(b) of the GATT 1947. In the *Thai Tobacco Case*,[4] the Thai Government took measures to restrict the sale of tobacco domestically and also its import from the United States for the reason that tobacco created risk to health. Upon a petition by the US that the Thai measure violated Article XI of the GATT, the panel considered the matter and judged that the Thai measure fell under Article XX(b) since smoking tobacco was harmful to health and a policy to reduce smoking was covered by Article XX(b). However, the panel stated that the measure in question must be "necessary" to accomplish this purpose and to satisfy "the necessity test," there should be a circumstance in which there was no other alternative way which was less trade restrictive. In the view of the panel, the Thai measure did not meet this standard and it was struck down as a violation of Article XI of the GATT.

In the *Tuna/Dolphin* Case,[5] the US Government imposed an import prohibition on tuna and tuna products from countries which did not take

[4] *Thailand–Restrictions on importation of and internal taxes on cigarettes*, adopted on November 7 1990, BIASD 375/200.

[5] *United States–Restrictions on imports of tuna*, circulated on September 3 1991, not adopted, BISD 395/155.

steps to protect dolphins when their fishing vessels harvested tuna. In this case, the Panel held that the imposition of an import ban on tuna was not necessary to accomplish the purpose of protecting dolphins and that the US measure was contrary to Article XI of the GATT. In the *US Gasoline Case*,[6] the US Government imposed restrictions on the domestic production and sale of gasoline and also on imports to prevent air pollution caused by the emission of harmful substances from automobiles. The Panel and the Appellate Body held that, although the US policy to prevent air pollution was covered by Article XX(b), the import restriction did not meet the necessity test since there would have been less trade restrictive alternatives.

As mentioned above, panels and the Appellate Body interpreted the necessity test restrictively and, unless it was proven that there was no less trade restrictive alternative, a measure would not enjoy exemption from the prohibition of the GATT even if it is categorized as a measure to protect the life and health of humans, animal and plants. *This narrow interpretation of the necessity test makes it difficult for this provision to apply to measures to protect product safety including food safety.*

In this respect, the *Asbestos* case[7] is interesting. The French Government prohibited the use and import of asbestos because it contained material which created the risk of cancer. Canada alleged that this amounted to a prohibited discrimination of Canadian asbestos since there were three other domestic products which had similar features, but which were allowed to be used. The Appellate Body upheld the French decree primarily on two grounds: (1) asbestos and similar products which could be used as building materials were not "like products" because those who used these substances (e.g. builders) were conscious of the hazard of asbestos compared with other similar substances and this should be taken into consideration when judging whether asbestos and other substances were like products. (2) The prohibition of asbestos could be covered by Article XX(b) of the GATT 1994. Article XX(b) covers product and food safety issues. With the ruling of the Appellate Body in the *Asbestos case*, this provision is now probably more useful today than before.

[6] *United States–Standards for reformulated and conventional gasoline*, Appellate Body and Panel Report, adopted on May 20 1996, WT/DS2/9.

[7] *EC–Measures affecting asbestos and asbestos-containing products*, Report of the Panel, September 18 2000, jWT/DS135/R; Report of the Appellate Body (AB-2000-1), March 12 2001, WT/DS135/AB/R.

3. *The SPS Agreement*

The Agreement on Sanitary and Phytosanitary Measures (SPS) specifically addresses issues of food safety and international trade. The SPS tries to balance the need to protect the life and health of humans, animals and plants with the need to prevent excessive control of international trade under the name of protecting life and health. The SPS allows Members to take "SPS measures" to protect the life and health of humans, animals and plants by imposing the prohibition of imports on certain items and the requirement for labeling with regard to some products. However, the SPS requires that Members take such SPS measures only to the extent necessary to protect life and health. SPS measures cannot be maintained unless they are supported by sufficient scientific data established by appropriate risk assessment (Art. 2.2 and Art. 5 SPS).

SPS measures taken by Members must be based on international standards, guidelines and recommendations if there are any. If a SPS measure is based on an international standard, guideline or recommendation, it is presumed to be necessary to protect the life and health of humans, animals or plants and compatible with the SPS and the GATT (Art. 3.2 SPS). The SPS recognizes the *precautionary principle* only in a limited way. According to the SPS, Members can take a provisional SPS measure when there is not enough scientific evidence to support it; however, the Member must endeavor to obtain additional information regarding the measure and must review it in due course (Art. 5.7 SPS).

4. *The TBT Agreement*

The TBT Agreement (hereafter TBT) provides that domestic mandatory standards need to be based on international standards if there is any with regard to product safety, product testing and product representation. Provisions of the TBT generally apply to food safety matters unless such matters are covered by the SPS.[8] Therefore, depending on the nature of the issues, the TBT can be applied to domestic standards which deal with food safety. According to the established WTO jurisprudence, mandatory domestic standards must be based on international standards regardless

[8] Article 1.5 of the TBT Agreement states: "The provisions of this Agreement do not apply to sanitary and phytosanitary measures as defined in Annex A of the Agreement on the application of Sanitary and Phytosanitary Measures."

of whether the domestic standard came into effect before the taking effect of the TBT or *vice versa.*[9]

The *Sardine Case*[10] is a case which deals with food representation issues. Although this case did not deal with food safety issues directly, holdings of the Appellate Body in this case may have some bearing on food safety issues. Involved in this case was a regulation of the EC which provided that the word "sardines" could be used only on canned foods made from fish caught in the Black Sea, the North Sea and the Mediterranean Sea. The Codex Alimentarius which was an international standard regulating food representation provided that, although the word "sardines" could be used only in connection with canned foods made of fish caught in those areas, the word could be used for canned foods made of fish of a similar type caught in other areas as long as the prefix "X" was attached such as "Peruvian sardines" or "Pacific sardines" etc. In this sense, therefore, there was a difference between the EC regulation and Codex Alimentarius.

Peru brought a claim against the EC in the WTO and argued that the EC regulation was inconsistent with Article 2.4 of the TBT which requires that a mandatory domestic standard needs to be based on an international standard if this exists or its enactment is imminent. Both the Panel and the Appellate Body held that the EC regulation was contrary to Article 2.4 of the TBT. The EC argued that this regulation was necessary to ensure that consumers in the EU would not be led to believe that all canned foods with the label "sardines" are made from fish caught in the Black Sea, the North Sea and the Mediterranean Sea. However, the Appellate Body rejected this claim by stating that the EC claim was not based on substantial evidence.

As mentioned earlier, the TBT applies regardless of whether the domestic standard in question was enacted before the taking effect of the WTO or later. *This suggests that domestic standards for food safety to which the TBT applies need to be revised whenever new international standards come into being.*

II. The EC *Beef Hormones* case

Although there were some GATT panel reports on health matters before the coming into being of the WTO such as *Thai Tobacco* mentioned earlier, so far there are only five cases which have been handled by the Dispute Settlement

[9] See the *Sardines Case*, below.

[10] *EC–Trade description of sardines*, Report of the Appellate Body (AB 2002-3) September 26 2002, WT/DS231/AB/R.

Body of the WTO in which SPS issues were raised. These are: *EC Hormones*,[11] *Australian Salmon*,[12] *Japan Apple (I)*,[13] *Japan Apple (II)*[14] and *GMO* which will be discussed later. The *Australian Salmon* case dealt with the issue of the health of salmon and the *Japan Apple* cases were concerned with the quarantine of agricultural products. Therefore, the only cases in which food safety and SPS issues were dealt with were *EC Hormones* and *GMO*.

In *EC Hormones*, the EC imposed a ban on the domestic sale and imports of beef taken from animals treated with six kinds of hormones. An international standard formulated by the Codex Commission stated that, with respect to two hormones, beef product involved no recognizable risk as long as the residue of hormones remained within the limit stated in the standard. The US and Canada filed a complaint with the WTO alleging that this measure was contrary to the SPS. The Panel stated that the measure in question was contrary to the SPS and the EC appealed. The Appellate Body upheld the Panel's finding and held also that the EC measure was contrary to the SPS. A number of legal issues were discussed in the Panel and the Appellate Body reports.

First, the EC argued that its measure was based on the *precautionary principle* and should be justified. The Panel and the Appellate Body, however, stated that the precautionary principle was not recognized as a principle in international law. Also Article 5.7 of the SPS incorporated a provisional precautionary principle into the SPS and any application of a precautionary principle which allowed a wider scope of precaution than this would not be permitted.

Secondly, with regard to the *burden of proof*, the Panel held that it was incumbent on the party that had imposed a SPS measure to adduce evidence that there was a sufficient risk assessment. The Panel also held that it was the responsibility of the party that had invoked a measure not based

[11] *EC–Measures concerning meat and meat products*, Complaint by Canada, Report of the Panel, August 18 1997, WT/DS48/R; EC–Measures concerning meat and meat products, Complaint by the United States, Report of the Panel, August 18 1997, WT/DS26/R/U.S.A.; EC–Measures concerning meat and meat products, Report of the Appellate Body, February 13 1998, WT/DS26/AB/; WT/DS/48/R.

[12] *Australia–Measures affecting importation of salmon*, Report of the Panel, June 12 1998, WT/DS18/R; Australia–Measures affecting importation of salmon, Report of the Appellate Body, WT/DS18/AB/R.

[13] *Japan–Measures affecting agricultural products (Apples)*, Report of the Panel, October 27 1998, WT/DS76/R; Report of the Appellate Body (AB-1998-8), February 22 1999, WT/DS76/AB/R.

[14] *Japan–Measures affecting the importation of apples*, Report of the Panel, July 15 2003, WT/DS24/R; Report of the Appellate Body, November 26 2003, WT/DS245/AB/R.

on an international standard to justify it. The Appellate Body reversed both of the Panel's holdings. The Appellate Body stated that the party challenging a SPS measure of another Member had to prove that the measure was contrary to the SPS and also that the measure could not be justified by a provision for exceptions. In this way, the Appellate Body imposed a stringent responsibility on a complaining party to prove that there had been a violation of the SPS on the part of the defending party and to prove that there was no justification for deviating from general principles.

Thirdly, the matter involved in this case was *highly scientific* in nature. The Panel sought the views of scientists and they filed their views concerning the risk involved in hormone-treated beef. The majority of the scientists stated that, as long as the residue of hormones remained within the range stipulated in the Codex standard, there was no recognizable risk. One scientist stated that there was still a risk that one out of one million people who ate beef in which the residue of hormones remained within the range of Codex standard might get cancer. The Panel accepted the majority view and held that the EC measure was not based on a proper risk assessment. The EC appealed this holding to the Appellate Body and argued that the Panel had violated Article 11 of the Dispute Settlement Understanding by ignoring the view of the minority scientist. The Appellate Body upheld the holding of the Panel in this regard but *stated that, under some circumstances, a minority scientific view with regard to food safety issue could be accepted.*

This decision raises an *important evidentiary issue.* Although it may seem sensible that a majority view with respect to food safety should be accepted, under some circumstances, it may be justified to accept a minority view with regard to a food safety issue. *Especially if a human life issue is involved, the abundance of precaution should be taken* and even a minority view holding that a substance might involve risk to human life and health should be worthy of respect. Article 5.3 of the SPS states that, "in assessing the risk to animal or plant life or health, Members shall take into account as relevant economic factors including the costs of control in the importing country and the relative cost-effectiveness of alternative approaches to limiting risks." Note that the word "humans" is absent from Article 5.3. *A contrario* interpretation is that the SPS does not allow economic factors such as cost to decide whether a measure to protect the life and health of humans is justified whereas, with regards to animals and plants, such economic factors can be an important test. Therefore, *in the SPS, human life and health cannot be dealt with on the basis of cost-effectiveness as that of animals and plants.* This implies that the SPS makes a distinction between human life and health on one hand and those of animals and plants on the other and that the standard of proof for a risk in a substance related to food with regard to humans is different from that for animals and plants.

Fourthly, although the legal aspects of the *EC Hormones* case were resolved by the adoption of the Panel's report and the report of the Appellate Body by the Dispute Settlement Body of the WTO, this case raises an *important political issue.* In the European Communities, the ban on hormones was the result of long-standing discussion and consideration within the Communities. This was discussed at the level of national governments and in the decision-making bodies of the European Communities such as the Council of Ministers and the EC Commission. Therefore, the ban on hormones, in a sense, reflected the democratic decision-making process of the European Communities. There is a *sentiment in Europe that an important political decision which reflects the political process of Europe should not be so easily overturned by an international organization.* Of course, there is the counter-argument that the European Communities acceded to the WTO Agreement and should be bound by it. Legally this is the correct answer. However, this shows that an intervention of WTO disciplines into domestic policies of Members may create political tension and, if it goes too far, may cause non-compliance with WTO disciplines.

III. The GATT 1994 and the SPS in relation to GMO issues

As far as the GATT 1994 and the SPS are concerned, any control of food product with genetically modified organisms (hereafter GMO) content for food safety reasons must comply with the requirements contained therein. As mentioned earlier, the SPS requires that a SPS measure must be based on an international standard. If this is not the case, an SPS measure must be justified by scientific evidence that there is risk involved in the GMO product in question. Although different states enforce a variety of measures (e.g. labeling requirements on GMO related substances) there is no uniform international standard to regulate measures taken by trading nations. This is due to a lack of consensus about desirability and the extent of the control to be exercised on GMO products. This situation has already created a trade conflict between the US and the EU.

1. A GMO dispute between the US, Canada and Argentina and the EC

In 2003, the US, Canada and Argentina brought a claim against the EC in which they argued that the EC had violated provisions of the SPS by imposing a moratorium with respect to the approval of the import of agricultural products produced with biotechnology. The EC adopted procedures for the approval of such product.[15] However, according to those countries, the EC imposed a moratorium on approval in 1998 and has maintained it ever since. In essence, the claimants argued that the EC is in violation of the provisions of the SPS because of an undue delay in approval, lack of transparency in the procedure and lack of sufficient scientific evidence to justify the delay in approval.

The Panel issued an interim report on February 7 2006, which was secret (it was delivered only to the Parties involved) but which was leaked,[16] while it was assumed that the final report would be circulated to WTO Members not later than the end of September 2006.[17] According to this interim report, the Panel did *not* examine, whether: (1) biotech products in general are safe or not, (2) the biotech products at issue in this dispute are "like" their conventional counterparts, (3) the EC has a right to require the pre-marketing approval of biotech products and (4) whether the EC approval procedure, as established by three EC instruments, was consistent with the EC obligations under the WTO Agreements (para. 8.3). Instead, it was emphasized that specific or general moratoria on GMO might be justifiable – depending on the circumstances – if new scientific evidence comes to light which conflicts with existing scientific evidence and which is directly relevant to all biotech products subject to a pre-marketing approval requirement, until an appropriate assessment of the new evidence is done (see para. 7–1527).

The report of the Panel was adopted on November 21 2006 in which the Panel ruled that the moratorium adopted by the EC amounted to undue delay of procedure and was contrary to Article 8 of the SPS Agreement and Annex C.1(a) thereof which prohibits undue delay of approval procedure.[18] The Panel also held that the safeguard measures taken by six members of the European Communities which prohibited the sale and import of GMO products were not based on proper risk assessment and

[15] *EC–Measures affecting the approval and marketing of biotech products*, WT/DS291, 292 and 293.

[16] See Friends of the Earth Press Release of February 28 2006 (www.foe.org/news/releases/February2006/wto2282006.htm) and the WTO-Report www.foeeurope.org/biteback/WTO_decision.htm. For a first analysis of this interim report, see www.foeeurope.org/publications/2006/WTObriefings.pdf.

[17] Cf. WT/DS291/31 of March 31 2006.

[18] WT/DS291/R; WT/DS292/R adopted November 21 2006.

were, therefore, contrary to Article 5.1 of the SPS Agreement and that these measures did not satisfy the requirements for temporary precautionary measures as stipulated in Article 57 of the SPS Agreement.

This Panel report was not appealed by any party and was adopted as published. Although this report did not make rulings on some important issues such as whether or not GMO food products and non-GMO food products were "like products," it is the first case in which the Dispute Settlement Body dealt with the issues of whether GMO products were subject to SPS disciplines. It was recognized that GMO issues would come under the disciplines of the SPS Agreement and, in this sense, established an important precedent.

Only the concrete application of the *de facto* EC moratorium between October 1998 and August 2003 violated WTO law: in this interim report, the Panel concluded that the general *de facto* moratorium resulted in a failure to complete individual approval procedures without undue delay, and hence gave rise to an inconsistency with Article 8 and Annex C of the SPS Agreement (para. 8.6). Concerning the complaints against nine safeguard measures taken by several EC Member States, in the form of prohibitions imposed on particular biotech products which had been formally approved for use within the EC, this was regarded as a violation of Article 5.7 of the SPS Agreement, as these national measures were not based on a risk assessment as required under Article 5.1 of the SPS Agreement. This was also regarded as a violation of the second and third requirement of Article 2.2 of the SPS Agreement (paras. 8.8 and 8.22). The Panel identified that most of the national studies were missing the likelihood element (i.e. "probability of entry, establishment or spread of diseases and associated biological and economic consequences"). However, the EC was of the opinion, that the "process of review within reasonable period of time" (Art. 5.7) of the EC Members has to be based on a precautionary aspect, since "irreversible, life-terminating damage to human health" is at stake here, while "the GMO technology is still at the frontiers of science" (para. 7.3297).

2. GMO and scientific evidence

If there is no effective international standard, guideline or recommendation with respect to the GMO, a Member of the WTO intending to impose a ban on import or otherwise restrictions on it must provide risk assessment in connection with GMO and adduce evidence that the GMO in question involves substantial hazard to life and health. However, at this stage of scientific development, there is no positive evidence that GMO products will generate risk to human life and health. Under these circumstances, if a Member of the WTO takes a measure to prohibit or restrict the import of a GMO product, this may cause a trade dispute between the exporting Member and the importing Member. The importing Member may try to defend its position by invoking the *precautionary principle.* As stated earlier, however, the precautionary principle is recognized in Article 5.7 of the SPS only in a limited way so if Article 5.7 were used to justify the measure, the justification is only temporary and should be reviewed in future with the view to its ultimate abolition.

One alternative way to defend its position may be to rely on the precautionary principle embodied in another international agreement (i.e. the Cartagena Protocol) which was formulated under the United Nations Biodiversity Convention. The Cartagena protocol allows a Member to take a measure to prohibit or control imports of GMO products even if there is no scientific evidence. *In this sense, the Cartagena Protocol permits the precautionary principle more widely than the SPS.* This brings us to the question of what is the relationship between the SPS on one hand and the Cartagena Protocol and the United Nations Biodiversity Convention on the other.

IV. The relationship between the GATT/SPS and the Cartagena Protocol

The Preamble of the Cartagena Protocol states that the Protocol and the other international agreements including WTO Agreements are mutually supportive and the Protocol does not restrict rights and obligations of the participants under other international agreements. This suggests that if a nation is a Member of the WTO and, at the same time, a Member of the Cartagena Protocol, the rights and obligations of both Agreements apply to that Member. However, what happens if there is conflict between rights and obligations of one agreement with those of the other?

Such a conflict may arise between the SPS and the Cartagena Protocol. As stated earlier, the Cartagena Protocol allows a wider scope for the precautionary principle than that allowed by the SPS. There may be a situation where a Member of the Protocol takes a precautionary measure to prohibit imports of a GMO product without a clear evidence of risk to human life and health and another Member challenges this measure in the WTO. One of the parties to the dispute may be a Member of the WTO and the Cartagena Protocol or both of them may be Members of WTO and the Cartagena Protocol. To avoid such a conflict of obligations, several proposals are worth being considered.

1. Article 3.2 of the SPS

Article 3.2 of the SPS states that if an SPS measure of a Member is based on an international standard, guideline or recommendation, such a measure is presumed to be in compliance with WTO Agreements even if it is not supported by scientific evidence. Annex A 2(a)–(c) of the SPS identifies that standards promulgated by the Codex Alimentarius Commission, the International Office of Epizootics and the International Plant Protection Convention are such international standards. In order for any standards formulated and promulgated by the Cartagena Protocol and the United Nations Biodiversity Convention to be qualified as an international standard in the above sense, it must be recognized by the SPS Committee by consensus.

There are two major problems with respect to this approach. First, a decision of the SPS Committee to recognize standards established by the Cartagena Protocol as an international standard, guideline or recommendation must be made by consensus. This may be difficult to achieve due to the differencing views among major trading nations on GMO matters. The US, which is the major trading nation, did not sign the Cartagena Protocol and is not likely to vote for an adoption of any standard formulated by it as a qualified international standard in the sense of the SPS. Secondly Article 3.2 of the SPS creates only a presumption that a SPS measure based on an international standard conforms with WTO agreements. It does not state that such a measure is "deemed to be" in conformity with WTO agreements. Therefore, such a presumption may be overturned if it is challenged by sufficient evidence and persuasive claims. *If the precautionary principle as provided in the Cartagena Protocol is introduced into the SPS through the above procedure, it may amount to a de facto amendment of Article 5.7 of the SPS, since this would change one of the basic principles of the SPS.* There would be a strong criticism that such a major change in the SPS should be discussed and voted on at Ministerial Conferences. Therefore, whether such a major change to the SPS is allowed without any amendment process is not certain.

2. Article XX of the GATT

Article XX (b) of the GATT provides exemption from the GATT disciplines any measure necessary to protect human, animal and plant life and health. The Preamble of the SPS states that the SPS is an elaboration of Article XX(b) and, therefore, Article XX(b) and the SPS can be read together as one instrument. It may be claimed, therefore, that the exemption provided in Article XX(b) applies to any measure taken in accordance with the SPS. Therefore, if a SPS measure is challenged under any provision of the GATT, the defending party may invoke Article XX(b) and argue that the measure is exempt from the disciplines of the GATT.

However, this is not as easy as it looks. If Article XX(b) and the SPS are be read together, the consequences may be as follows. If a GMO measure is authorized by the SPS, it is also exempt from GATT disciplines by virtue of Article XX(b) of the GATT. However, can a measure which infringes the SPS be rescued by Article XX(b)? If the SPS is an elaboration of Article XX(b), whatever is authorized by the SPS should be regarded as being "necessary" to protect human, animal or plant life and, therefore exempt from GATT disciplines. If one follows this logic, however, *a measure not permitted by the SPS is not covered by Article XX(b)*, as the SPS is nothing but an elaboration of Article XX(b). Therefore, it is by no means clear if a measure which is not authorized by the SPS is still exempt by virtue of Article XX(b).

In order to remedy this situation, one would have to say that the scope of Article XX(b) is wider than the SPS and even items that are not permitted by the SPS could be exempted from obligations of the GATT under Article XX(b). This interpretation would in fact weaken the effectiveness of the disciplines of the SPS and may destroy it altogether.

3. International negotiations of the Doha Round

Paragraphs 31–33 of the Doha Declaration are concerned with environmental issues. Paragraph 31 states that Members negotiate on: "(i) the relationship between existing WTO rules and specific trade obligations set out in multilateral environmental agreements (MEAs)." It continues to provide "The negotiations shall be limited in scope to the applicability of such existing WTO rules as among parties to the MEA in question. The negotiations shall not prejudice the WTO rights of any Members that is not a party to the MEA in question . . ." Paragraph 32 provides, in part, that ". . . the negotiations carried out under Paragraph 31(i) and (ii) shall not add to or diminish the rights and obligations of members under existing WTO agreements, in particular the Agreement on the Application of Sanitary and Phytosanitary Measures, nor alter the balance of these rights and obligations, and will take into account the needs of developing and least-developed countries."

This ambiguity of the meaning of the Doha Declaration raises several issues.

(1) The negotiation will take place only with regard to the applicability of existing WTO rules as among parties to the MEA.
(2) The rights of WTO members that are not members of the MEA will be unaffected by the result of the negotiations.
(3) Generally the results of the negotiation will not affect the rights and obligations of members under existing WTO agreements in particular the SPS Agreement.
(4) The needs of developing and least-developed countries will be taken into account.

The terms of reference of the negotiations are primarily focused on clarifying the relationship between WTO Agreements and MEAs as among members of the WTO as well as the MEAs. It does not cover the relationship between WTO Agreements and the MEAs as between WTO members that are members of MEAs and those that are non-members of the MEAs. Therefore, the effect of the result of negotiations will be rather limited. If a dispute arises between Country A, which is a member both of the WTO and the MEA and Country B, which is a member of the WTO but not of the MEA, it will not be covered by the result of the negotiations of the Doha Round.

Although the Doha Development Agenda includes terms of reference of negotiations on the relationship between WTO Agreements (especially the SPS), there are many difficulties for negotiation, including agricultural issues. It is highly unlikely that any meaningful negotiations will be held on this issue in the near future.

4. Amendment of Article XX of the GATT 1994

However, the ultimate solution of the issues discussed above is an amendment of Article XX (i.e. the addition of a provision which would provide that measures which implement the UN Biodiversity Convention and the Cartagena Protocol would be exempt from the application of GATT provisions). This would be *Article XX(k) of the GATT 1994 providing that measures which implement environmental protection under MEAs would be exempted from the application of GATT provisions.* This option requires the adoption of a resolution to amend Article XX and requires the consensus of the WTO Members. Such a consensus may be difficult to achieve. There may be claims by some WTO members that such a drastic proposal is outside the scope of the Doha Declaration. The chances of this option being adopted are rather slim.

5. Understanding for interpretation

Another option is an adoption of "understanding for interpretation" with respect to the applicability of Articles XX(b) to measures designed to implement provisions of a MEA agreement including the Cartagena Protocol. Here, the WTO members consider the adoption of an understanding of interpreting WTO Agreements in which they would agree *that a measure taken by a WTO member for implementing a MEA agreement is given presumption that it falls under Article XX(b) or Article XX(g)* as the case may be. Such a presumption is given only under certain conditions. *Conditions* for such a presumption should include, *inter alia*, the following:

(a) Any country should be allowed to join the MEA as long as it shares the common objectives of the MEA.
(b) There should be a sufficient number of participants in the MEA which reflect the interests of major supplier and consumer countries of products affected by measures implementing the MEA.
(c) The content and scope of trade measures which will be used to implement the MEA should be clearly defined. Also the procedure for executing such measures should be clear and transparent.
(d) Trade measures implementing the MEA should not be arbitrary and discriminatory with regard to countries under the same or similar conditions. Also these should not be employed in a way that they constitute a disguised restriction of international trade.
(e) The purpose of the MEA should be protection of environment including the protection of life and health of humans, animals or plants as well as the conservation of exhaustible natural resources.
(f) Trade measures employed to implement the MEA should be related to the objectives of environmental protection and this relationship should be reasonably close and real.
(g) The scope of trade measures based on the MEA should not be too wide in proportion to the purpose of protecting environment.

Understanding of interpretations incorporating the above principles can be promulgated as "*decisions*" of the WTO in accordance with Article IX:1 of the Marrakesh Agreement or Article XXV of the GATT 1994. It can also be announced as a "*declaration*" of the WTO. Either way, the understanding would be non-binding and exhortative. However, it is expected that WTO members will abide by these principles. Also panels and the Appellate Body dealing with disputes in which the relationship between WTO Agreements and MEAs is at issue are encouraged to follow them. In this understanding of interpretation, national measures complying with the principles incorporated therein should be given a presumption of satisfying the requirements of Articles XX(b) of the GATT 1994 and the presumption can be rebutted.

This non-binding understanding of interpretation is not a complete answer to the question of how to resolve conflict between disciplines of WTO Agreements and measures implementing MEA, but it is probably as much as one can hope for given the sharp division of views among WTO members on this issue today.

6. Waiver

Another way to avoid conflict between a measure on GMO which is authorized by the Cartagena Protocol which may come into conflict with WTO Agreements is to obtain a waiver under Article IX:3 of the Marrakesh Agreement. Using this approach, a WTO member implementing a provision of the Cartagena Protocol and the UN Biodiversity Convention through measures which may come into conflict with provisions of a WTO agreement seek a waiver from the WTO in accordance Article IX:3. If a waiver is granted, the Member's obligations under the GATT 1994 or any other WTO Agreement are waived to the extent of the conditions incorporated in the waiver.

However, a waiver is only an *ad hoc* and temporary measure and can be granted only by a three-quarters majority at the General Council of the WTO. Article IX:3 states that the waiver is granted to deal with "exceptional circumstances." To characterize a food safety measure on GMO products as "exceptional circumstances" seems to be at odds with the importance of food safety policies today. Although the use of waiver may be necessary as a temporary measure, it is hardly a permanent resolution of conflict between WTO provisions, the Cartagena Protocol and the UN Biodiversity Convention.

V. Conclusion

It is hoped that this short review of food safety issues reveals that there are many unresolved problems in this area. Some problems may be resolved through *"creative interpretation" of WTO Agreements* and other international agreements. However, much is left to future negotiators to decide what accommodation can be given to the domestic regulatory framework for food safety in the WTO regime.

17

Trade and the environment: With particular reference to climate change issues(*)

SHINYA MURASE**

I. Introduction

The *Doha Declaration* addresses the issue of 'Trade and the Environment' in paragraph 31, which states as follows:

> (i) [The] relationship between existing WTO rules and specific trade obligations set out in multilateral environmental agreements, negotiations limited in scope to the applicability of such existing WTO rules as among parties in question. The negotiations shall not prejudice the WTO rights of any Member that is not a party to the MEA in question.
> (ii) Procedures for regular information exchange between MEA Secretariats and the relevant WTO committees, and the criteria for granting of observer status.
> (iii) The reduction or, as appropriate, elimination of tariff and non-tariff barriers to environmental goods and services.

To the disappointment of many of the experts in the field, the Declaration has defined the scope of negotiation so narrowly by limiting to the relationship between WTO and MEAs (multilateral environmental agreements) *only* in such cases where the countries concerned are parties to *both* WTO and MEA. In other words, the paragraph does not cover the cases where one of the countries is not a party to a MEA, such as the United States or Australia in relation to the Kyoto Protocol on climate change.

Nonetheless, it would be a great step forward if the Doha Round successfully reaches an agreement in formulating a viable scheme for the coordination between trade rules and the rules for the environment even in

* This study was conducted in part by the generous grant from the fellowship of the Center for Global Studies (Abe Fellowship) of 2004. This is a revised and updated version of an article pre-published in the *Manchester Journal of International Economic Law* 2 (2005) issue 2, 18–38.

** Sophia University, Tokyo.

a limited way, since it will certainly have a favourable effect on resolving the issues, perhaps by way of analogy, among the WTO members involving non-parties to a MEA.

This section first addresses the question of co-ordination between WTO and MEAs in a broad, general perspective, and then take up the problems of Kyoto Protocol as a concrete example of MEA. In this presentation, both topics will be considered mainly from the *lex ferenda* perspectives.

II. GATT Article XX and MEAs

1. Relationship between WTO/GATT and MEAs

First, it may be appropriate to review the relationship between WTO/GATT and MEAs. It may be recalled that the GATT (General Agreement on Tariffs and Trade), as it stood from 1947 until 1994, was not really an international organisation, but was merely a loose combination of treaty-based relations among States. It would not even have been regarded even as an international regime at least at its initial stage. The GATT lacked an institutional mechanism which otherwise would have assured a substantial degree of normativity. It goes without saying that in 1947 when the GATT was drafted the environment was not a prominent issue.

The World Trade Organization (WTO) was created in 1995 by the Uruguay Round negotiations as a fully-fledged international organisation, with an international legal personality and effective, transparent institutional apparatus. The GATT is now an annex, together with other annexed agreements, to the Agreement Establishing the WTO, which makes it clear in the first paragraph of its preamble that its aim is to reconcile trade goals and environmental needs 'in accordance with the objective of sustainable development', indicating a stronger and integral link with general international law, with international environmental law in particular.

As recalled, it was the *Tuna/Dolphin* dispute before the GATT panel that sparked a heated debate on 'trade and the environment' worldwide in 1991.[1] This was the case in which the US, in order to protect dolphins, took measures to prohibit imports of tuna that had been caught by Mexican fishermen on the high seas – a dramatic replay of a century-old story of the

[1] *US Restriction on Imports of Tuna* (*Mexico* v. *United States*), 30 *ILM* (1991), 1594.

Bering Sea fur seals arbitration.[2] The GATT panel found that such 'extra-jurisdictional' application of domestic environmental law should be rejected under GATT as undermining the multilateral framework of world trade and concluded that trade measures taken by the US were not consistent with GATT provisions. After the establishment of the WTO in 1995, its Committee on Trade and Environment (CTE) began discussing the issue, and a consensus grew that any unilateral, extra-jurisdictional measures must be denied. As far as *non-treaty-based* measures are concerned, it seems clear that they are not generally regarded as GATT-consistent.[3]

What about *treaty-based* measures? The GATT panel noted in the above *Tuna/Dolphin* case that the US had not exhausted all other efforts available under international law to protect dolphins: 'The United States had not demonstrated to the panel that it had exhausted all options reasonably available . . . in particular through negotiations of international cooperative agreements.' *This suggests that the US actions may have been considered differently if it had been taken pursuant to a recognised international environmental agreement.* The claim for an Article XX exception would have, effectively, been considered to have a greater legitimacy if it had been made within the specific context provided by a recognized MEA.[4] If certain trade measures, such as the restriction of imports or levy of high tariffs, are taken in accordance with a multilateral environmental agreement (MEA), would they be considered permissible under the GATT? Between the GATT and an MEA, which is supposed to prevail over the other in case of a conflict? This is the crux of the problem that the present writer wishes to pose in this chapter. Before discussing the issue of compatibility, however, we should confirm our basic understanding of the legal framework of WTO/GATT relevant to the problem of trade and the environment.

2. The legal framework of the WTO/GATT regime

To consider first the procedural aspect of WTO/GATT dispute settlement, the central question here is whether the WTO dispute procedure

[2] Shinya Murase, 'Conflict of International Regimes: Trade and the Environment', Kalliopi Koufa, (ed.) *Protection of the Environment for the New Millennium*, Institute of International Public Law of Thessaloniki, *Thesaurus Acroasium*, Vol. XXXI, 2002, 297–340.

[3] Shinya Murase, 'Unilateral Measures and the WTO Dispute Settlement', in Simon S. C. Tay & Daniel C. Esty, (eds.) *Asian Dragons and Green Trade: Environment, Economics and International Law*, Times Academic Press, 1996, pp. 137–44.

[4] UNU/IAS, Global Climate Governance: Inter-linkages between the Kyoto Protocol and Other Multilateral Regime, 1999, p. 24.

can be regarded as '*a self-contained regime*'. It may be recalled that the notion was first referred to in the judgment on the *United States Diplomatic and Consular Staff in Tehran*, in which the International Court of Justice held that the resort to unilateral countermeasures by the injured State was excluded from the diplomatic law except for those measures specifically prescribed.[5] It may also be recalled that the debate at the International Law Commission in elaborating draft articles on State Responsibility, particularly in the context of the most controversial point whether the aggrieved State should exhaust all the available dispute settlement procedure before taking countermeasures.[6] One of the primary concern of the international community during the Uruguay Round of negotiations was to block and contain unilateral measures by the US and other powerful States, and from that perspective, the new WTO dispute settlement mechanism has attained a significant improvement toward a self-contained regime.

The former GATT dispute system had a number of defects, such as delays in the establishment of panels and in the appointment of panel members, delays in the completion of the panel reports, blocking of the adoption of panel reports and non-implementation. It was essentially based on the principle of consensus, and had strong elements of conciliation procedure rather than judicial settlement. In the WTO, by contrast, the dispute procedure is centrally administered by the Dispute Settlement Body (DSB) in accordance with the Understanding on Rules and Procedures Governing Dispute Settlement, or Dispute Settlement Understanding (DSU). The DSU has incorporated the '*negative (reverse) consensus rule*' in the establishment of a panel and in the adoption of reports of panels and the Appellate Body. This enables WTO dispute settlement to proceed automatically, unless there is a consensus to the contrary (which is, of course, most unlikely). The DSU has also set out *a strict timetable* for each key stage of the proceedings in order to ensure speedy completion, adoption and implementation of the rulings, which are closely monitored by DSB.[7]

Thus the GATT dispute settlement system has been substantially strengthened and '*judicialised*' under the WTO, which has attained a rule-

[5] *ICJ Reports 1980*, p. 43.

[6] Oscar Schachter, 'Dispute Settlement and Countermeasures', *American Journal of International Law*, vol. 88, 1994, pp. 471–7; Yoshiro Matsui, 'Countermeasures in the International Legal Order', *The Japanese Annual of International Law*, No.37, 1994, pp. 1–37.

[7] John H. Jackson, *The Jurisprudence of GATT and the WTO: Insights on Treaty Law and Economic Relations*, Cambridge University Press, 2000.

oriented, binding system of adjudication with compulsory jurisdiction over virtually the entire body of WTO law. Article 23 of the Dispute Settlement Understanding makes it clear that States are obliged to refrain from taking any unilateral action against alleged impediments to trade and to seek recourse to WTO's dispute settlement procedure. The intention of the drafters was clearly to move toward a self-contained regime, with the notion that unilateral measures can be effectively 'contained' and that resort to such measures is prohibited.[8]

The WTO dispute settlement system has so far demonstrated great success, and the number of cases filed and settled during the past ten years since its establishment has already far exceeded the number of cases referred to the GATT dispute settlement during its forty-odd years of existence. However, it is still open to question whether the WTO system of dispute settlement can be regarded as being completely sealed and self-contained regime. It can fairly be said that the system works as a self-contained regime as far as a given dispute concerns trade matters arising *within* the GATT system, such as tariff rates, anti-dumping and subsidies, namely, those disputes arising under the 'covered agreements' of WTO as provided for in Article 23 of the DSU. When it comes to the kind of disputes in which the GATT trade system is challenged from *outside*, such as trade *and the environment*, the WTO dispute settlement will face certain difficulty, *since the subject matter has not yet been covered by the WTO' s annexed agreements, with the result that WTO members may not be presumed to be bound by the DSU* at least for disputes that are predominantly environment-related rather than trade-related.

This leads us to consider the substantive law aspect of the problem on trade and the environment in the WTO. The most pertinent provision is GATT Article XX, which is an exception to the most-favoured-nation (MFN) clause of Article I, the supposed cornerstone of GATT. Article XX provides for 'general exceptions' and its paragraphs (b) and (g) are the most relevant to our discussion. Article XX provides:

> Subject to the requirement that such measures are not applied in a manner which would constitute a means of arbitrary or unjustifiable discrimination between countries where the same conditions prevail, or a disguised restriction on international trade, nothing in this Agreement shall be

[8] P. J. Kuyper, 'The Law of GATT as a Special Field of International Law', *Netherlands Yearbook of International Law*, vol. 25, 1994, pp. 227f.

> construed to prevent the adoption or enforcement by any contracting party of measures:
>
> ...
>
> (b) necessary to protect human, animal or plant life and health;
>
> ...
>
> (g) relating to the conservation of exhaustible natural resources if such measures are made effective in conjunction with restrictions on domestic production or consumption.

Obviously, this provision is far from satisfactory for the protection of the environment. One may question, first of all, if these paragraphs are really applicable to the measures taken for the protection of the environment. The legislative history of the GATT Article XX does not reveal any significant signs of concern for the environment, except in the very limited area of sanitary and phytosanitary measures for the protection of human health, animals and plants, which are related to customs regulations applied at the border. How is it possible to make these paragraphs applicable to the broad objective of protecting the environment of a particular country, or extend it to cover the protection of the global commons? This is the very question underlying the issue of compatibility of MEAs with GATT.

Naturally, it is necessary to interpret the GATT articles not only from their text and legislative history but *also in light of the 'subsequent practice' of States* (Vienna Convention on the Law of Treaties, Article 31, paragraph 3), and from that perspective, the findings of dispute settlement panels and the Appellate Body are very important. Nonetheless, the defects of GATT provisions in respect of environment-related trade measures are too obvious.

It was for this reason that the WTO has set up the Committee on Trade and Environment (CTE) to consider and elaborate applicable rules. Despite the high expectations of international community, the CTE and the Ministerial Conference have failed to reach any substantive consensus and no new rules have yet to emerge.

As noted earlier, the procedures under the WTO certainly have improved. But such procedural improvement goes only halfway toward a self-contained regime. Substantive law reform is crucial for the WTO to become fully self-contained. *The lack of substantive rules pertaining to environmental protection may well be considered a reason for not submitting certain disputes to WTO*, because there is no point on relying on the

WTO when no remedies can be expected therefrom based on the existing WTO law. The mandate of a WTO panel or the Appellate Body is to interpret and apply the existing law, namely, covered agreements, and such a panel or the Appellate Body would and should certainly exercise judicial restraint when facing new areas of law. It therefore seems inevitable that, at least at the present stage, there are important gaps discernible in the multilateral trading system dealing with the legal problems of trade and the environment.

Before offering his own proposal regarding a method of filling this existing gap, the present writer wishes to point out the modalities of the conflict between MEAs and the GATT, which is the central question of this section.

3. *Modalities of conflict between WTO/GATT and MEAs*

A conflict between the GATT and an MEA could take various forms: (a) a conflict of *basic constitutional principles*; (b) a conflict in the *methods of regulation*; (c) a conflict arising from the *means taken for domestic implementation of MEAs*; and (d) finally, a conflict arising out of the *means taken to ensure effectiveness of MEAs*.

First, *there are explicit or inherent differences between the GATT and an MEA on the level of basic constitutional principles*. The basic norm of the GATT, as expressed in its Articles I and III, is 'equal treatment and non-discrimination' and if there are exceptions to this principle, they are recognised only on the specifically prescribed basis, whereas MEAs for the protection and use of the global environment are based on the principle of 'common but differentiated responsibility' according to which developed States bear special responsibility (Principle 7 of the Rio Declaration), while the special situation and needs of developing countries are given special priority (Principle 6).

Thus, for example, the UN Framework Convention on Climate Change and the Kyoto Protocol impose on Annex I parties (industrialised, developed countries) targets for the emission reduction/restriction of greenhouse gases (GHGs), with no such obligation prescribed for developing countries. As a result, goods produced in developing countries enjoy comparative advantages in the markets of developed countries. Since the WTO/GATT law requires that all members be placed, in principle, under the same privileges and obligations, the Annex I countries may assert to impose, in accordance with the WTO rules, countervailing measures or labelling requirements on these goods to reduce such advantages enjoyed by the developing countries under the Convention and the Protocol.

Such a voice will be stronger in view of the fact that the total amount of GHG emissions from developing countries will be higher than that from developed countries from around 2010–20. It will be recalled that the US Senate passed a resolution in 1997 to the effect that unless there is 'meaningful participation' by major developing countries, most notably, China, India, Indonesia, Brazil and Nigeria, the US would not be a party to the Protocol. Eventually, the Bush administration 'unsigned' the Protocol in April 2001 for the same reason.

Secondly, *there may be a difference in the methods of regulation between the GATT and MEAs from which a conflict may arise.* One of such questions is *processes and production methods* (PPMs) used in MEAs. This kind of regulation was not known to the GATT, which applies its rules primarily on *products.* In the long history of GATT practice, it was not until 1987 that the GATT was faced squarely with the question of PPMs for the first time. In the course of negotiating the Montreal Protocol on Substances that Deplete the Ozone Layer, the committee that drafted the Protocol's Article 4 relating to the trade restriction with non-parties to the Protocol discussed the question of compatibility of the PPM requirements with the GATT. It was understood then that such requirements were permissible under the GATT law. As a result, Article 4 of the Montreal Protocol provides not only for the restriction of CFCs themselves and goods containing CFCs, but also of goods which are produced with CFCs even where the goods do not contain them, if the restriction is deemed feasible after a certain period of time. It is this last category of regulations that concern PPMs.

In the context of global warming, it is possible to imagine a wide range of measures that may be contestable under the WTO rules. A party might impose equivalent energy efficiency standards on domestic and imported refrigerators and automobiles. Or a party might ban the national production or import of rice grown under methane intensive cultivation methods or wood harvested under non-sustainable forestry practices. All these measures are related to the question of permissibility of PPMs under the WTO/GATT.

The *Tuna/Dolphin* and the *Shrimp/Turtle* disputes were cases involving PPM regulation. There was nothing wrong with either the tuna or the shrimp *as products.* Presumably, they were clean, healthy tuna and shrimp. The concern of the United States was that the methods and processes of harvesting tuna and shrimp allegedly caused the incidental killing of dolphins and turtles. It should be noted however that dolphins and turtles are not the species protected by treaties,[9] and the fishing nets and equipment used were not of the type prohibited by international law. In other words, the PPM regulations in question *were not treaty-based unlike the above-mentioned Montreal Protocol*, which led to the decision in these two cases that they were not GATT-consistent.

Nonetheless, the *Shrimp/Turtle* ruling by the WTO's Appellate Body[10] seems to have broken new ground for PPM requirements under the GATT law, for better or worse. The complaint brought by India, Malaysia, Thailand and Pakistan concerned in this case the prohibition by the United States of the importation of certain shrimp and shrimp products because fishing vessels of these countries did not use turtle excluder devices (TEDs) or equally effective means of protecting turtles from shrimp-trawling activities. The Appellate Body implicitly indicated in its finding that such a PPM requirement might not be inconsistent by its very nature with GATT Article XX(g), although it held that the measures in question be considered unjustifiable under the chapeau of Article XX because of insufficient efforts made by the United States to secure a multilateral acceptance of its exclusionary programme.

Although there is not yet a universally accepted interpretation of the *Shrimp/Turtle* decision, *an argument has been advanced that PPMs may no longer be considered incompatible with the GATT.* If that is the case, however, the Appellate Body appears to have *exceeded its competence* as a judicial organ that is supposed to interpret and apply the existing law and not create a new law. The present writer believes that the Appellate Body's judicial legislation is not acceptable while the CTE, as the WTO's legislative body, has been considering the topic on PPMs for a number of years now without reaching a consensus.

With regard to a difference between the GATT and MEAs on the basis of the methods of regulation, there may be another possibility of conflict. The method of regulation presupposed in the WTO/GATT has been the direct administrative regulation generally called 'command and control' such as the imposition of tariffs and the restriction of imports. However,

[9] The sea turtles are covered by the 1973 Convention on International Trade in Endangered Species (CITES), but the CITES is an instrument which restricts *international trade* and, strictly speaking, is not an instrument for the *protection* of such species. Concerning the PPM issue see also Taira, chapter 18 in this book.

[10] *United States–Imports. Prohibition of Certain Shrimp and Shrimp Products.* See Jutta Brunee and Eellen Hey, (eds.) 'Symposium', *Yearbook of International Environmental Law*, vol. 9, 1998, pp. 3–47.

in the field of international environmental law, there has been increasing support for the use of 'economic instruments' that are considered more cost-effective. As a method of indirect regulation, these instruments include deposit-refund systems, charges and taxes, emission trading and financial assistance and they are premised to use market mechanisms to realise the environmental objectives. They have been incorporated in some of the MEAs, most notably in the Kyoto Protocol, an issue which will be discussed in some detail later.

The third type of conflict between the GATT and MEAs is one that may arise out of the means of domestic implementation. Within the bounds of an MEA, a State party may take different means and measures for its domestic implementation to fulfil the objectives of the MEA in question. This may create a situation where the domestic measure is challenged by another State under the relevant rules of WTO/GATT. As it will be explained later, this is exactly the situation that countries may face in respect of national implementing legislation taken in accordance with the relevant MEAs. For example, a national system on the allocation of permits for tradable emissions that is set up in implementation of the Kyoto Protocol but that actually works in favour of domestic firms may well be contested as being GATT-incompatible by exporting countries.

Fourth and finally, a conflict can occur when an MEA incorporates certain measures to ensure its effectiveness by way of sanctions either on non-parties or on non-compliant parties. Article 4 of the Montreal Protocol has already been referred to above, which provides for restriction of trade with non-parties. The discussion currently going on in respect of compliance mechanism under Article 18 of the Kyoto Protocol is posing the problem of sanctions on the parties that have not complied with the commitments set out in the Protocol, which will be discussed later.

4. Co-ordination of conflicting regimes

As described above, there are diverse implications involved in the problem of 'trade and the environment'. Together we have come to a conclusion that clear criteria need to be established for co-ordination between an MEA and the WTO. However, an MEA and the WTO are independent treaties on an equal footing, and between the two there is no supremacy over the other. If there is an overlap and a resulting conflict regarding the same subject matter, theoretically co-ordination in the form of dispute settlement should take place at a forum other than the MEA or the WTO to maintain impartiality. There should be at least an equal chance of selection between the two for dispute settlement. However, on the environmental side, there is no counterpart to the WTO's compulsory dispute settlement procedure, and therefore a dispute on 'trade and the environment' is more likely to be submitted to the WTO rather than that under an MEA, which is possible only on a consensual basis. It is more than *desirable that a World Environment Organization (WEO) be established* as a counterpart of the WTO with a view to attaining an equal footing between the two regimes.

With regard to methods to accommodate MEAs into the GATT, there has been a division between *ex post* and *ex ante* approaches. The former is based on the idea that the existing GATT provisions are adequate to deal with the question and that any clarification can be provided, as necessary, *ex post*, either through the WTO dispute settlement or through the use of a waiver procedure. The latter *ex ante* approach includes an amendment of the existing GATT provisions, such as the insertion of the term 'environment' into Article XX(b). None of these suggestions have attained full support among the WTO members.

This writer's own suggestion in this regard is to consider *an amendment to the effect of incorporating into the GATT an 'approval procedure'* similar to the exception for international commodity agreements of Article XX(h). This proposal has become the core of the position taken by Japan's Environmental Protection Agency (EPA, now the Ministry of the Environment) on the basis of the recommendation made by an EPA advisory group in March 1999. However, due to certain differences among Japan's Ministries (which is not surprising to those steeped in Japanese policy making), at the present this remains as the EPA's only provisional proposal. Those who have been watching and involved in the process hope that this proposal will be formalised as Japan's official proposal for consideration at the CTE, or at the WTO's ministerial meeting at some point in future.

The gist of this proposal is to insert, as a new subparagraph (k) of Article XX of the GATT, the following provision:

> (k) undertaken in pursuance of obligations under any multilateral environmental agreement which is submitted to the Ministerial Meeting and not disapproved by it.

This is a combination of *ex post* and *ex ante* approaches and in my view, this proposed method is most appropriate for harmonising the conflicting obligations of free trade under the WTO/GATT on the one hand and the protection of the environment under MEAs on the other. In my view, it will satisfy the requirement of assuring legal stability and predictability, while at the same time maintaining flexibility. If it is difficult to add this language as an amendment to existing GATT provisions, the above provision *could be incorporated in a binding 'Understanding' to be annexed to the WTO Agreement.*

There are some thirty MEAs with trade measures awaiting the formulation of objective criteria. New environmental agreements like the Kyoto and Cartagena Protocols are being elaborated with similar trade measures. Furthermore, increasing number of cases are expected to be brought before the WTO panels and the Appellate Body. It is therefore strongly hoped that the international community will reach a consensus on this important agenda as soon as possible.

What the present writer has attempted to do here has been to find out a method of co-ordination between two multilateral treaties, an MEA and the GATT. Questions regarding the overlap of two multilateral treaties is basically a matter that can be settled in accordance with the principles laid down in Article 30 of the Vienna Convention on the Law of Treaties regarding 'application of successive treaties relating to the same subject-matter'. However, the issue on 'trade and the environment' is not *merely* a conflict of treaties. It is a conflict of 'regimes'. Since a regime is comprised of multiple treaties and non-binding instruments, a conflict between one regime and another, – the trade regime and the environmental regime – cannot be solved simply as a matter of co-ordination of individual treaties.

From the present writer's perspective, the conflict of international regimes should be considered first as a question of their *external accommodation* on the basis of opposability. Confrontation between respective regimes can be seen as a clash of opposability. As recalled, the component element of opposability is effectiveness and legitimacy. The issue on trade and the environment is in fact the *on-going competitive process between the two regimes in terms of effectiveness and legitimacy.* In case of conflict between the two, one regime, either trade or the environment, will have to prevail over the other, and that will depend on which regime is regarded as more effective and more legitimate.

Needless to say, such a confrontation of international regimes is not desirable. It is therefore necessary to achieve *internal accommodation* within each regime. The environmental regime should try not only to passively obstruct but also actively incorporate the legitimate interests of free trade, while the trade regime should try to accommodate the legitimate concerns for environmental protection, both within their respective regimes. *In this way, it is hoped that both regimes can be transformed to be 'mutually supportive'.*

While some aspects of the Kyoto Protocol have already been touched on, it may be appropriate next to concentrate on the Kyoto Protocol, or more specifically, the so-called Flexibility (Kyoto) Mechanisms, and their relationship with the WTO/GATT regime.

III. Kyoto Protocol and WTO/GATT

1. The climate change regime and international trade

It may be recalled that it was especially a hot summer in 1988 when heat and drought hit large parts of the United States as well as some areas of Europe. That heat and drought supplied the driving force for action on the global warming issue. However, there was striking differences of positions among States surrounding the issue. Not only was the usual decisive division between developed and developing countries exhibited, but also conflicting positions in each group were more than evident in the negotiating process of the 1992 Framework Convention on Climate Change. In particular where conflicts related to energy production and consumption patterns, levels of technological development in the use and conservation of energy and resources and the specific vulnerability to climate change. Developed countries were far from being united, with the US alone in publicly opposing the specific targets and timetables. Germany and Japan were at the forefront viewing the Convention as an instrument for gaining a longer-term competitive advantage by requiring the further development, production and dissemination of innovative new technologies. Developing countries were also divided. The oil producing countries, led by Saudi Arabia, strongly opposed any substantive obligations in the Convention. The large industrialising developing countries, such as China and India, were concerned that their economic development, including use of large coal reserves, should not in any way be limited. Countries with extensive forests, such as Brazil and Malaysia, were concerned that the primary emphasis of the Convention should be on limiting developed countries' emissions and not on protecting or enhancing developing countries' sinks (forests). And developing countries particularly vulnerable to the effects of climate change, such as the thirty-seven member Alliance of Small Island States (AOSIS), sought a Convention with strong and enforceable commitments and an emphasis on the adverse effects of climate change. It was in these complex economic and environmental interests that the emergence of a climate change regime had to be worked out in the form of the Framework Convention in 1992. These same situations remained when Kyoto Protocol was drafted in 1997.

Before getting into the problems of the Kyoto Protocol, it is important to point out a certain intrinsic similarity between the WTO/GATT and the climate change regimes. It was suggested that both regimes are based on the common recognition that the problems that they are dealing with, whether trade barriers or the GHG emissions, need to be treated *as a continuing process* and under the framework within which the relevant issue links could be adequately co-ordinated in each round of negotiations. Thus the idea was proposed by David Victor in 1991 for the creation of a General Agreement on Climate Change, or GACC, modelled after the GATT, intended to provide for allowable contributions to global warming set for individual nations or groups of nations.[11] Under the system, it was envisaged that the level of emissions would be lowered through interactive and highly flexible rounds of negotiations in the same way as, say, tariff and non-tariff barriers have been lowered under the GATT.

Although a GACC was not realised, elements of the GATT model are nonetheless discernible in the Framework Convention on Climate Change. In fact, among the principles guiding the Parties, the Convention provides that 'policies and measures to deal with climate change should be cost-effective so as to ensure global benefits at the lowest possible cost' (Article 3, para. 3). While the developed countries assumed specific commitments, recognising that 'return by the year 2000 to earlier emission levels [unspecified] would contribute to modification of longer-term emission trends' (Article 4, para. 2), it was the intention of the Parties that a protocol or protocols would stipulate future targets and timetables for GHG emissions in developed countries for the post-2000 period. Thus, the Kyoto Protocol was elaborated to cover the first phase of this period with an expectation that similar protocols will be worked out in future for succeeding periods. These arrangements may not be as institutionalised as the WTO/GATT round of negotiations, but the *considerations underlying the climate change regime for the continuous efforts to stabilise and lower emission levels can be seen as quite similar to the WTO/GATT principles.*

[11] David Victor, 'How to Slow Global Warming', *Nature*, No. 349, 1991, pp. 451–6.

While the topic under consideration is the 'conflict' between an environmental regime and the WTO/GATT regime, as far as the climate change regime is concerned, co-ordination between the two may not seem to be much of a problem because of the similarity which was just mentioned, and because of the fact that the Kyoto Protocol has incorporated a new type of flexible economic instruments based on market mechanisms. It should be noted that a number of specific policies and measures promoted by the Kyoto Protocol, as a means of achieving its environmental goals, are not only consistent with measures promoted by the WTO Agreements, but result in mutual support. Some of the ways in which the Kyoto Protocol aims to achieve its goal of reducing GHG emissions include the promotion of the 'progressive phasing out of market imperfections, fiscal incentives, tax and duty exemptions and subsidies in all GHG emitting sectors that run contrary to the objective of the Convention and application of market instruments' (Article 1, subparagraph (a) (v)). This is very much in line with the objective of the progressive removal of trade restrictions and distortions.[12]

Nevertheless, it is possible that at the practical operational level the Kyoto Protocol may pose certain intricate problems of conflict with WTO/GATT rules, though this will largely depend on how its mechanisms are defined, designed and actually implemented. A potential point of conflict hinges upon the issue of discrimination. While the fundamental objective of the WTO regime is to remove any form of discrimination that may act as a barrier to free trade, the market mechanisms within the Protocol are dependent upon discrimination by distinguishing between developed and developing countries, between signatories and non-signatories, and between different manufacturing technologies and processes.[13] The Kyoto (Flexibility) Mechanisms are examined here from this angle.

2. The Kyoto Mechanisms

The key Annex I countries agreed to take on substantial targets for emission reduction/limitation in Kyoto, which was indeed the most ambitious environmental commitments ever set by an international agreement. However, it was recognised during the Kyoto negotiations that many

[12] UNU/IAS, *Global Climate Governance: Inter-Linkages between the Kyoto Protocol and Other Multilateral Regimes*, 1999, p. 13. [13] *Ibid.*, p. 12.

developed countries would find it difficult to achieve their target reductions solely on the basis of domestically implemented policies and measures. The reason for their acceptance despite such practical difficulties can be attributed in part to the availability under the Protocol of a number of unique market-based flexibility mechanisms. Essentially, these mechanisms constitute ways in which developed countries can supplement their domestic efforts to achieve their emission reductions by implementing specific projects and policies outside their countries.

These most innovative Kyoto Mechanisms can be grouped into two types: One is the project-type mechanism, namely, the *Joint Implementation* (JI, Article 6) and the *Clean Development Mechanism* (CDM, Article 12). The other is a mechanism called *Emissions Trading* (Article 17). All three mechanisms rely on existing economic forces to make them viable. It is considered that the Protocol will work most efficiently if parties or related private entities are allowed to acquire or invest in emission reduction opportunities in whichever countries they are cheapest to achieve. In effect, this approach will allow Annex I emitters to acquire parts of each other's assigned amounts or to invest in projects that generate 'emission reduction units' within each other's territory. These parts of assigned amounts or emission reduction units can then be used *as credits* to offset domestic obligations or international commitments under the Protocol. If these mechanisms are designed properly, it is considered that they may provide both the incentives and the means for countries to comply.[14]

Because some of the practical and operational details relating to the implementation of the Protocol's flexibility mechanisms have yet been made fully available, the elements of possible conflict with WTO/GATT may simply be hypothetical and speculative. Nonetheless, some potential points of conflict have become already apparent.

First on JI and CDM: While there is a difference between the two in that the Joint Implementation mechanism covers transactions between Annex I parties, and the Clean Development Mechanism runs between Annex I and non-Annex I parties, the nature of the operation of these project-based mechanisms is quite similar in the sense that the amount of emission reductions achieved through these activities may be offset against the party's assigned emissions. Articles 6 and 12 provide the

[14] Jacob Werksman, 'Compliance and the Kyoto Protocol: Building a Backbone into a "Flexible" Regime', *Yearbook of International Environmental Law*, vol. 9, 1998, pp. 48–101, at p. 50.

opportunity for Annex I parties to transfer or acquire emission reduction units (ERUs) resulting from joint implementation projects under Article 6, or to use certified emission reductions (CERs) resulting from CDM projects undertaken in accordance with Article 12.

It is believed that an industrialised country such as Japan can make a significant contribution in JI and CDM activities. From the bitter experience in the 1950s and 60s of disastrous pollution and the two 'oil shocks' experienced in the 1970s, the public and private sectors in Japan have made tremendous efforts to achieve the most energy-efficient style of industry, and as a result, Japan now enforces the world's strictest standards for exhaust emission controls for both factories and automobiles. For instance, through progress made in fossil-fuel and facilities improvement programmes, the volume of sulphur oxide and nitrogen oxide emissions per unit of electricity generated in fossil-fuel plants has been reduced drastically, with the result that SOx emissions during the 1980s was one-eighteenth that of the average of five leading OECD countries and NOx emissions was one-seventh. Thus, Japan's efforts for energy conservation have been carried through to the near maximum, and to reduce emissions by one-tenth of a percent would require a tremendous amount of investment. It can be expected that the same amount of money, if used under the proposed JI or CDM programmes for replacement or improvement of non-efficient plants and facilities in a technologically less-developed country, would contribute to dramatically reduce the volume of GHGs emitted in that country.

Despite such utility, JI and CDM may not be without a problem in respect to WTO/GATT law. Depending on how the specific rules on the operation of these mechanisms are elaborated, they may, at least in part, be deemed incompatible with relevant WTO rules. Although the WTO/GATT is not directly applicable to investment *per se*, it may nonetheless be applicable to trade-related aspects of investment activities. Therefore, a potential for conflict with the GATT may arise if, for example, a party hosting a CDM project is encouraged or required by the Protocol to expressly discriminate between investors or investment-related goods on the basis of the status of their home country in several ways: Annex I versus Non-Annex I parties, Complying versus Non-Complying parties, Party versus Non-Party, etc.[15] Thus, for example, it may be questioned whether the industrial plants to be exported to the

[15] UNU/IAS, pp. 31–2.

host country under the CDM scheme could be duly exempt from the importing State's obligation to extend MFN tariff rates and other benefits to other countries imposed under the GATT. From the GATT's point of view, such transactions should be treated as exceptions to the MFN principle and should be authorised in the same way as, say, the preferential treatment under the Generalised System of Preferences granted for developing countries.

Second, the Emissions Trading under Article 17 of the Kyoto Protocol: This has introduced a completely new 'product' to be traded called '*certified emission credits*', or CECs. Under the system, one Annex B party will be allowed to purchase the rights to emit GHGs from other Annex B parties that have been able to cut GHG emissions below their assigned amounts. Structured effectively, this market-based emissions trading approach, pioneered in the US Sulphur Allowance Trading Programme, can provide an economic incentive to cut GHG emissions while allowing the flexibility needed to promote cost-effective actions.

When the GATT was created in 1947, 'trade and the environment' was not an issue, let alone the 'trading of air pollution' among its parties. First we must ask whether emissions are identifiable as something that can be traded on international markets, and that can be under the jurisdiction of the WTO/GATT. *Is a CEC really a good* to be covered by the GATT? If we can recognise a certain physical element in a CEC, it is argued that it may be characterised as a good, similar to hazardous waste or used oil, which would then entail application of the GATT. However, waste is not normally considered as a good because of its lack of commercial value (unless it is intended for recycling). Some argue that a *CEC is a service* rather than a good by characterising it as the right to emit and as a permit or credit that is a negotiable instrument. For this reason, they consider a CEC to be a sort of financial service covered by the General Agreement on Trade in Services (GATS). The apparent artificiality of these arguments notwithstanding, either the GATT or the GATS, which work on similar principles, will be applicable to emissions trading to the extent it has an effect on trade. Depending on the size and effectiveness of the system, emissions trading will certainly have significant impacts on international trade as has been the case for other trade-related environmental measures.

Questions on the compatibility with the WTO are raised by the very fact that the Kyoto Protocol restricts the trading of emissions only to Annex B parties, which could be seen as barrier to trade particularly from the perspective of non-Annex B parties, namely, developing countries.

Some of these countries have large inventories of emission credits which they might wish to trade on an emissions 'credits' market, but could only do so by becoming Annex B members. There is also a possibility of discrimination if the eligibility for participation in the market is linked with compliance: for instance, if the selling party were in compliance with its emission requirements, the trade would be unrestricted, while if, by means of a monitoring and verification process, a potential for non-compliance were recognised, then the trade would be banned or the seller would be sanctioned for trading while out of compliance.[16] Such a system would certainly pose delicate compatibility problems with the WTO principle of non-discrimination.

The crucial aspect of the emissions trading system is also the allocation of permits within the domestic market, which could raise the issue of compatibility with the WTO rules. Various forms of allocation have been debated including 'upstream', 'downstream' and 'hybrid' models.[17] No matter how national trading systems are designed, importers and domestic producers of fossil fuels should be treated equally in obtaining emission allowances under the like-product provisions in the WTO. It is feared, for example, that governments might allocate permits in such a manner as to favour domestic firms against foreign rivals, violating the GATT principle of *non-discrimination.*[18]

[16] UNU/IAS, p. 16.

[17] An 'upstream' trading system would target fossil-fuel producers and importers as regulated entities, and therefore would reduce the number of allowance holders to oil refineries and importers, natural gas pipelines, natural gas processing plants, coal mines and processing plants, making administration of the system easier. However, since such firms would simply raise prices, an upstream system would provide no incentive for energy end-users to develop disposal technologies, an aspect deemed critical in searching for long-term solutions to climate change problems. In contrast, a 'downstream' trading system would apply at the point of emissions. As such, a large number of diverse energy users are included. However, such a system would be more difficult to administer, especially concerning emissions from the transportation sector and other small sources. Alternatively, a national trading system could be modelled as a 'hybrid' system, which is similar on the one hand to a downstream trading system, in the sense that regulated sources at the levels of energy users are also limited to utilities and large industrial sources, but which, on the other hand, like an upstream trading system, would require fuel distributors to hold allowances for small fuel users and pass on their permit costs in a mark-up on the fuel price. As such, small fuel users are exempt from the necessity of holding allowances, and yet the rise in fuel price will motivate them to reduce fuel consumption or switch from fuels with high carbon content such as coal to fuels with a low carbon content such as natural gas. Zhong Xiang Zhang, 'Greenhouse Gas Emissions Trading and the World Trading System', *Journal of World Trade*, vol. 32, no. 5, 1998, pp. 219f. 225–6.

[18] Zhong Xiang Zhang, *ibid*, pp. 226–7.

All of these flexibility mechanisms adopted by the Kyoto Protocol must be elaborated in detail and with care and a view to avoiding potential conflict with the WTO as much as possible. It is imperative to bear in mind that the Kyoto Mechanisms are available only as supplementary means to domestic efforts to reduce/limit GHG emissions by Annex I countries. They will never be the mainstream measures contemplated by the Protocol. Certain domestic measures intended to curb global warming might again pose intricate compatibility problems with the WTO.

3. Certain domestic measures

The Kyoto Protocol provides in general terms that Parties be bound to adopt policies and measures in a manner to promote sustainable development. The Protocol, however, stops short of specifying the *methods* by which to attain the objectives through domestic policies and measures. Such actions are to be taken in accordance with national circumstances, and the selection of appropriate methods is left largely to the discretion of individual States. It is conceivable that the validity of certain measures by a State come to be challenged by other States for not being mandated under the Framework Convention and the Protocol. *Measures that are not clearly treaty-based thus pose delicate problems, as they might be categorised, at worst, as tantamount to unilateral measures by individual States.*

Nonetheless, active debates have been going on in various countries with regard to such domestic policies and measures. Examples are policies or measures to enhance energy efficiency, protect and enhance sinks and reservoirs, promote research and development, increase the use of new and renewable forms of energy and environmentally sound technologies, phase out fiscal incentives and exemptions in GHG-emitting sectors, and promote the application of market instruments, to name but a few. Energy, carbon and other taxes, mandatory and voluntary standards, subsidies for environmentally friendly production processes, labelling and certification schemes are also mentioned. All of these domestic measures employed to reduce emissions will certainly have a bearing on world trade, and accordingly, potential conflict with the relevant WTO principles and rules.

There are some specific cases of domestic environmental policies worthy of mention. First, some Annex I countries have already established domestic legislation, either in mandatory or voluntary forms, regarding energy efficiency requirements and standards for the product and/or processes and production methods (PPMs). Japan, for example, revised its Law Concerning the Rationalisation of the Use of Energy (Energy Conservation Law) in 1998, which imposes strict emission controls on factories, construction, machinery, automobiles and electric appliances. The Law has introduced the so-called 'top runner approach', under which standards are set at the levels meeting or exceeding the highest energy efficiency achieved among currently commercialised products. To take a specific case of gasoline-fuelled passenger vehicles, it was expected that fuel consumption would be improved by about 23 per cent from 1995 levels by 2010 (this target was actually achieved by 2005). Importation of such automobiles that are not sufficiently energy efficient may be restricted under the Law. These requirements and standards may however be deemed inconsistent with the WTO agreement on technical barriers to trade (TBT), unless they are specifically accepted as legitimate exceptions to trade liberalisation clauses. In fact, the US and the EU have reportedly noted their concern to the Committee on TBT; expressing certain reservations to Japan with respect to the specific provisions of the Energy Conservation Law for fear that *they might be used for the protection of domestic automakers against European and American firms*. It should be noted, however, that no inconsistency is discernible under the Appellate Body's interpretation of the relevant provisions of TBT which was given in the *Asbestos* and *Sardines* cases.[19]

To consider the potential trade-distorting effect of certain domestic legislation, another interesting Japanese law, the Law Relating to Recycling of Disposed Household Electric Appliances established in 1998 may be of interest. Its primary objective is waste management rather than emissions control, but it has an important aspect of conservation of resources through recycling and thus a certain bearing on emissions reduction. Interesting about this law is that it requires not consumers or municipalities but rather the *producers* of household electric appliances (such as TV sets, refrigerators, air-conditioners and washing machines) to *recycle* their products after consumer use upon disposal by the consumer. This means that the producers must design their products so as to facilitate recycling and also that they must set up effective networks for collecting disposed appliances. Similarly in 2004, the Law Relating to the

[19] Shinya Murase, 'Japan's Measures on Global Warming and the TBT Agreement', in Survey and Research on Co-ordination of Trade and Environment, GISPRI, 2004 (in Japanese) pp. 81–92; See also, Mitsutsune Yamaguchi, 'Implementing the Kyoto Protocol Commitment and their Impacts on Trade: Focusing on Japanese Automobile Fuel Efficiency Standards', *Keio Economic Studies*, vol. 41, no. 1, 2004.

Recycling of Automobiles was enacted so as to include automobiles for recycling. These are exactly the policy adopted by the OECD called '*extended producer responsibility*' (EPR). It is reported that the European Union has recently decided on even tougher recycling requirements.[20] These measures may be challenged, however, as being inconsistent with the TBT agreement in the same way as the energy efficiency requirements described earlier, particularly by prospective foreign producers and exporters of those products.

These energy efficiency or recycling measures may also be coupled in some cases with certain subsidies or tax reductions, in which case the same benefits may, in principle, have to be extended to foreign imports in order to be compatible with the WTO/GATT. There have been debates about the use of subsidies in the form of financial support for investments with the objective of developing technologies and goods that reduce emissions. The WTO Agreement on Subsidies prescribes three kinds of subsidies: prohibited (red light), actionable (yellow light) and non-actionable (green light) subsidies. *Environmental subsidies are generally considered to be non-actionable*, though they can be actionable if they are regarded as substantially trade-distorting, in which case certain countervailing measures become permissible under WTO law.

Finally, some Annex I countries may decide to implement a carbon tax or environmental tax as a way to combat climate change. Taxes are considered effective tools for achievement of environmental goals, particularly in the context of global warming, creating incentives for polluters to limit activities that cause GHG emissions. However, taxes raise inevitable questions concerning competitiveness, and therefore an effective system for border tax adjustment is indispensable to offset tax-related production costs. This is one of the major topics discussed at the WTO/CTE that needs to be resolved.

IV. An alternative regime on climate change and WTO/GATT

With the desertion of the US from the Kyoto Protocol, the original landscape of the global warming issues has changed considerably, though the Protocol came into effect in February 2005 with Russia's accession. While the US may be condemned for its 'selfish betrayal' of the *bona fide* efforts of the international community, there are many now who question the

[20] EU: Directive on Waste Electrical and Electronic Equipment, June 2000.

basic approaches adopted by the Protocol, most notably, its rigid imposition of national caps and its purported enforcement of sanction in case of non-compliance.

1. Non-compliance of the Kyoto Protocol

The Kyoto Protocol requires industrialised parties to limit and reduce GHG emissions by quantified amounts and within a specific timeframe as set out in Annex B, according to which, for example, Japan is obligated to reduce 6% of its total emissions as compared to the 1990 level, the US 7% and the EU 8%. It should be noted that these numerical targets were set out in a top-down manner as a political compromise and were not in any way based on the objective criteria of bottom-up figures. The year 1990, selected as the base year for comparison, is quite unfair for countries such as Japan which reached the level of substantive achievements in energy-saving technologies, while it is quite advantageous for the European countries that were still halfway toward that level, not to mention Germany's unification which created extremely favourable 'bubbles'. The problem of non-compliance for the Kyoto Protocol is focused on these commitments by developed countries, since most of these industrialised countries appear to be having difficulty in meeting the assigned numerical targets. This was evidently another reason for the earlier departure of the US from the Protocol.

Article 18 of the Kyoto Protocol provides that 'appropriate and effective procedures and mechanisms to determine and to address cases of non-compliance' be established. It is, however, reminded that '[a]ny procedures and mechanisms . . . entailing binding consequences shall be adopted by means of an amendment to this Protocol'. There are two schools of thoughts about the responses to non-compliance that are contemplated under this Article. One view advocates *'soft' compliance management*, which favours primarily facilitative and promotional approaches by rendering *assistance* to non-compliant States, modelled after the Montreal Protocol's non-compliance procedure. The other view takes a *'hard' enforcement approach* to coerce compliance by imposing *penalties or sanctions* on non-complying parties. Financial penalties and economic or trade sanctions have been proposed along these lines.[21]

[21] Jacob Werksman, (see fn.14), at 48 *et seq.*; 'The Negotiation of a Kyoto Compliance System', in Olav Schram Stokke, Jon Hovi and Geir Ulfstein, (eds.), Implementing the Climate Regime: International Compliance, Earthscan, London, 2005, pp.17–37.

These measures, if incorporated, will certainly come in conflict with WTO/GATT rules on trade liberalisation.

However, it is hard to believe that this latter approach can be a realistic option. The authority to impose coercive measures would certainly entail 'binding consequences', and so it will not be possible to establish such measures without an amendment of the Kyoto Protocol as is clearly stipulated in the second sentence of Article 18. An amendment means a change of the carefully balanced compromises achieved in Kyoto, not to mention another cumbersome ratification procedure that many States may not be willing to take when the Kyoto Protocol itself is facing difficulty in collecting the necessary number of ratifications to enter into force. Even if such coercive measures are introduced into the system, it does not appear that it will work effectively for the reasons based on the very nature of the global environmental regimes in which confrontational approaches do not seem to be appropriate.

The COP-7 meeting at Marrakesh in November 2001, nonetheless, adopted an enforcement approach by a decision (Decision 24/CP.7) to the effect that the level of reduction/limitation of GHG emission be 'deducted' from the second commitment period for those non-complying Annex I countries. The rate of deduction has been set as 1.3 times of the amount of the emission that has not been complied with, *the sanction that should be applied by the Enforcement Branch.*

There are a number of problems that should be pointed out about this 'decision'. First, the establishment and jurisdiction of the Enforcement Branch fall under the 'binding consequences' entailing 'amendment' of the Protocol in accordance with Article 18 of the Protocol. Second, the deduction of 1.3 times the non-complying amount also comprises of the 'binding consequences' entailing 'amendment' of the Protocol. Third, since the amount of the reduction/limitation for the second commitment period has not been decided on yet, it is meaningless to talk about the reduction therefrom. It should be pointed out that the temporal scope of application of the Kyoto Protocol is to extend only to 2012, the end of the first commitment period. Clearly, a decision of the Conference of the Parties cannot be equated with an amendment of a treaty provision. Any consensus reached at the COP-7 meeting should have therefore been deemed merely as a provisional political agreement which itself has no legal significance.

Nonetheless, the First COP/MOP meeting of the Kyoto Protocol in Montreal in November–December 2005 (held after its coming into effect in February 2005) adopted the following decision on

'Procedures and mechanisms relating to compliance under the Kyoto Protocol':

> *The Conference of the Parties serving as the meeting of the Parties to the Kyoto Protocol, . . .*
>
> 1. *Approves and adopts* the procedures and mechanisms relating to compliance under the Kyoto Protocol, as contained in the annex [Decision 24/CP.7] to this decision, without prejudice to the outcome of the process outlined in paragraph 2 of this decision;
> 2. *Decides* to commence consideration of the issue of an amendment to the Kyoto Protocol in respect of procedures and mechanisms relating to compliance in terms of Article 18, with a view to making a decision by the third session of the Conference of the Parties serving as the meeting of the Parties to the Kyoto Protocol.

While it was decided that the issue on the amendment be resolved at a later stage, the meeting clearly endorsed the basic approach taken at Marrakesh which was, in the opinion of the present writer, highly undesirable from the policy perspective and highly problematical from a legal point of view.

2. A new mechanism modelled after the WTO/GATT

It has become increasingly evident that the Kyoto Protocol as it stands now will not adequately work as an instrument to combat global warming, even if it comes into effect. Almost certainly, it will not sustain after 2012 when the so-called first commitment period is to end. We would even be able to predict the worst conceivable scenario in 2012 that everybody is condemning everybody else. Developing countries will condemn the non-compliance of the developed countries. Developed countries condemn developing countries for non-cooperation. There will also be condemnation among developed countries. And naturally, all the parties will condemn the US for having deserted from Kyoto. In order to avoid such a situation, *we should seriously consider the possibility of establishing a new, alternative, regime as early as possible*, as the negotiations for the second commitment period have now commenced.

Let us summarise what the problems are: *First of all, it was a mistake that the Protocol provided for the absolute numerical national caps as binding commitments for industrialised countries.* Such a binding system is simply not feasible, not only from the practical point of view but also from the logical standpoint. Governments can enter into agreements and will comply with the obligations incorporated therein that are within their reach (e.g. levying carbon tax) but they cannot be directly responsible for the activities, economic or otherwise, outside their mandate (such as limiting the amount of CO_2 emissions from various sources of a country) unless they are under the strict and all-encompassing State planning similar to the former socialist countries or those States under the wartime control. In this sense, we can fairly say that the Protocol has wrongly attempted to impose on the market-economy industrialised countries those binding commitments that have no guarantee to be complied with in the first place. *In other words, the Kyoto Protocol should have set the caps as non-binding goals* rather than binding commitments. As was stated earlier, to adopt the enforcement approach for non-compliance is only to duplicate a mistake on top of the original mistake.

The second mistake was the numerical quantification of such commitments. While the general target of 5% reduction might have been legitimate, the individual national targets (such as 6% for Japan and 7% for the US and 8% for European countries, etc.) were set quite arbitrarily without any objective foundations. These targets were politically agreed on in a top-down, deductive manner rather than accumulating objective figures, sector by sector, in a bottom-up or inductive manner. The result was that those percentages were unfair for Japan, unfeasible for the US and quite advantageous for Europe if considered together with the so-called 'EU bubbles' and the base year of 1990. Such unfair and unfeasible elements would be detrimental to the incentives to comply by the industrialised nations outside Europe.

Thirdly, the Kyoto Protocol was concerned primarily with short-term achievements, while global warming is something that should be tackled over the long term, say fifty or one hundred years. The Protocol's basic approach was to set a timeframe of some ten years, and to assess the result of achievement by individual nations at the end of each commitment period, which is to be reflected for the level of commitment to be allocated at the following period. This kind of mechanism may work well in some quarters domestically, but it is rather difficult to imagine that it will work as effective machinery in the international community. No legal link has been established between the first and second commitment periods in the Kyoto Protocol. Naturally, the nations cannot agree on the binding substantive commitments lasting for fifty or 100 years, though they can probably agree on establishing certain procedures such as the one to be elaborated later in this chapter.

The fourth point is well known and it has already been touched on. It is now clear that *'meaningful participation' by major developing countries* such as China, India, Indonesia, Brazil and Nigeria should be inevitable, at least after 2012. Korea and Mexico, now OECD member countries, should be regarded as having 'graduated' from the status of 'developing countries'.

The present situation surrounding the Kyoto Protocol *appears quite similar to the circumstances after the adoption of the UN Convention on the Law of the Sea* (UNCLOS) in 1982. It may be recalled that the US and other industrialised countries strongly objected to Part XI of the Convention on the deep-sea mining which was deeply influenced by the ideology of planned economy. The developed countries refused to ratify the Convention while the ratifications from the developing countries were piling up by which time the Convention came close to entering into force by the early 1990s. In the meantime, the developed countries, led by the US, concluded the so-called mini-agreement for the development of the mineral resources of the deep sea. This was, in a word, a situation of parallel existence of two conflicting treaty regimes. It was apparent that the UNCLOS regime would face a serious paradox of collapse by the very entry into force of the Convention, because of the obvious fact that developing countries alone would not be able to support the regime financially. It was the UN Secretary-General's efforts for conciliation between the developed and developing countries that eventually saved the Convention by 'freezing' (i.e. in effect, terminating) the Part XI.

In any event, it seems quite possible that the Kyoto Protocol will not be sustainable beyond 2013. If our assumption is valid, then, *what kind of new mechanism can be envisaged for an alternative regime to Kyoto Protocol?* In the present writer's view, it should incorporate the following elements: First, the new regime should be a mechanism that is capable of assuring continuous efforts by all nations lasting for a long term of fifty or 100 years. Second, instead of imposing rigid obligations on States by way of absolute caps, it should guarantee flexibility by which special requirements of individual nations can be accommodated. Third, however, the new regime after the Kyoto Protocol cannot go back to the level of soft law or even to the level of the UNFCCC. It should contemplate the adoption of some sort of binding commitments while maintaining the flexibility just mentioned. Fourth, rather than the top-down approach, we should consider the bottom-up approach based on the objective criteria accumulated in various sectors within the State. Fifth, the regime should have a steering organ in which major State parties have special powers and responsibilities, the one similar to the Antarctic Treaty Consultative Meetings.

As a concrete example based on the above considerations, it may be appropriate to venture the following proposal: A new regime could be worked out after the WTO/GATT model as it was already referred to earlier. 'Greening the GATT' has been a popular theme: Conversely, *attention should be given to 'GATT-isation of an MEA'*. It is believed that *GATT-isation of the Kyoto Protocol* is inevitable in view of the fact that the Protocol is, in essence, much more of an economic and energy treaty than an environmental treaty. The word, GATT-isation which was 'invented' only recently as this chapter was in preparation, has a very good association with the Japanese word, *Gattai*, which means 'merger' or 'accommodation' and I am hoping to disseminate this word as a slogan for my proposition!

The WTO/GATT has been very successful for the past fifty odd years in realising free trade, through lowering tariffs and non-tariff barriers. The GATT is a framework that combines bilateralism with multilateralism. Under its request–offer system, country A requests country B, for example, to lower tariffs for automobiles, offering the latter in return to lower its tariff for steel products. If the agreement is reached bilaterally between the two countries, the results are extended to all the other contracting parties on an MFN basis. Countries continue negotiations until the target is reached. Thus, the Kennedy Round negotiations in the 1960s, for example, started with the goal of reducing 50% of the tariffs for all the industrial products, ended with the result of some 36% average reduction, which was nonetheless a great success. In the course of such intergovernmental negotiations, the representatives from the related industrial sectors, such as the automobile and steel industries and those from the consumer side, are no doubt involved substantially. *Introduction in this process should also consider the 'pledge and review' system* similar to the one adopted by OECD code for the liberalisation of capital movement.

This is in the present writer's view the model scheme that can be used for the reduction of GHG emissions. The result of the negotiations would be binding on states, but in a different form from the absolute national caps embodied in the Kyoto Protocol. The process is continuous and flexible, which lasts in principle until the set goal is achieved, like the 5% overall reduction target. For developing countries, we can always consider the possibility of granting preferential treatment (another important GATT experience) which should be subject to individual scrutiny rather than the unqualified, sweeping system of generalised scheme applicable to all developing countries.

As high tariff rates are preferable for the protection of domestic industry, States are inclined to be negative toward lowering the emission level for protecting the domestic industry. However, in the context of GATT, countries soon realised that lower tariffs would be desirable for the public interests of the international community which is also beneficial for the long-term national interests of each State. Although admittedly the distance between the individual national interest and the international public interest in the context of global warming is not as close as trade, it is believed that countries have realised the linkage much more acutely than before.

Finally, a reference should be made to the recent *'Asia-Pacific Partnership on Clean Development and Climate' (AP-7)* inaugurated in January 2006, partnership between Australia, Canada, China, India, Japan, Republic of Korea and the US, which is to focus on technology development related to climate change, energy security and air pollution. Eight public/private task forces are to consider: (1) fossil energy, (2) renewable energy and distributed generation, (3) power generation and transmission, (4) steel, (5) aluminium, (6) cement, (7) coal mining, and (8) buildings and appliances.[22] So far, it appears to be merely *a loose 'coalition of the willing' with modest, voluntary commitments*, but it is important that the partnership includes a State which departed from the Kyoto Protocol (the US) and those developing large emitter countries (China, India and Korea) as well as developed country parties to the Protocol (Australia, Canada and Japan). As was the case in the 'mini agreement' for the deep sea mining activities in the 1980s, *this may create a situation of coexistence of dual regimes*. However, it may create a more positive climate that encourages healthy competition between the regimes, which will certainly influence the process of building a better, more workable mechanism for the period after 2013.

Additional References

Baumert *et al.* (eds.), *Building on the Kyoto Protocol: Options for Protecting the Climate*, World Resources Institute 2002.

McKibbin and Wilcoxen, *Climate Change Policy after Kyoto: Blueprint for a Realistic Approach*, Brookings Institution 2002.

Murase, Perspectives from International Economic Law on Transnational Environmental Issues, *Recueil des Cours de l'Academie* vol. 253, pp. 283–431.

Victor, *The Collapse of the Kyoto Protocol and the Struggle to Slow Global Warming*, Princeton 2001.

[22] www.dfat.gov.au/environment/climate/ap6/index.html.

18

Live with a quiet but uneasy status quo?–An evolutionary role the appellate body can play in resolution of "trade and environment" disputes

SATORU TAIRA*

I. Introduction

How is it possible to reconcile trade liberalization with environmental protection? This is among the most urgent questions facing the new trade round negotiation, the Doha Development Agenda, of the World Trade Organization (WTO).[1] In particular, the issue of the permissibility of process-and-production-method- (PPM-) based trade measures under the WTO law is the most difficult and controversial one afflicting WTO lawyers. The problem can be described in a nutshell: *can a trade ban on a product imposed because of the fact that the PPM of that product is harmful to the environment be consistent with WTO law?*[2]

* Professor of Graduate School of Law, Osaka City University, Osaka, Japan. The first version of this chapter was prepared for the Osaka International Symposium, The Social Responsibility of Legal Profession in the Age of Globalization, Commemorating the Fiftieth Anniversary of the School of Law, Osaka City University, July 5–6 2003.

[1] The Doha Ministerial Declaration adopted on November 14 2001 (WT/MIN (01)/DEC/1, November 20 2001), which launched the new trade round negotiation called the "Doha Development Agenda," provides the mandate for negotiation, among others, "with a view to enhancing the mutual supportiveness of trade and environment, on the relationship between WTO rules and specific trade obligations set out in multilateral environmental agreements." *See* Paragraph 31 of this declaration.

[2] There are many comments and articles on this problem. *See*, among others, Markus Schlagenhof, *Trade Measures Based on Environmental Process and Protection Methods*, 29 *JWTL* 123 (1995); Robert Howse & Donald Regan, *The Product/Process Distinction – An Illusory Basis for Disciplining 'Unilateralism' in Trade Policy*, 11 *EJIL* 249 (2000); *Robert E. Hudec, The Product-Process Doctrine in GATT/WTO Jurisprudence, in* New Directions in International Economic Law: Essays In Honour of John H. Jackson 187 (Marco Bronckers and Reinhard Quick (eds.), Kluwer Law International, 2000); Sanford E. Gaines, *Processes and Production Methods: How to Produce Sound Policy for Environmental PPM-Based Trade Measures?*, 27 *Colum. J. Environ'l L.* 383 (2002); Steve Charnovitz, *The Law of Environmental "PPMs" in the WTO: Debunking the Myth of Illegality*, 27 *Yale J. Int'l L.* 59 (2002); Satoru Taira, *Trade and the Environment: The*

The purpose of this chapter is to trace what the panels and the Appellate Body of the WTO have done in settlement of disputes concerning the above problem and to think about a possible evolutionary role that the Appellate Body can play in resolution of "trade and environment" disputes.

In order to do this, the chapter first considers generally the essential characteristics of the problem of so called "trade and environment" and then identifies a special problem which is raised by these characteristics in the context of the dispute settlement system of the WTO (II). Second, on a more substantial level, this chapter will consider what a trade related environmental measure (TREM) based on a PPM is and will then identify the issues of its possible inconsistency with the WTO law (III). Third, we will trace how the panels and the Appellate Body have disposed of these issues in practice and also make some analysis of a new approach adopted by the Appellate Body in interpreting the WTO law in two recent cases (IV). In conclusion, this chapter will consider a possible evolutionary role that the Appellate Body can play in the resolution of "trade and environment" disputes by evaluating this new approach (V).

II. The characteristics of the problem

1. The characteristics of the problem of "trade and environment"

The essence of the controversy concerning the problem of "trade and environment" is summarized as follows.

On the one hand, *environmentalists argue* that the values of free trade conflict with the values of environment. According to them, trade liberalization creates new market opportunities and enhances economic activity. Trade also generates wealth, which allows consumers to acquire higher economic outputs. But freer trade and economic growth, if they go without fair payments of the costs ("*internalization*"[3]), result in

Possible Consistency of PPM-Based Trade Measures with GATT 1994, in Trilateral Perspectives on International Legal Issues: Conflict and Coherence 309 (Chi Carmody, Yuji Iwasawa & Sylvia Rhodes (eds.), American Society of International Law, 2003).

[3] "Internalization" means inclusion of pollution-related damages into a product's price. As to the "Polluter Pays Principle," Principle 16 of the Rio Declaration states:

> National authorities should endeavour to promote the internalization of environmental costs and the use of economic instruments, taking into account the

the unsustainable consumption of natural resources and waste production and lead to increased pollution and other environmental harm ("*externality*"[4]). Trade agreements contain market access provisions that can be used to override domestic environmental regulations. Environment represents a higher order and a more emergent value than trade. TREMs to enforce environmental standards are justified as leverage to promote worldwide environmental protection, particularly to address global or transboundary environmental problems and to reinforce international environmental agreements as in treaties designed to protect the ozone layer,[5] manage hazardous waste trade,[6] and preserve endangered species,[7] without regard to disruption to trade or any cost–benefit analysis. *Countries with lax environmental standards have a competitive advantage in the global market place* and put pressure on countries with high environmental standards to reduce their environmental requirements. TREMs make it possible for these countries to avoid such a pressure. *In the context of the North–South problem*, TREMs are also justified by the urgent necessity not to make the South follow the way the North took at the crisis of the global commons.[8]

On the other hand, *free traders mainly argue* as follows. Environmental values and trade values are complementary and the latter serves the former. If the consumption of a country's environmental resources is correctly priced, liberal trade improves a country's overall welfare and leads to a more efficient use of natural resources. Increased economic growth stimulates the demand for environmental

Footnote 3 (*cont.*)

> approach that the polluter should, in principle, bear the cost of pollution, with due regard to the public interest and without distorting international trade and investment.

The Rio Declaration on Environment and Development, June 14 1992, *reprinted in* 31 *ILM* 876 (1992).

4 As to a definition of "externality", Samuelson, for an example, states:

> [A]n externality is an effect of one economic agent's behavior on another's well-being where that effect is not reflected in market transactions.

Samuelson and Nordhaus, Economics (16th edn 1998) at 331.

5 Montreal Protocol on Substances that Deplete the Ozone Layer, September 16 1987, 26 *ILM* 1550 (1987).

6 Basel Convention on the Control of Transboundary Movements of Hazardous Wastes and Their Disposal, March 22 1989, 28 *ILM* 657 (1989).

7 Convention on International Trade in Endangered Species, March 3 1973, 993 UNTS 243.

8 *See* Schlagenhof, *supra* n. 2, at 123; *see also* Jeffrey L. Dunoff, *The Death of the Trade Regime*, 10 *EJIL* 739–40(1999); Esty, Greening The GATT: Trade, Environment and the Future, Institute for International Economics, at 43 (1994).

protection, generates additional income to pay for it and leads to improved environmental standards and protection techniques. The problem is not the harm that free trade does to the environment, but the harm that TREMs do to free trade. TREMs undermine the concept of comparative cost advantages[9] upon which the basic principles of liberal trade rest and bring inefficiency and the reduction of economic welfare.[10] *In the context of the North–South problem*, TREMs of the North applied to imports from the South can be equated with the unilateral exportation of the North's own environmental policy to the South. They infringe the sovereign right of developing countries to dispose of their own natural resources. Many environmental problems in the South can largely be attributed to lower income levels and the complex problems of poverty. TREMs would make it more difficult for those countries to earn foreign exchange income from their exports and, therefore, will disturb their economic development. They would aggravate environmental problems in these countries.[11] Free traders criticize, stating that environmentalists have not proved the causal link between the deterioration of the environment and free trade and that they also have not established that TREMs are the most efficient way to change the environmental policy of the exporting country. Trade *per se* is not the source of environmental problems, but rather various forms of "market failures"[12] and "government failures".[13] Therefore, TREMs cannot be the appropriate instrument to achieve environmental goals. There is also a danger that unilateral TREMs become a disguised protectionist instrument for domestic competitors seeking relief from international competition.[14] The use of TREMs may also undermine the

[9] The theory of comparative cost advantages can be briefly explained as follows: the difference of resource endowment among nations makes the difference of the cost of production and results in comparative cost advantageous and disadvantageous industries in each country. In this case, each country should specialize its production in the comparative cost advantageous industries to make international division of production. By doing so, the most effective and proper use and allocation of resources can be realized. Then, if countries can, by free trade, exchange the products that are fruits of international division of production, all these countries can maximize their economic welfare.

[10] *See* Schlagenhof, n. 2, at 123–4. [11] *Ibid.*, at 124.

[12] For example, the failure to internalize external costs or the absence of the concept of "right to environment" as a property right. *Ibid.* at 124, n. 11.

[13] For example, agricultural subsidies leading to excessive use of chemical fertilizer polluting soil and water. *Ibid.*, n.12.

[14] *Ibid.* at 123–4; *see also*, Petersmann, *International Trade Law and International Environmental Law, Prevention and Settlement of International Environmental Disputes in GATT*, 27 JWT 43, at 43 and 48 (1993).

cooperation necessary for the continued functioning of the trade regime.[15]

Despite this controversy between environmentalists and free traders, respecting both the environmental value *and* the trade value seems to be essential for the sustainable development and welfare of human beings. Both values should not be considered as inherently conflicting, but as mutually supportive or complementary.[16] *And in this sense, the essence of the problem is how to best strike a balance between the environmental value and the trade value.*

However, trying to strike a balance between these two values presents issues that are among the most "contested" in trade policy and are currently contested in a way that appears to remove them from the legal domain, and place them squarely in the political domain. Professor Dunoff expresses appropriately this point as follows:

> To be sure, many trade policy issues are contested in the sense that they are subject to disagreement and dispute, but the claim here is that the many "trade and" issues are "contested" in a much more fundamental way. They are "contested" in the sense that fundamentals of the debate – say, the balance to be struck between economic and environmental interests – are "up for grabs" and that participants in these debates acknowledge the legitimacy of disagreement over these fundamental issues. In this sense, the question of basic GATT policy towards tariffs is not contested, while that of GATT policy regarding, say, competition [*or environmental*] issues, is highly contested.[17]

2. A special problem raised in the context of the dispute settlement system of the WTO

If we grasp the problem of "trade and environment" as having such characteristics, a special problem is also raised in the context of the dispute settlement system of the WTO. When a WTO negotiating body considers the problem of "trade and environment," it is both expected and appropriate for it to declare that it has weighted and struck a balance among all appropriate interests and values, and resolved political and policy issues through consensus or at least a majority process.[18] But, as Professor

[15] *See* Dunoff, n. 8, at 740.

[16] See para. 31 of The Doha Ministerial Declaration, n. 1, for the mutual supportiveness of trade and environment.

[17] See Dunoff, n. 8, at 754–5. Italics added by this author.

[18] *Ibid.*, at 754.

Dunoff accurately pointed out, the same is not true for the WTO dispute settlement panels and the Appellate Body. According to him, while there has long been debate over whether GATT dispute settlement should be a legalistic, rule-based system or a more flexible diplomatic mechanism, the WTO Dispute Settlement Understanding (DSU) represents an unequivocal victory for the legalists. WTO panels and the Appellate Body are not intended to be simply another forum for the political settlement of controversial value conflicts. Rather, they are to apply settled law to the facts, to resolve disputes according to pre-existing principle. *The legitimacy of the dispute settlement system would be undermined if panels and the Appellate Body were understood to engage in either policy-making or deal-making.*[19]

But once disputes concerning the problem of "trade and environment" are submitted to the dispute settlement system of the WTO, panels or the Appellate Body would be in effect asked to draw a principled line in the midst of larger political struggles. Professor Dunoff continues to say, following the above cited expression:

> [I]t is precisely this contestedness that renders it almost impossible for panels and the Appellate Body to apply any nuanced test in a manner that appears to produce consistent results. Inconsistent results in these controversial areas would invite the criticism that the outcome are simply political . . . And any perceived "delegalization" of WTO dispute settlement proceedings would threaten to delegitimize these proceedings.[20]

Indeed, it should be noted that even the WTO's Director-General pleaded recently that *the WTO not be asked to serve as "judge, jury and police" on international environmental matters.* He warned that:

> [a]sking the WTO to solve issues which are not central to its work, especially when these are issues which governments have failed to address satisfactorily in other contexts, is not just a recipe for failure. It could do untold harm to trading system itself.[21]

Given the institutional constraints on WTO panels and the Appellate Body, and the highly politically controversial characteristics of the problem of "trade and environment," it is argued that it is politically

19 *Ibid.*, at 754; *see also* Daniel Bodansky, *The Legitimacy of International Governance: A Coming Challenge for International Environmental Law?*, 93 *AJIL* 596, at 606 (1999).

20 *See* Dunoff, at 755.

21 'WTO cannot be "Judge, Jury, Police" of Environment Issues, Top Official Says,' *BNA International Environmental Daily*, March 18 1998, *reproduced ibid.* at 756.

naïve to urge WTO panels and the Appellate Body to "struggle openly" with the value conflicts raised by the problem of "trade and environment."[22]

Then, the questions are as follows: Should the WTO panels and the Appellate Body refuse to decide disputes concerning the problem of "trade and environment" when such disputes are submitted to them? *Should the WTO lawyers "live with a quiet but uneasy status quo"*[23] *until a WTO political body decides a matter?*[24] By tracing what panels and the Appellate Body have done in settlement of the "trade and environment" disputes, these questions will be considered below.

III. Trade-related environmental measure based on a PPM

1. Substantial issue to be considered here

Among the substantial issues related to "trade and environment", that of consistency of a TREM based on a PPM with the WTO law has been addressed by Panels and the Appellate Body. In order to trace and evaluate how they have addressed this issue, it is convenient first to consider here *a TREM based on a PPM.*

2. Two categories of PPM

As domestic environmental problems become more serious and world concern about the global environment grows, there is increasing recognition that "production externalities" arising from a PPM in a production process of a product often affect the environment more significantly than "consumption externalities" coming from the use and consumption of a product. As a result, in addition to environmental regulations on products, States have also had a tendency to concern themselves with how a product is produced, manufactured, or obtained.

PPMs can be placed into two categories, *depending on whether the resulting product causes an environmental effect during its consumption or production.*[25] Some PPMs cause "consumption externalities." They

[22] *Ibid.* [23] *Ibid.*

[24] Professor Dunoff answers affirmatively to these questions. *See also* Claude E. Barfield, Free Trade, Sovereignty, Democracy: The Future of the World Trade Organization (AEI Press, 2001) 45–56.

[25] *See OECD Conceptual Framework for PPM Measures*, in OECD, Trade and Environment: Processes and Production Methods, at 149–62 (1994).

change the product's performance to such an extent that the product causes, or threatens to cause, damage to the importing country's environment when it is consumed, used, or disposed of. It is sometimes said that these PPMs are "materialized" into the product as such. This category of PPMs is directly related to the physical characteristics of the product concerned and is called *a "product-related-PPM."* For example, pesticides used on food crops may produce harmful chemical residues; cattle raised on growth hormones can produce meat with hormone residues.[26]

On the other hand, the second category of PPMs causes environmental effects in the production process of a product, but neither transmits such effects to the product itself nor affects the product's characteristics. These PPMs may lead to "*production externalities*" not only in the producing country, but also by their spillover effect in other countries and even in the global environment. This category of PPMs is therefore called a "*non-product-related PPM.*" Examples include, as referred to below, the practice of catching tuna by fishing methods causing high dolphin mortality and the incidental capture of large numbers of sea turtles by shrimp trawling. In addition, methods of cutting woods without a program of sustainable development and cleaning of semi-conductors and other electric parts with CHCs are also among these PPMs.[27]

3. TREM based on a PPM regulation

In international trade, *product-related PPMs* are less problematic in that importing countries that are also consumption countries can regulate them through internal regulations on the product as such. As long as imported products are treated the same as domestic like products, they will meet the discipline of "national treatment" under Art. III of GATT 1994.[28]

Non-product-related PPMs should be properly regulated by process standards in producing countries. But if a PPM regulation of a producing country is insufficient or ineffective, other countries that suffer from production externalities due to transboundary spillover effects may want to enforce their own regulation to halt the damage caused by the PPM in issue. It is here that a TREM plays its role as a measure to regulate the

[26] *See* Thomas J. Schoenbaum, *International Trade and Protection of the Environment: The Continuing Search for Reconciliation*, 91 *AJIL* 268, 288 (1997). [27] *Ibid.*

[28] *See* Schlagenhof, n. 2, at 126.

non-product-related PPM. Indeed, the TREM normally takes a form of import regulation by an importing country of the good produced by the PPM in question, but the purpose of the TREM in this case is to make the producers of the producing country stop using the PPM in issue, and thus, without any agreement among concerned countries, this TREM would be seen as extraterritorial and unilateral application of a regulation of this importing country and criticized as so called *"eco-imperialism"* because the TREM is equated with an unilateral imposition of an environmental standard by the importing country.

The problem becomes further complicated when a non-product-related PPM causes production externalities in a more extended jurisdictional scope. The more the number of affected countries increases, the more difficult it becomes to agree on a suitable sharing among the affected countries of the required internalization of environmental externalities because of the difference of policy stances of the countries concerned on the environmental problem. Thus, *the circumstances under which TREMs based on a PPM are taken can be distinguished according to the degree of attainment of agreement among the countries concerned*:[29] one country may be obliged to take a TREM *under a multilateral environmental agreement* (MEA), while another may *unilaterally* take a TREM arguably based upon some general principles of international law, such as the principle of state responsibility for transboundary environmental harm. And even in the former case, it is necessary to take note that if the target country of the TREM is not a party to the MEA, the TREM taken against it cannot escape from being criticized as an unilateral measure. The next sections focus on TREMs based on a non-product-related PPM and consider the issue of their consistency with the WTO law.

IV. The issue of consistency of a TREM based on a PPM with WTO Law

1. *Identification of some substantial issues*

As there are a variety of circumstances under which TREMs based on a PPM are taken, it will be expected that the appraisals of TREMs under international law and the WTO law are delicately different case by case,

[29] *See OECD Conceptual Framework for PPM Measures*, n. 25, at 157.

each depending of circumstances. For present purposes it is sufficient to identify simply some substantial issues that may be raised when a TREM based on a non-product-related PPM taken unilaterally by one nation, whether by virtue of a MEA or not, is appraised under the GATT 1994.

Since a TREM based on a non-product-related PPM is usually in the form of import regulation of the product in question in the importing country, the most relevant agreement as to the framework of regulation under the WTO law is the GATT 1994, which is the core of the regulations of trade in goods among the WTO agreements.[30] The GATT provides, as the basic principles for constructing the liberalized world trading system, non-discrimination principles and trade liberation principles, including the general prohibition provision of quantitative restrictions and other non-tariff measures. The GATT, however, permits departures from these principles in exceptional cases that meet certain criteria.[31] Where a TREM based on a non-product-related PPM is taken unilaterally by one nation, such a TREM may well raise issues of inconsistency with, among others, the "*product-based regulation approach*" and the "*multilateralism*" in the framework of regulation under the GATT.

2. Inconsistency with the "product-based regulation approach" under the GATT

Non-discrimination principles of the GATT are: the most-favored-nation principle of Article I and the national treatment principle of Article III. The former *prohibits discrimination among "like products" coming from different states of origin.* The latter *prohibits discrimination between domestic and foreign "like products"*. The "product-based regulation approach" appears in the criteria of *likeness* according to which the concept of "like products" is defined. The GATT itself does not define the

[30] Among the WTO agreements, the Agreement on Technical Barriers to Trade (the so-called TBT Agreement) is also relevant here. This agreement, in respect of technical regulations, not only provides non-discrimination principles like as the GATT (Article 2.1), but also provides that they shall not be more trade restrictive than necessary to fulfill "legitimate objectives" including protection of the environment (Article 2.2). However, since a technical regulation is defined as a "document which lays down product characteristics or *their related processes and production methods* (emphasis added)" (Annex I), it is interpreted that regulations of non-product-related PPMs are excluded from this definition. As a result, it should be noted that the TBT Agreement is interpreted as not to be applied to the regulations of non-product related PPMs. *See* Schlagenhof, n. 2, at 132.

[31] *See* Article XX of the GATT.

concept,[32] but certain kinds of criteria have been adopted as a legal practice through many dispute settlement panel cases. These are: (i) the nature and physical characteristics of competing products as they appear at the importer's border; (ii) tariff classifications based on them; (iii) the product's end-use; and (iv) the consumers' taste and habits.[33] With the exception of this last criterion, the finding criteria of likeness are pursued in the character of a product itself, and the factors involved in production, especially the PPM, are made irrelevant for the like-product determination. Indeed, product-related PPMs are in fact taken into account as far as they are materialized into the character of the product, but non-product-related PPMs are not taken into account at all. As a result, discriminating based on the difference of the PPM between products that are found as "like products" by the criteria other than the PPM, will be not permitted. As far as one product produced by a PPM harmful to the environment and another product produced by a PPM friendly to the environment are considered to be "like products," these products must be treated equally.

3. Inconsistency with the "multilateralism" under the GATT

Article XX of the GATT provides general exceptions to the trade liberalization principles of the GATT and permits under certain conditions deviation from these principles to realize certain values that have priority over trade values. Among these values are included the environmental values. Therefore, there is a room for TREMs based on a non-product-related PPM being legalized under the GATT by fulfilling the requirements of this Article, even if they are otherwise against the trade liberation principles under the GATT.[34] It is, however, in the interpretation and the application of this Article XX that the "*multilateralism*" *in*

[32] However, under Article 2.6 of the so-called Antidumping Agreement (Agreement on Implementation of Article VI of the General Agreement on Tariffs and Trade 1994), there is a definition of the term like follows:

> Throughout this Agreement the term 'like product' ('produit similaire') shall be interpreted to mean a product which is identical, i.e. alike in all respects to the product under consideration, or in the absence of such a product, another product which, although not alike in all respects, has characteristics closely resembling those of the product under consideration.

[33] For these criteria, some panels and the Appellate Body have referred to the Working Party Report on the Border Tax Adjustments adopted December 2 1970, BISD 18S/97.

[34] The relevant part of Article XX is as follows:

> Subject to the requirement that such measures are not applied in a manner which would constitute a means of arbitrary or unjustifiable discrimination between

the framework of regulation under the GATT has been prominently expressed. Since TREMs based on a non-product-related PPM are, as are already said, essentially unilateral and extraterritorial in their nature, there is strong probability that such TREMs cannot fulfill the requirements for applying these exceptions and thus cannot acquire legalization under Article XX.

V. Approaches adopted by panels and the Appellate Body

1. Approaches adopted by the panels in the Tuna/Dolphin cases

Here, let's trace how panels and the Appellate Body have actually disposed of our issues. The famous *Tuna/Dolphin* cases of 1991 and 1994,[35] which triggered the controversy of the problem of "trade and environment," were just concerned with the inconsistency of a TREM based on a non-product-related PPM with the GATT 1947. In these cases, panels declared a US embargo on tuna caught by a fishing method causing high dolphin mortality to be inconsistent with the GATT 1947 and seemed to typically adopt the "product-based regulation approach" and the "multilateralism" in the framework of regulation under the GATT 1947.

The 1994 Panel noted in relation to the application of Article III providing the national treatment obligation that "Article III calls for a comparison between the treatments accorded to domestic and imported like products, not for a comparison of the policies or practices of the country of origin with those of the country of importation."[36] The Panel, therefore, implied that according different treatments to like tuna products based on a criterion of a harvesting method which "could not have any impact on the inherent character of tuna as a product" would not be permitted under Article III.[37] This means nothing but that the Panel

> countries where the same conditions prevail, or a disguised restriction on international trade, nothing in this Agreement shall be construed to prevent the adoption or enforcement by any contracting party of measures:
>
> . . .
>
> (b) necessary to protect human, animal or plant life or health;
>
> . . .
>
> (g) relating to the conservation of exhaustible natural resources if such measures are made effective in conjunction with restrictions on domestic production or consumption;
>
> . . .

[35] *United States–Restrictions on Imports of Tuna (hereinafter Tuna I)*, in 30 *ILM* 1594 (1991); *United States–Restrictions on Imports of Tuna (hereinafter Tuna II)*, in 33 *ILM* 839 (1994).

[36] *Tuna II*, para.5.8. [37] *Ibid.*, para. 5.9.

adopted the "product-based regulation approach" and that *invoking non-product-related PPMs as a base for denying likeliness between products would not be permitted.*

The 1991 Panel, after having found the US embargo to be inconsistent not with Article, III, but with Article XI[38] continued to examine further the possibility of legalization of the embargo under Article XX. As to the territorial scope of (b) and (g) of Article XX, on which there is no express indication in the texts, the US argued that (b) and (g) were applicable to a measure protecting environmental values outside the jurisdiction of the invoking country (like as dolphin in this case).[39] The Panel, however, dismissed these arguments and said as follows:

> [I]f the broad interpretation of Article XX (b)[and (g)] suggested by the United States were accepted, each contracting parties could unilaterally determine the life or health protection policies [and the conservation policies] from which other contracting parties could not deviate without jeopardizing their rights under the General Agreement; The General Agreement would then no longer constitute a multilateral framework for trade among all contracting parties.[40]

Further, the 1994 Panel declared clearly that Article XX as an exception to obligations under the GATT permitted no deviation from the "multilateralism" of the GATT as follows:

> If Article XX were interpreted to permit contracting parties to deviate from the obligations of the General Agreement by taking trade measures to implement policies, including conservation policies, within their own jurisdiction, the basic objectives of the General Agreement would be maintained. If however Article XX were interpreted to permit contracting parties to take trade measures so as to force other contracting parties to change their policies within their jurisdiction, including their conservation policies, the balance of rights and obligations among contracting parties, in particular the right of access to markets, would be seriously impaired. Under such an interpretation *the General Agreement could no longer serve as a multilateral framework* for trade among contracting parties.[41]

In short, these panels said that if the provision of Article XX were interpreted *as permitting extraterritorial measures, one state could unilaterally decide its environmental policy* and other states, which did not comply

[38] *Tuna I, supra* n. 35, para. 5.18.
[39] *Ibid.*, paras. 3.36 and 3.42.
[40] *Ibid.*, paras. 5.27 and 5.32.
[41] *Tuna II*, n. 35, para. 26. Italics added by this author.

with this policy would be denied their right under the GATT and that this would lead to the collapse of the multilateral framework of the GATT. It should be noted that the both panels refused the unilateralism to keep the "multilateralism" under the GATT. According to these panels, *TREMs based on a non-product-related PPM having such a unilateral and extraterritorial character were doubtlessly incompatible with the "multilateralism" under the GATT.*

Thus, according to the panels of *Tuna/Dolphin* cases, TREMs based on a non-product-related PPM encounter obstacles of the 'product-based regulation approach' and the 'multilateralism' of the GATT and cannot acquire their consistency with the GATT.

From our perspective, it is also interesting to note that the 1991 Panel underlined that its task was limited to the examination of this matter "in the light of the relevant GATT provisions,"[42] and added in its concluding remarks that the adoption of its report would not affect "the right of the CONTRACTING PARTIES acting jointly to address international environmental problems which can only be resolved through measures in conflict with the present rules of the General Agreement."[43] This Panel itself *raised the question of whether the panel was the appropriate place to frame an appropriate rule to accommodate the opposing policies involved* or, alternatively, *whether this task belonged more appropriately to a political organ.*

2. New approaches adopted by the Appellate Body in the asbestos and Shrimp/Turtle cases

Two recent WTO cases, however, deserve attention in that they imply that the above approach adopted by the *Tuna/Dolphin* cases should be amended. First, in the *Asbestos* case of 2000,[44] Canada challenged a French ban on asbestos in construction materials. Asbestos has been long known to be a deadly carcinogen. Canada argued that the asbestos it exported was a "like product" to the substitute products used in construction in France, therefore deserving of no less favorable treatment under the national treatment obligation of Article III of the GATT. In this case, the Appellate Body made a noteworthy ruling that implies the amendment of the above "product-based regulation approach" under Article III.

[42] *Tuna I*, n. 35, para. 6.1. [43] *Ibid.*, para. 6.4.

[44] *European Communities–Measures Affecting Asbestos and Asbestos-Containing Products (hereinafter Asbestos)*, Report of the Panel, WT/DS135/R, September 18 2000 Report of the Appellate Body, WT/DS135/AB/R, March 12 2001, *adopted* April 5 2001.

In assessing the "likeness" between asbestos and the substitute products, the Appellate Body noted first that "a determination of 'likeness' under Article III:4 is, fundamentally, a determination about the nature and extent of a competitive relationship between and among products" in the marketplace.[45] Setting this forth as a premise, the Appellate Body pointed out that the evidence relating to the health risks associated with asbestos might influence consumers' behavior and might be relevant in assessing the competitive relationship in the marketplace between allegedly "like" products in this case.[46] The Appellate Body, thus, reversed the Panel's conclusion that the asbestos and the substitute products are 'like products' under Article III.[47]

This ruling suggests that *the evidence relating to environmental harm of a product may influence consumers' behavior and competitive relationship of the product in the marketplace* and that *the likeness of an environmentally harmful product and an environmentally non-harmful product may be denied*. This further implies that *even in the case of a product made by an environmentally harmful non-product-related PPM, if consumers can identify such a PPM,*[48] *the likeness of the product and other product may be denied*. If so, TREMs based on a non-product-related PPM may after all be able to avoid the inconsistency with Article III.

Second, in the *Shrimp/Turtle* case of 1998,[49] India, Malaysia, Pakistan and Thailand complained about a US ban on the importation of shrimp caught by trawlers that do not employ a special device in their nets to protect sea turtles from being trapped and killed. Once again the problem of the unilateral and extraterritorial TREM based on a non-product-related PPM was the central question. In this case, the Appellate Body also made a noteworthy ruling that implied alleviation of rigorous application of the "multilateralism" under Article XX, and showed its flexibility permitting a unilateral TREM under certain conditions.

[45] *Asbestos*, Report of the Appellate Body, paras. 99 and 103.

[46] *Ibid.*, paras. 113 and 122. [47] *Ibid.*, para. 126.

[48] Eco-label is a way to identify such a PPM.

[49] *United States–Import Prohibition of Certain Shrimp and Shrimp Products (hereinafter Shrimp/Turtle)*, Report of the Panel, WT/DS58/R, May 15 1998; Report of the Appellate Body, WT/DS58/AB/R, October 12 1998, *adopted* November 6 1998; *United States–Import Prohibition of Certain Shrimp and Shrimp Products: Recourse to Article 21.5 of the DSU by Malaysia (hereinafter Shrimp/Turtle 21.5)*, Report of the Panel, WT/DS58/RW, June 15 2001; Report of the Appellate Body, WT/DS58/AB/RW, October 22 2001, *adopted* November 21 2001.

In its 1998 report, the Appellate body, in examining whether the TREM in this case was justified under Article XX, considered that the requirements of the chapeau of Article XX maintain a balance between the right of a Member to invoke any of exceptions, on the one hand, and the substantive rights of the other Members under the GATT1994, on the other hand[50] and also observed that the chapeau of Article XX is but one expression of the principle of good faith.[51] According to the Appellate Body, the United States failed to engage shrimp exporting countries in serious negotiations with the objective of concluding an international agreement for the protection and conservation of sea turtles, before enforcing the ban in this case.[52] By this and other reasons, the Appellate Body concluded that the TREM in this case failed to meet the requirements of the chapeau of Article XX, and, therefore, was not justified under Article XX of the GATT.[53]

Afterwards, the US corrected its discriminative application of the measure and negotiated an international agreement for the protection of sea turtles with the appellant and further offered technical assistances to the appellant in order to comply with the 1998 recommendations and rulings of the Dispute Settlement Body. The Appellate Body in the phase of the compliance examination under Article 21.5 of the DSU moved further forward and observed that *the chapeau of Article XX does not necessarily require the conclusion of an international agreement, but only the serious and good faith efforts for the conclusion of it.*[54] *After all, the unilateral TREM of the US in this case was permitted under Article XX* and therefore did not violate the GATT.

This ruling may suggest that a TREM based on a non-product-related PPM, even if it is unilateral one, would be permitted under the GATT under certain conditions. If so, this case would show that the "multilateralism" under Article XX adopted by the panels of *Tuna/Dolphin* cases was withdrawn.

VI. A concluding remark: An "evolutionary" role of the Appellate Body?

Given the highly controversial characteristics of the problems of "trade and environment," some people argue that panels and the Appellate Body

[50] *Shrimp/Turtle,* Report of the Appellate Body, paras. 156 and 159.
[51] *Ibid.*, para. 158. [52] *Ibid.*, paras. 171–2. [53] *Ibid.*, para. 184.
[54] *Shrimp/Turtle 21.5, supra* n. 49, paras. 124 and 134.

should not decide disputes concerning such a problem and avoid being involved in political conflicts between environmentalists and free traders. These people argued that any perceived "delegalization" of WTO dispute resolution proceedings would threaten to delegitimize these proceedings.[55]

One of the *Tuna/Dolphin* panels, as noted above, also expressed some doubt about the appropriateness of the panel's deciding disputes concerning TREMs based on a non-product-related PPM. According to this panel, its task was limited to the examination of the matter "in the light of the relevant GATT provisions."[56] After all, the panels of this case came to a conclusion unfavorable to environmental values by adopting the "product-based regulation approach" and the "multilateralism" in the framework of regulation under the GATT. The result of this case provoked deep antipathy against the GATT among environmentalists worldwide and threatened to delegitimize the GATT itself. It triggered the very controversy of "trade and environment."

In such a context, the behavior of the Appellate Body in two recent cases, *Asbestos* and *Shrimp/Turtle*, is noteworthy. The Appellate Body implied the possibility of breaking through the barriers of "product-based regulation approach" and "multilateralism." The door is slowly being opened for TREMs based on a non-product-related PPM. Its rulings were more environmentally sensitive and welcomed by environmentalists.[57]

However, the door is also being opened for "unilateralism." This has caused some to suspect that the Appellate Body may have exceeded the jurisdiction and mandate set out in the DSU. After the *Shrimp/Turtle* decision, many developing Members of the WTO criticized the case and argued that the Appellate Body added to or diminished certain rights and obligations present in the covered agreements, and in so doing encroached upon the rights and responsibilities of the Members.[58] According to the DSU, the Appellate Body cannot add to or diminish the rights and obligations provided in the covered agreements.[59]

The WTO dispute settlement system depends on Member confidence. It will only remain legitimate and effective if the Members believe that the Appellate Body is interpreting the covered agreements as negotiated, as

[55] *See* n. 24. [56] *See* nn. 40 and 41.

[57] One commentator says that "the Appellate Body's decision is sound from a political and policy perspective." Arthur E. Appleton, *Shrimp/Turtle: Untangling the Nets*, 2 *JIEL* 477, 495(1999). *See also* Gary Sampson, Trade, Environment, and the WTO: The Post-Seattle Agenda, at 110 (Overseas Development Council, 2000).

[58] *Sampson ibid.*, at 110–11; Barfield, n. 24, at 48–9; Appleton *ibid.*

[59] *See* Article 19.2 of the DSU.

opposed to modifying them.[60] There is a divergence of opinion on whether the Appellate Body modified the rules of GATT in the two recent cases. If the Appellate Body remained, however, interpreting, instead of modifying the rules of GATT "*in the light of contemporary concerns of the community of nations about the protection and conservation of the environment,*"[61] its rulings may well deserve praise as an "*evolutionary" interpretation.*[62] When we realize that due to the WTO's insistence on consensus decision making, the political bodies of the WTO were often unable to legislate clear rules resolving policy differences between Members, *the evolutionary ruling of the Appellate Body, as far as it remains being within its jurisdiction and mandate, should be appreciated affirmatively.* In this sense, it can be remarked that the Appellate Body does not need to "*live with a quiet but uneasy status quo*"[63] in the "trade and environment" disputes.

[60] *See* Appleton, n. 57, at 496.

[61] *Shrimp/Turtle*, n. 49, Report of the Appellate Body, paras. 129–30 Italics added by this author.

[62] As an example of 'evolutionary' interpretation of the rules of international law, *see Case of the Aegean Sea Continental Shelf* (*Greece* v. *Turkey*), International Court of Justice, paras. 78–80, at 4 (1978).

[63] *See* n. 23.

19

Health, environment and social standards in the Doha Round: Comparison of visions and reforms needed and results achieved

LUTZ STRACK[1]

A. Introduction

With the successful conclusion of the Uruguay Round (1986–1994), and the subsequent creation of the World Trade Organization (WTO) on 1 January 1995, a new era in world trade began.[2] The Uruguay Round has significantly increased the role given to the rule of law in the international trading system.[3] The new WTO agreements and provisions are more precise and more detailed than the old General Agreement on Tariffs and Trade of 1947 (GATT 1947).[4] The enlargement of trade areas covered by the WTO as opposed to the previous GATT 1947 reduces the scope remaining for unilateral action by individual states. The WTO plays an important role in ensuring that domestic regulations do not become *de facto* barriers to trade or hide protectionist policies.

At the same time, the interdependencies among countries in the world economy are becoming more intense, a phenomenon commonly labelled 'globalisation'.[5] Trade, investment, capital flows, technology and communication will continue to move us towards a more integrated, even

[1] Legal Affairs Officer, Parliament of the Free and Hanseatic City of Hamburg, Germany. The author alone is responsible for any shortcomings contained, the facts mentioned and the opinions expressed in this chapter. The author would like to thank Arthur Steinmann for his very useful comments. This chapter was written in September 2006 and updated in October 2007.

[2] See generally *J.H. Jackson*, The World Trading System: Law and Policy of International Economic Relations (2nd edn 1997), 44.

[3] See *P.-T. Stoll and F. Schorkopf*, WTO–Welthandelsordnung und Welthandelsrecht (2002), 39.

[4] General Agreement on Tariffs and Trade (hereinafter GATT 1947), 30 October 1947, 61 Stat. A-11, TIAS 1700, 55 UNTS 194.

[5] See generally *J.H. Jackson*, Global Economics and International Law, *JIEL* 1 (1998) 1; *P. Sutherland*, Globalisation and the Uruguay Round. In *J. Bhagwati and M. Hirsch (eds.)*, The Uruguay Round and Beyond (1998), 143.

borderless, world economy ('global village'). Impediments to international exchange such as tariffs and political barriers lose importance, the economic distance shrinks, and a greater number of countries will participate in the world trading system.[6] Globalisation of the world economy clearly presents national economic policy makers with enormous opportunities and challenges. For example, trade liberalisation during recent years has opened up new markets for many agricultural commodities and products. Some view globalisation as a process that is beneficial, a key to future world economic development, and also inevitable and irreversible. Others regard it with hostility, even fear, believing that it increases inequality within and between nations, threatens safety, health, food security, environment, employment, living standards and thwarts social progress.

Many have seen in the powerful impetus of globalisation the undermining (or perhaps the end) of the sovereignty of states as power flows out of the formal decision-making process of the state and into the hands of international organisations. There is some fear that globalisation increasingly constrains the ability of democratic communities to make unfettered choices about policies that affect the fundamental welfare of their citizens, including those of health, environment and social standards.

As the world becomes increasingly integrated in this way, it becomes less possible for different policy areas to be handled independently of each other. The *linkages between international trade and non-trade concerns (so-called 'trade ands')* have been the focus of much debate in the last decades.[7] Thereby, three issues are always on the top of the agenda: trade and health, trade and environment, as well as trade and social standards.[8]

The need to incorporate these highly controversial non-trade concerns in multilateral trade negotiations has been noted several times by some of the world's major trading countries. The breakdown of the Third WTO Ministerial Meeting in Seattle, USA, in December 1999 provided an opportunity to review the alleged shortcomings of the current WTO framework and to recognise the interests of developing countries and

6 See *H. Siebert*, What does Globalisation Mean for the World Trading System? In *The WTO Secretariat*, From GATT to the WTO: The Multilateral Trading System in the New Millennium (2000), 137, 138.

7 See generally *L.A. DiMatteo, K. Dosanjh, P.L. Frantz, P. Bowal & C. Stoltenberg*, The Doha Declaration and Beyond: Giving a Voice to Non-Trade Concerns Within the WTO Trade Regime, *Vanderbilt J. of Transnat'l Law* 36 (2003), 95.

8 Another major topic in this context is trade and development, which is discussed extensively above in Part 1 of this book and is therefore excluded here.

civil society in the future work. The Fourth WTO Ministerial Meeting in Doha, Qatar, in November 2001 provided a good opportunity for negotiations on a wide range of new subjects, and other work including issues concerning the implementation of the present WTO agreements.[9] This new trade round should maximise potential for positive synergies between trade liberalisation, health and environmental protection as well as economic and social development.

This chapter will review the current Doha Round of trade negotiations, often characterised as a 'development round', and will provide *some insight as how the WTO can better accommodate the three concerns of health, environment and social standards.*[10] Beside the main Doha Ministerial Declaration,[11] the separate Decision on Implementation-Related Issues and Concerns[12] and the Declaration on the TRIPS Agreement and Public Health[13] will be discussed. The following analysis is *divided into four sections*: Part B discusses trade and health, and is itself divided into human, animal or plant health and public health. Part C examines trade relating to the environment. Finally, Part D analyses social standards and their complex relationship with the WTO. The conclusion (Part E) is that health, environment and social standards are serious public concerns, which can no longer be ignored on the global level. The good news is that all three issues are on the Doha agenda and are still being discussed. The bad news is that there are some significant shortcomings and only narrow mandates concerning these issues, so the outcome of the negotiations should not be prejudged. So far, the WTO has failed to take the concrete actions needed to address those concerns effectively and to deliver serious input to an open and rule-based trading system to achieve development that is healthy, as well as environmentally and socially sustainable.

[9] Implementation issues have been big in talks at the WTO since the adoption of the Uruguay Round agreements. Increasingly developing countries began to focus on implementation by addressing the 'implementation of existing agreements' to redress apparent imbalances, because of the view that the Uruguay Round agreements have failed to create anticipated benefits.

[10] This chapter will not examine institutional and dispute settlement reforms as well as so-called 'other Singapore issues' addressed in the Doha Round. Neither will it provide an overview of the WTO provisions nor of the WTO 'case law' in the relevant fields.

[11] Adopted on 14 November 2001, WT/MIN(01)/DEC/1, 20 November 2001.

[12] Decision of 14 November 2001, WT/MIN(01)/17, 20 November 2001 (Doha Decision). This separate Decision divides up 'implementation issues' into a set of issues agreed in Doha, and a set of 'outstanding issues' (including many of the more important ones for developing countries), which will be negotiated as part of the single undertaking.

[13] Adopted on 14 November 2001, WT/MIN(01)/DEC/2, 20 November 2001.

B. Health

Trade liberalisation can affect health in multiple ways. Sometimes the impacts are direct and the effects are obvious, for example, when a disease crosses a border together with a traded product; other times the effects of trade liberalisation are more indirect, for example, when the use of certificate trading helps to reduce pollution. A medical or scientific definition of 'health' does not exist. According to the World Health Organisation (WHO) health 'is a state of complete physical, mental and social well-being and not merely the absence of disease or infirmity'.[14]

In the Doha Round, the health issue has *two aspects*: First, the influence of international trade on *human, animal or plant health* (I), and second, the influence of international trade on *public health* (II). Both aspects of health are linked to different WTO agreements: Human, animal or plant health is primarily addressed in the SPS Agreement.[15] Public health is primarily linked to the TRIPS Agreement.[16]

I. Human, animal or plant health

Besides the SPS Agreement, which is probably the closest match between trade and health, the protection of human, animal or plant health is addressed in other WTO agreements as well, *inter alia*, in Arts. XX (b) GATT 1994,[17] Art. 2.2 TBT Agreement,[18] Art. XIV(b) GATS,[19] Arts. 8.1 and 27.2 TRIPS Agreement. No actual definition can be found, but the

[14] Preamble to the Constitution of the WHO as adopted by the International Health Conference 1946, signed on 22 July 1946 and entered into force on 7 April 1948. The definition has not been amended since 1948.

[15] Agreement on the Application of Sanitary and Phytosanitary Measures (hereinafter SPS Agreement or SPS), 15 April 1994, WTO Agreement, Annex 1A, reprinted in 33 *ILM* 1125, 1144 (1994); OJ 1994 No L 336, 40.

[16] Agreement on Trade-Related Aspects of Intellectual Property Rights (hereinafter TRIPS Agreement or TRIPS), 15 April 1994, WTO Agreement, Annex 1C, reprinted in OJ 1994 No L 336, 214, and in 33 *ILM* 125, 1197 (1994).

[17] General Agreement on Tariffs and Trade 1994 (hereinafter GATT 1994), 15 April 1994, WTO Agreement, Annex 1A, 1867 UNTS 187, reprinted in 33 *ILM* 1125, 1153 (1994); OJ 1994 No L 336, 11. See Generally *P.T. Stoll and L. Strack*, Art. XX(b) GATT 1994. In *R. Wolfrum, P.T. Stoll and A. Seibert-Fohr (eds.)* WTO – Technical Barriers and SPS Measures (2007), 96.

[18] Agreement of Technical Barriers to Trade (hereinafter TBT Agreement), 15 April 1994, WTO Agreement, Annex 1A, reprinted in 33 *ILM* 1125, 1154 (1994); OJ 1994 No. L 336, 86.

[19] General Agreement on Trade in Services (hereinafter GATS), 15 April 1994, WTO Agreement, Annex 1B, reprinted in 33 *ILM* 1125, 1168 (1994); OJ 1994 No L 336, 191.

SPS Agreement specifies the scope of sanitary and phytosanitary (SPS) measures in its Annex A:1.[20]

1 Visions and reforms needed

SPS measures and the application of the SPS Agreement are of increasing importance to the movement of goods in agricultural trade. This importance is expected to increase, for all WTO Members. The SPS Agreement is serving its purpose to the benefit of both importing and exporting Members. It provides a multilateral framework of disciplines to guide the enactment and enforcement of SPS measures in order to minimise their negative effects on trade caused by differences in national protection policies.[21] It also provides a framework for bilateral arrangements and protocols (such as for recognising each others' veterinary measures). The impact of the SPS Agreement on health also brings an emotional side to the debate. These can obscure otherwise clear protectionist policies. To counter this problem the WTO has committed to finding the truth behind the science and evaluating the evidence in an objective fashion.

SPS measures are criticised by some who claim the SPS Agreement is too invasive and deny them sovereignty over domestic regulation. Others assert that the SPS Agreement does not go far enough and domestic health regulation is often a form of protectionism. Those who have criticised the SPS Agreement for restricting democratic control over standards are concerned that weak international standards will jeopardise life, health, safety and welfare on the domestic level. Others have mounted challenges to the very idea of restricting the national choice of preferred levels of risk and safety by subjecting standards to international consensus.

[20] See generally *H.-G. Kamann*, Das Übereinkommen über die Anwendung gesundheitspolizeilicher und pflanzenschutzrechtlicher Maßnahmen. In *H.-J. Prieß & G.M. Berrisch (eds.)*, WTO-Handbuch (2003), 211, 215; *T. Makatsch*, Gesundheitsschutz im Recht der Welthandelsorganisation (WTO) (2004), 55. The definition of 'SPS measure' is likely to remain contested in the future, see also the *EC–Biotech Panel* Report, WT/DS291–2931R, 29 September 2006, para. 7.147.

[21] See generally *J.J. Barceló III*, Product Standards to Protect the Local Environment – the GATT and the Uruguay Round Sanitary and Phytosanitary Agreement, *Cornell Int'l L.J.* 27 (1994), 755; *D.A. Wirth*, The Role of Science in the Uruguay Round and NAFTA Trade Disciplines, *Cornell Int'l L.J.* 27 (1994), 817; *J. Pauwelyn*, The WTO Agreement on Sanitary and Phytosanitary (SPS) Measures as applied in the First Three SPS Disputes. EC–Hormones, Australia–Salmon and Japan–Varietals, *JIEL* 2 (1999), 641; *D.G. Victor*, The Sanitary and Phytosanitary Agreement of the World Trade Organization: An Assessment after Five Years, *NYU J. of Int'l L. & P.* 32 (2000), 865; *O. Landwehr*, Globalisierung, Freihandel und Gesundheitsschutz–Trade and Health (2000); *F. Wiemer*, Produktsicherheit und freier Warenverkehr in GATT/WTO (2001).

Developing countries protest that drafting and agreeing the relevant international standards promoted in the SPS Agreement (Art. 3) lack their input and are dominated by the interests of developed countries or multinational companies. The inability of developing countries to adequately fund their delegations to attend SPS meetings is certainly also a concern.[22] Adding their voices to the debate are environmentalists, non-governmental organisations (NGOs), and local regulatory officials who feel excluded from negotiations of a topic that directly affects them.

Obviously, *the SPS Agreement has some weaknesses*. For example, Members are supposed, where possible, to accept that different SPS measures used by other governments, which provide the same level of health protection, can be equivalent to their own. The SPS Agreement requires this in Art. 4, but does not say how it is to be achieved. The main question is how to establish that an exporting country's measures are equivalent to those used in the importing country. In the WTO, developing countries in particular, said that developed countries are not doing enough to accept that actions they are taking on exported products – in particular inspection and approval procedures (Art. 8) – are equivalent to the importing developed countries' requirements, even when the measures are different, because the measures provide the same level of health protection.

A number of Members, developing countries in particular, said *the SPS Agreement is too vague on some points*, for example, it uses phrases such as 'a reasonable period of time' (Art. 5.7) or 'where identical or similar conditions prevail' (Art. 2.3). Some wanted to see this clarified and tightened through a ministerial declaration or some other means. Two issues are the advance notification Members should provide when they draft new SPS measures, and the time developing countries should be allowed to adapt their exports to developed countries' new SPS measures. Developing countries would also like some voluntary commitments turned into mandatory ones (*e.g.*, by using 'shall' instead of 'should'), like the whole of Art. 10 SPS, which deals with special and differential treatment.

22 On international standards and protectionism, see also *L. Strak* Internationale Standards als Mittel geg Protektionismus im Gesundherts- und Pflauzenschutz? In *A. Steinmann, F. Höhue and P.T. Stoll (eds.)*, Die WTO von neuen Heransforderungen (2005), 45. A growing number of Members have been participating in meetings of the SPS Committee (Art. 12 SPS), but effective participation, including adequate preparation in anticipation of meetings as well as timely follow-up, is still a problem for many developing countries, and in particular least-developed countries, which lack skilled staff, appropriate infrastructure and adequate capabilities.

In addition to seeking clarification on the above issues, a number of developing countries have expressed concern about their lack of resources for implementing the SPS Agreement. Among the burdens are the difficulties in monitoring new measures in their export markets in both the public and private sector, and the *difficulty of demonstrating sufficient scientific evidence* (Art. 2.2) to justify their own SPS measures or challenge those of others. These developing countries are calling for both technical assistance, and more time to comply.[23]

The SPS Agreement has attempted to use scientific evidence as the objective basis by which measures should be judged (Arts. 2 and 5). Nevertheless, people's fears and scientific evidence do not always correlate and so measures intended to protect human, animal or plant health are often contentious. Additionally, the recent debate surrounding some *food safety and animal health issues* – including the long-standing GATT/WTO dispute over the use of hormones in beef production[24] – raises the question of whether the SPS Agreement's preference for scientific evidence goes far enough in dealing with possible risks for consumers. In the highly contentious debate over Genetically Modified Organisms (GMOs), for example, some NGOs argue that the SPS Agreement affords countries inadequate flexibility to manage scientific uncertainty and risks to human health.

A phrase that has emerged in that debate is the *precautionary principle*, which addresses the problem of regulatory decision making in the face of scientific uncertainty in order to prevent potential harm.[25] This principle would permit a nation to err on the side of caution when faced with

[23] So far, most developing countries still have incomplete or out-dated SPS legislation with poor enforcement capacity.

[24] *EC–Measures Concerning Meat and Meat Products (Hormones)* (hereinafter *EC–Hormones)*, Complaint by the United States, Report of the Panel, WT/DS26/R/USA, 18 August 1997; Complaint by Canada, Report of the Panel, WT/DS48/R/CAN, 18 August 1997; Report of the Appellate Body, WT/DS26/AB/R, WT/DS48/AB/R, 16 January 1998. See *M. Hilf and B. Eggers*, Der WTO-Panelbericht im EC/USA-Hormonstreit, *EuZW* 1997, 559; *B. Eggers*, Die Entscheidung des WTO-Appellate Body im Hormonfall, *EuZW* 1998, 147; *G. Goh and A.R. Ziegler*, A Real World Where People Live and Work and Die – Australian SPS Measures After the WTO Appellate Body's Decision in the Hormones Case, *JWT* 32 (1998) 5, 271; *D.E. McNiel*, The First Case Under the WTO's Sanitary and Phytosanitary Agreement: The European Union's Hormone Ban, *Virginia J. of Int'l L.* 39 (1998), 89; *R. Quick and A. Blüthner*, Has the Appellate Body Erred? An Appraisal and Criticism of the Ruling in the WTO Hormones Case, *JIEL* 2 (1999), 603. See also Matsushita, chapter 16 in this book.

[25] The specific content of the precautionary principle is, however, still controversial. See generally *H. Hohmann*, Precautionary Legal Duties and Principles of Modern International Environmental Law (1994); *D. Freestone and E. Hey (eds.)*, The Precautionary Principle

uncertainty on specific risks, or by using non-legal terms, indicates that it is better to be safe than sorry. The precautionary principle is based on the premise that science does not always provide the information necessary to take protective action effectively or in a timely manner; undesirable and potentially irreversible effects may result if action is not taken until science does provide such information.[26] To some extent, Art. 5.7 of the SPS Agreement addresses the precautionary principle.[27] However, as compared with other international, regional and national legal developments, Art. 5.7 appears to be much more rigid, as it is confined to provisional measures in situations of insufficient scientific evidence, while imposing a duty on the Member at hand actively to seek additional and better information and to review the measure accordingly. Therefore, some Members have said that they would like the precautionary principle strengthened,[28] and it has been discussed in the SPS Committee, but there have been no proposals for altering existing WTO provisions so far.

2 Results achieved

In the *Doha Ministerial Declaration (para. 6)*, ministers strongly reaffirmed their commitment to the objective of sustainable development. They also recognised that, under WTO rules, countries should not be prevented from taking measures for the protection of human, animal or plant life or health, or of the environment at the levels it considers appropriate, subject to the requirement, *inter alia*, that such measures not be discriminatory. Furthermore, ministers confirmed that non-trade concerns – without specifying them – will be taken into account in the current agriculture negotiations (para. 13).

With regard to specifically the SPS Agreement, the Doha Decision (para. 3.1) allows a longer time-frame for developing countries to comply with other countries' new SPS measures (Art. 10.2 SPS): Where a phased

and International Law: The Challenge of Implementation (1996); *Primosch*, Das Vorsorgeprinzip im internationalen Umweltrecht, *Zeitschrift für öffentliches Recht* 51 (1996), 227.

26 See *E. Hey*, The Precautionary Principle in Environmental Policy and Law: Institutionalizing Caution, *Geo. Int'l Envtl. L. Rev.* 4 (1992), 303, 308.

27 *EC–Hormones*, Report of the Appellate Body, WT/DS26/AB/R, WT/DS48/AB/R, para. 124. This finding has also been endorsed in *EC–Biotech*, Report of the Panel, WT/DS 291–293R. para. 7.87. See *C. Henckels*, GMOs in the WTO: A Critique of the Panel's Legal Reasoning in *EC–Biotech*, *Melbourne J. Int'l Law*, 7(2) (2006) 278, 293.

28 For example the European Union (EU), G/SPS/GEN/168, 14 March 2000. The evolution of the precautionary principle suffered a setback in *EC–Biotech*, Report of the Panel, WT/DS291–293R, paras. 7.76–96. This ruling makes it more difficult for an importing Member to justify an SPS measure in a case of scientific uncertainty.

introduction is possible, the longer period for developing countries for compliance is now understood to mean, normally, at least six months. Where a phased introduction is not envisaged, but a Member has specific problems complying, the trading partners shall consult, 'with a view to finding a mutually satisfactory solution to the problem while continuing to achieve the importing Member's appropriate level of protection'.

Additionally, para. 3.2 of the *Doha Decision on Implementation-Related Issues and Concerns* (Doha Decision) defines the phrase 'reasonable interval' between the publication of a country's new SPS measure and its entry into force (Annex B:2 SPS): This means, normally, at least six months, subject to certain conditions. But particular circumstances and the actions necessary to implement an SPS measure must also be taken into account. If the SPS measure contributes to trade liberalisation, it should not be delayed unnecessarily.

In the lead-up to Doha, the SPS Committee settled the implementation issue of *equivalence* by deciding on some outline steps that are designed to make it easier for all WTO Members to make use of the SPS Agreement's equivalence provisions (Art. 4).[29] In the Doha Decision (para. 3.3), ministers instruct the SPS Committee to develop expeditiously the specific programme to further the implementation of these equivalence provisions immediately.

The Doha Decision (para. 3.4) instructs the SPS Committee to review the operation and implementation of the SPS Agreement, pursuant to Art. 12.7 of the SPS, at least once every four years. In the follow-up, the SPS Committee undertook the Second Review of the SPS Agreement in 2004–2005.[30]

The Doha Decision (para. 3.5) notes the actions taken by the WTO Director-General to help developing countries participate in setting international SPS standards more effectively, including efforts to coordinate with the relevant organisations and to identify needs for technical assistance in the field. The Members go on to urge the WTO Director-General to continue with this, and to give priority to least-developed countries.

Finally, the Doha Decision (para. 3.6) calls for Members to provide financial and technical assistance to least-developed countries so that they can respond adequately to new SPS measures that significantly could

[29] G/SPS/19, Rev. 2, 23 July 2004.

[30] G/SPS/36, 11 July 2005. The First Review of the SPS Agreement was completed in 1999, G/SPS/12, 11 March 1999.

obstruct their trade. It also calls for technical assistance to help them implement the SPS Agreement as a whole.

3 Conclusion and outlook

There is no doubt that *the SPS Agreement has been one of the most significant achievements of the WTO*, and a very successful global effort to reduce trade distortions caused by differences in national health policies. The SPS Agreement contains both promises and pitfalls. Several of the SPS Agreement's 'core provisions' were included in the Biosafety Protocol.[31] Some of its fundamental concepts, like risk assessment and precautionary measures, are not identical, but are quite similar to the SPS Agreement.[32] Thus, the provisions relied upon in the SPS Agreement to strike a delicate balance between legitimate health and fair trade concerns are particularly noteworthy as a 'model' for future multilateral agreements. However, it is equally clear that during any new round of trade negotiations, some aspects of its operation and implementation will be hotly debated. Nevertheless, the SPS Agreement has never been a 'hot topic' at WTO ministerial meetings so far.

Obviously, the SPS Agreement could have been drafted more clearly, and further clarification is needed.[33] Some countries see the required clarification as part of improving the implementation of the SPS Agreement; others say it involves interpreting or modifying the SPS Agreement and therefore it should be included in new trade negotiations. So far, no Member has formally asked to reopen the SPS Agreement or has proposed significant changes to the basic provisions like the science-based requirements (Arts. 2 and 5), the encouragement of harmonisation

[31] Cartagena Protocol on Biosafety to the UN Convention on Biological Diversity (hereinafter Biosafety Protocol), adopted on 29 January 2000, entered into force on 23 September 2003, reprinted in 39 *ILM* 1027 (2000); OJ 2002 No L 201, 48. See generally *B. Eggers and R. Mackenzie*, The Cartagena Protocol on Biosafety, *JIEL* 3 (2000), 525; *K.M. Graziano*, Biosafety Protocol: Recommendations to Ensure the Safety of the Environment, *Colo. J. of Int'l Env. L. and Pol'y* 7 (1996), 179; *P.E. Hagen and J.B. Weiner*, The Cartagena Protocol on Biosafety: New Rules for International Trade in Living Modified Organisms, *Geo. Int'l Env. L. Rev.* 12 (2000), 697; *A. Steinmann and L. Strack*, Die Verabschiedung des 'Biosafety-Protokolls'–Handelsregelungen im Umweltgewand?, *Natur und Recht* 7 (2000), 367.

[32] See *P.-T. Stoll*, Controlling the Risks of Genetically Modified Organisms: The Cartagena Protocol on Biosafety and the SPS Agreement, *YIEL* 10 (1999), 82; *L. Stökl*, Der welthandelsrechtliche Gentechnikkonflikt (2003), 264.

[33] See *K.C. Kennedy*, Resolving International Sanitary and Phytosanitary Disputes in the WTO: Lessons and Future Directions, *Food & Drug L.J.* 55 (2000), 81, 102; *T. Cottier*, Risk Management Experience in WTO Dispute Settlement. In *D. Robertson and A. Kellow (eds.)*, Globalization and the Environment (2001), 41, 57.

with international standards (Art. 3), or the obligations for transparency (Art. 7). *Although many Members are unhappy with particular aspects, there may be insufficient consensus on any specific change.* Moreover, there are generalised fears that a rewrite of the SPS Agreement could create new problems.

In the SPS Committee, specific progress has been made on a number of critical issues it has decided to address, including the development of guidelines and recommendations on regulatory consistency (Art. 5.5), equivalence (Art. 4), inspection, monitoring and transparency (Art. 7).[34] However, Members recognise that more work can be done by the SPS Committee to ensure an effective implementation of the SPS Agreement. At the April 2003 meeting, the SPS Committee adopted a principle of applying *special and differential treatment for developing countries* (Arts. 9 and 10).[35] This was based on a Canadian proposal whereby Members agree to consultations whenever a developing country identifies a problem with a new or modified SPS measure.[36] Furthermore, at the March 2004 meeting, the SPS Committee finalised its *Decision on Equivalence*.[37] This Decision is aimed at helping developing Members to prove that their products are as safe as those in developed countries.

The Doha Round is striving to address myriad issues underlying the SPS Agreement, but the most progress to date has been on the needs of developing countries. In September 2002, the WTO initiated a global programme to enhance the expertise and capacity of developing countries to participate in negotiations and implement international SPS standards. The programme, called the *Standards and Trade Development Facility (STDF)*, joins the efforts of the WTO, the WHO, the Food and Agriculture Organisation (FAO), the World Organisation for Animal Health (OIE) and the World Bank.[38] The strategic aims of the STDF are to increase participation of developing countries in forming international standards and improving their human, animal and plant health situation,

[34] For a good summary see G/SPS/36, 11 July 2005. On development of guidelines and recommendations on regulatory consistency in Art. 5.5 SPS, see G/SPS/15, 18 July 2000.

[35] G/SPS/R/29, 17 June 2003, para. 112; G/SPS/35, 7 July 2005. Generally, special and differential treatment is addressed in para. 44 of the Doha Ministerial Declaration and in para. 12.1 of the Doha Decision.

[36] G/SPS/33, 2 November 2004, G/SPS/33/Add. 1, 6 February 2006.

[37] G/SPS/R/33, 7 May 2004, para. 102. The Decision aims to speed up recognition of equivalence of SPS measures for products previously traded or those for which information already exists.

[38] Already at the Doha Conference, the Executive Heads of these five organisations issued a joint communiqué committing the institutions to explore new technical and financial

and thus their ability to gain and maintain market access. In addition to facilitating international trade, *SPS capacity building, notably in the area of food safety*, can result in improved health conditions for local markets and so favour economic and social development. The STDF is both a financing and a co-ordinating mechanism. It provides grant financing for developing countries seeking to comply with international SPS standards and a forum for dialogue on SPS technical assistance issues among its five partner organisations.

Few issues are raising as many concerns about food safety and consumer protection as that of biotechnology and *GMOs*.[39] The EU has a moratorium on the approvals of new GMOs, and has also passed laws mandating labelling requirements.[40] In August 2003, the WTO established a panel in a complaint against the EU's *de facto* moratorium on the approval and marketing of biotech products developed through recombinant DNA technology and measures related to the import and/or marketing of specific biotech products taken by several EU Member States.[41] The US, Canada and Argentina argued that the moratorium violates several provisions, *inter alia*, of the SPS Agreement, since the prohibition of GMO imports is not legally or scientifically justified. The EU responded that market authorisation had been granted to numerous GMOs, with applications pending for others.[42] The long awaited outcome of this 'hard

mechanisms for co-ordination and resource mobilisation to assist developing countries in the establishment and implementation of appropriate SPS measures. Building on this commitment, work already underway in the five organisations and developing country demand for enhanced capacity building programmes in the areas of food safety, plant and animal health, the partners formally adopted a business plan for the STDF on 10 September 2004.

39 Although Members have notified a large number of regulations related to GMOs to the SPS Committee, most of the discussion on the subject has been in the TBT Committee with the focus on labelling regulations. See, for example, EC Regulation 1830/2003 of 22 September 2003 concerning the traceability and labelling of genetically modified organisms and the traceability of food and feed products produced from genetically modified organisms, OJ 2003 No L 268, 24. Concerning food safety and GMOs see Matsushita, chapter 16 in this book.

40 EC Directive 90/220 of 23 April 1990 on the deliberate release into the environment of genetically modified organisms, OJ 1990 No L 117, 15; EC Directive 2001/18 of 12 March 2001 on the deliberate release into the environment of genetically modified organisms, OJ 2001 No L 106, 1; EC Regulation 258/97 of 27 January 1997 concerning novel foods and novel food ingredients, OJ 1997 No L 43, 1.

41 *EC–Measures Affecting the Approval and Marketing of Biotech Products*, Complaint by the United States, WT/DS291; Complaint by Canada, WT/DS292; Complaint by Argentina, WT/DS293. See also Matsushita, chapter 16 of this book.

42 Nevertheless, individual EU Member States may provisionally restrict or prohibit under certain conditions the use and/or sale of an approved GMO in their own territory if these

case' did not clearly show if the SPS Agreement really protects human, animal and plant health, or if it merely facilitates international agricultural trade and even forces globalisation. Definitely, the findings of the Panel in *EC–Biotech* will have an impact on ongoing regulatory and policy discussions on trade and sustainable development at both national and international levels. The decision illustrates the limits of the WTO dispute settlement system in dealing with complex and multifaceted issues that involve polarised views and ethical concerns. There is a risk that a WTO ruling on such controversial issues may be regarded as lacking legitimacy and the WTO could be accused of exceeding its scope of competence.

II Public health

Public health refers to all organised measures (whether public or private) to prevent disease, promote health and prolong the life of the population as a whole. While also covered by Art. XX(b) of the GATT 1994 and the SPS Agreement, the focus of the following analysis is the complex relationship between public health and the TRIPS Agreement.

1 Visions and reforms needed

The public health debate is an issue of real and urgent concern to developing countries. It needed to be addressed in a serious and sensitive manner. The public health debate grew out of fear and frustration by least-developed Members, mostly in sub-Saharan Africa, over their inability to effectively *combat devastating infectious diseases* (such as HIV/AIDS, malaria and tuberculosis). It is these countries' sense of vulnerability and helplessness that must be addressed, not as a trade issue but as a capacity-building issue. They needed to have confidence that the TRIPS Agreement in general, and pharmaceutical patent protection under the TRIPS Agreement in particular, would not stop them from exercising their responsibilities to address health crises and fight infectious diseases.

In the lead-up to Doha, it became clear that the WTO has to respond to concerns about the possible implications of the TRIPS Agreement for access to medicines. There are *acute disparities in pharmaceutical access*

Footnote 42 (*cont.*)
EU Member States have detailed grounds for considering, based on new or additional information or scientific evidence, that the particular product poses a risk to human health.

between developing and industrialised countries. Developing countries make up approximately 80% of the world's population, but only represent approximately 20% of global pharmaceutical consumption. Among the many barriers to drug access are the potential consequences of the TRIPS Agreement. Many developing countries have recently modified their patent laws to conform to the TRIPS Agreement, given the 2005 deadline for least-developed countries (Art. 66). On 30 November 2005, WTO Ministers agreed to extend the deadline to 1 July 2013, or to the date a country is no longer 'least-developed' if this is earlier. Safeguards to protect public health have been incorporated into the TRIPS Agreement (the most important being compulsory licensing, parallel imports and measures to enable the early introduction of generics). However, in practice, governments may be reluctant to exercise such rights given concerns about the international trade and political ramifications, particularly in the area of trade sanctions.

2 Results achieved

In the *Doha Ministerial Declaration (para. 17)*, ministers stressed that it is important to implement and interpret the TRIPS Agreement in a way that supports public health, by promoting both access to existing medicines and the creation of new medicines. They therefore adopted, in a concession to developing countries,[43] a separate *Declaration on TRIPS Agreement and Public Health.*[44]

This separate Declaration emphasises that the TRIPS Agreement does not and should not prevent Members from acting to protect public health

[43] At the Doha Conference, the US and the EU made a bargain with developing countries in order to obtain negotiations on some issues which the US and EU advocated. However, the developing countries had demanded that the reference to the issue of the TRIPS Agreement and public health in the Ministerial Declaration should set out the common understanding that 'nothing in the TRIPS Agreement shall prevent WTO Members from taking measures to protect public health', followed by an endorsement of the clarification and interpretation of the TRIPS Agreement, which was to be contained in a separate declaration. This has not been reflected in the Doha Ministerial Declaration.

[44] Neither ministers nor the WTO secretariat have, however, explicitly defined the legal status of this Declaration. An unofficial explanation of the Declaration, available on the WTO website, states that the Declaration provides 'important guidance' to individual Members and WTO dispute settlement institutions in the interpretation of the TRIPS Agreement. The argument can be made that the Declaration is a strong political statement and a 'subsequent agreement' between the parties regarding the interpretation of a treaty or the application of its provisions, under Art. 31.3(a) of the Vienna Convention on the Law of Treaties. However, the exact legal status of the Declaration will not be clear until its practical application has been observed by future WTO panels and the Appellate Body.

(para.4). It reaffirms governments' right to use, to the full, the TRIPS Agreement's flexibilities to avoid any reticence the governments may feel (para. 4). The Declaration clarifies some of the forms of flexibility available, in particular compulsory licensing and parallel importing (para. 5).[45] Ministers agreed to extend exemptions on pharmaceutical patent protection for the least-developed countries until 1 January 2016 (para. 7). They finally assigned further work to the TRIPS Council to establish a means of providing additional flexibility, so that countries unable to produce pharmaceuticals domestically can obtain generic supplies of patented drugs from other countries (this is sometimes called the 'paragraph 6 issue', because it comes under that paragraph in the Declaration).

3 Conclusion and outlook

Now that the landmark Public Health Declaration has been achieved, Members should move beyond the sterile debate of the past. They should drop calls for tiered pricing and re-export bans, issues that are seen by the developing world as new obligations and that wrongly carry public health issues into the trade arena. It is also time to debunk the myth that compulsory licensing for export is the answer to providing affordable medicines. This issue has properly been returned to the TRIPS Council to fine-tune the balance that needs to be found in the intellectual property system. At Doha, neither the least-developed nor the developing countries with generic drug industries made a serious push on compulsory licensing for export, probably because it is becoming apparent that the generic producers are not really interested in the least-developed countries as a viable market for their generic drugs.

The Public Health Declaration was partially an effort to interpret Art. 31(f) of the TRIPS Agreement, which states that compulsory licensing shall be 'predominantly for the supply of the domestic market'.[46] Given that the majority of developing countries lack the domestic capacity or technical expertise to manufacture on-patent pharmaceuticals, the

[45] The Declaration specifically reaffirms Member countries' rights to determine the grounds on which compulsory licenses may be issued, to determine what constitutes a national emergency or circumstance of extreme urgency and to determine their own regime for the exhaustion of intellectual property rights.

[46] Art. 31(f) TRIPS applies directly to countries that can manufacture drugs – it limits the amount they can export when the drug is made under compulsory license. It has an indirect impact on countries unable to make medicines and therefore wanting to import generics. They would find it difficult to find countries that can supply them with drugs made under compulsory licensing.

interpretation of this terminology is crucial for ensuring access to medicine for the poor in many developing countries. On 30 August 2003, the WTO issued an interim solution, the *Decision on the Implementation of paragraph 6 of the Doha Declaration on the TRIPS Agreement and public health*.[47] This Decision which can, at best, be described as a political undertaking temporarily waives Art. 31(f) of the TRIPS Agreement, permitting countries with local manufacturing capacity to issue compulsory licenses to produce and export drugs to countries without adequate manufacturing capacity, in return for a pledge from countries to use the Decision 'in good faith in order to deal with public health problems and not for industrial or commercial policy objectives'. Eligible importing countries include least-developed countries or a country that can demonstrate insufficient or no manufacturing capacity for the purpose of meeting its needs. A country may be reluctant to notify the WTO of its intention to operate as an importer under this Decision, as a result of economic and political pressure.[48]

C. Environment

Probably, there is no issue which inspires more intense debate among WTO Members than the issue of trade and the environment – an issue which has been analysed exhaustively from all points of view.[49] The debate on trade and environment started a few years ago ('greening the GATT')[50] it is over-burdened with suspicion and strained by misunderstandings

[47] WT/L/540 and Corr. 1, 1 September 2003; WT/GC/M/182, 13 November 2003.

[48] A number of countries announced that if they use the system it would only be for emergencies or extremely urgent situations. See also WT/L/641, 8 December 2005.

[49] See, for example, *J.H. Jackson*, World Trade Rules and Environmental Policies: Congruence or Conflict?, *Wash. & Lee L. Rev.* 49 (1992), 1227; *A. Diem*, Freihandel und Umweltschutz in GATT und WTO (1996); *F. Altemöller*, Handel und Umwelt im Recht der Welthandelsorganisation WTO (1998); *M. Hilf*, Freiheit des Welthandels contra Umweltschutz, *NVwZ* 2000, 481; *J. Scott*, On Kith and Kine (and Crustaceans): Trade and Environment in the EU and WTO. In *J.H.H. Weiler (ed.)*, The EU, the WTO, and the NAFTA (2000), 125; *H. Hohmann*, Der Konflikt zwischen freiem Handel und Umweltschutz in WTO und EG, *RIW* 2000, 88; *J. Neumann*, Die Koordination des WTO-Rechts mit anderen völkerrechtlichen Ordnungen (2003), 112; *T. Cottier, E. Tuerk & M. Panizzon*, Handel und Umwelt im Recht der WTO, *ZUR* 2003, 155; *S. Puth*, WTO und Umwelt. In *M. Hilf and S. Oeter (eds.)*, WTO-Recht (2005), 577. See also Murase and Taira, Chapters 17 and 18 of this book.

[50] See generally *D.C. Esty*, Greening the GATT: Trade, Environment, and the Future (1994); *D. Zaelke, P. Orbuch and R.F. Housman (eds.)*, Trade and The Environment: Law, Economics, and Policy (1995); *M.M. Weinstein and S. Charnovitz*, The Greening of the WTO, *Foreign Affairs* 80 (2001), 147.

that need to be addressed. The debate was, to some extent, formalised in the 1994 Decision on Trade and Environment that accompanied the adoption of the WTO Agreement.[51]

Some environmental issues such as climate change, or the protection of the ozone layer, are global in nature, they affect every country on the planet. Others, such as the disposal of wastes, or the protection of endangered species, can also involve interactions between many different countries. Since trade is the most immediate and pervasive means by which countries interact, it is understandable that trade issues can arise in the context of global environmental issues. This might be because measures taken to protect the environment have an impact on trade, or because trade is itself part of the way a particular environmental issue is addressed (e.g. the shipment of waste for recycling in other countries). In formulating trade policy, it is therefore important that the potential environmental impacts of proposals are recognised, and the most environmentally beneficial outcomes possible are desired. Increasingly, efforts to govern these types of interlinkages are being broadened to encompass not only the environmental pillar of sustainable development, but also the social and economic pillars.

I Visions and reforms needed

The development of a worldwide environmental policy has resulted in an increased use of trade measures for environmental purposes. Unfortunately, due to the vagueness of the WTO rules in this area and the different approaches taken by its Members, many 'grey areas' remain, which often lead to trade disputes.[52] The new round must clarify relations between the WTO rules and the principles adopted by its Members to formulate their environmental policies. Environmental considerations should be reflected throughout any negotiations. Moreover, WTO rules, like Art. XX(b) or (g) GATT, allow its Members considerable scope to

[51] Adopted on 15 April 1994, MTN.TNC/W/141, 29 March 1994. This Decision reflected many of the current issues at that time in its broad mandate, covering all areas of the multilateral trading system. See generally *G. van Calster*, The World Trade Organisation Committee on Trade and Environment: Exploring the Challenges of the Greening of Free Trade, *Eur. Env. L. Rev.* 5 (1996), 44; *S. Charnovitz*, A Critical Guide to the WTO's Report on Trade and Environment, *Arizona J. of Int'l & Comp. L.* 14 (1997), 341.

[52] See, for example, *US–Gasoline*, Appellate Body Report, WT/DS2/AB/R; *US–Shrimp*, Appellate Body Report, WT/DS58/AB/R; *Brazill–Retreaded Tyres*, Report of the Panel, WT/DS332R.

adopt measures to protect the environment, provided they are not discriminatory.[53]

Such trade measures for environmental purposes, including those pursuant to multilateral environmental agreements (MEAs), are a complex and critical topic and are the most controversial.[54] These range from issues of hierarchy and compatibility between the multilateral trading system and MEAs to the comprehensive framework of the MEAs, which combine a mixture of incentives and trade measures to deal with environmental externalities.

MEAs are agreements among governments that co-operatively share environmental problems. During recent years, the importance and scope of MEAs has increased dramatically as the international community struggles to address increasing global environmental problems such as the spread of toxic pollutants, biodiversity loss, protection of the ozone layer and global warming. There are now over 200 MEAs to co-ordinate the activities of states on issues related to environmental protection in an effort to achieve sustainable development.[55] About twenty of these include provisions that can affect trade, for example, they ban trade in certain products, or allow countries to restrict trade in certain circumstances. By applying general principles of international law, analysts have argued that a MEA might trump WTO rules as being a more specific obligation and because the later treaty prevails.[56] Nevertheless, this view still has not been endorsed by the WTO, and the possibility exists that a WTO panel would disregard parallel obligations between parties to a WTO dispute if these are outside the WTO agreements. So far, no measure affecting trade taken under a MEA has been challenged in the GATT/WTO system. Nevertheless, the challenge is to determine the means by which legal stability and prediction can be assured, while at the same time maintaining flexibility in accommodating obligations under MEAs within the framework of the WTO.

[53] See generally WT/CTE/W/203, 8 March 2002. See *N. Matz-Lück and R. Wolfrum*, Art. XX(g) GATT 1994. In *R. Wolfrum, P.T. Stoll and A. Seibert-Fohr (eds.)*, WTO–Technical Barriers and SPS Measures (2007), 141, 156.

[54] See generally TN/TE/W/10, 3 October 2002; *D. Brack*, Reconciling the GATT and Multilateral Environmental Agreements with Trade Provisions: The Last Debate, *RECIEL* 6 (1997), 112; *N. Matz*, The Relation between International Agreements for the Protection of the Environment and the GATT. In *T. Zhenghua and R. Wolfrum (eds.)*, Implementing International Environmental Law in Germany and China (2001), 163; *P.-T. Stoll*, How to overcome the Dichotomy between WTO Rules and MEAs, *ZaörV* 63 (2003), 439.

[55] WT/CTE/W/160/Rev.2, 25 April 2003, Annex 2.

[56] See generally *R. Wolfrum and N. Matz*, Conflicts in International Environmental Law (2003), 152.

Additionally, there is considerable debate over other environmental issues such as the extent to which the WTO agreements allow trade restrictions based on specifications related to process and production methods (PPMs). Members disagree, for example, over the extent to which the TBT Agreement allows Members to differentiate between identical products that are produced in different ways. Can a country treat products differently because the production methods used have different environmental impacts? Another concern was raised by a number of developing countries about goods being exported to them in situations where their domestic sale in their exporting countries had been either prohibited or severely restricted on environmental grounds. Such concerns have fuelled fears among environmental and civil society groups that the Uruguay Round agreements may threaten environmental quality. Nevertheless, until today, only a handful of environmental cases ever came up.

II Results achieved

In the Doha Round, for the first time in a multilateral trade negotiation, *the environment is on the agenda.*[57] The environmental issues in Doha differ significantly from each other, and therefore are best discussed individually. *Briefly, the main issues, as keyed to the Doha Ministerial Declaration, are*:

(1) Ministers agreed to launch negotiations on the *relationship between existing WTO rules and 'specific trade obligations' set out in MEAs* (para. 31(i)). The negotiations will address how WTO rules are to apply to WTO Members that are parties to environmental agreements, in particular to clarify the relationship between trade measures taken under MEAs and WTO disciplines. However, the Doha mandate is a very narrow one, namely, the status of specific trade obligations in MEAs when all parties to a potential dispute are party to both the MEA and the WTO – this case is truly the least controversial and the least likely to lead to an actual dispute. Moreover, there is no mandate to clarify the relationship to non-parties to MEAs and to specify *non-specific* trade obligations.

[57] For details see *M. Lehner*, Welthandel und Umweltschutz im Lichte der Doha Agenda. In *A. Steinmann, F. Höhne and P.T. Stoll (eds.)*, Die WTO vor neuen Herausforderungen (2005), 11.

(2) Furthermore, ministers agreed to negotiate *procedures for regular information exchange between secretariats of MEAs and the WTO* (para. 31(ii)). Currently, the Committee on Trade and Environment (CTE) holds information sessions with different secretariats of the MEAs once or twice a year to discuss the trade-related provisions in these agreements and also their dispute settlement mechanisms. The new information exchange procedures may expand the scope of existing co-operation. Generally, cooperation between the WTO and relevant international environmental and development organisations should be promoted (para. 6).

(3) The Doha negotiations aim to develop *criteria for observer status in WTO (*para. 31(ii)). Overall, the situation concerning the granting of observer status in the WTO to other international governmental organizations is currently blocked for political reasons. The mandate is only designed to deal with environmental, and not all, organizations.

(4) Ministers also agreed to negotiations on the *reduction or elimination of tariff and non-tariff barriers to environmental goods and services* (para. 31(iii))[58] such as air filters or consultancy services on waste-water management. The open-ended reference regarding environmental goods and services is very troubling.[59] So far, the discussions have been marked by disagreement between developing and developed countries – the former argue that a single non-environmental end use should suffice to disqualify a product from consideration for being an 'environmental good', the latter counter that this would exclude all but a handful of items.

(5) Ministers agreed to clarify and improve WTO rules applying to *fisheries subsidies* that have caused huge problems for community and small fisheries in developing countries (paras. 28 and 31). The issue of fisheries subsidies has been discussed in the CTE for several years.[60] Some studies demonstrate that these subsidies can be environmentally damaging if they lead to too many fishermen

[58] Negotiations on market access for environmental goods and services take place in the Market Access Negotiating Group and 'special sessions' of the Services Council.

[59] This language was sponsored mainly by the EU, which is known to be pushing strenuously on behalf of several huge EU-based water companies for expansion of WTO rules to promote the commidification of bulk water, which has enormous environmental and democratic governance implications.

[60] For details see *D.K. Schorr*, Fishery Subsidies and the WTO. In *G.P. Sampson and W.B. Chambers (eds.)*, Trade, Environment, and the Millenium (2000), 143.

chasing too few fish. The negotiations are aimed at helping to reverse this dangerous trend. However, again there are caveats in the Doha text. The negotiations will only 'aim to clarify and improve WTO disciplines on fisheries subsidies' without aiming to stop their use by Members to deplete the fisheries of West Africa and other regions.

(6) The effect of environmental measures that impede market access, and those situations (so-called *'win-win-win' situations*) in which the elimination of trade restrictions and distortions would benefit trade, environment and development (para. 32(i)).

(7) The CTE is to look at the *relationship between the TRIPS Agreement and the UN Convention on Biological Diversity*[61] (paras. 19 and 32(ii)). There is also to be continued work in the CTE on the impact of *eco-labelling* on trade and its relationship to existing WTO rules (para. 32(iii)). Parallel discussions are to take place in the TBT Committee. Finally, the CTE has to review the environmental and development aspects of the Doha negotiations with the objective of having sustainable development appropriately reflected (para. 51).

III Conclusion and outlook

The inclusion of several environmental issues on the Doha agenda is *an important development pregnant with possibilities for the WTO to improve its own environmental profile* as well as to help other environmental efforts. In the past, the trade and environment debate in the WTO have proceeded in a desultory fashion.

In addressing the linkages between trade and environment, WTO Members should not operate on the assumption that trade rules are an answer to environmental problems. *However, trade and environmental policies can complement each other* – environmental protection contributes to the preservation of natural resources on which economic growth is premised. From the point of view of developing countries, where poverty is a major concern and a serious obstacle to environmental protection, the opening up of world markets to their exports can be part of the solution. Trade liberalisation for exports of developing countries,

[61] Adopted on 5 June 1992, entered into force on 29 December 1993, reprinted in 31 *ILM* 818 (1992); OJ 1993 No L 309, 1.

along with financial transfers and technical assistance, may help developing countries generate capacities to protect the environment and work towards sustainable development.

All WTO Members would benefit from *clarification in two key areas.* First, *eco-labelling schemes* should be devised in a transparent way. They must be WTO compatible, and not create new trade barriers. Second, in discussing the *relationship between WTO rules and MEAs*, it is essential that both sides of the debate be involved. MEA secretariats and UNEP (which acts as the secretariat for certain MEAs) should be *granted observer status in the CTE* where the issue is being negotiated and WTO Members should agree that MEAs should mesh seamlessly with international trade.

With regard to MEAs, the *Doha Ministerial Declaration* includes the statement 'the negotiations shall not prejudice the WTO rights of any Member that is not a party to the MEA in question'. That gives, for example, the US a let-out clause on MEAs they have not signed, such as the Biosafety Protocol. The Doha text also provides an incentive for countries not to sign up to MEAs in the future, thereby benefiting from international action without being bound by any of its provisions, by *creating a free rider loophole* excluding countries that have not signed on to a MEA from whatever safeguards for a signatory's implementation of such rules might be provided. After all, the GATT/WTO CTE has been examining the MEA question since 1994, with very little to show for it. The most likely outcome is that the Doha negotiations will produce only *a general statement about the putative mutual supportiveness of MEAs and trade rules.* However, whether the WTO is on a path to achieve such a common-sense outcome is doubtful.

One solution could be an authoritative Interpretation of Art. XX(b) and (g) of the GATT 1994, stating that specific trade obligations taken under MEAs will be deemed compatible with (b) and (g), and that a complaining government bears the burden of proving that such a trade measure is a violation of the chapeau of Art. XX GATT 1994. An analogous accommodation should be reached for Art. XIV(b) of the GATS. Furthermore, *the Interpretation should state that no WTO dispute can be invoked until the complaining party exhausts any specific dispute settlement procedure in the relevant MEA*, if it exists. If a dispute goes forward to the WTO, the Interpretation should further state that a panel shall seek the advice of the Parties to the MEA upon request of either party to the WTO dispute. Finally, as with all WTO panels that consider environmental issues, some would like to see a new requirement in the Dispute Settlement

Understanding (DSU)[62] that the panels should have the necessary expertise.[63]

D. Social Standards

In the past decades, the links between international trade and social standards have become a key issue in the relations between industrialised and developing countries, and therefore figure prominently in the vigorous trade and development debate as well. Concerns about social standards and their impact on global trade and international competition are not new. The development of international labour standards in the nineteenth century and the creation of the International Labour Organisation (ILO) in 1919 were centrally related to commercial considerations.[64] The GATT 1947 also contained a reference to national measures relating to products of prison labour in its Art. XX(e). However, the ambit of this exception is very limited: Firstly, it does not address the practice (prison labour) itself, but only refers to the products; secondly, in keeping with the overall interpretation of exceptions, Art. XX(e) has been interpreted narrowly and as such only to 'prison labour', excluding all other forms of labour rights infringements.

The current heightened interest in social standards is, *inter alia*, related to globalisation. Accelerated global economic integration provides great opportunities for economic growth and employment. But it also poses challenges to ensure that the broadest number of producers and workers benefit from the globalisation process and that *international competition occurs on the basis of accepted social standards.* To emphasise only the opportunities from globalisation, without addressing the concerns of producers and workers, would be self-defeating and makes it more difficult to maintain the consensus necessary to pursue a trade liberalisation agenda. Enterprises originating in developed countries realised that they have to implement corporate social responsibility measures in order to sell their products, particularly when exported into the markets of developed countries. However, some economists also have shown that

[62] Understanding on Rules and Procedures Governing the Settlement of Disputes, 15 April 1994, WTO Agreement, Annex 2, 869 UNTS 401, reprinted in 33 *ILM* 1125, 1226 (1994); OJ 1994 No L 336, 234.

[63] Such a provision could be modelled on para. 4 of the GATS Annex on Financial Services, which states that panels for disputes on prudential issues and other financial matters shall have the necessary expertise relevant to the specific financial service under dispute.

[64] See *A. Blüthner*, Welthandel und Menschenrechte in der Arbeit (2004), 139.

low social standards do not provide developing countries with unfair advantages in their exports, nor do they drive foreign direct investment.[65]

Although existing codified social standards vary from country to country – depending on the stage of development, per capita income, political and social conditions – efforts have been made in the past to identify and achieve consensus on a group of social standards that ideally should apply universally. In the WTO, the key phrase is '*core labour standards*'; essential standards applied to the way workers are treated. The term covers a wide range of things from abolition of child labour and forced labour, non-discrimination in employment, to the right to organize trade unions and to strike.

I Vision and reforms needed

The intense debate on trade and labour standards has attracted much public interest and has been with the WTO from the beginning.[66] In April 1994, when ministers gathered to sign the Marrakesh Agreement[67] that formed the WTO, nearly all governments expressed a view on this complex issue. But there was no consensus among Members at that time, and thus no basis for an agreement on the issue.

Advocates for including labour standards on the WTO's agenda of future work maintain rights including the freedom to bargain collectively, freedom of association, elimination of discrimination in the workplace and the elimination of workplace abuse (including forced labour and certain types of child labour). In the past, several Members have suggested that a WTO working group should be established to examine the link between trade and core labour standards. Other Members have suggested that a working group involving a number of international organisations be established to examine the social issues that are affected by globalisation. But developing countries have another view. They believe

65 See, for example, *R.M. Stern and K. Terrell*, Labour Standards and the World Trade Organization, Discussion Paper No. 499 (August 2003), University of Michigan.

66 See generally *P. Stirling*, The Use of Trade Sanctions as an Enforcement Mechanism for Basic Human Rights: A Proposal for Addition to the World Trade Organization, *Am. U. J. Int'l L. & Pol'y 11* (1996), 1; *S.H. Cleveland*, Human Rights Sanctions and International Trade: A Theory of Compatibility, *JIEL* 5 (2002), 133; *A.E. Appleton*, The World Trade Organisation: Implications for Human Rights and Democracy. In *K. Koufa (ed.)*, Human Rights and Democracy for the 21st Century (2000), 421. *S. Puth*, WTO und Sozialstandards. In *M. Hilf and S. Oeter (eds.)*, WTO-Recht (2005), 637.

67 Marrakesh Agreement Establishing the World Trade Organisation (hereinafter WTO Agreement), 15 April 1994, reprinted in 33 *ILM* 1125, 1144 (1994); OJ 1994 No L 336, 3.

that attempts to introduce labour standards into the WTO represent a thinly veiled form of protectionism which is designed to undermine the comparative advantage of lower-wage developing countries. These countries say that workplace conditions will improve through economic growth and development, which would be hindered should developed countries apply trade sanctions to their exports for reasons relating to labour standards. Application of such sanctions, they argue, would perpetuate poverty and delay developmental efforts including improvements in workplace standards.

At the *First WTO Ministerial Conference in Singapore in December 1996*, the issue was taken up and finally addressed in the Ministerial Declaration.[68] Ministers stated:

> We renew our commitment to the observance of internationally recognized core labour standards. The International Labour Organization (ILO) is the competent body to set and deal with these standards, and we affirm our support for its work in promoting them. We believe that economic growth and development fostered by increased trade and further trade liberalization contribute to the promotion of these standards. We reject the use of labour standards for protectionist purposes, and agree that the comparative advantage of countries, particularly low-wage developing countries, must in no way be put into question. In this regard, we note that the WTO and ILO secretariats will continue their existing collaboration.[69]

At the *Third WTO Ministerial Meeting in Seattle in 1999*, the issue of labour standards was perhaps the most divisive topic on the agenda. In the run-up to the Conference, both the US and the EU put forward proposals for addressing the issue inside the WTO.[70] At the Seattle Conference itself, the US, EU and other developed countries fought to get the issue addressed in a working group, and succeeded. Debate in that group was intense and there was strong disagreement among Members. Although officials from both Members said they did not envision the use of trade sanctions in the context of labour standards, both proposals were fiercely opposed by developing countries. Some US officials believed that trade sanctions might one day be used in retaliation for violations of labour standards. Developing country delegates hardened their resolve and, although there was serious debate on how the issue might be dis-

[68] Adopted on 13 December 1996, WT/MIN(96)/DEC, 18 December 1996.

[69] Existing collaboration between the WTO and ILO secretariats includes participation by the WTO in meetings of ILO bodies, the exchange of documents and informal cooperation between the two secretariats.

[70] WT/GC/W/382, 1 November 1999; WT/GC/W/383, 5 November 1999.

cussed inside an international framework, consensus on any role for the WTO on the question of labour standards was not achieved.

Since the Seattle Ministerial Meeting, governments from around the world *have turned their attention to the ILO as the appropriate forum for addressing the question of labour standards.* During the June 2001 meeting of the ILO Governing Body, the Working Party on the Social Dimension of Globalisation reached several agreements on how it might proceed with its work.[71] It was agreed informally that the technical capabilities of the Working Party needed to be addressed and that key issues for further discussion needed to be decided in advance. There was general agreement that trade liberalisation, employment and investment, with special emphasis on poverty reduction, should be issues taken up by the Working Party. There was also general agreement that a permanent forum for exchange of views should be established. High-level meetings could be arranged on an *ad hoc* basis. Members agreed generally as well that the ILO contribution to an integrated policy framework on the question of globalisation needed to be enhanced, and that a major report on the social dimension of globalisation could be written.[72]

The actions taken in 2001 follow on from the *1998 adoption of the ILO Declaration on Fundamental Principles and Rights at Work.*[73] It states that ILO Members endorse some basic principles included in ILO core conventions. These are the fundamental workplace rights and include: freedom of association and effective recognition of the right to collective bargaining; elimination of all forms of forced or compulsory labour; the abolition of child labour and the elimination of discrimination in respect of employment and occupation. ILO Members agreed to respect and promote these core conventions even if they have not ratified all of them. The Declaration makes it clear that these rights are universal, and that they apply to all people in all states, regardless of the level of economic development. It particularly mentions groups with special needs, including unemployed and migrant workers. It recognises that economic

[71] ILO Governing Body, 281st session, June 2001, Doc GB.281/WP/SDG/1.

[72] There was also the idea that a global commission of eminent personalities could be formed to examine the social aspects of globalisation, but no agreement was reached on this point. Among the ideas discussed was that the report on globalisation could be written by this commission and that the commission could be launched under the aegis of the UN Secretary General. Additionally, there was discussion that the commission might be serviced by a secretariat, under the ILO organisation, that could include representatives from the secretariats of other interested organisations.

[73] International Labour Conference, 86th session, Geneva, June 1998.

growth alone is not enough to ensure equity, social progress and to eradicate poverty.[74]

ILO Members also agreed to *prohibit and eliminate the worst forms of child labour.*[75] These practices were defined as all forms of slavery, child prostitution and pornography, forced recruitment of children for military purposes, the use of children for illicit activities such as the trafficking of drugs, and work which is likely to harm the health, safety or morals of children. ILO Members recognised that child labour is largely a function of poverty and that the long-term solution to the elimination of exploitative and harmful child labour is through sustained economic growth.

II Results achieved

At the Doha Conference, one group of developed countries stressed the importance of labour standards. They also favoured the WTO recognising efforts undertaken on this subject in the ILO through the text. Several developing countries wanted to delete references to the ILO. Some wanted all references to the issue deleted completely because it already had been dealt with at the Singapore Ministerial Meeting.

The *Doha Ministerial Declaration (para. 8)* states, offering little comfort to those wishing to introduce labour standards into the WTO: 'We reaffirm our declaration made at the Singapore Ministerial Conference regarding internationally recognised core labour standards. We take note of work under way in the International Labour Organisation (ILO) on the social dimension of globalisation.'

However, the dropping of the final sentence from the draft text of the Declaration, which reads: 'The ILO provides the appropriate forum for a substantive dialogue on various aspects of this issue', was hailed as a victory by labour rights activists, who argued that the final text at least does not exclude the WTO from taking part in such a 'substantive dialogue' in the future.

[74] As a follow-up, the ILO issues annual reports including information gained from governments which have not ratified all conventions on any changes that may have taken place in national Laws or regulations which may impact on these fundamental labour rights.

[75] This does not mean stopping all work performed by children. International labour standards allow the distinction to be made between what constitutes acceptable and unacceptable forms of work for children at different ages and stages of development. It has been estimated that less than 5% of child workers in the developing world are involved in export-related activities.

III Conclusion and outlook

When discussing trade and social standards, it is important to keep in mind the essential purpose of trade. As the Preamble of the GATT 1947 and WTO Agreement state, the purpose of increased trade is to raise standards of living and to ensure full employment. Trade liberalisation is not an objective to be pursued in the abstract, it is pursued to promote faster economic growth, which in turn can result in better and more jobs, improved labour conditions and higher living standards. To deny the links between trade and social standards is to fundamentally deny the very foundation upon which trade liberalisation has been built.

Therefore, it is vital for the WTO to address the relationship between trade and social standards. *A multilateral approach through the WTO working together with other international organisations is the best way to address the social dimension on a global level.* In the absence of such a multilateral approach, pressure will build to advance these concerns in ways that may be less preferable for the global trading system (such as bilateral and regional agreements). Further, failure to address the social dimension in the WTO may lead to precisely the result that critics of the trade and social standards debate say they want to avoid: an increase in protectionist pressures. The goal is to promote improved social standards worldwide, not to introduce new forms of protectionism into the trading system. In this spirit, it must be recognised that some countries may need assistance in adhering to international social standards. Therefore, *Members from developed countries should increase the capacity of the ILO to provide technical and financial assistance to its members*

Social standards are not subject to any WTO rules at present save for Art. XX(e) GATT 1994,[76] and while the issue continues to be deeply important for some developed countries, it seems unlikely that in the WTO – where consensus is required – social standards, or human rights in general, will be taken up in any official way in the near future. Thus, *the lead role of monitoring social standards continues to lie with the ILO. However, the ILO has been given little real enforcement power.*

[76] In recent years, lit. (e) has attracted attention as the only exception in Art. XX GATT 1994 explicitly applying to production-based trade restrictions. The provision has been used as an argument for and against the applicability of other Art. XX GATT 1994 exceptions to production-related measures. In addition, proponents of a human rights-respective trading system have identified Art. XX(e) as a way to open the door for the integration of human rights into WTO law. See generally *G. Marceau*, WTO Dispute Settlement and Human Rights, *EJIL* 13 (2002), 753; *S. Hörmann*, WTO und Menschenrechte. In *M. Hilf and S. Oeter (eds.)*, WTO-Recht (2005), 647, 660.

One solution would be to include a new 'social clause' in the binding WTO rules, for example, an amendment to Art. XX GATT 1994, incorporating the core labour rights developed by the ILO.[77] Another approach seeks the *aid of the WTO dispute settlement institutions* to create an interpretation that extends coverage of existing clauses to social conditions. For example, the 'social dumping clause' (Art. VI GATT 1994), or the 'public morals exception' (Art. XX(a) GATT 1994), could be invoked to justify trade sanctions against products that involve the use of child or forced labour. When doing so it could be argued that attempts to enforce social standards through trade sanctions are likely to cause economic harm to most exporting developing countries, at least in the short to medium term, while doing little or nothing to improve their social standards. Indeed, under wholly plausible circumstances, this approach could be seriously counterproductive and reduce social standards overall ('race to the bottom').[78]

In the context of implementation and enforcement of social standards, it is interesting to note that the WTO has made some progress on specific trade obligations for human rights. In November 2002, participants in the so-called Kimberley Process[79] expressed their intent to implement an international scheme of certification for rough diamonds to help break the link between armed conflict and the global trade in rough diamonds. Therefore, several Members requested a waiver, according to Art. IX of the WTO Agreement, from WTO rules to give legal certainty to domestic measures taken under the Kimberley Process aimed at curbing trade in 'conflict diamonds' while supporting the legitimate diamond trade.[80] The explanation for this development may be that the Kimberley Process also

[77] See *A. Blüthner*, Welthandel und Menschenrechte in der Arbeit (2004), 402.

[78] Furthermore, many economists also have also pointed out that in addition to the possible adverse impact on workers in developing countries by forcing them out of their jobs without providing a viable alternative, consumers in developed countries may have a more limited choice of products and face higher prices for the goods available. On the 'public morals exception' of Art. XX(a) GATT 1994, see *N. Wenzel*, Art. XX(a) GATT 1994. In *R. Wolfrum, P.T. Stoll and A. Seibert-Fohr (eds)*, WTO – Technical Barriers and SPS Measures (2007), 80, 89.

[79] In May 2000, Southern African diamond producing states met in Kimberley, South Africa, to come up with a way to stop the trade in 'conflict diamonds' and to reassure consumers that the diamonds they purchase have not contributed to violent conflict and human rights abuses in their countries of origin.

[80] The Kimberley Process Certification Scheme as such does not constitute a trade measure in WTO terms. However, it invites participants to adopt trade measures; therefore, the question of WTO conformity arises on the level of national implementation of such measures. The WTO waiver decision exempts – from 1 January 2003 until 31 December 2006 – trade measures taken under the Kimberley Process by Members that would subsequently

promotes the interests of several African governments and of the world diamond industry. The Kimberley Process provides that each participant should 'ensure that no shipment of rough diamonds is imported or exported to a non-Participant'.

E. Summary and conclusions

The question remains whether the troubled Doha Round really represents a substantial step forward in the incorporation of health, environment and social standards into the WTO.

In sum, the Doha Ministerial Declaration, and its accompanying work programme, is vaguely worded and adopts few substantive reforms of the WTO framework. Nevertheless, *the Doha agenda has the potential to significantly improve growth and development throughout the world.* The WTO needs to build on the positive experience of Doha, especially when exploring development issues as vehicles for growth and stability. Members need to continue to engage with and listen to all trading partners, at all levels of development, and devise strategies that respond to their individual trade and development needs. Furthermore, Members need to continue capacity-building efforts to help developing countries address problems in implementing existing WTO agreements. Members also need to ensure that ongoing initiatives in other fora are complementary to and build on successes in Doha. The WTO can no longer ignore the work done by other international organisations like WHO, the United Nations Environment Programme (UNEP) or the ILO. Thus, the provisions relied upon in the SPS Agreement to include international SPS standards (Art. 3) are particularly noteworthy as a 'model' for future multilateral negotiations. For many of the most sensitive topics, co-operation in other fora can reinforce progress in the WTO and ensure that Members do not load excessive burdens on the trading system.

Some of the perceived problems with the SPS Agreement are that it relies too heavily on a vague set of risk assessment provisions (Art. 5), that it fails to take into account the importance of consumer considerations in

join from GATT 1994 provisions on most-favoured-nation treatment (Art. I:1), elimination of quantitative restrictions (Art. XI:1) and non-discriminatory administration of quantitative restrictions (Art. XIII:1). See WT/L/518, 27 May 2003. The agreed Waiver recognised 'the extraordinary humanitarian nature of this issue and the devastating impact of conflicts fuelled by trade in conflict diamonds on the peace, safety and security of people in affected countries and the systematic and gross human rights violations that have been perpetrated in such conflicts'.

managing risks, and that it discourages the application of the precautionary principle. There is a strong need to clarify the scope of the 'strict' SPS Agreement, especially after the not appealed decision of the Panel in *EC–Biotech*. In fact, issues like animal welfare, food radiation, or GMOs are crucial. How these will be addressed in the future is unclear. Only NGOs have questioned the handling of GMOs in general, and the relationship between the SPS Agreement and the Biosafety Protocol in particular.[81] *Astonishingly, none of the SPS problems have been addressed in the Doha Round seriously*. Instead, it seems that Members prefer a clarification of these issues by the *dispute settlement institutions* of the WTO on a case-by-case basis rather than by multilateral trade negotiations. But *ad hoc* dispute settlement decisions alone are not a proper solution to the impact that WTO rules, as currently interpreted, may have on measures to protect human, animal or plant health.

The Public Health Declaration is an important political statement which has enormous value in reassuring least-developed and developing countries that all Members support their efforts to fight life-threatening diseases and that the TRIPS Agreement is not a bar to those efforts. In articulating the flexibilities of the TRIPS Agreement, the Declaration gives least-developed and developing countries facing real health crises greater confidence that they have the necessary authority to address them. Equally important, the Declaration reaffirms the importance of intellectual property protection and affirmatively acknowledges that the TRIPS Agreement is part of the solution to public health needs, not part of the problem.

It must be emphasised *that the long-lasting trade and environment debate confronting the GATT/WTO will not be resolved at a single ministerial meeting*. Future conferences will provide an opportunity to refocus and catalyse the WTO environmental discussions so that they lead to a positive outcome in the long run. Before and during the Doha Round there has been little effective progress with respect to clarifying the relationship between trade provisions pursuant to MEAs and WTO rules. It is

[81] See, for example, *EC–Biotech*, Report of the Panel, WT/DS 291–293/R, para. 7.75; *S. Charnovitz*, The Supervision of Health and Biosafety Regulation by World Trade Rules, *Tul. Envtl. L.J.* 13 (2000), 271; *A.H. Qureshi*, The Cartagena Protocol on Biosafety and the WTO – Co-existence or Incoherence?, *Int'l & Comp. L.Q.* 49 (2000), 835; *N. Bernasconi-Osterwalder*, The Cartagena Protocol on Biosafety: A Multilateral Approach to Regulate GMOs. In *E. Brown Weiss and J.H. Jackson (eds.)*, Reconciling Environment and Trade (2001), 689; *L. Stökl*, Der welthandelsrechtliche Gentechnikkonflikt (2003), 237; *M. Böckenförde*, Grüne Gentechnik und Welthandel (2004).

doubtful that another organisation will be able to tackle the complex relationship better than the WTO, although there is an obvious need to strengthen global environmental institutions in general. But a convenient balance of trade and environment can only be achieved through consensus and negotiations, as the WTO Members need transparency and predictability.[82]

Overall, the Doha Ministerial Declaration fell far short of demands for an effective WTO commitment to begin a process to address the relationship between global trade and social standards. The Doha Conference showed, once again, that a considerable number of developing countries *oppose any discussion of social standards.* In their view, the inclusion of social standards would limit the potential for boosting trade. This would restrict the welfare benefits of trade and would have the counterproductive effect of undermining sustainable development.

When looking at all three controversial issues at the same time, it becomes clear that there are some common elements and difficulties. The WTO should not set standards, but should be actively involved in enforcing them. *Many advocates of enforceable standards want them to become part of the WTO rules so they can be enforced by trade sanctions*, but it is at least questionable if the WTO is the appropriate forum and if its dispute settlement institutions are properly suited to arbitrate complex disputes over health, environmental or social standards. Another major problem with enforcing health, environmental or social standards through the WTO is the *lack of clear definition of what those standards should be, how compliance should be measured, and who should determine whether they have been violated.* In many developed countries there is the fear that negotiating and adopting standards on the global level encourages a *downward harmonisation*, or a 'race to the bottom'. In contrast, for many developing countries the pace and scale of trade liberalisation may

[82] The Uruguay Round did not lead to a provision similar to Art. 104 North American Free Trade Agreement (NAFTA), which provides certain rules for solving possible conflicts between the provisions of NAFTA and MEAs like the Basel Convention on the Control of Transboundary Movements of Hazardous Wastes and their Disposal, which came into force in 1992, reprinted in 28 *ILM* 649 (1989); OJ 1993 No L 39, 1. Accordingly, it remains the task of the WTO organs to solve similar conflicts under WTO Law. At least in theory, a WTO panel might have to examine the impact of, e.g., the Basel Convention within a WTO dispute settlement proceeding between signatories to the Convention. See generally *H. Hohmann*, Implementation of the Basel Convention on Hazardous Wastes in the EC and Germany: Improvement or Impediment of its Enforcement? In *T. Zhenghua and R. Wolfrum (eds.)*, Implementing International Environmental Law in Germany and China (2001), 141.

overwhelm the capacity to develop and enforce international standards; in such circumstances, global trade may exacerbate the consequences of poor domestic policies.

The WTO must continue to strike a delicate balance between the shared, but sometimes competing interests of promoting international trade and safeguarding legitimate government regulations. *In the long run, the WTO* cannot operate in isolation from the concerns of the world in which it exists and, therefore, *can no longer exclude health, environment and social standards* – especially if public confidence in the WTO and the global trading system is to be strengthened. All Members need to promote a better understanding of the concerns involved through a substantive dialogue between all interested parties, including civil society. The absence of an explicit recognition of these important issues in the WTO contributes to weaken and jeopardise the multilateral trading system. Ignoring the actual and potential linkages to trade *provides an incentive to deal with these issues outside the WTO*, contributes to the proliferation of regional and bilateral trade agreements, and stresses the decay of the most-favoured-nation (MFN) principle. Finally, it may be helpful to remember that *all three issues are directly linked to sustainable development* – the ultimate objective of the Doha Round. Therefore, concrete suggestions on how the promotion of complementarity and mutual supportiveness of policies can contribute to the objectives of sustainable development are needed.

PART FIVE

Conclusions

20

Some personal conclusions

HARALD HOHMANN

In order to stimulate some discussions on the issues of the Doha Round, let me summarize and comment some aspects of the nineteen chapters as follows.

Aspect 1: Future of the Doha Round

There are a lot of indications that the Doha talks will be continued and resumed in the near future; there may be questions about the size of the final package. Because of the principle of Single Undertaking, which is also applicable for the Doha Round, nothing is agreed until everything is agreed. Thus the agreements reached so far in the Doha talks (see Chapter 1b) are conditional on the conclusion of the entire DDA negotiations themselves. This is why resuming and concluding the Doha Round is imperative for the world community. On the other hand, if a WTO Member wishes to implement a few of these agreements now, it must not wait until the entire DDA negotiations are legally binding. *Peter Mandelson* (Chapter 1a) reminds us of the high chances of Doha: largest liberalisation of fair trade in history, elimination of all remaining industrial peaks and a very substantial development component and sees a win-win situation for industrial and developing nations.

Aspect 2: Development aspect 1: Agricultural access

A significant reduction in tariffs and in the high level of domestic subsidies and especially of export subsidies in industrialized countries, which may increase the market access of some developing countries, is a key issue to most developing countries. Under para.13 of the Doha Declaration, the WTO Members have agreed to a three-band system for reductions in domestic support, with higher linear cuts in higher bands, and the EU Members have agreed to ensure the parallel elimination of all forms of export subsidies by the end of 2013. Nonetheless, the bottleneck that remains is the proportion of the cuts in domestic supports and tariffs, and the treatment and percentage of tariff lines to be covered under "special" or "sensitive products" (see Chapters 1b, 2 and 4). Thus, developing countries would gain a lot, if the Doha Round is resumed. Two caveats: one: Liberalization in industrial products and services is more likely to be the key to a successful pro-development conclusion of the Doha Round than the reform of agricultural market access (see Chapter 3a). Two: Trade liberalization may lead to poverty reduction, but market access must be complemented by domestic policy reforms and capacity building (see Chapter 4).

Aspect 3: Development aspect 2: NAMA and services access

The NAMA (non-agricultural market access) negotiations have concentrated on improved access to developed country markets, *inter alia*, by reduction of tariff peaks for products originating in developing countries, improved opportunities in South–South trade, and improved market access for LDC products, as well as by the request of developing countries to have some flexibility that would allow them lower tariff cuts or exempt a number of tariff lines from new bindings or reduction commitments ("preserving policy space," "protecting infant industries," "non-preferential preference erosion" etc.). Service production is the dominant economic activity in nearly every country in the world, including not only labour-intensive traditional services (e.g. construction, distribution, social services), but also modern services (e.g. telecommunications, financial services, business services, transport and logistics), which often have a large impact on a modern infrastructure of a country. Service negotiations are taking place on two fronts: market access and rule-making. The market access segment consists of negotiations on new or improved commitments for inclusion in Members' schedules of specific commitments under GATS and the re-negotiation of current MFN exemptions. The rule-making negotiations are concentrated on emergency safeguard measures, government procurement and subsidies. Concerning NAMA, the WTO Members decided to implement para.16 of the Doha Declaration (the elimination of high tariffs for products of export interests to developing countries) by using a Swiss formula, which requires that the highest tariffs are more cut than the lowest. In addition it was agreed that developed WTO Members – and those developing WTO members in a position to do so – shall provide duty-free and quota-free market access for nearly all products (at least 97%) originating from LDC' s (the "Everything but Arms Initiative"). These are two remarkable Doha results, even though there has not been much success in the other questions up to now (see Chapters 1b, 2 and 4); only very recently, chances for a NAMA agreement have been raised. There are thus big potential gains in the NAMA negotiations for all developing countries: developed countries will reduce high tariffs the most, followed by a few large emerging countries. However, LDC' s are not required to make any commitments, but they will profit from the duty-free market access (see Chapter 3a). Concerning services, in the long run it may be possible to come to market access solutions for developing and developed countries alike, if rules for labour-intense and modern services are equally integrated into the framework of negotiations (see Chapter 3a). To achieve this, high asymmetric levels of commitment for WTO Members may be needed (see Chapter 4).

Aspect 4: Development aspect 3: S&D, technical assistance and poverty reduction

While capacity building, technical assistance and poverty reduction of the developing WTO Members were soon accepted principles of the Doha Round, a lot of open questions remained concerning S&D (special and differential treatment) of developing countries. While there was always some S&D language in the WTO Agreements (e.g. longer transitional periods for developing countries) for some specific situations (see Chapter 4), the introduction of this as a general principle was new. What does it really mean to grant some flexibility to a developing country? It could mean flexibility concerning time (i.e. longer transitional periods for developing countries) or flexibility concerning the contents of a duty (i.e. some duties must not be fulfilled at all by developing countries). In the latter case, questions may arise about whether this is consistent with the multilateral system of WTO rules. What has been agreed upon during the Doha Round are the decisions in favor of LDC' s, as contained in Annex F of the Hong Kong Declaration (more chances will be given to requests of waivers by LDC's, providing duty-free and quota-free access for 97% of the products from LDC's, temporary deviations from WTO duties for LDC's etc.; see Chapter 5). A lot of work must be done on how other developing WTO Members should become beneficiaries of S&D, possibly through dispute settlement (see Chapter 5). Not only improved market access, but also some form of S&D may be required to fight against poverty within the WTO – here, some differentiation between different levels of development is helpful – and for a successful fight against poverty, adjustment measures/domestic reforms (fiscal, monetary, investment, social, educational and democratic reforms) and some form of capacity building/technical assistance is an urgent *must* (see Chapter 4).

Aspect 5: Trade policy aspect 1: NAMA

The main source of conflict with the Swiss formula, which implements the NAMA-approach of para.16 of the Doha Declaration (see Aspect 3), is the amount of the two coefficients (one for developing, one for industrialized nations), as they will determine the extent to which tariffs are reduced and hence the scope of genuine market liberalization. Another bone of contention is the proposed flexibility for developing countries concerning full or partial exemption from tariff reductions. Both of these issues are pivotal to the establishment of concrete NAMA modalities (see Chapter 6b). Paragraph 16 of the Doha Declaration speaks of the reduction or elimination of tariffs, but does not explicitly refer to sectoral tariff elimination; the July 2004 package and the Hong Kong Declaration have underlined the need for sectoral tariff elimination, but such a specification has not yet occurred. That sectoral tariff elimination is of the highest importance, for the improved access of non-agricultural products can be demonstrated by the chemical industry. Today, the average bound chemical tariffs are relatively low in industrialized countries (between 2 and 6%), but they are quite high in emerging countries (between 20 and 40%). Thus, the goal of getting real market access in emerging countries will not be achieved (see Chapter 7). It is advisable to address some non-tariff barriers within the NAMA negotiations or under a mediation mechanism at WTO level, (e.g. export duties, double pricing schemes, "buy national" campaigns, fiscal incentives, tax and duty exemptions, (see Chapter 7)). It is safe to assume, that substantial new commitments concerning trade in services will only be realized following, or in conjunction with, an agreement on NAMA and agricultural matters.

Aspect 6: Trade policy aspect 2: Improvement of "rules"

The issue of the improvement of rules concerning anti-dumping and subsidies remains extremely complex. Especially developing WTO

Members have proposed tightening these anti-dumping rules (i.e. reflecting exporter interests) while others have cautioned against making the rules too difficult for developing country investigating authorities to implement, thereby reflecting their interests as users. Proposals concerning rules on subsidies are differentiated among developing country Members and certain other factors. This diversity is reflected in proposals concerning if and how subsidy disciplines might be strengthened, and on proposed changes to the S&D treatment provisions of the Agreement on Subsidies and Countervailing Measures. In the area of fisheries subsidies, certain developing country Members favor very strict disciplines with few exceptions and limited S&D treatment, while others seek broad exemptions from any new disciplines (see Chapter 2). There has at least been one success. Members in the Negotiating Group on Rules approved a draft Decision establishing a Transparency Mechanism for RTA (Regional Trade Agreements). This requires early announcement of the RTA by the RTA members to the WTO Secretariat (cf. Chapter 1b). By contrast, competition rules had a short-lived career in the WTO negotiations – it was identified in Singapore 1996, but dropped in Cancun 2003. The worldwide expansion of competition law has meanwhile found a more accommodating forum: the International Competition Network (see Chapter 9).

Aspect 7: Trade policy aspect 3: Trade facilitation

There is now consensus, that the following aspects are integrated into trade facilitation: a periodic review of trade restrictions with the aim to standardize and minimize them, harmonization of national trade restrictions with international obligations, publication of all trade rules (including rules on fees) and notification of new rules to other WTO Members, the introduction of some simplified export procedures, the introduction of auditing schemes and of pre-shipment customs notifications, the simplification and harmonization of customs procedures (regional customs cooperation, mutual recognition of equivalent standards, electronic transfer of customs clearance, Single Window), simplification and the harmonization of transit, import and export procedures (periodic review of the appropriateness of these trade restrictions, mutual recognition of equivalent standards, close customs cooperation, Single Window), non-discriminatory legal rights of affected traders to appeal against customs or other trade agency rulings and decisions within standard set times, uniform administration of national customs and trade regulations (e.g. by establishing a central body within the government), establishing objective criteria for the application of fees and charges for trade operations, and establishing objective criteria for the tariff classification of goods (see Chapter 8). Because of S&D, these rules are combined with longer transition periods for development countries and with capacity building. Based on this consensus, the time will soon be ripe for the conclusion of an Agreement of Trade Facilitation.

Aspect 8: Development and trade policy aspect: Sustainability of the DDA

A recent study on the Sustainability Impact Assessment (SIA) of the DDA[1] came to the conclusion, that there are potential aggregate economic welfare gains to be made from the trade liberalization measures, but they will be different for the groups of developing countries: While the major exporting developing countries (e.g. Argentina, Brazil, Uruguay) and the highly protected developing countries (e.g. Egypt and India) will clearly be economic beneficiaries, this is more doubtful for LDCs and low-income developing countries. Whether they can achieve even a modest gain from the DDA depends on adjustment measures, (e.g. whether they can respond to higher import prices). Only under these conditions will domestic production expand and domestic prices may ultimately fall, implying a long-term gain for the economy; otherwise, economic and social consequences will be negative. The DDA impact of trade liberalization on social and environmental welfare – especially on poverty reduction – will be more favorable in some large developing countries (e.g. India and China), while in some of the poorest countries the social situation may worsen – at least in the short- and medium-term – if no effective social and educational adjustment measures are taken (see also Chapter 4). To avoid such negative effects, the study highlights the importance of trade-related technical assistance to build the capacity to (i) formulate a locally owned trade policy, (ii) participate in trade negotiations, and to (iii) implement trade agreements and establish a trade-related infrastructure. For this, the Aid for Trade capacity building program under para. 57 of the Hong Kong Declaration is of the highest importance, to make the

[1] C. Kirkpatrick and others from the Impact Assessment Research Centre at the University of Manchester, *Sustainability Impact Assessment of Proposed WTO Negotiations, Final Global Overview Trade SIA of the DDA, Final Report*, May 2006, especially at iv–vi and at 45, available at: www.sia-trade.org.

DDA a win–win situation for industrialized and developing WTO Members alike. This is also extremely important for the trade policy of industrialized WTO Members (see Chapter 6a); the establishment of the Integrated Framework for Trade-Related Technical Assistance to the LDC (IF) and of the WTO technical assistance program (cf. Chapter 4) are good examples of this. In order to achieve economically and socially sustainable results under the DDA, economic and social rights (including the fulfilment of basic needs and the right to a modest environment) must be integrated in the same way as civil and political rights. Thus the aim should and must be integrating economic, social and environmental concerns as well as human rights in the DDA program, at least in the medium or long term (see Chapter 10).

Aspect 9: Dispute settlement aspect 1: More transparency and more state control

Several proposals have been made to make the WTO dispute settlement system more transparent: early release of Panel reports, public access to Panel hearings, a non-state actor' s rights to submit *amicus curiae* briefs or to participate as observers in Panel proceedings. These are helpful proposals for greater global acceptance of Panel decisions. They would give an expert or an NGO the chance to add helpful specific issues to a dispute which might otherwise be ignored by the Panel's lack of expertise. More critical in my view are the proposals aimed at increasing flexibility and member control of the dispute settlement. While proposals like more flexibility in the determination of the reasonable implementation period under Art. 21 para. 3 of the DSU, or having the ability to suspend appeal proceedings (or having the enhanced ability to suspend panel proceedings) – both would be in favor of more consultations – are to be welcomed, doubts arise, when such a proposal aims to give more state control over the Panel procedure (e.g. the proposal that a deletion by mutual agreement of some findings in the panel or AB report which are regarded as unnecessary or unhelpful should be allowed). That would endanger the difficult balance between the ineffective political decision-making procedures of the WTO and the comparatively effective adjudication of the Panels (see Chapter 12). All proposals that carefully advance the current dispute settlement process, like raising the number of the members of the Appellate Body or introducing time-tables for Panel procedures or a remand procedure at appeal stage, are to be welcomed. The only question is whether these kinds of reforms can be achieved using the dispute settlement practice (i.e. by panels experimenting with new procedures, which should later be codified in the DSU (see Chapter 11)) or whether it should be reached directly by a reform of the DSU (see Chapter 12).

Aspect 10: Dispute settlement aspect 2: Special interests of developing countries: Funding/legal assistance and effective counter-measures

Far-reaching proposals on collective coercion or on transferring an authorization to retaliate against other WTO Members have been made by developing countries that lack sufficient retaliatory power. It is quite clear that those ideas that require major changes to the DSU, or even to the case of the dispute settlement altogether, will not find support. Thus it is very likely, that the ideas of collective retaliation, retroactive monetary compensation, tradeable rights to suspend concessions, or provisional preventive measures will not be accepted (see Chapter 12). While these ideas from developing countries have no chance of realization, one aspect of S&D – creating an independent unit to provide legal assistance to developing countries – was realized in July 2001 by the creation of the Advisory Centre on WTO Law. The ACWL has provided more than 200 legal opinions to developing countries and LDC's; two-thirds of the developing countries that have participated in the panel proceedings as complainant or respondent have decided to become Members of the ACWL. The ACWL offers its services free of charge to Members of the ACWL – but exclusively to developing countries among the ACWL members – who must pay a membership fee ($300,000, $100,000 or $50,000 depending on the level of development, while industrialized members fund this activity with $1m), and to LDC' s, which must not take any steps to become members of the ACWL (see Chapter 14).

Aspect 11: Role of social rights in world trade

There is hardly a clear legal basis for a trade-based enforcement of human rights at work. Even if it would be possible to provisionally justify those measures under Art. XX(a) GATT, the necessity test sets up a high hurdle on the way to GATT conformity, and the wording of Art. XX(e) GATT is limited to "prison labour." One solution would be to enact a new "social clause," an interpretative agreement concerning the application of Art. XX GATT, which would include the four core labour rights developed by the ILO in its Declaration of 1998 (freedom of association, elimination of forced labour, abolition of child labour, elimination of discrimination in employment) (see Chapters 15 and 19). Another way would be to solve the issue within a dispute settlement case by – as I would call it – a "harmonious interpretation" of WTO Law alongside other applicable international law (see Art. 31 para. 3(c) of the Vienna Convention on the Law of Treaties),[2] namely with general principles of law, here with the four core labour rights of the ILO which today may be regarded as universally accepted general principles of law.[3] Such an interpretation would also find support by para. 8 of the Doha Declaration ("*We take note* of work underway in the ILO on the social dimension of globalisation"), since this formulation ("we take note") is more or less identical with the requirements under Art. 31 para. 3(c) of the Vienna Convention ("any relevant applicable rule of international law *shall be taken into account*"). When this interpretation is done narrowly in such way to give effect to the four core labour rights of the ILO, of which the WTO Members must take account anyway, it may be possible to have a good argument against the idea that the WTO cannot protect human rights, until the WTO Members have agreed to extend its mandate into this area (see Chapter 13). I think, para. 8 of the Doha Declaration already contains a certain extension of the WTO mandate. It is possible (and likely), that in the near future not only the ILO, but also the WTO may be regarded as a – second – best forum for the protection of these four core labour standards. Another question is, whether a "cooperationist" policy model addressing the social dimensions of globalization, namely the UN Global Compact, may be more effective for the protection of these four labour standards, since it is a voluntary and market-based approach towards putting human rights principles into practice (see Chapter 15).

Aspect 12: Role of health in world trade

One of the results of the debate on protection of health within the Doha Round was the Declaration on TRIPS and Public Health, which reaffirms a government's right to use, to the full, the flexibilities of TRIPS for protection of public health, in particular by allowing compulsory licensing and the parallel import of medicines which are urgently required for abating diseases like AIDS etc. Thus, the acute disparities in

[2] Thus Hohmann, Der Konflikt zwischen freien Handel und Umweltschutz in WTO und EG. In *Recht der Internationalen Wirtschaft* 46 (2000), 88 *et seq.*, at 89.

[3] For this interpretation, under what circumstances customary law and general principles of law are emerging in international law, see Hohmann, *Precautionary Legal Duties and Principles of Modern International Environmental Law*, London (1994), 166 *et seq.*

pharmaceutical access between developing and industrialized countries may be solved in the short or medium term (see Chapter 19). More open are some of the questions concerning the protection of health and food safety. While a few of the vague formulations in the SPS Agreement could be solved by clarifications during the Doha Round, and while during the Doha Round a global WTO program to enhance the capacity of developing countries in forming, interpreting and implementing international SPS standards was started (see Chapter 19), the open questions concentrated especially on the relationship between Art. XX(b) GATT and the role of the precautionary principle for health/food safety concerns and its relationship to the SPS (see Chapters 16 and 19). The narrow interpretation of the necessity test makes it difficult to apply Art. XX(b) GATT to food safety issues, and since the SPS recognizes the precautionary principle only in a limited way, the question arises whether it is possible to come to a different interpretation of Arts. 3.2 and 5.7 of the SPS with the help of other international rules (e.g. by the wider interpreted precautionary principle under the Cartagena Protocol (see Chapter 16)). I personally would instead make a plea for a "harmonious" interpretation of the duties under Art. 3 para. 3 of the SPS with another applicable rule of international law (Art. 31 para. 3(c) Vienna Convention), namely the precautionary principle, which has now established as a principle of customary international law,[4] with the result that the requirements of scientific justification under Art. 3 para. 3 of the SPS are a bit lessened, when great risks to human health cannot be excluded, as in the *Hormone* or the *GMO cases*.[5] A similar proposal states that in cases where human life is at risk, already minority opinions may be sufficient to justify a national health measure (see Chapter 16). Another question is whether an Understanding for Interpretation of conditions which are required for justification under Art. XX(b) and (g) of the GATT is helpful (see Chapter 16).

Aspect 13: Environmental protection and world trade

In para. 31 of the Doha Declaration, the environment was on the WTO agenda for the first time. Ministers agreed to launch negotiations on the relationship between existing WTO rules and "specific trade obligations" set out in MEAs, to negotiate procedures for regular information

[4] See Hohmann (n. 3), at 333 *et seq.* (344). [5] Cf. Hohmann, (n.2), at 98.

exchange between secretariats of MEAs and of the WTO, and to develop criteria for observer status of these secretariats within the WTO. Currently, the WTO Committee on Trade and Environment (CTE) holds information sessions with different secretariats of MEAs once or twice a year; this exchange may expand the scope of existing cooperation. Since the negotiations on the relationship between WTO and MEA rules has had little success up to now, one solution (Solution 1) would be an interpretative statement of Art. XX(b) and (g) GATT, stating that specific trade obligations taken under MEAs will be deemed compatible with Art. XX(b) and (g) GATT, and that a complaining government bears the burden of proving, that such a trade measure is a violation of the chapeau of this provision (see Chapter 19). An additional question is whether this presumption of compatibility depends on the fulfilment of several conditions (see Chapter 16). Very similar is the proposal to amend a new Art. XX(k) GATT (see Chapter 17). Another solution (Solution 2) is an "evolutionary interpretation" within a dispute settlement procedure by a Panel, which may be better suited than decisions by a political body, as far as the Panel remains within its jurisdiction and its mandate (see Chapters 13 and 18). One proposal for this is the "harmonious interpretation" of the WTO rules with the provisions of the MEA concerned, in *Sea Turtles* with provisions of CITES, UNCLOS and Agenda 21, which all required a protection of these sea turtles also by unilateral measures.[6] Under this interim result, the panel was obliged to think twice, whether the unilateral protection of sea turtles was justified, at least exceptionally, under Art. XX(b) and (g) GATT. A third way (Solution 3), which seems to be more complicated, would be to interpret the rules of the WTO and of the MEA as "mutually supportive," and if this is not possible to work for a new codification of some rules of the MEA, as demonstrated by the Kyoto Protocol (see Chapter 17). An additional open environmental question is whether WTO Law allows trade restrictions based on specifications related to production and process methods (see Chapter 18).

To sum up, the survival of our children depends on the question of whether we will be able to solve the global economic, social and environmental concerns as well as human rights concerns in an integrated way in the long run. For this, the implementation of the DDA will be decisive.

[6] See Hohmann, (n. 2), at 98.

INDEX